ANTHONY EDEN

Robert Rhodes James was born in India in April 1933, the youngest son of a senior Army officer, and was educated at Sedbergh School and Worcester College, Oxford. In 1955 he was appointed a Clerk in the House of Commons and in 1963 was elected a Fellow of All Souls College, Oxford. Between 1968 and 1973 he was Director of a research institute at the University of Sussex, of which he is an honorary Professional Fellow. He is a Fellow of the Royal Historical Society and the Royal Society of Literature, and an Honorary Doctor of Letters of Westminster College, Fulton, Missouri. Between 1972 and 1976 he was Principal Officer to the Secretary-General of the UN, and in December 1976 was elected Conservative MP for Cambridge. He has served in the present Government at the Foreign and Commonwealth Office and as Liaison Officer for Higher Education, and is Chairman of the History of Parliament Trust.

His first book was a biography of Lord Randolph Churchill (1959), which received widespread praise, and was followed by award-winning books on the House of Commons (1961), on Lord Rosebery (1963), and what is still considered the definitive history of the 1915 Gallipoli campaign (1965), while his *Churchill: A Study in Failure 1900–1939* (1970) is recognized as the first serious and successful analysis of Churchill the man. *The British Revolution, 1860–1939* (1976 and 1977) and his authorized biography of Prince Albert (1983) added to his formidably early-gained reputation as a historian and biographer. The British critic Paul Johnson has described Robert Rhodes James as 'a phenomenon', moving easily and impressively in the worlds of scholarship and public affairs.

Robert Rhodes James was married in 1956 to Angela Robertson. They have four daughters and live near Cambridge.

Robert Rhodes James

ANTHONY EDEN

PAPERMAC

First published 1986 by Weidenfeld and Nicolson Limited

First published 1987 in paperback by
PAPERMAC
a division of Macmillan Publishers Limited
4 Little Essex Street London WC2R 3LF
and Basingstoke
Associated companies in Auckland, Delhi, Dublin, Gaborone, Hamburg, Harare, Hong Kong, Johannesburg, Kuala Lumpur, Lagos, Manzini, Melbourne, Mexico City, Nairobi, New York, Singapore and Tokyo

British Library Cataloguing in Publication Data

James, Robert Rhodes
  Anthony Eden.
  1. Eden, Anthony   2. Prime ministers——
  Great Britain——Biography
  I. Title
  941.085′5′0924   DA566.9.E28

ISBN 0-333-45503-7

Printed in Hong Kong

IN MEMORIAM

SERENA BOOKER

1955–82

Contents

Illustrations

(*Unless otherwise indicated, all the photographs are from Lady Avon's collection
   and are reproduced with her kind permission.*)

MAP

Preface

When the long life of Anthony Eden, first Earl of Avon, ended in January 1977 the tributes paid to him in both Houses of Parliament were of notable warmth and eloquence. The then Prime Minister, Mr James Callaghan, and another Labour Member of Parliament, Dr Marcus Lipton – who had been at Oxford with Eden – spoke of the man they had known and respected in the 1930s when, in Winston Churchill's celebrated phrase, he had seemed 'the one strong young figure standing up against long, dismal, drawling tides of drift and surrender, of wrong measurements and feeble impulses'. To many of a later generation, recalling only Eden's brief and ill-starred premiership and the Suez crisis of 1956 that ended his career, these sympathetic tributes and obituaries came as a considerable surprise. As Dr Sidney Aster wrote in his study of Eden, 'It is a cruel fate, even by the harsh standards of politics, to be remembered by one failure and not by numerous achievements.' But even over that 'failure' – Suez – there has developed a realization over the past thirty years that the verdict may have been too hastily reached.

Although Anthony Eden was born eleven years later than my father, he was of the same generation that served in, and narrowly survived, the First World War, and whose lives and attitudes were shaped by that searing experience. Both saw the England and Europe of their childhood, which seemed so permanent and indestructible, utterly changed; then, in 1939, they had to go through the whole ghastly business again. Both were brought up in a world in which the internal combustion engine had only just been invented and manned flight was a derided vision; both died in the 1970s, in a totally transformed world and country.

I admired Anthony Eden from a distance as a child and young man, and when in 1955 I became a junior official of the House of Commons I saw him at close range as Prime Minister. I never knew him well, although he was very kind to me in my study of Churchill's career up to 1939, but I had always found his brand of humane, liberal and progressive Conservatism, born in the trenches on the Western Front in 1916, the only version that appealed to me. This remains so.

I had also glimpsed, in public and in private, the complexities of his personality that made him such a deeply interesting, as well as attractive, man. I certainly never accepted the dismissive, even hostile, attitude towards him of so many political commentators and some historians, and always considered that his policy over Suez deserved a more sympathetic understanding than it has usually received. I was interested to see, in Eden's last years, the tide turning in his favour, and the success of his three volumes of memoirs and his minor classic *Another World*, published in the last year of his life, demonstrated how highly he was regarded.

Several studies of Eden were published in his lifetime, of which the best was the relatively brief but sympathetic biography by Dr Sidney Aster, published in 1976. In 1981 Dr David Carlton published a very much longer biography that was, to my eyes, consistently and mystifyingly hostile to Eden throughout his career, and often unfairly so. Neither, of course, had access to Eden's own papers.

No biographer should embark on this very difficult task if he is an unqualified admirer of or implacably hostile to his subject. In my experience as a practitioner in this uniquely English aspect of literature and historiography I have invariably found that I have passed through various stages of attitude before reaching a balanced judgement on my subject. True political biography is not simply a record of a man's life. It is a portrait, which is only possible if there is a core of understanding and sympathy; that is not the same as adulation, which is as perilous a defect as hostility, and leads to equal distortions.

In order to present a fair portrait, the biographer must try to know everything, even though he may not publish everything. In Eden's case, I have, as Rosebery wrote of Churchill's biography of his father Lord Randolph Churchill, been 'threading a living crowd'. Many people closely involved in Eden's life – public and private – are alive; in other cases their close relatives are. So in dealing with relatively recent events I have had to use some discretion and tact without – unless wholly unwittingly – falsifying anything. If I have omitted some of Eden's comments on others, I have attempted to be fully objective about Eden himself. His own memoirs are, like all political memoirs, self-justificatory, but even in these the careful reader will notice more self-criticism than is customary, and this is even more evident in his drafts and 'Files For My Biographer'. Not many politicians describe a major speech of their own, as he did, as 'disastrous'.

The historian of modern times does not lack paper material, but politicians of the twentieth century do not write as many or as revealing letters as did their predecessors, and the telephone, which may be a boon for the transaction of political and official business, has been a lamentable innovation from the point of view of the political historian. Diaries are always of value, but as authentic records of what actually happened they should be handled with caution. And human memories are fallible.

Eden wanted a biography of himself to be written, and his personal and official papers are formidably substantial. With only brief intervals, he kept a daily diary from the age of twelve until shortly before his death; he seems to have kept virtually every letter he received, copies of his replies, and memoranda. His brother, Sir Timothy Eden, destroyed many of their mother's papers on her death in 1945, and Eden himself burnt some very personal letters at one point. But in both cases the destruction was far from complete and, so far as I can determine, did not include anything of public or political content. He was a tenacious holder of confidential official papers, as was Churchill. In my experience of political biography, only Lord Rosebery was a more assiduous retainer of documents or a more indefatigable diarist and note-taker.

When his widow, Lady Avon, asked me to undertake this task, a substantial part of her husband's papers had already been sent to the Library of Birmingham University, where they have been meticulously collated and catalogued under the supervision of Dr Benedikz and his colleagues, but a large amount remained at the Avons' house in Alvediston, Wiltshire. These were being examined and catalogued by Miss Serena Booker, who had been recommended to me by my friend Mr Alastair Horne, but the project was not only seriously delayed but most tragically shadowed by her murder in Thailand in September 1982. Her remarkable knowledge of, and feeling for, the political period of Eden's life, and her warm personality and enthusiasm, impressed all who knew her. Thus it is to her memory, with sadness and gratitude, that this biography is dedicated.

After her tragic death, her work was carried on with great skill by Mr Julian Jackson, now a Reader in History at Swansea University; I am very grateful to him. As I do not believe that research itself can be delegated, I have undertaken all of it myself. The burdens of an active political career and especially the concerns of Cambridge have meant that it has taken far longer than is usual. Our close friend, Mrs Gillie Coutts, has again done the bulk of the production of the final preparation with characteristic meticulous care, wonderfully assisted by my wife, my second daughter Emma, and my secretary Mrs Andrews.

My first and greatest debt is to Lady Avon for asking me to undertake this biography, for placing her husband's papers unreservedly at my disposal, and for many kindnesses, for which I am deeply grateful. I have also received assistance and papers from many others, particularly Nicholas, the second Earl of Avon, and Lord Eden, Anthony Eden's son and nephew respectively. Nicholas Avon was very kind to me, and generous both in allowing me to see and use family papers and in providing invaluable reminiscence and advice. It was a profound shock to his many friends and parliamentary and ministerial colleagues when he was compelled to retire from the Government in the spring of 1985 because of severe ill health, and his death on 17 August of the same year at the age of fifty-four deprived us of a good friend and a considerable public servant. He had felt the triumphs and misfortunes of his father's political career very deeply, and had begun to create his own career in politics when he fell grievously ill. He saw his father with a far greater clarity than is usual in such a relationship. I much admired his devotion to the memory of his mother – whose brother, Sir Martyn Beckett, has also been very helpful to me. So have a considerable number of former colleagues, officials and friends of Eden, but as they gave their help on the strict understanding that it would be in confidence I will not name them individually, but express to them collectively my most warm appreciation of their kindnesses and assistance.

I am particularly grateful to the Marquess of Salisbury for permitting me to quote from Eden's correspondence with his father, and to Sir John Colville and the Churchill Trustees for a similar kindness over Eden's correspondence with Sir Winston Churchill. As most of the documents in Eden's papers relating to the Suez crisis are covered by the 'thirty-year rule' relating to official papers, I have sought, and received, special permission to quote from them, for which I am most grateful. The Librarian of the House of Commons, Dr Menhennet, and the staff of the Library have been characteristically helpful at all stages of this project.

This, accordingly, is the portrait of a man. It has been my purpose that it be sympathetic, but not uncritical, and, above all, fair. I have no doubt that more documents not yet available for inspection or publication will be discovered and published about Eden's life and career, and that judgements may have to be amended in the light of these. There will be further, and different, assessments. This is in the nature of historiography. 'Definitive' biography is no more attainable than 'definitive' history, but when the biographer is dealing with events that are so recent, and on which the material is so large, this qualification is particularly necessary.

Robert Rhodes James

The Stone House
Great Gransden
Near Sandy
Bedfordshire

PART ONE

Morning

[1]

Childhood, 1897–1914

In his seventies Anthony Eden, by then the first Earl of Avon, was driving along the Great North Road, south of Rushyford in County Durham, when, on a whim, he decided to see Windlestone Hall, his family and childhood home, now sadly reduced by the exigencies and circumstances of the twentieth century to anonymous and institutional purposes. He had not seen it for forty years.

I turned in from the south up the drive to Windlestone. There it was, apparently intact; the roof whole, the windows glazed. Yet what had been spacious and elegant was now gaunt and vacantly lonely. The curved and squat outlines of some Nissen huts crowded up against the north front windows, and the lake had lost its limpidity under a green mask.

My eyes travelled sadly along the avenue that led to the chapel. Here was frank ruin. The building lay open to the sky with the family memorial plaques removed from the walls and taken to my brother's new home in the heaths of Hampshire. The avenue of yews down which I had so often walked was still intact; only as I peered I realized they were not yews at all but ilex trees.*

This visit was a mistake. Eden was dismayed and saddened by the spectacle of the wreckage of his family's creation and the now lost surroundings of beauty and drama that had provided the setting for his strangely starred childhood.

Anthony Eden never returned to Windlestone, but it is truly there that this account of his life and fortunes must begin.

The Eden family had been established in County Durham, in the district of Eden – consisting of the parish of Castle Eden and Little Eden – from which they drew their family name of De Eden, at least since the twelfth century, and in all probability earlier. Robert de Eden, who died in 1413, was 'the man from whom the present race of Edens is undoubtedly descended',† and became a significant owner of property in the County. John Eden, who died in 1588, further increased the family estates as a

---

* The Earl of Avon, *Another World, 1897–1917*, p. 11.
† Robert Allan Eden, *Some Historical Notes on the Eden Family*, p. 17.

3

result of a prosperous marriage, which included the purchase of the Windlestone estates.

All this was put to terrible hazard when Robert Eden, the eldest son aged twenty-one, joined the 1569 rebellion of the northern counties which had broken out under the leadership of the Catholic Earls of Westmorland and Northumberland. The death of Queen Mary, and the triumph of Protestantism, had been viewed with horror in the north of England. Westmorland and Northumberland, wrongly confident of Spanish and Scottish support, and with what appeared to be substántial numbers of eager volunteers, destroyed the odious bibles and prayer books in Durham Cathedral, and declared against Queen Elizabeth and for the Roman faith. The folly of the enterprise was that the Queen's cousin, Mary Queen of Scots, already in effect her captive, was strongly opposed to it, rightly calculating that it was deeply to her personal and political disadvantage. The rebellion was a fiasco, and the vengeance of Queen Elizabeth's servants was harsh. Lord Sussex, the Lord Lieutenant, had the rebel prisoners brought to Durham, where their fate was certain and swift. 'I gesse', Sussex wrote to Sir William Cecil, 'that it will not be under six or seven hundred at the least that shall be exequuted of the common sorte, besides the prisoners taken in the felde.' On one day eighty men of 'the meaner sorte' were hanged in Durham alone, and 233 elsewhere in the County. The 'prisoners taken in the felde' met a similar fate.

Fortunately for the Edens, Lord Sussex was averse to hanging men of stature like 'Robert Eden, of West Auckland, gentleman'. If it was a bad time to be a rebel and a Catholic, it was salvation to be rich. Thus money changed hands for the Royal Exchequer, and Robert Eden was released 'upon sufficient bonds' for his future good behaviour. His wife Jane, clearly also a person of Catholic spirit, was arraigned before the Ecclesiastical Court of Durham for indulging in Popish practices in the Church of St Helen's, Auckland; the charges levelled against her were grave indeed, but although the verdict of the Court has not survived, the fact that she was to outlive her husband fifteen years later demonstrates that she at least shared his capacity for survival.

This inclination to live dangerously was certainly inherited by their grandson, Robert Eden. When the Civil War opened, he at once declared for King Charles I and, with other Durham gentry, raised a regiment, in which he rose to colonel. His son John followed his steps and also commanded a regiment of foot for the King, a thousand strong, while his brother Gascoigne was a captain in a regiment of horse; indeed all the Eden adult males were actively involved on the King's side.

As in the case of the former Robert Eden, it was again the losing one. On this occasion, the penalties for being a Delinquent were disgrace and sequestration of estates, recoverable only on payment of a heavy fine. For Robert Eden, this was £132, calculated on the basis of a sixth of the annual value of his estate, reckoned at £800. Even this sum seems to have caused him difficulty; in November 1652 he appeared as one who had 'not compounded, or had not paid this compositions', and the trees of Windlestone were cut down and sold. Family tradition has it that Cromwell's soldiers inflicted this barbarity, although it is very possible that it was done by Robert Eden himself to meet the financial demands of the Protectorate.

But Eden's loyalty was to be rewarded. When King Charles II resumed the throne in 1660 he was one of the sixty-seven gentlemen of England and Wales deemed fit to receive the honour of becoming a Knight of the Royal Oak, but nothing more; there were seven such Knights – which did not carry a title with it – in County Durham, and the value of his estates was assessed at £1,000 in 1660, a very formidable sum at that time. He died in 1682, and was succeeded by John Eden. The great and expanding prosperity of the Edens, so closely jeopardized twice in a century, resumed its progress.

At some stage Barbara Villiers, Lady Castlemaine, later the Duchess of Cleveland, the most famous of the mistresses of King Charles II, mysteriously became involved in the Eden story. This can only have been with Robert Eden, eldest son of John, whose baronetcy in 1672 at the early age of twenty-eight, when his Cavalier father was still alive, was to seem inexplicable to the Reverend Robert Allan Eden, the earnest and scholarly family chronicler for, as he comments, 'at that early age Sir Robert, who had not as yet entered upon public life, could have done nothing to gain it for himself'. The key to this remarkable preferment may well have been Barbara, of whom Bishop Burnet justifiably wrote that she was 'always carrying on intrigues with other men, while yet pretending she was jealous of him [the King]'. Her most famous conquest, after the King, was John Churchill, the future Duke of Marlborough, but it would appear that another was Robert Eden, who was reading for the Bar in London and was called to the Middle Temple in 1670. His family was in high favour at Court, and he was then twenty-six years of age. If there is nothing in the family legend, why did he mysteriously receive high honours at such an early age? If the King wished to honour the Eden family, why confer the baronetcy on the son and not the father who had raised and led a regiment for the cause? And why did Barbara's portrait find its way into the possession of Sir Robert and the Eden family?

Anthony Eden disliked this portrait and was sceptical when told that she was an ancestress 'until many years later when, in the course of an official visit to Sweden ... I was presented with an elaborate genealogical table tracing my descent to a saintly early Swedish king. The connecting link, incongruously enough, was Barbara.'

Robert Eden was certainly fecund, his wife bearing him eight sons and seven daughters, but as his eldest son was born in 1677 the claim for Barbara Villiers being Anthony Eden's 'ancestress' looks somewhat threadbare, although a distinct mystery remains. It is certainly pleasant to reflect that the ancestors of Winston Churchill and Anthony Eden both enjoyed Barbara's favours. Robert Eden became Member of Parliament for the County in 1679, which he represented for six Parliaments until 1713. In that year he was succeeded by his son, John, who became, in 1721, the second baronet.

This Eden was clearly a lively parliamentarian, successfully taking on an outrageous Bill introduced in the Lords by the Bishop of Durham to transfer the rights in mines in the County to himself and his Dean and Chapter. The Bill passed the Lords, and Eden led the fight against it in the Commons. When it perished, Eden's already considerable local popularity soared, and his return home was a veritable triumph.

But it was his grandchildren who truly spread the fame of the Edens beyond County Durham and the House of Commons. Robert (1741–84) became Governor of Maryland and, being the second son, a baronet in his own right; William received an Irish and then an English peerage, with the title of Baron Auckland; Morton, the eighth son, entered diplomacy, rose to become an ambassador, and received an Irish peerage as Lord Henley. One of the three sisters of this remarkable generation married a future Archbishop of Canterbury, and another was Emily Eden, the authoress of *The Semi-Attached Couple* and of a diary of particular charm while she was assisting her brother in India when he was Governor-General. The parliamentary representation was continued, but not by the fifth baronet. Robert Johnson Eden (1774–1844), described as 'a shy man of retiring habits' who sold property at Preston-on-Tees which had been in the family's possession since the fourteenth century, pulled down the old house at Windlestone and built anew, to the designs of Bonomi.

This was to be the home of the Edens until, under infinitely sad circumstances, it was sold in 1936. It was laid out 'on a handsome plan, with extensive offices, and plantations'. Built on a commanding position on the brow of the hill, in yellow stone in the then-favoured classical style, the cost is unknown, but has been thought to be over £100,000. A descendant has given a portrait of Windlestone in the moonlight:

On the brow of a hill a long, low, porticoed house stood empty in the moonlight. A park, crossed by a silver chain of ponds and splashed here and there with inky shadows on its grey grass, swept up to a sunk fence where a close-cropped lawn fell away from the house to meet it. Behind the dull ochre mass of the building a further hill stretched upwards yet to a crest of wind-torn beeches.

This Eden, who never married, gave to his descendants a home of quiet dignity. The library was its finest room and was unaltered by his successors. For Sir Robert Johnson Eden, 'Building and books were his obsession. An only son, and his mother being an heiress, he could afford to indulge himself,' and Anthony Eden has recalled it thus:

On three sides of the room from floor to ceiling the walls were books, cut across three-quarters of the way up with a gallery with brass balustrading. The shelves had been let into the walls and divided by delicate mahogany pilasters. The only breaks in the vista of bindings were the mahogany door into the room from the East Hall, and a very fine eighteenth-century mantelpiece, presumably a survivor from the old house, in the west wall.

In the corner were several rows of skilfully designed dummy books, one above the other. In one of these rows a catch was concealed which the initiated could press to open a door on a small staircase which led to the gallery, giving easy access to the higher shelves.

The interior was to be further improved by more pictures and more books, and the gardens and the park by new plantings; but the house, and the rolling fields and trees that were its setting, were the creation of this modest, gentle, bibliophile Eden.

On his death, in 1844, all – baronetcy, estates and wealth – passed to his cousin Sir William Eden, grandson of Robert Eden, the first baronet of Maryland, who had acquired that position as the eventual result of a highly judicious, but none the less happy marriage to the daughter of Lord Baltimore in 1765 at the age of twenty-four. That family possessed the Lord Proprietary of the Province of Maryland, and exercised 'almost kingly' power there before the ungrateful American colonials were to bring this agreeable state of affairs to an abrupt end. Robert Eden, nominated and in effect appointed by the Baltimores, became Governor of Maryland in 1768, and in 1769 arrived with his wife and family at Annapolis to assume the position at an uncomfortable time for relations between the Colonies and the British Crown.

Maryland, however, did not share the discontent and rebelliousness of other provinces, and Eden was both popular and respected. But the tides of history were too strong even for a good governor and a relatively quiescent and loyal province, and in 1776 a British warship had to rescue him from the wrath of the revolutionary army after some dispatches to him had fallen into their hands. The Committee of Safety at Baltimore had been peremptorily ordered to seize their governor, but had adamantly refused. Even this remarkable action of personal loyalty could not obscure

7

the fact that the situation was menacing. He suffered the somewhat characteristic Eden fate of being on the losing side, although he received a baronetcy for his endeavours. His property in Maryland, which he had received on his marriage, was confiscated, and when he returned in 1784 to seek its restitution he succumbed to a severe fever.*

His brother William Eden (1744–1814) was the most successful of all – a Member of Parliament for Woodstock in Oxfordshire (whose last representative in that lively but compliant pocket borough, the virtual property of the Marlboroughs, was Lord Randolph Churchill), an effective ambassador and a member of the Younger Pitt's Government. Created Baron Auckland, his son George was also MP for Woodstock, and rose to become Cabinet Minister with the positions of President of the Board of Trade, First Lord of the Admiralty and Governor-General of India.

Meanwhile, Sir Frederick Eden, the grandson of Sir Robert, and the third baronet of Maryland, perished as a soldier at the age of sixteen in the siege of New Orleans in December 1814. And thus his brother William, at the age of eleven, succeeded him as fourth baronet and, in 1844, inherited the older baronetcy of West Auckland and the Windlestone estates.

Timothy Eden has painted a touching portrait of his grandfather Sir William, a traveller, scholar, linguist, artist, art-collector and romantic. But when this good and gentle man eventually came to Windlestone at the age of forty-one, resolved – newly married to Elfrida Iremonger – to be the best of fathers and most prudent of landowners, tragedy struck. In Timothy Eden's words:

So Sir William Eden lived his sober life as he had planned it, and had children and saved money for his children. But suddenly great trouble and sorrow came to him. One after another his children died. Within the space of a few years he lost two sons, including his heir, and four little girls – Elfrida, Rose, Blanche and Caroline.

The portraits of the girls still smile happily from the walls of their old home. They are extremely pretty children, with ringlets framing their pink cheeks, and all were painted out of doors, in little black shiny shoes, white socks, billowy skirts and large floppy hats. Elfrida, the eldest, sits on the ground beneath a large tree, her hands clasped demurely in her lap; Blanche, the smallest and the pudgiest, clutches a large bunch of blue grapes; Helen, the darkest, who lived to grow up and marry, trips across the grass with a bird in her fist and a long curling feather in her hat; Rose and Caroline are playing with a fawn.

Their father built a chapel for them in the grounds: no terrible affair of Victorian gothic, marbled and stained glass, such as might be supposed, considering the

---

* See B. Steiner, *Life and Administration of Sir Robert Eden*, for the most detailed account.

8

dangerous date, but a simple classical building of sandstone with a green copper dome. His taste was always restrained and correct.*

William Eden's anguish can be seen in the inscription on their tomb:

> Oh! not in cruelty, not in wrath
> The Reaper came that day;
> An angel visited the green earth
> And took the flowers away.

The grass withereth: the flower fadeth

'He lived for five years after this, still conscientiously performing his duties,' as his grandson Timothy wrote. 'Every afternoon at half-past two o'clock he mounted his grey pony and rode around the estate. He entertained his neighbours, though sparingly, subscribed generously to the restoration of his parish church, and went into the local town "to see about this accursed election business".' The deaths of his children, which had broken his spirit, also made him more irritable. In Timothy's account, he became

exasperated with the stupidity of his wife, a beautiful, God-fearing but stiff and narrow-minded woman. He was troubled, too, about the boys. The youngest [Charles] was sickly,† and William, now the eldest and in the army, was very hot-tempered and apt to be rude to his mother whenever he was at home. This was natural, but it could not be permitted. Moreover the boy had become engaged to a quite impossible girl – impossible, that is, in those days, for she would be more than welcome for her money in these – but 'That woman', said his father sternly, 'shall never sit in your mother's chair', and the engagement was broken. Altogether 'Dear Willy' was the source of much anxiety.

This tragic, 'very well-read man of refined and artistic tastes',‡ died suddenly on 21 October 1873. He was buried with his six children in his Windlestone Chapel; perhaps significantly, when his widow died in Bournemouth nine years later, she was buried there and not at Windlestone. The troublesome 'Dear Willy', aged twenty-four, succeeded him 'to carefully collected riches and a parsimoniously controlled estate'.

Sir William Eden certainly inherited his father's artistic interests and irritability, but had a far more volcanic temperament. Born in 1849,

---

* Timothy Eden, *The Tribulations of a Baronet*, pp. 9–10 (hereinafter referred to as *Tribulations*).

† He died in 1902 at the age of forty. One of his two surviving sisters, Helen, had died young in 1874.

‡ Robert Allan Eden, *Some Historical Notes on the Eden Family*, p. 46.

educated at Eton, as were virtually all Edens – and in his case, very unhappily – he thankfully entered the army in 1868, but retired in 1874 when he succeeded to the baronetcy and Windlestone. As Anthony Eden later wrote ruefully, 'William Eden had a comfortable income, but he liked to spend it.' Much of it was spent on the Windlestone estate and house, and a great deal on pictures and books. In Anthony's words: 'Nothing was stinted anywhere within or without the house, so that if there were no shortages, there were also no savings.'

Frustrated by his father's veto of his first choice of a wife, in 1886 he had married Sybil Frances, daughter of Sir William Grey. It is, alas, true that 'The Voice that Breath'd o'er Eden' was sung at their wedding at St Paul's, Knightsbridge, on 20 July 1886. She had wanted to marry Francis Knollys, the confidant of the Prince of Wales, but the Prince forbade it. This linkage with the family of the Great Reform Act of 1832, when Edens and Greys had stood together, must have appeared highly appropriate.

The new Lady Eden was certainly very beautiful, but she was also very strange in character, particularly about money matters. Her children, for reasons which will become only too clear, were very guarded in their references to her in their reminiscences. 'I suppose her way of life, her reactions and her behaviour would nowadays be considered eccentric,' Anthony was to write. 'Then they were quite conventional, and they were appreciated.' She swiftly achieved, and held to the end, the affection of the people of the County at all levels which nothing, not even scandal that shamed and troubled her children so deeply, seemed able to destroy. Years after her death Anthony would meet old people in County Durham who spoke with genuine warmth and gratitude of his mother's kindnesses. 'I think my mother preferred the simpler relationship which existed between donor and recipient to the more complicated one between mother and child,' Anthony was to record – no doubt truly, but with conspicuous coldness.

Lady Eden was justly famed for her beauty. 'Lady Eden is but little seen in London, but when in town is greatly admired,' enthused the Society reporter of *Woman* in 1893. 'It is left to her to be the almost sole remaining example of the pure Madonna type of loveliness, now so rarely seen.' The artist Henry Bacon declared that 'there is no more beautiful woman in all England,' and *Madame* extolled her virtues as one of the leaders of Society, 'this warm-hearted, kindly woman'.

Her generosity, also, became legendary, as contemporary local press reports reveal: 'Lady Eden is always busier than usual about this time distributing meats and warm clothing to all who need them'; 'Lady Eden has, this Christmas [1896], with her usual generosity, distributed a large amount of beef and plum puddings amongst the poor in Shildon, Coundon, and Merrington, as well as sending tea, tobacco, and toys to the Bishop Auckland Workhouse. There has also been a bullock killed and distributed among the workmen on the Windlestone estate.' She launched the appeal for a cottage hospital for miners in Bishop Auckland, to be called the Lady Eden Cottage Hospital, and made a generous donation. It was opened by her friend the former Liberal Prime Minister Lord Rosebery. She reorganized the Bishop Auckland branch of the Society for the Prevention of Cruelty to Children and demonstrated much concern for waifs and strays. Indeed, she was always making generous donations and, not surprisingly, was greatly loved in County Durham.

The trouble was that this fabled generosity rested on very slender financial foundations. Her husband was a generous man, and meanness was something he abhorred. Windlestone was run in style, with all profits put back into the estate, and he gave his wife a most generous allowance; but it was not generous enough for Lady Eden's very expensive personal tastes and her lavish gifts to others. The gifts of beef, for example, were never paid for. At some point, and it is impossible to know precisely when, she turned to moneylenders to meet her costs. They were delighted to respond, at dizzying and dreadful rates of interest. To repay them, she borrowed more, heedless that the interest rates had risen even further. The poor people of County Durham adored her; the avaricious and eager County Durham moneylenders hardly less so. It was a recipe for catastrophe, and catastrophe duly followed.

When the crash came in 1921, her counsel had to inform the King's Bench Court what had happened before 1914. Although she had had a personal allowance from Sir William Eden of £3,000 a year,

she had got into the web and was borrowing from one moneylender to pay off another. All these moneylenders were sharing each other's transactions and it was fairly plain that they were in close contact with each other and knew perfectly well what was going on. Lady Eden was sent from one to another. She was of no business capacity whatsoever, and had no business memory. She did not even remember the agreed terms upon which a loan was made.

This action, brought at the initiative of her children, resulted in an agreement that the lenders should return to the Windlestone estate all monies that Lady Eden had borrowed which had been in excess of 60 per cent interest per annum. From this disaster there was to be no recovery, in spite of valiant endeavours. By her profligacy and improvidence she was not only to destroy Windlestone but totally to alienate her children.

Anthony was born in the heady years of Windlestone in 1897. His christening was celebrated at Windlestone very lavishly and expensively by Lady Eden, 'the elite of the district being present' and three hundred other guests. For occasions such as this the baby Anthony, his brother Tim and Windlestone itself were to pay a terrible price.

William Eden was an extraordinary man, whose portrait has been drawn by both Timothy and Anthony, with great vividness in both cases, although Timothy's is the longer, more lyrical and more tender. Anthony was somewhat frightened and bewildered by him, while Tim was not. Some contemporaries and later critics have portrayed William Eden either as a madman, or as an eccentric with very enlightened and advanced tastes, or as an erratic tyrant cursing the world, explosive and incomprehensible. Although each element in such caricatures has justification, they do not provide the complete and true portrait. In Tim's words: 'While the love of art and the love of sport were coexistent and continual in his nature, with advancing years and intensified sensibility the delight in all things beautiful, the joy in artistic achievement, the raging sorrow for artistic decay, tended increasingly to prevail.' He quarrelled violently, and publicly, with Whistler over a portrait of Lady Eden, a dispute of much ferocity, which fascinated contemporaries and makes excellent reading; but the fact was that he was in the right on the matter. With many talents – indeed, quite exceptional ones – he achieved depressingly little, which was probably the true cause of his later tempestuousness and eventual resigned melancholy. But in Tim's words again: 'We are constantly regaled nowadays with the stories and memoirs of small men hitting bull's-eyes. Let us for a change, consider him who shoots a splendid arrow wildly at the skies.'

Both Timothy and Anthony have recorded memories of William Eden's outbursts that especially amused them. Tim recalled one day marked for shooting, with a house full of guests, pheasants waiting in the woods, keepers and beaters at the ready, but all plans destroyed by pouring rain. 'Oh God!' he exclaimed bitterly as he watched through the window the rain streaming from the sky, 'Oh God! How like You!'

Anthony's story has a similar theme:

My father had a fixed obsession that on any day when he wished especially for fine weather, the Almighty would send a downpour to vex him, much as Lord Salisbury, when Prime Minister, was convinced that bishops died to spite him. On this day the rain was true to tradition, beating down on hounds, huntsmen and loyal followers. As my father came through the front hall to join them, his eye fell on a barometer hanging on the panelled wall. He walked up to it and tapped; it read 'Set Fair'. He tapped again; it still replied 'Set Fair'. He took it off the wall, walked through the front door to the flight of steps and sent it clattering down before the assembled company, saying, 'Go and see for yourself, you damned fool!'

Tim had another favourite:

'Do we shoot hens, Willie?' called out one of the guns after he had reached his place in the line.

'Yes!' shouted back his host. 'Shoot hens! Shoot everything! Shoot the Holy Ghost if He comes out!'

A young neighbour of Sir William's was invited to lunch at Windlestone and arrived in justifiable trepidation. Sir William was charming, until at lunch the butler, House, wheeled in a covered trolley. When he lifted the cover to reveal a large and excellent loin of lamb, Sir William shouted, 'Not bloody lamb again!', seized it and threw it out of the window. House, who had evidently experienced this before, meekly wheeled out the empty trolley. The family and guests lunched off vegetables, while the young guest reflected that all he had heard of Sir William appeared to be well-founded.

The trouble was not that William Eden did anything indifferently, but that he did everything he attempted supremely well. Under his care and eye Windlestone became a house of rare beauty. He had 'created Windlestone, as only an artist could, as a personal harmony', Anthony was to write in grateful recollection

The Impressionists kept company with the Old Masters, the graceful Hepplewhite dining-room chairs might have been bought, but others had been rescued from a loft over the stable buildings to which they had been relegated in Victorian days, and the splendid William and Mary leather screen had been discovered above some cupboards in the old laundry.

And, as the house glowed with light and beauty, so did the garden and the park. Trees were cut down and others planted at carefully planned angles until they became one of the glories of Windlestone. The garden was soft, for William Eden hated harsh colours, and was scented with lavender, rosemary and sweet briar. He had inherited a beautiful house, but it, and its surroundings, were transformed by his eye, his ravaging search for beauty and perfection, and his constant vigilance.

As a magistrate, he had a reputation for administering robust, stiff, but fair justice from the Bench, not without comment.

A witness said complainant's own son kicked her. *Sir William Eden*: You can go, we don't believe you.

Thus reported the *Darlington Echo* of 17 August 1897. On 9 September the admiring *Auckland Chronicle* warmly approved a sentence of fourteen days in prison for hitting a child: 'Ill-usage of dumb creatures, women or children will find no apologist in Sir Wm Eden.' The *North Star* of 14 December 1897 recorded a wholly characteristic exchange:

Mr Proud, on behalf of the accused, David Morrow:

If I am prepared to call half of Shildon to show that the man was not drunk, surely that would have some weight on the Bench?

Sir William Eden: Call them.

Mr Proud: Well, I scarcely know what to do.

Sir William Eden: Well, call your witnesses. Call the whole of Shildon if you like. I will hear them.

Four witnesses were then called on behalf of the defence, each stating that in their opinion the defendant was sober.

The Bench imposed a fine of 7s 6d, including costs.

This was a regular imposition, and he was widely known as 'Old Seven and Sixpence' or 'The Bloody Baronet', but with affection, and he was by no means always on the side of the police.

He was also recognized as the best horseman in the County, if not in the entire North; on form, one of the best shots; and an amateur boxer of the first rank. He was himself, although an amateur, certainly a water-colourist of very high quality. Into everything he attempted, he hurled himself with almost demonic energy and success – but he did too much, and at too fierce a pace. He was full of paradoxes, with a kindness and shrewdness too often ruined by impatience, anger at contradiction and personal rudeness, unhappily mixed with a perilous susceptibility to flattery. Tim had faithfully catalogued his father's astonishing complexities with rare insight: 'Nature had showered upon him with an uncontrolled hand her gifts and her curses alike, and without control he received them all, and without control he expended them.'

Lady Eden bore five children. John, the eldest son and the heir, always known as Jack, was of sunny temperament and utterly untroubled by his father's vagaries. Marjorie, the eldest child and the only daughter, was Sir William's favourite and could do no wrong. Then came Tim, born in 1893; Robert Anthony, the subject of this biography, four years later, on 12 June 1897; and Nicholas, three years later.

There has been family conjecture whether Sir William Eden was in fact the father of Anthony. There is a certain element of mystery over this matter.

The history of 'The Souls', that group of men and women in the late 1880s and early 1890s, described by Consuelo, Duchess of Marlborough with some waspishness as 'A brilliant company, a select group in which a high degree of intelligence was to be found happily allied to aristocratic birth', has been often related and analysed. Its core was certain families – the Wyndhams, Charterises, Tennants, Custs, Windsors and Grenfells – but one of its strengths was that it was not exclusive, and was something more than a coterie. It first came together in the mid-1880s, with Lady Elcho (Mary Wyndham) and Mrs William Grenfell (later Lady Desborough) as the principal hostesses at Stanway and Taplow Court. The vivacious Tennant sisters, especially Margot, who was to marry Asquith, were the principal catalysts. A future prime minister, Arthur Balfour, was the acknowledged and revered leader; George Curzon, who possibly, although this is contested, actually coined the phrase 'The Souls', was the group's heroic figure, with Harry Cust and George Wyndham, once described as 'the handsomest man in England', and a rising literary and political star, as strong contenders.

Although the Souls were not promiscuous, they admired romance and passion. Curzon fell deeply in love with Sibell, the widow of Lord Grosvenor, and was plunged into gloom when she married George Wyndham; Wyndham's cousin Wilfrid Scawen Blunt competed closely with Harry Cust as a formidable seducer of beautiful women, and although Balfour's relationship with Lady Elcho may not have been physically sexual, it was certainly extremely close. For all their fervent protestations about the high-minded nature of the Souls – a nature which is undeniable – hedonism was certainly not excluded, and romantic letters and poems, whether or not fulfilled in practice as in spirit, much admired.

Frances, Countess of Warwick, who was later to reappear somewhat dramatically in Anthony Eden's life, spitefully commented that the Souls 'were more pagan than soulful'. She thereby touched a very real and sensitive point, which had particular relevance to George Wyndham, of whom it has been written that he 'seemed, at the beginning of his career, to possess more promise than is perhaps good for any man'. Margot Tennant described him as 'among the best-looking and most lovable of our friends', and he was widely admired for his looks, charm, excellent company, athleticism and sensitivity. His occasional writings were much admired, to modern eyes quite excessively, as Anthony Eden himself discovered when he tried to read them. After Eton and Sandhurst, Wyndham served in the Sudan Campaign with the Coldstream Guards, was elected to Parliament for Dover in 1889 and was Balfour's Private Secretary, confidant and protégé. He once described himself as 'an anarchistic barbarian, wallowing in the sixteenth century, hankering after the thirteenth, with a still ruder relish for the pagan horseflesh of the Sagas', which may be regarded as one of the odder self-portraits. Charles Whibley, his close friend and editor of Wyndham's *Essays in Romantic Literature*, wrote of him, with no greater clarity, as being 'by character and training a romantic. He looked with wonder upon the world as upon a fairyland.' But there was no question that he was rich, amusing and genuinely interested in literature, and it is not to be wondered that he was seen by so many as the coming man, nor that he was so fascinating to women, and his conquests so many.

Sir William Eden was a highly improbable associate of the Souls, being, for all his artistic interests, considerably too Bohemian, eccentric, outspoken and difficult for such gilded company. The fact that he also managed to live simultaneously and happily in the world of hunting, racing and shooting was not attractive to the Souls, who despised and reviled such occupations. Quiet intellectual conversation, and the give and take of courteous dialogue, were certainly not William Eden's strong suits.

But Sybil Eden, in contrast, was bewitched by the Souls, and hovered on their fringes. She had lost Francis Knollys, was bored by Windlestone, which was very much Sir William's domain, and was perplexed by her strange husband. In her unpublished memoirs, an extremely odd compilation of fragments, she wrote of her marriage and husband: 'While, with his turbulent spirit around, we could never live placidly, on the other hand we could never lie still or vegetate. And so we did have our days of unforgettable happiness.' But this palpable lack of enthusiasm is transformed when she writes of George Wyndham:

Among my dearest friends were the handsome and debonair George Wyndham and his wife Sibell Grosvenor. The former used to call me 'copper-head' because of the tints in my hair. I might call him my political god-father, for he it was who first interested me in politics and helped me with my feeble speeches and initiated me into the beauties of literature. He was a frequent and ever-welcome guest at Windlestone and one of Nicholas's godfathers.

George Wyndham was a great personality with the soul of a poet. I don't think there has ever been anyone in the world quite like him – such good looks, such vitality, such imagination, and so generous a disposition. I think he even saw politics with the eye of an artist, and politics broke his heart. I always wished he had abandoned politics and given his life to literature. The world would have been the richer and the better, for he spent himself with such lavish prodigality.

I feel we were greatly privileged in having him as a friend. I used to love it when he stayed at Windlestone or when he asked us to little quiet dinners to his home in London, and after dinner read aloud to us in his beautiful voice extracts from Shakespeare's sonnets or from his book on Ronsard. Those were golden moments in my life.

The concept of Sir William listening patiently while Wyndham recited Shakespeare or read extracts from his tedious essay on Ronsard is not an easy one to accept, and some unknown hand has excised the last paragraph from Lady Eden's forlorn endeavour at autobiography; in the margin is her unmistakable handwriting, 'Why has this been scratched out?'

As always, Tim Eden expressed the difficulty about his father perfectly:

He was a true and loyal friend, a shrewd adviser with a knowledge of the world, a man largely capable of sympathy and love, and sadly needing it; but his uncontrolled rages terrified and drove away an approaching friendship as a bird is scared to a distant branch. His intolerance of the opinions of others not only hurt their natural vanity but ·made any reasonable discussion impossible. His personal and direct rudeness was offensive to the most patient. His constant and exaggerated irritation with the minor details of life, and the volcanic expression which he gave to his acute suffering from incidental noises, sights and smells – mere nothings which the normal man passes over unnoticed – though amusing at first, become quickly wearisome, if not alarming. . . . Thus any friendly intercourse with him, though brightened with unique and delightful compensations, could never be reposeful. It was bound to be a guardedly attempted, difficult, dangerous and exciting experiment. . . .

Perhaps above all things he was simply, profoundly, and thoroughly egotistical, with the natural, guileless and uncontrolled egotism of a child, and, like all egotists, he was incapable of tolerance for the slightest symptoms of the same disease in others.

Thus a less probable additional member of the Souls is difficult to conceive; his wife was a different matter.

After his mother's death in 1945, Tim conducted an indiscriminate and perhaps unfortunate destruction of her papers, but some fragments from George Wyndham survive. There is a letter to 'Dearest Sybil' in which he writes: 'Even a scolding from you is better than nothing! What I want is a sight of your face. My dear, I had not one minute of time to dispose of as I pleased. . . .' And there is a poem dedicated to her, and written for her:

> Because I love, and death threatens, but I shall never
> Take into darkness my adored,
> I will build a city that shall last for ever,
> And fight for it with my sword.
>
> Youth soon grows old; life lags for death to end it;
> Love only is beautiful and still new:
> I will cradle it in store and set steel to defend it,
> And forget fear and be true.

'He had a faultless instinct for the best in poetry,' Lady Eden rhapsodized, on somewhat dubious foundations if we may judge by this endeavour: 'Love and beauty were so evident in every phrase and aspect of his life; they breathed through all he did. . . . He was a soul from another world.'

It would be very foolish indeed to assume from fragments of an artless attempt at autobiography many years later, and one surviving poem and one letter, that Wyndham and Sybil Eden were lovers in 1896. If the Windlestone visitors' book is an accurate guide, Wyndham was not at all a regular visitor. It is true that Sybil Eden was beginning the process that was to cause her family such public and private shame by feckless borrowing from eager moneylenders at appalling rates of interest, and there is no doubt that the Eden marriage had proved disappointing to both partners by this point. She certainly spent much time in London in 1896, the public explanation being 'a severe operation' in June, about which no other information has survived. Also, it is true that Anthony was physically wholly unlike his brothers and sister. 'He is a Grey, not an Eden,' Sir William remarked, in Anthony's hearing. As he grew up, his physical resemblance to the young George Wyndham, and the similarity in their voices, was so extraordinary that belief that he was Wyndham's son grew.

On such matters it is impossible to be absolutely certain, but Anthony Eden himself, when he learned of the persistent rumours, did not discount them completely; indeed, he found them both amusing and interesting. But he did not really believe them. His mother had a reputation not only for astounding financial ineptitude and irresponsibility but also for flirtatiousness and fantasizing, and he doubted whether anything more was involved. He certainly knew of his mother's deep feelings for Wyndham, but doubted whether they were returned. At Wyndham's death in 1913, when Anthony was sixteen, he wrote to Lady Eden from Eton that 'I was afraid George Wyndham's death would be a dreadful shock to you – it certainly does seem a great shame. There is a good notice of him in the [Eton] Chronicle which I will send you.' Wyndham was Nicholas Eden's godfather, which demonstrates nothing more than friendship, but it is interesting to find Anthony on the Western Front in 1918 carefully reading a biography of Wyndham.

That Sybil Eden was infatuated by Wyndham is beyond doubt. But so were many others. The extravagant hopes placed in Wyndham's political fortunes were to be most cruelly disappointed. Torn, as he always had been, between literature and art on the one side of his ambitions, and politics and power on the other, he became overwhelmed with dark pessimism. Lady Plymouth became more important to him than his wife, and it was with her, in Paris, that he died in June 1913, 'not yet fifty, exhausted by drink and disappointment'.*

But if he was the father of Anthony Eden, which is far from being impossible, what is incontestable is that Wyndham had no influence whatever on Anthony's childhood and development, whereas Sir William Eden, in his very strange way, certainly did.

Although Anthony came to dread Sir William's infrequent visits to him at Eton, and was always relieved when he was away from Windlestone and

---

* Max Egremont, *Balfour*, p. 225.

life could assume some normality, he admired his qualities as an artist, landscape gardener, countryman and scholar, and, although frightened of him and his variable moods and temper, loved him. Sir William Eden was not a man who invited neutral opinions; for all Anthony's apprehensions of him ('How I *hated* his visits to me at school,' he told Robert Carr years later), his view was very positive. He saw the qualities and accepted the defects, whereas too many others took exactly the opposite view. For his mother he was to develop emotions not far removed from hatred, and she never occupied a place in his heart and affections remotely comparable to that which Sir William did. George Wyndham was a very distant shadow compared to Sir William in Eden's childhood and early manhood.

Anthony Eden grew up at Windlestone, surrounded by so much that was beautiful, with brothers and a sister he loved, yet in a loneliness which is very evident in his own records, and in his subsequent recollections. It is very possible to be solitary and yet happy, and if it is possible to summarize an existence so simply, this is clearly a fair portrait of Anthony Eden's childhood. 'I was very fond of Windlestone,' he has written. 'As I knew it would never be mine, my affection was not possessive. I loved its spaciousness and the knowledge that within it I could find beauty, reading and entertainment for any mood.'

When he was three there was a financial setback after it was discovered that Sir William's agent had absconded, leaving many unpaid bills and much complication. Sir William resolved to deal with the matter himself and, characteristically, dispatched his entire family and the appropriate retinue of servants to Europe. Anthony later vividly recalled their stays in Nice, Paris-Plage and Dresden. The children, including Anthony, were taught French and German, and the lessons continued when the family was recalled to Windlestone. This precocious introduction to languages was to be one of the greatest boons his otherwise odd parents could have given him. Then there came an English governess and tutor, a Miss Bromhead, always known in the family as 'Doodles', who stayed with the Edens for thirty years. He learned to ride and to shoot, revered Jack from a distance, adored Marjorie, and was closest to 'little Nicholas'. Although his parents were distant beings, he gradually realized the importance of pictures, books, trees and flowers. Sir William never bullied his children into appreciating these things; indeed, apart from Marjorie, he was not much interested in his children. He simply provided beauty because it was his passion, and although they all loved Windlestone, it was Anthony who was the most receptive to the treasures put before him, particularly the pictures which Sir William collected with remarkable discernment. It was from him that Anthony developed his eye for pictures and his lifelong fascination with art and artists, although he never was in the same class as Sir William as an artist. If it was a highly unconventional childhood, it was a deeply happy one.

In the account he wrote of Windlestone life when he was old, Anthony Eden has recaptured that life perfectly. The riding, the shooting and the pleasures of a substantial estate and of the personalities of those who served the family were conventional enough for a child of his class in those days; what were not conventional were the books, the paintings, the evenings of boxing at Windlestone, or the welcome visits of the most famous champion of the time, 'Bombardier' Billy Wells, of whom Sir William had been an early promoter. Wells contrasts with other welcome visitors who included the actress Mrs Pat Campbell, Walter Sickert, George Moore, Max Beerbohm and, occasionally, George Wyndham. Amateur dramatics were encouraged, and the children staged their own performances, both at Windlestone and in the local village hall. For all the strangeness and irrationality of Sir William, which particularly bewildered and often frightened Anthony and Nicholas, it was a remarkably civilized and balanced upbringing.

Sir William, above all, had no trace of snobbishness or condescension. His care and friendship for everyone who worked for him were genuine, and they knew it, just as they knew that his frequent wild rages were equally genuine. His rudeness was usually reserved for people of his own class, who could answer back – and often did. Sir William's headlong progress was thus marked by many broken friendships. 'I still go on', he once wrote, 'loving my enemies and abusing my friends' (to one he once wrote, 'You are lucky to have 15 friends – I wish I had 5'), but to those who were his faithful servants he showed another side. To one, who had retired, he wrote:

Buck up, Walker!

I am so glad you are better. We can't spare you yet. We must both jump into the bottomless pit together.

His few letters to his children were similarly brief and to the point. This, to Nicholas:

My dear little Nicholas

You treat me very badly. Poor Daddie!

You never even wrote to thank me for the rabbits. Have they choked you, or what?

How are you dear boy? Well & happy?

Yr devoted
Daddie

When he heard that Anthony was unhappy at school, there came this:

My dear old Anthony,
    Be not downcast, oh my soul! Hope thou in the Lord! You are not a waster,
thank God. You may yet be as great and good a man as

                                        Your affectionate
                                            Daddie.

Then, although he was a Conservative, and a strongly pro-Joseph
Chamberlain Protectionist one at that, with a deep distrust of foreigners,
he had a healthy suspicion of most politicians. He chaired the local Conservative Association with gusto and with no nonsense about democracy.
But, even in this sphere, he was idiosyncratic and his own man. Unlike
other Conservatives of the time – including Balfour and Wyndham – he
had no fears about the uprising of The Masses against his own world, and
was genuinely more at home with his workers and servants than with his
very rich neighbours, many of whom owed their vast wealth to the brutal
exploitation of the Durham minefields.
    When shown Sir William's pictures, including what Eden proudly called
'my own immaculate Degas' – this was Degas' *Washerwoman*, which hung
over his desk between a Corot and a Mark Fisher – one of these neighbours,
Lord Londonderry, muttered, 'You know, something ought to be done
about it. Willie actually gave good money for these things.' William Eden
was tolerated in County Durham for his enlightened management of his
estates and his brilliance in the hunting field and as a shot; his artistic
enthusiasms were a matter of bewilderment and incomprehension to the
County magnates, while Eden considered that he lived among barbarians.
This did not lead to close friendships. He had no time whatever for religion,
was a convinced atheist, thought consistently ill of God, and was not a
conspicuous figure in local religious circles.
    As Tim and Anthony and Nicholas well knew, Sir William 'could not
endure, for long, even the presence of his own children. He had not the
patience to suffer their moods and tears. He was incapable of placing his
intellect on a level with theirs. Their casual irresponsibility irritated him'
(Marjorie being the great exception). What he actually gave them was an
incomparable setting for their talents. 'Undoubtedly they were right who
said that he was not a fit companion for children, and he realized it himself,'
Tim has written.

Whenever the holidays returned, he fled from his house like a hunted deer, and
not chiefly from his children, but from all the paraphernalia of children – tutors
and their pipes, tennis-parties, Christmas trees, 'the babe of Bethlehem and all
that!' . . . But he was fond of his family. They could cause him intense unhappiness,
throw him into unreasoning rages, but they were never indifferent to him. He gave
them the best of everything – education, food, clothes, shooting, ponies. Though

he often expostulated, he never seriously grudged even extravagance on their behalf.*

Jack was the outdoors son, uninterested in the other glories of Windlestone; the festivities for his coming-of-age in 1911 lasted for three days of lavish celebration, and he then disappeared into the cavalry. The lovely Marjorie married young, to Lord Brooke (Guy), when Anthony was ten. Then Tim went first to preparatory school at Sandroyd, thence to Eton, almost, although not quite, as extrovert as Jack.

The outstanding beneficiary of the Windlestone world was Anthony. It took an exceptionally sensitive and nervous little boy into the realms of art, literature, languages and the joys of the English countryside at an early age, with enduring consequences. He was brought up in a home in which class distinction and snobbery were unknown, in which the sense of service to the community was exceptionally strong, and in which outspokenness and the strong expression of views were admired. 'It all seemed so permanent,' he later wrote wistfully of his childhood. And so it seemed to all of them. He was certainly not to know that it was only by chance that he did not himself inherit Windlestone.

One aspect of Anthony Eden's character which those who knew him best appreciated the most was his kindness, which was evident as a child. When he was seventy-eight, he received this letter from May, a former kitchen maid at Windlestone:

Dear Sir Anthony
I have followed your life quite a lot and I have just read of your loss of your cattle and thought I would like to say I am sorry. You will never remember me as your life has been very full and eventfull, but I am the young girl you were extremely kind to in your lovely mother's home, many years ago.
It was a time of great stress to me as I had left home to be able to earn a living and except for the kindness and compassion I received after my near disaster when there was so much distress for me at the hands of Lady Eden's cook. I would just like to say your kind words and gentle manner to me when I was able to return and help in the house, away from the kitchen, has played a big part in my life.
I am almost 70 years old, but you were my hero always....

In one of his very few subsequent references to his formal education, Anthony Eden wrote, 'I never pretended to like school and my years there were far from the happiest of my life.' His first school was the South Kensington Preparatory School in Rosary Gardens, off the Old Brompton Road. The headmaster regarded Anthony, at the age of five, as 'very

* Timothy Eden, *Tribulations*, p. 45 and pp. 46–7.

interested and bright'. It was a very small school, with sixty boys. This was followed by Sandroyd School in Cobham, where he was reasonably happy and successful, and where his headmaster wrote of him to Lady Eden: 'He is rather young for his years still & wants more determination to go his own way. He has begun to develop in this way. His soft heart balanced by a little more grit & energy will make a strong as well as a loveable character of him.'

His own letters from Sandroyd were characteristic of somewhat bored boys incarcerated at an early age in a boarding school and longing for the holidays. Thus, 10 April 1910:

Dear Mummie,
    Hoorah, Hurrah, Hurrah !!!!!!!! only 3 more days. Hurrah !!!!!!!!!!!!!!!!!!! It is a horrid day to-day. There is absolutely no news.

> Your beloved,
> Anthony

Another may suffice:

We had a concert last night it was very interesting. Mr Langdon was very good and sung some very funny songs.
    We played a match last Saturday which was most disastrous to us we *lost* 3–1 it is the first match we have lost this season.
    We had some fireworks on Friday November 5th, they were awfully good there were some rockets and several other things

Inspired by their uniforms while watching the Royal Military Tournament, Anthony had declared his ambition to join the Royal Horse Artillery and seek a military career; Cheltenham was deemed the most suitable school for an aspiring gunner. This absurd idea for a boy with poor eyesight and with intellectual tastes was roundly denounced by Tim, who was enjoying himself at Eton and campaigned vigorously for Anthony to join him. At the right moment his House tutor, Ernest Lee Churchill – inexplicably known as 'Jelly' to the boys – provided a vacancy, and in 1911 it was decided that Eton was infinitely more appropriate. 'For this conclusion I am grateful in retrospect,' he later wrote; 'the independence and freedom of choice which Eton encouraged were some compensation [for school life]. I preferred Greek to Latin and French to either, while rowing and sculling on the river were a constant enjoyment.'

But Eton notably failed to make that enduring impression, amounting almost to love, that it has inspired so often in others. This was at least partly because so many of his few real friends, as at South Kensington and

Sandroyd,* were to be killed so soon; many memories therefore became painful. But his letters home and his diaries, which he began to keep in earnest in 1912, reveal both his dislike of the sheer tedium of school life in contrast with the joys of Windlestone and a strong interest in politics.† This admixture is best illustrated by representative entries:

11 January 1913: Home Rule Bill passed by House of Commons.

27 January: Awfully hard to keep a diary at school because it is always the same every day. There is nothing to say to-day.

29 January: This half is going quite quickly, but I wish it would go quicker still. I am simply longing for next holidays.

30 January: Home Rule Bill rejected by House of Lords by a huge majority.

28 April [Windlestone]: Time approaches shall soon have to go back to that Hell.

30 April [Eton]: Back again, alas! to thirteen weeks of pining, slavery, & misery.

13 September [Eton]: Perfectly foul being back after 8 weeks' holidays which have simply fled.

8 November: Reading [by-election] result declared. Perfectly splendid; coupled with West Lothian it should prove a smashing blow to the Radicals.

9 January 1914: Mr [Joseph] Chamberlain retired from West Birmingham. The greatest Imperialist has therefore retired entirely from public life although he has not taken an active part in politics for some years now. He was the last great figure in English politics – there is now no one left deserving the name of 'great'.

The doctor's report noted that Anthony was 'A healthy well nourished boy of good physique. He is inclined to hold himself badly and to be round shouldered. The teeth are, I understand, having the necessary attention. The vision is very defective, due to an error of refraction.'

E. L. Churchill was an admirable and sympathetic tutor, and his reports to Lady Eden provide the best portraits we have. In July 1912 he wrote:

* In the 1914–18 War, seventy-two Sandroyd boys, almost all contemporaries of Eden, and including his brother Nicholas, were killed in action or died of wounds. In the case of the South Kensington Preparatory School, by the end of 1917 it had lost sixty boys killed, and had won eleven DSOs and twenty-five MCs. The Eton losses in boys killed in 1914–18 was 1,157. There are no figures for those wounded. These cold statistics may give some impression of what the 1914–18 War meant to that generation. Out of twenty-eight boys in the Eton Middle Fourth in 1914, of whom Eden was one, nine were to be killed, including a particularly close friend, L. N. Kindersley.

† 'The counting of the votes in a parliamentary election is my first political memory,' he wrote in the early 1960s. 'This was in 1910 at Bishop Auckland and I was twelve years old. The two principal candidates, Liberal and Unionist, walked white-faced round the tables as the ballot papers mounted up. The Liberal won with a fair majority, the third candidate, who was Labour, being a long way behind. As we stood on the balcony where the results were announced, I heard him declare: "One day Labour will win." Incredulous we were, but he was right.' (Avon, *The Reckoning*, p. 3.) At Sandroyd he stood as Conservative candidate in the school elections – successfully.

'So at present he is at any rate a son of whom you may be quite proud. Of course he will not get through life without giving us some anxiety. But for the moment I veritably think there is no cause for any at all & a great deal of cause for satisfaction with him.' But in December 1912 he was reporting that 'his work is spoilt by careless mistakes', that he was highly critical of Eden's 'inattention, untidiness, and forgetfulness' and 'his tantrums', but he also cited the verdict of Anthony's French tutor, Charles Gladstone, that 'He is keen & intelligent & it has been very pleasant working with him.' In April 1913 Churchill was still critical of Anthony's 'fits of inattention & slackness', but went on:

He is a nice bright, intelligent fellow, with much that is very likeable about him in all sorts of ways. You need be under no doubt that he is all right in serious matters. But he is rather volatile in disposition, & has to solidify his character. But he is so sweet tempered & pleasant in all his relations with me that it is not hard to get as much out of him as I think fit.

In July 1913, Churchill reported to Lady Eden:

He has quite ceased to be petulant or childish, & is getting much more thoughtful & steady. As I have said before, he is a very good boy, & I like him. His weakness was – I am not at all sure that it is fair to say is – a certain heedlessness & lack of restraint. That seems to be becoming a thing of the past, & I hope you no longer find him in any way difficult to manage in the holidays, & that he has grown out of the 'tantrums' of which he used to give exhibitions from time to time at home.

Anthony was certainly a highly strung boy; Lady Eden had written to him while he was at Sandroyd, 'Darling little boy, I want you to keep watch over your tongue. It runs away with you & will be getting you into trouble if you are not careful.' Now, in December 1913, Churchill was reporting that 'what he wants above all things is discipline. He has not yet entirely controlled his temper, though much better in this respect than he was.' So concerned was Churchill at this aspect of Anthony's personality that he believed that the boy should be threatened with having to leave Eton if he failed to pass his School Certificate examinations, as

Some such incentive he wants now rather badly.... I have tried to impress on him that it is his duty to live for others rather than for himself. It is a lesson that does not come very easy to him. But I am not without hopes that the idea has got well into his head & will bear fruit. But much depends on his having to exercise a good deal of self-restraint in the coming year or two.

It must have been very difficult being an Eden son and at a school he disliked, although he never hated it as much as some of his letters and diaries might convey. He was simply indifferent to Eton, and his poor eyesight precluded him from gaining eminence at any sport in a House that was exceptional in its sporting achievements. But at this time he was moderately successful at rowing, and certainly very promising. The occasional visit of Sir William Eden did not assist matters. He received one on 7 December 1912:

We walked up the street and he stood and cursed the [Queen Victoria] Memorial at the top of his voice. Then he came to my room and had a look at it & then we went to the Chapel, which he did not like, and then thank heaven he went away. While in my rooms he loudly abused Ashley for being drunk or something.

In November 1912 there was a tremendous family dispute between Sir William and his brother-in-law Robin Grey. The latter, a Free Trade Conservative, wanted the Conservative nomination for a County Durham constituency; Sir William, the arch-Protectionist, was determined to deny it to him. Anthony took his uncle's side, describing his father as 'stupid and obstinate', and was delighted when Grey's cause prospered: 'I am *so* glad that the old man got ragged. He will be an utter fool if he goes on opposing Robin now because everyone is against him.' This was evidently a very major family row if it involved the active participation of a boy of fifteen, but his letters and diaries only really come to life when politics were discussed. 'I wonder if we shall win Bolton? I think not, because the Radical is a local man and very popular, though a shocking speaker; but I think we are practically certain to win Bow and Bromley.' He rejoiced at the downfall of the Liberal, Charles Masterman, wrote to his mother (29 May 1913), 'Aren't the by-elections *splendid*?', and abhorred Asquith, Lloyd George and Winston Churchill – especially Churchill. He startled his mother on a train journey to the North by giving her full and accurate information from memory of the Members of Parliament of every place they passed, with their exact majorities. His subsequent disclaimers of much interest in politics until the early 1920s are emphatically refuted by his childhood letters and diaries.

His vehement support for Robin Grey had a strong, and very interesting, personal element. Here was a dashing romantic – very good-looking, and, as Anthony admiringly noted in later years, 'he had also been something of a rolling stone, his activities ranging from growing oranges in Florida, which failed, to an admiration for Dame Nellie Melba, reputedly more successful'. What a splendid Member of Parliament he would have made! But when the nation next went to the polls he had been a prisoner of war for four years and Sir William was dead; their intense and futile feud belongs simply to the fading records of this extraordinary family.

Now even Windlestone became more remote to Anthony. Sir William's London peregrinations had ended in Duke Street, where the house adjoined the Cavendish Hotel, in which the famous Mrs Rosa Lewis reigned. Her robust and Bohemian attitude to life, her many loves and immense kindness of heart had a great appeal to Sir William, and he had a door driven through the wall so that he could dine quietly there. Subsequently he moved into a ground-floor room which looked on to a small courtyard and was known thereafter, until the hotel was demolished after the Second World War, as 'Sir William Eden's Room'. His future daughter-in-law was shown it many years later. It had been kept as it had been in Sir William's time, and she was struck by its melancholy seediness. Lady Eden established herself in a house in Sussex, near Battle, where most family holidays were now spent.

It was obvious that Sir William was fading with heart weakness, but family controversies remained fierce. There was a stormy meeting between him and Jack over the latter's allowance – as Jack had inherited his mother's relaxed view on matters financial – and an even more serious controversy over his fiancée, Pamela Fitzgerald, which engagement Sir William vehemently opposed. This matter was not resolved when August 1914 intervened. Perhaps most grave of all was when Jack, a cavalry officer, threatened to refuse orders to act against Ulster units in the deteriorating situation in Ireland and to send in his papers. In this he was not alone, but Sir William was incensed and threatened to disinherit him totally. Anthony, who revered Jack, took his brother's side. Years later, recalling the incident in the margin of Winston Churchill's *Great Contemporaries*, he noted that he now realized that Sir William had been absolutely right on this matter. 'I was then 16 & surprised at his violence. Now I should endorse it.'

The summer of 1914 also remained etched in Anthony's memory. He was now a member of 'Pop', the Eton Society, and an active debater of some merit and effectiveness, the details carefully recorded. He was increasingly enthusiastic and successful on the river and his House boat rowed at Henley. Churchill reported sadly in July that all Anthony's masters' reports were favourable, but his examination results were consistently 'all bad'.

In Pupil-room he has seemed to me to be just as usual, working quite well & distinctly intelligent without being brilliant, or nearly so; my own idea is that he is going on nicely, has had his mind fixed more on rowing than on Latin or Greek, perhaps: but deserves a good report.

It was an especially beautiful summer. The Conservatives won the Ipswich by-election ('Splendid victory', Anthony exulted in his diary). He was a member of the Eton College Officers' Training Corps, due to hold its annual camp in July, but of far greater importance were the river, and the Eton and Harrow cricket match. 'It all seemed gaiety, sunshine, and good food,' he later wrote nostalgically. There was what he described as 'a proud but fearsome' lunch with Jack at the Cavalry Club:

Jack was very much my hero but I was intimidated by his altered and dashing appearance which included a new moustache and a monocle. I was also over-awed by the large club room and the many friends who came up to ask about regimental polo prospects for that weekend, to the point when my words hardly come at all. I suspect that we were both relieved when the time came to pay the bill and leave in his Austro-Daimler for Lord's.*

On 14 July Anthony's diary recorded: 'Have forgotten who preached – some weird Bishop or other. Did last Sunday Questions on the half. Rather long & boring. Murder of Austrian Archduke has caused rather a sensation & has angered the Austrians against Serbia who are supposed to have arranged the murder.' He later wrote of his family that 'without being in any sense Jingo we were very much aware of the growing menace of war' in 1914, and the campaign for military conscription waged by the aged Field Marshal Lord Roberts was often discussed. Jack was a professional soldier in the Twelfth Lancers, Uncle Robin Grey was a dashing pilot in the Royal Flying Corps – altogether appropriately – and Nicholas was about to go to Dartmouth to begin his chosen career in the Navy. Anthony was preparing for the Eton Officers Training Corps annual camp and manoeuvres. But so few believed that war would actually occur that Tim, studying for the Diplomatic Service and improving his knowledge of the language in Germany, was not summoned home.

The diaries resume, this time in camp. Although the talk was of war and the European crisis, the platoon commander dismissed them.

23 July: Austrian Note presented to Serbia with 2 days' time-limit. Most humiliating terms asked.
24 July: Sir Edward Grey suggests mediation by four Powers and asks for extension of time limit. Things looking rather black.
25 July: It looks like a European war.

The entries now become more detailed and concerned. 'Looks very bellicose! ... Ranger & I wandered about trying to secure latest war news.... Rumours of war between Russia & Germany – if so we are in for it alright.'

And so it was to be. He returned to Battle to find that his mother was in London seeking news about Tim, 'who is unfortunately caught in Germany'. As it happened, this almost certainly saved his life; at the time, his internment seemed, to himself and to his family, an appalling disaster. The first blow of war had fallen on the Eden family. It was the end of childhood.

* Avon, *Another World, 1897–1917*, p. 51.

[2]

Education by War, 1914–19

For the biographer, speculation on how matters might have been different is one of the most perilous of indulgences. As Winston Churchill wrote of the Gallipoli Campaign, 'The terrible "ifs" accumulate.' It is, therefore, fruitless to speculate how the life and personality of Anthony Eden would have developed if the Great War had not occurred, that cataclysm which devastated Europe, slaughtered millions of its young men, and destroyed the world and family in which he had been brought up and which had seemed to him so permanent, so unchanging and unchangeable. The facts are that it not only totally transformed his own personal world, but left permanent and crucial marks on his character which were never eradicated. It represented his true education.

The beginning of the Great War on 4 August 1914 – which, an Eton master confidently told Anthony Eden, would last only a few days – found the Eden family, with the exception of Anthony, actively involved in various ways. Jack's cavalry regiment was part of the British Expeditionary Force sent to France; Guy Brooke was in the Warwickshire Royal Horse Artillery, which he had formerly commanded, and Marjorie became a nurse; Nicholas was at Dartmouth, unhappy, but eager for his chance to go to sea; Lady Eden was developing plans for turning Windlestone into a wartime hospital; Tim was languishing in a German internment camp; Uncle Robin Grey, flying what to Anthony seemed terrifyingly fragile aircraft, was in France with the Royal Flying Corps and soon in action.

Anthony Eden was too young to join the Army, and in any event his eyesight precluded him even from applying for Sandhurst. He consulted E. L. Churchill about what he should do, and then wrote to his mother:

M'tutor told us the other night that the best we could do was to go on with our work & games the same as usual for another year & then if the war is still going on, which he said he thought was quite probable, we could offer our services. That seems to me to be the best plan – what do you think?

Sir William Eden was now fading fast. Anthony later wrote:

I liked to be alone with my father. He would then usually treat me as an equal, rather than embarrass me as a witness or butt. However, my last visit to

Windlestone in his lifetime was a tragic experience. There were no guests in the house, nor children, and I had never known it without both. It was the early autumn of 1914, the rooms and the passages were hushed and sombre as though someone were dead in the house already, my father hating noise.... My father was himself by this time scarcely mobile, a wheel-chair in the house and a bath-chair in the garden was the best he could do. At times his thoughts wandered, but more often he was mentally alert and very good company....

The days of my last visit to Windlestone in my father's lifetime were soon gone, as is the way with holidays when one is young. I saw him alive only once or twice more, in his last illness in London in the following February. He told Nicholas and me, the 'little boys' as he still called us, that we could have his guns: 'I shall not need them any more.' I only heard him express regret once, that he could no longer hold a brush to the paper. His eyes saddened and he looked towards us, but without seeing us any longer.*

On 18 October Eden wrote in his diary, 'Uncle Robin is missing.' His flimsy aircraft had been shot down, but he had crashed without serious injury behind the German lines and been taken prisoner. He was to prove a lively guest of the Kaiser. After many attempts he succeeded in escaping and had almost reached the Dutch border when he was caught. The Germans, on the grounds that he was both a difficult customer and a cousin of Sir Edward Grey, placed him in solitary confinement. The Edens were proud of him. Then, on 20 October, Anthony wrote in his diary:

M'tutor told me after twelve that Jack had been killed in action probably at dawn on Sunday morning. Poor Mummie she will feel it dreadfully. No details to hand as yet. Let off all work after twelve. Played in a House game in the afternoon. Wrote to Mummie.

To her he wrote:

Dearest Mummie,

M'tutor has just told me. How dreadful for you. I will do what I can & whatever you want of course.

Poor little Mummie. You are having a fearfully trying time just now. But we must all do our share & the greater the share the greater honour if it is nobly borne.

Poor little Nicholas, too! I fear it will be a sad blow to him but we must all take our share.

I will do all I can but I wish Tim was home to help comfort you.

Please excuse my writing.

I cannot realize it properly yet.

God bless & reward you.

from your very affect. & sympathetic son,
Anthony

* Avon, *Another World, 1897–1917*, pp. 57 and 59.

Three days later he wrote to her: 'I hope you are not going to make yourself very ill over this, for, after all, Jack would be the first to cry out against it if you did.'

There was a memorial service at Windlestone, which had a strange sequel, as Eden later related.

I never saw Pamela [Fitzgerald] until after Jack had been killed when she journeyed to Windlestone for the memorial service which was held in the chapel. I admired her grace and elegance and her fair beauty and felt an almost reverential respect for her as the girl Jack had loved. When the time came to return to London it fell out that I was to drive her to Darlington to catch the express. 'Yes,' commented my mother sharply, 'and then you can flirt all the way to London.' I was shocked, because Pamela was for me on a pedestal, and angry because my mother had not understood this.

Although he met her only on this occasion, as she died young in 1918, Eden never forgot her.

The first fury of the war had produced casualties on a scale that no one had remotely envisaged. Already, boys Eden had known well at Sandroyd and Eton had been killed, the *Eton College Chronicle* was filled with obituaries, the original British Expeditionary Force had been grievously mauled, and the Secretary of State for War, Lord Kitchener, was calling for massive voluntary recruitment – with spectacular results. There was a new urgency to the training in the Eton OTC, and Eden himself was impatient to become involved, to the dismay both of his mother and of his housemaster. Meanwhile, life had to go on, with gloomy reports from Lady Eden about the sad situation at Windlestone:

I can't get reconciled to it [Jack's death], Darling, it hurts me day and night.... Oh! Anthony, *how* it hurts.

Life is really dreadful here. Melancholy isn't the word for it, not a soul to speak to, not a sound, empty rooms, memories crowding on me – every stick and stone reminding me of Jack. It's hardly bearable.

He [Sir William] has just woken up very X – very imbecile. Here is the conversation:

Dad: What time is it?
Me: Nearly 2 o'clock.
D: What shall I do?
Me: Get up now.
D: What then?
Me: Get dressed.
D: What then?
Me: Luncheon.
D: What then?

Me: Bath Chair – go out.
D: What then?
Me: Come in – have Tea.
D: What then?
– this repeated 6 or 7 times from the beginning. I longed to hit him!! It is now
2.15 & we have just succeeded in getting him up. – He ought to be shut up
somewhere.

This glum theme was often repeated in her letters in that dismal autumn.
'Did not sit up to see the New Year in,' Anthony wrote in his diary for 31
December. 'It has been an awful year and thank God it is over. Let us
hope that 1915 will be more lucky for the Eden family and the British
Empire.' At Eton, Churchill noted of Anthony: 'He seems to me distinctly
more serious-minded than he was. Of course, his danger is a lack of ballast:
but he is still young & seems to be sobering down a lot. There has been
enough to make him of late.'

Sir William was not even given the blessing of dying in his beloved
Windlestone, but was taken to London. 'He is *quite* mad today,' Lady Eden
wrote to Anthony, '– very difficult to manage.'

From Eton, Anthony tried to console her: 'Poor little Mummie. I am
afraid you are absolutely worn out, and it will really [be] a relief when the
end comes. I will speak to m'tutor about the clothes for the funeral, and
will order them tomorrow morning.... Cheer up, darling.'

Sir William's ordeal – and that of his family – ended on 20 February.
When his body was brought back to Windlestone, on the railway journey
he knew so well, the porters at Darlington station asked to be allowed to
carry his coffin from the train to the waiting hearse. This they did, and so
Sir William Eden returned home.

Anthony Eden's later judgement on William Eden put him in a more
charitable light than his childhood letters and diaries would indicate.
'Daddie goes up to London to-morrow, for which mercy Tim & I are truly
thankful,' he wrote at Windlestone on 11 June 1912. The gulf between
himself and Sir William had been considerable. Sir William took no interest
whatever in Anthony's formal education, perhaps partly because he had
hated Eton and had bitter memories of the floggings which in his day had
been so conspicuous a feature of Eton life. When Anthony won a divinity
prize he was appalled. Anthony explained that it had been for Greek
Testament. 'But he was not to be comforted and all those holidays I was
introduced sadly as "my son who is going into the Church", or sometimes
as "my son who is going to be a bishop".'

It was only later that Anthony and Tim, with better perspective, could
fully appreciate what a remarkable and many-faceted man William Eden
had been; by then they had gained a far better appreciation of the grievous

limitations of their mother. For both of them throughout their lives the memories of their father at Windlestone lived with them, and Anthony was to write in his old age:

Although my father spent so much of his life on horseback, I think of him on foot, returning from one of his frequent walks with Cradock to some wood or farm, hazel stick in hand, or sitting on a bench in the garden with his brother Morton or some other guest.

Tim's valediction must not be omitted:

He had written his last indignant letter, he had given his last order to the gardener, he had painted his last picture, he had fired his last shot. He had fought his fight for truth and beauty. He would plan and admire and criticize and quarrel no more....

He died at the end of an age, at the dawn of another. He died, and all that he loved died with him. His blue garden in that summer of 1915 was singing more than the death of its master. With the droop of its bloom and blossom drooped and fell a regime, an order, a manner of life. Death did not now mean for this place, as it had meant in the past, a mere change from master to master. It meant destruction as violent and as complete as the bursting of a volcano.*

The deaths of Sir William and Jack meant that the baronetcy and Windlestone now reverted to Tim, incarcerated in misery in Germany. The house became a hospital and convalescent home for wounded soldiers, and although the estate seemed well endowed none of the sons had any knowledge of their mother's fatal depredations, and it was not to be for some time that Tim was to be able to assess the complexities and burdens of his unexpected inheritance. Lady Eden had an annual income of £2,000 from her husband's estate but this, again, was not to be enough. Paintings and other objects began to disappear mysteriously and the Durham moneylenders still hovered happily.

She was, understandably, cast down by her misery. She wrote to Anthony from Windlestone on 23 May 1915:

Miss Brown is down here to give me a little massage & through her Jack sent me a message to say he is always near me – that he is perfectly happy – so glad he passed over as he did because it was such a glorious Death. I will tell you all about it when I see you. He told me he was looking after Tim. Oh! Anthony Darling how near we are really to the Spirit World could we but realize it – cleanse ourselves of earthly faults & failings. We put it from us instead of drawing it nearer to us. It is illogical to limit thought-power to the earth's sphere.

---

* Timothy Eden, *Tribulations*, pp. 185–6.

Anthony's impatience at Eton life was not lessened by a severe attack of influenza which coincided with his father's death, and by only fragmentary letters from Tim and Nicholas. Tim had difficulty in getting letters out, but in normal circumstances he was a splendid correspondent, while 'little Nicholas' was not. His few letters to Anthony were of his dislike of Dartmouth and his enthusiasm to go to sea and into battle.

Anthony's diaries and letters were now dominated by the war. 'The news does not seem very cheerful, and the casualty lists are appalling,' he wrote to his mother on 28 April: 'Fancy giving the command [at the Dardanelles] to an incompetent driveller like Ian Hamilton!'* 'We have just heard that another 2 boys from m'tutor's have been killed. 21 & 19 years old. It is *ghastly*,' he wrote on 9 May. He raged at the incompetence of the Asquith Government:

It really would be incredible except in England. We really are a wonderful nation! Why can't W. Churchill look after those sort of things [Navy ships] instead of making strategical plans about which he knows nothing at all? (Diary, 16 May 1915)

I should like to hang, draw, & quarter Haldane, Asquith, Winston Churchill & McKenna. Ye Gods! *What* a quartet! (Letter, 14 May 1915)

Within days of this outburst Haldane had gone from Government, and Churchill from the Admiralty, while Asquith survived as Prime Minister. Eden's bleak views on Winston Churchill were to endure until, in 1924, he met him. Even then, and for many years after, there were strong reservations in his attitude to this astonishing man until their destinies unexpectedly converged.

His desire to leave Eton and join the Army – 'the sooner I get out the better so that I can get settled in before the cold weather sets in', he wrote to his dismayed mother – was shadowed by the problem of his eyesight. He had suffered from shortsighted astigmatism since childhood and, although this is never shown in photographs, wore spectacles ('my new glasses suit me perfectly' is one entry). In fact, his eyesight was not particularly bad, and he was an excellent shot, but it was not up to Army standard for officers.

Meanwhile, the slaughter went on while Anthony led his House crew to victory in the Eton Aquatic Cup. 'You fool,' E. L. Churchill said to him when Anthony reiterated his intention to leave Eton, 'you won't be any use at the war, but you could be of some help in the House four.' Churchill

* General Sir Ian Hamilton had been given command of the Mediterranean Expeditionary Force on 12 March; the landings on the Gallipoli Peninsula had taken place on 25 April.

wrote to Lady Eden that 'He really is a good boy – much more serious minded than he was, & capable of prolonged & vigorous application to his business.... the capacity for amusing himself with a book is one not to be despised.' This last comment was in response to a complaint by Lady Eden about Anthony's love of reading, which she found both irritating and incomprehensible, as Sir William would not have. Churchill entirely supported Lady Eden in her opposition to Anthony joining the Army:

Anthony is not precocious at all. To send him out to stand a winter campaign at 18 + seems to me unfair to him & useless to the country – nay, worse than useless, for it will but add one to the number who need looking after.... I do want to urge the inadvisability of doing anything which has its aim & object his being got to the front this year. (21 June 1915)

In his diary Anthony wrote (13 July): 'This really is a terrible war.' To his mother, 23 July: 'Three people from m'tutor's have been killed this week. One a great friend of Tim's, [A. C.] Hobson, wounded & missing believed killed. He came out on the launch with us one 4th June. Do you remember?'

In his own later account Eden characteristically made no reference at all to his eyesight, which could have provided him with a perfectly honourable and honest excuse for not joining the Army; indeed, in any normal test he would have failed, as he and Marjorie – who had made her own enquiries and was a qualified nurse – both knew. Nor, later, was he to make any reference to the fact that he won the Military Cross. Those who have written of his 'vanity' should avert their gaze from such matters.

Marjorie's enthusiastic activities on her brother's behalf caused much anger from Lady Eden. This was perfectly understandable; in a very short time she had lost a son and her husband, her brother was a prisoner of war, Tim was interned at Ruhleben, and Nicholas was in the Navy. But Marjorie was an indefatigable intriguer on Anthony's behalf, laying siege to senior officers and officials in the War Office and to politicians. There was talk of the Coldstream or the Grenadier Guards – 'if Anthony goes on probation to the Grenadier Gds,' Marjorie reported, 'then the Col. merely applies for him. We can easily get at the Col.' – or of joining her husband, Guy Brooke, in the Warwickshire Royal Horse. Although Eden never subsequently disclosed the fact, the deadly impediment remained his eyesight. 'Mummie darling,' Marjorie wrote on 28 May, 'I have just returned from the War Office – & this is what I have found out – the eye test for Sandhurst is *supposed* to be the same as any other but might possibly in reality be a little severer.'

Then Kitchener decided to re-form the Yeomanry Regiments, and the Earl of Feversham became the commanding officer of the Yeoman Rifles, the 21st Battalion of the King's Royal Rifle Corps (the Sixtieth Rifles). Feversham, who had been a Member of Parliament for a Yorkshire constituency until he inherited his title, lived at Duncombe Park in Yorkshire, and was a close family friend of the Edens. His remit was to recruit the sons of owner or tenant farmers in the North, with the promise that those who volunteered would serve together and not be sent to strange regiments from other areas.

Feversham was married to Guy Brooke's sister, Marjorie, always known as Queenie in the family, and she and Eden's sister were not only sisters-in-law but close and dear friends since long before they married. Thus Eden not only knew 'Charlie' Feversham well but the latter was delighted to have the opportunity of having in his new command a young man he knew and admired, a countryman like himself, a County Durham man, who had served in the Eton Officers' Training Corps, and whose praises were sung to him by his wife and sister-in-law. The eyesight problem was ignored or, rather, neatly circumvented. As Eden wrote, the medical test 'was hardly more than a formality carried out by our family doctor, a well-read Irishman for whom my father had much affection'. Feversham drove over to Windlestone to seek the approval of Lady Eden in her role as one of Anthony's guardians. This she very reluctantly gave.

And thus, in this somewhat unusual manner, did Robert Anthony Eden become, at the age of eighteen, a second lieutenant in the 21st Battalion, the Yeoman Rifles, of the King's Royal Rifle Corps. His pay was to be £120 a year, with a £50 kit allowance, and three shillings a day for billeting when this was necessary. As a younger son he had received little from his father, and this modest sum represented his entire income.

Nineteen fifteen had been a terrible year for the Allies. The conflict on the Western Front had acquired an especial horror of its own, as the high hopes of a decisive war of movement congealed into the writhing and stinking trenches, the first use of gas, and the ever-increasing power of artillery pounding not only the ground and the flesh, but the nerves of man. The machine-gun, the bomb, barbed wire and the artillery were the masters of the field, against which men hurled themselves with tragic futility. The casualty lists grew to unparalleled levels, and the supply of volunteer recruits began to fade with the decline of the first ardour.

The Asquith Liberal Government groped for a way out of this morass, and in the event made matters even worse. Ill-led, divided and embroiled in a war whose scale was unprecedented, it lurched towards the Gallipoli Campaign, which consumed the lives of over 46,000 British and Allied troops and countless wounded in seven months before the venture had to be abandoned in December. By this time, the Liberal Government had fallen in May, with the First Lord of the Admiralty, Winston Churchill, its most conspicuous victim. Huge quantities of men and matériel went to Salonika, where their presence proved to be wholly irrelevant. In Mesopotamia the British Empire soldiers found themselves involved in a campaign of much suffering and loss. At sea, the long-awaited total defeat of the Germans did not occur, and their submarines inflicted great destruction and fear. At home, with the Zeppelins bombing, debates raged about whether conscription should or should not be introduced. The Russians marched and counter-marched from one catastrophic defeat to another, and on the Western Front the British and French commanders never lost their obstinate faith that with only more guns, more shells and more men would they secure decisive victory, while the Germans, too overstretched on too many fronts, dug themselves in deeper, improved their defences and contested every yard. Only on the Verdun sector were there plans for a major German advance, where they, also, were to learn how the balance of advantage had swung so decisively from the attacker to the defender. Millions of shells and bombs, thousands of millions of bullets, were expended; hundreds of thousands of men perished; by the end of 1915 nothing had been achieved by any of the belligerents.

No one had expected anything like this, but the lessons of the Western Front, with the troops 'chewing barbed wire' as Winston Churchill described it in an unheeded War Council memorandum, had not percolated into the British Army. Training was rudimentary and brief, and there was none on trench warfare. Lloyd George as Minister of Munitions was making his reputation with great speeches about his great achievements, of which the troops saw only limited evidence. The British fought with great courage – a highly expendable quality – but as amateurs.

This was the grim context of Anthony Eden's arrival into the Army, a minor participant in Sir Douglas Haig's grand strategy.

Eden's first experience of the Army was a strenuous officers' course near Ipswich, and it was not a pleasant one. 'I was relieved when I got through it after a fashion,' he later wrote, but at the time his opinions were more forcefully expressed in his letters. 'We are kept at it, and I am getting very sick of my company and Capt Wootton whom everybody hates. He is a typical schoolmaster of the bullying type,' he wrote to his mother on 17 November, and then, on 30 November:

Ld Feversham may say 'come here' or he may say go and get some more recruits, or he may say 'take a week's leave'....

There has been a lot of 'telling off' since I came back but I have not yet been on any of the black lists so far, but I should be alright, but then [one] never knows.

There is far too much favouritism about the business to suit me.

One of Eden's first tasks was recruitment for the platoon which he would command. Driving around County Durham in Sir William Eden's yellow Benz, he found that his endeavours were hardly necessary, as volunteers were applying as soon as news of the formation of the battalion had circulated, but he was able to persuade at least one reluctant employer to permit an eager young volunteer to put himself forward.

In retrospect, it can be seen that this policy was a mistake in that in one major misfortune many of the young men of a village or town would be lost, in some cases an entire generation. Tragically, this is what so often happened, but the advantage of the Yeomanry concept was that the officers and men had much in common, and often knew each other well, so that many of the frictions and animosities that occur in an Army unit drawn from entirely different backgrounds and parts of the country were not present. It is perhaps difficult to pass a true judgement, except to note that the spirit and comradeship in the Yeomanry regiments were outstandingly high and the relationship between officers and men exceptionally close and good, facts that gave to them a special quality which the young Anthony Eden never forgot. In a Guards regiment he would have been among strangers; in the Yeomanry he was among friends, so that every loss suffered had a very personal impact.

We went out to do a night march last night and then do an attack. The whole business was a complete washout. We never saw the enemy till we were coming home, one hour later than we should have been. I don't know who was responsible for the blunder but I do know that it was not our party that went wrong.

I think that it was Capt Wootton's mistake, but he was in a devilish temper today so I expect it was his blunder. I narrowly escaped trouble, and it was only because of my 'good character' as he put it that I got off. Lots of others caught it pretty hot. (Letter, 4 December 1915)

It was a relief to return to the battalion, based at Helmsley. In later years Eden marvelled at how hopelessly inexperienced they all were, but at least they were fully aware of their own ignorance. 'We knew nothing,' he wrote, 'and there were few at hand to teach us.' But they were all very young and came from the same part of England, which helped to create bonds that were to prove remarkably durable among the survivors. One friendship which was of great importance to Eden was with Corporal Reg Park, his platoon corporal, who took his duties with great seriousness. Gradually the platoon developed into a real unit, to Eden's pleasure and pride; for their part, the men developed a real affection and respect for their very young officer, generally known as 'The Boy'. It was the first real achievement of his life, and a fine one for someone of eighteen, barely out of school and noticeably shy, although Eden's temper and impatience could also make him formidable. In old age, those days had to him a glow about them which is understandable; at the time, his letters reveal frustration rather than pleasure, in spite of his devotion to his platoon. On 14 November he and Marjorie went to hear Ben Tillet, the former Socialist trade union leader, speak: 'He was quite wonderful,' he told Lady Eden, 'and he spoke very straight. I am afraid that things are going very badly, not at the fronts, but at home. Everyone is very down here.'

His Army career, and his life, very nearly came to an end when he was sent on a bomb course in Aldershot in December. These bombs were of an exceptional crudity, consisting of a jam tin, a priming charge of explosive, a detonator with a fuse, and sharp stones or fragments of metal; one lit the fuse (not easy in pouring rain) and threw the contraption in the general direction of the enemy. Eden, strangely enough, enjoyed the bombs: 'Very ingenious little things,' he wrote to his mother. 'They make the devil of a mess.' Fortunately, the Mills bomb had been invented, which was to prove one of the most lethal weapons of modern warfare, but ignorance of the power of explosives extended to Eden's tutors, as he has related:

We were to witness a demonstration and were shown a steel rail and a pound slab of TNT. The explosive with its detonator was placed under the rail and we were shepherded lower down the slope to watch the experiment. The fuse was lit and in a few seconds a convincing bang resulted. Then things began to happen. I was vaguely conscious of a cry close beside me, and of men falling and of an order to stay where we were by the officer in command. It was soon evident that some could not obey that order.*

Two men had been seriously injured, and one killed. 'It has of course damped the ardour of the men – and of the officers!' Eden told his mother, but it had certainly made him vividly aware of the perils of explosives, a lesson which he never forgot.

While still on the course, Eden was told that his battalion was moving to Aldershot and that he must await it there. The purpose was three months of intensive training, installed in the grim Victorian Peninsular Lines which had seen far better days. Eden was miserable. 'Thank God 1915 is coming to an end at last. What a ghastly year!' was his valediction on 31 December. His experience of the intense training did not raise his spirits. 'We are worked like sin here' (25 January); 'We are still fearfully handicapped by a shortage of rifles. They don't seem yet to have enough in spite of Lloyd George's gas.' To his mother he wrote urgently on 27 January: 'I must have a pair of field glasses at once. There is a need for haste about it. I also want a prismatic compass.' Such was the condition of the British Army after eighteen months of war.

* Avon, *Another World, 1897–1917*, p. 69.

'Nothing seems settled at present about our destination, or anything else,' he wrote to Lady Eden. 'I hear different stories every day.... Cheer up, darling, let us hope that this war will not last for long now.' The weather was vile, and the training concentrated upon open warfare, in complete defiance of all experience on the Western Front. The Sixtieth Rifles may have been raw, but they had heard enough to know what the realities were. 'Aldershot had taught us only a smattering of what we most needed to know,' he later wrote; at the time his comments were more virulent. There was a final grand parade, inspected by the King, and the battalion was deemed fit for the front line. Eden had a brief leave at Windlestone, principally to see Nicholas, who had now received orders to join his ship. He had not enjoyed Dartmouth, and expressed considerable doubts about the abilities of the officers under whom he now had to serve. Nicholas left for HMS *Indefatigable*, Anthony for Ploegsteert Wood, south of the Ypres Salient, one of the ugliest sectors of an especially ugly Front.

'One lovely afternoon towards the end of June, when we were in the support line,' Eden later wrote,

Bob [Iley, Eden's runner] sought me out and told me that the colonel was at company headquarters and wanted to see me there at once. Off I went, somewhat puzzled as to what this summons could be about. I found Charlie Feversham alone outside our company headquarters' dugout, looking glum. 'I want a word with you, Anthony,' he said, and led the way into the bay of a neighbouring unoccupied trench.

A quiet lull in the wood, a brilliant summer's day and Charlie standing there disturbed and unhappy.

It was to inform him of the death of Nicholas.

The war had brought to Lady Eden's life the misery of Jack's death, the anguish of Tim's internment, her brother's imprisonment, the death of her husband, and very justifiable concern about Anthony, now in high danger in France. Guy Brooke had just been injured in France. Nicholas must have seemed safe. He was just sixteen, a midshipman for whom Admiral Beatty in his letters to Lady Eden forecast 'a distinguished career in a very distinguished if somewhat arduous Service'. But his reports from Osborne (which he hated, writing from 'this desert isle') recorded that he had 'lots of abilities, but not much application and lacks ginger and general interest in things that are going on'. At one point, in April 1914, there had been formal notice that unless Nicholas's record improved drastically he would be removed; it did, and after Dartmouth he was ordered to HMS *Inde-fatigable*, a battle-cruiser in the Grand Fleet. He was ecstatic and in his letters to his mother and Anthony glowed with pride in his ship and excitement at the prospect of a great naval battle.

It took place, off Jutland, on 31 May 1916, very shortly after Anthony Eden's battalion had arrived in France. Much has been written about that extraordinary battle, but from the point of view of the Eden family the real event was that a German salvo struck *Indefatigable* at the very beginning of the battle-cruiser's action shortly after 4 p.m. She blew up and capsized with total loss of life.

For three days, nothing was known, until the Eden butler, William House, called personally at the Admiralty for information. In Lady Eden's papers is the customary Admiralty enquiry form submitted at the entrance by House. It seeks information about Midshipman W. N. Eden RN, with the words, 'What news please?', and is marked on the back: 'Regret to state this officer is killed in action.' Formal telegrams and letters of regret followed, including one from the King, but this dun-coloured enquiry form, kept by Lady Eden all her life, and subsequently by Anthony, was the first confirmation of her fears.

If Lady Eden was understandably distraught at this latest tragedy, so were Nicholas's surviving brothers and sister. Anthony wrote tenderly to his mother and Marjorie, but it was to Tim that he poured out his distress.

He was now in the front line, and his first scribbled pencil letter was 'interrupted by a few unfriendly shells'.

I long to hear from you, Tim, just so that I know you are alright. I know how fearfully upset you will have been at losing Nicholas, especially as you will be so lonely that you have only too much time to think. Out here we have one great boon to be thankful for – we are so busy that our minds are fully occupied.

Tim was indeed deeply saddened by the loss of his youngest brother, and Anthony wrote to him, again in pencil, from his odious dugout.

As you say, Thank God we have got remembrance.

Jack and Nicholas are with us still, with *all* of us, and around us all, helping in our struggle until our time comes, be it soon or later, when we are called to join them.

Now, Tim dear, this is for your private ear alone.

Should I be killed before I see you again, remember this always – I shall be with Jack, Nicholas, and Daddie, and although I may be for a time here in this earth I shall be with the others. I shall be *so* happy with them, I *know* I shall.

I can barely write tonight, I am in such a curious mood.

I feel almost hysterical, it all seems so cruel, and yet I know they are all much happier in paradise.

But my heart aches at times most terribly at the horror of it all.

Don't be in too much of a hurry to come out here. This war will not be over for a long time yet, I am afraid.

There was another memorial service at Windlestone. Of the four sons, now only Tim and Anthony were left, and the latter was about to pass through his ordeal.

In *Another World* Eden made a notable contribution to the literature of the Great War, although he was very modest about himself and his own courage, of which there is much evidence. The schoolboy had to grow up very quickly, as had so many others.

At first 'Plugstreet', where Winston Churchill had just served as the commander of the 6th Royal Scots Fusiliers, who vacated the line to be replaced by the 21st Battalion, was deceptively quiet. The weather was good and the trenches were dry. There were night patrols in No Man's Land, some shelling, and much random firing and shrapnel, which was not taken seriously until one of Eden's platoon, Private Spence, received a slight flesh wound, which was regarded by his mates as the perfect light 'Blighty' wound which would return him to England and his family. Eden had only recently been discussing with Reg Park – now a full sergeant – whether to make Spence a lance-corporal. A few days later Eden was told that Spence had died of his wound. In his old age he wrote: 'This was our first sharp contact with sudden death and we were utterly miserable. The passage of years had never blunted it. We had yet to learn that it was the chance deaths in the trenches which left a sharper imprint than the wholesale slaughter of a battle.'*

The front line became livelier, and there were more casualties. Eden had the opportunity of long talks with Reg Park and another corporal, Norman Carmichael. They discussed politics, agreeing that their country could never be divided on class lines after the war when this experience had been shared by men of all backgrounds. Eden never forgot these talks 'on still summer nights in Plugstreet Wood'. They, and what now happened, formed the crucial part of his real education.

Reg Park was the next of Eden's true friends to be killed, by a chance shell, 'and I lost a friend I have never forgotten'. He was replaced as sergeant by Bert Harrop, a Yorkshireman who was a novelty to the battalion in that he was a regular soldier of considerable experience. Another man whom Eden greatly respected was Major Hon. Gerald Foljambe, a professional whose dislike of incompetence and folly at the highest levels and outspokenness on these matters probably debarred him from the most senior posts he merited. It was Foljambe who now summoned Eden to tell him that divisional headquarters were anxious to identify the Germans opposite them. This could be done only by night patrols in No Man's

---

* Avon, *Another World, 1897–1917*, p. 79.

Land, which was barely one hundred yards wide. Eden was to command the first of these.

He laid his plans carefully. With three riflemen, they would cut the German wire and then jump into the German trench and either capture or kill, but certainly identify, the sentry. Harrop and two other riflemen would cover them from a carefully chosen position in No Man's Land. Secrecy and surprise, on a night with little moon, were the key elements.

Eden's account, although written many years later, deserves to be given in full:

The first moves went according to plan. We worked our way across no-man's-land without incident, and Pratt and Liddell began to cut the enemy wire. This was tough and rather thicker in the long grass than we had reckoned. Even so we made good progress and there were only a few more strands left to cut, so that we were right under the German trench, when suddenly, jabber, jabber, and without warning two German heads appeared above the parapet and began pointing into the long grass. We lay flat and still for our lives, expecting every second a blast of machine-gun fire or a bomb in our midst. But nothing happened. After a little more jabber, the heads disappeared and all was quiet again.

We lay without moving for what must have been nearly an hour. There were no abnormal noises from the German line nor was the sentry on patrol. Less than four minutes of wire-cutting would complete our task and I had to decide what to do next. I touched Pratt and Liddell to go on.

The job was just about done when all hell seemed to break loose right in our faces. The German trench leapt into life, rifles and machine-guns blazed, Very lights soared up and the place seemed to us as light as day. Incredibly none of this bombardment touched us, presumably because we were much closer to the German trench, within their wire and only a foot or two from the parapet, than the enemy imagined possible. As a result the firing was all aimed above and beyond us, into no-man's-land or at our own front line.

Once more we had dropped down into the long grass and made no move until the firing ceased and the Very lights dimmed a little. Then I signalled to my small section to begin to crawl back. Our first blow was the old field ditch, a German machine-gun sputtered down it at intervals, so there was no choice but a slow creep back across the open, praying that no Very light would expose us too clearly. All went well for a while, and we were about fifty yards from our front line when I heard what seemed a groan at my left hand. Signalling to the others to go on I moved a few yards to investigate. There I found Harrop lying in the lip of a shallow shell-hole bleeding profusely from a bad bullet wound in his thigh and two riflemen trying to help him.

Harrop was weak from loss of blood, but still calm and decided. As we fixed a tourniquet on his leg he kept insisting, 'Tighter, tighter, or I'll bleed to death.' If he was to have any chance, we must get him back to our line without delay. The question was, how. The firing was now sporadic rather than intense, but as I crouched beside Harrop I knew we must have a stretcher if we were to get him in before dawn. I said so, and one of the two young riflemen with Harrop, Eddie Bousefield, at once volunteered to go.

In a few minutes he was back in our line, had collected a stretcher and a fellow rifleman, and rejoined us without being spotted. Then came the difficult decision. We had only fifty yards to go, and even though stooped, we would all four have to stand up to carry Harrop's stretcher. The longer we waited the better the hope of the night growing quieter, but the worse for Harrop and the more extended the risk for us all. I wanted to get it over with, and we did. To this day I do not know whether the enemy saw the stretcher and held his fire, or saw nothing in the flickering Very lights. There was a chilly feeling down our spines anyway.*

Eden's account characteristically omits to mention the fact that this act of outstanding courage and leadership led to his immediate recommendation for the Military Cross by Foljambe and Feversham. The only immediate result was what Eden subsequently described as 'an agreeable citation by the divisional commander on a small piece of paste-board'. It has survived. It states in print 'I wish to place on record my appreciation of', and then, in ink, 'your consistent good work as Bombing Officer & on Patrol, May–Sept 1916', and adds 'NOTE – It does not follow that your name will be submitted to higher authority.' It may well have rested there had not Feversham's successor, Talbot Jarvis, who put great value on obtaining decorations for his men, successfully repeated the application.

There were other patrols at Plugstreet, and Eden has written with warm admiration of the riflemen – especially 'Tiger' Pratt and Tom Liddell – who were his regular companions on these perilous ventures. For their part, their admiration for 'The Boy' and confidence in him were total. Sergeant Harrop survived the war, although his wounds required many operations, and so did Pratt; Liddell was killed within a few days of the Armistice in 1918.

But these grim experiences were only the prelude to the nightmare of the Battle of the Somme.

One lesson of 1915 had at least been learnt. Some battalions had lost virtually their entire officer complement, from commanding officers to subalterns, and strict orders were now given that regiments had to look to their future. Commanding officers were not to advance with their men, and the number of officers to be sent into action was to be limited. These orders were greatly resented, but when the tumult and misery of the Battle of the Somme ended it could be seen that there was much justification for them.

Eden's battalion, at Plugstreet, had not been involved in the opening stages of that terrible battle, which began on 1 July; on that day alone the

* Avon, *Another World, 1897–1917*, pp. 89–91.

British casualties were 57,470 of whom 19,240 were killed or died of their wounds. But the Allied commanders persevered. In the words of Cyril Falls:

So it went on, Haig imperturbable and nursing the hope that by mid-September the German resistance would be so reduced that a powerful assault might lead to a break-through. August was the month of attrition at its height: continuous, heart-breaking milling at close quarters, minute gains at best, each ending with groups of crumpled corpses strewn about the objectives.*

The Yeoman Rifles were not yet engaged, and Eden and his battalion were now out of the line and training. 'Our training was strenuous, the weather was glorious and we became very fit,' he later wrote.

Looking back on those days, I suppose that I was never again to see a battalion so primed in all respects during more than two years of war which were to follow. While we knew that the field exercises we were put through must lead to some action somewhere, we knew nothing more and it is fair to say that our mood was eager rather than apprehensive.

Then the blow fell. Each company had to leave behind two officers and two senior sergeants as well as a percentage of junior non-commissioned officers. Eden was astounded and enraged to be told that he was to be one of them. 'I had been with my battalion since its early days, I had helped recruit my platoon, I could not desert them in their first major action,' he later explained. He appealed to Feversham, without success. 'We have to take some thought for the battalion's future' was the reply. When the battalion did move to the front, Eden contrived to ride up with the letters to Delville Wood. The mail was well received, Eden less so, Feversham being friendly but peremptory. Eden never saw him again.

One exciting and remarkable novelty was the arrival of the first tanks, which, as Eden recorded, were first assumed to be 'an improved form of water container'. The appearance of these remarkable weapons of war – although few in number – immensely heartened the commanders and men. General Rawlinson wrote in his diary:

The Chief [Haig] is anxious to have a gamble with all the available troops about September 15, with the object of breaking down German resistance and getting through to Bapaume.... We shall have no resources in hand save tired troops, but success at this time would have a great effect throughout the world, and might bring the Boche to terms.... It is worth the risk.†

Had the tanks – the true war-winner – been available in greater numbers and concentrated rather than dispersed, subsequent events would have been very different.

---

* Cyril Falls, *The First World War*, p. 172.
† A. H. Farrar-Hockley, *The Somme*, p. 184.

On the following morning, 15 September, the battalion attacked at Delville Wood. What then happened had a grim familiarity. The casualties were great, the valour impressive, the gains non-existent. Feversham was among those who were killed, having ignored the orders about commanding officers leading the attack. The battalion suffered 394 casualties, of whom 127 were killed. Eden had to come up to read the roll. There were many gaps. Foljambe became the colonel, and his first action was to appoint Eden adjutant, the previous one, Honey, having lost an eye in the battle. It was a remarkable promotion, Eden becoming one of the youngest adjutants in the British Army. His first task was to prepare the battalion's casualty return; each had been a friend.

He wrote to his mother:

Mummie darling,
A very sad letter for you to-day I am afraid.
The Colonel was killed yesterday afternoon & my company commander & Wates (do you remember him dining with us at Farnboro?) Coke badly wounded. Major Paget badly wounded although not with us. Capt Honey hit in the eye. I think that is all those you know. I am in reserve & quite alright.
My company suffered worst I'm afraid, so try & make some room at the hospital for them.
They fought like heroes.
Do do all you can to get hold of them & give them a really good time. They deserve it.
I have seen things just lately that I am not likely to forget. Poor Coates is finally bad I'm afraid. Hit in the stomach.

Afternoon
Have seen one or two of our wounded. All wonderfully cheerful & brave. There will be lots of applicants for Windles. Please make *every* effort to get them in. . . . The Colonel was wonderful, as brave as a lion.
These are rather depressing days darling, but if I can come through, which I feel sure I shall do, I see leave looking ahead.

One good development in an otherwise bleak year for the Edens was that Tim had been repatriated from Germany and was back at Windlestone. It was usual in such cases for repatriated men to sign an assurance that they would not serve in the armed forces, but in Tim's case no such assurance seems to have been given or requested, and Tim was preparing to join the Army, to his mother's understandable unhappiness; nor was Anthony at all encouraging. He wrote to Tim on 24 September:

Many thanks for your letter which I received safely yesterday.
All is well with me at present except that I have not got a Blighty but I hope that will not be too long delayed.

46

You will have heard about the Colonel being killed & the loss of nearly all our best officers. The battalion fought splendidly & made its name with the people out here, but of course not with the press!!

All the officers in my unit were hit, but the men carried on splendidly in spite of the adverse circumstances of which I shall speak some day. When I get home, Tim my lad, I shall be able to tell you a thing or two. Truth far more surprising than the fiction of the wonderful heroism of the officers & men and the wonderful folly of 'others'....

If you get one of our wounded at Windles you might have a talk to him.

Don't be in a hurry to join up, but wait till I get some leave or a Blighty.

The battalion, not brought back to anything like its full strength, received information that another attack was planned, in which it would be in support. Foljambe insisted on a personal reconnaissance of the front line, accompanied by Eden. They found chaos, and would have been killed if a shell that landed between them had exploded. The German positions looked ominously good, and the ground over which their brigade was due to advance very exposed. Also, the weather had now changed, and as Eden wrote, 'The rain had added the final touch of sordid misery to the Somme battlefield.'

The march of the battalion to the front line was in itself a hard experience. Long before it had reached its initial position, struggling along a congested track in the rain and mud, one officer and three men had been killed in Eden's proximity and several wounded. When the attack actually began, the previous experiences were exactly repeated, casualties were heavy, and no progress was made. That morning Foljambe had reproved Eden for wearing his revolver on his left side. As he was moving around, trying to find out the situation, Eden suddenly realized that a large piece of shrapnel had hit the revolver; the wound would have been far more serious than a 'blighty'. Foljambe received a DSO for his gallant work that dreadful day and night, and Eden was later recommended for the same award. Again, his modest account gives no indication of his own courage nor of this recommendation.

Units were now inextricably mixed, and communications were difficult, often impossible. The relief units were not from the battalion, and had been badly shelled on their way up. Foljambe told brigade headquarters that his men, or rather those few who remained, were in no condition to launch another attack. By chance, an officer had come across Feversham's body, and Eden took a small burial party to find it. With considerable difficulty they did so, just as dawn was breaking and the first shells began falling. 'Sadly we set about our task. I read a few lines from the burial service, which someone had lent to me at headquarters, Dale* set up the

---

* Tom Dale was a pioneer sergeant, who had been brought up on the Feversham Estate.

wooden cross, we gave our commanding officer a last salute and turned away, leaving him to Picardy and the shells.'

'We had a pretty hellish time, I can tell you,' he wrote to Marjorie on 11 October, 'and I was never so glad to get away from somewhere.... I am quite whole, but absolutely done'; and, again to her on 9 November: 'It really is a horrible war. There goes a burst of shell, ours I think, I shall be glad when I never hear another of their beastly shrieks or see another burst!'

The Yeoman Rifles as such had virtually ceased to exist. On top of the September losses there now had to be added six more officers and 180 other ranks. Throughout the action no one from brigade or divisional headquarters had been in, or anywhere near, the line. 'This did not go unnoticed by the riflemen,' Eden noted. The rain was unceasing, the billets miserable, and the remnants of the battalion shuttled around various inhospitable places in cattle-trucks. At the time, and later, Eden marvelled at the patience and confidence of his men. Not before long they were back in the line, to relieve the Australians in the Ypres Salient. 'Six days in the line, followed by six in support in Ridge Wood, six more back in the line and then the same period at "rest" in a camp at La Clytte, became our established pattern.'*

Eden's mixed emotions can be seen in a letter to Tim on 24 December:

One hears great rumours of peace, but of course that cannot be yet. The Germans are just beginning to feel uncomfortable, and they have to go through hell and worse. All the same I think that 1917 should see the end of it all, and Germany really broken. A peace with Germany as she is now would satisfy nobody's conscience. A peace now would mean that all the lives that have been sacrificed have been sacrificed in vain. However, I think that one can trust Lloyd George to deal with peace agitators.

But to Marjorie he wrote on the same day that 'it is impossible to do anything except sit still and wish that the war was over'.

In the trenches, as Eden later wrote, 'Political figures were not discussed and certainly not liked. Lloyd George† was the most generally accepted and those campaigning against conscription the most condemned.' Those who, like Lord Lansdowne, urged a negotiated peace were, ironically, the most disliked of all.

---

* Avon, *Another World, 1897–1917*, p. 121.
† As an immediate result of skilful intrigue, but in reality in response to parliamentary and public dissatisfaction with the conduct of the war, Lloyd George had replaced Asquith as Prime Minister early in December 1916.

Eden was now one of the few survivors of the initial battalion. Not many of the original officers were left, and too many Durham men he had personally recruited had been killed. Now they had to endure a savagely harsh winter, which was triumphantly survived by the huge and voracious rats, and in which Eden continued his duties as adjutant, coping with administration and nightly visits to companies in the line. He described this period as one of 'cold monotony laced with funk which was trench warfare in winter. There was so much waiting in the trenches. Waiting through the hour before dawn for stand-down, waiting for the battalion which was to relieve us, waiting for rations and for letters, waiting for leave, or the blighty wound, or....'*

There was a leave, in London and at Windlestone, which was, although welcome, not entirely happy. Like so many other soldiers, Eden found the bustle and glitter of London uncomfortable, and Windlestone held too many memories. On return, he discovered that Foljambe had been recalled to be an instructor, and was replaced by Colonel Talbot Jarvis, a brave fire-eater, described by Eden as 'lion-hearted but not adaptable and liable to be put out by the unexpected'. After virtually a year in the line, Eden had developed an intense dislike 'with growing fervour the whole business of being shot at, whether by shell or machine-gun, but particularly shell. What depressed me most was that I could see no hope of improvement ahead.' But when the battalion thankfully came out of the accursed line at the end of March 1917, having, in Bob Iley's words, 'filled one cemetery and well on the way to filling another', it was for more training for yet another offensive.

This time, everyone was impressed by the thoroughness of the training and preparation for the attack, in such notable contrast with their previous experience. The purpose of the assault was to dispose of the Ypres Salient, and the Second Army – including the 21st Battalion – was to capture the dominating German positions on the Messines–Wytschaete line. What was alarming to Eden was the realization that their part was going to be especially dangerous, making their attack from the St Eloi craters in a heavily mined area where No Man's Land was only fifty yards, but what impressed him was the care and thought of his general, Sir Herbert Plumer, in the planning and preparation. This was not going to be another amateur foray into oblivion. As will be seen, Plumer was also greatly impressed by Captain Eden.

On 5 June the battalion began its move into its battle positions, eagerly welcomed into the trenches by the rats. The headquarters' runners, including Bob Iley, strung up their rations by a rope from the roof of their

---

* Avon, *Another World, 1897–1917*, p. 125.

dugout; the rats scrambled along the roof and down the rope; when the runners awoke their rations had gone.

On 6 June the British artillery barrage crashed upon the German positions; when darkness fell the Germans responded, and 'the whole small area was soon a blazing inferno', in Eden's account. At 3.10 a.m. the New Zealand miners, whom Eden deeply admired, exploded their mines, the biggest explosion to date in military history, 470 tons of explosive going off simultaneously, and the riflemen charged; 'for the rest of the day our attack succeeded beyond our wildest dreams'. 'The show was simply splendid, and I thoroughly enjoyed it, contrary to my expectations,' he wrote to Marjorie on 11 June. The battalion gained all its objectives, took 130 prisoners, and this time, while the German losses were very heavy, those of the battalion were only seven killed and sixty-four wounded in twenty-four hours.

But it was then moved to the left in Ravine Wood, where progress had not been as spectacular, and this time the attack was fiercely resisted, with heavy casualties. The elation of Messines quickly evaporated under severe shelling: 'I could not help seeing how haggard and spent our best officers and NCOs looked,' Eden wrote, 'and I was miserable. The red-eyed stage was back again.' These were, as he later recalled, 'hideous days'. The battalion went into action with nineteen officers and 487 other ranks; their casualties were 282, of whom ninety-one were killed; Jarvis was one of the thirteen officers wounded. 'It is difficult to extract a very clear story from the meagre accounts of the fighting,' the regimental history sombrely records of this new disaster.* Then, one shell alone wrought terrible destruction just as the battalion was being relieved after six days, killing more of the survivors of the original battalion. To lose officers and men at this moment, after a great victory and grim ordeal, was unbearable, and, as Eden wrote, 'our eventual return to our support line was carried out in a daze'.

Throughout, Eden had been in the forefront of the fighting, and he had, once again, been extraordinarily lucky not to have been among those killed or wounded in the fighting or by the shells that had caused such havoc. Indeed, he and Jarvis had been only yards away from the final shell; fortunately for them they had been in a pill-box, which 'shook and swayed' in the blast, but which saved them. Throughout his life, Eden pondered on the extraordinary number of very near misses he had experienced, while so many of his friends had been killed or severely wounded. His own courage and fortitude were beyond all question, and, once again, he was recommended for the DSO – again unsuccessfully. The Yeomen who

---

* Major-General Sir Stewart Hare, *The Annals of the King's Royal Rifle Corps*, p. 239.

survived, and they were few, have testified to his bravery. After a year of intense fighting, he himself was amazed to be still alive, and unwounded. Bob Iley was another survivor, but few others remained of that happy battalion that had travelled to France what seemed an eternity ago.

In the midst of his immediate preoccupations, a storm had arisen at home.

Tim had now assessed the dreadful condition of his inheritance, and had come to the painful but necessary decision that in order to save Windlestone as a house and estate some of its contents would have to be sold. What is, unhappily, a familiar story then followed. Jack's death had complicated the legal position appallingly, and Sir William Eden had not changed his will – in which Jack was the principal beneficiary – so that, after the payment of death duties and other charges, principally Lady Eden's huge debts (or, to be precise, some of them), there was confusion over what was the property of the three surviving children. As the new baronet, Tim considered that it was all his; Marjorie and Anthony did not. Many painful letters were written and responded to. On 17 July Anthony wrote to Marjorie:

You will have got my letter about Mama by now. It is not worrying me much, except that she will probably go on telling lies about me, probably starting with Grannie [Grey].... I shouldn't worry about Tim. He isn't worth it.... [He] has seized all Jack's things and all Daddie's and I have not the most trifling article that ever belonged to either of them!

Yes, the Cabinet changes are the limit. I haven't heard anybody express approval of them yet.... I shall certainly not go to Windlestone again under the present regime. I certainly shouldn't take any trouble about Tim.

This was severely unfair on Tim, as Anthony later realized, but the real trouble-maker was, as always, Lady Eden. 'You will have to watch Dear Mama carefully,' he wrote to Marjorie on 30 October, 'because she has the most extraordinary idea of what is legal and what isn't! ... I know that Dear Mama is all out for Tim, and she won't hesitate to hide or swindle where she can.'

The storm passed, but it was an unhappy augury of problems to come, which were to place strong strains upon Anthony Eden's relations with his mother and Tim.

In May Eden had been asked whether he was interested in becoming a junior General Staff Officer at Second Army Headquarters. With the Messines attack imminent, Eden had refused. 'My place is in the regiment at my age,' he wrote to Marjorie; 'I cannot help thinking that I ought to stay here' (10 May). But Jarvis urged him to postpone rather than to reject the offer. He had been adjutant for over a year, and was now the only combatant officer to have served continuously with the battalion since it had been in France. After the battle Jarvis urged him again, and this time Eden accepted.

This was only a brief interlude. He did exceptionally well, and in the early spring of 1918 was appointed brigade major with the 198th Infantry Brigade, to see more action, although this time on the advance, with relatively light casualties. It is clear from Eden's letters home that although the heavy losses in the Yeoman Rifles, and his own experiences, had scarred him and certainly had not improved his temper, his commitment to the war and to victory was as strong as ever.

On 23 December he wrote to Lady Eden:

Mummie darling,

Many thanks for your Christmas letter which arrived safely today.

What on earth has come over everybody? Did you read X's* speech in the House? I never read such wait and see twaddle in all my life. He says we want men badly, and them at once, and then proceeds to adjourn for a month, meanwhile nothing is done. Can *we* adjourn for a month! My God! it does make my blood boil. Have we not one single politician who is really out to do his best, holiday or no holiday, or are they all an unscrupulous set of narrow-minded, self-satisfied crassly ignorant notaries! My God! it does make me see red. Then they start criticizing the Army! My God, if they would mind their own business and do their own job and let the Army run the fighting we should bring the Germans to their knees.

Everything is alright here in our little world. All we want is a firm backing from England.

What about Ireland? Not a word about conscripting them. There are a quarter of a million of the finest fighting men in Europe to be had for the taking and we do nothing.

We do deserve to lose this war, and if we go on like this we *shall* lose it in spite of our soldiers and because of our politicians. Excuse this outburst but sometimes I am so angry when I think of this that I nearly burst....

The band has just been playing Christmas carols (I hope the Hun didn't hear) which though very nice makes me rather homesick.

Much love, your very affectionate son

Anthony

To Marjorie (to whom he had written on 12 November to say that 'I am reading "George Wyndham Recognita", which I am rather disappointed in so far') he wrote on the same day in the same terms: 'Lloyd George has made a very stupid speech in the House, I see. I wish they would muzzle, or drown, or murder all these infernal politicians until after the war.... My God, they are brutes and murderers, they make me see red at times.'

* Lloyd George.

But we then find him writing to Marjorie on 3 January:

Please don't be so pessimistic about the war. It is only the beastly papers that talk such rot. I am sure that we have only got to stick it another year and then we shall have the Germans beaten. We want more men. One last great effort and not peace talk is what is needed now. Peace now would mean another war in another five or ten years' time! Just think of it.

In fact, the 'last great effort' came from the Germans in March. The Russians were out of the war, there were several difficulties and mutinies in the French Army which had had to be dealt with by the most Draconian measures, and the Americans had not arrived in sufficient strength to be a factor as yet. The full storm of the reinforced German Army fell upon the British Fifth Army, and made very considerable and frightening gains. Ground won over three years at terrible cost was lost within hours, and for several days it seemed that the Germans were unstoppable. 'What a war!' Eden wrote to Marjorie on 11 April. 'It seems to be raging everywhere at once. This *must* be the Germans' last throw, and if they cannot break us they must give in – and they cannot break us. I am glad that Lloyd George is facing things at last, but what a pity all these measures were not taken a year or even six months ago.' A week later he wrote to her that 'The House of Commons seems to be more out of touch with the war than ever. They seem to be the last people in the whole country to realize that this is the final struggle and that the fate of even their own beastly skins hangs on the result.'

Eden's judgement proved to be right, but the division found itself in much hard fighting before the tide definitely turned, and the Allies began to advance again. But the going was so difficult, and German resistance so fierce, that on 28 September Eden wrote to Marjorie, 'The news is wonderful, isn't it? Personally I feel quite sure that it will all be over by next June, if not sooner.' On 13 October, after the capture of what remained of Le Cateau, Eden wrote to Marjorie that 'We had some very hard fighting, but on the whole I was surprised at the extent to which the Germans have deteriorated. Their morale is on the whole very bad.' But, on 23 October:

I am afraid that this war is nothing like as nearly over as people in England seem to imagine. The last German division we had any dealings with fought very well indeed. We hammered them very badly but there was no 'Komerad' business about them. They fought as well and as treacherously as any Huns I have known. I only heard of one lot surrendering and they picked up their arms and shot our fellows in the back at the first opportunity. Of course we did not want many prisoners after that.

The end of the war came with unexpected speed. Defeat in the field, mutiny in the Navy, uprisings and fighting in the German streets, and the fall of the Kaiser, heralded the Armistice on 11 November. Eden's regiment was in the fighting almost to the end. 'I quite agree with you about the League of Nations,' he wrote without prescience to Marjorie on 1 November. 'I don't like the idea at all myself. Anyhow you will never get me to have anything to do with any German ever again.'

Ten days later, at 11 a.m., an eerie silence fell on the battlefields, an unforgettable experience for those who had fought for so long and so hard. Millions had fallen, countless more had been irreparably scarred physically and mentally. To have survived, and as in Eden's case, to have survived with distinction, was in itself an achievement. With only relatively brief interludes, he had been in the fighting for twenty-nine months. He had lost two brothers, and scores of friends from school and County Durham. His Yeomen were almost all gone or wounded. On 12 November he wrote to Marjorie:

Well, it is all over. I sincerely hope for the best. I am not altogether satisfied that we have not fought the war in his country [Germany], but all the same it is wonderful and I don't care a *damn* what anybody says, the result is not due to Lloyd George – Foch – internal trouble in Germany – the intervention of America, or anything else – but it is due to the BRITISH ARMY.

I really don't know whether to stick to soldiering after the war. I am afraid that it will be a dreadfully slow game for a bit until the next war comes!

Perhaps the best comment of all on Eden's war experiences was written many years later by himself:

These events* could not, however, have for me the same close personal character of comradeship as life with the Yeoman Rifles, where we had enlisted together, trained together, fought together. The more beastly and dangerous the conditions, the more this association seemed to count....

It may be that as the years were also for some of us the years when we were very young, we have been apt to confuse the two and even to feel a sigh of regret when thinking of that time. The truth is that grief, and the sadness of parting, and sorrows that seem eternal are mitigated by time, and they leave their memories and their scars and we would not have it otherwise....

I had entered the holocaust still childish and I emerged tempered by my experience, but with my illusions intact, neither shattered nor cynical, to face a changed world.

Anthony Eden now felt, as did so many others, emotions of exhaustion and anti-climax. After over two years of almost incessant activity and danger, there was now suddenly nothing to do. For all the perils and losses, the fear and discomfort, the experiences he had had of comradeship,

* The closing months of the war.

equality and hope for the future had made it an unforgettable period in his life. The return to normality was, accordingly, particularly difficult. Also, in his case there were gnawing doubts about the future, and difficulties with Tim. Peace – or at least an armistice – had been declared between the two brothers, but Lady Eden remained impossible. 'I had a letter from Mama yesterday', Eden wrote to Marjorie on 18 March, 'saying that she could expect no more consideration from me or you or from the trustees, and that Daddie at his worst had never treated her like that. She has fairly got up on her hind legs about it. I am sorry, but I cannot see how it was to be avoided. She is really too unreasonable, and will not discuss matters sanely'.

But Tim had the option – however repugnant – of selling Windlestone, its estates and farms, and the bulk of the contents; Anthony Eden did not even have this. Marjorie was married to a rich man, and although she was tenacious about demanding what she considered to be hers, she had no serious financial difficulties. Thus, of the three surviving children, Anthony was the only one with virtually nothing, and the children also faced the need to provide for their mother who, although impossible, selfish and wholly unreliable, could not be left destitute. The prospects, accordingly, were bleak. Eden's income from his father's trustees, based on the sale of Sir William's personal possessions, was going to be very modest indeed, and the prospect of peacetime soldiering was not attractive, even if – which was doubtful – the Army were to offer him a permanent commission. Everyone assumed that it really *had* been 'the war to end all wars' and that the huge British Army would be reduced to its pre-war modest size; a professional army requiring only professional soldiers. There remained the problem of the stringent eyesight requirements.

There was the possibility of politics, and three days after the Armistice Eden wrote to Tim:

I can't make up my mind whether to stay in the Army or not. I think not on the whole but I don't suppose that I shall be able to get out altogether till next Spring. At the present moment I am thinking very seriously of standing for Parliament. I am told that Spennymoor is perfectly hopeless and so I have asked Dear Mama to enquire who is standing for B[ishop] A[uckland] and if nobody is to suggest me.

He wrote to Marjorie on 15 November that 'I have been thinking rather seriously of standing for Parliament at the next general election. Don't laugh! It is a choice of that or staying in the Army.' Tim had inherited his father's extreme Conservatism, had developed a horror of Bolshevism, and expected bloody revolution in Britain. 'Anthony, I understand, is going to stand for Parliament,' he wrote with much gloom to Marjorie. 'Personally,

I think we shall all get our throats cut if we don't clear out of England soon. The difficulty will be to find a safe country to go to! I have no desire to be shot in a cellar or roll down Park Lane in a tumbril! What do you think of this?' Marjorie and Anthony thought it was nonsense.

The prospect of Eden standing for Parliament was swiftly dashed. Eagerly capitalizing on victory, the Lloyd George Coalition called a general election with indecent speed and cynicism and rode to overwhelming victory after one of the most discreditable campaigns in modern political history, while Eden could only look on from afar.

The next few months were to be among the most frustrating in Eden's life. 'Life is very dull here at present and I cannot but feel I am wasting my time,' he wrote to his mother on 8 February 1919, and went on:

I do nothing, literally nothing, from morning till night. An hour a day is about all the work I have to do, and that is as dull as it can be. . . .

I can't make out a bit what my position is at present, except that I don't get the bounty of 31/– per week! Trust Winston Churchill for that.* My services are apparently indispensable for the time being but we are being demobilised very quietly & the future is very uncertain. If I only had a job to go to I could soon get out, although I am that unfortunate most exploited person the Staff Officer. Any news of a job?

The Army is really *non bon*. They have thousands more officers than they want and so they don't want me – besides which I could never like the Army as a profession except in war-time. So there – what else is open?

The report on Eden by his commanding officer in January 1919 described him as 'A young but capable and energetic Brigade Major. Cool and resourceful in battle and possessed of a staying power his appearance doesn't suggest.' It describes him as physically 'delicate', and adds that 'considering his age he has a good knowledge of soldiering but a staff course would be of value if he is intending to stay on in the Army'.

This was now definitely not Eden's intention. 'Regular commissions in the Army are now practically unobtainable,' he noted. In order to keep his troops reasonably contented as they waited impatiently for demobilization, and to keep himself occupied, he was reduced to organizing concerts and plays 'to amuse the men'. 'There is absolutely no news here,' he wrote on 13 February; on the 24th he reported that 'Life is perfectly deadly here . . .

---

* Churchill, about whom Eden's comments in his letters and diaries were invariably hostile, had become Secretary of State for War and Air in January. He found a critical situation in the Army: what seemed to many men to be a grossly unfair system of priorities for demobilization had actually caused mutinies in several units and street demonstrations by soldiers. Churchill handled the crisis admirably. His 'bounty' for soldiers not demobilized was not available to officers.

they seem to be making a pretty good mess of the peace conference. I wish President Wilson were at the bottom of the sea.'

Lady Eden considered that he should stick to the Army as a career, and Eden replied on 19 February:

I am bored to death and feeling very depressed, and so I write to you!

This morning at 4 a.m. I said farewell to the 350 men from the Inniskillings off home to be demobilized. With them went about the only regimental officer I care much about so now I am bored *and* lonely. I do detest these partings and breaking up of friendships. Heaven only knows how long the remnant of us will be kept hanging about. I hope not long. The sooner it is all over the better.... The General is away and I am tired of the other occupants of our mess. Altogether, I am in a charming temper! This is such an utterly purposeless existence.

Eden was manifestly depressed not only about his current boredom but about his future. He was already twenty-two, had no money, no job, no future in the Army even if he had wanted one, no qualifications and no discernible prospects. In this situation he was not alone, and he could not see the way ahead. To Lady Eden he wrote on 26 February:

Now, darling, please don't talk *rot* about my future.

It is no earthly use my hanging on here any longer than I can help. There is no possibility of my getting a regular commission even if I wanted one – which I don't, and I am only wasting time here.

No: I do not want to go up to Oxford – I should hate it after this. After all for the last year at any rate I have been ordering other people about and holding a position of great responsibility. It would probably be good for me to go back & wear a gown & attend lectures, but it would certainly drive me mad. No – I do *not* like the idea of the Bar. Too sedentary.

There seem to be three alternatives –

(1) B[ishop] A[uckland] at the next election.

(2) Civil Service in East Africa.

(3) Foreign Office, of which there is a large political side which I should like to get on to after having seen something of the world.

Voilà, darling! What an outburst!

Think over what I have said. Those are the only three alternatives I will consider.

A thousand blessings.

Eden's duties were indeed tedious, but the winding up of his brigade was also an infinitely sad experience. 'I think I have done my share – three years – but it seems much more, & is full of a host of memories. It is a depressing finish & rather different to the triumphant ending I expected! Sneaking out amidst a shower of paper & indents!' (11 May). He briefly visited Cologne in March ('For the first time I felt we had really won the war,' he recorded) and then went to Louvain in Belgium, the first attested scene of German destruction. 'It stamps the Germans for ever as entirely lacking in love of the beautiful and as a brutish monster beneath a veneer of civilization,' he wrote angrily.

His impatience with his mother became increasingly evident in his letters to her. Thus, on 5 March:

I have not heard from you for ages. Why don't you *ever* write? Tim has not written since he has been demobilized – of course if he doesn't want to write he needn't, though it hardly seems polite. He already owes me three letters & he *can't* be busy if he only works from 12 till 4.

Life is *deadly* dull here – But what is the use of telling you that? You don't seem to care if I vegetate here for ever. If this life goes on much longer I shall certainly go mad.

Your affectionate & *very* bad tempered son,
Anthony

But on 9 May he received definite news of his departure to England for demobilization, and on the 26th he arrived at his appointed camp in Wiltshire. His luggage did not. His discharge papers truthfully recorded: '*Occupation:* None.'

[3]

Post-war and Politics, 1919–29

It is not at all clear from Eden's own papers why he changed his mind and decided to accept a place offered to him at Christ Church, Oxford, to read Oriental Languages in October 1919. In her unpublished memoirs Lady Eden took the credit, recording that he had remarked, 'What, go back to school?', which, as his doubts were very evident in his own letters at the time, is probably authentic. There was also the factor that he had little else to do.

Eden subsequently wrote little about his three years at Oxford. He made a few friendships, but was not active either in college or university life. His initial reactions were certainly sardonic: 'I matriculated* yesterday. Rather a farce I thought. We were all marshalled into a room and, disguised in a cap & gown, received a dog-Latin blessing from a bibulous-looking old fogey – for which blessing £3.3 please!'

He founded the Uffizi Society, whose purpose was 'to discuss Painters and Painting, past and present' (certainly a broad remit), with Lord David Cecil, R. E. Gathorne-Hardy and another Christ Church contemporary, Henry Channon (known widely, although for mysterious reasons, as 'Chips'). Other members were Victor Cazalet, Edward Sackville-West, Christopher Hussey, John Maude, Lord Balniel and Henry Studholme, each of whom was destined to attain high distinction. Eden was the President and gave the first paper, on Italian art. He subsequently gave one on Cézanne, which has survived, and is of very high quality and perception. Eden described Cézanne as 'the father of modern Art', and interspersed Cézanne's varying life, his controversial relationship with Zola, his tempestuous character and his art. Many years later, as an Oxford undergraduate myself, I heard it described by a Christ Church tutor, J. C. Masterman, as one of the most remarkable papers he had ever heard delivered by an undergraduate.

Eden's collection of pictures began at Oxford and grew gradually, and eventually included works by Corot, Monet, André Derain, Degas, Picasso, Braque, Marie Laurençin and Gwen John. Each was bought cheaply and was chosen simply on Eden's eye for a picture and his enjoyment of it. He

---

* Formally enrolled into the university.

also greatly liked Sir William Eden's watercolours of Windlestone which he had inherited, and so he created a collection that was very personal, which said much about the collector and his taste. It remains, and it was when I first saw it and experienced Eden's modest pride in it that I became aware of this aspect of his personality and of the wholly benign side of the influence of Sir William Eden.*

To his own considerable surprise, Eden discovered that he was a scholar, and became fascinated by his chosen subjects. His tutor in Persian was Professor Richard Paget Dewhurst, and in Arabic the eminent Professor Margoliouth, a scholar of the very first rank, though his Arabic was reputed to be so pure as to be unintelligible to Arab audiences. They liked Eden very much, and he them, and Dewhurst forecast for him a very distinguished future. No one had given him such academic praises or encouragement before, and the results were dramatic. He became President of the Asiatic Society. His presidential address to the Society included this passage on Persian literature:

It is the charm and melody of its verse, with its depths of mystic richness, its descriptive and varied vocabulary, the subtlety of its thought, couched in a language as beautiful as it is expressive, that gives it its unique power.

Dewhurst admired Eden's intense application, and saw without any disapproval the fact that he totally ignored almost every other facet of university life. He also noted Eden's close interest in politics, and told colleagues that he would be Foreign Secretary before he was forty.

In 1919, as in 1946, most of the undergraduates were, like Eden, far older than is normal, and many had served in the war. They were dominated by the feeling that they had already lost vital years of their lives and had much time to retrieve. It was also clear that the post-war economic environment was going to be harsh, and good degrees were going to be essential. Eden was far from being alone among his contemporaries in his solitariness and resolute application to work.

But his letters also demonstrate that he was not particularly happy with his Oxford contemporaries. 'This place is perfectly heavenly,' he wrote to his mother, 'except for unpleasant earthly ones who swarm all over the face of the earth & mar its beauties with their grating voices & hideous clothes.' He complained to Tim about the 'unceasing intrigue and narrow-minded petty politics. It all seems such a waste of time and energy & yet everybody seems to thrive on it. I suppose that it was the same before the war but it is bathos now after.' It was for this reason that he had nothing

---

* See Denys Sutton, 'A Statesman's Collection', *Apollo Magazine*, June 1969, for a detailed and sensitive account of Eden's pictures.

to do with the Oxford Union, that so-called foundation for a political career, but he had certainly not lost his appetite for politics.

Eden's natural Conservatism had survived the war, but now had little in common with that of Sir William Eden, and certainly nothing at all with the egregious hard-faced Tory right-wingers who crowded the Government benches after the Coalition landslide of 1918. There was talk of a separate National Party, which Eden, significantly, briefly thought of joining. He was also, very briefly, attracted to the Ultra-Tory Canning Club. He spoke to the University Labour Club and reported to Tim that he 'was very freely heckled. It was really rather amusing, the first terror once over. On Friday evening I have got to speak at a Primrose League Concert at a place called Great Milton. But, enough of politics.'

He had also developed a propensity for falling in love. The most serious was with Molly Cecil, the daughter of the Bishop of Exeter, whom he very much wanted to marry. But his passions were unrequited. To Tim, he poured out his anguish: 'I am still hopelessly in the toils. You are probably much amused at the wretched fate of a confirmed bachelor. If you knew Molly, perhaps you would not be too surprised. I am longing for your opinion of her. I am afraid that I have but little chance. My rivals are too numerous. However, one can but hope.' 'I am very much in love,' runs another forlorn letter to Tim; 'a d—d uncomfortable proceeding & yet pleasant withal.'

Tim, battling with the problems of saving Windlestone and in the process of taking his mother's creditors to court to reduce the levels of their usurious interest rates, was very sympathetic from afar, but Miss Cecil's heart was not engaged. 'I am sure Molly *must* say "yes" eventually,' Eden enthusiastically wrote on 30 September 1920. But on 15 October she announced her engagement to Francis Manners. 'Until this came I still had hopes,' Eden wrote to his mother, 'but I suppose now – Ah well. But life can be hard when it tries.' This rejection hurt very much, and he returned with even greater zeal to his studies, to be rewarded by an outstanding first-class degree and a lifelong love of Oriental language, literature and history. He always bore his very real erudition lightly, and was particularly modest about his very keen eye in artistic matters. With very little money he was beginning to collect pictures, and in his appreciation – as with Cézanne – he was notably ahead of contemporary taste. He was grateful to Oxford, and especially to his tutors, but he had not particularly enjoyed himself there any more than he had at Eton, and was impatient to leave. Politics beckoned.

By 1921 the confusion surrounding Eden's inheritance as a younger son was settled. He was to receive £7,675, which was all his capital, but on excellent advice he invested £5,000 in Reyrolle; the income from this was to provide him with steady, if modest means, which in 1922 amounted to £706 after tax. Out of this he had to pay for everything, including his Oxford fees, but in the context of the times he could consider himself reasonably well off for a single undergraduate.

But in 1921 there was much industrial unrest, and the real possibility of a general strike, and Eden to his dismay was recalled to the colours to command the Spennymoor detachment of the defence force, stationed in Barnard Castle, where Eden had jaundice in early June. This not only disrupted his time at Oxford, but threatened his examinations, on which there was anxious correspondence with, and between, his tutors. At one point it appeared that he might have to have special deferment, or even a special examination, but the strike faded away, the Spennymoor detachment was disbanded, and Eden could return to his studies. He was then free to take part in a lively cross-European journey with David Cecil and another friend, which began in Holland, and went on through Germany, Austria, to Budapest on the Danube, Rumania ('David talked too much. . . . Incredible scene over my revolver at Roumanian frontier. I managed to preserve it with considerable difficulty'), to Costanza, and thence by boat to Constantinople. The purpose of this 'Uffizi' voyage was the study of pictures and houses, and Eden bought a Maratti for £46 and a Constable for £200. Returning from Constantinople, their boat was turned back after leaving the Dardanelles and ordered back to Constantinople, having been taken over by the Greek Government; 'our consternation can better be imagined than described,' he noted, together with pithy and heartfelt accounts of the lamentable food and bad cabin arrangements. No doubt it was an adventure, and enjoyable, but one gains the distinct impression from Eden's diaries that it went on too long, and that the turbulent post-war Balkans had been ill chosen for a holiday.

By the beginning of 1922 he was definitely interested in a County Durham seat. He tried out his oratory in the Oxfordshire villages, thus receiving 'my baptism in the crude give and take, often tedious, sometimes stimulating, of a public meeting'. If he had ever seriously thought of the Diplomatic Service as a career – which is very doubtful – he had now definitely rejected it. He had read Lord Curzon's classic volumes, and realized that Parliament was an alternative approach to foreign affairs, which by now had become his dominant interest.

Now came a stroke of considerable good fortune. The Parliament elected in 1918 would have to be dissolved in 1923, and by the spring of 1922 it was evident that the lustre had left the Lloyd George Coalition and Conservative restiveness at its continuation was matched by the fact that the Labour Party was likely to present, for the first time, a serious challenge to the established parties. From Oxford, Eden eyed the possibilities carefully and, although deeply involved in his final studies, kept closely in touch with Tim about the possibilities in County Durham. To Tim he wrote on 3 April from Oxford:

I am glad that you agree about Spennymoor. I am not really very keen but I feel that I ought to try. Both the others are so very undesirable.

No candidate has yet been found for Sedgefield but I am not anxious to stand there. Burden has made such a mess there that I hear on all sides that his successor will have a very difficult task to keep the seat. There is little credit to be obtained there whereas if I can manage to win Spennymoor it really will be something of an achievement. It is very difficult to weigh the chances. One thing is certain – Batey will be in the first two. It will be a fight between him and me. Conservatism v. Extreme Labour. A worthy cause if ever there was one.

I am going into Durham next Wednesday to address the joint committees of the division and to be adopted if they think fit.

To Lady Eden, he wrote on 3 April that he had agreed to accept the nomination if it was offered:

There is no money & no organisation but they are very enthusiastic. When my name was suggested to a joint meeting of Committees, both Liberal & Conservative, & it was explained to the Liberals that I was a strong Conservative the chief Liberal man at once got up & said it did not matter a damn what I was, they would support an Eden.... If I can scrape 10,000 votes I should win. It will be a very close thing.

A splendid deal was struck. Mr Atterley-Jones would stand in Bishop Auckland with Conservative support; Eden would stand in Spennymoor with Liberal support. No one fully appreciated how fragile was the existence of the Conservative–Liberal alliance nationally, and both were to be the victims of machinations elsewhere.

On 12 April Eden wrote to his mother, who was in Spain, about the meeting in Durham Masonic Hall, in which gloomy context his political career began:

Very wet evening – 70 invited, nearly 60 appeared.

A dear old man called Askew in the chair.

Robson secretary.

Askew explained the object of the meeting.

Then I addressed them – I then retired. They proposed and seconded me. The invitation was then extended to me unanimously.

They were very nice & most *enthusiastic*. I wish that you & Tim could have been there. *It could not have been a better meeting.* Several women. All very keen. The Liberals were as enthusiastic as the Conservatives.... Robson summed up by saying to me, 'You have never seen such an enthusiastic meeting in the Bishop Auckland division.' I certainly have not....

And thus did it begin.

His political baptism came considerably earlier than he had expected.

In spite of a sharp decline in its popularity and position, and much Conservative discontent, the position of the Lloyd George Coalition had looked strong at the beginning of 1922, but a series of reverses and errors of judgement made the Conservative rank and file increasingly restive. When Bonar Law reappeared from apparent retirement to castigate its foreign policy and the hitherto virtually unknown Stanley Baldwin turned against Lloyd George, the Conservative mutiny became a full-scale and triumphant insurrection. At a Party meeting at the Carlton Club on 19 October, addressed by Austen Chamberlain and Balfour on behalf of remaining in the Coalition and by Baldwin and Bonar Law in favour of fighting the next election as an independent party, the latter won by 185 votes to 88. Lloyd George resigned that afternoon, and Bonar Law – after insisting on a Party meeting to elect him Leader of the Party – became Prime Minister and formed a government from which the principal Conservative Coalitionists (Austen Chamberlain, Lord Birkenhead, Balfour and Sir Robert Horne) stood contemptuously aloof. It was certainly not a government of all the talents, but it sufficed; Parliament was dissolved immediately, and the general election was held on 15 November.

The Labour Party, although it had done badly in the 1918 general election, was now truly a force to be reckoned with, especially in the North-East, and Eden's early optimism in Spennymoor quickly receded. So lively were some of his meetings that a survivor of his platoon came, 'as I had heard there was going to be trouble'. But Eden experienced nothing worse than much derisive heckling and noise, whereas in Dundee Winston Churchill was being howled down and venomously assailed. Churchill had just had a serious appendix operation, and had to campaign in a wheel-chair; he later believed that if he had not been so obviously incapacitated he might have been physically attacked, so high were feelings. On one occasion Eden was able to restore good humour in a rowdy meeting when he was accused of being 'one of the idle rich', upon which he pulled out his empty pockets. The genuine respect that his family enjoyed in the area gave him an easier ride than many other Conservatives and Coalition Liberals had, but it was certainly a lively initiation.

Eden's Election Address and his speeches stressed his local connections and his strong support for law; he also emerged as an opponent of restrictions on the sale of alcohol ('the thin end of the wedge to introduce prohibition') and as an advocate of the reduction of the beer duty, which can hardly have lost him many votes. But he also urged industrial peace and conciliation, better pensions and the abolition of the hated means test for benefits. It was a significantly liberal programme, but the Labour tide in County Durham was much too strong, and Joseph Batey won easily with 13,766 votes to Eden's 7,567. At a time when, although the Conservatives won the election overall, Labour was sweeping the North and winning 142 seats in the new Parliament, there was no disgrace or personal humiliation in such a result.* With 345 seats, as opposed to Labour 142, Asquithian Liberals 60, and 57 (Lloyd George) National Liberals, and with Churchill among the ranks of the fallen, Bonar Law had achieved a very comfortable majority, and seemed to be destined to rule for at least four years. Eden was very quickly to discover what an astonishingly hazardous and unpredictable profession he had entered.

He had not really expected to win Spennymoor, and was not noticeably downcast by his defeat. The causes of the depression with which he began 1923 ('A very delightful day with which to open this very ominous & uncertain year,' he wrote in his diary on 1 January) were lack of serious employment, continuing concern about his finances, and regular disappointment in love.

Eden's desire to marry seems rather strange in the light of his modest finances and indecision about his future, but it was very real, and after the disappointment over Molly Cecil he had for a time high hopes of marrying another lady, but again his feelings were not returned. With great kindness she wrote to him gently, and almost classically, 'I do like you most awfully as a friend, but I am not in love with you,' and that was that. Eden was plunged into deep gloom. 'The evening was one of terrific depression,' he lamented to his diary.

The sense of my loss was truly felt. In many ways no marriage could have been more successful. There was between us that sympathy which cannot be explained or understood unless & until it is felt. And now – the future stretches out bleaker and more desolate than ever. My own fireside is unattainable, happiness more than ever distant. I wonder whether she feels any of this?

Another with whom he was briefly smitten later told him that she would have married him had he not been a poor younger son, which at least had the merit of candour.

His mood was not improved by boredom at Windlestone, Tim's success in love and happy marriage, and difficulties with his mother. 'Mama in an

---

*Lord Peart recalled in the House of Lords on Eden's death: 'When I was a small boy – I must have been eight years of age or younger – I can remember him fighting his first election in 1922, in Spennymoor. My school was a polling station and, peeping over the wall, I could not help being impressed by the tall Conservative candidate, with his handsome face, black hair and moustache. He came from an old North County Durham family with a great history of public service. He was linked with the history of my own county; he was part of it.' (House of Lords, 18 January 1977)

unamiable mood' runs one entry; 'Mama read me extracts from Papa's letters after dinner, which did not help my reading' is another. The sons conspired to persuade her to go abroad for six months. There was some desultory political activity: 'After lunch we motored into Durham for Unionist conference. A waste of time. Lord L[ondonderry] spoke, not as well as usual, but very directly. I fear that it will be of very little use. We passed a series of resolutions that will have very little result.'

He was invited to meet the Executive Committee of the Hartlepool Conservatives at the end of February, '& was not very much impressed'. He spoke for the successful Conservative candidate in a by-election in Darlington and canvassed: 'Quite good fun but incredibly tiring.' He made inquiries about the possibility of a candidature at Sedgefield; his interest was welcomed but 'There remains the difficulty of fixing up finance.' He kept links with Spennymoor, and noted poor meetings, low attendance, no money (the Association had an overdraft of £25), and a 'dictatorial' agent. He heard Leo Amery speak, and noted that he was 'good & sound ... but lacked genius'. On 14 May he spoke at a meeting at Chilton, 'which was a farce. Only the Chairman and Secretary were present.'

The boredom of his life at Windlestone is best described in his complete diary entry for 13 May:

A day in which I read a little in compensation for many unproductive days. A story or two and a considerable proportion of Gibbon's autobiography, which gave me the greatest pleasure. He is indeed unsurpassed as a master of English prose.

A few walks were interspersed, and a few letters were written.

From this he frequently fled to London, where he had a small flat, and assisted his finances by writing articles for the *Saturday Review*, which can best be described as well researched and thoughtful rather than inspired. Indeed, until his old age, when he surprised everyone by writing *Another World*, Eden's capacity for writing was limited, even on artistic subjects on which his knowledge and enthusiasm were manifest. His style was clear, but deficient in excitement, and sometimes came perilously close to the banal. But he was young, he tried hard, and the modest income he derived from journalism was important. 'I am seriously thinking of giving up politics, and reading and writing for the future,' he wrote on 4 June. 'We shall see how the writing goes.' On 10 June he recorded that 'George Moore came to lunch. He was in very good form. He does not talk as good English as he writes'; Eden's problem, ironically enough, was the reverse.

Laboriously, he tried to augment his very modest, but very enlightened, collection of pictures.

... Tim lunched with me. Walked to Grafton St to see Bonnard Exhibition but it was closed so we went on to the Alpine Gallery – [Augustus] John.

Interesting. One picture, Head of a Girl, brilliantly painted on a rough canvass, I liked. Otherwise nothing I cared about. He is a brilliant draughtsman at times, but very uneven. His colouring is crude and vulgar. And why try and paint like El Greco? A twentieth century drunkard from Chelsea and essentially of the age, blunt and worldly in his conception, vulgar in his inner self, trying to paint like the sixteenth century mystic. Incongruous indeed. (Diary, 19 May)

The difficulties with Lady Eden were interminable.

Mama came to lunch, half an hour late! in an odious temper.... I thought Mama's attitude perfectly detestable all day and I am convinced that she has no intention of giving Tim any list of her debts.... I believe her to be a very unscrupulous and untruthful woman. (Diary, 21 May)

But these were not the total picture of Eden's activities and interests.

It would be pointless to pretend that Eden was not immensely attracted to beautiful women, nor they to him. In spite of his eagerness to marry, at this time he also involved himself in a passionate relationship with a beautiful and talented singer and actress. It began when he went to a performance of John Gay's *Polly*, a sadly inadequate endeavour to repeat the triumph of *The Beggar's Opera*, but it was 'Polly' herself who enraptured Eden. He became a regular attender, noting on his second visit: 'We were in the front row, too near to obtain a fair view of the performance, but I was not sorry as it enabled me to see "Polly" herself. She is very attractive – clever, a beautiful voice, & great charm.' Two days later: '... then to Polly – more delightful & charming than ever ... very fascinating'. Matters swiftly proceeded, and evenings with 'Polly' became regular events, and there was a brief but evidently exciting affair. When Eden confided to Marjorie, his sister was, not surprisingly, horrified; Tim took a more relaxed view. But there is no evidence at all that the hearts of either were engaged. As Eden wrote: 'I saw her after the first Act as before and said "good-bye" very regretfully. I think that she felt it too, but she was very charming as usual and looked very beautiful.'

This was a passing matter, fervent while it lasted, but no more. The contrast with boredom at Windlestone, oppression over finances ('Another fall in Rio Tinto to 36 +. D—m the things. I wish that I had sold them when they were 40 –. I was a bloody fool not to take the profit') and desultory political meetings in County Durham can only have been delightful. Tim's judgement was the correct one.

Despite Eden's occasional wistfulness for a life of writing and art, he had certainly not abandoned his political ambitions. In May, Bonar Law, having been told by his doctors that he had terminal throat cancer, resigned the premiership. 'Very heavy blow for the present Govt.,' Eden wrote on 21

May. 'I wish that [Austen] Chamberlain could step into his shoes. I mistrust these die-hards – they are an ignorant and unbalanced crew and will ruin the party if once they gain control.' To general surprise, the dying Law was succeeded not by Lord Curzon, and certainly not by Chamberlain, but by the almost unknown Stanley Baldwin. The Coalition die-hards whom Eden so despised remained in their isolation. But the Government had a large parliamentary majority, and no election apparently loomed. While these great events convulsed the political world, Anthony Eden had fallen in love again.

There are few more attractive personalities in Anthony Eden's life than Sir Gervase Beckett. He was a successful banker, part-owner and Chairman of the *Yorkshire Post*, a Member of Parliament for North Leeds, the owner of a fine property at Kirkdale, and a man of notable sweetness of character; and if shrewd in business he had a warmth of heart that made him not only respected but beloved. His second wife was Queenie, Charlie Feversham's widow, who had particular reason to love Anthony and whose friendship with her sister-in-law, Marjorie Brooke, remained very close. Beckett thought well of young Eden, who liked him immensely and knew him as 'Ger' for some time as a friend before he had really noticed his young daughter, Beatrice, with any seriousness. He was, after all, recovering from the shock of other failed romantic missions, was baffled about his future, and although Ger was so much older there was a strong rapport between the two men, which was destined to survive many changes of fortune, to the immense credit of both. Ger Beckett was a wonderful man, with a keen eye for talent and promise, and, although devoted to the memory of his first wife and to his four children and Martyn (the child of his second marriage), was a highly objective father. He had been impressed by Eden's war record and his valour in contesting Spennymoor; he marked him down as a young man of great promise. Eden found in him a friend and counsellor to whom he became devoted.

Beatrice was young – aged eighteen – was very beautiful, and had an impulsive but glowing personality of immense warmth and unconscious sensuality. Eden only began to observe this in the June of 1923, when she begins to replace the lost 'Polly' in his diaries: 'Beatrice looked very beautiful in a black dress with a green shawl,' he wrote admiringly on 14 June. She invited him to stay at Kirkdale on 7 July, and Eden's feelings deepened. He tore himself away for more political meetings in County Durham; Chilton on 19 July was successful, and 'Came home in high glee.' Port Clarence on 26 July was less so: 'Blowing a hurricane and clouds of dust and dirt flying about.' On the 28th he was back at Kirkdale with Tim to see Beatrice again: 'she looked lovely and I was so pleased to see her again.... Tim was much impressed. Held on to her hand for a second when I said goodbye.' On the next day he wrote: 'I wish I had more courage. Sometimes I think she cares, sometimes I am not sure. We spent the greater part of the day together.'

Contrary to some snide hints then and later, there was no calculation in this romance. Eden was certainly keen on becoming married, and Ger Beckett was an influential Conservative MP and newspaperman, but although Eden had known Beatrice for such a short time, there is no questioning his ardour, as his diary demonstrates:

The greatest day of my life. After a night of doubt & sorrow – almost – I made the plunge and proposed at an unearthly hour of the morning. Beatrice was angelic. She looked so beautiful leaning up against a table in the oak room that I could bear it no longer. Thank God it was a swift act of folly. No set speeches, nothing – just one word & then incoherent rattlings that were perfectly intelligible to her heart. Never can there have been a worse-formulated proposal – never can there have been a happier man at the result.

Beatrice accepted and I gained the promise of the most beautiful, the most lovable, the truest and the best woman in the world.

Ger seemed quite pleased and very very nice indeed. (31 July)

Ecstatic days ensued at Kirkdale. 'Happiness and delirious delight such as I have never known,' Eden wrote in his diary on 1 August.

I have indeed won a treasure, perhaps the rarest on earth. A beautiful woman, with the character of an angel and a heart of gold – & she actually loves me. I have added cubits to my self respect in the last twenty-four hours. My head will soon be disproportionately large! In the intervals of delirium contrived to write letters and send off telegrams. We went for a ride at some time. I have never taken less interest in my horse or the scenery. They were just not [there] – Beatrice was – and joy beyond description.

He described 2 August as 'A day of wild delight.'

The engagement was not universally greeted in the two families with the joy that radiates out of Eden's diaries. There was the matter of Beatrice's age, which Eden dismissed as 'fatuous'. There was the fact that they had known each other for such a short time. There was also the matter, about which Eden probably did not know at the time, that Beatrice, also, was 'on the rebound', having formed an attachment considered so unsuitable by her father that she had been hastily sent on a heavily chaperoned visit to Egypt. Although the Becketts had no idea what was in store for Eden, they knew that Beatrice was massively uninterested in politics, and had a wayward nature that was intensely appealing but also made them wonder whether marriage at this early stage was right for her. Her devoted half-brother Martyn considered then, and after, that she would have been happiest in a Yorkshire landowning marriage. The Becketts loved Eden, and were always staunch to him, but even at this very early stage there were doubts which were perfectly expressed in a letter to Eden by Ger on 9 August:

My dear Anthony,

The task that you found hard in writing to me was also not really necessary. Nevertheless I appreciate it, & assure you that you have well expressed what I know you feel.

I am not good at playing the heavy father, but cannot say how much I am anxious for the happiness of the children. I look upon it (as it is) as a sacred trust; & ever since their Mother's death I have done what I could to be faithful to it. I may have made mistakes in my methods, & have found sometimes unexpected obstacles in my way; but I have always tried singly to carry out what I believe she would have wished. I feel quite sure that she would have welcomed you as the husband of her beloved Beatrice, & therefore I am more than content.

I think you are right in your estimate of Beatrice's feelings & temperament; &, were you my son, I should feel quite happy that you had chosen – that best of boons – a good wife. I can't say more than this as it is everything, if one has brains to appreciate it & patience to prove it.

You will remember that she is young & not expect her too soon to give up 'childish things'; she must be allowed for a time to feel, think, & speak as a child; but I am sure that as she comes on she will never be wanting in her loyalty, faithfulness, & love towards you. Such as her Mother, & life after death (in my belief) largely consists & persists through the spirit inherited.

And so I wish you both the best of all things, knowing as I do that these lie in your own possession, if you choose & determine to keep them in your grasp.

Ever your affectionate

Ger

From Kirkdale, Beatrice wrote to her fiancé:

Antonio Mio,

I wonder how you are getting on?

I hope successfully & *not overworking yourself*.

Please don't darling – it does worry me so much. I *hate* seeing you with dark lines & a white face – it honestly frightens me, beloved. . . .

And, again:

Darling, I *hope* you are not too tired – you know, Antonio, you really must *not* do too much. I shall be so annoyed if you are so tired you are not fit to speak to me (!) at the wedding! And you wouldn't like me to be annoyed, would you?

Her letters always began, 'I love you, I love you, I love you'.

70

The wedding was provisionally arranged for 1 November at St Margaret's, Westminster, and the young couple went eagerly house-hunting, both assuming that they would continue to live in the North. Ger knew the financial difficulties of his future son-in-law, and wanted, tactfully, to help. 'Ger told me that he proposed to hand over 2000 shares in his bank to me and I could either buy the house or rent it from the income derived thereby. He really is the most amazingly generous person I know, or have ever known' (30 August). 'I am happy, madly happy, in her love' was one of many similar outpourings in Eden's diary at this wonderfully happy time.

Wedding preparations and house-hunting in Yorkshire and County Durham were now startlingly disrupted by a totally unexpected event.

Early in October the sitting Conservative Member for Warwick and Leamington, Sir Ernest Pollock, was appointed Master of the Rolls and automatically vacated a seat that had been only cursorily contested in 1918 and not at all in 1922. This time it was to be very different. George Nicholls, a former farm labourer and Radical MP for North Hampshire between 1906 and 1910 and Mayor of Peterborough, came forward as the Liberal candidate, and the flamboyant sixty-two-year-old Countess of Warwick, the mother-in-law of Marjorie, announced herself as the first Labour candidate Warwick and Leamington had experienced, and declared that she would tour the constituency in a carriage 'drawn by four milk-white steeds'. She had been converted to Socialism by Robert Blatchford, who had denounced one of her lavish social extravaganzas at Warwick Castle in his journal *The Clarion*, and whom she had subsequently met. Her family, knowing her close relationship with King Edward VII and capacity for spending money, tended to ascribe this dramatic change to a desire for expiation for past misdeeds rather than to concern for the downtrodden masses. In this they probably misjudged her. But it was certainly bizarre to see this former leading member of the notorious 'Marlborough House Set' and the wife of the fifth Earl of Warwick sallying forth from Warwick Castle bearing the banner of Socialism. It was certainly highly embarrassing for her family.* 'What a heartless female Lady W is,' Eden noted in his diary after a talk with her daughter Queenie Beckett.

It is not clear from Eden's papers how or why he became the Conservative candidate for a constituency so far removed and different from his own area, and about which he knew nothing. His diary at this time is intermittent

---

* The fifth Earl of Warwick died in 1924 and was succeeded by Guy Brooke, Marjorie becoming the Countess of Warwick. Her mother-in-law died in 1938, one of the last acts before her death being a warm letter of congratulation to Anthony Eden on his resignation as Foreign Secretary.

and the only entry for 19 October is 'Heard by wire an invitation to contest by-election at Warwick & Leamington.'

What had happened was a familiar enough story, but it was crucial for Eden's fortunes.

A local worthy had put himself forward confidently for the nomination. The trouble with local candidates is that they tend to be rather too well known in their area, and in all politics it is considerably easier to make enemies than friends. This was what happened in Warwick and Leamington, and the local worthy was rejected by the Conservative Association. Time was pressing, and an appeal was hurriedly dispatched to Conservative Central Office for possible candidates on the Party list, with a strong preference expressed for one who had already fought an election, it already being obvious that there was to be no repetition of the easy saunter to which Sir Ernest Pollock had become accustomed. Eden had fought a seat, and was not committed to any constituency, unlike many of his contemporaries, and he was accordingly drawn to the attention of the constituency association. The key roles were played by the local chairman, Lord Willoughby de Broke, who was twenty-seven, had also won a Military Cross in the war, and was eager to have someone of his own age who had served with him, and by Marjorie. Doubts about Eden's inexperience and youth were set aside. Indeed, he was virtually the only candidate, and the combination of his charm, handsomeness and sincerity convinced the Warwick and Leamington Conservatives that their search was over. In politics, as in everything else, luck is vital. At the age of twenty-six, Eden had found that most cherished of objectives, 'a seat for life', which he was to represent for thirty-three years.

Although Eden's wedding was not to take place until 5 November – in the middle of the campaign – the complicated family involvement in the by-election was a delight to the press and a source of acute embarrassment to the Warwick and Beckett families.

Thus, by the mysterious processes of political Providence, Beatrice found herself involved in a major by-election, with her wedding taking place in the middle of the contest. Ger Beckett made a generous contribution to Eden's expenses, and a thoroughly lively electoral battle then ensued.

Warwick and Leamington was then a geographically large constituency – over two hundred square miles – and in its industrial and social composition utterly different from County Durham. Also, there was the new factor that since the last contest nearly 20,000 women were entitled to vote, and there was much speculation about whether they would be attracted by the rarity and novelty of a woman candidate. The Conservative Government, although competent enough, notably lacked sparkle, and the Liberals, anticipating a split vote, were in good heart. The general feeling was that, in the special circumstances that seem to attend every by-election, the Conservatives, with no local organization of any note, and unaccustomed in that constituency to contested elections, could be in difficulties.

There was swift and widespread agreement that they had at least chosen an outstandingly attractive candidate. He looked older than he was, his war record – almost essential for a Conservative candidate in 1923 – spoke for itself, and he had already acquired that almost mesmeric hold over women audiences that was to be the wonder and despair of his envious colleagues and opponents for the rest of his career. He was undeniably a glamorous candidate, with his beautiful, if somewhat bewildered, fiancée at his side, and although by no means a riveting speaker he easily held his audiences, who were conspicuously more docile than the Durham miners. Nicholls, no doubt wisely, concentrated on the discontented and ill-treated agricultural workers; the Countess of Warwick conducted a campaign that can best be described as idiosyncratic; it was in a sense before her time, the spectacle of the immensely wealthy flaunting and advocating extreme Socialism not being as familiar then as it was subsequently to become.

The Countess was unable to fulfil her pledge to campaign with four 'milk-white steeds', but did so in her carriage drawn by two cobs, one bay and the other chestnut. On one occasion her progress was involved in a procession of animals advertising 'The Garden of Allah' in Leamington, which included 'two camels, a pair of mules, a small donkey and a foal, and many onlookers took it for granted that she was part of the show'.*

What Dennis Bardens has felicitously described as 'the Eden charm . . . integrity plus friendliness' was considerably more important than the content of his Election Address and his speeches. But what is surprising to modern political eyes was the virtually wholly uncritical attitude of the local and national newspapers. When asked at a meeting about his views on divorce, his reply that 'it is rather hard that you should ask me about that already' was widely applauded. Thus he became used, too early, to an immensely favourable and almost deferential press, for which a heavy price was to be exacted in later years. But in 1923 the political sun shone for him.

The battle of the hustings was only briefly interrupted by Eden's wedding on 5 November, a day of great happiness: 'Beatrice looked incredibly beautiful in her wedding dress,' the bridegroom wrote: 'This was not only my opinion but that of everybody. Many people said that she was the most beautiful bride ever seen. *I* thought so.'

The honeymoon was spent with friends in Sussex, and lasted only two days, as polling day in Warwick and Leamington lay two weeks ahead.

* Dennis Bardens, *Anthony Eden*. In his old age, Eden told me the same story – totally confirmed by local papers – with much glee and laughter.

Beatrice was immensely proud of her handsome husband, on the verge of becoming a Member of Parliament, and was always to remain so, but this was to be both an unfortunate, and unhappily a characteristic, beginning to a marriage on which both embarked with intense ardour and no doubts. Throughout his life Eden hated elections: 'There are those who enjoy them, and those who endure them,' he once wrote; 'I belong to the latter category.' But he loved politics, and was to come to love the House of Commons, two passions that Beatrice, valiantly though she initially tried, could never share.

They were also not rich, as Eden glumly noted on 21 October:

Everything seems to be going well except the financial situation, which still causes grave anxiety! 70 odd days of this year remain to be struggled through & with little over £100 with which to do it. It is not a pleasant outlook unless a few cheques come in as wedding presents, or unless I could sell my car but nothing of the kind has happened so far.

Then, as the by-election approached its climax, there was a thunderclap.

The economic situation had continued to deteriorate. Unemployment was over 11 per cent, and, particularly with Neville Chamberlain* in the Cabinet, talk of protective tariffs was heard again, and was a dominant topic at the Imperial Economic Conference in London in October. But no one was prepared for Baldwin to raise the issue at the Party Conference on 25 October by reminding his audience of Bonar Law's pledge – which most people had either forgotten or had not noticed – that there should be no fundamental change in fiscal arrangements in the lifetime of the existing Parliament. By raising the banner of Protection, Baldwin convulsed the political world. There was, it has been argued, no need for a general election, but there were tactical considerations, not least that of taking the issue away from Lloyd George. The Conservative Protectionists, led by Chamberlain and Amery, were enthusiastic for an appeal to the country on the issue; tacticians saw the merits of a swift election. On 12 November the Cabinet agreed, and Parliament was dissolved.

The news caused consternation at Warwick and Leamington, with the candidates and their supporters panting into the last days of the campaign, with polling day on 22 November looming with blessed promise of deliverance. Now, everything had to be stopped, and then restarted. The sense of let-down was universal, but was particularly hard on the Conservative candidate and his wife. After a break of six days, the Edens were back on the seemingly endless slog around the villages through fog and frost.

* The son of Joseph Chamberlain and the half-brother of Austen.

On the eve of poll, Eden spoke to four meetings in one evening, and estimated that he had made eighty speeches since the marathon had begun. His final appeal to the electors of Warwick and Leamington at least had the merit of brevity:

I am a Conservative, and a supporter of the Prime Minister. I stand for the protection of British industries. It is also the only country with a vast army of unemployed.

On polling day itself, 6 December, the constituency was again enveloped in a fog so thick that there was a last-minute alarm about the turnout.

But all went well when the count took place on 7 December. On a 75 per cent turnout Eden had a majority of 5,203 over the Liberal, and Lady Warwick, with only 4,015 votes, came a very poor third. The campaign had lasted over six weeks, and Eden, although elated, was exhausted, with a heavy cold. After lunch at Oxford, 'which Beatrice had never seen before', the Edens returned in triumph to London to have 'A quiet and very happy evening'. Apart from one brief visit to attend a dinner in Leamington ('Left Leamington by the 9.28 train with the greatest energy') the Edens went to Kirkdale for Christmas, where the snow fell heavily, and Eden directed and starred in a family performance of *The Importance of Being Ernest*; there was some shooting, and much dancing. On 31 December Eden wrote in his diary:

This brings to a close a most eventful year in my life. One which opened under omens & auspices by no means favourable and closes leaving me a happier man than I dare to confess even to myself.

Above all it has given me the blessings of a wonderful and beautiful wife. Even when I was engaged to Beatrice I hardly realized what a treasure it was that I had found. So far our married life has been one of the greatest happiness. It will be my fault if it does not continue so. Politically I have risen from the undignified position of an unknown & ignominiously defeated candidate for a little-known constituency to be a member by more than 5000 majority for one of the most historic seats in England. To many my name is now familiar. The future is now in my own hands. Financially things have not been so bright, but I am in a sounder position now than I was at the beginning of the year, & I close with a good balance. This however was only possible by Ger's amazing generosity.

Good-bye, dear 1923. Thank you!

Baldwin's decision to go for an early election did not look justified when the results were declared. The Conservatives had lost nearly ninety seats, and although still the largest Party in the House of Commons (258) they were in a minority in the event of a Liberal–Labour coalition. Labour, with 191 seats, had dramatically and definitely emerged as the principal challenger to Conservative domination; the Liberals, shakily reunited, had

158 seats, with Winston Churchill again among the unsuccessful candidates; this was to be his last appearance in the Liberal colours. Baldwin refused to resign either the premiership or the Party leadership until and unless the Opposition parties combined against him in Parliament.

This was the uneasy situation when Anthony Eden took his place in January 1924 as MP for Warwick and Leamington.

Eden wrote many years later:

At the age of twenty-six, I knew little except war and schooling. War I hated for all I had seen of it among my family and friends, for the death, muck and misery, the pounding shell-fire and the casualty clearing stations. I was ready to support any effort to stop it coming again, but I was no pacifist, not from any motive of doctrine, but because I was convinced that pacifism on our part would not prevent war. In this mood I went to Westminster, earnest but only sketchily informed.*

The first days of being a Member of Parliament are the most delightful of all. There are many moments in a campaign when a new candidate wonders whether all this clatter, public meetings, canvassing, travelling, always being polite and becoming exhausted in the process, is really worthwhile. For most of the successful, these doubts disappear when one actually arrives at Westminster. Everything is bewildering, one gets lost in the seemingly endless and purposeless corridors of the vast Palace, the procedure and customs appear archaic, unfathomable and extraordinary; but everyone is immensely kind to the new Member, and the excitement of having actually reached the objective sustains him for the initial weeks until it becomes evident that politics, like any job, has its tedium, frustrations and uncongenial colleagues. Finding one's place in such circumstances takes time.

Warwick and Leamington was to prove a superb base for Eden's career. The modern Conservative insistence that the MP live in or very close to his constituency did not then exist, and the demands made by the constituency upon Eden were, by today's standards, very modest indeed. It was possible in the inter-war years to achieve a reputation as a diligent MP by responding promptly to the few letters constituents wrote, subscribing to local charities and Party functions, and making the occasional visit to the constituency, heralded and regarded as a major event. A respectful local press reported Eden's speeches in and out of Parliament at some length, and hardly ever made criticisms. The modern Member of Parliament can also see that Parliament itself was infinitely less demanding in time and activity, so that it was possible for a politician to live a civilized existence, with evenings at home or being entertained, opportunities for

* Avon, *Facing the Dictators*, p. 4.

extensive travel abroad, and weekends free for reading, friends and family, and thought. The parliamentary recesses were long and frequent. The Warwick and Leamington Conservatives took good care of constituency problems, gave Eden their constant support, and remained faithful through all vicissitudes.

These sterling advantages, denied to so many politicians, did have their price. The task of representing a marginal constituency is an arduous one, and gives to the MP a daily tension and concern which compel him into constituency activity. In that process he learns much about human problems and concerns, most of them apparently humble but of real importance to the individual. Eden, the most humanly sympathetic of men, did not have this experience in representing Warwick and Leamington. He worked immensely hard, and was a devoted MP, but the circumstances of his constituency made it rather too easy to become remote from the day-to-day practical realities of ordinary people by concentrating upon international affairs and general issues.

In the 1920s, politics, especially Conservative politics, was a rich man's profession, and remains so to this day. The parliamentary salary of £400 was worth very considerably more in 1924 than it would be today, but this must be put into perspective. Thus in January 1924 Eden's meticulously kept accounts for the month show expenditure of £202, and his parliamentary salary £23 (Parliament had not met until 8 January). His monthly parliamentary salary was £32, and was to remain at this dismal level – except when he was in Office – for over twenty years.* His total income before income tax, from his modest family trust and his own investments and sales of shares, for the whole of 1924 was £1,162, and his literary income was £63. Beatrice had a small allowance from her father, and Ger Beckett was always very ready to help in emergencies – insisting, for example, on meeting Beatrice's hospital bills when she had a miscarriage. Thus the young Edens were far from penury, but London was not a cheap city, nor were politics a cheap profession at a time when every item of expenditure, including stamps for constituency correspondence, came out of the MP's own pocket. Nor was journalism very remunerative; Ger arranged for Eden to write an occasional article in the *Yorkshire Post*, and the fee varied between a maximum of ten guineas to only five; the *Saturday Review* paid two guineas!

The Edens' first London home was 2 North Street (now Lord North Street) which they rented for £250 a year. The political prospects for the Conservative Party were somewhat uncertain, with another general election

---

* In fact, as a result of the October general election, during which MPs were not paid, Eden's actual income as an MP in 1924 was £311.

looming. This would involve further expense, and the Edens' financial position was already distinctly worrying, but they were happy and excited, deeply in love, and regarded as an exceptionally handsome and intelligent couple, much welcomed on the London scene, with which they were both, especially Beatrice, unfamiliar.

Eden's papers and diaries were principally concerned with the financial and logistical problems of being a newly married MP. He recorded his first day in the House of Commons:

8 January 1924
Went round to the House at 2.30 (after lunch with Ger Beckett) and was successful in finding seats for the election of the Speaker. I was very much interested. Speeches by Baldwin, Lloyd George and Ramsay MacDonald. Baldwin was very much the best, short, clear, and dignified. He has a pleasant voice. McD reeked too much of the soap box, emphasizing the last words of every sentence as though for rounds of applause. Ll G unimpressive, but I am told that he is never at his best upon such occasions as these. He had a very poor reception.

The Baldwin Government had resolved to meet Parliament, and the Debate on the Loyal Address lasted until 21 January, recorded by Eden as 'a fateful day at the House'. It fell by seventy-two votes, and Britain had her first Labour Government on the morrow, with Ramsay MacDonald as Prime Minister. While this administration was in the process of being created, the Edens fled London and the chaos of their new home for a second honeymoon at Sidmouth. There were then post-election festivities and meetings in Warwick and Leamington, and the return to London and politics.

After losing the election so unexpectedly, Baldwin's leadership had been called into question:

Beatrice and I motored to Hotel Cecil for the Party meeting. A large attendance. Baldwin spoke better than usual, but not a word, or even a hint, of resignation. Balfour proposed a resolution of confidence in Baldwin. An excellent speech: very much the best of the day. Austen also spoke, and well, a very loyal effort. A few criticisms, most of them badly, and some of them inaudibly, expressed, and the meeting came to an end. Considering all things: a very successful gathering. (Diary, 11 February)

Eden's maiden speech was made on 19 February in support of a motion favouring strong air defence proposed by a Conservative colleague, Sir Samuel Hoare. It was startlingly brief for such an occasion, lasting barely five minutes, and was – very unusually for a maiden speech – heckled with cries of 'No! no!' from the Labour and Liberal benches when he declared that 'Attack is the best possible form of defence.' By this, as he explained, he meant that 'we should have the means at our disposal to answer any attack by an attack'. The next speaker, Captain Wedgwood Benn, made no reference at all to Eden's speech, no doubt being offended at Eden's derision of his Party rolling on their backs like a terrier 'and waving their paws in the air with a pathetic expression'. Eden's sentiments might have been admirable, but it was a poor speech, and certainly broke the convention that a maiden speech should be uncontroversial. Not surprisingly, little notice was taken of it.

He had made the mistake of speaking virtually unprepared, and in response to what he described in his diary as 'a sanctimonious & unimpressive' speech by the Under-Secretary for Air, 'which drove me to speak.... I was terrified, and did not I thought acquit myself with any credit. But the House was very generous & cheered me very well when I sat down.' On the next day he continued to be miserable, realizing that the congratulations he received only came from kindness to a new Member. 'It was "thin",' he gloomily wrote of his speech, 'and I missed a great opportunity, but perhaps that is just as well in a maiden effort.' What he could not realize then, although he later did, was that his early espousal of strong air defence was to serve him well. He had also learned, the hard way, that the House of Commons does not appreciate unprepared and somewhat shallow and perfunctory interventions on serious matters. This was the most important lesson of all, and one which he took immediately to heart. He was to continue to be, throughout his long parliamentary career, a severe critic of his own performances, over which he took immense trouble. The fact that the career of one of the most skilled and sensitive parliamentarians of modern times began with what was almost a fiasco may give comfort to others who have experienced that deep sickness in the stomach which follows a manifest failure in the House of Commons, and which no amount of kindness from family and friends can quickly assuage. Eden's maiden speech was not a disaster, but although he would not wish his biographer to linger over it, the important point was that he learned from it. He knew little or nothing about air defence in February 1924; henceforth, although many of his speeches may have lacked sparkle, they were invariably based on deep knowledge and preparation, which the House of Commons recognized.

It had been a salutary beginning.

Politics were in a curious condition at this time. There was a widespread feeling that the first Labour Government, owing its existence to the Liberals, should be given a fair chance to prove itself. The Liberals themselves remained acutely divided, and the former Coalition Conservatives, although reconciled, were still critical of their supplanters.

Winston Churchill was still out of Office, having fought the 1923 election as a Liberal, but was beginning the process that was to make him first a 'Constitutionalist Anti-Socialist' candidate and then, later in this strange year, virtually a Conservative again. Eden, who barely knew him, and who retained his wartime prejudices, regarded this as a somewhat cynical performance, which indeed it was.

One prejudice was removed by experience of the House of Commons. Asquith was, as an orator and parliamentarian, still formidable, and Eden was immensely attracted to him. As he later wrote: 'His speeches were models of lucidity and brevity, with the English language at its best. In an age when prolixity was already becoming a substitute for conviction, he never wasted a word.'* He also swiftly became an admirer of Baldwin, whose advice to him and the few other new Conservative MPs was to treat Labour with respect. Eden was a very ready pupil in this matter, and the war and Spennymoor had taught him a great deal; the House of Commons taught him even more.

Eden's own memoirs say virtually nothing about this period of his life. In fact, after the misfortune of his maiden speech he worked to retrieve his position, and made his first speech on foreign affairs on 1 April. But he also spoke on air defence again, on housing, and on army marriage allowances, on each occasion from a basis of knowledge and in a style notably different from his first efforts, which he was later to develop into one modelled on Asquith and Baldwin, but which became uniquely his own.

The life of an MP then could be an agreeable one. The Edens experienced all the difficulties of moving into a new home, and Eden was a regular attender of the House, although his diaries emphasize how undemanding politics could be in those days.

28 February
Wrote letters in the morning and lunched at home.

House in the afternoon. [Conservative] Committee on Foreign Affairs. Not very interesting – a sub-committee was formed about Russia.

Beatrice came to tea at the House – Ger joined us.

Dined at the Londonderrys: a large party, about sixteen. I sat next to Lady Masserene. I quite like her.

Played Bridge. I won 30/-! Not so bad. Went on to dance at Sassoons. A great crowd there & some dreadful people.

Home about 1 a.m.

At this time, at Ger's suggestion, Eden wrote a political article for the *Yorkshire Post*, which was published on 3 March; 'this fills me with the hope that I shall get the job of writing for them every week. It will be a

---

* Avon, *Facing the Dictators*, p. 6.

considerable financial help.' On 7 March, at a royal function, 'the King was very affable, sent for me and talked for quite a long time'. This was their first meeting.

Eden started to ask questions in the Commons on foreign affairs, was bored by committee work, and experienced the usual miseries of being a back-bencher, noting on 20 March: 'A long sojourn in the House in an attempt to get in on Air Estimates. Was eventually successful about 7.20 p.m. A better speech than any as yet, delivered in a very thin House. Quite a good cheer when I sat down; but it is awful to have to wait for hours and hours in order to get in at all.' There are frequent references to 'a dull day in the House', 'House not very exciting', or 'a fairly interesting debate'. Wisely, he used committees for practising his speaking, although without much enthusiasm. Yet the 1 April speech was a real success. He had worked very hard on it, 'but it should have been better', he lamented. It was praised publicly by the Prime Minister and privately by Baldwin. On 24 April he spoke again, on the limited subject of diplomatic buildings, but it was experience. North Street had not been a success, and in May the Edens took the lease of 1 Mulberry Walk, which was to be their London home for several years.

It is not difficult to recognize from Eden's diaries and letters a somewhat bored back-bencher, more dutiful than many in his attendance in the House, and considerably more attentive to his constituency than most. He was consistently worried about his finances, and found the *Yorkshire Post* articles a necessary chore. The only political gleam of solace was that the Labour Government was getting into severe difficulties, and its position increasingly precarious. The less satisfactory side was that Conservative Central Office, because it regarded Warwick and Leamington as absolutely safe, decided that the local Association must raise its own money when the general election came. Some help was offered, as the Principal Agent, H. E. Blain, wrote that 'Captain Eden himself is a young man of the type that we are exceedingly anxious to encourage to stand for Parliament, and I should be grieved if anything I said to him was in any way a discouragement.'

Although politics are the most notoriously unpredictable of all occupations, it was clear that the life of the first Labour Government would not be long. Parliament rose on 7 August after MacDonald had announced the Anglo-Russian Treaty, regarded as one of his major achievements, though one not approved by Eden, who described it in his diary as a treaty 'with the Bolshies'. But he also thought the Conservative opposition a political error. He went on a brief political foray to Wales, which he hated ('A miserable waste of time ... Swansea, a terrible place. The station thronged. I do not like the Welsh. Under-sized little humbugs with radical instincts'). Returning to Kirkdale was much more agreeable, with reading, driving around the countryside, and the agreeable country-house life that Eden, throughout his life, loved; there was a parliamentary visit to Northern Ireland, of somewhat vague purpose, with a regular procession of huge feasts, and there were more articles for the *Yorkshire Post*. Then, with an eye on the forthcoming elections, he and Beatrice went to Warwick and Leamington for some discreet electioneering, but on this visit Eden discovered 'some terribly bad slums' which shocked him: 'Really a disgrace. If we get back to power we simply must make a success of our efforts to fight this slum evil.'

Parliament resumed in high tension on 30 September. Liberal unhappiness over keeping Labour in office had been greatly increased by the treaty with Russia, but it was a relatively minor issue that sealed the Government's fate. The Attorney-General, Sir Patrick Hastings, had initiated a prosecution against a Communist, J. R. Campbell, for an inflammatory leaflet directed at the Army, but under Labour pressure had dropped it. The Conservatives, and many Liberals, alleged that this was further evidence of Communist sympathies, whereas a more rational explanation was that it was simple political incompetence; it was certainly a good issue on which to drive Labour out.

Not called for the whole of 1 October, Eden was fortunate on the next day, being called in a full House immediately after Lloyd George, whom Eden had the temerity to criticize strongly. This speech went well in the prevailing atmosphere, and Eden was immensely relieved. 'Many congratulations were showered upon me, and I received a very hearty cheer when I sat down.' On the next day, however

After lunch walked with Tim to the Carlton Club where I read the papers, all full of gloomy predictions of an immediate general election. It will be maddening for us if we have one this autumn. I have no idea where the money to fight it is coming from. But there is always hope.... *The Times* had a good report of my speech: the best that there has been so far.

On the 6th his fears deepened:

A general election seems more and more imminent though there is just a possibility that the Liberals & the govt. may agree to a judicial committee to inquire into the Campbell case, and that the Liberals may run away from their present attitude towards the Russian agreement. I dread the idea of an election. I think that we shall have another stalemate, and personally the thought fills me with dismay.

By the 8th he was trying to seek ways of persuading the Liberals not to contest his seat, as 'an election is now almost certain'. It was announced on the following day, the Liberals having deserted Labour: 'Feel thoroughly depressed at the prospect of another contest.' There was a disagreeable meeting with Blain, who had done nothing about the Liberals and could not provide any money.

Thus, with very marked reluctance, Eden returned to the hustings again. His experience of the Commons had been brief, and not notably distinguished, and the cost of the campaign was as daunting as the gloomy prospects of speeches and canvassing. He was surprised by the enthusiasm of the local Conservatives and by excellent meetings.

None the less, he expected a considerably lower majority, as Labour had decided not to contest the seat. 'As the count went on the size of the majority staggered us. . . . I can only suppose that many moderate Liberals voted for me.' Eden's victory, with a majority of 6,609 over Nicholls, was part of the national pattern. Four hundred and nineteen Conservatives were returned, to 151 Labour and 40 Liberals, Asquith being among the defeated, his career ended, to Eden's personal regret. Baldwin formed his second administration, which, to universal astonishment – fully shared by Eden – included Winston Churchill, returned to Westminster as 'Constitutional' MP for Epping, as Chancellor of the Exchequer. Eden had only once met this *bête noir* of his childhood and youth, and found the appointment both amazing and bad; historians have tended to agree with this judgement, and this was the one great office Churchill held that he did not adorn.

Eden's main preoccupation was with Beatrice's pregnancy, now in its eighth month. The baby came unexpectedly and suddenly early in the morning of 13 November, after a difficult confinement. But the baby boy – to be christened Simon – was well, and Beatrice soon recovered. Originally they had thought of calling the boy Nicholas, but Eden felt that it would remind him too painfully of his dead brother and might bring bad luck; alas, in spite of the change of name, Simon was to have the same ill fortune as his dead uncle, but at the time there was much rejoicing and happiness.

The political situation was less propitious. Eden entertained high hopes of becoming a parliamentary private secretary to a minister – the lowest rung on the political ladder – but although he made his wishes known, and had good friends, he was unsuccessful. Also, the cost of the election had been £905 – a very much larger sum proportionately than is permitted today – and this was a severe additional burden, because a significant part would have to be paid by him personally. He had, in fact, very little to do, apart from his regular newspaper articles, writing letters, doting on Simon, casual reading and fretting about his investments, and occasional visits to his constituency. He now found that to be a back-bencher in a huge government majority, surrounded by new and unknown faces, was disconcerting and frustrating. 'I can see that this is going to prove a pretty deadly Parliament, from my point of view,' he glumly wrote on 15

December. An offer to go on a parliamentary visit to the Persian oilfields was, accordingly, accepted with alacrity. Meanwhile, he was becoming impressed, in spite of himself, with Churchill's speaking ability, and deeply disappointed by being overlooked by the Whips as a PPS. He had coveted the Foreign Office – where Austen Chamberlain, another of the forgiven, now reigned – but the job went to his friend Roger Lumley. 'Too maddening for words,' Eden wrote, 'as I would have given anything to have had that particular job. No other department interests me as much & Austen is a good man to work with. Damn & damn & damn!' Even the Persian trip at one point seemed in jeopardy, until the Anglo-Persian Oil Company telephoned to confirm that he would be going. 'So ends a very eventful year,' he wrote on 31 December.

My first year of married life heralded with the advent of a son & heir, & yet another general election! The former is a very great joy & happiness unqualified. The latter, in its result, better than I had dared to hope, & not [the] least benefit, promising at least four years without any more. These things apart the year has been rather mixed. Politically, whereas I did make some sort of a name in the last Parliament, all that has to be done afresh in the new, with the added difficulty of being one of an overwhelming majority. Also, principally through muddling, I have failed to secure a PPS job. All that is bad. Worst of all is Finance. I have spent nearly £1500 this year, apart from political expenditure which is also very heavy. This is some £400 more than I can afford.... We cannot afford another year such as this. I need hardly add that married life has been such a complete & unqualified success as to need no comment!

Eden began his long voyage to the Middle East on 5 January, reaching Alexandria after a rough voyage from Marseilles, then on to Cairo where he thought the Sphinx by moonlight 'quite intoxicating in its beauty. Huge, baffling beautiful & bewitching it overwhelms description,' and he reached Jerusalem on the 13th. His route took him by boat from Haifa to Beirut, and then by car across Lebanon to Damascus, and thence to Baghdad, a somewhat odd itinerary to modern eyes, but one that made use of the very few roads (and tracks that passed for roads) in that beautiful, and at the time largely uninhabited, area. There was a meeting with the formidable Emir Feisal, formerly and briefly King of United Syria (which included the Lebanon) and in 1920 appointed King of Iraq by the British. Eden considered him 'a man of a very fine presence with the natural shrewdness of the Arab & his acquisitiveness, but I doubt whether very much more. Reminded me of the Czar of Russia & suspect that his fate may be similar.' Abadan in the Gulf, which Eden was to know only too well in later years, struck him as 'a Swansea on a small scale'; he found the technical conversation as he toured the then modest refinery beyond his understanding, but the political situation infinitely more interesting. With a small and somewhat primitive camera, he took many photographs on this trip, which have survived. What is striking about these otherwise somewhat poor snapshots is how modest the installations were; but there was much drilling. These were early days in a development that was to revolutionize the area – quite literally, as it happened – and to make the Middle East a key part in British foreign policy, but Eden was impressed by the obvious potential as well as by the probable precariousness of the regimes created by the British and French. Although he found this journey interesting, the first of so many to this area, travelling was a long and uncomfortable process, and by 4 February he was writing in his diary: 'Long to conclude the journey & to arrive home again & see Beatrice & Simon once more.' This homecoming occurred on 10 February, but owing to a muddled telegram Beatrice had not expected him and was at the theatre. Yet the reunion delighted them both, the Stock Exchange had risen, and Eden found that his shares were now worth £10,031, 'the first time into five figures!' he noted, and national politics were resumed.

Immediately on his return there was an unexpected development. He was asked to become PPS to Godfrey Locker-Lampson, Junior Minister at the Home Office. Eden was not very interested in the subject, but accepted. On 17 February he walked to the Home Office to begin his official career.

In those days PPS appointments were usually done personally by a minister, and what the job entailed depended entirely on the persons concerned. Also, the PPS, on issues outside his minister's responsibility, was a free agent and not considered to be, as he is now, on 'the payroll vote'. Eden developed the habit of going to the Home Office on most mornings, and quickly had the confidence of Locker-Lampson. The Home Secretary was Joynson-Hicks, universally known as 'Jix'. He was regarded by most as a preposterous figure, so a considerable burden fell on his junior colleague, who was delighted to have Eden to assist him, while Eden from time to time asked parliamentary questions on Middle East matters. It was not an especially exhilarating time, but rescue was at hand when he was invited to attend the Empire Press Conference in Australia and New Zealand as the representative of the *Yorkshire Post*.

As Eden had only made one speech since the new Parliament had met – on unemployment on 26 March, 'and not very well' – and had been away for six weeks in the Middle East, his eagerness to leave for a much longer period gives some indication of his boredom with domestic politics and with his Home Office work. In order to economize he gave up smoking – one of many unsuccessful ventures – and there were unhappy rows with Tim and Lady Eden over the Windlestone furniture and contents; but the *Yorkshire Post* came through with an offer of £500 to cover Eden's expenses in return for articles on his travels, and Mulberry Walk would be let. This offered a very welcome alternative to assisting Locker-Lampson on subjects like taxi-cab fares, with which Eden was massively bored.

Apart from his constituency duties, which he took seriously, and usually – although not always – enjoyed, this had been a rather arid period of Eden's life and political career. The Edens' social life in London was a remarkably full one, but was almost entirely non-political, and Eden was already clearly demonstrating that he was not by temperament either a 'House of Commons man' nor very interested in close friendships within politics; the exceptions were almost always men he had known before he became an MP. On 11 July he and Beatrice left for their long journey to Australia on *The Empress of France*, headed for Quebec, and thence by train to Vancouver ('A desperate place. All sky-scrapers & electric signs') before boarding another ship for the leisurely crossing of the Pacific. They arrived in Auckland on 16 August, and Eden's love of New Zealand began with a much publicized trip to the top of Mount Eden ('I am very proud of my mountain').

Eden's articles in the *Yorkshire Post*, subsequently published in book form under the title *Places in the Sun*, caused him much trouble – he regarded them as a tedious chore and distraction – and were understandably less caustic than his diary entries. But there was much irony in his opening claim that 'The twentieth century is a century of world politics. The fencing of the nineteenth century, admirably adapted to the pages of a history book, is broken down. We can cozen ourselves no longer. The politics of the Pacific are not one whit less important to Great Britain than the politics of the English Channel.' The travelogue part of his articles – a large proportion, unhappily – no doubt had its interest to readers in Yorkshire, though the dutiful statistics on imports, exports, products, facilities and immigration cannot be described as arresting. But Eden's warnings about the perils of industrial disputes, strikes and the import of 'a more extreme Socialism than they have known' into Australia were realistic and prophetic, and his enthusiasm for Empire was manifest and genuine. They returned by way of Ceylon, then through the Red Sea, through the Suez Canal ('The Egyptians cheeky & the town [Port Said] without charm'), and reached Mulberry Walk on 28 November and a happy reunion with Simon.

Domestic politics were resumed without enthusiasm:

To the Home Office in the morning where nothing of any great interest in progress & all quiet at Office of Works.... Heard that Locker-Lampson had been transferred to the Foreign Office: he asked me to go with him but I could not make up my mind. Certainly shall do if he keeps Office of Works but not enough work for me otherwise, though interesting.

But on the following day he spoke briefly on Imperial matters, and noticed that Baldwin and Churchill stayed to listen. He himself was disappointed: 'I don't seem to be able to get going in that place, the bored atmosphere makes it difficult especially when the House is nearly empty.' But he did discover that one cause of poor reporting of his speeches was his habit of turning his back on the Press Gallery, which made him almost inaudible to the reporters. Another lesson had been learned.

Yet the frustrations remained. Locker-Lampson recommended Eden to the Chief Whip for a vacancy in the Whips' office, but was told that there were those with longer service whose claims could not be overlooked. Eden was very disappointed, and Ger Beckett advised him strongly to stick to Locker-Lampson; the latter, however, urged him not to go to the Foreign Office, as it would prevent him from speaking in the House on foreign affairs matters.* This was indeed wise advice, for on 21 December Eden made by far the best speech he had made so far, which was warmly praised by ministers from Baldwin down.

This speech was the direct result of his visit to the Middle East, as the debate was on the subject of a League of Nations arbitration on the boundary of Iraq, which was accepted by the Government but involved a prolongation of the British Mandate in Iraq. Labour criticized this; right-wing Conservatives criticized the League, supported by the *Daily Express* and *Daily Mail*. Eden strongly supported the British presence in Iraq, denouncing those who urged a policy of

scuttle, like flying curs, at the sight of our own shadow. Hon. Members know that if we pursued a course like that our name would be a jibe in the mouth of every tavern-lounger from Marrakesh to Singapore. It might take centuries to recover.... In the East [democracy] is a forced growth, an importation, and foreign to the soil. Consequently, it needs many years more to develop and many more to grow to be understood by the people.

But what really startled the House was his assault on the Beaverbrook and Rothermere press for encouraging Soviet ambitions in the area: 'Are we to see Bolsheviks perusing the columns of the *Daily Express* and Noble Lords bustling to Fleet Street in Russian boots?' Deriding these mighty figures was not then politically fashionable, and certainly not politically wise, but it certainly got considerable press coverage, only the *Daily Telegraph* ignoring it.

'Pleased with the reception but I should have done better' was Eden's characteristic comment in his diary. But Christmas at Kirkdale was the happier for this success. '1925 has been a lucky year for us,' he wrote in his valedictory diary entry. 'We began it with some anxiety. I shall always

---

* David Carlton, *Anthony Eden*, p. 19, incorrectly states that Locker-Lampson's transfer 'took Eden into the department in which he had pre-eminent interest'.

remember it as one of the happiest as well as one of the most successful of my life.... Politically the year has been good, unexpectedly so. It started doubtfully, with the essential difficulty of making a name afresh in a new Parliament that "knew not Joseph".' He now considered, in retrospect, that working at the Home Office had been 'invaluable experience' but there were great advantages in being a free-lance. 'I may truly say that 1925 has established me on the road to a career, & I hope to useful work. We are on the ladder. Even finance, still our weakest point, has shown better results than in 1924.'

The Baldwin Government also looked upon 1925 with satisfaction. At home, Baldwin had crushed a right-wing Conservative move to capitalize on the Conservative victory by introducing swingeing anti-trade-union legislation, and the major error by Churchill to return to the Gold Standard at the pre-war parity of $4.86 was perceived as such by only a few economists, most notably Maynard Keynes and Hubert Henderson. Abroad, Austen Chamberlain had returned in triumph from Locarno with a non-aggression pact between Germany, France and Belgium, guaranteed by Britain and Italy. The Treaty of Locarno seemed, at the time, a masterpiece of international diplomacy. Europe was at peace, prosperity was rising. For a while, the sun shone.

But it was not shining on everyone. The remarkable feature of the 1920s in Britain was that whereas there was great and increasing prosperity in many areas – demonstrated by the fact that by 1927 there were nearly two million registered private motor cars – in the old industries in the North there was inexorable decline. Unemployment never fell below one million – proportionately a higher figure at that time than in the 1980s – and serious industrial unrest was a constant preoccupation of Baldwin's. One per cent of the population owned two-thirds of the national wealth, and three-quarters of the people of Britain earned less than £100 a year. Rural and urban poverty, concentrated principally in the North, where coal and cotton, shipping and steel, the pre-war giants, languished, were palpable and grim. But both Churchill and Philip Snowden were dedicated Free Traders, and they ruled the Treasury from January 1924 until November 1931. There were ministers – notably Leo Amery and Neville Chamberlain – who were strong believers in Protection, but neither held key positions, and the result of the 1923 general election seemed to emphasize that Protection had little public support.

The condition of the miners had become even worse as a result of the return to the Gold Standard, which had substantially raised the cost of British exported coal; this, together with the recovery of the Ruhr coalfields, had a catastrophic effect. The mine-owners responded by the classic methods of revoking agreements on wages and working conditions, reducing wages and increasing the working day. So intense was the reaction, while Eden had been in Australia at the end of July, that a general strike seemed probable. Baldwin was able to fend off the crisis with a special subsidy to the industry and a Royal Commission headed by Herbert Samuel. This bought time, but the fundamental crisis was wholly unresolved. It was another grim winter.

Baldwin's political problem was that a substantial number of his supporters and even ministers – notably Churchill and Birkenhead – saw the situation very differently. This very important and vocal element had deplored the compromise of July 1925, and expected – and in many cases actually thirsted for – a decisive confrontation with the trade union movement. They despised Baldwin's moderation, and were fearful of the menace of Socialism. Those younger Conservative MPs like Duff Cooper and Harold Macmillan who represented poor constituencies – Oldham and Stockton-on-Tees – and Eden, who did not but knew what conditions were in the North-East, were strong Baldwin supporters. But even they recognized that a general strike could only be seen as a major political challenge to the elected Government, a challenge which must be resisted if it came.

In cold print, Eden's speech of 21 December 1925 does not read very impressively, but, as so often happens in the Commons, it made a great impression at the time, and marked Eden down as a future Foreign Secretary. Baldwin agreed to write the Foreword to *Places in the Sun*; Samuel told him that his speech had put him in the first place for the next vacancy in the Government; others spoke of it as the best speech by a government back-bencher in the Parliament. One suspects that its real impact was that it was made by a member who had actually visited the area, and clearly spoke from experience of a place unknown to most members and even to ministers. For good or ill, it had placed him in the foreign affairs category, in which, with one brief interlude, he was to remain for the rest of his political career.

For Eden, 1926 opened with a miserable visit to Windlestone, when he and Tim fell out badly – 'he [Tim] has a conceit which is fast becoming unbearable and manners which it would be difficult to label. A pity. A life less idle would be good for him. . . . I am profoundly glad to have nothing to do with Windles' – but the fact was that Eden cared deeply about Windlestone and Tim's management of the estate, far more than he usually admitted to himself. A visit of several days to his constituency was more cheering, but when Parliament resumed he made the mistake of speaking again on the Middle East. It was well received, but as he shrewdly noted, 'the House is easily tired, and likes to be surprised', and the press reports were not as full or as enthusiastic as in December. But he was now in great demand to speak to Conservative Associations, and on 23 March spoke in the Commons at the request of the Government, again on foreign affairs, and specifically on disarmament proposals.

This was a major debate opened by Lloyd George, followed by Chamberlain, Ramsay MacDonald and Lord Hugh Cecil, whose speech Eden described in his account as 'very brilliant' and difficult to follow. But Eden spoke clearly and well, and was warmly congratulated by Churchill, who was becoming a wholly unexpected admirer, although not yet a friend. Duff Cooper, with whom Eden's relations were destined to be complex, was also highly complimentary, and *The Times* was laudatory. A major speech in Bristol on 25 March was also widely reported and praised, and Eden's diaries for this period are full of travels and speeches to Conservative audiences. He was still writing his articles, and putting the final touches to his first book.

The Samuel Committee reported on 11 March. Parts of the proposals were positive for the industry, but it also recommended the immediate reduction of wages. The owners were unimpressed by the former, the miners were incensed by the latter, their leader A. J. Cook coining the memorable phrase, 'not a penny off the pay, not a minute on the day'. Negotiations continued throughout April, with little movement on either side. On 1 May the agreement ran out, and the owners responded with their standard answer, the lock-out. On the same day, a special union conference placed authority in the central Council of the TUC and approved a general strike on 3 May.

Eden was heavily pressed with finishing *Places in the Sun* ('Finances this year are so tight that I want every penny & want it badly') and a heavy constituency speaking tour ('All together the worst managed meeting I have ever been at [at Driffield]. I like young Braithwaite & he spoke well, his father then proceeded to undo all the good he had done with a real politician's speech. Made me shudder. They will lose the seat if they can & I think they can'), and it was when he was in Stratford on 1 May that he heard the news of the strike: 'Damn! & that puts it mildly. Everybody seems to have imagined somehow that there would be a settlement at the last moment. The other unions including the Railways threaten to come out on Monday night so we are now in a pretty kettle of fish. Still, there has been no wild talking & hope persists.' But, back in London on the 2nd, 'the outlook is indeed very black'.

The Government and the TUC had stumbled into confrontation, and 3 May was a day of considerable confusion. 'Cannot resist an impression of unreality,' Eden wrote, but at midnight the General Strike was on. This impression continued in the following days, and Eden joined up as a special policeman. Throughout, Eden was a firm supporter of Baldwin's essentially moderate and calm handling of the crisis, in contrast with Churchill, whose newspaper *The British Gazette* adopted a considerably more robust approach. As a 'special', Eden was sent to Fulham for a meeting of railwaymen, who were 'very quiet and orderly'. Although the General Strike swiftly ended, just in time, as tempers were rising, the miners held out, the owners being relentless. Churchill, ever magnanimous in victory, tried hard to effect a fair compromise, but to no avail.

Eden was also preoccupied with finishing his book, and was indignant when Baldwin altered his Foreword 'at the dictation of the Colonial Office which is a pity & has made it less complimentary'. But this was overshadowed by a crucial event in his life.

In the middle of July Eden's friend Roger Lumley, who was Austen Chamberlain's Parliamentary Private Secretary, mentioned to Eden that he was going to Australia on a parliamentary delegation, which would mean that he would be away for six months, and asked Eden if he would take on his position. Eden hardly knew Chamberlain at all; 'always correct and polite, but he seemed an aloof figure to us', he later wrote. But although this had been the job he had coveted most, now he was not so sure. Only shortly before he had spoken well and with modest authority in a debate on Germany's entry into the League in which the other speakers had been Lloyd George, Chamberlain, MacDonald, Hugh Cecil and Sir John Simon; the fact that he had been called to speak in such senior company was itself an indication of the growing respect for his ability and knowledge, and Eden had briefed himself very carefully for this debate. Eden wrote:

A very full House & each of the first three speeches lasted nearly an hour. I followed Ramsay having been in a state of indecision as to whether to get up or no until the very last moment, & having been bothered by Nancy [Astor] coming in & chattering in my ear just as I wanted to listen to Ramsay. Had really very little to say & felt that my remarks were very disjointed but House for some reason very kind & cheered me at the end I think better than they have ever done.... It is a nervously & physically prostrating business.

If he became a PPS he would be debarred from speaking on foreign affairs, and Eden did not like the prospect of having to remain silent in the House for the rest of the Parliament. But Lumley recommended him warmly to Chamberlain – who was doubtful – and Baldwin himself was enthusiastic, while Locker-Lampson spoke to Chamberlain of Eden's qualities and promise. Locker-Lampson later said of Eden that 'He was very ambitious, but in a good sense and as every young man ought to be.' 'After much thought & discussion decided to accept Austen's invitation,' Eden wrote on 14 July. 'Saw him after Questions. He was very friendly & pleasant, more so than I had expected.... The great gain is that I shall have opportunities to learn which hereafter may be useful.'

Eden came to like and admire Chamberlain, and their relationship became warm and close, but the disadvantages of the job were made clear very soon.

4 August
Austen spoke to me about Geneva. He evidently wants me to come & said he was very sorry he could not ask Treasury for anybody extra but would I like to come on my own. In fact same words as I received by message. I had not the courage to tell him that I could not afford to go! It so obviously did not occur to him & muttered words about Scotland conveyed still less.... Beatrice advises a letter & a letter I think it shall be.

Thus Eden missed his first experience of working at the League, but in the following year he did accompany Chamberlain to attend the League Council. Meanwhile, in November he paid his first visit to Chequers, where the rising Canadian politician Mackenzie King and the South African Prime Minister were fellow guests. Characteristically, Eden's account concentrates almost entirely upon the pictures. *Places in the Sun* had been well reviewed, but sales – barely two thousand – were disappointing, particularly as 1926 had been another bad year financially. 'Politically the year has been fair for me,' he wrote. 'We have made some progress but at no very great or startling rate.... I have perhaps added a little, though not greatly, to my reputation.'

In fact this was another turning-point. Chamberlain's reputation was very high, and the League of Nations at its zenith, particularly now that it included Germany, and Eden now found himself the Foreign Secretary's confidant, lunching and dining with Aristide Briand of France and Gustav Stresemann of Germany, and learning about the proceedings of the League and negotiations at Foreign Secretary level. He wrote at the time that this 'has given me an insight into foreign affairs which may prove valuable later on'. As meetings of the League received considerable publicity, photographs of the young Captain Eden became more frequent, and Chamberlain's approval of him grew, particularly as Eden's reports to him on parliamentary affairs while he was abroad were models of lucidity, to the point that when Chamberlain became seriously ill in November 1928 and had to go on a long convalescent sea voyage, Eden was asked to speak in a major Commons debate on Anglo-French naval agreements, following

MacDonald. Both at the time and later Eden was very critical of his own performance, but others were not. It was another advance.

Eden now divided his time almost equally between the House of Commons, the Foreign Office and the City, where he had developed a close association with a leading stockbroker, Harry Lucas, whose firm developed into Warburgs, and his diaries and papers of the time are notably more concerned with financial rather than political matters. Health, however, intruded with a grumbling appendix and much pain, which gradually subsided, it being decided by his doctor that an operation was not necessary – a decision that Eden was later to regret deeply, when the trouble recurred in 1947. But the real problem was an ulcer, and Eden endured months of pain and drugs, and at one stage was told that he would have to diet all his life.

Although Eden did speak on other subjects, he was now becoming identified with foreign affairs and being seen as a specialist with high promise. This was to make him, but was to have its disadvantages, as was his close relationship with Baldwin. His rapid rise also made him an object of jealousy and resentment, which would not have mattered had he not been perceived by many political contemporaries as aloof and unclubbable, moving in somewhat grand circles. 'He is highly polished, has the bearing and manner of an aristocrat that gives him distinction in a House where the aristocrat is so much rarer than in Parliaments of the past,' a political correspondent wrote of him, but added: 'He is intensely interested in politics, takes his parliamentary duties most seriously, devotes much study to political questions, and spares no labour to make himself efficient.' The former was more noted than the latter. Many years later General Ismay wrote that he had thought Eden one of fortune's darlings, attributing his success to charm and a lucky flair, until he worked with him at the Foreign Ministers' meeting in Moscow in October 1943 and realized his diligence, thoroughness and sensitivity.

It might have been thought that he would have had much in common with two other Old Etonian Conservative MPs who shared his detestation of the Party's right wing, Harold Macmillan and Duff Cooper, but he did not form any real friendship with them, then or later. That he dressed well and was an admirable host and a keen and fastidious collector of pictures gave some the entirely false impression that he was wealthy, just as his interest in beautiful women gave others the idea that he was a playboy, whereas he worked very hard, was constantly worried about money, bought his pictures at very low prices, and found in his son Simon a wonderful companion and friend. Also, not many realized that what was ascribed to aloofness or even arrogance was shyness and an innate defensiveness, and few appreciated the difficulty he had with his journalism – principally for the *Yorkshire Post* – which was vital for his income. 'Ger tells me that Mann* is very pleased with my writing & says he must "raise me to a higher scale of payment". Splendid!' (9 February 1927). He found the Foreign Office work fascinating, and Chamberlain an increasingly agreeable master, but he was in effect an unpaid junior minister without the title.

Eden's own financial difficulties, with a modest income in the most precarious of professions, were not reduced by the many problems caused to Tim, Marjorie and himself by their mother. Lady Eden had proved herself to be hopelessly improvident and demanding, and when Tim had returned from the war to inherit Windlestone he discovered that she had personal debts of over £20,000 and had sold or pawned family possessions that were not hers to dispose of. Tim settled her very formidable debts, and he and his brother and sister arranged to provide her with virtually free accommodation at Windlestone and an adequate personal income. 'She . . . should really not be badly off,' Tim wrote to his brother on 1 June 1927, 'with reasonable care & without worry. Of course, she will not exercise reasonable care, but that we cannot help.'

Tim's forebodings, shared by Anthony and Marjorie, proved only too justified. Until her death in 1945, Lady Eden was a constant source of difficulty and embarrassment to her children. She developed a strong dislike for Tim's wife, going out of her way to be unpleasant to her, and when Tim bought back her personal jewellery and presented it to her she promptly pawned it. Tim, as he frankly admitted, had inherited 'the Eden temper', and there were many explosions. But in the circumstances his conduct was saintly, although Anthony and Marjorie often took a different view. Indeed, their mother's antics and demands put a very considerable strain on the relations between Tim, Anthony and Marjorie, and their correspondence on occasions became very fierce and acrimonious, particularly when Marjorie temporarily withdrew her contribution to her mother's income. In view of Lady Eden's conduct this was not unreasonable, but as it put the full burden upon the brothers they were indignant, although Anthony took Marjorie's side. After the dismal episode of the court case about their mother's debts, already referred to, she piled on additional agonies, of which by far the worst was her use of money raised for charity, which could have had the most grievous consequences if it had ever been known. Again, her children came to the rescue, but very angrily.

---

* Arthur Mann, editor of the *Yorkshire Post*, an early admirer and friend of Eden, who was to prove totally loyal in all vicissitudes. Eden's increased fee for his weekly 'Political Notes' rose from £3 to £4!

The fact was, as Eden once noted, Lady Eden was, if not actually immoral (referring to the rumours of his own paternity), certainly amoral; for her the normal unwritten (and written) laws of conduct simply did not apply. Allowance had to be made for the personal losses she had suffered in the war, but the real havoc she had wrought upon Windlestone and the family fortune had occurred before 1914. Everyone thought her a marvellous old lady, generous and kind – except her children. There is no point in detailing these controversies, which were constant during Lady Eden's life: what was remarkable was that the deep affection between her three children was not permanently affected. They were united in their angry despair at their mother's selfishness and irresponsibility, and there was one moment when a terrible scandal threatened the reputations of them all and the family, which was only narrowly averted. There were occasions when these strains led to intense scenes and letters between them, and when 'the Eden temper' flared violently; but the bond held, so far as the three were concerned.

Lady Eden did not write or concern herself with Eden's illness ('I think it disgusting not to have written to you but one can only suppose she is queer in the head,' Tim wrote to him on 3 August). Tim was very troubled, and urged his brother to seek the best medical advice: 'You should leave no stone unturned to recover your health,' he advised on 20 September. 'It is vital to you & your work, which must not be interfered with at the outset of your career. Do not reconcile yourself to any depressing diagnosis. All doctors make mistakes and there is a very great deal in the determination to recover one's health.' His prescription was rest 'deck chairs & a French novel & to hell with the rest of the world' – and sustenance – 'the future PM of England must drink his bottle of port & eat his stuffed turkey!'

The chief victim of these misfortunes and difficulties was Tim, and the more one reads his letters the more one warms to him. In addition to Lady Eden's aggravating performances, Tim was desperately trying to save Windlestone under bleak circumstances, not successfully but with admirable good humour. 'Why don't you come here for a bit?' runs one letter to his brother: 'It is years since you have honoured me with a visit. The air is good, & we can watch Mr Taylor & his syndicate shooting our pheasants, or the South Durham Hunt breaking our fences, or the adjutant of the Durham Light Infantry riding in our park, or Mr Atkinson planting cauliflowers in our herbaceous border. There is no lack of entertainment' (1 October 1927).

Eden so loved Windlestone that the situation especially depressed him. 'A lovely day & Windlestone as beautiful as it is melancholy,' he wrote in September 1928. 'Impossible to explain sense of sorrow that hangs over everything. It cannot be neglect for it is all well kept. It is a tragedy that it cannot be lived in & taken care of as it should, but Tim is so unbusinesslike that no method is possible & with the coal trade so bad, the outlook is dark indeed.'

Wholly unlike Anthony, Tim was not a natural country gentleman. To his brother he lamented: 'The Bench, the cart-horse, the saw-mill – what a life! I am afraid I am a Bohemian & loathe the ordinary round of humanity. I shot at Raby [Castle] the other day: enjoyed the shooting & all very nice people – but not a thing in common. Crops & salmon & prize sheep. And yet I cannot bring myself to part with this beautiful place. Curse on't!'

But Anthony, although often angered and frustrated by his brother, always enjoyed his letters, which filled pages with reports of Windlestone, his family, local dramas and the chronic problems created by their mother. Thus, a report towards the end of 1927:

Dear Sir,

This has been a very bad summer. The hay has only just been carted & the corn is in many instances not yet led & in some not even cut. The turnips are inundated, the potatoes will shortly be rotten. The fence on Dunn's farm is being renewed with exquisite stakes symmetrically cut from South Agnew plantation. 'Sammy' the cart-horse has been pronounced unfit for further work except on the land. James Battley was fined 7/6 at Bishop Auckland the other day for being drunk and disorderly. There was a grand frost last night of 0.02 degrees, the wind is in the NW & more rain is falling. The tenants are, very rightly & properly (since who but he is responsible for the weather?) demanding a reduction of rent from their landlord.

Yours agriculturally,

Timothy Eden

Nineteen twenty-eight was a year of tragedy for the Eden family. Guy Warwick died after a long and miserable illness, and Eden was troubled by Marjorie's bad relationship with her son Fulke, who succeeded to the title. Then, on 14 October, Beatrice's second pregnancy ran into unexpected difficulties when she contracted pneumonia; Eden recorded on the 15th:

Further examination in the morning revealed further causes for anxiety, so B was moved to a nursing home just before lunch. Consultation there with yet another specialist & a decision to operate.

Operation successful but little boy only lived a quarter of an hour. The sweetest little baby, quite lovely. Heartrending. However the great thing is that B is safe & going on very well.

Rather a miserable night.

The boy was to be named Robert.

18 October

I think the most wretched day I have ever been through. The funeral of Robert in the morning. Quietly & well done, poor little chap.

In the morning learnt that Beatrice had slight congestion of one lung. In the afternoon she held her own, but the evening brought a terrible crisis. The doctors most anxious & a lung specialist called in. I think the last saved her life. He insisted on a doubling of the dope – 'She must sleep at all costs.' Poor darling she is having a terrible time & I don't think I ever spent a worse hour than between 6 & 7. The specialist gave us hope – if little else.

The crisis passed, but with much sadness for the parents.

At the end of 1928 Eden ruminated in a personal – and understandably sad – note on the year, dogged by illness and the consequent doctors' bills – Ger Beckett stepping in to meet Beatrice's – and by the deaths of his son and brother-in-law, and concluded that while it was interesting to be Austen Chamberlain's PPS he was not wholly convinced that the League would work, and that from a personal point of view a period in Opposition would be more fruitful. But he did not expect it. What was significant was his close personal link with Baldwin.

12 March [1929]

PM came into my room & we chatted in the evening. Charles informed him of a short Cabinet Agenda for tomorrow. He shook his head & turned to me. 'Short agendas do not necessarily mean short Cabinets, as you will learn, Anthony, when you are a Cabinet Minister & I am being wheeled about in a bath chair.'

Early in 1929 Beatrice went on a lengthy visit to the West Indies to recover from her pneumonia and the loss of Robert, and was away for three months, returning just in time for another election campaign, which was certainly not her favourite experience, nor her husband's.

In spite of the unexpected revival of the Liberals, the Conservatives went into the 1929 general election in May with high confidence of success. Eden noted that his meetings were 'well attended and enthusiastic', although 'I fear Liberals have made headway.' But on election night on 30 May he recorded 'A grim evening listening to disastrous results' on the radio, and when he went to his own count on the following morning he found his supporters prophesying a greatly reduced majority 'and many of them covering fears of worse. Indeed it was not until within an hour of the close that we felt certain of a majority.' In fact Eden was easily returned with a majority of 5,460, but elsewhere the Conservatives had done poorly, and Britain had her second Labour Government. Thus Anthony Eden's first tentative experience of the Foreign Office was abruptly ended.

PART TWO

Noon

[4]

Rising Star, 1929–34

The 1929 defeat was a wholly unexpected reverse not only for the Conservatives but for Anthony Eden, and his disappointment was not assuaged by a kind letter from Austen Chamberlain to tell him that, had the Conservatives won the election, he would have become his Under-Secretary at the Foreign Office. 'I was surprised and pleased at such a possibility,' he later wrote, 'but saddened that the opportunity had been denied me. It seemed to me then that it would not come again and that my political career was over, so strong did the Labour Party appear in the first flush of victory and so raw was my experience at thirty-two.'

Eden subsequently wrote very little about this period of his life, although more than he did about the period 1945–51, no doubt believing that the readers of his memoirs would be more interested in his experiences in Office than in Opposition. This was unfortunate, as it was in both periods that he had the time to develop his political thinking and, certainly after the 1929 defeat, to establish at some hazard his personal political position.

Eden joined a small group of Conservative MPs – the forerunners of the 1951 One Nation group – which met weekly to dine and work together closely in the cause of liberal Conservatism. Its most brilliant and influential member was a young Scotsman, Noel Skelton, who coined the phrase 'a property-owning democracy' which Eden never forgot, and was to use to great and enduring effect in a much later Opposition period. Other members were Oliver Stanley, William Ormsby-Gore, Walter Elliot and W. S. ('Shakes') Morrison. Skelton died young, but all the remainder were to be Cabinet ministers, and Morrison to become Speaker of the House of Commons and Governor-General of Australia. As a group, they were particularly receptive to Baldwin – and he to them – in Eden's words 'sharing our youthful ideas for a progressive Conservatism which would have positive aims'. Stimulated by this company, and especially by Skelton, Eden launched on a series of speeches urging the expansion of private ownership of property as widely as possible, 'to enable every worker to become a capitalist'. He advocated co-partnership in industry, share options for workers and greater personal incentives; what was to become standard Conservative philosophy after 1945 was, in 1929, almost revolutionary, and certainly anathema to those Conservatives who now gathered to bring down Baldwin.

To the regret of his biographer, Eden neglected his diary in the last months of 1929 – his only entry in the election campaign demonstrating his lack of foresight about the result, in which he was not alone. But at the end of the year he wrote:

1929 has been above all a happy year. Thank you very much. Not perhaps very successful, certainly not financially, nor politically triumph[ant] but in both passable, & in happiness real. We seem both to have enjoyed ourselves – perhaps too much. All three – mercifully – in good health throughout the year. In this a pleasant contrast to its predecessor.

In politics I have at least survived the ordeal of an unhealthy General Election & the present Parliament afford[s] opport mities. Certainly my political stock has not gone back in 1929, but my financial stock has! This year has been poor financially. The only consolation is that it might have been very much worse, as for many others it has been calamitous. Despite placing small additional sums to reserves these are lower than a year ago & a very real attempt must be made in 1930 to improve our financial position. If this proves unsuccessful we shall have to alter our mode of life somewhat.

But above all we can write that we are a happy family. The trips abroad were as successful as enjoyable. All together a good year 1929 – thank you very much. If we never fare worse we shall have no cause to complain, even though we never be either millionaires or Prime Ministers.

Eden's admiration and affection for Baldwin were undiminished by the election defeat, but a significant number of his colleagues were not so charitable or forgiving. The Conservative Party on the morrow of defeat is not an agreeable spectacle, and 1929 was no exception. But, in addition to the chagrin of losing Office, there were other, and more ominous, strands.

The most serious was the revival of the old Protectionist–Free Trade schism, given additional drama by the unexpected intervention of Lord Beaverbrook and his newspapers advocating Empire Free Trade, which was in effect Imperial Protectionism by another name. Neville Chamberlain and Leo Amery were both ardent Protectionists, and had strong support within the Party. Baldwin, recognizing the dangers, sought a compromise, but without success. Beaverbrook sponsored Empire Free Trade candidates at by-elections, and the hopes for a *modus vivendi* in March 1930 – which Eden ardently supported – were swiftly dashed. Baldwin was compelled to drop the Party Chairman, J. C. C. Davidson, but his critics were out for a larger target. Twice Baldwin was compelled to seek motions of confidence in his leadership, a sure sign of declining authority. Then, on 31 October, the Government, in the name of the Viceroy of India, Lord Irwin, announced that the granting of Dominion Status for India was inherent in the 1917 Montagu proposals and that an Anglo-Indian Conference would be convened. The right wing of the Conservative Party, with the fading Lord Birkenhead (who died in 1930), Churchill and the former Viceroy Lord Reading at the fore, erupted; Baldwin temporized; 1930 was a bad year for His Majesty's Opposition.

It was not a good year, either, for the Member for Warwick and Leamington. After entering City broking, he was surprised to find how much he enjoyed the work, although his health continued to trouble him. 'Have been far from well these last few days. The old internal trouble again with much pain & some bad nights. Better today a little' (14 February). He was, like Baldwin, a compromiser on Protection, but not a hopeful one: 'A sensible compromise is in our grasp. But I fear such counsels will scarcely obtain a hearing now' (30 January). Nor did they. In the Commons – in the days long before the modern novelty of the Shadow Cabinet – he was often asked to respond from the front bench on foreign affairs, but as he was generally a supporter of the policies of the Labour Government – conciliation with Europe and the United States, the reduction of German reparations, the resumption of relations with the Soviet Union and the pursuit of disarmament – this was not a burdensome task, nor a particularly exciting one at a time when the first shock waves of the collapse of the American economy were reaching the British and European shores. None the less, Eden's courteous questions and interventions, clearly based on real knowledge, made a greater impression than he himself realized. But the prospect of four more years of this, with constant Party bickering and cabals against Baldwin, was not exhilarating. He felt lost, and often despondent.

13 April
Margot Oxford [Asquith] came to lunch. She had proposed herself and was all together delightful. We were alarmed, but needlessly so as nobody could have been kinder. She spoke much of my father, as all do whoever knew him, & scarcely at all of my mother. Much of politics, urging Oliver [Stanley] & I and one or two others to go out with courage on our own, & warning us of the peril of newspaper support.

A holiday in France gave some relief in April: 'A rest & respite abroad is necessary, for there has been much & heavy work as well & I am tired' (17 April).

Eden's diaries, somewhat spasmodic though they were in this year, give a clear portrait of a somewhat aimless existence, and frequent pain from 'this infernal complaint', as the ulcer responded reluctantly to treatment.

'The session has been generally a disappointing one for almost everybody,' he wrote on 1 August. 'We have spent so much time wrangling over uninteresting clauses in the Finance Bill. For me, if I had not increased my debating reputation, at least it has not fallen off, & actually I think that

I have spoken better, even though the Press has heeded me less, or no more.' At Warwick and Leamington, meanwhile, there were now fears of a Beaverbrook-inspired Empire candidate; 'we should be able to withstand it,' Eden wrote, somewhat doubtfully. The house in Mulberry Walk had to be sold, not very well, but as Eden told Beatrice, 'even a diminutive bird in the hand is something'. The Edens moved to 17 Lower Berkeley Street; 'it looks very well, & will prove I trust a cheerful home, & beautiful & convenient. We are very fortunate to be able to possess it, & shall be happier if we can afford to live in it!' (17 August). Then, with Beatrice pregnant again, Simon contracted scarlet fever, and the family was placed in strict isolation: 'This is not entertaining. Invitations refused.' Eden was now writing leading articles for the *Yorkshire Post* as well as his regular articles. Arthur Mann's political approach was considerably more robust than Eden's, and he sadly noted that 'I can never be so violently opposed to compromise.'

The fears that Beatrice might contract Simon's scarlet fever had proved unfounded, and on 3 October she gave birth to another son, who, curiously enough in view of previous sentiments, was called Nicholas. The joy of this event at least temporarily eased Eden's concerns about the deteriorating political situation, his finances and his own health.

The Baldwin Must Go campaign had raged throughout the summer and early autumn of 1930 and even to his own small but devoted group of supporters it seemed that his leadership was doomed. Although the Labour Government was beginning to wilt as unemployment rose and the economic skies darkened, the plight of the Conservative Party appeared definitely worse. The drum-beat of the Beaverbrook–Rothermere press was constant and daily, and as their newspapers were read by a very large number of Conservative voters and loyalists, this relentless persistence of criticism, derision and abuse was having a real effect, not least on Baldwin himself, a considerably more sensitive man than was realized at the time.

Early in October the issue was argued in the correspondence columns of *The Times*, and on 6 October a letter from Eden was published:

If the Conservative Party jettisons Mr Baldwin it will sacrifice its greatest electoral asset. But that is not, of course, the sole reason why many of us would deeply regret to see Mr Baldwin relinquish the Leadership of the Conservative Party. So long as Mr Baldwin leads the Conservative Party so long will its 'right' wing be unable to dominate the party's counsels and narrow its purposes – of this the Trade Disputes Bill was a sufficient example; so long also will confidence persist that the Conservative Party can remain truly national, both in the sources of its strength and in the objectives of its policy. Nor, with Mr Baldwin as its Leader, will the Conservative Party ever sink to become the creature of millionaire newspaper owners or a mere appendage of big business.

'This turned out to be a shrewd judgement,' a somewhat hostile biographer has written,* but at the time it seemed politically suicidal. 'I gave public support to S.B. in his difficulties, from principle not expediency,' Eden wrote in his diary on 31 December. 'I thought at one time I had backed the wrong horse.' And so it seemed at the time. But Eden's small group was defiant. As Eden later recalled:

It was typical of the times that at a party meeting held to discuss the leadership, one of Stanley Baldwin's critics should complain: 'At every luncheon party you go to you hear criticism of him.' Noel Skelton cried out from the gallery: 'But what do you hear in the back streets?' We might not have known as much about back streets as we thought, but at least we knew it was their confidence we must win and their conditions we intended to improve. We meant to realize the property-owning democracy, though few in our party had much confidence in our faith and the opposition was derisive.†

In his customary personal assessment of the year in his diary, Eden concluded with guarded optimism: 'The year has been nationally so bad that the personal events scarcely expect to be good. Yet in certain respects it has been so. Politically our stock is definitely higher than at the beginning of the year. Have only made a few speeches in this Parliament, but they seem to have been fairly successful.... S.B. thanked me [for his support] & I have been on much more intimate terms with him and perhaps of a little more account in counsels of party than previously.'

On his financial affairs, Eden was less gloomy than usual, but then added that 'The worst feature [of 1930] has been my health which, in the last weeks of the year particularly, has been unsatisfactory. The old pain back again. Almost every night restless, and some almost sleepless. It begins to depress me. Creates a longing for sunshine & peace, satiates ambition, quenches energy, favours a sluggishness which is constitutionally stronger than many know.'

Nineteen thirty-one opened with the Conservative Party still in deep discord, and Baldwin's leadership in peril. Churchill now emerged as the most definite and outspoken Conservative opponent of the policy on India which Eden supported, using language so fierce and intemperate that his departure from the Opposition front bench at the end of January came as no surprise. What no one could have anticipated – least of all Churchill himself – was that this exclusion was to last for eight years. Churchill's

* Carlton, *Anthony Eden*, p. 27.
† Avon, *Facing the Dictators*, pp. 13–14.

recollections of India were dim, and his excoriation of the limited British policy of modest Commonwealth Status has not stood up well to retrospective judgement, but the crucial political point was that he had now linked himself with the section of the Conservative Party whose dominant motivation was hatred of Baldwin, those who belonged to the ultra-right that Eden so despised, and who – apart from India – had little in common with Churchill's other political views. It was a terrible error of judgement which was to have dire consequences for Churchill personally and for British and indeed world history. Inevitably, it also severely shadowed his relationship with Eden, as Churchill's concept of loyalty required a totality which Eden, and the great majority of the Tory Party, could not give him on this issue. Duff Cooper later described this deep rift as 'the most unfortunate event that occurred between the two wars'.

Duff Cooper himself played a major role in Baldwin's salvation in March. The assaults by Churchill and the Beaverbrook–Rothermere press were at their height when a by-election occurred in the St George's, Westminster, constituency. Baldwin had already come close to resignation, and at one point considered fighting this by-election himself, but eventually decided against it. Duff Cooper relinquished the safe seat for which he had been adopted to be the Baldwinite banner-bearer. There followed a campaign noted by the *Annual Register* for its 'unusual scurrility', in which Eden campaigned for Duff Cooper and in which Baldwin turned on Beaverbrook and Rothermere with devastating effect – 'What the proprietorship of these papers is aiming at is power, and power without responsibility – the prerogative of the harlot throughout the ages' – and won easily. This was the turning-point. Beaverbrook came to terms, and Baldwin's critics in the Party relapsed either into sullen acquiescence or hastened to proclaim their fealty – Churchill, unhappily, being the exception. Never again, until the difficult summer of 1936, was Baldwin's leadership in any serious danger.

But it had been a very close thing. Eden strongly backed Baldwin, while in the meantime experiencing the chronic frustrations of the back-bencher: 'Spent two whole days in a vain attempt to get called in the Electoral Reform debate. Such seems to be always my fate these days. An irritating waste of time' (3 February). Eden's frustrations were compounded by his duodenal ulcer, and by dismay and apprehension at the continuing feuds and bitterness in the Conservative Party. On 4 March he did speak in the House on India, and recorded: 'At the end S.B. asks me to come to his room. He is depressed & worried. We go through drafts of his speech for Friday on India. It is on this subject that I cannot disagree with him that the party is more die-hard than he or I. Later same evening, on account of what Billy [Ormsby-Gore] tells me, write urging him not to resign on any account.'

During his illness, which persisted for some time, Eden's diary had been fragmentary, but it was now renewed:

5 March
(Statement on India). Immensely relieved personally. Irwin has done splendidly – almost a miraculous achievement.... S.B. delighted & scarcely able to retain his joy. Some thought he should have congratulated Edward [Irwin] there & then, but he told me he had had enough India Committee trouble for a time & it was perhaps wise not to rub salt into sores. Our die-hards are very angry. Bracken's* face as red as his hair, Jix taking defeat as badly as the ill-bred do, but the party as a whole assessing the position pretty soundly.

On the next day, however, Eden found himself to his embarrassment – and to the fury of the Whips – on the same side as the ultra-right 'forty thieves' on the issue of co-partnership in industry, for very different reasons. The Whips accused Eden and his friends of being 'conspirators' against their own front bench, Eden's notorious temper flared, 'leaving thereby a nasty taste. Page-Croft's† speech a nightmare – what an unpleasant fellow that is. A bland manner & a natural crook under it – whether he practises or not.'

Baldwin, however, was less troubled than his Whips by this independence, as he knew that Eden was with him on the main issues of India and his leadership. 'Now he will be able to go after we have won St George's', Spender-Clay‡ triumphantly told Eden on 12 March. 'Why should he?' Eden wrote. 'He is the only statesman we possess. Unhappily we have too few who can recognize one, still fewer who will fight for one. Old women are too numerous in our party. S.B. spoke to me after his speech of some important work he wants me to do. Cannot be written here but naturally flattered.'

This work was in fact membership of an all-party group consisting of MacDonald, Lloyd George and Eden whose purpose was the preparation for the forthcoming Disarmament Conference, a truly remarkable recognition of Baldwin's belief that Eden was a coming man. As he later wrote: 'This was my first experience of discussion at the Cabinet level, and I liked it.' On 26 March he spoke in the House on the subject, and was warmly congratulated by Austen Chamberlain, among many others; Eden referred to it in his diary as 'The best debating speech I have yet made', and it was noted with approval in the national and local press.

What was not noted with approval in Warwick and Leamington was his support for Baldwin. He had spoken twice for Duff Cooper, but when he

---

* Brendan Bracken, MP for North Paddington, and a vehement Churchill ally and friend.
† MP for Bournemouth.
‡ MP for Tonbridge.

spoke to his constituency executive he found his chairman hostile to Baldwin and his own reception was 'not too kindly'. 'I feel tired & battered,' he gloomily confided to his diary on 28 March. He did not approve of the compact with Beaverbrook: 'I am not enthusiastic. Almost alone I disapproved of the last, & I am no more disposed to approve this when he & Rothermere are Beat [after St George's]. The former is constitutionally incapable of "staying put", the latter the foulest influence in British public life today.'

Eden, accordingly, was now publicly, and strongly, aligned against Churchill, Bracken and Beaverbrook, to the great annoyance of many in his own constituency Party. The Beaverbrook–Rothermere press picked him out for special, and hostile, attention. Neville Chamberlain was not the only prominent Conservative who was convinced that Baldwin was doomed, and was reaching, somewhat impatiently, as Eden noted, for the crown. Eden was on the other side from Chamberlain on virtually all issues, at a time when Baldwin's fortunes were at their lowest. For an ambitious young politician this was a foolhardy position to be in, and yet one greatly to his credit. The long-term consequences of this rift were impossible to foresee.

These severe political worries and his ill health, which persisted throughout the spring and early summer of 1931, had additional personal concerns. Beatrice was away from London a great deal, and the financial worries were constant. His careful estimate for the year's expenditure was £1,745, and the actual was £1,828, 17s. 10d. His income from his investments and parliamentary salary was £1,205, so that with his *Yorkshire Post* review income and that from the City job he was only narrowly able to meet his obligations.

But at this point the condition of the Labour Government suddenly became notably more hapless than that of the Conservative Opposition. The international economic tides now battered Britain, unemployment continued to rise terribly, and in February the Chancellor of the Exchequer, Philip Snowden, had agreed to the appointment of a Committee on National Expenditure chaired by Sir George May, thereby in effect handing over the Government's responsibilities to an independent forum that was hostile to the fundamental purposes of the Labour Party, in itself one of the most extraordinary acts of abandonment of ministerial responsibility in modern political history. By the end of July, when May was due to report, unemployment was over three million and withdrawals from London were running at nearly £2.5 million a day. All Europe and the United States was reeling under what Churchill described as 'the economic blizzard' – which had nearly ruined him, also – but what mattered in British politics was that a Labour Government pledged to the abolition of unemployment was in office, and evidently helpless and without answers.

Eden's close involvement with MacDonald made him seriously alarmed about the Prime Minister. On 19 May, while he was reading a newspaper in the Commons Library, as he recorded in his diary:

Ramsay came up & poured forth his indignation against our party for putting so many amendments down on the order paper to the Finance Bill. 'Obstruction is written across it in red letters,' he exclaimed. 'I would have been prepared to do a deal. But how can I in the face of this? It ties my hands with my own people' – & much more to the same effect. I told him I had not even seen the Order Paper. Actually I had no idea what he was talking about for some time.

On 19 June Eden had another odd conversation with MacDonald: 'All of course about himself.... Ramsay always creates the impression in conversation that, not only do all the cares of the world rest upon his head, but nobody can ever have been Prime Minister of England before.'

By concentrating upon disarmament and foreign affairs, this was a successful summer for Eden, as the Labour Government tottered to its downfall. Baldwin had survived the threat to his leadership, now it was MacDonald's turn; it is not often that the fortunes of two leaders have been reversed so swiftly. Eden now was one of the minor beneficiaries of this transformation – and one of the more deserving ones. On 29 June he made 'on the whole I think the most successful speech I have yet made in the House [on disarmament]. Won the warmest approval of those who count there even if the Press ignored it.'

This speech, in fact, had less to do with disarmament than rearmament, particularly for the air force. 'The seeds of war psychology still exist in Europe. I even doubt whether during the past two years what is usually called the spirit of the League has grown in strength in Europe. On the contrary, the probability is that it has weakened. I do not wish to be alarmist, but I do not think that anyone who studies the European situation today can be otherwise than anxious about it....' Eden emphasized the weakness of the Royal Air Force, the fact that other nations had sharply increased their expenditure on air armaments while that of Britain had been reduced, although 'it is the air defence of this country that will most concern future generations.... There will be no heroics in a war where the safest place will be the front line, if there is one, and the most dangerous the houses of our civilian population.' These warnings were so notably out of tune with contemporary emotions about war to a nation obsessed with its economic turmoil that it is not surprising that the speech was generally unreported. But in the small world of the House of Commons it was noted with approval for its style and thoughtfulness, if less so for its content.

There was a certain, and significant, dichotomy in Eden's attitudes at this time. He was a strong believer in an arms agreement, if only for financial reasons, so far had Britain fallen behind others. But he remained sceptical about long-term German ambitions, and believed that for Britain to have a major role in Europe it had to be militarily strong. There was no fundamental illogicality in this dual approach, and in 1931 the future of Europe, racked by the economic crisis, was indeed very difficult to foresee. But, so was that of British politics.

In 1929 it had seemed to Eden that he was doomed to another four or five years of back-bench Opposition, that most futile and dispiriting of all political activities for an ambitious young politician. If the Baldwin Must Go movement had succeeded – as it very nearly did – his personal fortunes would have crashed with those of his leader and patron. Even at this stage, his relations with Neville Chamberlain were not close, and certainly nothing like as close as they were with Baldwin. But now his luck dramatically changed.

The Report of the May Committee was published after Parliament rose for the Summer Recess. Its picture of the British economy was bleak; its proposals Draconian. The former caused panic among foreign investors and a run on sterling; the latter split the Labour Cabinet and Party fiercely. There were confused meetings with bankers, between ministers, and between the Party leaders – excepting Lloyd George, who was recovering from an operation. The Opposition now in effect dictated to the Cabinet by rejecting its proposals for economies of £56 million. In these desperate and chaotic circumstances the King intervened by summoning Herbert Samuel for the Liberals – who favoured a National Coalition Government – and then Baldwin. It would have been the other way around, except for the fact that Baldwin was lunching at the Travellers' Club and had left no word of his plans. When he did see the King it was to be asked if he and his colleagues would serve in a National Government headed by MacDonald, as Samuel had proposed. Put in these terms, Baldwin virtually had no choice but to respond positively, although personally he was not enthusiastic. Had Lloyd George been well, and part of the compact, the answer would have been definitely negative.

The Cabinet was now completely split on the Opposition parties' demand for cuts of £78 million, and MacDonald asked them all to place their resignations in his hands. They did so, under the impression that they would be succeeded by a Conservative–Liberal Coalition headed by Baldwin. But the King, with flattery and skill, appealed to MacDonald as 'the only man to lead the country through this crisis', and Baldwin – urged not only by the Liberals but by Neville Chamberlain – acquiesced at the crucial meeting called by the King at Buckingham Palace on the morning of 24 August. Thus was born the National Government, which described itself as not 'a Coalition in the ordinary sense of the term, but co-operation of individuals', whose task was solely to resolve the economic crisis. Labour ministers were too stunned to protest initially, although the majority, after they had recovered, considered that they had been misled and betrayed by their leader. Snowden and J. H. Thomas joined MacDonald in the new Cabinet, which was dominated by the Conservatives. Such was The Great Betrayal, for which MacDonald has never been forgiven by Labour.

These extraordinary events now transformed Eden's prospects and career. The difficulty about coalitions is that the need to share ministerial offices – in those days considerably fewer than they are today – means disappointment to many who would have had good reason to expect Office in a purely party government. In these circumstances Eden was not sanguine of his chances, but on 27 August, after a nervous morning at art galleries – a characteristically soothing foray at a moment of acute nervousness and strain – he lunched with Austen Chamberlain, who himself had hopes, soon to be dashed, of high Office in the new Government. Eden recorded in his diary:

[Austen] told me there was a chance I might go to F.O. That he had spoken strongly to Reading & that S.B. had agreed to his doing so. He hoped something would result but S.B. had given away so much to the Liberals it was impossible to say. He – S.B. – apparently greeted my name with more enthusiasm than any other. The F.O. in a national govt. with the S of S in the Upper House is higher than I hoped for & I do not expect that I shall get it.

Saw Walford Selby later in the evening who told me that he had thought it all settled that I was going. That 3 names were put forward & that he & Van* plumped for me at once. However I have not heard a word. Our people very bitter against S.B. for letting Libs have W[ar] O[ffice].

On the next day 'the summons came'. 'S.B. could not have been kinder,' Eden wrote that evening. 'He told me that he wanted me to go to the F.O., where he had intended to send me for a spell himself if our party had been returned, and added that he regarded me as "a potential Foreign Secretary" in about ten years' time and that was why he wanted me to have the experience as soon as possible.'

But it was not to be that easy. MacDonald wanted his son Malcolm to take the post, and it was very possible that Eden would have to accept the only other vacancy, as Junior Minister at the Dominions Office. This was a serious disappointment:

* Sir Robert Vansittart, Permanent Under-Secretary, Foreign Office.

He [Baldwin] had sent for me because he did not wish me to think during the weekend that I had got nothing. Ramsay's son had been going to the Dominions Office but 'one of them shall be yours'. I thanked him and told him that I had not counted on anything in a coalition, knowing what his difficulties must be. He said he was afraid some of his late colleagues had sore heads, but he could not help that, he was there unhappily for that purpose among others. I told him that I would prefer the F.O. of the two. He said 'Of course you would of course you would', and added that he hoped this might still be possible. We had some general conversation in the course of which he showed me the draft of his letter to M.P.s urging constant attendance. Finally he showed me out with the words: 'I hope this may be the beginning of a long and successful but', with a laugh, 'I won't say prosperous career. This is not in politics.'

The Edens spent the Saturday and part of Sunday the 30th at Kirkdale. 'A quiet & restful day at Kirkdale,' Eden noted. 'Lovely weather. Bad night. Some pain. Had to take drug. Hope *that* trouble [the ulcer] doesn't start again now.' It is more than likely that tension over his future was a contributory cause; the Foreign Office was so close, but it was not yet his, and his fate was being debated elsewhere. MacDonald was, after all, the Prime Minister, and Baldwin only Lord President of the Council; if MacDonald insisted upon Malcolm going to the Foreign Office, Baldwin would have had to concede, and Eden was not particularly interested in the Dominions Office. It was not his field and was, politically speaking, a backwater. He tried to soothe himself by reading Trollope's *Framley Parsonage*; there was no news, no telephone call. On the Sunday afternoon he apologized to Ger Beckett and Beatrice, and returned anxiously to London.

31 August
Lunched at Carlton where Sam Hoare* & Neville C. joined me at round table. No sensational news. Sat at home all afternoon expecting to hear something, but nothing until dinner time when [Geoffrey] Fry [Baldwin's Private Secretary] rang up, first to tell me to go to S.B. at 9.30 [and] then to say it wasn't necessary as nothing yet to tell. And so ends another day of suspense. Read George Moore's 'Aphrodite in Arlis'. A little disappointed in it. Does not capture a fresh atmosphere.

The next morning passed slowly with no news until:

A message from Geoffrey Fry about 12 telling me to come & see S.B. He told me that the F.O. was mine all right & advised getting to work as soon as might be. The trouble is that the appointments may not be out for some days.

Saw Walford [Selby] & Van, both very friendly. Decided I should come to the Office tomorrow afternoon.

* Sir Samuel Hoare, MP for Chelsea.

Lunch at Carlton then on to City where I cleared up papers & said goodbye – or more likely au revoir – to Mortimer.* A quiet evening at home. Read Pepys. I am very fortunate to get the F.O. Nothing could have suited me better & everybody there very friendly.

It was indeed a remarkable opportunity, achieved for Eden by Baldwin personally, as MacDonald's fascination with foreign affairs, and his considerable ability for them, had made him desperately eager for his son to go to the Foreign Office. As matters turned out, Malcolm MacDonald proved to have a flair and aptitude for Dominion matters that was to endure far beyond the end of Empire and to enable him to play a unique role in that process and in the difficult aftermath. So, as it happened, all proved to be for the best for both young men – and for so many others.

Eden had deserved his good fortune, through his dedicated hard work on foreign affairs and for his staunch loyalty to Baldwin when things had been bad and the prospects gloomy for both. Those who believe that success in politics goes to men who chop and change and seize the immediate advantage should ponder on this episode.

It also provides us with another view into Eden's personality. He was volatile, and often hot-tempered; his apparent suaveness may have irritated many – as it did – but those who experienced his outbursts saw what they thought was another man, not appreciating the inner tensions and capacity for hard work that could make him so impatient. But he valued loyalty very highly, as he valued his self-respect. He had stood by Baldwin not because of personal advantage – at many times there had been no advantage at all, very much the opposite – but because he believed in him and in his view of Conservatism and the national interest.

On 3 September Eden wrote in his diary:

Tommy [Dugdale, Baldwin's Parliamentary Private Secretary] called on me unexpectedly at breakfast. We walked down to the F.O. together. A morning of work there, reading up China & the Shanghai concession negotiations. Lunched at Carlton.

Back at F.O. in the afternoon when more reading. There are many threads to pick up & the task is likely to occupy one fully – until the govt. goes out! Dined at home & read Pepys & some Kipling stories.

The first National Government lasted only until 6 November. Eden's Foreign Secretary was Lord Reading, who was obviously a *locum tenens*, and an early general election was inevitable, although not before hesitations and changes by MacDonald about the Liberal involvement which Eden recorded with exasperation in his letters and diaries. When it came, the National candidates – predominantly Conservatives – had a majority so large that it was dangerous, and Labour was reduced to a diminutive and

* Roger Mortimer, stockbroker.

forlorn minority group. Eden's own majority was over 29,000, and when the election was over Reading was replaced by the Liberal Sir John Simon, a man of undoubted intellect but with a reputation for calculating deviousness and irresolution which Eden came to experience and dislike profoundly. But his opportunity had arrived.

If post-war British foreign policy has any theme, it was to avoid the circumstances that had brought disaster in 1914. Thus the emphasis was on non-commitment – especially in Europe – wary association with the League of Nations, and disarmament. The concept of maintaining the balance of power had been tacitly abandoned. As William Strang later wrote with truth: 'We behaved as though we could play an effective part in international affairs as a kind of mediator or umpire without providing ourselves with the necessary arms and without entering into firm commitments, whereas the truth was that, for lack of international solidarity in face of the common menace, we were in mortal peril.'[*]

The 'mortal peril' was to be provided by Nazi Germany after 1933, but one of the Nazi skills was to play upon British guilt feelings about the terms imposed upon Germany by the 1919 Peace Treaty at Versailles, for which Maynard Keynes bore a considerable responsibility, and about the lunacy of the intolerable reparations demanded from Germany at French insistence. But to those of Eden's generation the pre-war arms race seemed to be the principal cause of catastrophe. Thus, if disarmament – or, at least, the control of armament – could be achieved, so could peace. This approach was not only idealistic but made practical sense, as Churchill had argued throughout his tenure as Chancellor of the Exchequer. What did not make sense was for Britain to urge such a course on others while pursuing, in Strang's words, 'an almost Cobdenite non-interventionism'.

In retrospect, we can see clearly now that the events of 1929–31 had delivered a mortal blow to the post-war European economic recovery and political stability, and especially to the Weimar Republic in Germany. Self-confidence had also been shattered in the United States, which was entering one of the darkest and most unhappy periods in the history of the Republic, and in Britain the National Government was more obsessed by domestic than international concerns except insofar as the latter affected the former. The buoyancy of the 1920s, and the high hopes of Locarno, had gone, and were never to return. Europe was at the beginning of a dark and terrible night.

But few at the time, even those who recognized how badly the political situation had worsened under the pressures of the economic disasters of the previous two years, realized how ominous the future was. Not many

[*] Lord Strang, *Home and Abroad*, p. 154.

people outside Germany had heard of Hitler, and those who had done had little understanding of how profound was the threat posed by the Nazis to Weimar. The Soviet Union, with its own grievous internal problems, was internationally quiescent. Mussolini was generally regarded as a moderate, reasonably benign and·useful anti-Communist Italian leader. Franco was an unknown Spanish officer, Haile Selassie an unknown feudal monarch of an unknown country. Any well-informed person, surveying the European scene at the end of 1931, could see a multitude of problems and much cause for concern, but can be easily forgiven for not anticipating that within three years the situation would have changed so catastrophically.

That Britain herself would be at war within eight years was not dreamed of. Churchill's Ten-Year Rule still limited British military expenditure based on the premiss of no war for a decade, and Churchill himself was at this time so preoccupied with India that it was not until 1933 that he began to give public expression to his alarm at European developments. The more the British looked back at the Great War, the more futile it all seemed, and the great success of anti-war books and poetry – especially the writings of Siegfried Sassoon, Edmund Blunden and Robert Graves – testified to this mood. It would be unwise to describe it as pacifist in the full sense; it was more a combination of hatred and fear of war and a strong belief that it need never happen again. In these circumstances the faith placed in the League of Nations was immense. The mood was for Protectionism in economic matters and the minimum of European entanglements. There was little – if any – pressure for rearmament.

This was the context of Anthony Eden's arrival into international diplomacy, and it was clouded by his poor relationship with Simon.

Here was a man of undoubted intellectual qualities marred by a personal manner that many found unappealing, and some deeply objectionable. Eden was soon regretting the departure of Reading. Simon's real weaknesses were his ignorance of international diplomacy and procrastination, which Eden found exasperating from the beginning of their official collaboration.

Matters were not eased by the fact that MacDonald remained keenly interested in foreign affairs, whereas Baldwin, Eden's mentor, was largely indifferent to them. Eden's youth, inexperience and junior position did not give him a strong position in Parliament or the Foreign Office, where from the beginning he was patronized by the Permanent Under-Secretary, Sir Robert Vansittart. 'Young Eden, straight from charm-school and pushed by both Baldwin and Chamberlain, got his first experience of international conferences,'* he later wrote with much condescension after they had separated.

* Robert Vansittart, *The Mist Procession*, p. 346.

He . . . omitted nothing to ensure his promotion. His appearance went far to ensure that he would get what he wanted, and that was a lot. He was ambitious, but not self-seeking, if by that we mean search for a self rarely found. . . . Desirous and deserving of praise, he avoided suspicions of brilliance or originality and pruned protrusions with sense. He said the right thing so often that he seemed incapable of saying anything else.*

This obnoxious and patronizing valediction from an embittered and ultimately totally unsuccessful diplomatic grandee says more about Vansittart than it does about Eden. The judgements of Sir John Colville on men and events are controversial, but that on Vansittart has proved fully justified. He was, as he has written, 'a man of striking intellectual ability, profound literary knowledge, and poor judgement'. Other comments have been even more severe.

Relations were also not improved by the fact that Vansittart was very rich, very opinionated and, as Permanent Under-Secretary, very powerful. As his memoranda, minutes, letters and later writings showed, he was also vain and intolerant. He clearly saw no particular reason to be considerate to a minister so much junior to him in years and experience, and behind all the letters beginning 'My dear Anthony' and 'My dear Van' one senses from the beginning an antipathy that was to develop into something deeper and far more serious. One also gains the clear impression that Eden, while being very much aware of Vansittart's real qualities and knowledge, was never awed by him and had views – which he later articulated strongly – about a senior official who behaved as though he were the Foreign Secretary and his political masters mere temporary minnows swimming in his personal lake. Relations were usually courteous, but never close.

The long-awaited Disarmament Conference, in preparation for years, eventually met in February 1932. Eden was not a member of the British delegation, and he watched with dismay the acrimonious opening exchanges between the Germans and the French. The proposals placed no serious arms limitations on any country except Germany, which refused to be thus discriminated against. So, as the Conference ground along, hopelessly divided and paralysed even over detail, Eden's impatience became more marked. He wrote in his diary on 6 July:

A good deal of friction during the early part of this week between Cabinet at home and Liberal Ministers at Geneva. The trouble with Simon and Samuel is that they are hopelessly chameleon. The colour of the Cabinet at home, of Geneva there. They have no minds of their own, though unlimited ingenuity. Finally Simon telegraphed a suggestion for no more capital ship construction after 1936 to be

---

* Vansittart, *The Mist Procession*, p. 429.

hinted to the Americans to please them.... This proposal was dropped after some heat had been engendered at home, and probably irritation at Geneva.

Our proposals were finally announced this afternoon, and reasonably well received though of course shorn of the effect they would have had if announced six months ago, as they could and should have been. They would not have been announced even now but for strong pressure by S.B. The handling of this country's disarmament policy has been weak and timorous from the start.

The British problems were compounded by the fact that MacDonald was taking such keen interest in the matter, and on 12 July Eden recorded in his diary that:

We were a good deal astonished and confounded to learn at F.O. yesterday that ... P.M. and Simon had concluded a pact with France. This in its original form could well have been interpreted as a revival of the Entente. It included a proviso for mutual discussion between F[rance] & E[ngland] whenever Germany approached either about the Treaty of Versailles. None of them seem to have realized what they had done. Even Runciman* to whom I spoke seemed to think it wholly harmless: 'underlining a present personal relationship' he called it. None of them seemed to appreciate that such underlining is either significant or superfluous. Moreover almost the worst feature was that Germany & Italy knew nothing of it: that the agreement was kept secret. Luckily we were able to water it down very much. The great would be wiser to keep in touch with their expert advisers at these times. If you pay a F.O. it is as well to use it. Van was, not unnaturally, very distressed at this clumsiness, & somewhat chagrined that the office should thus have been ignored.

On 26 July Eden set out his more fundamental concerns in his diary:

Several conversations with Simon in these days about the disarmament position. At one stage I wrote him a brief minute on the subject setting out the alternatives that confront us.

The truth is that the hesitation of HMG as personified in this instance by Charlie L[ondonderry] and Eric [Drummond]'s† influence over the P.M. has not only resulted in our missing a chance but has landed us in a position of the utmost difficulty. If the Cabinet had finally summoned up significant courage to over-ride the Air Ministry and had offered the total abolition of the military and naval air arm we should (1) if the proposal had been accepted by the conference (by no means improbable as some profess to believe) have raised ourselves from fifth place among the air powers to equal first: because where there is no armament all are equal. Removed the most serious existing menace to the safety of London: saved ourselves a considerable expenditure. (2) If the proposal had been refused we should at least have convinced the world, and not least important our public opinion at home of our sincerity. As it is we have made the worst of all worlds.

---

* Walter Runciman, President of the Board of Trade.
† First Secretary-General of the League of Nations.

The P.M. would not come down on either side of the fence despite all S.B.'s pressures. The latter was the leader of the plan and its most vigorous advocate. The compromise to 'talk it over' with the French was futile in the extreme. The only chance of getting the plan accepted was to make it ours and champion it. Simon ought to have refused the tentative half measure.

Now we are in this unhappy position. If the Conference begins again in the autumn we shall be on the defensive against the Hoover plan ... and we shall soon be made to appear the obstructionists at the conference and then we shall catch it – deservedly – at home. This quite apart from the unhappy effect on world recovery of the failure of the Conference.

Simon talked over with me his letter to the P.M. in which he proposed to write to the Admiralty stating their own case when the conference resumed. It was not in the least clear what he meant by this so I asked him.

S: 'Well, I don't agree with Admiral Pound: if they want to state their case in this way let them do it for themselves.'

A: 'I agree with your view, but surely that is the wrong way to put it to the P.M. You have won a breathing space: the Cabinet has now one more chance to decide upon a positive disarmament policy.'

S: 'It will never do it.'

A: 'It should surely none the less be urged to do it. Whoever speaks for the Admiralty plans you will be blamed if the conference fails.'

S: 'I don't like my position. It does not seem to me fair that whatever the services want I have to defend [them] however impossible their positions. Well anyway, what do you suggest?'

A: 'That the Cabinet should be reminded that there is now no alternative between decision upon positive contribution when the conference meets again – if it does – and a large measure of responsibility for its failures.'

S: 'Yes, but what do you suggest? We know all that. But the Cabinet must have some plan. What can we offer?'

A: 'What we wanted to offer from the first: the total abolition of the naval and military air arm.'

S: 'Well, I see what you mean. We must try and put something to that effect in the letter' – (he walks up and down) – eventually 'How would this do' & he dictates a paragraph to the effect that the Cabinet will have to face the alternatives which will confront us at the conference in the event of our being unable to contribute something constructive. Not so strong as I had hoped but none the less showing that we are not blind to the big issues.

Simon's difficulty is not so much in making up his own mind as that once he has made it up – or at least has seemed to do so (perhaps that it is the truth it is not really made up). Anyway he will not fight for his own policy. He expects the Cabinet to find his policy for him. That they will never do. They want to be told. The only result of present procedure is F.O. pushed into the background, which is not good either.... Poor Simon is no fighter. Nothing will make him one.

As this reveals – which his own memoirs do not – Eden was a considerably more radical and enthusiastic disarmer than has been realized, and he was later to advocate, with Baldwin's strong support, a British proposal to ban all bombing aircraft. But although he was prepared to go much further than he seemed willing later to admit, his fundamental point was absolutely right. The British had no policy, and the Conference was slithering into disrepute and towards total failure. What would happen then?

What Eden saw as lamentable British dilatoriness was made worse by the fact that Germany's Brüning Government had fallen, and with it, it was subsequently believed, the last chance of real disarmament. The truth was that the tardy British proposals foundered on French insistence on long-term British security commitments which the British could not give. The Germans withdrew in September, refusing to return until and unless they were given equality of rights, and the argument now became how to bring Germany back to the Conference. Although this was achieved in December, it was all too late. Eden always believed that if the negotiations had been conducted by the British from the beginning of 1932 with real urgency it was possible that this disaster could have been prevented. This is very debatable, but Eden's contention that the attempt should have been made with greater vigour cannot be denied. But neither Simon nor Vansittart shared his enthusiasm or concern, and his protests had little effect.

After spending his holiday at Kirkdale and Windlestone, followed by a spell on the Riviera, Eden returned to the charge in September, preparing with Vansittart a paper which Simon said he liked, only then to qualify his approval. There was still no British disarmament policy. Eden subsequently wrote that he went to Geneva as a substitute delegate to the Conference on 2 November, but he was in Geneva to attend the League from mid-September.

On 10 October he noted, 'A long weary morning in the Assembly, approving reports of little significance'; when the Disarmament Conference did meet early in November, Eden was sent there 'without a single syllable of instruction or advice'. He became increasingly disillusioned with the problem of getting Simon to make up his mind. On 29 October, back in London, he wrote that 'If the Cabinet will not have it [the Eden–Vansittart paper] Simon should ask them to send someone else to Geneva. I told him this – but that he should not ask me to go!' But on 31 October:

Simon went off to the Cabinet like a scalded rabbit, really in a pitiable state. I heard afterwards that he was wretched in Cabinet, running round in circles. However, ultimately a drafting committee was set up. But this last week has been most exacting for Van & I. It is not possible to do more than give and make material to fight with: no one else can give him [Simon] guts.

Eden went to Geneva on 2 November 'to hold the fort and to provide an audience for the French'. He had had a discussion with Simon, who spoke of nothing except Persia and cursed the fact that he had been forced to abandon an entire weekend of constituency engagements. It was a somewhat bizarre introduction to the international stage.

Things got worse when Simon himself arrived in Geneva on 14 November:

Simon arrived. In comparatively cheerful mood in the morning. We had a long talk on various matters and he expressed himself as pleased with what we had been doing. This however did not last long.

He found that an attack on him had appeared in *Manchester Guardian* which had not been shown him. This peeved him and still more the excuse that he had been too busy to be shown it. Then we went to see Drummond who told him of a Manchurian rumour as to our policy spread by the French ... tiresome but of course by no means unheard of in this wicked world and Drummond only wanted authority to deny it. However it had the worst possible effect upon Simon who could talk of nothing else (and *Manchester Guardian*) and who sank back into unrelieved gloom. Lunch with him and [the American] Norman Davies which was entertaining as a study in incompatibility of temperaments.

The situation was not only farcical but hopeless. Germany would not be involved unless there was equality of rights on rearmament; meanwhile, German armaments, as the British and French well knew, were already in excess of the limits imposed by the Treaty of Versailles. The French proposals were as unacceptable to the British as they were to the Germans, and the British themselves vacillated while Eden fumed. He was relieved to return to London on 18 November, where he had a fierce struggle with the Treasury and the Governor of the Bank of England, Montagu Norman, over a crucial Portuguese order for warships to be built in British yards. If this plan to increase Portuguese armaments seemed in odd contrast with the Disarmament Conference the fact was that Portugal presented no threat to international peace and the Vickers and Yarrow yards desperately needed the work. Eden wrote that he was 'Depressed by power exercised by wizened and cold-blooded officials'; Montagu Norman, he added, 'whatever his merits is a neurotic'. Eventually he secured the support of Neville Chamberlain; as Eden wrote, an order of over one million pounds 'is an important political issue this winter ... the Treasury are only convinced I have shares in Vickers!' But on 26 November he had to return to Geneva to endeavour to extricate something, by now convinced that unless there was progress by Christmas the operation would be a total fiasco.

Eden had succeeded in impressing MacDonald as well as Baldwin about the urgency of the situation, and MacDonald came to Geneva on 2 December with Simon to concede the German demand for equality of rights. This made Eden uneasy, as 'equality' needed to be defined, and he noted that 'the Germans hold all the cards'. When Hitler came to power in January 1933 the truth of this was only too evident.

This had been a time of intense frustration for Eden. He had a Prime Minister for whom he had admiration, but who was clearly past his best, and who looked and sounded out of touch with realities, at home and abroad. He had a Foreign Secretary whom he neither liked nor trusted, whose irresolution was chronic and incurable, and who left to Eden much of the work normally taken on by the Foreign Secretary himself. He had been plunged without instructions or a policy into European power politics at a notably difficult time. He shared with Sir Alexander Cadogan, the chief adviser to the British delegation, not only impatience with Simon's inability to make up his mind on anything, but also alarm at the real prospect of the collapse of the Conference. And so, at the end of 1932, he resolved to try again.

The difficulties facing the Foreign Office were not confined to Europe. Late in 1931 the first serious Japanese incursion into Manchuria occurred, and, as the Foreign Office Minister involved, it was Eden's responsibility to answer Parliamentary Questions on the matter. The American Secretary of State, Henry Stimson, favoured declarations on territorial changes caused by force, but both he and the President, Hoover, opposed the use of force itself. As British interests in the area were far greater than those of the United States, and were more valuable, these declarations without reality were hardly impressive. Eden recorded in his diary on 28 January:

Later a summons to a conference about Shanghai. Wellesley* extremely confident that all is over & reluctant to make any response to American offer. He may be right in the latter but I felt in my bones he was wrong about former. A little later in Van's room when there was more disquiet – because Lindsay† had not delivered our modified message of agreement at USA (an exceptional course, but he I suppose thought our measure of agreement insufficient) and because the Jap chargé d'affaires had confessed to the navy's irritation at the possibility of a Jap attack on a point in the international settlement – Wellesley asked me what I feared. I replied bombardment of Shanghai. He roared with laughter & said nothing was less likely. Incident was closed: we were flogging dead horse. Half an hour later came first news of Shanghai bombardment. We drafted telegram of warning to Tokyo on what we knew so far, & eventually left about 8.30, Simon with a bad headache & heavy cold. I have a fear – against all the experts – that the Jap objective is Shanghai & the valley of the Yangtze.

* Sir Victor Wellesley, Head of the Far Eastern Department, 1925–36.
† Sir Ronald Lindsay, British Ambassador to the United States.

On the next day he wrote that 'The dept. has been singularly misinformed. The Shanghai position is bad & looks like growing worse. . . . Secretary of S. in bed all day.'

The options before the British Government were in reality very limited, as Vansittart minuted on 1 February: 'we cannot contemplate, in any circumstances, the severance of economic and diplomatic relations [with Japan] unless we are eventually prepared for war.' It was this stark fact that made the Stimson 'initiative' so unrealistic, as are subsequent claims that the failure of the British to act in support of China against Japan was an early example of 'appeasement' – a word not then in the political coinage – of dictators. What was not known until much later was that Eden was strongly in favour of refusing to recognize the Japanese puppet state of Manchukuo established in Manchuria. Simon was not only critical of China but favoured unilateral action (if any) whereas Eden was convinced that only a collective response to Japanese aggression and ambitions had any hope of success. If the United States had been a member of the League, the situation might have been different.

In spite of the frustrations and disappointments of 1932, Eden's interest in the subject of disarmament, and the physical problems of having a Foreign Secretary shuttling to and from Geneva by boat and train prompted MacDonald at the end of the year to suggest to Simon that Eden should be made Lord Privy Seal and appointed to the League, although he added that 'My doubt consists mainly in whether Anthony's guns have got big enough yet for this important position.' Other names mentioned, without enthusiasm for this post were those of Lord Hugh Cecil and Austen Chamberlain, but Simon preferred an Assistant Foreign Secretary in the Cabinet with standing duties in Geneva, and had no objection to Eden in this role. Nothing came of any of these suggestions, but the result was that Simon, to his great relief, was spared the Geneva scene, which was left to Eden.

In one sense this decision, taken so casually, was the making of Eden's career. The light of international publicity and interest shone very brightly on the League and Geneva at that time, and Eden quickly found himself regarded as a significant rising young international politician. The failures of 1932 had not diminished hopes – however unreal – that there could still be international disarmament, and Eden's evident conviction that this might be possible, his positive approach and his developing strengths as a diplomat attracted attention and admiration. His great qualities of hard work, attention to detail, professionalism and political skill, and a remarkable sensitivity to people and atmosphere, made a strong impression. The facts that he was so handsome, well read and an excellent linguist were also noted. In a somewhat drab scene, populated by so many older and duller men, and with shadows looming everywhere, he stood out as an exciting exception. At the beginning of 1933 he was almost unknown; by the end of the year he was being hailed as a rising star, better known through photographs, films and press reports than most members of the Cabinet. Few such opportunities have occurred to a young politician.

But there was a price to be paid. His frequent absences put further strains on a marriage that had been in difficulties for some time. Colleagues at home were not universally gratified by his sudden fame. He became dangerously remote from the House of Commons. And, for a time, he became so involved with the League that its fortunes became perilously linked to his own.

From the moment Eden had, at Oxford, decided to immerse himself in foreign affairs, but to take the political 'Curzon' route rather than that of the professional diplomat, he had chosen his own destiny. It is sensible for a young and ambitious politician to specialize and to become recognized in the House of Commons as a man worth listening to on his own subject. It was never true that Eden was uninterested in other subjects – those who thought so and then met him were usually surprised and impressed by his thoughtful understanding of domestic matters. But he had chosen his own field of specialization and concentration. It was a decision that had much to commend it, but politically it had its disadvantages.

What is so impressive is how hard he tried, under circumstances we can now see were impossible. He was the Geneva delegate, but he was only a junior minister, with a Secretary of State who provided, as Cadogan wrote, neither 'a chart [nor] a Captain'. Indeed, Simon showed so little interest that Eden developed the habit of consulting Baldwin directly before he did Simon. As Eden wrote in his diary on 17 January after a meeting in Paris with the British Ambassador, Lord Tyrrell, 'Simon is no better at delegating authority than at doing things himself.' Meetings with Simon were not satisfactory or rewarding, and Eden himself was at first very reluctant to take the assignment; Baldwin agreed with him, but added characteristically that 'we had probably better carry on as we were for the present' (diary, 14 January). When Eden saw Simon in Geneva on the 18th – where he had gone with great reluctance 'for appearance's sake' – Eden could only report: 'Eventually & with much difficulty induced him to talk of disarmament. He stone-walled for as long as he could & talked of every other subject first.'*

---

* Carlton, *Anthony Eden*, p. 29, states that 'To judge by the tone of Eden's memoirs, one might imagine that the working relationship between him and Simon were marred throughout by personal coolness and fundamental disagreements. The contemporary records do

Geneva provided Eden with his first opportunity of working with Alexander Cadogan, whose task during 1932 had been immensely difficult. Cadogan considered that the Foreign Office gave him scant advice and demonstrated little real interest; the Service Ministries were at best unenthusiastic; and his opinion of Simon was not high. In Eden, however, he found a young minister who really cared about the Conference, writing of him that 'He seems to me to have a very good idea of what is right and what is wrong, and if he thinks a thing is wrong, ten million wild horses won't make him do it.'* Between them they prepared what was known as the MacDonald Plan, presented by MacDonald in March, which laid down figures of armaments for each country. For a brief time it seemed to have some chance of rescuing the Conference and, had it been agreed a year earlier, it might have. But Hitler was now in power, and irresolution reigned in London and Paris.

Political difficulties were not the only ones:

9 February
Lunched with Dutchman. While I was there John Simon dragged me to telephone box & tried to dictate sentences of my speech re air disarmament. I said I had no one to take 'em down. No pencil, speech already typed. He was not pleased & turned me on to Charlie [Londonderry]† who was more reasonable although his own service is at stake. They both wanted to make explicitly a statement about bombing for police purposes. I said right time was air committee, if set up.... Simon unhelpful, but I eventually convinced Charlie far enough for him to ring off. On return to hotel foyer telephone message that I 'must' specifically mention police bombing. Decided not to. Furious with Simon for making no attempt to defend me against service depts. He was worse than they.

Still more furious the next day when I discovered that P.M. had said in reply to a question in H of C on the same afternoon Air Committee was proper place. The very argument I had used with Simon & he had refused to accept.

15 February
While I was in Political Commission this afternoon long awaited instructions from Cabinet on tomorrow's Air proposal by us arrived. They are satisfactory, *but* attached to them was a request by Simon that to please Charlie L I should include six items, each of which is irrelevant & silly & two of which would kill our efforts at the start. I was very angry.

---

not, however, bear this out.' As will be seen, the records demonstrate only too clearly that the Eden–Simon relationship was poor from the beginning, and deteriorated. In his memoirs Eden was politely cool about Simon, but did not quote from his own diaries and letters to show how low an opinion he actually held of his Secretary of State.

* David Dilks (ed.), *The Diaries of Sir Alexander Cadogan, 1938–45*, p. 8.
† Secretary of State for Air.

Fortunately Simon had gone to address the electors at Southampton, so I was able to ring up [Sir Maurice] Hankey* [to] state the facts with some energy and ask him to speak to the P.M. He was most sympathetic & did so. P.M. replied that he knew I intended to carry out instruction of Cabinet (by inference not Simon & Charlie) & that he had perfect confidence in my handling of the situation. Hankey told P.M. that no work had been done by Cabinet Cttee on control of aviation. P.M.: 'And why haven't you seen to it?' Hankey: 'Because I can't get Simon to function.' P.M.: 'He must function. Committee must meet tomorrow.' P.M. added that he had hoped Cabinet Minister could have come out to serve on Committee. This would not now be possible, but he was so pleased with the way I had handled things out here he wanted me to do it. This is a compliment I would rather have been spared because it means long battle with Air Ministry also are all here. However . . .!

Relations with the Foreign Secretary worsened when Simon announced in the Commons that Eden was acting on instructions, whereas, as Eden angrily wrote, 'I have had no instructions. Nor had I any on Saturday. I acted on my own initiative, telling Van that I was doing so.' Eden also found the Air Ministry officials 'more trouble & less help than all other depts put together'. He considered that only MacDonald and Baldwin appreciated what a burden he was carrying, and it was indeed remarkable that so vital a conference had as its British representative such a junior and young minister, often denied instructions and with little support at home. When he was telephoned from London with a complaint about one of his interventions he merely wrote 'Balderdash', but he was surprised and moved when there was 'an instantaneous revolt of our delegation' after rumours had spread in March that he was going to be recalled to London. What was even more disconcerting was that when MacDonald and Simon arrived in Geneva the Prime Minister could talk of nothing except the need for rearmament, especially in warships, citing the inability of Britain to respond to the Japanese bombardment of Shanghai. 'But we cannot defend Shanghai against Japan without a fleet very much larger than we have today, & we cannot afford that anyway,' Eden wrote in his diary after lunch with MacDonald and Simon. 'It was a depressing luncheon with the Tory eager for disarmament, the Liberal sceptic & silent, the Socialist vehemently reactionary. Age is a bigger barrier than Party in these days.' 'We are cutting an inglorious figure,' Eden wrote to Baldwin, '. . . we have no scheme, only conditions. . . . Attempts to secure any helpful contribution [from the Air Ministry] are as exhausting and ineffective as beating one's fist into a row of pillows.' Baldwin sympathized, but matters drifted on as before.

* Secretary to the Cabinet.

A new complication was that the Italians, hitherto helpful, now began to cause deliberate delays, even wooing MacDonald with an invitation to go to Rome to see Mussolini, which attracted the Prime Minister greatly, but which Eden postponed. Mussolini had conceived his own plan for a Four-Power Pact, and the Italian representative at Geneva, Aloisi, was instructed to hamper the Conference.

Eden's draft Convention was indeed radical, and cleverly balanced the French obsession with security and German demands for equality. France would be allowed 200,000 troops in Europe and another 200,000 outside it, Germany was eventually to have 200,000 troops in Europe, air bombing would be outlawed, there would be limitations on naval power and qualitative reductions in armaments. It would operate over a period of five years, there would be a permanent Disarmament Commission, and all signatories would join a consultative pact. MacDonald, with whatever reservations, introduced this in a rambling speech to the Conference on 16 March. It was absolutely doomed, but there is much to be admired in Eden's enthusiasm for his plan, its scale and skill, and his absolute sincerity, which radiates out of his diaries, letters and telegrams. He had also mastered the technical complexities remarkably quickly, as became clear to the House of Commons when it debated the subject on 23 March.

This was a significant debate for another reason. Churchill had become so locked in his battle with the Government over the Government of India Bill that his speeches had concentrated on this topic to the exclusion of almost everything else. But the rise of Hitler, and the clear evidence of an aggressive mood in Germany, had drawn his interests and energies towards this new menace. In a speech on the Air Estimates on 14 March he challenged Baldwin's claim that 'the bomber will always get through' and called for strong air defence. About the Geneva proposals he was less than complimentary:

There is the same kind of helplessness and hopelessness about dealing with this air problem as there is about dealing with the unemployment problem, or the currency question, or the question of economy. All the evils are vividly portrayed, and the most admirable sentiments expressed, but as for a practical course of action, solid footholds on which we can tread step by step, there is in this great sphere, as in other spheres of Government activity a gap, a hiatus, a sense that there is no message from the lips of the prophet. There is no use gaping vacuously on the problems of the air.

Churchill was so discredited that this deeply impressive and excellently researched speech made few, if any, converts, but it marked the beginning of one of the longest and most admirable political campaigns conducted by any British politician. Although Eden at this point honestly believed that there was still a chance of agreement at Geneva, and his youthful optimism was infinitely more in tune with the spirit of the time than Churchill's concern, their personal paths had begun to converge. On 23 March Churchill returned to the attack with an even greater speech in which he was scathing about the MacDonald Plan and the Prime Minister's introduction of it. The Disarmament Conference was denounced as 'a solemn and prolonged farce', MacDonald's visit to Mussolini, on which he had insisted, was compared to the visit to Canossa; when he dwelt upon the alarming realities of what was going on in Germany, he said, to general hostility, 'Thank God for the French Army.' It was a fine speech marred by the personal invective which so often diminished the effect of his greatest speeches in the 1930s, but it was both realistic and prescient.

To Eden there fell the responsibility of replying to this Philippic. He obviously had to be loyal to his Prime Minister and Foreign Secretary and to support his own draft Convention, in which he genuinely believed. But, as his diary records, this was a last-minute decision:

Attempted to do some work upon a speech in the morning, but interruption owing to telephone message from Geneva that conference was to go on sitting & discuss our plan. Simon would not decide which of us was to go until late in the evening, when, as an outcome I suspect of P.M.'s insistence he said he would go himself. . . .

Eventually decided about 7 p.m. that I should wind up & Simon not speak. I think latter was disappointed. Fortunately for me Winston had overdone his attack. Two entertaining incidents with him. First he came & said he was very sorry he could not stay to hear my reply but had to go to Eaton [Hall]. I replied that I understood that but of course he could not expect me to say less in his absence than in his presence. He agreed. An hour later he came back & said, somewhat shamefacedly, that he had decided to stay. I did not spare him but he was very pleasant about it & we had a drink together afterwards, he eventually leaving for Eaton & I sending my love to —* which he undertook to deliver, adding '& I shall tell her what a good speech you made.' House seemed to like my speech better than I had dared to hope. I believe that I have made more lively ones & better in earlier Parliaments. Maybe it is the advantage of the Front Bench.

Eden's task had been facilitated by Churchill's claim that MacDonald was personally responsible for the European situation, and by his denunciation of personal diplomacy at high levels which, he argued, should be left to professional diplomats and ambassadors. But although Eden rejected Churchill's 'fantastic absurdity' in accusing MacDonald, it was impressive that in what was in effect an impromptu speech Eden should display such great knowledge of the subject.

Yet, privately, he was beginning to lose hope. The Germans were increasingly hostile and negative, the Italians slippery, and although Eden

* A particularly close lady friend of Eden's.

came to like Arthur Henderson greatly, as President of the Conference he had many limitations. But the real problems were not technical or procedural, but political. In March Japan left the League, the London Economic Conference was a failure, and the French were becoming deeply alarmed at the German situation and rearmament. These fears were only too justified, and Eden also became convinced that the Germans were totally uninterested in his Convention. He worked hard to make it a reality, but as his letters to Baldwin and his diaries show, his optimism waned throughout the summer and autumn of 1933. On 23 April he wrote that 'there is I think just a fighting chance of success [but] not more'; this faint optimism did not last long. By 2 May he was writing that the German position was 'indefensible'; on 12 May when Eden was 'Feeling very tired myself & beginning to sleep badly', Simon was complaining of ill health but refused to go away ('The effect of his presence for the present is that we have no Foreign Secretary, only the appearance of one which is worse than none'). And there was the tiring shuttling between London and Geneva, either by long train journeys or by flights that took over four hours in what now appear to be alarmingly small and flimsy aircraft.

There were more difficulties with Simon ('Cold feet as usual; did not want to come out or do anything that I could discuss.... Second conversation at the end of which Simon undertook to come, most unpleasantly. This job can be hell'). When Simon did arrive on 14 October Eden considered him to be

in characteristically bad state, snappy & scared to death. It is very difficult to feel anything but contempt for the man at these times. It is not only 'nerves' at the speech which we might all suffer or excuse but I truly believe an utter lack of moral courage. It has its consequences.... Speech unctuously delivered. In the afternoon news of German departure. The conference was becoming a sham so that it is perhaps just as well now. All the same I should not like Simon's conscience about the earlier part of last year when Brüning was still in power. We missed the bus then, & could never overtake it.

This was only too clearly true. The London Economic Conference, intended to provide an international response to the economic crisis, collapsed; the Japanese had left the Disarmament Conference. Eden worked hard throughout 1933, but the reality of German determination to rearm and the attitude of the Nazi Government, combined with British and French indecision, made it a fruitless business. On the same day that the Germans left the Disarmament Conference Hitler announced that they would also leave the League. But the British decided to try to persuade them to return, while concern at German rearmament was being reflected in new action in London. With infinite reluctance and timidity, the British began to rearm.

Throughout these negotiations, meetings and travels that had no result, Eden had won warm opinions for his energy and enthusiasm, although few realized how despondent he had become. Both *The Times* and the *Daily Mail* wrote that he should be in the Cabinet, either as Lord Privy Seal or even as Foreign Secretary, to Simon's distress: 'Simon in an awful state about press campaign,' Eden noted on 19 November. 'Kept pulling cuttings from his pocket about me & would talk of nothing else!'

It would indeed have been remarkable if Eden had received such swift promotion, but the contrast between the energetic and skilful junior and the vacillating and indecisive Foreign Secretary was as striking to Mac-Donald and Baldwin as it was to journalists and the House of Commons. And in this case the press was well informed, as Eden discovered.

19 December

P.M. sent for me as I was about to dress for dinner with Dick Cavendishes. He explained that it was essential to have F.O. representative in Lords. After careful consideration this was the offer he would make to me. He was determined not to have two F.O. ministers in Cabinet. Previous experience had proved to him that it did not work he argued. He would however like me to accept the office of Lord Privy Seal without a seat in the Cabinet. My work to continue as present. Appointment would be announced on 1st January if I agreed. Baldwin & Simon concurred.

I thanked P.M. & told him I wanted a few hours to think it over & consult S.B. He readily agreed.

I saw S.B. after dinner & we had a long talk. He was pleased with solution & confessed that they had had much trouble in arriving at it. He himself had suggested a K.C.B. for me! He thought that Sir Anthony would sound well! I reminded him that if the idea was Geneva status I was quite happy as I was & nobody troubled about status there.

The difficulty was that Eden's lack of seniority precluded him from becoming a Privy Councillor; also, he would not even be a member of the Cabinet Committee that decided the policy he would be expected to carry out. 'The world may soon forget this & put upon me more responsibility than I bear. However, F.E.'s* motto never refuse – & the cash will be useful to the needy!'

For all his reservations, this was a definite advance, and put Eden well ahead of his contemporaries; his Privy Councillorship was to come six months later – the only Honour he regarded as worth having. Thus 1933 had ended better for him than he had anticipated, but Europe was, as he noted, 'sullen and suspicious'. Of the fact that Germany was rearming there was no doubt; disarmament was in practical terms a dead issue.

---

* F. E. Smith, first Earl of Birkenhead.

Alarms were growing in Austria and France, and even in pacific Britain there were stirrings of a response to these grim new realities.

'The [news of the] Privy Seal appears & the Press is kind to the animal in its new shape,' he wrote on 1 January 1934, and on the 6th he received his Seals of Office at Sandringham.

5.30 we arrive, we find an Archbishop, pregnant with sermon, on the station platform. We are bowed through a booking office, panelled, flowered & carpeted.

The front hall at S[andringham]. Beatrice advances. Only King & Queen, two waiting. We hover round belated tea, rapidly exhausting gambits of conversation.

King summons me to his study. Contrive to kneel on right knee holding testament in right hand – gymnastic difficulty, Equerry attempts to read oath, but loses spectacles and becomes incoherent. I advance to footstool, kneel again. H.M. produces collar box, hands it, extends hands to be kissed. What should I do? Out of practice in Norfolk atmosphere, so I bungle. Ceremony is at length over, then I am seated in a chair, while for an hour H.M. discourses on foreign policy. Very kind, but I still suffering from shock.

Dinner. We are clocked off beforehand. Boys one side (average age 80) girls the other (average age Aunt Blanche). I stray into wrong pen, by accident (not lechery). Confusion. Equerries rush. I am rescued from temptation.

Everybody very kind, but I fear Charles 11 should have been our King. We are very sleepy but where are our Sweet Nells & spoilt Monmouths?

That evening Sir Stafford Cripps, combining a brilliant legal intellect, high principles and extreme Socialism, delivered a public assault on 'Buckingham Palace influence', though he exonerated the King personally.

7 January
Paraded for Church at 11 a.m. After it was beckoned to the King's side and he launched out into a tirade against Cripps' speech which broke out again at intervals throughout the day. The excuse only made it worse. 'What does he mean by saying that Buckingham Palace is not me? Who else is there, I should like to know? Does he mean the footmen? D'you see the fellow says there is going to be a General Election in August? Who is he to decide that? D—d cheek I call it. I have seen moreover in one of his earlier speeches he says that if Labour gets back with a clear majority (which please God it never will) then a Trade Union Congress is to tell *me* who is to be the Prime Minister. I'll see them d—d first. That is my business and I'll send for whom I like' etc. I treated Cripps as beneath contempt & harmful only to Cripps. King agreed 'but this will give you material. You'll have to answer him.'

We went for a walk round stud in afternoon with Duchess of York & Princess Elizabeth. Both charming.

This was Eden's first meeting with the future Queen Elizabeth 11. 'Everyone very kind,' he wrote, 'but I should never make a Court flunkey.'

Eden found that his appointment had caused great pleasure in Warwick and Leamington, but that John Simon was distraught at the excellent publicity it had received, and particularly was 'in a frenzy' about a favourable leading article in the *Daily Mail*: 'Was not summoned to attend a Cabinet Committee on disarmament, & Simon's jealousy is now so rampant that I feared I should only feed it by suggesting it.'

Infinitely more congenial was Eden's new Parliamentary Private Secretary, Lord Cranborne, known to his family and friends by his childhood nickname of 'Bobbety', the brother of Lord David Cecil, and MP for South Dorset. As has been mentioned, Eden had few friends in politics, but Cranborne was to become an outstanding exception. He was a man of high convictions and standards, did not mince his words or opinions on all matters that interested him, and had a political courage that often amounted to recklessness. His intelligence, kindness and strength of character made him immensely attractive to Eden, and they were intimate political and personal friends until Cranborne's death, when they were both old men and had travelled far together. Given the fiery temperament of each it would be incorrect to say that they always agreed, but on the big issues they were to become almost inseparable, and their trust and friendship were very strong and very deep.

As Anthony Eden's work intensified and his reputation grew, so did his separation from his wife and children. I do not know when it was that Eden discovered that Beatrice was having affairs with other men, but it was depressingly early in their marriage. He was deeply wounded and distressed, but at some point they came to a tacit agreement that each would go their own way, that the fabric would hold until it became intolerable. It would be wholly wrong for the biographer to begin to apportion blame on either; he can only record with sadness what actually happened, and use his discretion about those involved in the infidelities that now characterized the marriage. Fragments from Beatrice's surviving letters at this time are undated, but they reflect her increasing loneliness.

I read your doings daily. Great Britain always seems to have something bright and intelligent to say!

I'm lunching with Tommy [Dugdale] tomorrow. Rather annoyed he didn't ask me to dine! If you're not back before Sun[day] don't forget it is Simon's birthday & he'd no doubt appreciate a letter – we are having his party on Tuesday....

Darlingest
I simply have no news at all, but I thought you might like to see my superb writing & know that none of your family are dead or dying! I have enjoyed getting your

letters & have carried out your orders.... All our love, darling – it was fun, your hectic visit. Come again sometime! Devotedly ... I've got to go to Leam[ington] on Wednesday for this bloody YMCA thing....

All my congratulations Darling. I think it was the best speech I've heard you make. All the other ladies were delighted too. Au revoir, & be a bit more peaceful after that effort!
All love, B.

... I feel so lost without you – there seems to be nothing really mine to do at all – then I keep half forgetting you're away, & when I'm not rushing about I sort of think vaguely & deliciously how marvellous it would be [for you] to get back....

Eden's own diaries and papers are, mercifully, not entirely limited to politics and international conferences. He conducted lively, and somewhat indiscreet, correspondence with his numerous lady admirers, with whom his relations were in the main blameless, although not entirely in all cases, and one could have become serious. She was a singularly beautiful and intelligent young woman, and she clearly idolized Eden. Matters might have become very serious indeed had not the lady left a letter from him on her dressing table which her mother then read. In a wonderful letter to Eden she apologized abjectly for calling everything off, as 'it not worth risking my happiness & a lot of yours.... I always knew something horrid would happen, but I've thought of every way, but I'm terrified.... Please Anthony dearest don't let your love turn to real hate.' It never did, but this was a clear indication of how things were going wrong with Eden's marriage, for this was no casual flirtation.

By 1934 there were real difficulties. Eden's almost constant absences and his all-consuming interest in politics, which Beatrice did not share in the slightest nor understand, were part of a much deeper problem. Beatrice Eden was delightful, with a warmth and kindness that were very appealing, and she was a devoted mother. Indeed, as parents the Edens were superb. Eden was captivated by Simon and loved his cheerful companionship when this was possible; Beatrice tended to be closer to Nicholas. But no one could accuse Beatrice of having intellectual tastes, and her friends and companions reflected her own cheerful gregariousness and enjoyment of fun; one can see how wise is the assessment of her brother Martyn that she would have been happier with an extrovert Yorkshire landowner, surrounded by children and animals, rather than married to a highly strung, ambitious politician with intellectual tastes for books and pictures, who worked too hard at things Beatrice did not comprehend, and whose hot temper, which was totally unpredictable, in itself caused understandable strains and rows. Love had turned too quickly to companionship and friendship, and they increasingly moved in different worlds. The infidelities on both sides were not the cause but the symptom of real trouble, though the bonds of affection and respect were, blessedly, never to be wholly broken.

Eden had become, somewhat unexpectedly, a great favourite of King George v, and his diaries and letters spring into particular life when he describes their meetings.

2 November 1934
King sent for me to talk of Scandinavia.

It was amusing to be announced by Sim [Lord Feversham], & to be his only duty for the day. Nothing epoch-making about our conversation except that King told me, with some indignation, of his drink renunciation that had come about during the war. It seems that Ll G came to him much troubled about heavy drinking among munition workers. It was having an influence on output. Could not an example be set? The King was reluctant, asked for more information, said he would consider it, whereupon Ll G went out & told everyone he had agreed. Then he had no choice. A scurvy trick, H.M. thought. All this arose from a passing reference to Ll G & Haig controversy.

Had some conversation with [Sir Clive] Wigram* before & after. Not pleased with municipal elections. His hope was Govt would get back, S.B. & elder men then carry on for a year or two, then hand over 'to you & Oliver [Stanley] & the younger men'. 'That I know', he added, 'is what the King wants to see, too.'

Royal interest in Eden extended to the Prince of Wales.

7 November
Prince of Wales summoned me for 5.30. A whisky & soda & a talk about Scandinavia & other matters. South America was his favourite topic, & as to domestic politics he regretted absence of [W.S.] Morrison from Nat. Govt. I agreed. He shows a shrewd appreciation of men & matters & is probably more receptive than the King. Very friendly & I liked him.

The diaries also demonstrate the bitterness of his relations with Simon:

7 November
He was exceptionally unpleasant before going to Cabinet. All his confidence of yesterday had evaporated. Felt icy. 'This what comes of having Conservative colleagues. Let a true Conservative make the speech, like Sir Philip Sassoon. Anyhow I won't' etc. etc. I retorted that it was not Conservatives who were reactionaries in this. In fact had he supported [us] in Cabinet then we might have secured better attitude on Geneva draft articles. But he never helped us at all. Truth is he will not say 'boo' to [Viscount] Hailsham† or perhaps he has no real

* The King's Principal Private Secretary.
† Secretary of State for War.

convictions of his own. Anyhow he could not have been more offensive & relations chilled for the rest of the day!

To Eden's unconcealed satisfaction Simon made a bad speech in the Commons on the following day, and then blamed the failure on Eden and the Foreign Office in a note to Baldwin. The latter called Eden in for a private talk, in which all his sympathies were with him, and against Simon. But Baldwin was not Prime Minister, and could not engineer a reshuffle. Eden came away with the clear impression that it was Baldwin's wish that he, and not Simon, should be Foreign Secretary; from this conversation much difficulty was to flow.

The British Memorandum of 29 January 1934 accepted a limited degree of German rearmament, and Eden, accompanied by Cranborne, was sent by the Government on an exploratory mission to Paris, Berlin and Rome on 16 February. 'Politically poor France is in an unhappy state and her troubles are by no means over,' Eden reported to Simon, with considerable understatement for France was still reeling from the riots caused by the Stavisky Affair. This, an issue not usually remembered today, involved elaborate fraud, the disappearance of several million francs of publicly subscribed bonds, violent public riots, the fall of the Government, and the distinctly mysterious death of Serge Alexandre Stavisky himself in refuge. Eden found intense demoralization in Paris and mounting fear of the Nazi paramilitary units, the SA and SS: 'there are now no doubt many influences here that do not want a [disarmament] convention, though none that dare say so,' Eden wrote. 'Dominant impression is France's unhappy internal political state. I fear much trouble ahead. This govt. cannot last long: there is the rot of corruption in the whole Parliamentary system' (17 February).

These convulsions in France, whose effects on national morale and public confidence in democratic institutions were profound, had brought to the premiership the veteran Gaston Doumergue and Louis Barthou as Foreign Minister. Eden regarded the former, as he told Simon, as 'a gay and gallant old gentleman' but 'Barthou I did not like. I thought him bristly and foxy. I should think a nasty old man at heart,' and their discussions were not useful. Eden was concerned by the fact that the French Ministers were poorly informed about the new British proposals; a more dispassionate observer might feel that Eden gave inadequate attention to the political turmoil that they were passing through in their own country.

But Barthou's name brought to Eden other memories, and he was already demonstrating his extraordinary, and what one of his private secretaries described as 'almost encyclopaedic', knowledge of people and events. It was Barthou who, in 1922, at the Reparation Commission, had moved for the official notification of the German default on timber deliveries. This was in itself a trivial matter, but it was deliberately calculated to raise the issues that had led to the Franco-Belgian military occupation of the Ruhr in January 1923, which Eden regarded – rightly – as a cataclysmic event that gave an immense impetus to the revival of German militarism, to the destruction of Weimar, and, eventually, to Hitler's rise to power. Just as Eden loathed Prussian arrogance and brutality, so also did he despise the merciless Clemenceau generation that had been resolved to ruin and humiliate Germany and its fledgling democracy. In the front rank of that generation stood Barthou.

Moving from this dispiriting atmosphere, Eden travelled by train all day to Berlin. He noted in his diary: 'The journey was interesting, more especially the first part which took us through the battlefields. The Ruhr gave few signs of life, & Essen boasted scarcely a smoking chimney. So that though the Germans are no doubt rearming they are not doing so "au grand gallop", I am convinced. May be that they will have enough to do internally during the next few years.' His meetings with Hitler in Berlin seemed more promising. 'He is a surprise. In conversation quiet, almost shy with a pleasant smile. Without doubt the man has charm. I am told, however, that we saw him at his best' (to Baldwin, 21 February). In his diary he wrote on the 20th:

Chancellor himself was friendly & talked at considerable length. I am told that he was quieter than usual. Certainly he listened to what I had to say.

The man is clearly much more than a demagogue. He knew however what he was speaking about & seemed to me more sincere than I had expected. He has even a suspicion of a sense of humour, & at close quarters resembles the average Austrian much more closely than appears from his posters.

To Beatrice he wrote:

Yesterday was very interesting. After a morning spent with Neurath, Blomberg (General) & Von Bülow (an unpleasant Van), we repaired to see Hitler in the afternoon. The interview lasted two hours & he & I were the only ones to speak.

Dare I confess it? I rather liked him. He was quiet, rather shy in manner, & only worked up into the demagogue when he began to speak. Even so he was never too fervent, though near it. There is nothing of the Prussian in him, much more of the typical Austrian & he is more like Dolfuss than Hindenberg.

I am told that he was unusually quiet this time, no doubt somebody had told him that Englishmen do not like being shouted at. Moreover the fact that he had to stop to be interpreted from time to time helped to quieten him.

The interview took place in a magnificent room, as in a stage palace, & we approached through miles of passages, heavily guarded, & everybody saluting, even the typists, so that I had difficulty not to giggle. . . .

On the 21st Hitler lunched at the British Embassy: 'I sat next Chancellor. We talked freely enough with the help of an interpreter and my limited German. Hitler thawed materially, especially when we discussed the war which he likes to recall like most Germans. We discussed the various sectors where we had each been on. I took the chance to rub in that ex-soldiers should be the last even to wish for another war. He assented heartily.' Eden concluded from these discussions that 'the new Germany of Hitler and Goebels [sic] is to be preferred to the old of Bülow', as he reported to Simon. Hitler appeared to make substantial concessions on the SA and SS and to accept international supervision. He would not accept Versailles, which had been signed under duress, but would honour other agreements that had been 'freely' agreed.

Eden was encouraged, although depressed by the new atmosphere in Berlin. As he later wrote: 'At these meetings Hitler had not made the grim impression upon me which I recorded a year later.' Hitler had appeared to accept French military superiority, Locarno and limitations on the SA and SS; only on aircraft development was he unhelpful. 'I think we can trust the Chancellor not to go back on his word,' Eden wrote to MacDonald. Vansittart strongly disagreed, but Eden's belief that there was a possibility of *some* measure of compromise on limitation of armaments with Hitler early in 1934 cannot be derided or dismissed totally. At the time Eden was in effect disowned by the Foreign Office, an article in the *Observer* – clearly inspired by Vansittart – declaring that 'He is not competent either to negotiate or to prepare for negotiation.' In his diary Eden described the reaction from London as 'profoundly irritating ... showing Simon & Van's manifest mistrust in all I am doing. It is really hopeless to attempt to work for such a man. He is not only a national but an international calamity.... A wretched business.'

As Eden had been given only an exploratory role, without precise instructions, his reaction was understandable; what now seems so extraordinary is that such an important task was entrusted to a thirty-six-year-old minister who was not in the Cabinet. As he later wrote, 'my authority was slender enough without being undermined'.*

As he later freely admitted, Eden had initially misjudged Hitler, but he was far from being alone in this.† His judgement was affected by Hitler's

---

* Avon, *Facing the Dictators*, p. 75.

† Even Churchill, as late as the autumn of 1937, was publicly comparing Hitler to one of those men who 'when their life is revealed as a whole, have been regarded as great figures whose lives have enriched the story of mankind. So it may be with Hitler', and that 'One may dislike Hitler's system and yet admire his patriotic achievement. If our country were defeated, I hope we should find a champion as indomitable to restore our courage and lead us back to our place among the nations.'

apparent difference from the old Prussian militarist type he had hated, and by the fact that he was also a survivor of the Western Front. Eden always liked, and got on especially well with, soldiers, and his reminiscences with Hitler about their miserable shared experience made a considerable impression upon him. Unlike others, he soon appreciated the reality of this man and his capacity for evil: in February 1934 he was not totally deceived, but he believed that it would be possible to do real political business with him.

In this he certainly reflected British public opinion. It was only gradually that the true character of Nazi Germany became clear, and even then people could not believe that it would again embark on a policy of aggrandizement that would lead to a crisis. The British were disillusioned with war, and the economy was only slowly recovering from 1929–31, so that even the modest rearmament plans of the MacDonald Government were hotly opposed. As has been rightly written of the national mood, there was a 'spontaneous solidarity . . . and unquestioned assurance that good sense and calm would win in the end'.* Baldwin's instinct that the need to rearm was 'a horrible thing to have to say', and was 'a terrible conclusion' was shared by many. Churchill, now thoroughly alarmed and aroused, was an unrepresentative voice, but although he pressed for greater urgency and expenditure on rearmament and much closer ties with France – an especially unpopular stance – even he did not accept the inevitability of war, and in public praised Eden's endeavours.

Eden himself was angered by his treatment by London. He had a Prime Minister who, if not technically senile, had long ceased to live in the real political world; a mentor, Baldwin, who gave him general and personal support, but no real guidance; and a Foreign Secretary he neither liked, admired, nor trusted. They had not only put a heavy responsibility upon him, but now were being obviously unsupportive.

Eden's meeting with Mussolini in Rome on 26 February was even more controversial. Eden always indignantly denied that it went badly and that Mussolini derided him; indeed, the official British account confirms his own description that the discussion was 'crisp and easy', and he described Mussolini as 'lively, friendly, vigorous and entertaining'. But on German rearmament he was wholly unhelpful and unsympathetic to the British and French view, although not negative on the main issues. What Eden did not discuss was Mussolini's true assessment of where Italy's interests lay, and in Paris he made no progress at all. He returned to London on 1 March a very disappointed man, and in reporting to the House of Commons on the 14th he emphasized that without agreement on the lines he had

* F. S. Northedge, *The Troubled Giant*, p. 385.

advocated the result would be a desperate arms race. This was precisely what happened.

There was to be a long postscript of meetings at Geneva, the preparation of papers, gleams of hope and disappointment, and much hard work, but if there ever had been a chance of limiting German armament and checking Italian ambitions it had definitely gone. The French were now convinced of the futility of the operation; the German and Italian dictators ignored it. At the last session of the Disarmament Conference at the end of May the last rites were delivered.

For Eden personally the disappointment was acute. He had devoted two years of his life to the search for disarmament, and had clearly been unsuccessful. The physical and intellectual strains had been severe. But his endeavour had been recognized and his name made. If he had received earlier and stronger support from his own Government and Foreign Secretary; if the French had not become paralysed by their internal crisis; and if there had been any clear objectives in British foreign policy, things *might* have been different. But the story of how Europe tumbled downhill from 1933 is replete with might-have-beens and lost opportunities.

Eden had become so identified with the League, with disarmament and with the quest for peace that it was especially significant when in his public speeches he emphasized the folly of unilateral disarmament – which he had never advocated – and the need for effective rearmament, especially in the air. He had a particular claim to be listened to carefully. In a broadcast he said that 'at no time has the outlook been as black as it is now'. It was to become considerably blacker. The period of pacific illusions was over. That of ugly *realpolitik* had come.

But before 1934 ended, Eden's perseverance and developing diplomatic skills raised him from the understandable pessimism of his failure on disarmament. Early in October he was sent on an official tour of Sweden, Denmark and Norway. On the evening of 9 October he was told that King Alexander of Yugoslavia had been assassinated by a Macedonian at Marseilles; Barthou had also been wounded, and should have survived but for a gross medical blunder. Eden had disliked what he called Barthou's 'foxy chauvinism' and consistently negative attitude towards his disarmament package. 'It is the Barthous of this world who have made Hitler inevitable' was another of his comments, and he was concerned by Barthou's proposals for closer relations between France and the Soviet Union. Eden supported the successful moves to bring Russia back into the League, but the bilateral Franco-Soviet Treaty had worried him. Barthou's oratorical style – even at its most dangerously witty as on 31 May when he had poured scorn on the British disarmament proposals in Geneva, a scorn clearly more designed to delight his French constituents than to make serious progress – was not always helpful. Many historians have seen Barthou in a much more favourable, indeed admiring, light as the one European politician who saw Hitler clearly and was intent upon an encircling anti-German coalition with his so-called Eastern Locarno. Others, with greater justification, have recognized his laudable objectives but have been highly critical of his tactics.

Eden's immediate reactions are recorded in his diary of 9 October:

News reached us during the evening of murder of Alexander & Barthou. Particularly sorry about the latter on personal grounds. He may have been foxy, & something of a scamp, but he had courage, perhaps the most essential quality in a Foreign Secretary at this time. Moreover, having learnt that Anglo-French co-operation had to be, he had vigour enough to make such co-operation real. He was not mean in friendship as French politicians so often are. As I wrote at the time, Anglo-French relations at the close of the Assembly were better, essentially franker, than I have ever known them. Moreover Barthou's foreign policy, whether wise or not, was essentially personal. It certainly could not succeed were it not backed with vigour. I can see no obvious successor. Personally I regret a man who had become, I think in truth, a friend.

As for the King, it is difficult to foretell consequences: the potential dangers are clear enough.

They were indeed, and to most it was all too terribly reminiscent of Sarajevo, as both Italy and Hungary had designs on Yugoslavia, and the complicity of each was suspected and canvassed. With the possibility of a Balkans war, this was one of the occasions when the League justified the high hopes placed in it. In response to a Yugoslav request the League resolved to appoint a *rapporteur* to mediate in the crisis. It is a measure of Eden's considerable reputation at Geneva that he was pressed on all sides to take the post. This he agreed to do, albeit with heavy misgivings.

What then happened was a classic example of behind-the-scenes diplomacy and persuasion. The finger of suspicion pointed very definitely towards the Hungarians, but while Eden had great sympathy for the Yugoslav call for retribution and censure, which at one point looked very close to an ultimatum, a censure by the League of the Hungarian Government would have precipitated another crisis; in any event, the evidence of governmental responsibility was not conclusive. His resolution censured 'certain Hungarian authorities' for negligence in acts concerning the murders; called for the Hungarian Government to conduct its own inquiry and to report back; and invited the League Council to investigate the whole question of terrorism and to draft an international convention on the matter – a proposal eerily familiar in the 1980s. This resolution was produced at a midnight meeting of the Council on 10 December, and was unanimously approved, to widespread relief. The crisis faded away, and

Eden's reputation soared even higher, not least in Budapest and Belgrade, where the formula was received with relief. Both considered that honour had been satisfied. Eden's skill had lain in confining the hostility between the two nations to a specific issue and ignoring all other differences; containment worked.

This important exercise in peaceful diplomacy coincided with the equally serious issue of the Saar.

Under Versailles the Saar coalmines had been ceded to France, and a large area was placed under the control of a League Commission for fifteen years, to be ended by a plebiscite on the question whether its overwhelmingly German population wished to remain under French or German government. This would have to take place in January 1935, but although the League had organized the conduct of the plebiscite it was not in the Nazi tradition to permit elections to take their course, and a campaign of blatant intimidation was employed to secure a pro-German majority. Hitler publicly, and skilfully, identified the return of the Saar as the last significant obstacle to reconciliation with France; Barthou had made a strong stand on the matter. But his successor, Laval, came up with an attractive compromise that an international military contingent including French and German forces should supervise the elections and keep order.

Up to this point the British had not taken any particular interest in the matter, but after a conversation at Geneva with the League Commissioner in the Saar Eden became convinced that unless something was done on the lines Laval proposed there would definitely be bloodshed, terror and intolerable intimidation by the Germans. But he was not at all attracted by Laval's proposal to have only French and German troops, which could only make the situation more inflammable.

This crisis was the genesis of the first international peacekeeping force. Baldwin fully shared Eden's conviction that it was the only answer and that the British should be involved. The Cabinet had some misgivings. 'Continual harassment from London over unimportant details,' he wrote irritably on 7 December when he was grappling simultaneously with the Saar and the Yugoslav-Hungarian question. 'A peevish & patronising telegram from Simon to which I wrote a tart rejoinder I afterwards tore up.... J.S. sent a message through News Dept. in F.O. to their man here [Michael Wright] that he is much dissatisfied with handling of news at Geneva and which gives impression that initiative had come from Geneva whereas work was really done in London!' Eden was authorized to make the offer, which he did at the League Council on 5 December; the Laval proposal was dropped, and contingents of Britain, Italy, Sweden and the Netherlands moved in within two weeks. It was widely hailed as yet another coup for Eden, as it was.

When the plebiscite resulted in a 90 per cent vote for the Germans, relief at the end of the crisis obscured the fact that Hitler had successfully recovered, at very little cost, territory lost by Germany in 1920, and his own reputation in Germany received a crucial boost at a very difficult time when he was brutally eliminating the SA. The plebiscite would almost certainly have gone in his favour, but his methods should surely have alerted more people than they did to the true nature of Nazism. At the time it seemed an admirable example of international co-operation and a demonstration of the importance of the League.*

To the applause Eden received he was fully entitled. His developing maturity and sensitivity were striking, and if he was generally perceived as the one man who actually made the League work this was the truth, although the Beaverbrook press remained hostile to the League and to Eden personally. It was perhaps unwise for Eden to remark in a speech in Edinburgh that 'it is impossible that Lord Beaverbrook and silence could be on no more than nodding acquaintance'.

Thus ended an exhausting but personally triumphant year. But now even fiercer storms arose, that were to engulf the League of Nations and all dreams of the peaceful settlement of disputes. The League era was ending. With his new emphasis on the need for Britain to rearm, Eden recognized it.

---

* By a supreme irony, the next occasion when there was a genuine international peace-keeping force was in November 1956.

[5]

Foreign Secretary, 1935–8

Britain entered the crucial year of 1935 with a virtually leaderless Government and no discernible direction in her foreign policy, while the European situation relentlessly became more menacing and complex. In January, the increasingly powerful and sinister Pierre Laval travelled to Rome to settle outstanding matters between France and Italy, in Africa as well as in Europe, including proposals to cede French territory adjoining the Italian colonies of Libya and Eritrea, and thereby giving Mussolini a clear licence to develop his ambitions for Abyssinia, which had been worrying Eden for several months. The British decided that, on balance, improved Franco-Italian relations should be encouraged, and further attempts should be made to deal with Germany.

By now, Eden was becoming highly sceptical of any of these possibilities. As he wrote in January, 'Germany is now well on the way to rearmament, she is no longer afraid of a "preventive war" against her and in a few years – four I am told is the popular figure in Berlin – she will be strong enough to ask, in a tone which will not brook refusal, for her desiderata.' His mood was now one of bleak realism, but he was wholly unheeded. Ingenious proposals for meeting German claims and coming to reasonable terms were unobjectionable in themselves, he pointed out, but as they were not accompanied with military strength and political resolution – and with a general election approaching – their chances of success were forlorn. The one advance made in the year was the Anglo-German Naval Treaty, in which Eden was not involved, and, although the Germans made concessions, the overall result was not to their disadvantage.

Eden's own official position remained equivocal, and his relations with Simon were as bad as ever. After characteristic indecision by Simon, it was Eden who forced the pace when, through the intercession of the Swedish Government, the British were invited to Berlin for direct discussions; another invitation was received from the Russians for a British visit. After some typical dithering, it was decided that Eden and Simon should go to Berlin, and Eden then to Russia.

But on 4 March the British Government issued a White Paper on defence in entirely new, welcome and unexpected terms about the reality of German rearmament and the militarist mood in Germany. But, although the language was admirable, it was accompanied by an increase in the Estimates of only £10 million. Even this raised a political storm and the abrupt postponement by the Germans of the Simon–Eden visit. Although the period of wishful thinking was ending among those most involved in the realities, it was not ending elsewhere in Britain, and the failure of the National Government to educate public opinion about these realities now exacted a heavy price. On 9 March the existence of the Luftwaffe was coolly announced by the Nazis, and on 16 March the introduction of German military conscription and the formation of an army of thirty-six divisions – developments in total and flagrant defiance of the Treaty of Versailles. But although the British Cabinet protested, it also asked if the Germans wished the Simon–Eden visit to go forward. The Germans accepted this supine gesture, to the justified anger of the French; Eden, deeply unhappy about the state of affairs, was sent to Paris to calm them down. In this he partially succeeded, but the episode was only too typical of British division and timidity.

When he got to Berlin, Eden considered that Hitler's personality had notably deteriorated since their first meeting. Eden has described the meetings in detail in his memoirs; they lasted seven hours, and there were no German concessions and no progress whatever. Eden considered Hitler 'negative and shifty' and thought his tone conspicuously hostile, even contemptuous. It was only when he sat near Eden at a typically overblown and vulgar Nazi dinner and they discussed the war again that the mood changed. Only on naval matters was there any political progress made at all, and Hitler staged one of his notorious storms over the alleged treatment of Germans in Lithuania. The hours moved into days; nothing was achieved at all.

In the train on his long journey to Moscow with Cranborne, Eden brooded on this grim fiasco, and concluded that the chances for a general settlement in Europe had gone, and that what was urgently needed was the unity of the major powers in reaffirming their full commitment to the League Covenant and accepting the consequences of aggression, of Mussolini as well as of Hitler. He argued that this was the only language they could understand, but the Cabinet did not agree. Above all, it was Hitler's dramatic claim that German air strength had reached parity with Britain's, although untrue, which carried a very plain message. In Britain, for the first time, Churchill's remarkably well-informed warnings began to be taken seriously by more Conservatives, although the general mood remained pacific and hopeful.

Eden was the first British minister to visit the Soviet Union since the Russian Revolution, and his relations at Geneva with the Russian Foreign

Minister, Maxim Litvinov, had always been conspicuously good; Eden's warm welcoming of the return of the Soviet Union to the League had been appreciated, and he found Moscow's reception very different from that which he and Simon had received in Berlin. Eden had no illusions about the Soviet system, but he was completely free from the fierce hostility and prejudice against anything Soviet that characterized the bulk of the Tory Party. Eden did not see the impossibility of reasonable Anglo-Soviet relations, and was untroubled about ideology; he also recognized that the Soviet leadership was alarmed about growing German military strength and Eastern intentions; having read *Mein Kampf*, Eden was able to confirm that their fears were fully merited.

Eden's first meeting with Stalin was the key event. It was nearly cancelled, as Eden insisted on having his own interpreter, the British Ambassador, and for a time it appeared that the meeting might never take place. In the event it did, in itself a tribute to the esteem the Russians had developed for Eden and their genuine interest in better relations with the British. Eden has related, from notes he kept at the time:

As we entered I saw standing there a short, thick-set man with hair *en brosse*. He was in a grey tunic, with rather baggy dark trousers and calf-length black boots. I never saw Stalin in anything but a variant of this uniform. He always appeared well laundered and neatly dressed.

Stalin impressed me from the first and my opinion of his abilities has not wavered. His personality made itself felt without effort or exaggeration. He had natural good manners, perhaps a Georgian inheritance. Though I knew the man to be without mercy, I respected the quality of his mind and even felt a sympathy which I have never been able entirely to analyse. Perhaps this was because of Stalin's pragmatic approach. It was easy to forget that I was talking to a Party man, certainly no one could have been less doctrinaire. . . . I have never known a man handle himself better in conference. Well-informed at all points that were of concern to him, Stalin was prudent but not slow. Seldom raising his voice, a good listener, prone to doodling, he was the quietest dictator I have ever known, with the exception of Dr Salazar [of Portugal]. Yet the strength was there, unmistakably.

Stalin told Eden that he thought the international situation more dangerous than it had been in 1913, as then there had been only one potential aggressor, Germany, while now there were two, Germany and Japan. The answer to Germany was genuine collective security, with which Eden entirely agreed, although he had to listen to strong hints about the danger of hesitant policies conducted by certain countries. Eden tried to emphasize the difficulty experienced by a democracy such as Britain, with a concerned public opinion and many non-European interests. Eden was impressed by Stalin; the Russians were impressed by him, although evidently less so with his Government. What was clear was that Soviet fears of the Germans were real, and that they had no illusions about the League unless it had unity and strength.

This visit was also Eden's first experience of the contrast between the wretchedly poor condition of Russia and her people and the lavish Soviet hospitality to official guests. When he visited the Opera he was placed in the Imperial Box and the orchestra played the British National Anthem, for the first time since the Revolution (and to the fury of King George v when he heard about 'my anthem' being played together with the 'Internationale'). Both Eden and Cranborne were struck by the consideration of the Russians as hosts, even granting Eden the opportunity he craved to see the famous private collections of French Impressionists, then despised as 'bourgeois art' by their hosts. Eden travelled by train to Warsaw, very tired, but convinced that progress had been made, and that there was a real chance of a sensible Anglo-Soviet relationship; the fact that the agreed communiqué stressed that there were no conflicts of interest between the two countries on any of the main issues in the international field was itself a considerable advance in attitude. In their preoccupation and work, however, the small British delegation had operated independently, without consultation with London. 'It was not until we had pulled out of the station and were immured in our train for the long journey to Warsaw that we realized that we had kept London in the dark and that Whitehall was not likely to be particularly pleased by our failure.' It was not.

Eden returned by way of Warsaw, where he met total rejection of any Polish involvement in any Eastern European Pact by the Foreign Minister, Colonel Jozef Beck: the mood was one of complacency, determination not to be involved and, Eden sensed, impermanence. He could not persuade the Poles that the Russian offer of collective security in Eastern Europe and joint resistance to German demands was in their own interests. In Prague, in contrast, he found the Czechs, particularly the Foreign Minister Eduard Beneš and Jan Masaryk, enthusiastic and positive.

Berlin had been, if not a disaster, highly revealing; Moscow had been genuinely encouraging, with the strictly controlled Soviet press warmly extolling the visit and its achievements; Warsaw was depressing, and Prague heartening. The elements for a strong combination against Nazi and Italian expansionism clearly existed, if the British and French Governments were resolved to establish it. This was the difficulty.

Eden's return flight from Prague was through very bad weather, and, in his own words, 'we were hurled about with a seismic violence' which he never forgot; eventually the plane landed precariously at Cologne, by which time Eden was exhausted. He was put to bed in a hotel, and a doctor was sent for. Although he was allowed to return to London by train and boat, further medical investigation pointed to the possibility of a minor heart attack, certainly some heart strain, and the urgent need for six weeks' rest. Contrary to some versions then and later, it was not a heart attack at all, there was not even heart strain, and there were no ill effects. Eden's health throughout his life had its low moments, but his constitution was exceptionally strong, and there was never anything remotely wrong with his heart; if there had been, he would never have recovered from his later ordeals.

But, not for the last time, he was ill-served by his doctors, and the immediate result was to put him out of action at a vital time. He could not even report to the Cabinet on the results of his mission except by a paper that urged League support and mutual-assistance pacts to counter the German demands. His lowly status in the Government remained such that little positive attention was given to his advice. The drift continued.

Lamentably, his convalescence meant that he could not go as part of the British delegation to the Anglo-French-Italian conference at Stresa, which was now headed by MacDonald and Simon. Eden had become alarmed by the evidence of mounting tension between Italy and Abyssinia, fomented by the former, and both MacDonald and Simon agreed with him that the matter must be raised with Mussolini: in the event it was not even discussed. Nor was an ominous paper submitted by the French about German activities in the demilitarized Rhineland. Stresa merely gave the impression of a collective front against Germany, not the reality, and these two key matters had not even been raised. Eden rightly considered that it was a tragically lost opportunity, and the failure to warn Mussolini against his obvious military build-up on the Abyssinian borders and to underline the complaints of the Emperor Haile Selassie gravely compromised the position of Britain and the League.

There was much to be said against the manner in which Abyssinia had been administered since Ras Tafari had in 1928 proclaimed himself Emperor Haile Selassie 1. Indeed, there was very little to be said in its favour: it was a desperately poor, ethnically riven, slave-owning and corrupt tribal oligarchy. But the fact was that it had been, since 1923, a member of the League, and the Italians had signed a treaty of non-aggression and co-operation in 1928. Churchill was justified in saying in 1935 that 'no one can keep up the pretence that Abyssinia is a fit, worthy and equal member of a League of civilized nations', but it *was* a member of the League and, for all its administration's faults, a sovereign independent nation, as Mussolini had accepted in 1928. It was certainly ironical that in the dimunitive, and far from blameless, Selassie – 'The Lion of Judah' – anti-Fascism found its first hero. But history is the history of ironies.

The British dilemma was that they were anxious not to alienate Mussolini to the point of pushing him in the direction of Hitler; he was important in guaranteeing the independence of Austria, and the Royal Navy was uneasy about the prospect of a hostile Italian Navy in the Mediterranean; Laval had no compunction at all in paying the Abyssinian price in return for the Franco-Italian alliance, and similar views were prominent in the British Cabinet and the Foreign Office, particularly in the case of Vansittart. Eden understood the value in buying Italian co-operation, but was beginning to baulk at the price. He believed, and argued, that instead of the vague and oblique warnings that Simon conveyed to the Italians and French about British public opinion, his attitude, as he wrote in his diary, 'is nothing like stiff enough. Italy's request was a diplomatically phrased demand for a free hand in Abyssinia. This should have been strenuously resisted, emphasis laid on our support of the League, etc.'

Very late in the day, when Eden's colleagues – even Simon – realized how serious the matter was, Eden was again sent to Geneva to persuade the Italians to accept the right of the League Council to institute arbitration proceedings, and for both them and the Abyssinians to agree not to use force. This difficult task was accomplished with characteristic skill, but Eden remained deeply troubled about Italian intentions. To one letter of warm congratulations on this technical triumph, Eden replied, 'I do not myself feel that we have achieved so much. There are, I fear, greater troubles ahead.'

Eden was now eager to become Foreign Secretary. Reconstruction of the Government was being actively canvassed as MacDonald's period in the premiership drew, at long last, mercifully to an end. Simon was to become Home Secretary, and Eden felt that he had earned his position, as did the Foreign Office itself, several of his colleagues and much of the national press. He had become internationally the best-known member of the British Government, and was now, interestingly, the subject of increasingly hostile comment in the German and Italian newspapers. For four years he had carried the principal burdens, but without the authority, and with an inadequate Foreign Secretary whom he did not even like.

Nor was this only his opinion. The *Contemporary Review* of September 1934 called him 'one of the coming men of the Conservative party. ... He is liked and trusted by all those with whom he comes into contact, and he will in time prove a great Foreign Secretary', and on 20 May 1935 the *News Chronicle* declared that:

The obvious man for this all-important position is Mr Eden. His courage, his newly revealed force of character and the extraordinary confidence which he has won in the capitals of Europe mark him out instantly on merit as the best candidate. He has enemies in the party – some jealous of his swift advance, others disliking what they regard as his League complex and his lack of patriotic insularity.

Eden also considered that Baldwin, about to replace MacDonald as Prime Minister, had in effect promised him the position. He saw Baldwin on 16 May and made his view plain that he was not prepared to continue under a new Foreign Secretary on the old lines as a League of Nations subordinate. But now Eden's youth and other political and personal considerations intruded. Neville Chamberlain had not yet moved as far as he was later to do in his desire to placate Mussolini, but the tone of Eden's attitude towards the Italian dictator concerned him, as it did others, and he recommended Hoare; *The Times*, under Geoffrey Dawson's editorship, was now developing the line that was to make it temporarily notorious, and Baldwin was susceptible to Dawson. Hoare had just finished an exhausting period as Secretary of State for India, and had won glowing opinions – although not from Churchill – for the successful carrying of the Government of India Act. If Baldwin had taken serious interest in foreign affairs the inadequacy of Hoare's experience would have been clear; on character grounds alone it was a bad choice, and Eden was not the only politician who disliked and distrusted the ambitious and slippery Hoare. But he looked, and seemed, 'safe'; he was not being castigated by the German and French press as Eden was; he was older; he deserved a break from the India Office. All such usual lamentable arguments and excuses were employed for a bad appointment, and Eden was to be placated with entering the Cabinet as Minister for League of Nations Affairs.

On 21 December 1936, Eden had a long talk with Baldwin, at the latter's request, about Hoare. By then, the scales had fallen from Baldwin's eyes. Eden told him that 'Sam's manoeuvres were clear. He was a born intriguer & wanted to be P.M. "Well, he must be mad. He hasn't the least chance of it & wouldn't get 50 votes in the Party. I am tempted to write to him & shall certainly speak to him," he wound up. I have never known S.B. so outspoken about Sam' (diary). But the revelation had come a year too late.

Eden was deeply disappointed and angry at having been treated in this way, and he eventually accepted only on the assurance that the arrangement would not last for very long – as indeed it did not. He also realized that, for all his achievements and publicity, or perhaps because of them, he had surprisingly few political friends in influential positions. Although he did not say so, he also felt that Baldwin should have especially recognized his past loyalty to him. His only comfort was that Cranborne, equally resentful on Eden's behalf, was to become his Under-Secretary.

But Eden was at least in the Cabinet, and his immediate tasks were to placate the French over the Anglo-German naval agreement limiting warship construction – in which he was successful – and to try, on Cabinet instructions, about which he was not enthusiastic, to avert the Italian invasion of Abyssinia by a direct approach to Mussolini to offer to cede British territory in Somaliland to Abyssinia in return for the latter ceding territory to Italy.

The chances of this enterprise succeeding were not high, and were reduced further when an accurate account of the Government's proposals appeared in a British Sunday newspaper. Mussolini was not prepared to consider it. Eden denied that his private discussion with Mussolini again became heated, as has been claimed on several occasions by Italian sources, but his own record demonstrates that Mussolini was wholly indifferent to Eden's requests and warnings, and Eden concluded that 'There was a gloomy fatality about his temper which I fear it may be beyond the power of reasoning to modify.' Even less successful was a second meeting on the following day – for which Eden was very late, having been lunching at Ostia with Mussolini's son-in-law Count Ciano and a number of attractive ladies; this tardiness was entirely Eden's fault, and persuaded at least one Italian present that neither he nor his mission was serious.* Eden returned utterly convinced that the Italian dictator was determined to have his colonial war against Abyssinia and was impervious to British and League opinion; when Eden told him that British information was that Selassie would fight, Mussolini was arrogantly dismissive. The Italian press, briefed by the regime, was openly and noisily contemptuous of Eden and his mission.

The general situation had not been improved at all by the fact that Laval had become Prime Minister of France as well as Foreign Secretary and had no intention of endangering Franco-Italian relations over Abyssinia. What then followed were disjointed attempts by the British to prevent war, while the Italians stalled until everything was ready for it. But in London Vansittart also represented, with great vigour, another point of view, which was that nothing should compromise the anti-Hitler alliance which was his dominant priority, and that to alienate Mussolini over so relatively petty a matter as Abyssinia, where there were no direct British interests, would be lunacy. This view he pressed upon Hoare and others with much fervour,

---

* 'We thought he was just a playboy,' this Italian later related. 'He kept Il Duce waiting, just because he was enjoying a party. His officials kept urging him to leave, but he kept postponing it, as he was enjoying himself.' The story is true, but the cause of Eden's reluctance to see Mussolini was much deeper than mere enjoyment of attractive company, as the Italian later realized. None the less, it gave a bad impression, and contributed to the hostile Italian opinion of Eden, and thus has a certain historical significance.

and he had his effect. Thus British pressure upon both the Italians and the French was negligible, and Ministers were genuinely alarmed that if Britain fulfilled her obligations under the Covenant there would be an unnecessary war, or at best a high level of crisis, with the Italians. Eden argued that what was now at stake was the whole position of the League and the manner in which the nations did or did not act collectively against clear aggression, but his was a minority voice. At virtually every level, political, diplomatic and military, there was an almost total lack of any intention to do or say anything that might involve Britain in a crisis with Italy. Eden did his best to urge a more robust approach in his discussions with his colleagues and Laval, but to no avail. Had he actually been Foreign Secretary, it is just possible that he might have had some effect. He was not even able to achieve the relaxation of the British arms embargo to Abyssinia, Cranborne being one of his few supporters. When Ministers contemplated the possibility of the League imposing economic sanctions on Italy if she invaded Abyssinia, they became as apprehensive as Laval. What they did note, however, was that public opinion in Britain was stirring, and the League of Nations Union was becoming vocal.

It was this political factor, with a general election imminent, that led to the unexpected strength of Hoare's speech to the League on 10 September. Both Eden and Cranborne were surprised by it, as Hoare went far beyond the instructions Eden had had to work with. Indeed, they tried to modify the text, for, although Hoare's ringing support for the League and collective security was practicable for Mussolini's African ambitions, there were perils in implying a readiness to intervene by force in other disputes, notably in the war between China and Japan. But Hoare was insistent, and the speech was a sensational success. The only logical interpretation was that Britain would stand strongly against acts of international brigandage. The French were uneasy, and there were doubters in Britain, but the speech, accompanied by the dispatch of a large British naval force to the Mediterranean, seemed to have only one meaning. However, the Government combined support for the League with further attempts to remain close to the Italians – an impossible position. Baldwin's own position was clearly expressed in a speech in the Commons in May: 'the moment you are up against sanctions you are up against war.' And, although the celebrated – or notorious – Peace Ballot organized by the League of Nations Union overwhelmingly supported the use of force in collective security, ministers were concerned by the lack of British military strength, and, politically, by the overtly and often strident pacifism of the Labour Party. The worst of all possible policies was to try to bluff Mussolini, yet this was the one that was chosen. There was nothing of substance behind

Hoare's speech. His real formula, and his own words, was 'negotiation with Italy and respect for our collective obligations under the Covenant, based on Anglo-French co-operation'.

Eden, while doubtful – and rightly – about Laval's constancy, urged that the pressure on Mussolini must be maintained, while Hoare was instructing him to delay any discussions on sanctions and was pleased by 'the somewhat altered atmosphere produced at Rome by the combination of pressure and friendly message'. When Selassie ordered his troops to withdraw from his frontiers to deny Mussolini a pretext for aggression, he also asked for impartial observers to be sent by the League. Eden, and the majority of the League Council, agreed with this; his Government did not. Eden was instructed to be cool towards it, and to state that there would be no British observers; so the request was diverted into a sub-committee of experts to consider the matter! Meanwhile, the British were again looking at territorial concessions to Mussolini in Eden's absence. The contrast between Hoare's heroic statement at Geneva and his actual policies was already becoming obvious, although it was unknown outside the Government.

Eden was in Paris on 3 October when the Italian invasion of Abyssinia began with the bombing of a hospital storehouse flying the Red Cross. When Eden saw Laval that evening the latter told him that it was still possible to negotiate with Mussolini by giving him a mandate for the whole of Abyssinia except for those areas inhabited by the Amharic races – namely, a mandate for nearly three-quarters of the country, including Addis Ababa. Eden told him firmly that the British could not agree to such a proposal to reward the aggressor. Hoare's reaction was less positive, but Eden was permitted to go to Geneva for the crucial Council meeting, where he took the lead by proposing a special committee to advise whether the Italians were in breach of the Covenant: it ruled that they were, and had resorted to war, which meant, under the terms of Article xvi of the Covenant, that they must '*ipso facto* be deemed to have committed a war against all other members of the League'. The French representative on the committee was Alexis Léger, the head of the French Foreign Office, whom Eden liked and trusted and who in turn supported Eden; but he had incurred Laval's wrath for agreeing to the committee's ruling. In order to save Léger, Eden complained to Laval, who had belatedly arrived in Geneva, that Léger had caused much difficulty. 'Laval's brow cleared,' Eden later wrote. 'He looked relieved and said: "We will have a talk." We settled down to a discussion of sanctions [under Article xvi] with Laval at his ease and Léger, for the time being at least, secure.'*

---

* Avon, *Facing the Dictators*, p. 277.

Laval had no enthusiasm whatever for economic sanctions against Italy, unlike Eden, who was now pressing hard, and there was timorousness in London. But in both countries the spectacle of the brutal invasion of a desperately poor and ill-armed African nation by a European Fascist state had aroused a public reaction reminiscent of 1914. In Italy the Abyssinian adventure was received with ecstatic enthusiasm. Mussolini's much publicized appearances from his Rome balcony, in full uniform and wearing a steel helmet, brought enormous and exultant crowds as vast as any addressed by Hitler. Support both in Britain and France for strong action by the League was overwhelming, and impressed even Laval. Eden had no doubts, and on 9 October fifty states in the League Assembly agreed to apply sanctions, only Austria and Hungary demurring. 'Since it is our duty to take action,' Eden said in his speech, 'it is essential that such action should be prompt. That is the League's responsibility – a responsibility based on humanity: for we cannot forget that war is at this moment actually in progress.' So great was the enthusiasm for his achievement that Eden was presented with the Freedom of the Borough of Leamington, and there was even talk that he would be unopposed at the forthcoming general election. When he spoke in Coventry on 28 October there were twenty-five thousand applications for three thousand places.

It seemed that the League had passed the most crucial test in its brief history. Mussolini stood condemned and, it was thought, would pay dearly for his harsh and unprovoked aggression. The British Government found itself overwhelmingly supported. Eden warned that what mattered was the *effectiveness* of sanctions, on which he was not optimistic, knowing full well how thin was Laval's support, and in the days after the Assembly decision it became even thinner.

The key was oil. Other sanctions would only have limited effect, but oil seemed to be decisive. The possibility certainly caused alarm in Rome, and all pressures were applied to prevent such sanctions. The grandson of Garibaldi, an old friend of Hoare, came to London to warn the Foreign Secretary of the consequences. Oil sanctions could only be effective through a British naval blockade in the Mediterranean, which in itself alarmed the Admiralty, and would be impracticable without strong French support, which was clearly impossible under Laval. As Hoare later wrote of his discussions with Laval, 'we both excluded the idea of war with Italy as too dangerous and double-edged for the future of Europe'.* Thus London became frightened about a Mediterranean war, and Eden found himself under strong personal criticism for going too far. In public, Hoare defended

* Viscount Templewood (Hoare), *Nine Troubled Years*, p. 168.

him, but Eden clearly noted the signs of disapproval. And when would sanctions take effect? Delay on this matter was a further encouragement to Mussolini, now talking of starting a European war if he was subjected to such pressures. Vansittart was emphatically on the London side, throwing his formidable position and powers of persuasion into overruling Eden's insistence that the arms embargo to Abyssinia must be lifted; the British Government, over Eden's protests, adopted the pathetic French compromise that arms should be prohibited to *both* belligerents. As the Italians had no need of British or French arms, and the Abyssinians were virtually defenceless, the cynicism of this compromise spoke for itself.

These vital decisions – if they can be so described – took place in the context of a general election. It was one that Eden regretted on foreign affairs grounds, and his fears were justified. Baldwin stressed that Britain could only act over Abyssinia if there were full concert with other members of the League, and this could result in a naval blockade and even war. His speeches and the Conservative Manifesto, drafted by Neville Chamberlain, put much emphasis upon British military weakness; while this made the case for rearmament, it also sent another message. Baldwin's celebrated speech to the Peace Society on 31 October, with its evocative talk of 'the level evening sun over an English meadow, with the rooks tumbling noisily home into the elms, the ploughman "with his team on the world's rim, creeping like the hands of a clock", one of those garnered memories of the long peace of the countryside', also dismissed the notion that he had ever encountered governments possessed of 'the malevolent qualities' of 'leading reluctant or unsuspecting people into the shambles' of war. It was a fine speech, and a deeply moving one, but in the context of a war raging in Africa, of Germany rearming with furious speed and making demands for a plebiscite in Austria and for 'justice' for the Sudeten Germans in Czechoslovakia, and of a divided and feeble France, it was markedly irrelevant to the realities. Labour's raucous campaign against rearmament of any kind was also profoundly unhelpful. Eden consoled himself that he knew that Baldwin, with characteristic skill and subtlety, was seeking his mandate for rearmament, and he got it. The Government lost only 80 seats of its huge 1931 total, receiving 53.6 per cent of the vote, with the Conservatives winning 432 seats, Labour 154 and the Liberals 20. Ramsay MacDonald and Malcolm lost their seats, but were speedily returned to the House of Commons.

The election won, with Eden himself easily re-elected, the search for compromise over Abyssinia continued, with Laval making the running. Oil sanctions would have made Mussolini at least think, if not pause. There was a barrage of Italian public and private threats concerning the terrible consequences of such an act, which Laval exploited with much skill. Italian troops were moved to the French border, Mussolini threatened to leave the League and break the Franco-Italian Alliance. London was wavering, Paris was engaged in a policy of calculated procrastination, repeating Italian threats that an oil embargo would be an act of war. Eden found again that his original instructions to be firm were being whittled down by London. He personally had little confidence in Hoare, who was irresolute and disloyal, as well as secretive and shallow. Vansittart was eager for an Anglo-French settlement with Mussolini almost on any terms, and Hoare swung to his viewpoint. Matters were not helped by Hoare's poor health and fainting fits which clearly required a holiday if he was not to suffer a serious decline. It was arranged that he should go to Switzerland, breaking his journey on the way in Paris, at Laval's request.

By this point Eden was virtually the only member of the Cabinet who really believed that oil sanctions would work and must be imposed if the League Powers were to give real help to Selassie. He had lost on the arms embargo, and as he saw the drift of argument in the Foreign Office – principally Vansittart, who was closely in touch with the Italian Ambassador Dino Grandi – and in the Cabinet, he realized he was in danger of losing this one as well. He did not believe that Mussolini would go to war over the oil sanctions issue, and the continuing delay was having a bad effect not only on European Governments and public opinion, but also on the United States – a factor to which he attached great importance, although his colleagues did not. Hoare's real problem was his irresolution, strong one day, nervous the next. He seldom confided in Eden. He was an ambitious career politician but an innocent abroad. Eden knew this, but even he did not anticipate what was now to happen.

Hoare had no instructions to negotiate with Laval, whom he first met on 7 December. The meeting seemed to be general, and reasonably satisfactory, although Eden was uneasy when he read the record of the meeting and was surprised to learn that another was now planned. But the report he received on the evening of the 8th was that Hoare was on his way to Switzerland and that he and Vansittart were 'well satisfied with the day's work'.

When Eden saw the actual document Hoare and Laval had initialled he was astonished and appalled. The two Foreign Ministers had agreed to proposals 'which might serve as a basis for a friendly settlement of the Italo-Ethiopian dispute' giving Mussolini half the country, with no concession whatever for the Abyssinians except a corridor to the sea, derided by *The Times* as 'a corridor for camels'. At first, Eden thought that there must be something else, perhaps military matters of Anglo-French co-operation, which had been omitted from the amazing document sitting on his desk. But there was not.

The Hoare–Laval Pact was leaked in Paris. A storm of unparalleled ferocity now arose, Duff Cooper later writing that no single episode in his political career, not even Munich, aroused such public anger. The British press was quick to see what it meant. So was the League of Nations Union. So was the Conservative Party. Eventually, the Cabinet and the Prime Minister saw it too. Hoare, skating in Switzerland, wholly failed to realize the enormity of what he had done. His great September Geneva speech now marched back to engulf him.

Eden's first response was to resign, but he was persuaded not to by Lord Stanhope, the Foreign Office Under-Secretary in the House of Lords, who pointed out that neither of them knew enough about what had been agreed, and that the Cabinet had not authorized Hoare to negotiate, let alone sign a piece of paper written in French (Hoare's French was very limited). Baldwin should have recalled Hoare at once, but he did not – a cardinal error. There was instead a desperate effort to save Hoare. Laval now raised his price by insisting that if the Emperor rejected the new proposals there would be no oil sanctions. Vansittart was still defending the Hoare–Laval position. Eden argued that it must be decisively rejected.

He now had full public opinion, the press and Parliament on his side. All the references in speeches made by ministers in the general election about collective security and the sanctity of League commitments were exhumed by Labour and Conservative alike, and the Conservative Foreign Affairs Committee met in a bitter and ashamed temper. Eden had to go to Geneva to face the wrath of Britain's allies; he did his best to defend the indefensible, trying to emphasize that these were only proposals that were 'neither definitive nor sacrosanct'. But it was hopeless. He urged Hoare to return home, only to find that Hoare had had another fainting fit, had fallen on the ice and broken his nose, and was in bed. He did not see the urgency of the matter. With this comment he was finished. Baldwin belatedly summoned him home at once, nose or no nose; the retreat from Hoare–Laval now became an undignified stampede. Eden reported from Geneva that his own position was becoming untenable. On 18 December Hoare resigned; on the next day, in the Commons, Baldwin made one of his worst speeches, Hoare made a resignation statement, and Baldwin pronounced the Pact dead.

If the Government and Britain were humiliated, so was the League. Laval's cunning duplicity and Hoare's inexperience and folly had dealt its authority a devastating and, as it transpired, mortal blow. Throwing Hoare to the howling mob could only be a temporary palliative to British opinion. A dictator had won a great victory. His air force and troops butchered their way into Abyssinia, in one of the most ghastly one-sided campaigns in modern history, where the ranks of the dead, maimed and blinded were literally uncountable. It marked the lowest point of British prestige abroad since the worst days of the South African War.

Eden always believed that this had been entirely unnecessary. He considered that a reasonable agreement with Mussolini could have been effected if firmness and consistency had been shown, and that, in spite of Laval, the Anglo-French alliance could have been maintained and even strengthened. But what had happened was, as has been rightly written,

a disaster of the first magnitude. It went far to destroy what confidence [the British and French] had in each other and dug yet deeper the gulf of mistrust between their peoples and their governments and between both countries and Soviet Russia. It split Britain and France immediately from Italy, now to become a pawn of the Reich, and showed them before the world's eyes as 'willing to wound and yet afraid to strike', dubious as allies and inconsiderable as enemies.*

This was the miserable context in which Anthony Eden, at the age of thirty-eight, became Foreign Secretary. He had wanted the job very much in May, but he did not want it now. In this he was genuine. In a note he wrote in old age he gave as his reasons his total loss of confidence in Vansittart, his strong feeling that neither the Prime Minister nor the Cabinet had given him backing when he was warning against the perils of their policies, which he had no reason to suppose they would change. And he disliked succeeding to what he called 'a wretchedly disordered heritage'. In May, much could have been done to prevent the Abyssinian disaster; it had now occurred, and the League was enfolded in chaos and disillusionment. The position of the British Government at home, for all its huge parliamentary majority, looked precarious, and the Conservative Party was severely rattled. Everywhere he looked he saw dangers about which he had warned to little avail. These were solid reasons for not wishing to accept this poisoned chalice, but I believe that there was another reason – lack of self-confidence in his own capacities. His self-assurance was deceptive, as Baldwin had always understood.

His advice to Baldwin was to recall Austen Chamberlain, who had been a strong opponent of Hoare–Laval and whose consistent warnings since 1933 on the German menace had been eloquent, right and perceptive in a period of self-delusion. Baldwin dismissed the suggestion on the grounds of age. Eden then proposed Halifax, but Baldwin would not consider a Foreign Secretary in the Lords. There was then silence. In Eden's account:

* Northedge, *The Troubled Giant*, p. 425.

Eventually he turned to me and said: 'It looks as if it will have to be you.' Feeling by this time somewhat hurt at this eliminative method of being appointed, I replied that six months before I would have been very grateful for the chance to be Foreign Secretary, but that now I felt quite differently about it. Baldwin nodded understanding at this, and so this strange interview ended with my words being taken as tacit acceptance.

Eden's diary for 23 December reads:

A Sandringham day. Cold & foggy.
Travelled to S & back to receive seals.
King friendly, Queen more so. Had an audience before ceremony. H.M. very down on plan of Paris. Said he had told Sam. 'Poor fellow - no more Coals to Newcastle, no more Whores [Hoares] to Paris!' Anxious I should not part with Van.

The King was coughing heavily, and was dead within a month. Eden was the last Foreign Secretary to receive the Seals from him. He was destined to be Foreign Secretary under four Sovereigns, but at the time 'I took stock of our battered fortune.'

Eden's personality had become established, and was not to change significantly for the rest of his life. He had many admirers, but, inevitably, he had his enemies and detractors. There were those who envied him his rapid advancement, and ascribed it to what was called either his 'Ronald Coleman' or his 'Noël Coward' glamour and style – on which Brendan Bracken was particularly derisive – rather than his abilities. There were others who, more seriously, thought that he had been over-promoted too young for his own good. There were those who actively disliked him for a variety of reasons, distrusting his debonair charm, and unimpressed by his speeches or writings. There were those who liked him personally, and even admired him, but did not see in him much strength of character or resolution. So it usually is in politics.

Those who worked closely with him have given varying accounts of the experience. All, admirer or critic, agree completely on his phenomenal capacity for work and the extraordinary range and depth of his knowledge of foreign affairs and diplomacy, the histories of countries and the personalities of their rulers. The American John Winant wrote of him that 'He was one of the best-trained diplomats I have ever met. He had no use for shoddy politics whether at home or abroad.'* In this respect he was unquestionably the most 'professional' Foreign Secretary since Lord Salisbury. Also, he bore this knowledge lightly, as part of his intellectual

---

* John G. Winant, *A Letter from Grosvenor Square*.

and political equipment, which made it even more impressive. He was intellectually restless; as Alexander Cadogan frequently complained (and, in spite of outbursts of frustration, he was an admirer), 'Anthony always wants to *do* something.'

Such a political master or colleague can be inspiring or infuriating, although in Eden's case the former was stronger: Nicholas Henderson spoke for very many Foreign Office officials when he wrote:

I was always treated by him with sublime courtesy. Given to gusts of impatience and prone to constitutional irritability, he was nevertheless a most considerate man to those dependent on him – indeed his occasional outbursts had the effect of rendering his politeness more human. Such was his personality that he could get the most out of people – and that applied, incidentally, not just to FO officials, but to foreign statesmen as well.*

Pierson (Bob) Dixon, described by Henderson as 'the paragon of Private Secretaries' – an opinion Eden himself would have strongly endorsed – fully echoed his tribute, although also not glossing over the fact that Eden could become very angry and explosive on occasions. What is intriguing about this aspect is that some who worked closely with him had little experience of these celebrated brief storms; others who did ignored them, treating them, quite rightly, as part of the man; others resented them very deeply. 'He seemed to be two men,' one who worked under him has told me; 'one was charming, kind and deeply impressive – the other impossible.'

The fact was that Eden was an exceptionally tense, lonely and shy man, and the unhappiness of his marriage – his diaries now hardly ever mentioning Beatrice at all – and his dedication to his work accentuated these aspects of his character. He loathed men's clubs and the male club atmosphere of the House of Commons – in later years he was to shock Winston Churchill deeply by refusing to join The Other Club, which he and F. E. Smith had founded, membership of which was considered by him superior to any honour short of the Garter, and refusing honorary membership of the Athenaeum – but his circle of real friends was surprisingly small. The charge of personal vanity, so often made, was in fact entirely unjustified, as was his alleged interest in clothes. He dressed well, but did not take the trouble over them that his detractors claimed, and was not particularly interested when his Homburg hat became generally known as 'an Anthony Eden'. To him it was just a hat. Those who knew him best knew that of all the epithets applied to him, that of personal vanity was the least true, but very shy people do often compensate for their shyness by trying to appear extrovert and even gregarious. He was highly strung,

---

* Nicholas Henderson, *The Private Office*, p. 15.

but it was characteristic of him that he seldom became angry when really important matters were involved, but did so over irritating trivialities, usually in his own home; very seldom did he lose his temper in public. What many ascribed to blandness was good manners and self-control.

Politics are what is called in the current jargon 'a high-stress profession' for all but the most callously ambitious and the most idle or ignorant. Reaction to this can take many forms, some beneficial, some malignant. Churchill took comfort in his home, his writing and his painting during his periods of what he called 'the black dog'; Baldwin, far more sensitive than he is usually depicted, had a profound feeling for the English country-side and literature; Neville Chamberlain had his fishing, his family and his passion for music. Eden indeed had his deep knowledge of art and books, and his as yet unrequited love affair with the joys of country living, but he lacked a satisfying marriage, that inestimable boon given to Churchill, Baldwin and Chamberlain; and, in spite of the façade, he had constant money worries. His work became too large a part of his life, as he later realized, to his bitter regret; he drove himself too hard, as he often drove those who worked for and with him. Some found this exhilarating, others did not.

His relationships with his Permanent Under-Secretaries were not always easy. Vansittart patronized him as well as disagreeing with him; and Eden wrote of him (16 November 1936): 'I fear that he is not balanced & is in such a continual state of nerves that he will end up making would-be aggressors think the more of us as a potential victim.' Alexander Cadogan, beneath an impressive veneer of professional suavity, could be testy, as his diaries demonstrate, but he was later to write of Eden: 'I don't think any Secretary of State I served excelled him in finesse, or as a negotiator, or in knowledge of foreign affairs. When something had to be done, Anthony would long to do it. That quality was perhaps carried to a fault; but on the whole a good fault for a Foreign Secretary. No one worked harder.'* This was very high praise from that very critical source.

One who came to know him officially very well once remarked of Eden that what struck him was that he had many political cronies but few real friends in politics. There is much truth in this, although not the whole truth, as his correspondence and diaries reveal so clearly. He did not spare much time for the 'club' aspect of the House of Commons, which Churchill so relished, and was not well equipped by temperament or intellect to endure fools gladly. None the less, his politeness was legendary, and he lost his urbanity only when provoked or in a dark mood. Very humanly, he preferred to have around him people he liked, but these were not

---

* Dilks (ed.), *The Diaries of Sir Alexander Cadogan, 1938-45*, p. 345.

invariably the most able or the most representative. This is very under-standable, but it has its political drawbacks. One cannot choose one's parliamentary colleagues, and it is often necessary to work with people who are uncongenial; this was not one of the political virtues at which Eden shone, and he often overestimated those he liked and underestimated those he did not. Thus his real political following in the House of Commons and in the Cabinet was, in contrast with his public following, remarkably small, as events were to demonstrate. Where it existed was usually in the Labour Party, among whose members he was always popular and respected. A former Labour MP has written:

Somehow, news that my stepfather had died reached Anthony Eden and he sent me a handwritten two-page letter of sympathy. In it he referred to his feelings at his own father's death. I was very moved. As a backbencher from the opposite side of the House, I felt the letter confirmed my belief that Eden really cared about people. As long as he lived, I remained one of his admirers and I hope history will be kinder to him than his contemporaries were.*

Others who worked closely with him also noticed this feature. 'I would say that AE's familiars were few, and his circle of consultation narrow among his parliamentary colleagues,' one has recorded. This observer also noticed his 'impatience' with fellow MPs, in spite of which 'he did not drop his guard with outsiders'. Although Eden had chosen politics as his career, and pursued his ambitions, and worked harder at his profession than almost any of his contemporaries – Churchill being the great exception – he already gave the clear impression, which was the truth, of distancing himself from partisan politics and certainly from partisan politicians. His occasional ventures into this area were unenthusiastic, and, as Ursula Branston, who worked with him ten years later, has written, 'AE had quite a high degree of tolerance towards opposing views.' He never forgot Baldwin's advice about the dangers of patronizing the Labour Party, and went to considerable trouble to avoid phrases that might wound or offend or appear condescending. It could be argued that he went too far, and gave an impression not only of blandness but of weakness and indecision, but these were two crimes of which he was notably free of guilt. Combative politicians, revelling in the Party and House of Commons fray, accordingly found him difficult to understand, charming but aloof. Duff Cooper's comment on Neville Chamberlain had equal application to Eden: 'Ungreg-arious by nature, he never frequented the Smoking Room of the House of Commons, where Stanley Baldwin and Winston Churchill were familiar figures, often in the centre of groups which included political opponents.'†

* Lord Tonypandy, *George Thomas: Mr Speaker*, p. 66.
† Alfred Duff Cooper, *Old Men Forget*, p. 188.

His circle of political friends was accordingly very small, though it included men of the calibre of Bobbety Cranborne and J. P. L. Thomas, but not Churchill or Duff Cooper. This isolation was the result partly of calculation, but principally of temperament. He gave the impression of being an extrovert, but in reality was not.

Yet his public following outside Parliament was indeed remarkable by 1935. It was partly, although only partly, the appeal of his youth, good looks and freshness of style in an especially drab and depressing political era. Sir John Wheeler-Bennett later wrote of Eden at this time that 'Anthony was the Golden Boy, slim, handsome and charming. My generation looked upon him as typifying the generation who had survived the war to become the champion and defender of our pathetic belief in what proved to be ephemeral Wilsonian shibboleths of "a war to end war" and "let us make the world safe for democracy".' Much, although not all, of his contemporary press was highly favourable, at times adulatory. His speeches were undramatic, but were listened to attentively; that most critical of assemblies, the House of Commons, had become definitely impressed.

Eden's speaking style, which some critics have derided as banal, was in fact quite deliberately developed to be as simple and clear as possible. Ursula Branston has described the technique:

AE's style of working was decidedly informal, but in its way relentless. The draft of a speech, at first pronounced just what was wanted, was invariably reduced to snippets of paper littering the floor, and then put together again in much of its original form – save that a 'clever' phrase was likely to be thrown out and a cliché brought in, rather than blur his image of himself as a spokesman for the many as against the few. The process of arriving at the final version was both lengthy and exhausting; the method, if not the result, was Churchillian.

Eden was not yet the master of the House of Commons that he was to become, with that calm voice and easy good humour backed by detailed knowledge which could silence tumult and guarantee a respectful hearing, but he had travelled a very long way from his unfortunate maiden speech. He did not have the remarkable capacity of Duff Cooper, who could introduce his Army Estimates in a long and detailed speech without a single note; he certainly wholly lacked the orator's genius of a Churchill or a Lloyd George, and he did not attempt to emulate any of them. His style was essentially conversational, courteous and palpably sincere. It was this last quality, the greatest of all, that shone through speeches which, read in cold print, seemed somewhat pedestrian. It was also the secret – if secret it be – of his success on a public platform or on radio. Never then, or later, did Eden make any political capital whatever out of his war record, except to refer in general terms to what his generation had passed through, but others knew it, just as those who worked with him, and his family, knew of his capacity for sheer hard work and real kindness. Alas, he had not yet learned the importance of relaxation, which was to cost him dear in health and happiness.

Eden's obsession with his work was noticed by others, and Austen Chamberlain took him aside one day to tell him that his father, Joseph Chamberlain, had warned him when he was young not to become too absorbed in politics and to 'find a hobby'. Austen had taken up rock-gardening, but, although Eden had a passion for country life, he could not afford a country house and garden. His other love was art. His own collection, from modest beginnings, was in its way exceptional, and he had a remarkable eye for a picture, as he had for animals. When in his retirement he built up an outstanding Hereford herd his eye for a good animal won the admiration of professionals, who had first been sceptical about an amateur in their business. In 1935 Ramsay MacDonald invited him to Downing Street and told him that his seven-year period as a Trustee of the National Gallery was ending. He invited him to take his place. Eden did so with delight, and was a Trustee for fourteen years. The Chairman was Sir Philip Sassoon, whose immense wealth and style of living invited much criticism and some snobbish derision – 'a kind of Haroun al Raschid, entertaining with oriental magnificence in three large houses, endlessly kind to his friends, witty, mercurial, and ultimately mysterious', as Kenneth Clark described him. The brilliant and soaring young Clark was himself Director. Eden found the work personally enjoyable, and it gave him the opportunity to use his artistic judgement and move in the circles he most enjoyed. As he later wrote, 'Until I could afford a country home and a garden of my own, pictures provided the escape for me.'

Another was literature, including French and Persian, and especially Persian poetry, but Shakespeare was a lifelong favourite, and he would never go on a foreign journey without a precious copy of the Collected Works. He found the art and subtlety of that genius of endless fascination, and one of the few aspects of Winston Churchill that truly irritated him was that Churchill was only interested in the 'war' plays. To Eden, someone who 'knew his Shakespeare' at once entered a favoured club; his facility for quoting passages was remarkable, and never boring. He was an enthusiast, but always an interesting one.

He entered into his formidable responsibilities under lowering skies, but to many of his contemporaries he represented the hope of his generation, and theirs.

Few British Foreign Secretaries have taken office in circumstances so bleak, and which were destined to become even bleaker very quickly. For two years Eden had been pressing for a more energetic approach to rearmament, but by virtue of his junior position he had had little effect; as a result he now had to conduct foreign policy from a position of military weakness. Although Baldwin had roused himself briefly to get rid of Hoare (now campaigning hard and shamelessly for reinstatement), he seemed enveloped in lethargy. Eden recorded in his diary for 20 May: 'Talk with S. B. in the evening. Did not get much out of it save that he wants better relations with Hitler than with Musso – We must get nearer to Germany. "How?" I asked. "I have no idea, that is your job." '

The last Baldwin Cabinet was a dispiriting group. Many considered that Eden's appointment was an error, and there was no shortage of jealousy among his elders. To Eden's fury, it was then the practice of ministers to read and amend Foreign Office dispatches. After one particularly vigorous protest at this intolerable interference – in which Eden was strongly supported by Duff Cooper – Baldwin told him that of his twenty colleagues there was probably only one who thought he should be Minister of Labour but nineteen who thought they should be Foreign Secretary. Vansittart was another, and the initial attitude of the head of the Treasury, Sir Warren Fisher, was one of equal condescension. Fisher informed Eden that all his ambassadorial appointments had to be submitted to him as head of the Civil Service, for transmission to the Prime Minister. Eden absolutely refused, and raised the issue with Baldwin, who 'showed signs of acute discomfort, as he was apt to do if anybody mentioned anything unpleasant to him', and proposed that he should see Neville Chamberlain. Eden gained his point after some heated exchanges, but it was a significant episode. He was very definitely not among friends. Curiously enough, in the light of later events, he considered that the most realistic of his senior colleagues was Neville Chamberlain, who had become at least intellectually convinced of the need for rearmament, which he defended with speeches of stinging contempt for the pacifist Opposition. Eden got into the habit of calling on him at 11 Downing Street, and found him helpful and sympathetic.

With the war in Abyssinia assuming an ugliness and brutality that further inflamed British opinion, Hitler had read the lesson of the Hoare–Laval débâcle. In his first circulated dispatch to British Embassies in January Eden wrote:

Hitler's foreign policy may be summed up as the destruction of the peace settlement and re-establishment of Germany as the dominant Power in Europe. The means by which this policy is to be effected are two-fold: (a) Internally through the militarization of the whole nation in all its aspects; (b) externally by economic and territorial expansion so as to absorb as far as possible all those of German race who are at present citizens of neighbouring states, to acquire new markets for German industry and new fields for German emigration, and to obtain control of some of the sources of those raw materials at present lacking to Germany. The form and direction of this expansion is the one still doubtful factor in Germany's plans for the future.

This trenchant and perceptive document went to the British Ambassador in Rome. The British Embassy was not secure, and the Italians quickly had a copy, which they passed to the Germans. Denunciation of Eden personally had now become a standard feature of the Italian press and radio; now he had the Nazi press to contend with as well.

Eden was quite prepared to contemplate good relations with Germany and to make concessions, but only as part of an overall settlement that included Germany's return to the League and genuine arms reductions. He was not optimistic on either count. In his own words, his purpose was to secure 'the appeasement of Europe', by which he meant the maintenance of peace: it was only later that it became synonymous with a very different policy of unilateral concessions to the Fascist Governments. But the reality was that whereas a possible conflict with Italy had its dangers, these were nothing when compared with a conflict with Germany; and British public opinion, so vociferous over Italian barbarities in Abyssinia, remained notably unconvinced by Churchill's lonely and courageous warnings about Nazi Germany, as did the House of Commons. But just when Churchill was making real progress, and genuine alarm was aroused about the scale and level of German rearmament, especially in the air, he wrecked his position in December 1936 by supporting King Edward VIII in the Abdication crisis, for reasons that were entirely honourable but misjudged. When Baldwin accepted the argument for a Minister for the Co-ordination of Defence in March, the choice was the Attorney-General, Sir Thomas Inskip, of whom Neville Chamberlain wrote that he 'would create no difficulties. He would excite no enthusiasm but he would involve us in no fresh perplexities.' The disastrous appointment of such a pedestrian figure to what could have been a key position contained its own message, and one that could be clearly read in Berlin, Paris and Rome.

While Eden was grappling with the continued difficulties over oil sanctions, to which the Cabinet agreed with marked reluctance on 26 February, and with efforts to restore the League's shattered reputation and morale, Hitler struck.

Using the pretext that the newly agreed Franco-Soviet pact was a breach of Locarno, Hitler orchestrated a diplomatic and publicity barrage on the new French Government, threatening to occupy the demilitarized territory in the Rhineland. On Saturday 7 March he did so, with massive force amid wild enthusiasm. This blatant breach of Versailles and Locarno was accompanied by a cloud of vague promises for improved relations and new agreements. The enormity of what had been done was completely lost on the British people and the House of Commons, where there was no mood whatever for resisting the German move by force. For this was the only available option, and the political will to take it did not exist in Britain or in France. The French Foreign Minister, Pierre-Étienne Flandin, later claimed that only he and three other members of his Government favoured military action, although other colleagues have excluded him from this list. There was no plan for French reoccupation of the Zone, which now had over 90,000 German troops in position. It was a stark choice between war and acceptance of the *coup*. There were no voices for the former option in London. The British press and the House of Commons, while expressing some regret and criticism of the German action, were more impressed by the honeyed words from Berlin than by the action itself.

Hugh Dalton, no friend of Germany, stated in the Commons on 26 March on behalf of Labour (and not only on that behalf):

public opinion in this country would not support, and certainly the Labour Party would not support, the taking of military sanctions or even economic sanctions against Germany at this time.... Public opinion does, I think, draw a clear distinction between the action of Signor Mussolini in resorting to aggressive war and waging it beyond his frontiers, and the actions, up to date, of Herr Hitler which, much as we may regard them as reprehensible, have taken place within the frontiers of the German Reich.

There were those in France who favoured military action, provided it was collective. Eden knew that British opinion would not accept – and did not accept – that the reoccupation of their own territory by Germany constituted a *casus belli*. This was the reality. Flandin himself wrote of 'pitiful confusion' in his own Government, and when Eden and the new Lord Privy Seal, Lord Halifax (as Lord Irwin had now become), went to Paris they both came to the firm conclusion that Flandin's words bore little relation to French opinion or to the solidarity of his own Government.

Subsequently, Eden considered that Britain and France had made a terrible and fatal error in not confronting Hitler at this point, when in spite of massive rearmament he was in no position to be involved in war with Britain and France. But this was with hindsight; at the time the reaction in the League and among the Locarno Powers was one of acceptance, and of opposition even to sanctions against Germany. As Eden later wrote, 'There was nowhere a suggestion that we should have been sharper with Hitler, still less that we should have joined in military sanctions in the Rhineland or the Saar.' Eden's role was publicly to establish staff talks between the Locarno Powers, which particularly enraged the new German Ambassador Joachim von Ribbentrop, while in the Cabinet Kingsley Wood reported Conservative hostility even to this. Eden considered that the establishment of this military link between the allies was at least one positive result, and his speech to the House of Commons on 26 March combined firmness on the principle of international commitment with proposals for responding to German suggestions for establishing international security. Hitler did not even bother to reply to them. He had won his most important victory yet.

Eden's policy at the time, endorsed by the Cabinet, was firmly to discourage a strong French response and to try to reach 'as far-reaching and enduring a settlement as possible whilst Herr Hitler was still in the mood to do so'. It is very improbable that there was a genuine French will to react militarily, but it is certain that few in Britain would have supported it; even Churchill was speaking cautiously, and approvingly, of the Government. In retrospect, Eden was unhappy at the failure to resist Hitler on this issue, and at his own role, but given the actual situation it is possible to be more forgiving. When the proposed negotiations were spurned and the German demands grew, he learned a lesson that he never forgot.

The hope that Abyssinian resistance might cause severe internal difficulties for Mussolini now faded, and the Italian campaign – which included the use of poison gas – moved swiftly. With the fall of Addis Ababa on 5 May the policy of sanctions had manifestly failed, and Eden himself privately accepted that they could not be maintained.* He wrote in his diary after a Cabinet meeting on 27 May:

Majority seemed to be in favour of calling off sanctions then. Neville [Chamberlain] and I in minority that felt tenacious. Many thought problem consisted in discerning whether you could get anything in return for keeping sanctions on. Bobbety and I and William Strang [of the Foreign Office] had a conversation on the subject, after a longer meeting at which Van was also present. It is a desperately difficult decision. To some extent one is inevitably influenced by dislike of Italy & her methods. I am inclined to favour going on until Sept. because decision is one for League as a whole, & because the military situation is not yet clear. French might refuse. If so it would then be their responsibility. Very tired. Dinner in bed.

Chamberlain was not 'tenacious' for very long. The problem was more one of tactics than of principle, and the matter was in effect resolved by a

---

* An embarrassing situation arose when Selassie sought refuge in Britain and King Edward tried to stop him coming. Eden bluntly told him (21 May) that the Emperor could go where he liked. 'This did not all together satisfy & a concluding request that he should not be asked to see him' was agreed. Eden was rather shocked by the King's attitude, and when the Abdication crisis erupted in December he took a highly critical view of the King's conduct. Of his first audience with King George VI on 17 December he wrote, 'I am sure he is a trier, very like his father even in his writing & he may do very well given time to gain confidence.'

speech made by Chamberlain to the 1900 Club on 10 June, in which he referred to the continuance of sanctions as 'the very midsummer of madness'. He had not consulted Eden about the speech, but it was less of a snub than it has sometimes been portrayed; Chamberlain wrote to his sister, Hilda, that 'I did not consult Eden between ourselves because although I believed that he was entirely in favour of what I was going to say I knew if I asked him he was bound to ask me not to say it!' The continued French hostility to sanctions, the virtual collapse of Abyssinian resistance and the humiliations already suffered by the League made the decision inevitable. What was politically significant was that it was Chamberlain who had struck the blow, and not Baldwin or Eden. 'Chamberlain knew from that moment that he had the measure of Eden,' Lord Swinton wrote many years later; what Swinton had not realized was that Eden had come, reluctantly, to the same view. Only two Conservative MPs, Vyvyan Adams and Harold Macmillan, voted against the Government when the sanctions issue was debated in the Commons. It was an inglorious culmination to a singularly inglorious and tragic episode, which, rightly, further lowered the Government's prestige.

Eden now realized how unpleasant his inheritance had been. Within six months of becoming Foreign Secretary the Germans had torn up Versailles and had won a major bloodless triumph; Haile Selassie had been routed, and Mussolini's ambitions and vanity elevated.

The nightmare quality of the mid-1930s now became even more pronounced. Three days after the League had agreed to end sanctions against Italy, news came of a military revolt in Spain against the recently elected Popular Front Government. All civil wars have an especially foul character, and few more than this one. With startling speed the conflict spread throughout Spain and beyond its borders, the Germans and Italians pledging material support for the Nationalists, led by the hitherto unknown General Francisco Franco, and the Soviet Union committing itself to the Government Republican Loyalists. In both France and Britain ardent young men and women keenly identified themselves with the anti-Franco cause, for which many offered – and gave – their lives. Spain entered three years of blood and darkness, and the Powers took their sides.

There was little interest in the Conservative Party in becoming involved in this morass, and certainly not on the Loyalist side with its Soviet friends; the fact that Labour felt a strong commitment to that side merely confirmed their instinctive pro-Franco sympathies. Their dominant motive was crude anti-Communism – one of the most dangerous aspects of such thinking as there was on foreign affairs in the Conservative Government and Party throughout the period – and Churchill was for once representative of Conservative opinion in his initial approval of Franco and his urgings of a policy of strict non-intervention on Eden and the Government. The menace of Bolshevism was warned against by all Ministers. Although Eden's sympathies were more with the Republican side,* his task was to use British influence to contain the conflict.

A legend subsequently arose, in which there is no truth, that Eden was the driving force behind the formation of the international Non-Intervention Committee, which met in London for the first time on 9 September. In fact, it was the idea of the new French Prime Minister, Léon Blum, and his Government, to which Eden eagerly responded, not least because it was a personal pleasure to deal with a French Prime Minister who was so cultivated, civilized and decisive. Thus began a long and valuable personal friendship.

The effectiveness of the Committee has been derided by many historians, and certainly a body that contained Italy, Germany and the Soviet Union piously committed to non-intervention while becoming increasingly embroiled in the war lacks impressiveness, but at least Anglo-French unity was preserved. Eden himself had few illusions, describing non-intervention in the House of Commons as 'an improvised safety curtain' intended to reduce the possibility of a general war, and Baldwin commented that it was better to have a leaky dam than none at all. To the Labour Party and many young people this stance seemed craven and more likely to help Franco than the Republicans. To them it seemed as though the latter were fighting a kind of Holy War against Fascism; to many Conservatives it seemed that Franco was fighting a Holy War against Communism. The reality was less exalted. It was left to Eden to devise, maintain and explain a policy that was deeply dissatisfying to the partisans of both sides, though it was unquestionably the right one. But it did nothing to raise his prestige at home or abroad.

Eden's frustrations can be seen in his diary for 20 May:

Cabinet in a.m. Germany fairly satisfactory though Kingsley [Wood] rather tiresome. He knows nothing but speaks much. Outburst from Duff [Cooper] that Cabinet were always interfering in Foreign Affairs, result compromise, my policy thwarted. Much better leave matters to me & not interfere so much.

Long discussion on Egypt. Cabinet eventually agreed on my modified proposal which is better from Egyptian point of view since it allows reference to League.

---

* This was a contemporary, not a retrospective, view. He wrote in his diary on 21 November that 'I do not want even to appear to follow Hitler & Musso at the moment, but would prefer "to show a tooth" in the Medit: still less do I want to facilitate an attempt at a blockade that is maybe intended to starve Madrid [besieged by Franco].'

Several critical (all lawyers) & Hailsham dead against. S. B. told me later that H. had told Philip [Swinton] he would resign.

Baldwin's lethargy – which he shed dramatically when he was dealing with the tangled issue of the King's resolution to marry the twice-married Mrs Wallis Simpson, which culminated in the Abdication in December – was also vexatious to his young Foreign Secretary. Baldwin took a long holiday in the summer, and in the view of some of his colleagues seemed on the verge of a nervous breakdown. But his office issued a statement on 24 August that he was in constant touch with Eden on foreign affairs. Eden noted that 'his "constant touch" with me has consisted in one letter & one telephone this month, & these about my spending a weekend with him in S. Wales!' When on another occasion (5 June) Eden told him that the object of German foreign policy was to divide the British from the French, 'I think S. B. saw the force & was rather alarmed.' This was the domestic political context in which Eden had to operate.

Two other events in which he was involved were infinitely more positive. He was an active proponent of the Montreux Convention, signed on 20 July, which settled the issue of the passage of warships through the Bosphorus and Dardanelles in a way that was acceptable to Turkey; Britain's positive role in this played a significant part in further improving relations with Turkey, which was to play a major part in Turkey's subsequent attitudes. Eden also secured a 'gentleman's agreement' with the Italians concerning relations and forces in the Mediterranean. It was ignored by the Italians, but it marked an attempt to reduce the coldness of Anglo-Italian relations.

Even more important was the Anglo-Egyptian Treaty, which provided the basis for formal independence in return for British entitlement to defend the Suez Canal Zone, to be reviewed in twenty years' time. It certainly greatly improved the atmosphere in Cairo, which in itself worried the Italians, and was regarded at the time as an important and statesmanlike concession to political realities. Eden never considered full British withdrawal; indeed, the principal purpose was to preserve the British position while making sensible concessions to Egyptian nationalism, on the same lines as the Government of India Act.

These were positive aspects of 1936, but the review of that terrible year reveals few optimistic developments. The 'gentleman's agreement' was swiftly and cynically broken by the Italians, and on 8 January 1937 Eden proposed to the Cabinet that Britain should give the lead in establishing an effective international naval cordon around Spain. The new First Lord of the Admiralty was Hoare, who, having crawled back into office, was totally opposed to Eden's proposal: to Eden's dismay Baldwin, with whom he had discussed the proposal and who had seemed to agree to it, came down on Hoare's side. What Eden had in mind was 'a watch on non-intervention', to provide an international weapon to limit the arrival of equipment and men from other members of the Non-Intervention Committee. Eden was defeated. An emasculated version was later approved, which was notably ineffective. Spain continued to bleed, and the three principal 'Non-Interventionists' continued to intervene.

Writing in January 1937 in his diary Eden noted that 'nothing would be more foolish than openly to attempt to woo Mussolini away from Hitler ... however, I would much like an opportunity to call a halt to Germany and Italy in Spain.' But he urged limited commitments, and opposed one to fight for Czechoslovakia, as 'I do not believe we should at present secure national unity with such a policy. It may come, but for us to endorse it now would result in considerable division in our own public opinion. ... Therefore, however relatively unsatisfactory, we must hold the present position for the time at least.' Given the circumstances, this was probably the only possible option, but it contained its own perils. Non-intervention in the Spanish Civil War was justifiable; to become doubtful about other commitments in Europe was more dubious. But the way ahead was difficult to see.

The horror of Spain now became worse. In April the town of Guernica was bombed, with grim loss of life, the precursor of the fate of so many other cities. The aircraft were German, although this was, naturally, utterly denied by the egregious Ribbentrop. The fact of direct German–Italian participation pointed to a close relationship between Rome and Berlin, as was indeed the case. British Conservatism remained darkly hostile to the Soviet Union, while in some quarters it was becoming alarmingly sympathetic to the Nazi regime. The Berlin Olympic Games in the summer of 1936 had brought many British visitors to Berlin, who had returned deeply impressed. The reoccupation of the Rhineland seemed wholly forgotten, and the German and Italian Ambassadors in London worked assiduously at their protestations of peace, also spreading the word that the British Foreign Secretary was a major obstacle to real progress. On 12 January, in direct retort to Göring's celebrated definition of German policy, he told the Foreign Press Association that 'we definitely prefer butter to guns ... [but] no other policy but rearmament is open to us in a rapidly rearming world'. This found no response in the Cabinet, except from Swinton, Secretary of State for Air, but unhappily no friend or supporter of Eden's. When what was required was energy, there was lethargy; in place of dynamism there was bureaucratic dilatoriness. In Germany and Italy, Eden was becoming denounced as a warmonger; at home as a nuisance, constantly stating unpalatable facts.

Eden's position had never been strong in the Government; when Baldwin retired in May 1937 and was replaced by Neville Chamberlain, it was very weak. Had he been more of a politician, and not so heavily preoccupied by his many burdens, he might have noticed the signs, but he did not. He could only reflect that nothing seemed to be going right on the international scene. Nor, for his prospects, were they on the domestic.

Nineteen thirty-six had been a bad year for other reasons.

Eden had long been critical – on many occasions violently so – of Tim's management of Windlestone, although he appreciated, and sympathized with, Tim's real difficulties. It would have been better for their relationship if he had said this more often. He felt that Windlestone could have been saved if Tim had been more businesslike, sensible and determined. So did the Windlestone Agent. Tim and his wife considered Anthony's criticisms to be wholly unjustified, unfair and even cruel. As so often in family disputes, there was justice on both sides. Hot words had flown, as they did so often in the Eden family, but now Tim had decided to give up the struggle and to sell 'Windles'. Eden's indignation at the way he thought that Tim had mishandled his inheritance was derived less from an animosity towards his brother than from his anguish that his childhood home should be lost to the family. There were also angry disputes with Tim and Marjorie about pictures and furniture, in which Lady Eden characteristically joined. She had just narrowly avoided being involved in another major public embarrassment for the family, but it was intended that she should continue to live in a smaller house on the estate – whereupon she told the press that her son, the eminent Foreign Secretary, was throwing her out of her own house! Just to add to the family turmoil, she also let it be known that she was writing her memoirs with professional assistance, which would be available for publishers in due course. There were also strong hints that they would have a somewhat sensational nature. As Anthony surmised correctly, they would resurrect the rumours about George Wyndham, which were unwelcome.

Their mother's odious conduct had the effect of greatly reducing the anger between Anthony and Tim, but the loss of 'Windles' meant a great deal to Anthony – probably even more than it did to Tim. Eden had realized for some time how much he yearned for a home in the country, and how much he disliked London. Financially, such a home was impossible, although he was looking around, but another source of friction between himself and Beatrice was that she had expanded her taste for café society, which her husband increasingly detested. Kirkdale, for all the kindnesses of the Beckett family, was not his own home, where Windlestone had been, and in spirit still was. Its sale was a real, and intensely felt, wrench from the past, and he hated it.

He also knew, although he refused to accept the fact, that his marriage was now based on affection alone. The formalities were observed, the appearances maintained, but the only real binding link was their devotion to Simon and Nicholas, who were fully aware of the situation. Simon drew closer to his father, and Nicholas to his mother. The façade held, but it was only a façade. Eden's fundamental loneliness made his political responsibilities even more onerous. Beset by unhappiness, he hurled himself into his work with even greater ardour, as an antidote to private sadness.

Stanley Baldwin retired from the premiership to become Earl Baldwin of Bewdley immediately after the Coronation of King George VI in May, his reputation completely restored by his adroit and sensitive handling of the Abdication crisis, and his popularity high. Eden admired his achievement in creating national unity and his civilizing influence in the Commons and in public life, and when Baldwin was later vilified Eden would always firmly defend him. Although Baldwin's lack of interest in foreign affairs and rearmament has been exaggerated by his detractors, he never claimed that it was his principal concern, and Eden had often felt that his task would have been easier, and bad decisions prevented, if he had had a leader and then a Prime Minister who had had the knowledge and the inclination to throw his position and prestige on his side at critical moments. Also, Baldwin's age had definitely had its influence, and, although the pathetic drift of British policy since 1933 could not be blamed on Baldwin exclusively, Eden welcomed the prospect of a more dynamic Prime Minister who was actually interested in foreign affairs.

Neville Chamberlain had been Baldwin's heir for so long that his succession was a smooth and unanimous process, Churchill actually proposing his election as Leader of the Conservative Party. In some respects Chamberlain and Eden had much in common. Each was a rather lonely and shy man with strong views, who worked very hard, and to whom the House of Commons was a place of business rather than a political and social home. In private, Chamberlain was sensitive, kind and warm, and one can understand why those who knew him well were so devoted to him. Many years later Eden found at Chequers what he described as 'a charming and erudite monograph which he had written about the trees in the park', demonstrating a love of nature that Sir William Eden would have appreciated, and which Anthony Eden certainly did. Churchill, so long Chamberlain's opponent and detractor, was also amazed to discover how much they had in common when, for the only time, he penetrated Chamberlain's coldness and reserve, and found a very different man. Both Eden and Churchill, when later discussing Chamberlain, agreed that he was an enigma – hard on the outside, gentle within. Unhappily, they had to deal politically with the exterior man, who was hard indeed. Chamberlain's mind had its limitations, but when he moved on to a subject he was formidable, and his achievements as a social reformer and Chancellor of the Exchequer had been considerable and beneficial.

But these merits, and they were very real, were matched by less attractive characteristics. Unlike Baldwin, he could never resist exposing the errors and follies of his political opponents, and seemed to obtain an almost sadistic pleasure in doing so. 'Neville's manner freezes people,' his brother Austen wrote. 'Everybody respects him, but he makes no friends.' 'In manner he is glacial rather than genial,' Arthur Salter wrote of him in 1939.

He has neither the spontaneous ease of intercourse of some of his colleagues, nor the *fausse bonhomie* of others. It is unfortunate, and of some importance, that his expression often tends to something like a sneer, and his manner to something like a snub, even when there is nothing in either his intentions or his feelings to correspond. ... His instinctive attitude to a critic, even one who intends to be helpful and constructive, is to bear down, not to consolidate or to compromise. An opponent must be exposed; and a supporter who shows signs of independence must be disciplined.

William Strang described him as 'a man of cool, calm mind, strong will and decisive purpose, wholly devoted to the public cause and with a firm confidence in his own judgement'.

The last aspect was the key to his success, and to his eventual failure. He was not a man who welcomed, or often sought, advice if it was likely to be critical. His manner of dealing with people tended to be abrupt, and he had the disconcerting habit of forcing the other person to make the opening remarks in a discussion, often giving the clear impression that his valuable time was being wasted. A strong personality himself, he did not want others around him of comparable calibre. Thus there was no political hope for men like Churchill or Amery, and in retrospect it is clear that others in Office, notably Eden, Vansittart and Swinton, were doomed from the outset if they demonstrated any firmness of purpose and independence of mind. The role of Sir Horace Wilson, his former Chief Industrial Adviser, as his confidant on foreign affairs became more important than that of the Foreign Office, an institution in which he had little confidence and of which he had much suspicion, with the conspicuous and unhappy exception of the new British Ambassador in Berlin, Sir Nevile Henderson, who developed into a persistent, able and lamentable advocate of an Anglo-German settlement on any terms. Ironically, this appointment was at Vansittart's urging, and was to have dire results.

Initially, Chamberlain did not entertain any illusions about Nazi Germany, although he did about Mussolini, for whom his sister-in-law, Lady (Austen) Chamberlain, had a high regard. But the passage by the United States Congress of the Neutrality Act and the conspicuously pacifist tone of the Commonwealth Prime Ministers' Conference that took place immediately he became Prime Minister had a considerable influence. He was obsessed by the fear of another war, and consistently overrated German military strength. British rearmament was not proceeding as well or as rapidly as it should have, but instead of attempting to remedy this by, among other courses, the purchase of equipment from abroad, and appointing a minister who really cared about the subject, Chamberlain accepted the fact of British military inferiority, and freely negotiated from a position of weakness.

The other remedy, the one consistently and strongly argued by Eden, was genuine collective security in Europe and effective and binding guarantees and commitments, particularly with the French. Chamberlain abhorred foreign commitments, and saw the situation increasingly in bilateral terms, in a world in which reasonable men could find reasonable solutions to problems. Any alliance against Germany would, therefore, be provocative. As Halifax told the Cabinet in March 1938 after the German occupation of Austria, 'nothing was more likely to aggravate the difficulties of the present situation than any suggestions that our ultimate objective was to unite France, Italy and ourselves against Germany', a Chamberlainite statement of policy wholly different to that advocated and followed by Eden.

Chamberlain was not, as some of his detractors have alleged – although never Eden – an ignoble or ignorant man, but there was significance in his remark to Ivan Maisky, the Soviet Ambassador, in July 1937 that 'If only we could sit down at a table with the Germans and run through their complaints and claims with a pencil, this would greatly relieve all tension'. He considered the Americans 'a nation of cads' and believed that they 'have a long way to go before they become helpful partners in world affairs'. He despised 'the lethargy of the Foreign Office', and he described Eden's supporters as 'the Boys' Brigade'; when he got rid of Vansittart he wrote that 'Van had the effect of multiplying the extent of Anthony's natural vibrations and I am afraid his instincts were all against my policy. ... I suspect that in Rome and Berlin the rejoicings will be loud and deep.' They were.

Eden made a major, and inexplicable, misjudgement about Chamberlain, one of the worst mistakes in his life. He had seen much of Chamberlain since he had become Foreign Secretary, and believed that they were closer than any other two members of the Cabinet. He frequently called at

11 Downing Street on a Sunday evening for a quiet talk, and enjoyed Chamberlain's excellent hospitality, which he returned. He knew that Chamberlain would take an interest in foreign affairs, but he completely failed to realize until too late that Chamberlain was forming emphatic views of his own on dealing with the dictators and intended to have his way. The decision to get rid of Vansittart was taken very soon after Chamberlain became Prime Minister, and when J. P. L. Thomas was appointed Eden's Parliamentary Private Secretary in May it was made very clear to him by Warren Fisher and Horace Wilson that 'Vansittart was an alarmist, that he hampered all attempts of the Government to make friendly contact with the dictator states and that his influence over Anthony Eden was very great', and that his appointment 'might lessen the damage which had been done by the Foreign Office in general and by Vansittart in particular'. Thomas replied robustly to this extraordinary – and characteristic – attempt to use the post of PPS as an agent of Downing Street, but it was a clear warning sign that should have been noted more carefully. Eden also found that his relationship with Chamberlain changed after the latter became Prime Minister, but he was very slow to grasp the clear implications of what Chamberlain was doing, which was taking over the conduct and operation of foreign policy.

Eden was, admittedly, heavily occupied on many fronts. Although 1937 marked a lull between the horrors of 1936 and 1938, the Spanish Civil War still raged, with terrible atrocities on both sides and the active and brutal participation of German, Italian and Russian units; there was tension throughout Europe; and the Abyssinian rift had not been bridged. Eden worked immensely hard at all these subjects, and the House of Commons was exceptionally demanding. He had his hands very full at a time when the Foreign Secretary only had one Parliamentary Under-Secretary in the Commons and was expected to carry the main burden himself. Eden's exacting self-imposed conscientiousness over every aspect of foreign policy and affairs also clearly contributed to his inability to read the signs. As it happened, he had become as disillusioned with Vansittart as had Warren Fisher and Horace Wilson, although for very different reasons. Eden wanted to remove him because of personal dislike and Vansittart's indifference to Italian aggression, Downing Street because of his fierce and repetitive anti-Germanism. Eden's very high opinion of his Foreign Office staff excluded Vansittart and Nevile Henderson, but he did not appreciate the perils to his own position of a Whitehall *coup* to replace his Permanent Under-Secretary. What he effectively did do was to insist on the appointment of Cadogan rather than the congenial nonentity from the India Office that Fisher and Wilson had in mind. This proposal, also, should have alerted Eden to what was going on, but it did not, just as Chamberlain's brusque intervention in the 1936 sanctions crisis should have been recognized for what it was.

An essay could be written on why it is that so many modern Prime Ministers have been so dismissive of the British Foreign Service. Its standards of entry are exceptionally high, its record and experience are envied by other countries, and it has had a remarkable record of having been right on the big issues. All ministers in my experience who have served in the Foreign Office and then moved to other departments have – with the exception of the Treasury – been depressed by standards lower than those to which they had become accustomed in the Foreign Office. Like all human institutions, it has its weaknesses, but it is a machine of great power and influence abroad which several Prime Ministers have not only ignored but on too many occasions despised and distrusted. 'The Foreign Office' has too often been the scapegoat for policies which its leading members actually opposed or on which their advice was never sought. As will be seen, one of the real mysteries of 1956 is why Eden made the same mistakes as Chamberlain did in 1937–9.

Most revealingly, Chamberlain criticized a speech by Eden because it 'shows again a characteristic of the Foreign Office mind which I have frequently noticed before. They never can keep the major objects of foreign policy in mind, with the result that they make obstructions for themselves by endeavouring to give smart answers to some provocative foreign statement.'* Eden's policy towards Germany was to keep her guessing until British rearmament could enable him to negotiate from strength and to do everything possible to maintain the French alliance, while Chamberlain was impatient 'to get on better terms with Germany', with Rome as a lever. Within six months of becoming Prime Minister, Chamberlain was writing that the Foreign Office was 'coming along nicely, though I can see that if left to themselves there would be a danger of their letting pass the critical moment. ... As Chancellor of the Exchequer I could hardly have moved a pebble: now I have only to raise a finger and the whole face of Europe is changed!'†

A Prime Minister thinking on such lines, with a highly strung Foreign Secretary such as Eden, provided the fundamental cause of what then occurred.

It is doubtful whether Chamberlain set out to remove Eden from the beginning of his premiership – as he certainly intended with Vansittart – but what is plain is that he set out to run foreign policy in his own way and on his own terms. He certainly underestimated Eden's force of

* 6 November 1937. Quoted in Keith Middlemas, *Diplomacy of Illusion*, p. 79.
† *Ibid.*, p. 130.

character, as did so many others, just as Eden underestimated Chamberlain's capacity for quiet ruthlessness. It is significant that it was many years before Eden appreciated the extent of Chamberlain's guile, and was genuinely astonished when he discovered it. This might be ascribed to political naivety, but it was the result of Eden's assumption that politics was an honourable profession – with, admittedly, some very dishonourable participants – and of his reluctance to believe that someone he considered to be a friend as well as a close colleague could behave in such a way. Eden's judgement on people was usually cool and good, but in the case of Chamberlain it was totally wrong. And so, as he toiled devotedly at his tasks, the political tides were remorselessly moving away from him.

In addition to their differences on foreign policy, Eden's and Chamberlain's approaches to rearmament were seriously at variance, as Eden noted in his diary on 8 November:

Had a talk with N.C. in the morning about rearmament based on new Air Force paper. Told him of my conviction that rearmament must go faster, and that we should buy from abroad, if necessary. I know that some of my colleagues think we at F.O. insufficiently insistent in our efforts to improve relations with Dictator Powers. This, however, not true position. It was thought unless it were known that we were rearming effectively our efforts in International sphere today useless. N.C. did not, I think, share my view and clearly had the financial situation much in mind. I maintained that good financial position would be small consolation to us if London were laid flat because our Air Force had been insufficient. N.C. thought this was today too alarmist a view. Despite darkening international outlook, which he admitted, he did not think anybody was going to attack us for the next two years. It was necessary to follow a very cautious foreign policy.

After further talk N.C. undertook, however, to have a Cabinet Committee for discussion of the whole situation.

This was another ignored warning signal.

The tone and language of the Italian press and radio against Britain and Eden personally could not have been worse in the spring and summer of 1937, concentrating upon the British position not only in Europe but in the Mediterranean and Middle East. Nor was this all. The Italian Foreign Minister Count Ciano warned the British Ambassador in Rome that 'something more than a press campaign' would occur if Mussolini's just claims were not met, a warning that Drummond* took very seriously.

---

* In August 1937, Sir Eric Drummond succeeded his half-brother as sixteenth Earl of Perth. He had been an admirable, if excessively inconspicuous, first Secretary-General of the League of Nations, which had not endeared him to the Mussolini regime. As a junior member of his staff in Rome has written, 'Quiet, efficient, reserved and kindly ... I do not suppose he had ever met anybody like Mussolini and he was far too well disposed towards

Drummond's portrait of Mussolini was now of a paranoiac who genuinely believed in the prospect of a second Roman Empire, and there were ugly echoes of the campaign to bring Italian public opinion to fever pitch over Abyssinia in 1935. Reports of major Italian naval manoeuvres and the dispatch of two more divisions to Libya seemed to confirm these fears, which were also shared by Admiral Sir Dudley Pound, Commander-in-Chief of the Mediterranean, and by the British Ambassador in Cairo, Sir Miles Lampson.

Then, after a reasoned speech by Eden in the Commons on 19 July to the effect that Britain had no ambitions in the Mediterranean or Red Sea beyond maintaining the free and peaceful passage of her ships, the wily and skilful Grandi told Eden that this had been excellently received by Mussolini, who wanted nothing but friendship, and asked him to arrange a meeting with Chamberlain before he went on leave. Grandi then saw Leslie Hore-Belisha, the new War Minister, to tell him that Italy was convinced that the British were preparing to make war, which could only lead to more Italian preparations, and to suggest joint staff discussions. This was well received by Belisha, but Eden circulated a paper in which he ridiculed these protestations, and at his suggestion Vansittart prepared a detailed note for Chamberlain which specifically sought an explanation for the reinforcement of the Libya contingent, which would by August consist of 60,000 men, of whom 40,000 were white soldiers in motorized divisions, infinitely larger than anything the British could muster.

At the meeting with Chamberlain, Grandi read out a long letter from Mussolini, of which he did not leave a copy, and which was somewhat garbled by his own interventions, demanding British *de jure* recognition of the conquest of Abyssinia and arguing that the Libyan reinforcement was entirely in response to increased British expenditure on defence in the Mediterranean. To this Chamberlain responded sympathetically, and then wrote to Mussolini a letter markedly friendly in tone, which he deliberately did not show to Eden 'for I had the feeling that he would object to it'. As Eden had just described Mussolini as having 'the mentality of a gangster' this was undoubtedly true, but it was another warning sign that Eden did not detect. He was also puzzled by enthusiastic articles in the British press about the benign prospects for an Anglo-Italian agreement, which Vansittart traced back to Downing Street. 'By all means let us show ourselves ready to talk,' Eden wrote to Vansittart from his family holiday on Southampton Water on 4 August, 'but in no scrambling hurry to offer incense on a dictator's altar.' He reiterated his view that only strength would impress Mussolini. But he was surprised to see the copy of a letter

his fellow creatures to anticipate the cynical and ruthless attitude of the Italian dictator' (Charles Mott-Radclyffe, *Foreign Body in the Eye*, p. 15).

from Chamberlain to Halifax, who was in charge of the Foreign Office in Eden's absence, which declared that it was important to get the dictators 'in the right mood', in which case they would be perfectly reasonable men. As Italian aircraft and submarines were attacking British merchant ships and Mussolini was reinforcing what he described as 'the Italian legionary troops' in Spain, Eden found this interpretation difficult to comprehend. But, again, he did not realize that he was being deliberately by-passed, his opinions ignored, and a very different policy being actively pursued by his Prime Minister.

These attacks on British and French ships – which the Italians blandly denied had anything to do with them, although the evidence of their involvement was virtually complete – prompted Eden to propose Anglo-French discussions, which were expanded into a meeting of the Mediterranean powers. On 2 September a British destroyer was unsuccessfully attacked by an Italian submarine (although this could not be proved at the time) and then a British tanker was torpedoed and sunk off the Spanish coast. It was absolutely clear to Eden that these were Italian submarines – as indeed they were – and that Italy was in effect conducting an undeclared war while accusing the British of bellicose provocation. Eden recognized, as Chamberlain did not, that this was a classic strategy, which had worked before and would, if not checked, work again. The gulf between the two men now became a chasm, as Eden, very belatedly, began to realize.

Eden's concern at the Mediterranean situation produced his last achievement at the Foreign Office, and sealed his political fate. On the pretext that the Soviet Union would attend, the Germans and Italians refused to be involved in the Mediterranean conference, which was held at Nyon, near Geneva, on 10 September. Because Eden and the French had laid their plans carefully, it was over in four days with complete agreement to protect shipping routes by naval patrols, with provision for immediate counter-attack. The key factor was the strong attitude of the French, who, at a critical moment when it became clear that the eastern Mediterranean nations would not countenance Russian co-operation, offered more destroyers to patrol the Aegean. It was all settled by the 14th, to Italian astonishment and chagrin. The naval operations began at once, covering virtually the entire Mediterranean apart from the Tyrrhenian Sea, which was allocated to the Italians so that, in Eden's sardonic words, 'Mussolini could then send his warships to hunt his own submarines.' Firmness and collective security worked. All sinkings and attacks abruptly ended. In a broadcast from Geneva Eden spoke of 'a masked highwayman who does not stop at even murder' and of a 'gangster terror of the seas' which must be ended.

This triumph was badly received in Rome and at Downing Street, Chamberlain noting that 'we have had a great success at Nyon, but at the expense of Anglo-Italian relations.' Oliver Harvey, Eden's Private Secretary since January 1936, wrote in his diary:

A. E. saw the P.M. today (he had already had a very satisfactory letter from P.M. congratulating him on his success). A. E. anxious to ascertain his reactions as regards the next step *vis-à-vis* Italy, found him 'fed up' with the Italians and not at all disposed to run after them. The P.M. then said he was very annoyed to find A. E. was addressing a meeting at Llandudno on October 15th and wished him to cancel it as he would tire himself out; that he wouldn't allow his Foreign Secretary to be used as a 'party hack' and had forbidden the Central Office to ask him. A. E. protested that his health was all right and that he rather enjoyed it, and that 18,000 people had applied for seats. P.M. very firm and obstinate and said Llandudno in any case a bad place. When A. E. told Jim Thomas and me we were aghast and begged A. E. not to agree to cancel it as it would encourage rumours of difference between A. E. and P.M., apart from the fact that three or four speeches by him a year were invaluable and indeed indispensable for keeping public opinion informed of his foreign policy. A. E. agreed, and when lunching with P.M. later told him so. Jim Thomas meanwhile ascertained from Miss Maxse at Central Office* that she was horrified at this veto and put the worst construction on it, viz. that the P.M. wanted to deal with Foreign Affairs himself and to keep A. E. out of the picture. The P.M. had seen Hacking† and was apparently most obstinate and had said that anyhow October 15th was a bad date as he, P.M., meant to devote his Scarborough speech on October 12th to Foreign Affairs! Anyway, it has now been decided that Llandudno is to stand, but this episode is disquieting for the future.

This was the clearest signal yet. Unfortunately for his biographer, Eden's diary was kept very spasmodically at this time, but his subsequent recollection fully confirms Harvey's contemporary account, with the additional point that Chamberlain told him that he needed 'a really good holiday and must have rest'. At the time Eden was puzzled by this; what he did not realize was that this was the first he had heard of the whispering campaign, that almost certainly emanated from Downing Street, and in which Sir John Simon and certain Whips were deeply involved, that Eden was a sick man, severely overstressed. He now also found more difficulties with the Prime Minister and the Cabinet, both increasingly hostile to any Anglo-French initiatives and co-operation. With much justification, Eden considered this hostility to be an extraordinary reaction to the outstanding success of that co-operation at Nyon. Then Chamberlain rewrote a telegram to Washington on joint action with the United States in the Far East and completely changed its tone from acceptance to virtual rejection; Eden sent

* Miss Marjorie Maxse, Chief Organization Officer at Conservative Central Office.
† Sir Douglas (later Lord) Hacking, the Party Chairman.

another telegram of a more positive nature, but the damage had been done. All this was absolutely deliberate.

The attempt to prevent Eden from speaking in Llandudno is by no means an unprecedented fate for a Conservative politician who has fallen out with a strong-willed Prime Minister with control of the Party machine, although in this case the Party Chairman refused to accept the Prime Minister's urgings. Eden's speech – a defence of his policies, a denunciation of the dictators, a warm welcome to President Roosevelt's interest in co-operation with the democracies, and a condemnation of the folly of party politics at such a time – did nothing to improve his relations with Chamberlain, particularly as it was very well received.

On the day Eden made his speech, Harvey accurately summed up the Cabinet position:

There is no doubt he has more appeal than any of his colleagues. He has the H. of C. behind him as well as the country, but in the Cabinet he is criticized and thwarted by half his colleagues who are jealous of him and would trip him up if they had half a chance.

The worst ones are Hoare and Swinton: the first is consumed with ambition to be P.M., though God knows he'd land his party on the rocks in six months, and has never forgiven A. E. for succeeding him. Swinton is anyway a very second-rate politician.* Simon is slippery and evasive, a moral coward; yet incredible as it may seem, he also believes that he can become P.M.

Hailsham [Lord Chancellor] has had a stroke and should have been dropped at the reconstruction: he is a diehard and an obstructionist. ... Kingsley Wood is a severe critic of A. E. and is a pushing professional politician, De La Warr [Lord Privy Seal], Malcolm MacD (a good man), Elliot, Stanley, are all lightweights, though on A. E.'s side. Duff Cooper is bone-idle. Halifax is idle and pernickety. Most of the colleagues are 'dictator-minded' and hate to see us associate with France. A. E. had a very difficult time in the Cabinet on Wednesday when it was a question of our joining with France in a common attitude on the Italian reply. The Cabinet are in fact far to the right of the H. of C. and the country.†

In these bleak and hostile circumstances Eden took his case to the country. At Llandudno he had been greeted by cheering crowds and great enthusiasm, and on 20 November, in a speech in Leamington, he firmly stated that 'the rule of law should govern international relations, and not the rule of war'. He went on:

Our first task is to equip ourselves as a nation so thoroughly and so strongly that the whole world may see that we mean what we say, and that our conceptions of

---

* This was unfair. Swinton's difficulty was his extreme outspokenness and tendency to be over-critical of his colleagues: but he was no friend of Eden's.

† John Harvey (ed.), *The Diplomatic Diaries of Oliver Harvey*, Vol. 1, pp. 50–1.

international order have behind them adequate force. There can be no doubt that attempts to uphold international law have not benefited from the comparative decline of British strength in arms which has existed in recent years. The equilibrium is now being restored – nobody but a would-be aggressor will complain.

Another of Eden's concerns was mounting German complaints about the treatment of the Sudeten Germans in Czechoslovakia, and, although the Italian situation was a major preoccupation throughout 1937, it was the Nazis who were the real threat. Having recovered the Saar and the Rhineland without firing a shot, the same claims of harsh treatment of Germans by 'occupying Powers' were being employed in Czechoslovakia, with typical skill and ruthlessness. France was bound by treaty with Czechoslovakia, and Eden could see that here lay a matter that could precipitate European war, while the precarious condition of Austrian independence worried him. What was heartening was a very full meeting of the Conservative Foreign Affairs Committee at which some very robust things were said by back-benchers, especially Churchill, who praised Eden warmly for Nyon and for the general structure of his foreign policy. This was not approved in Downing Street.

Now came the clearest sign of all of what was going on. After an official dinner given by Eden for the Prime Minister of Yugoslavia, Halifax startled Eden – and Churchill, who was also present – by telling him that he had received an invitation from Göring to attend the International Sporting Exhibition in Berlin and would probably see Hitler. He added that he had told the Prime Minister, who had warmly approved. Although Eden was surprised, he saw no reason why he should attempt to veto the plan, and he agreed to it, albeit without much enthusiasm. There was no question of Halifax behaving in a disreputable manner behind the back of the Foreign Secretary. He and Eden got on well. Eden did impress upon Halifax and Henderson the need for warning comment on Austria and Czechoslovakia, but then was disconcerted to be told that Hitler would not be in Berlin but would be willing to see Halifax in his mountain eyrie at Berchtesgaden. Eden, in Brussels for the Nine-Power Conference on the Far East, to which he attached great importance as a result of the American presence, was alarmed by the impression 'of our being in pursuit of the German Chancellor' and instructed Cranborne to put this strongly to Chamberlain. This Cranborne did, without any effect at all; the Prime Minister was very keen on the visit. Eden's annoyance increased when the British press carried exaggerated and inspired reports on its importance, reports which certainly did not emanate from the Foreign Office. The *Evening Standard* of 13 November implied strongly that in return for a ten-year truce on the colonial issue 'Hitler would expect the British Government to deal him a free hand in Central Europe'. Chamberlain was adamant about Halifax's visit, writing tersely, 'But really, that F.O. I am only waiting for my opportunity to stir it up with a long pole.' Eden decided to take the matter up personally with Chamberlain at Downing Street on 16 November.

Eden was recovering from a brief, but sharp, attack of influenza, and was also becoming aware of how his authority was being challenged and of how a policy was being formed at Downing Street that was already causing alarm in Paris and was certainly contrary to his own. Eden was tense and suspicious, and he found Chamberlain at his worst, as his Parliamentary Private Secretary, Lord Dunglass,* has confirmed. Chamberlain did not particularly want to see Eden, and began by giving his opinion that Eden's visit to Brussels had been a complete waste of time; Eden retorted that it had not, and went on to complain strongly about 'the slowness, lack of imagination and drive shown by my colleagues in the matter of rearmament'. Chamberlain responded sharply to this, and both lost their tempers, Chamberlain ending the exchange by telling Eden 'to go home and take an aspirin!' When Eden returned, seething, to the Foreign Office he told Harvey that the meeting 'couldn't have gone worse'. A letter to Chamberlain, written when he had calmed down, set out his deep concerns about the Halifax visit and the pace of rearmament, to which Chamberlain replied by again ascribing Eden's concerns to his influenza. Eden's alleged infirmities were sedulously conveyed to the press and back-benchers by Simon and Hoare on Downing Street instructions. When Jim Thomas went to see Horace Wilson about the deteriorating relationship, he was told that Chamberlain 'was devoted' to Eden but he believed his policy of getting together with the dictators was the right one, that he was determined to persevere with it, and that 'he was saving A. E. from himself'.†

This brazen flouting of Eden's authority and the intrigues being carried out against him personally – of which he was well informed by Jim Thomas, who had turned out to be a very different kind of PPS to the one intended by Fisher and Wilson – now made him think, for the first time, that he would serve the cause better by being out of the Government. He now began to speak to Thomas and his Private Office of the possibility of resignation. He was talked out of it, but when such a thought enters a politician's mind it begins to take root; although Eden does not say so, it is my view that the disastrous meeting with Chamberlain began the process.

---

* Later the fourteenth Earl of Home, and then Sir Alec Douglas-Home, Prime Minister 1963–4.

† Harvey (ed.), *The Diplomatic Diaries of Oliver Harvey*, Vol. 1, p. 61.

When Eden read the full record of the talk between Halifax and Hitler his apprehensions increased. Hitler had given nothing, while Halifax, instead of being firm on Austria and Czechoslovakia, had actually said that there could be

possible alterations in the European order which might be destined to come about with the passage of time. *Amongst these questions were Danzig, Austria, and Czechoslovakia.** England was interested to see that any alterations should come through the course of peaceful evolution and that methods should be avoided which might cause far-reaching disturbances, which neither the Chancellor nor other countries desired.

Hitler said that Germany desired peaceful relations with her neighbours, but added, ominously, that it was up to the Czechs to treat Germans well. If Britain genuinely wanted better relations with Germany she should satisfy Germany's claims to her former colonies; he went on to say that he could not understand why the British had not shot Gandhi and thereby ended the unrest in India. 'This conception of trusteeship did not inspire me to make haste in granting Hitler colonial territories,' Eden later drily commented. The British did not know that Hitler had already given orders for the subjugation of Austria and Czechoslovakia, but it was obvious that this new method of conducting negotiations with a dictator was a disaster; 'I was mistaken in ever tolerating it,' Eden wrote in his old age. What had begun as a casual remark by Halifax about a visit to a sporting exhibition had become a direct, and very hazardous, amateur foray into a political minefield.

Matters became even worse when French ministers came to London at the end of November, to be told by Chamberlain that British public opinion would not countenance a war over Czechoslovakia and wanted a reasonable and peaceful settlement. He added, to Eden's dismay, that the Sudeten Germans were not getting fair treatment, like the British settlers in the Transvaal under Kruger in the 1890s, a somewhat astonishing analogy but a natural one from the son of Joseph Chamberlain, the true originator of the Jameson Raid and of the consequent disastrous Boer War. But it was a very revealing one. Chamberlain believed that his father and Cecil Rhodes had been absolutely right to use force to come to the aid of their nationals living in a foreign state, so why not the Germans? Eden, and the French, did not believe for a moment that Hitler was even faintly interested in the Sudeten Germans; they were an excuse to seize vital territory and fatally weaken Czechoslovakia. They were right.

Although Eden's personal relations with Chamberlain had been patched up, the gulf in approaches had widened again. Eden would not talk of

* My italics.

conceding on the former German colonies question without a general European settlement; Chamberlain was very interested indeed in using them as a bargaining counter for an Anglo-German settlement, a very different thing. On 5 December Eden told Harvey that he was convinced that his policy was now in a minority in the Cabinet, that his older colleagues were 'defeatist' on rearmament, and 'He wonders whether he could not serve his country better outside the Government.'

Harvey, who saw the situation very clearly, had written to him on 7 November that:

You are the only Foreign Secretary in sight. If you left the Cabinet the Government would fall. The Government is living on your popularity and reputation; you are not only entitled to but you are able to impose your terms. ... You are also receiving insufficient support in the Cabinet for your foreign policy; indeed, far from supporting you many of your colleagues, even the P.M. on occasions, seem mainly concerned in obstructing you. ... Your position is so strong now that the Cabinet would not dare let you go. They are imposing on your good nature because they do not think you will ever turn on them.

There was much truth in this analysis.

When matters reach such a stage, the catalytic event can often be something different from the main issue. Eden had gone to Brussels specifically to see American representatives on the situation in the Far East in order to concert action towards Japan, whose war against China now seriously threatened British and American interests. It was this attempt that Chamberlain had dismissed as 'a complete waste of time', but in December the Japanese bombed and sank an American ship and attacked British ships in the Yangtse River. Eden wanted to use this opportunity, with American public opinion thoroughly aroused, to send a substantial fleet to the Far East, leaving the Mediterranean to the French fleet; Roosevelt responded very positively. 'A. E. ... is much encouraged by this response,' Harvey wrote on 18 December. 'He feels strongly the need of bringing the Japs up short before they get further into China and make the position of Shanghai and Hong Kong untenable.' The Americans sent over a senior naval representative to take the matter further; Eden was delighted, although the Americans said they would wait for another incident before taking full action. Chamberlain was indifferent to the matter, his eyes fastened on his great rapprochement with Hitler and Mussolini.

By the end of the year Eden was both tired and depressed. Harvey noted on 5 December:

A. E. complains bitterly of defeatist attitude of all his older colleagues, including Inskip, in matter of rearmament and of attitude towards dictators generally. ...

A. E. is hoping to take six weeks' holiday and go to West Indies just after Christmas. P.M. to take on F.O. in his absence. This is rather alarming in view of intrigues, but as P.M. is now in agreement with A. E., perhaps all will be well. In any case, A. E. MUST have a holiday and now is a quieter season diplomatically than any other.*

The Vansittart matter was resolved satisfactorily by his being offered, and accepting, the honorific but in reality insignificant position of Chief Diplomatic Adviser, with Cadogan as his successor, Eden having won that particular battle at least. But the plan for the West Indies holiday was clearly impracticable; Eden then thought longingly about Madeira, yearning for sunshine, but with the American naval advisers due to arrive, this, also, had to be ruled out. He was worried too about Chamberlain's clear desire to give Mussolini – whom Eden was now describing as 'Anti-Christ' – his eagerly wanted *de jure* recognition of the Italian possession of Abyssinia and also of the King of Italy as Emperor of Abyssinia. The withdrawal of Italy from the League made it even more important that if Mussolini were to be given what he wanted, the price should be very high. Eden did not appreciate at all that Chamberlain was privately discussing with Grandi *de jure* recognition at virtually no price at all.

Eden took his wife and sons to the South of France on 3 January, and lunched with Churchill and Lloyd George on 5 January at Grasse. He wrote in his diary:

Both very friendly. Nothing particularly notable in the conversation, except that both strongly opposed to any recognition of the Italian conquest of Abyssinia. I told them something of our efforts to ensure co-operation with the U.S. Both seemed impressed with the progress that had been made.

As Eden later related, 'I played tennis and the days rolled uneventfully by, until the morning of Friday, January 14th, when I was called to the telephone to speak to Sir Alexander Cadogan.' His account in his memoirs of what then happened was culled from his diaries and notes, but the unpublished diary account is so much more graphic that it should be given in full:

Astonished to receive by telephone an urgent request to return to London at once. No details could be given by telephone, but bag was being sent to Marseilles. Started home that night. Bag unfortunately missed us and I received no information until I reached Folkestone after very stormy crossing, where I was met by Alex [Cadogan] and Oliver [Harvey]. . . .
Alex gave the messages from Washington which showed that Roosevelt was planning some form of initiative as a result of which he hopes to put forward plans

* Harvey (ed.), *The Diplomatic Diaries of Oliver Harvey*, Vol. 1, p. 63.

for the betterment of international conditions. There are one or two paragraphs in the Message which are not well-worded from our point of view, and there is also a certain vagueness about the proposals. All the same I attach so much importance to Anglo-American co-operation that I should myself be strongly in favour of responding to Roosevelt's appeal and promising to back it. The P.M., however, did not like it because he feared it might cut across our own attempts to improve relations with the Dictator Powers.

After some discussion with Alex we sent a telegram to [Sir Ronald] Lindsay explaining that I had been away and expressing hope that no final decision would be taken on one reply.

Also spoke to Ronnie on telephone, who explained that Roosevelt was undoubtedly disappointed at our reply. He advised me on the whole to wait until we received a written communication from the President, which was promised on Monday.

The journey itself had been rather more dramatic. With Harold Caccia, his junior Private Secretary, Eden had left Cannes by train for Paris – where he was quickly briefed by the British Ambassador Sir Eric Phipps on the domestic French political situation, which was not encouraging – intending to fly from there to London, but the weather was so bad that all flights had been cancelled. The Channel crossing was a particularly bad one, and the ferry crashed into Folkestone Pier, causing considerable damage. Eden later recalled that Cadogan and Harvey 'had troubled faces and a large file of papers'.

What had happened was that on the evening of the 11th, Sumner Welles, the American Under-Secretary of State, had conveyed to Sir Ronald Lindsay, the British Ambassador a most secret message from Roosevelt to Chamberlain to the effect that the President was so deeply troubled about the deteriorating international situation that he proposed to address the entire Washington Diplomatic Corps at the White House on the 22nd to point to the gravity of the situation and the manner in which smaller European states were being drawn reluctantly into the orbit of the dictatorships as a result of the loss of influence and cohesion of the major democratic nations. Lindsay had urged 'a very quick and cordial acceptance' of the Roosevelt initiative, not least because Britain was the only country that had been informed, and the British reaction was crucial. This was also Cadogan's advice when he conveyed the telegrams to Chamberlain at Chequers. The initiative had its technical defects, but the spirit behind it, of active American interest in the European situation and the need at least to begin the process of consultation and concerted action among the democracies, was the key new factor. Roosevelt was also looking towards Japan, but so was Eden.

But Chamberlain, who consulted only Horace Wilson, regarded Roosevelt's approach 'with the gravest concern'. His reply stated that 'it may be permissible to look forward to some improvement [in the European situation] in the immediate future'; he also looked forward to British acceptance of the *de jure* capture of Abyssinia and to conversations with Germany. The President's proposals could cut across such hopeful developments. It was, as Welles later wrote, 'in the nature of a douche of cold water'. It was in effect a rejection, one written in terms of complacency and superiority, and in which Chamberlain's fundamental contempt for the United States and his self-confidence that he had found the only course to success rang out. There are few more calamitous documents in modern international politics.

Eden later wrote that he was 'outraged' when he read Chamberlain's telegram; Harvey considered that Chamberlain had committed 'a colossal blunder', as did Cadogan and Cranborne. But there were other factors. Chamberlain had taken a major foreign policy decision without consulting his Foreign Secretary; he had also thrown in the news of imminent *de jure* recognition, which was anathema not only to Eden but to Roosevelt and American public opinion; nor was it, formally, British foreign policy. Nor had the Cabinet been informed. The Prime Minister had taken upon himself, in defiance of all advice save that of Horace Wilson, to rewrite the foreign policy of the Government. What was even more galling was that he had no doubt that he had done the right thing. As Chamberlain wrote:

The [Roosevelt] plan appeared to me fantastic and likely to excite the derision of Germany and Italy. They might even use it to postpone conversations with us, and if we were associated with it they would see in it another attempt on the part of the democratic bloc to put the dictators in the wrong. There was no time to consult Anthony, for in view of secrecy on which Roosevelt insisted in emphatic terms I did not dare to telephone.*

This explanation in Chamberlain's own detailed account of the crisis is revealing on all counts. One of his biographers, Iain Macleod, defended Chamberlain by writing that 'Eden was out of the country and in circumstances in which it was impossible to communicate with him', an extraordinary statement by a Cabinet Minister with knowledge of communications. Had the will to communicate with Eden existed, he could have been consulted securely from Paris or recalled to London. Cadogan had no compunction in using the telephone to alert him when he knew the full story. The fact was that Chamberlain had no intention of consulting his Foreign Secretary; had he wished to do so, the means were there. He deliberately chose not to use them, and then pleaded security concerns.

Eden dined with Cadogan and Cranborne after his arrival in London, and then not only spoke to Lindsay by telephone but telegraphed that the

---

* Memorandum by Chamberlain, quoted in Iain Macleod, *Neville Chamberlain*, p. 212.

President's 'disappointment at what he considers to be a negative attitude on our part ... was not the impression which it [Chamberlain's telegram] was intended to convey'. This was sent without any consultation with the Prime Minister.

On the following morning, Sunday the 16th, Eden drove down to Chequers. He wrote in his diary account:

He [Chamberlain] seemed in excellent health and spirits. Showed him the telegram which I had sent to Washington and which, I thought, he did not very much like. He did not, however, complain and we agreed that nothing further could be done until we received President Roosevelt's written message. I did, however, ask him whether he would like to endorse what I had telegraphed, but this I could not persuade him to do.

I then explained my own view that it was so important to secure Anglo-American co-operation, and that I would myself have wished to give a welcome to Roosevelt's initiative. He explained his fear that it would confuse our own efforts. I replied that I did not feel so optimistic about them nor thought it impossible to work on parallel lines. I added that I personally agreed with the appreciation of the European situation which Roosevelt's telegram showed. We then had some talk about our negotiations with Germany and Italy.

I told him my own views that we should do our best to improve Anglo-American relations and in the meanwhile our negotiations with Germany, but not at the present make any approaches to Italy. Every instinct was against recognition of conquest of Abyssinia at this time.

Then showed Neville file containing latest Abyssinian reports. I reminded him that last year when we made the so-called 'Gentleman's Agreement' with Italy Mussolini sent four thousand men to Spain a week after. I feared I had no more confidence in him now. Neville retorted that the position was different at this time. He added that he did not agree with me about Italy and that we had a wonderful chance of coming to terms about the future of the Mediterranean. I said that the less strong Mussolini was the less he appealed to Hitler. Our recognition of his Empire would, I thought, increase his authority, and, therefore, make him more attractive to Hitler. Undertook, however, to discuss the question fully with the French and to put his point of view to them as fairly as I could.

Eden later described the meeting as 'stiff' and 'profoundly unsatisfactory'. He did not know that Chamberlain was in close contact with Grandi, and, through Lady (Austen) Chamberlain, with Ciano, but for the first time Eden became fully aware of Chamberlain's ruthlessness, writing many years later that 'He was evidently determined to see the whole American business only in the context of his impending talks with the dictators. In this sense, Roosevelt, our French allies and I were all in the same boat. We were all held to be obstructing these negotiations, in which Chamberlain had dogmatic faith.'*

* Avon, *Facing the Dictators*, p. 555.

The baleful influence of Lady Chamberlain consisted not merely in giving her brother-in-law glowing accounts of Mussolini's eagerness to settle all differences amicably; she also in her letters regularly denigrated Eden, on all occasions described by the Italians as the only obstacle to a happy outcome. Others, including Chips Channon, reported back directly to Chamberlain in the same sense. Chamberlain wrote with marked irritation that all this – or what he knew of it – 'seemed to produce in Anthony only further suspicion'.*

Eden tried desperately to retrieve the Roosevelt initiative, but Chamberlain had effectively killed it. Roosevelt's major error had been to make it only to the British; had it been made more widespread, as was the eventual intention, there could have been strong international and national pressure upon the British Government to accept it, however reluctantly; as it was, very few people knew of it, and Eden had to preserve the extreme confidentiality of the approach.

Further discussions with Chamberlain only widened the gulf between them. After one on the 18th, Eden wrote in his diary:

There is, therefore, a fundamental divergence between us, the importance of which we both realize. . . . I fear that fundamentally the difficulty is that N. believes that he is a man with a mission to come to terms with the Dictators. Indeed one of his chief objections to Roosevelt's Initiative was that with its strong reference to International Law it would greatly irritate Dictator Powers.

There was then a bizarre meeting of the Cabinet Foreign Affairs Committee. Eden sat next to Inskip, and saw he had a note before him that read 'Eden's policy to line up the U.S.A., Great Britain, France – result war'. Chamberlain read long extracts from his sister-in-law's letters to justify his glowing expectation of an imminent rapprochement, and led Halifax, Simon, Inskip, Kingsley Wood and Hoare against the Roosevelt initiative. Totally outnumbered, Eden could only reiterate his position. Later that evening his only allies, Cadogan, Cranborne, Jim Thomas and Oliver Harvey, came to his house in Fitzhardinge Street. As they pointed out to him, the political problem was that Eden could not resign on this matter, as it had to be kept secret, and no one would know the cause of it. This Eden had to accept, but when Thomas saw Horace Wilson on the 20th and told him that the initiative might be leaked at the American end Wilson went into a towering rage and 'warned me that if America produced the facts he would use the full power of the·Government machine in an attack on AE's past record with regard to the dictators and the shameful

* Macleod, *Neville Chamberlain*, p. 213.

obstruction by the F.O. of the P.M.'s attempts to save the peace of the world'.* Thomas noted that 'The atmosphere was becoming intolerable.'

Many politicians would not have had a qualm about leaking the American plan, which would have caused a sensation and put the Prime Minister in an indefensible position as one who had curtly rejected an offer from a great democracy in order to continue direct negotiations with two dictatorships whose record was so contemptible. That this never occurred to Eden is as indicative of his character as Chamberlain's secret talks with Grandi – making use of the Conservative Chief Agent, the sinister and mysterious Sir Joseph Ball† – tell us much about him. Eden had been totally out-manoeuvred, but he had in his hand a political hand grenade which, if thrown, would have had shattering results. But he did not throw it. It remained unused. While his biographer may be proud of Eden's integrity and decency, the fact that such a leak might well have ended the developing Chamberlainite policy of appeasement to dictators that reached its apogee at Munich can only make him lament that it was never exploded. What Chamberlain and others ascribed to weakness on Eden's part was in fact something much better, but they had judged their man right: he would not stoop to conquer. I only wish he had. He continued to fight hard and honourably for a more positive response to Roosevelt, but Chamberlain utterly dominated the Foreign Affairs Committee. Eden was defeated at every point, and the Committee was so secure that the rest of the Cabinet was totally unaware that a crisis was taking place. When it broke, they were totally bewildered.

Duff Cooper was typical in this experience. As he later wrote, 'It is much to his credit that he [Eden] abstained from all lobbying of opinion and sought to gain no adherents either in the Cabinet or the House of Commons. Had he made an effort to win my support at the time he would probably have succeeded.'‡ At the key Cabinet on the 19th Cooper, like many others, could not understand what the fuss was about, and thought that 'if it were a question of now or never, it seemed to me to be better that the conversations should be opened without delay.' It was only later that he realized how

* Avon, *Facing the Dictators*, p. 563, quoting from Thomas's diaries. These were loaned to him, but the originals have subsequently not been traced after their return to his sister. There are detailed extracts in the Eden papers, which I have used.

† Iain Macleod, *Neville Chamberlain*, pp. 218–19, described Ball – then alive – as 'a man of honour and distinction', and dismissed Grandi's account of assignations in taxi-cabs. The contact was the legal adviser to the Italian Embassy; Thomas told Ball in writing that any information he received from this contact should be sent to the Foreign Office; Ball sent it directly to Horace Wilson. On 20 February Ball and the Italian contact, Dingli, did indeed discuss the matter in a taxi-cab ride from Waterloo Station to the Conservative Research Department, after which Ball telephoned Downing Street.

‡ Duff Cooper, *Old Men Forget*, p. 211.

deep were the differences and how important they were; at the time, it seemed not to be a resignation matter. Cooper had a Vansittart-like hatred and fear of Nazi Germany, and was all for accommodation with Italy, not realizing, as he later frankly admitted, that the issues were inseparable. It took the Rape of Austria to open his, and others', eyes.

The Chamberlain–Grandi talks continued, Lady Chamberlain continued to see Mussolini and Ciano, and the trusted and loyal Signor Secondo, the Deputy Chancery Servant at the British Embassy in Rome, continued to let in the Italian Secret Service at night to photograph top-secret documents, many of which were subsequently published as appendices to Ciano's diary! In modern espionage, perhaps only the brilliant placement of a Soviet agent as the personal confidant and amanuensis of David Ben-Gurion in the critical 1950s has been comparably devastating.*

Eden, relentlessly and regularly defeated in the Foreign Affairs Committee and deceived by his Prime Minister, of whom he was now deeply suspicious, took his argument to a meeting of the Junior Imperial League in Birmingham – a well-chosen venue – in which he declared fervently:

> if we are to have peace in your time it means that in any agreements we make today there must be no sacrifice of principles and no shirking of responsibilities merely to obtain quick results that may not be permanent. . . . We offer friendship to all, but on equal terms. For it is not by seeking to buy temporary goodwill that peace is made, but on a basis of frank reciprocity.

He also denounced defeatism – 'an ugly name for an ugly thing'.

Grandi was now openly contemptuous of Eden. When the latter invited him to see him at the Foreign Office, Grandi refused on the grounds that he was playing golf. But he was frequently at 10 Downing Street. Meanwhile, British Intelligence had not been as lax everywhere as the Secondo episode might imply, and from the sources thus obtained Eden knew that Hitler intended to seize Austria by force and that Mussolini had acquiesced and also intended to send more Italian troops to Spain. This, also, could not be made public, but it made the Chamberlainite approach even more lamentable. Grandi, at a meeting with Chamberlain and Eden at 10 Downing Street on 18 February, indignantly and piously denied all such evil rumours, gave the Italian version of events since 1935, and ended by declaring that the Anglo-Italian conversations should take place in Rome. Eden could not accept any of this, but Chamberlain clearly indicated that

---

* For a hilarious, although sombre, account of this disaster see Mott-Radclyffe, *Foreign Body in the Eye*, pp. 24–6.

he himself did. Indeed, Chamberlain had not wanted Eden to be present at all, but Eden had insisted.

After this extraordinary meeting, at which Chamberlain had accepted approvingly Grandi's version of recent history (as Eden noted, it sounded as though the British had invaded Abyssinia and that their submarines had been sinking Italian ships), Chamberlain told Eden that he intended to open the conversations with Mussolini at once, and that they would take place in Rome. When Eden protested, as he wrote in his diary:

N. C. became very vehement, more vehement than I have ever seen him, and strode up and down the room saying with great emphasis 'Anthony, you have missed chance after chance. You simply cannot go on like this.' I said, 'Your methods are right if you have faith in the man you are negotiating with.' N. C. replied, 'I have.'

Although Eden could not reveal the secret of his knowledge of the German-Italian agreement over Austria, Hitler had publicly summoned the Austrian Chancellor Schuschnigg to Berchtesgaden, berated him and ordered him to appoint the Nazi, Seyss-Inquart, as Minister of the Interior. This had been done. Chamberlain interpreted this as an impetus to his conversations with Mussolini, rather than the reverse, which was Eden's view, and told Wilson that 'I am determined to stand firm even though it means losing my Foreign Secretary.'

At the Cabinet on the 19th, Chamberlain put his case, and Eden replied, 'rather ineffectively I thought', Chamberlain recorded. History records otherwise on the facts of the case, but of the eighteen other members of the Cabinet fourteen supported the Prime Minister unequivocally, and only four expressed reservations. At that, after three hours' discussion, Eden said he must resign – 'whereupon there was a gasp of horror', Chamberlain's account relates.

With great skill and cold calculation, Chamberlain had made it appear as though his differences with Eden were really quite trivial, and certainly were not of principle. He pointed out that there was a golden opportunity, but it had to be taken *now*, rather than subjected to the caution of the Foreign Secretary, who had no objections in principle to talking to the Italians, but wished to do so on different terms with longer preparation. Eden's response was to repeat the Mussolini record, to take a different view to the Prime Minister on Grandi's assurances about the Italian attitude to German claims on Austria, and to argue that to appear to be running eagerly after Mussolini could only be seen as another surrender to the dictators. He felt he could not refer to the Roosevelt Initiative. Most of the Cabinet was baffled about what the row was all about. Again, Eden had been totally out-manoeuvred; even his few sympathizers, such as Duff Cooper and Malcolm MacDonald, were utterly bewildered.

Here, perhaps, Simon's sedulous campaign about Eden's nerves and health may have had their effect. He told Jim Thomas, and many others, that Eden was 'both physically and mentally ill' and needed six months' holiday; Thomas, barely politely, retorted that this was nonsense. In Thomas's graphic diary account, Simon 'popped his hat on his head, walked down the stairs and did not speak to me again until he had become Lord Chancellor in May 1940'.

Chamberlain would have been willing to accept Eden's resignation there and then, but the press had caught wind of a crisis; crowds were gathering in Downing Street to cheer Eden; the Chief Whip, Margesson, was becoming alarmed; and even Simon thought that Eden's resignation might bring the Government down. Eden's few friends in the Government wanted him to stay for more worthy reasons, but MacDonald for one recognized what Chamberlain really wanted.

There was a lengthy evening meeting and a following day of attempted mediation. On the morning of 20 February Chamberlain sent for Eden to ask if he had qualified his decision. It was only a formality. Eden replied that he had not. At the afternoon Cabinet both repeated their positions; this time Eden did refer to the Roosevelt Initiative – to the perplexity of most present, who had never heard of it – and Chamberlain admitted that the differences were deeper than simply one of timing. There was then a markedly confused and lengthy discussion, in which several suggestions were made for keeping Eden. This lasted for over three hours. A small mediation sub-committee was even formed. William Ormsby-Gore offered his office as Colonial Secretary to keep Eden in the Cabinet. Even the wily Kingsley Wood, alarmed by the political reverberations, suggested compromise. But it was hopeless, and merely prolonged the agony. At 7.30 Eden reiterated his view and returned to the Foreign Office to write his letter of resignation.

Eden was indeed tired after the events of the previous few days, but his resignation letter was so vague about what the differences were that it gave Chamberlain the further opportunity of replying that there were no fundamental differences involved and limiting the issue simply to that of the timing of the Anglo-Italian discussions: 'We had hoped that you would not feel this of sufficient importance to necessitate a parting which is painful to all of us.' When the letters were published in next morning's press there was renewed confusion about what it had all been about. Number Ten and the Whips' Office – some of whose members, notably James Stuart, Eden never forgave – stepped up the whispering campaign about poor Anthony's health, implying that he was on the verge of a nervous breakdown.

Two men who did know what was involved at once offered their resignations as well. Cranborne was incensed at the treatment his friend the Secretary of State had received; it was not true, as was sedulously averred, that he had been the strong man who forced a weak and ill Foreign Secretary to screw up his courage to resign, nor that it was the work of his Private Office, particularly Oliver Harvey. They had seen what was going on, but it had been Eden who had first broached the possibility of his resignation. Both Cranborne and Thomas were young men with hopeful political careers, Thomas being, as has been recorded, a protégé of Horace Wilson. Both resigned on the spot, and would not be moved. Their loyalty and sacrifice touched Eden profoundly, as did the sadness and pride of his officials.

That evening Cranborne and I dined together at my house. I think we both felt a sense of utter relief that the tensions and arguments of these last days were over.

One man, at least, understood the true cause of Eden's decision. Characteristically, Eden did not quote in his memoirs what Winston Churchill later wrote:

Late on the night of February 20 a telephone message reached me as I sat in my old room at Chartwell (as I often sit now) that Eden had resigned. I must confess that my heart sank, and for a while the dark waters of despair overwhelmed me. In a long life I have had many ups and downs. During all the war soon to come and in its darkest times I never had any trouble in sleeping. In the crisis of 1940, when so much responsibility lay upon me, and also at many very anxious, awkward moments in the following five years, I could always flop into bed and go to sleep after the day's work was done – subject, of course, to any emergency call. I slept sound and awoke refreshed, and had no feelings except appetite to grapple with whatever the morning's boxes might bring. But now, on the night of February 20, 1938, and on this occasion only, sleep deserted me. From midnight till dawn I lay in my bed consumed by emotions of sorrow and fear. There seemed one strong young figure standing up against long, dismal, drawling tides of drift and surrender, of wrong measurements and feeble impulses. My conduct of affairs would have been different from his in various ways; but he seemed to me at this moment to embody the life-hope of the British nation, the grand old British race that had done so much for men, and yet had some more to give. Now he was gone. I watched the daylight slowly creep in through the window, and saw before me in mental gaze the vision of Death.*

* Churchill, *The Gathering Storm*, p. 257.

War, 1938–40

Eden's resignation was a major national and international event, greeted with dismay in France and most of Europe, alarmed admiration in the United States, where not only President Roosevelt was looking anxiously at the European cauldron and Japanese expansionism, and much delight in Germany and Italy, although the Italian press under orders played the matter down so as not to make Eden an anti-Fascist hero. But, as Ciano happily noted, there was great satisfaction, much cheering, and many toasts were drunk.

In Britain, the Rothermere and Beaverbrook newspapers, and *The Times* and the *Daily Telegraph* were staunchly pro-Chamberlain, and, well briefed by Downing Street, made much of the fact that there would be no fundamental changes in foreign policy. There was a general welcome for Halifax as Eden's successor.* Only the *News Chronicle*, the *Daily Herald* and the ever-loyal *Yorkshire Post* took Eden's side, although even they were mystified about exactly why he had resigned.

But if the press reaction was mixed, the public response was extraordinary, and revealed how far, even at this stage, Chamberlain was misjudging the national mood. It was certainly not warlike, but British repugnance at the methods and successes of the dictators was beginning to grow. The cheering crowds outside Eden's house in Fitzhardinge Street were evidence that a significant number of people had had enough of humiliation at the hands of men who they realized to be brutal and evil. Eden, by his manifest integrity and his years of working, albeit vainly, for an ordered and reasonable world, had touched a particular chord. Eden had never been perceived as 'yet another politician', but as something different, and welcome. His enemies put it down to his good looks and bland speeches and unfair 'glamour', the epithets 'vain' and 'indecisive' being freely employed. The British people sensed something much better, honourable and brave. In this they were right. Cadogan, who had agreed with Eden over the Roosevelt Initiative, but not over the Italian negotiations, wrote to him:

---

* His Under-Secretary was R. A. Butler, who had made his reputation at the India Office since 1932.

You have had the most awful time any man could have. I think you had to take a decision on one of the most difficult questions with which any man could have been faced. It was a problem beyond my powers (and my distress at your leaving is increased by the fact that I haven't been able to help you) but I am convinced that you have done right because you have remained true to *yourself*. And you need never be ashamed of that. Nor, I think, will you regret it.

Personally, your going is a frightful wrench for me; as I hope you know what it meant to work for you. I owe you more than I can repay. You know that everyone in the office who worked with you was devoted to you, but that none was as much as myself in your debt.

Other letters of congratulation poured in from a very wide range of people, including rather surprisingly, the Archbishop of Canterbury, the dying Countess of Warwick, Gilbert Murray, his Australian friend Robert Menzies, and the artists Paul Maze and Muirhead Bone, from colleagues and from unknown citizens. In the first few days after his resignation Eden received over six thousand letters, and if there were any disapproving his decision they have not survived. Brendan Bracken wrote, 'The qualifications of a leader worth following must be courage, knowledge & resolution. You have shown all.' Attlee, in a particularly charming letter, thanked Eden 'for your unfailing courtesy to me during your tenure of the Foreign Office', and 'Jelly' Churchill, in retirement from Eton, wrote to say how proud he was of his former pupil. Perhaps most touching of all are the letters from Foreign Office officials, many of them quite junior at the time but destined to be eminent later, expressing their admiration and gratitude for his service as Foreign Secretary. Some obviously found it difficult to decide how to address him; some, defiantly, addressed him as 'My dear Secretary of State', making it plain that this was not accidental, and several ventured, with suitable apologies, to call him 'My dear Anthony', which moved and pleased Eden very much.

There was much excited speculation that he could bring the Government down. Tim, who before the resignation had urged him to 'stick to your guns' as the country 'will not stand that slimy, slithering brute Hoare for long. It is time these nonconformists, Parsons and old dodderers were put in their place', now wrote to express the hope that his brother 'will not be "gentlemanly" or anything tiresome of that sort'. Similarly Lloyd George urged him 'not to be too good a boy'.

This was also the advice of Churchill:

My dear Anthony,
Forgive me for intruding upon your immediate preoccupations. It seems to me vital that you should not allow your personal feelings of friendship to your late colleagues to hamper you in doing full justice to your cause, and above all you should not say anything that fetters your action in the future. You owe this not

only to yourself – which you no doubt feel the least part of this matter – but to your cause which is also the cause of England.

Yours ever,
Winston S. Churchill

Alle Zoll Recht Kommen!

This was echoed by many others, exultant at the emergence of a new national leader, in itself a remarkable commentary on disillusionment with the Chamberlain Government. But there were also close friends who urged him to be restrained and cautious, and not to widen his differences with the Government, several of them – very tactlessly – reminding him how quickly Hoare had returned to the Cabinet.

The scale of the public support Eden received surprised him considerably, but his own judgement and temperament led him to the 'cautious' rather than the 'attacking' course, whereas Cranborne's character took him to the latter. Thus, when they spoke in a packed House on 21 February, although Eden's speech was firm and good, Cranborne's was fiery. Eden could only refer obliquely to the crucial Roosevelt Initiative, and although he spelt out the fundamental differences in outlook and attitude between himself and Chamberlain that had caused the rift, it is one of those occasions when a speech reads better than it clearly sounded at the time.

He gave undue prominence to the questions of whether discussions with Mussolini should be opened before the ground had been prepared and before anti-British propaganda had ended, rather than on the issue of courting dictatorships which had demonstrated a total contempt for international agreements. He did say that 'We are in the presence of the progressive deterioration of respect for international obligations', but then said, 'In the light – my judgement may well be wrong – of the present international situation this is a moment for this country to stand firm.' The hint of uncertainty in that judgement was unfortunate and Tim was among those who were disappointed. What had happened, as Eden explained to Tim, was that in the tension of the moment, and trying not to read directly from his notes, a stronger qualifying passage had been omitted while he was on his feet. As Eden always suffered acutely from nerves while speaking in the Commons, and this was an especially tense occasion, this was very understandable. His decision not to reveal the crucial features of the Roosevelt Initiative was honourable, but of course left out one of the key elements in his rift with Chamberlain.

Harold Nicolson, who wrote at the time to his wife of the scene in the House that 'Those who have toadied and grovelled to Anthony all these years just kept silent', thought that Eden did not get the balance right; others were mystified as to what it had all been about, and it was left to

Cranborne to spell out, with some bitterness, the principles at stake. Ministers were relieved, Eden's friends and the Opposition were frankly disappointed. Channon, who had not heard the speeches, considered that Eden would not attack the Government very strongly, 'firstly because he is a gentleman, and secondly because he is too shrewd a statesman to burn his boats irretrievably'.*

Chamberlain's reply was simple, but revealing.

> The peace of Europe depends upon the four major Powers – Germany, Italy, France and ourselves.... If we can bring these four nations into friendly discussion, into a settling of their difficulties, we shall have saved the peace of Europe for a generation.... We must not delude ourselves. We must not try to delude small and weak nations into thinking that they will be protected by the League against aggression.

What Eden did establish, in a dramatic intervention in Chamberlain's speech, was that the Prime Minister was privy to information from the Italian Government through Grandi that was not available to the Foreign Secretary and Cabinet. The implications were clear, but Chamberlain evaded the issue by stretching the truth to its limits – and beyond. Eden, still unaware of the extent of Chamberlain's deviousness, did not press the point, and Chamberlain escaped.

Eden wrote to Tim:

> I got a very large measure of support from our benches and made our Party think, which was my main aim. Winston will be able to do the polemical stuff today better than I.... I am very unhappy at this time. Whatever one does is liable to be misunderstood and misinterpreted, and the real difficulty is that Chamberlain is absolutely open and sincere in everything he does, which only makes his naivete all the more dangerous. Winston is on the right lines in this matter, but he is desperately mistrusted by the Party. His attitude during the Abdication, for instance, did him much harm. All the same there are some good men among our own people, and we will do our best to spread the education.

Eden, at the time and later, strongly resented and disputed the whispers from ministerial sources, particularly from John Simon, that he was exhausted and overwrought. But the fact was that his friends and officials had been worried for some time about the effects on him of overwork, and one of the reasons many of his friends welcomed his resignation was for this cause, while recognizing that it was not, as his detractors averred, a major factor.

He had been in ministerial office for six-and-a-half years. This had involved a considerable amount of travelling and responsibility, and – more

---

* R. Rhodes James, *Chips, The Diaries of Sir Henry Channon*, p. 147.

important – he felt things deeply, was exceptionally conscientious and lacked the solace of a happy marriage. But his health was good, and although tiredness occasioned irascibility, it did not cloud judgement.

Eden saw the King on 22 February to surrender his Seals of Office, and was genuinely surprised when the Private Secretary, Sir Alexander Hardinge, told him that, having been privy to the telegrams and minutes, 'I should like to tell you that in my judgement you are right in all points', while the King told him that he had sympathy for his point of view and did not think it would be long before he saw him again as one of his senior ministers.

This was a very widely held opinion, but not one shared by Eden himself. He had no illusions about the gravity of what he had done and noted how quickly old 'friends' now avoided him in the House of Commons; he was somewhat embarrassed by some of his new admirers, particularly when a Communist faction tried to storm the Palace of Westminster to demand his reinstatement. Nor would he respond to invitations to join any group of MPs hostile to the Government. He was much more tired than he was prepared to admit then or later, and accepted Beatrice's urgings to have a holiday abroad. She knew better than anyone what resignation had cost her husband, and the effects of the emotional strain involved. There was also the financial cost of losing Office, which was a severe one, but which neither had considered should play any part in the decision.

The Commons debate went only reasonably well for the Government, and Chamberlain's final speech, in which he in effect buried the League of Nations as a useful element, played some part in causing over fifty Conservatives to abstain, the first real indication of the storm to come. Eden then made a bold move. He told his agent to book the biggest hall in Leamington, which was the public baths, and instructed that it should be a completely open meeting, not a Conservative one. Eden asked the President of his Association, Spencer Flower, to return from the South of France to take the chair, without knowing what his views were. Eden also asked for a vote of confidence, which understandably alarmed his agent even more.

When the Edens arrived, the crowd was estimated by reporters at some four thousand in the streets and one thousand in the main hall, with an overflow meeting of five hundred; there was a marked preponderance of young people. Flower, who arrived only just in time to take the meeting, made a strong unequivocal speech of support, which was tumultuously applauded, and Eden realized the mood of the audience. His own speech was long, and he denounced the allegation that he was a sick man. He stood by his decision to resign, and the need for fulfilment of international agreements and to stand firm. Oddly, it does not read as well as his

Commons speech, but here the response was totally different. The vote of confidence was carried by acclamation; the audience in the hall and in the overflow meeting rose to him. Years later he was to write: 'This was the most splendid tribute I have received in my public life.'

Eden's friends were not so fortunate. Cranborne found himself in deep trouble in South Dorset:

All my prominent supporters are furious, my executive have asked to see me, and I get the general impression that, at one or all of a number of meetings that I have next week, I am likely to be stoned. It shows how wise you were to be moderate. I merely let you know this in order that you may realize how strong feeling still is.

Jim Thomas was also in trouble: 'What a nuisance about your constituents,' Cranborne wrote to him with fellow-feeling. 'Really, I am fed up with the Tory machine, which becomes both more shortsighted and wrongheaded. My people seem quiet for the moment, except for an occasional snarl.'

In spite of the vote of confidence, Neville Chamberlain was very relieved when he read Eden's speech, writing to him that 'the dignity and restraint of your speech must add further to your reputation. I won't say more now than my personal feelings towards you are unchanged and I hope will always remain so.' At the time, Eden was rather touched by this letter. Later, when he knew more, his feelings were very different. It was not in his nature to personalize what he regarded as an honest difference of opinion on a major matter of policy, nor to widen these differences. In this, he differed greatly from other critics of the Government. Labour and the Liberals, who had writhed so long under Chamberlain's sneering contempt and condescensions, truly hated him, and he had made serious personal enemies on the Conservative benches. The Whips' Office, run by David Margesson, put a wholly excessive premium on loyalty, and the Deputy Whip, James Stuart – who has been well described as 'an intelligent reactionary' – was a bad influence, and no friend of Eden's. Chamberlain demanded blind and total support, and any deviation was taken personally. Margesson was a much better man than his enemies have averred, but the job of the Government Chief Whip includes that of reflecting the desires and prejudices of the Prime Minister, and this he did.

Thus, one of the most third-rate of modern British Governments was deliberately devoid of talent, intellect and independence, while on the back benches men of far greater ability viewed it, and its autocratic leader, with increasing distaste which in many cases became personal detestation of the Prime Minister himself. Brendan Bracken called him 'The Undertaker'. There were other, and even harsher, epithets, not least from Jim Thomas and Cranborne, while Churchill's immensely formidable fires smouldered.

But Eden, rightly or wrongly, could not or did not see the situation in this light. He had lost faith in Chamberlain's judgement, but did not propose to personalize issues of such gravity.

The Conservative parliamentary opposition to the Government's foreign policy, now gathering force, lacked unity or leadership. Churchill was widely regarded as, in Beaverbrook's phrase, 'a busted flush'; his personal following consisted only of his son-in-law Duncan Sandys, Brendan Bracken and Robert Boothby, and his own star was in the descendant after his Abdication débâcle. Leo Amery also seemed to belong to another era, and his speeches were notoriously dull and prolix. And when the younger Conservatives – originally known to the Whips as 'The Insurgents' and then as 'The Glamour Boys' – looked to Eden for anti-Government leadership, they found that Eden and his group were, at least initially, an acute disappointment.

Eden decided that he would not join, let alone lead, any anti-Government faction. He would keep his own counsel, and do what he thought best. There were those, like Thomas and Cranborne, who understood why he chose to take this course, and especially agreed that he should keep away from Churchill, but others did not. Eden himself was very much aware of this attitude, amounting in some cases almost to disillusionment, but he decided to wait upon events. He did not accept – nor did he welcome – the inevitability of war. He believed and argued that war *could* be avoided with firmness towards the dictators, greatly increased military strength, strong alliances and national unity. It was because of the latter factor that he refused to join Amery in his campaign for immediate military conscription, judging that it would arouse inevitable Labour hostility at a time when the Labour leadership and those Conservatives who felt as Eden did were coming together in their assessment of the capacity and resolution of the Government. It was a deliberate decision, in which self-interest was not involved; it certainly deeply disappointed many potential supporters, who put down to weakness of character or to personal ambition what was in fact the result of more complex calculations and concerns. But the result was that Ministers decided they had little to fear from him, and his personal position in Parliament and outside slipped.

In September 1941, when Churchill was Prime Minister, Eden Foreign Secretary again, and Beaverbrook, no longer an enemy but a Cabinet colleague and – although variable – a friend, Churchill took the two out to dinner at the Ritz. They dined on oysters and partridge, with champagne. There was much talk about the past, and then Beaverbrook, as Eden recorded in his diary,

girded at me for not understanding my strength when I resigned. He said that had I played my hand strongly I must have succeeded Neville. . . . My own feeling about it all was that I do not normally believe my own contribution at any time to be so overwhelmingly good as to be prepared to drive it *à outrance*. A fault in a politician, no doubt. I thought, as I listened to Winston and Max revelling at every move in their old games and even Winston, for all his greatness, so regarding it all, that I truly hate the 'game' of politics, not because I am better than these, God forbid, but because I lack the 'Spunk'.

This was the truth, simply and honestly expressed. There was no element of self-advancement in Eden's actions. But there was also the factor that the Conservative Party was not his spiritual home, nor was the House of Commons.

'He hates the old Tories and would rather join the Labour party if they remained dominant,' Oliver Harvey recorded of a conversation with Eden in 1941. Churchill's distaste for the Tories was probably even greater, but his undimmed personal ambition and detestation of Socialism and most Socialists were elements that Eden lacked. A particularly shrewd observer, Harold Macmillan, who knew Churchill and Eden so well, has remarked that both were aristocrats, but Churchill's American grandfather Leonard Jerome, a highly successful and ruthless operator, had given to Churchill a gambler's instinct and hardness that Eden lacked. Also, politics had been Churchill's whole life, and 'the great game' fascinated him, while it repelled Eden. If Eden was the nicer man – and often the wiser — Churchill was unquestionably the stronger. He saw war as virtually inevitable and was vehemently opposed to the Government; Eden thought that it was still preventable. While he disliked the Government, to the point of contempt, he would not be part of anti-Government cabal.

Another major obstacle to Eden working closely with Churchill at this time was that he still did not really know him very well or wholly trust his judgement. His early detestation of him from a distance has been recorded, but although this attitude had changed very considerably on closer acquaintance they had never become very intimate, either politically or socially. Eden had taken Baldwin's side against Churchill over India, and had been so absorbed with foreign affairs matters that while Churchill was beginning to launch his heroic campaign for rearmament Eden, while very supportive, had been engaged in his own concerns. When Eden became Foreign Secretary Churchill had written to his wife, 'I think you will now see what a lightweight Eden is', but he had changed his mind considerably, long before Eden's resignation. Eden had also changed his views of Churchill, but on both sides reservations remained. Also, while Churchill – with a few surprising waverings – was emphatic on Hitler and the German peril, he was considerably more sympathetic to Mussolini and Franco than Eden was, and had been notably sceptical about making an issue of Abyssinia. Their correspondence was not very great, although it was friendly. Churchill sent him copies of his biography of Marlborough as each volume appeared, which Eden greatly appreciated; they met relatively infrequently, and, in addition to the considerable difference in age, had very little in common except politically – and not always there did they agree. In 1961 Eden wrote in a private note:

Winston – character and tastes. No interest in nature or painting except his own and Daubigny because he had copied him, literature except history, Shakespeare except the wars. Hugh Cecil: 'Winston, you only became interested in the League when you thought it might lead to war.' Never seen Twelfth Night until his retirement. Not interested in fiction – nor poetry except Lays of Ancient Rome.

Far more important than these relatively trivial differences of taste and pleasure was that Eden had carved out his own career and was his own man with his own following, whereas Churchill had a very possessive attitude towards his supporters and friends. 'He demanded', as Violet Bonham Carter, who knew Churchill well, has written, 'partisanship from a friend, or, at the worst, acquiescence.' His egocentricity, which was to prove his salvation, was not attractive to everybody, and to many was positively repellent. Eden was never repelled, after he had come to know Churchill, but he regarded him uneasily. For his part, Churchill had come to admire Eden far more than Eden had realized, but the fact that he ended his few letters to him at this time 'Winston S. Churchill' says much about their relationship at this stage. To describe Eden's relationship with Churchill as 'filial' was absurd at any point, and especially in 1938. It could more accurately be applied to Eden's relation with Baldwin, with whom he had always been in close sympathy, and with whom he kept in close touch until Baldwin's death. Churchill, on the other hand, came to regard Baldwin as the author of his country's decline and – more justly – as being responsible for his own decade in the political wilderness.

Churchill was to deal especially harshly with Baldwin – far more so than with Chamberlain – in his memoirs, whereas Eden wrote in his diary on 15 October 1941 after dinner with Baldwin that 'I believe history will treat him more kindly than his contemporaries now do. He did much to kill class hatred and to unite the country. He did not understand the storms that raged without, but nor did he make Neville's mistake of believing that he did.' This remained Eden's view throughout his life. Churchill's highest tribute was to describe Baldwin as 'the greatest Party manager the Conservative Party has ever had', which, given Churchill's low opinion both of the Conservative Party and of its managers was the most insulting comment he could muster. Eden's verdict has stood the test of time better. There was also some significance in the fact that whereas Eden had greatly admired Asquith, Churchill had come to feel something very close to bitterness over the way Asquith had treated him in 1915, an emotion to which he gave eloquent expression.

Thus, in temperament, interests, background and in age – twenty-three years – Eden and Churchill were far apart in 1938; they were not a natural combination. Yet Eden felt that one of the great surprises of his life was how, after he had come to know Churchill really well after 1939, he found that they had an extraordinary telepathy. Each seemed to know instinctively what the other was thinking or about to say, and they were usually of the same mind – although not always coming to the same conclusion – even when separated and physically far distant. But it had not manifested itself yet, and although their perceptions of the looming disaster began to coincide in 1938, Churchill and Eden were far from being – or seeing themselves – as natural allies, or even particularly close friends. Only gradually did their destinies merge.

Immediately after the post-resignation debate Eden resumed his interrupted holiday in the south of France, he and Beatrice staying with Marjorie in her villa at Cap Ferrat. Churchill was also on the Riviera, and one evening they joined forces in the Cannes Casino, a more Churchillian than Edenesque expedition. By backing Number 17 at roulette they were highly successful: in one of the darkest moments of 1940, with everything going wrong, Churchill suddenly looked at Eden and remarked, 'About time Number 17 turned up, isn't it?' It was while Eden was 'reading the French newspapers and listening to the Vienna wireless that one day when I tuned in, I heard Hitler's entry into Linz, the hypnotized chants of the crowd, "*Ein Volk, ein Reich, ein Führer*", and Hitler's frenzied speech proclaiming the *Anschluss*'.

Here was another bloodless coup, clearly heralded with warnings of which the British Government had taken little note. On the very day of Eden's resignation Hitler had openly told the Reichstag of his demand for more territories on Germany's border, where over ten million Germans lived. The reference to Austria and Czechoslovakia could not have been more plain. Schuschnigg had announced on 9 March that an immediate plebiscite on Austrian independence would be held; the Nazi response to this brave stroke was an ultimatum to him to call the plebiscite off or be invaded. Schuschnigg offered to resign and postpone the plebiscite, but to no avail. Hitler personally rode in triumph into Vienna – itself, it must be remarked, an act of physical courage – and Austria's existence as an independent nation ended within hours.

Behind the German Army came the Gestapo, the anti-Jewish pogroms and the concentration camps. Schuschnigg was imprisoned, with many thousands of others. The iron hand fell, with a brutality that was to become all too familiar elsewhere. From Berlin, Henderson blamed Schuschnigg's 'ill-conceived and ill-prepared folly' for this unfortunate event. London accepted the situation, Chamberlain lamenting in his diary that all this unpleasantness might have been avoided 'if I had had Halifax at the Foreign Office instead of Anthony'. The eager pursuit of the conversations with Mussolini cont:nued; French alarm at the greatly endangered situation of the Czechs received a cool and patient response, but no commitment. Much credence was given to German assurances that they had no designs on Czechoslovakia; far too much was given to the alleged miseries of the Sudeten Germans. Even Cadogan wrote in his diary on 18 March 'F[oreign] P[olicy] C[ommittee] unanimous that Czechoslovakia is not worth the bones of a single British Grenadier. And they're quite right too!'* A version of appeasement wholly different to the one Eden had expressed two years earlier was now in favour, and gathered its dismal momentum.

The appeasement of Mussolini was another major step down this shameful path. Chamberlain and Halifax conceded *de jure* recognition of the rape of Abyssinia, in return for which Mussolini graciously promised to withdraw his troops from Spain *after* the Civil War. This Anglo–Italian Agreement was hailed in London as a mighty achievement; in private, the Italians were understandably derisive.

One of the most unfair calumnies against Eden, at this time and after, was that, because his principal concern was to return to the Government, he muted his criticisms. In fact, as he told Arthur Mann, he had lost all confidence in Chamberlain as a national leader, and considered the Government, like the Prime Minister, third-rate and too party-orientated: he wrote that 'It would be impossible for me to return to play the part of the ostrich, or to cheer on a party warfare which I regard as stupid, if not criminal, at this time.' Speaking to the Society of St George on 26 April, he emphasized 'the stupendous achievements' of the dictator states, and said, 'If we are to uphold our ideals, our conception of life, both national and international, if we are to see them prevail, then a comparable effort must be made by us, and an equal spirit be raised. Can any of us say that this is true of our country today?' To Mann and Churchill, whom he was now seeing regularly, he was speaking and writing about the formation of a National Party and a National Government, so deep was his disillusionment with the Conservative Party under Chamberlain. He wrote to Mann:

If we are to live, other than on sufferance, in the next few years a united national effort is called for on a scale comparable to that being put forth by the dictator countries. For this a national leader is called for. Neville Chamberlain has none of the necessary attributes. He is essentially a party man.

---

* Dilks (ed.), *The Diaries of Sir Alexander Cadogan, 1938–45*, p. 63.

In May a crisis arose over the Sudeten but faded deceptively, principally as a result of unexpected French vigour in their warnings, although it was also evidence of German military unpreparedness. Addressing his constituents immediately afterwards Eden declared:

Nobody will quarrel with the Government's wish to bring about appeasement in Europe. Any other intention would be as foolish as it would be wrong. But if appeasement is to mean what it says, it must not be at the expense either of our vital interests, or of our national reputation or our sense of fair dealing. Appeasement will be neither real nor lasting at such a price. It would merely make real appeasement more difficult at a later stage. There must always be a point at which we, as a nation, must make a stand and we must clearly make a stand when not to do so would forfeit our self-respect and the respect of others.

Eden saw much of Baldwin at this time. Baldwin warned him against getting too close to Churchill, as he would be perceived as a follower rather than a leader, to keep his own counsel, to bide his time, and to take his case to the country. Eden took this advice. Chamberlain on one occasion in May did strongly hint to him that he could rejoin the Government – suggesting the Admiralty – when the Anglo–Italian Agreement came into effective force. Eden merely responded that it would be better to wait on events. From that time until 3 September 1939 he had no further conversations with Chamberlain.

Eden's speeches in the country, contrary to the claims of his detractors then and later, became stronger.

You may gain temporary appeasement by a policy of concession to violence, but you do not gain lasting peace that way. It is a grave delusion to suppose that you can. Even more untrue is it to suggest that those who would have wished our country to have taken a firmer stand in the last six months on behalf of the principle of good faith in international relations would thereby have plunged this country into war. The very reverse is the truth.

But his appearances in the Commons were deliberately rare, and he watched events with much concern from a distance. One does not have to accept the criticisms of more vehement opponents of government policies that Eden was inactive to wish there had been more speeches of this kind, particularly in Parliament, even though their message was not overwhelmingly popular. Eden's acceptance of Baldwin's advice was perhaps taken too much to heart. But he could subsequently reflect that, in his public warnings on the crucial importance of supporting the French on Czechoslovakia and not trusting Mussolini or Hitler, he was proved to have been abundantly right.

But Eden underestimated his personal position. He calculated that not more than thirty Conservative MPs were hostile to the Government's foreign policy, and deduced from this that a campaign in Parliament was not practical politics; so he went to the country. As always, there were moments of self-doubt and a lack of self-confidence, although Lady Violet Bonham Carter's accusations of 'implacable fairness' and 'tepid impartiality' were inaccurate and unfair. He also hoped, and urged, that the British Government would actually do what it had unexpectedly said it would in May, that is to support the French over Czechoslovakia, and thereby inhibit Hitler's immediate ambitions. He knew all too well the state of British rearmament, which was not assisted when a disastrous failure in the Commons by the junior Air Minister, Lord Winterton, on 12 May allowed Chamberlain to seize the chance to dismiss Swinton. It was Swinton who had been responsible for ordering the Spitfire and Hurricane fighters into production on prototype evidence, for developing Radio Directing Finding (Radar), for constructing the 'shadow factories' which could be converted to aircraft production in time of war, and for ensuring a dramatic increase in pilot recruitment and training. He had many faults, but for these crucial decisions he should be remembered as one of the saviours of our nation. Had there been greater urgency and support, the British position would not have been so parlous. Now he was gone, and the pliant Kingsley Wood took his place; one of his first actions, at the behest of Lord Nuffield, was to cut down the shadow-factory programme.

If Eden exaggerated the military disparity in 1938 between Britain and France on the one hand and Germany and Italy on the other, he was not alone in this; Churchill's fearful warnings had convinced many others that Britain was in no condition to fight at that point. Calling for warlike policies without the means to carry them out may make good rhetoric and good subsequent reading; in Eden's view it was cruelly irresponsible. His memories of 1915 had taught him that lesson.

The fundamental problem with Chamberlain's foreign policy was that it was not, as Churchill alleged, irresolute but that it was immensely resolute. As Cadogan later wrote, Chamberlain had

an almost instinctive contempt for the Americans and what amounted to a hatred of the Russians ... another possible drawback was that he was, in a sense, a man of one-track mind. If, after much reflection no doubt, he decided on a certain move or line of policy, nothing would affect him.

Old-fashioned diplomacy and collective security were now considered as obsolete as the Anthony Eden Hat. Chamberlain was immensely pleased with the Anglo-Italian Agreement, while Ciano was noting (22 June) that Mussolini 'absolutely refuses to compromise – we shall not modify our policy towards Franco in the slightest degree and the agreement with

London will come into force when God pleases. If indeed it ever will.'
Mussolini sent another two thousand troops to Spain in June, and another
two thousand 'volunteers' in July, while arrogantly denouncing London for
having reneged on the Agreement. Chamberlain lamented that 'Mussolini is
behaving just like a spoilt child, and it is difficult to know how to deal with
him': as Eden had warned, the more Mussolini asked for, the more he got,
and the greater became his demands. He was not a spoilt child, merely an
avaricious and now overweeningly self-confident and cynical brigand.
Chamberlain considered that Spain was not worth risking difficulties over,
as it would jeopardize what he modestly described as his 'great influence'
on the Continent. Chamberlain was not an ignoble or unlikeable man, but
it was a supreme national and European catastrophe that he, Halifax and
Horace Wilson, applauded from Berlin by Nevile Henderson, should have
been in the positions they held in 1938–9. If rearmament had been pushed
vigorously and urgently, and vital alliances strengthened simultaneously
with dialogue with the dictators, there might have been more justification
for appeasement. But they were not.

Although Eden had decided that he could never serve in a Chamberlain
Government – and almost certainly never again in a Conservative Government – he did not fully appreciate the fanatical, quasi-religious zeal that
Chamberlainite appeasement had assumed since his resignation. The Foreign Policy Committee was in effect abolished – it did not meet between
16 June and the end of September – and foreign policy was in the hands
of Chamberlain, Halifax, Simon, Hoare, Wilson and Henderson, the last
of whom had cancer. With the exception of Halifax, Eden had no friends
in that regime. Nor did the Czechs.

Meanwhile, as Berlin reiterated, echoed by the egregious Henderson, the
only block to satisfactory relations between France, Britain and Germany
was the issue of the allegedly oppressed Sudeten Germans, whose spokesman Konrad Henlein was so persuasive that even Churchill was briefly
deceived by him when he visited London. Ministers became convinced by
the elaborate fictions of Sudeten exploitation by the harsh Czechs, described
by Nevile Henderson as this 'pig-headed race' led by Beneš, 'not the least
pigheaded among them'. Mentally, if not formally, the Cabinet's inner
group had decided by June to sacrifice Czechoslovakia, to meet what they
now regarded as the absolutely justified complaints of Hitler and Henlein.
The fact that the Sudeten Germans, who had heard something about what
was going on in Austria, had no desire for Nazi rule was not a factor. Once
again, a plebiscite might be embarrassing.

Eden's private endeavours to persuade the Government to impress upon
the Germans the inevitability of British involvement if France went to war

over Czechoslovakia were received politely by Halifax, but formed no part of British policy, while the new French leadership of Édouard Daladier and Georges Bonnet also lacked resolution. The attitudes of Nevile Henderson and *The Times* were dominated by the need to placate Germany. In a letter to *The Times* of 12 September Eden emphasized the dangers of lack of clarity and firmness in policies towards Germany. But the Government sent Lord Runciman to 'mediate' between the Czech Government and the Sudeten Germans. Hitler's threats became harsher. Then Chamberlain flew to Berchtesgaden on 13 September and the shadows deepened over Czechoslovakia; Eden's concerns increased, and Harvey found him 'miserable'.

Speaking in Warwick on 23 September he said that 'continued retreat can only lead to ever-widening confusion. The British people know that a stand must be made. They pray that it be not made too late.' But Chamberlain had gone to Godesberg, returning on the 24th with even stronger German demands, which now included military occupation of a far larger area than Sudetenland, and which Chamberlain conveyed to the Czechs. 'I was completely horrified,' Cadogan wrote; '– he [Chamberlain] was quite calmly for surrender. More horrified still to find that Hitler has evidently hypnotized him to a point. Still more horrified to find P.M. has hypnotized H[alifax] who capitulates totally.' As Cadogan had always been dismissive of Vansittart's anti-Germanism, was not pro-Czech and was fearful of war, this was a particularly significant reaction, and one in which he was not alone. This was a straightforward ultimatum, and when the terms became known there was so strong a revulsion – which Eden vehemently shared and conveyed to Halifax – that the Government stepped back. On his own initiative Duff Cooper mobilized the Fleet, as Eden had been urging.

War suddenly seemed imminent. There were startling evidences of air-raid trenches being dug in London parks, the distribution of gas-masks, and hastening plans for the evacuation of children from the capital. The crisis was wholly unexpected to the bulk of the population, and national morale was certainly not heightened by a lugubrious broadcast by Chamberlain on 27 September that was markedly egotistical and referred to 'a quarrel in a far-away country between people of whom we know nothing'. Phipps reported defeatism and anti-war feeling in France. What was not known was that Chamberlain was proposing more conversations with Hitler and Mussolini.

On the next day, in a tense House of Commons expecting a firm statement of support for Czechoslovakia and France, Chamberlain ended his speech dramatically. Having himself only just been informed, he announced that Hitler had just told him that he had delayed his mobilization and would meet with him, Mussolini and Daladier at Munich. There were wild scenes of relief and jubilation, Members leaping to their feet to cheer and wave order papers. Eden, Churchill, Amery and Harold Nicolson were among the very few who remained seated.*

Chamberlain flew to Munich in a blur of excitement and self-satisfaction. He virtually ignored Daladier, and the squalid business of the destruction of Czechoslovakia did not take long.

The German occupation of their desired territories – including the vital Skoda munition factories – would be spread over ten days, and the 'new' Czechoslovakia would be guaranteed by the Powers. On the following morning Chamberlain offered Hitler a brief document stating that the agreement was symbolic of 'the desire of our two peoples never to go to war with one another again', which Hitler gladly signed. This was brought back to London in triumph, to frenzied applause and relief, as 'peace for our time'. That Chamberlain genuinely believed this is incontestable. When Halifax, who no longer shared Chamberlain's illusions, urged him to widen the base of his Government and bring in Churchill and Eden, the proposal was at once rejected.

Those who reacted against the national hysteria and ecstasy at Chamberlain's supposed triumph were few indeed. Duff Cooper was the only minister to resign, and experienced, as did other Munich rebels, much hostility from Conservative Associations. As Harold Macmillan later wrote, 'The tide was . . . too strong and it was flowing against us in the Conservative Party, Parliament, and the Press.' There was even wild talk of an immediate general election to capitalize on the Prime Minister's popularity. To stand against all this required courage.

In the Munich debate the opposition emerged on the Conservative benches. The most dramatic and powerful speech was from Churchill, who declared, to a hubbub of protest, that 'We have sustained a total and unmitigated defeat.' Duff Cooper's resignation speech – derided by *The Times* as 'a damp squib' – was a devastating indictment of the folly, and worse, of the betrayal of Czechoslovakia. And there was a speech by Richard Law, the son of Bonar Law, that some felt was the best of all. Eden was more cautious; he praised Chamberlain personally, although he made it clear that he would not support the Government, saying that 'Surely the

---

* Many years later Lady Violet Bonham Carter related an episode on 29 September when the anti-appeasement Focus Group resolved to send a telegram to Chamberlain urging no more concessions, which Eden, contacted by telephone, refused to sign. When he read this Eden was baffled, checked his records, including his diary for 29 September and consulted Cranborne. He had no recollection whatever of such a request and strongly denied it, as did Cranborne. As Lady Violet disliked Eden, and perpetuated the myth that Eden's actions were motivated by personal self-interest, and her account was written so much later, it should be approached with scepticism.

House will be agreed that foreign affairs cannot indefinitely be continued on the basis of "Stand and Deliver". Successive surrenders bring only successive humiliations, and they, in their turn, more humiliating demands.' He reiterated his concerns about rearmament. It was a well-argued and thoughtful speech, but there was disappointment that it had not been stronger. He, Churchill, Amery, Cranborne and Macmillan were among the thirty Conservatives who refused to support the Government at the end of the debate.

There were those who were even more disappointed in Eden's post-Munich caution. Vyvyan Adams courageously resigned his seat to fight an anti-Munich and anti-Government by-election (which he won) but his pleas for Eden to send him at the very least a message of support were ignored; Lord Davies, an ardent League of Nations champion, wrote to him to say that 'During the last few months I have met many people who are beginning to lose confidence in you. Your stock has fallen appreciably. I wish to God it wasn't so, but there it is.' When the master of Balliol, A. D. Lindsay, stood as the anti-Government candidate, with Labour and dissident Conservative support, at the Oxford by-election against Quintin Hogg, he also appealed to Eden to speak for him, or to send nim a message; this Eden also refused. In his defence, it would have been very remarkable for a former Foreign Secretary to go so far so soon after his resignation. Harold Macmillan, whose independence had involved resigning the Conservative Whip, supported by the young Edward Heath, campaigned for Lindsay, but his position was not the same as Eden's. Hogg won, in a strange beginning to an illustrious and remarkable political career, in which he was destined to serve in the Eden Government, and to be Eden's choice as Prime Minister in 1963.

What Eden was now deliberately setting out to do was to establish a new position by emphasis on domestic matters and the need for a National Government. Speaking in Southampton within a fortnight of Munich, he said:

Now, when the world outlook is dark, the nation is beginning to feel once again the need for unity, comradeship and a joint national effort such as animated us in the war years. It is one of the most encouraging features of an otherwise not very encouraging future. There is a real danger that matters may so drift that England may become a nation where one half does not know how the other half lives. That would be very bad. There is a natural tendency to get used to evils that have been long with us – unemployment, for example. We have to cling tight to our faith, to be clear what are those things we prize so highly that we will not let them go.

In the Commons on 10 November he repeated this message, saying that if we had to make great sacrifices to meet the challenge of the dictators, as we must, England must be a country worth fighting for, in which expenditure on munitions must be equalled by that on housing, while the iniquities of the distressed areas and 'an army of unemployed' must be met and resolved. 'How could the national unity be realized unless made on behalf of an England that was free and united, an England of equal opportunity for all, regardless of class or creed, an England in which comradeship was the spirit of the nation, an England in which men refuse to rest content while poverty continues to be the lot of many?' Five days later the Eden Group tabled a motion demanding a more vigorous social policy and rearmament drive. The *Manchester Guardian* shrewdly remarked:

Mr Eden's campaign (for it is hardly less) is extremely significant. It is not cast in any party mould, and Mr Eden has no wish to change his party. It springs from the feeling that we have reached a point where the policy of the Government is an inadequate expression of the national will, and has lost the power to evoke a national response. If, as seems to be disastrously probable, Mr Chamberlain's dream of 'appeasement' by his present methods is cruelly dissolved, the country will not be without an alternative working faith which transcends our ineffectual party grouping.

The only thing wrong with this analysis was that Eden was seriously discussing with Cranborne, Amery and Thomas the possibility of not standing again as Conservatives; as will be seen, the proposal went a long way and was only interrupted by other events. He urged a National Government again upon Halifax on 11 October, and the mobilization of industry for rearmament; he found Halifax remarkably in agreement, but when he reported the conversation to Chamberlain the latter wrote that Eden 'leaves out, or chooses not to see for the moment, that the conciliatory part of the policy [towards Germany] is just as important as the rearming'. Hitler did not discourage these sentiments by stating in a speech on 9 October that if Eden or Churchill came to power 'we know quite well that it would be the aim of these men immediately to begin a new world war'. Five days later, at Cardiff, Eden said that British rearmament was still on a peacetime basis, whereas in the totalitarian states 'armaments are being piled up on a basis which we have hitherto only consented to adopt in time of war'. On 2 November he denounced the Anglo-Italian Agreement in the Commons. 'We are constantly giving, and they are constantly taking. I am reminded of the charity collectors in *The Hunting of the Snark*: they collect, but they do not subscribe.' When he denounced Nazi atrocities against Jews, of which hard and miserable evidence was now accumulating, he was further excoriated in the German press as being 'in association with the international conspiracy of Jews and Freemasons', his name again linked with that of Churchill.

There was then a surprising, but significant, brief interlude.

Eden had received an invitation to address the National Association of Manufacturers in New York, which he had refused, but on the urgings of the new American Ambassador in London, Joseph Kennedy, he was persuaded to accept. Eden made it clear that he was not prepared to denounce his own Government abroad. Indeed he had not uttered a denunciation even at a huge League of Nations rally in London, to the deep disappointment of his audience and his fellow speaker, Lady Violet Bonham Carter, who· subsequently said she felt like moving a Vote of Censure on Eden rather than a Vote of Thanks. But he told Kennedy he was prepared to speak on the international situation generally. This was agreed, and he, Beatrice, her half-brother Martyn and Lord Hinchingbrooke, acting as his secretary, sailed on the *Aquitania*.

The seas were terrible, and at one stage the captain told Eden that they would dock the day after his speech was due to be made, although he would make a special effort to arrive before that event. Meanwhile, Hinchingbrooke was coping with a deluge of cables from American institutions, universities, clubs and groups inviting Eden to address them. When they reached New York, Hinchingbrooke found even more cables, and a very large number of photographers and journalists. To their genuine surprise they found that Eden's name stood high in the United States, and although he only just got to the Manufacturers' Association dinner, and very late, his reception was overwhelmingly enthusiastic.

In his speech he spoke of 'the gathering storm', the perils of militarism and the precious importance of democracy in terms that caused even greater enthusiasm and applause, and that subjected Hinchingbrooke to more cables and letters of invitation, for Eden's speech was broadcast, and printed in full in the US Congressional Record. In Washington he was received by Sumner Welles and then by President Roosevelt. Their discussion was limited, but the gesture was not lost upon the American press. The sheer bulk of the press coverage of this very brief visit by a former British Foreign Secretary, who had been in the United States only once before, and that very briefly, was both extraordinary and important. The files on this visit are very substantial. When he sailed back to England, the *New York Times* wrote a glowing article entitled 'As a Friend Departs'.

Eden returned to find an inscribed copy of the fourth volume of Churchill's biography of Marlborough. In his letter of thanks Eden wrote that 'I only wish that I could pretend to find the news more cheerful. . . . I propose to dive into [the book] this very evening and seek to forget in its pages the haunting apprehensions of the present days.'

*   *   *

But appeasement had not run its course. Chamberlain and Halifax travelled to Rome, the former again manifesting his disdain for the French, from which the Italians drew the obvious conclusion. So did Eden. Speaking in Birmingham at the end of January at a large National Service rally he reiterated that force had become the sole factor in international politics and that it was perilous to live in a world of make-believe. But as Government – although not Foreign Office – Ministers repeatedly stressed, this was exactly their world; Hoare spoke of a new Golden Age of peace and well-being, and Chamberlain of a period of tranquillity in Europe. On 15 March Hitler's armies marched into Prague to complete the rape of Czechoslovakia.

Eden's policy of taking his case to the country rather than Parliament had impressed upon him the fact that the more strongly he spoke the greater was the applause and that the Munich euphoria had significantly faded. The invasion of Czechoslovakia definitely ended it. In a strong speech in the Commons on 16 March Eden pointed to the inescapable logic of the dictators' actions:

Is there any Member in any part of the House now who believes that after these events we shall have more than another brief respite, perhaps briefer than the last, before further demands are made, before another victim is arraigned and before that victim is again faced with the alternative of resistance or surrender?

But his call for collective co-operation by the democracies was dismissed scathingly by John Simon, who also denounced the principle of military commitments. The Eden Group was outraged, and now began to work more closely with Churchill. Collectively, they tabled a Commons motion calling for a National Government. Thirty-six Conservatives signed; the Government Whips organized a counter-motion supporting Chamberlain and strongly implying that Eden and his allies were trying to divide the nation. To such a stage had matters deteriorated. The members of the Eden Group were now talking of resigning the Whip and standing as Independent Conservatives. This may well have happened had not the Government abruptly changed course.

Having derided Continental commitments and abandoned them, the Government now hurriedly and unexpectedly announced an emphatic commitment to Poland. How such a commitment could be honoured militarily was not explained. On Good Friday Mussolini invaded Albania. The British made a mild protest. Hitler denounced and abrogated the Anglo-German Naval Agreement and the German-Polish Treaty and demanded Danzig. A limited measure of National Service was introduced by the British Government, but any possible impact this might have had was destroyed by the hard and lamentable opposition of the Labour and

Liberal Parties, who allowed their personal dislike for, and distrust of, Chamberlain to overcome their instinct for a more sensible approach. Even an admirer of Chamberlain, one of his Private Secretaries, John Colville, put his finger on the problem when he wrote in his diary that 'he suffers from a curious vanity and self-esteem which were born at Munich and have flourished, in spite of a good many wounds, ever since'.*

The Polish Commitment only made sense if it were matched with links with Russia. But Litvinov had gone, to be replaced by the dour Molotov, and Chamberlain viewed the possibility of an Anglo-Soviet Treaty with particular dislike. The sleep-walk continued. 'To hate war and to fear war is not the same thing,' Eden told a huge Paris audience early in May. 'No policy that is based upon fear, no policy that appeals to fear, is a policy that a great nation can follow and survive.' Chamberlainite appeasement has seldom been better described.

In these circumstances a somewhat unexpectedly glowing tribute to Eden came from Churchill in *The Strand* magazine; he described Eden as:

the only representative of the mutilated generation who has achieved a first-class political position and has held high and dominant office with significance and distinction.... This young, engaging figure, endowed with so much personal charm and agreeable manners, gathered a considerable influence of his own at Geneva in its fleeting hey-day.

Most interestingly, Churchill compared Eden with his own father, Lord Randolph, and with George Wyndham, both 'crushed' by the Tory Party machine, and commended

the strong fibre of his [Eden's] nature, and the resolute purpose of his mind. There is no one else of his age and experience who has a greater hold upon the sympathy and imagination of what may, in its widest sense, be called 'the liberal forces in England'.... It may well be that he will lead our country in days when leadership will even more be needed.

Since Eden still regarded Churchill with reservations – as Churchill well knew – this was very generous, but it was a widely held view. Eden himself, however, still did not see the way forward at all clearly. His diaries are, unhappily, very spasmodic at this stage, but to friends and to his family he gave a strong impression of believing that while war *could* still be prevented, if it came it would be on the worst possible terms; yet he was wholly unsure as to what part, if any, he was likely to play in it politically. As he later wrote:

I was not convinced what my own course should be. Even if asked to go back into the Government as it was at that time, I did not want to accept. I knew that my

* John Colville, *The Fringes of Power*, p. 117.

return would not be welcome to the Prime Minister and most of his senior colleagues; they would only tolerate it in response to public demand.*

His repeated calls for a truly National Government certainly had not helped his cause in the Conservative Party, and he was actively involved in his new preoccupation, the Territorial Army, which he had joined as a major in his old King's Royal Rifle Corps. Harold Nicolson, consistently depicting his own actions in a considerably more heroic light than they fully merited, wrote that Eden 'is missing every boat with exquisite elegance' – a somewhat hilarious comment from that source. But the reality was that the international and national political situations were remarkably confused, and Eden certainly was not the only person, in politics or out of them, who found the situation dark and perplexing. But, as his speeches and letters make absolutely plain, he had distinctly and publicly hardened against any further appeasement or concessions; this completely destroys the allegations of Nicolson and others, then and later, that 'Anthony wriggles and writhes.' 'To hate war and fear war is not the same thing' was a consistent theme of Eden's in public and in private, but he still hoped that, as he wrote to Arthur Mann at the end of July, 'If we can really make Germany believe that we will fight, then we may at long last be able to do something to prevent an outbreak of war.'

There were now several Conservatives opposed to Chamberlain who believed war to be inevitable, and some who actively wanted it. When Eden addressed a huge audience in Ealing on 1 July he noted that 'the tougher my words, the louder the cheering', but he continued to believe that if the British and French left the Germans with no doubt whatever that they would fight, war could still be averted. With all the great wisdom of hindsight, many commentators have derided this belief, but we now know that although Hitler remained absolutely committed to eastwards expansion and the subjugation of Poland he entered a period of uncertainty between April and August 1939. In a meeting with his senior military officers on 23 May he said that 'there must be no simultaneous conflict with the Western Powers' and spoke of a possible war with Britain with genuine apprehension as a life and death struggle, probably of long duration. 'Localizing' the war was his theme, and his objective. While he anticipated that war with Britain was probably inevitable, he did not want it at this stage.

As Eden had already seen, and repeatedly emphasized, the key was the Soviet Union, a point Hitler had already grasped but Chamberlain had not. In the Commons on 19 May Eden urged an alliance with Russia; at the beginning of June he offered to go to Moscow personally to negotiate

* Avon, *Facing the Dictators*, p. 61.

on behalf of the Government, and Halifax was not opposed. Chamberlain, while bowing very reluctantly to pressure, agreed to the dispatch of a delegation of officials led by William Strang that travelled *by sea* to Russia; but he would not permit Eden's involvement in a venture he regarded with distaste and scepticism. As Eden caustically commented in the House of Commons, 'These negotiations with Russia are always being forecast either in this country or in Paris as just about to finish but they never seem quite to reach their end. Indeed in this connection I am reminded of Rochefoucauld's definition of love and ghosts – everybody is always talking about it but nobody has ever seen it.'

Stalin was not slow to assess the signs, nor was Hitler. It is very probable that, at this stage, there was nothing the British could offer the Russians that could match what Ribbentrop (now Foreign Minister) had to offer – half of Poland and the Baltic states – but if Stalin and Hitler had been absolutely certain that the British would go to war over Poland it is just possible that they might have paused. Certainly, Hitler was wary, and Stalin's approach to all political and military matters raised cynicism to a high level; each, with good cause, hated and feared the other. As Alan Bullock has rightly written:

Hitler was now convinced that, if his approach to Moscow were to prove successful, he had hit upon the way of breaking the political deadlock, prising open the door barred by the British guarantee to Poland, and enforcing his will on the Poles without the risk of a general war.*

The tardy British and French Missions did not reach Moscow until 11 August, by which time the Russians had been persuaded by Ribbentrop. The increasingly anxious Italians were told to be quiet; Mussolini's belief that war could not be localized was brutally dismissed by Ribbentrop in a meeting with Ciano on 11 August at Salzburg, Ribbentrop saying that one of the two axioms of German policy was that 'the conflict will not become general'. Italian proposals for an international conference were contemptuously rejected; it was too late for such devices. In contrast, Stalin proposed stiff terms; Hitler eagerly accepted them. To his senior commanders on 22 August he said, with real conviction, that the chances of British and French intervention were slight. When the British, with totally unexpected resolve, reiterated their commitment to Poland in a strong letter from Chamberlain, which Henderson delivered on 23 August, Hitler went into an assumed rage – in fact he was more worried than he admitted. But by this stage it was all too late. The precise arrangements for the German invasion of Poland had been made; Ribbentrop and Stalin agreed

* Alan Bullock, *Hitler: A Study in Tyranny*, p. 475.

to the carve-up of Poland and the Baltic states on the 24th. On that day, speaking in the Commons, Eden warned that if there were

many people in Germany who believe that in the event of hostilities with Poland they may in a few short weeks or months obtain their military objectives in the East, and that, having seen that, they appear to believe that we should take no further interest in the matter ... they are making the greatest error in history.

But, even at this stage, Hitler was worried about the British reaction, and still attempted to neutralize Britain, so that he could have his 'localized war'. He offered a German guarantee for the British Empire, German assistance and a reasonable limitation of armaments, and said that he regarded Germany's western frontiers as final. It was all fraudulent, but it had a serious purpose; as Bullock has commented, it 'was a bribe in return for looking the other way while he strangled Poland'.* The British, while professing their willingness to come to an agreement, stood by their commitment to Poland, although in terms that certainly encouraged Göring and Hitler to believe that they could achieve their purpose. But this time Chamberlain, while still eager to avert war if at all possible, would not – and politically could not – make concessions that would betray the Poles. Yet, until he received the British ultimatum on 3 September, Hitler still thought that he could have his 'localized' war.

Eden now considered that war could not be indefinitely postponed, given the clear nature of Hitler's power and the use he intended to make of it, but he believed that it *could* be postponed temporarily if the British got close to the Russians and were unambiguous over Poland. Furthermore, his involvement in the Territorial Army reminded him too vividly of his experiences in 1915 of lack of equipment, arms and ammunition. He fully shared Churchill's alarm at the air balance. He differed from other Conservatives, the majority of whom believed that war could surely be averted, while the minority – and a very small one – now wanted it. Eden was a very solitary figure in instinctively feeling that, even at this late hour, resolution and alliance could at least delay war. We now know that his instinct was absolutely right, but he did not prevail.

Remarkable though it may now appear, in the midst of this relentless march towards war there was renewed and eager talk in the Conservative Party of a general election. One would have to occur before the late summer of 1940, and there were those who now argued that the autumn of 1939 would be a most propitious time. Eden wrote to Cranborne and Law on 12 August expressing his views:

I do not feel that I myself could, in these circumstances, support such an appeal [to the country]. There are, no doubt, many in the House and tens of thousands

---

* Bullock, *Hitler: A Study in Tyranny*, p. 489.

in the country, similarly placed. What then should our attitude be? Ought we to form a group of our own? Would we stand as Independent Conservatives? Would we seek to create a new party? What should our relations be with Winston?

Within three weeks these questions had been answered. Hitler invaded Poland on 1 September. Two days later Britain was at war.

The opening of the Second World War found Anthony Eden again at a military camp, as he had been at the beginning of the First, a most curious coincidence. Eden had been attached to the 2nd Battalion of the Sixtieth Rifles, which was part of the 1st (and only) Armoured Division. Once again, Eden experienced lack of equipment and training, only made up for by the fact that the men were enthusiastic and, he noted, much fitter and better fed than his young men of 1915. The fact that every man in his first detachment could swim, which would have been inconceivable in 1915, made the contrast even more marked to him. Not everything had gone wrong in the inter-war years. But when he spoke to the self-important and extravagantly publicity-conscious War Secretary, Leslie Hore-Belisha, about his division's inadequacies these were strongly denied; 'I continued my explanations, but he clearly had no patience with them and our interview ended badly,' Eden recorded. Given the explosive nature of both men, it is not hard to assess how badly it ended. On 1 September the Territorial Army was placed on active service, with Eden's battalion protecting key bridges.

Eden did not expect to be asked to join the Government, even after he heard that Chamberlain had been in touch with Churchill and that a reconstruction was in the offing, nor did he particularly want to. It would hardly be the National Government he had called for, but Churchill robustly told him his place was in the Government with him. It was also Churchill who directly asked Chamberlain if Eden was to be included, and was told that he would be.

But there was then an extraordinary hiatus, between 1 and 3 September with what seemed the real possibility of the Government reneging on the Poles. As these rumours swept Westminster, the mood became fierce and the position untenable until, late on the evening of 2 September in a ferocious thunderstorm that no one was to forget, the reluctant decision was taken to send a final ultimatum. Chamberlain's broadcast on the following morning announcing the outbreak of war was mournful, rather too egotistical for many, and utterly uninspiring. This time, there were no cheering crowds outside Buckingham Palace, and Churchill and Eden were still on the back benches, the former having heard nothing from Chamberlain, and Eden also completely in the dark as to the Prime Minister's intentions. In reality, the call for their reinstatement was loud and overwhelming, and in the circumstances could not be resisted. There was no pleasure on the side of the Conservative Establishment at their return, and there were those in the Whips' Office who resisted it to the end. But they had become the symbols of the end of appeasement, and on 3 September Churchill became First Lord of the Admiralty again, going back to the Office from which he had been dismissed in virtual ignominy in 1915; Anthony Eden, with some reluctance, agreed to become Dominions Secretary without a seat in the War Cabinet.

Eden had the advantage that he had travelled widely in the Empire and had met most of the principal personalities, and if the job was not quite the backwater he had feared he made little secret in his letters – particularly to Tim – and in his diaries of the fact that he was impatient and frustrated. One stroke of vital benefit was that South Africa, only narrowly, voted for participation in the war, Smuts returning to lead a new Government committed to belligerency, but under exceptionally difficult circumstances.

Eden's major contribution in the brief time he was in this Office was eagerly to accept the suggestion of Canada and Australia that their countries could best assist in the air: out of their discussion was born the Empire Air Training Scheme, which took tens of thousands of young Britons – including Simon Eden – and men from Australia and New Zealand to Canada, with similar programmes in Rhodesia and South Africa. At its peak the Canada schools were producing eleven thousand pilots and eighteen thousand aircrew a year, and the Rhodesian and South African pilots and aircrew were to be invaluable. Eden was less successful in persuading his colleagues to produce war aims, as the Dominions were seeking, but he took to France a group of five Dominion representatives, including Deneys Reitz of South Africa, whose classic book *Commando* about the Boer War, when he had served with Smuts, had been long admired by Eden.

Poland had been swiftly and cruelly ravaged, from the west by the Germans, from the east by the Russians. To special British fury, the Russians invaded Finland, to meet unexpectedly fierce resistance, but on the Western Front, nothing in particular happened. Fears of armadas of German bombers raining death on London did not materialize. German peace-feelers came out regularly and greedily, like a lizard's tongue. Only at sea, with the feared German submarines and pocket battleships at large, did it appear that there really was a war on. Dubbed 'the Phoney War' by an American journalist and 'the Twilight War' by Churchill, Eden and Reitz found the situation in France unreal and frightening, and reported back accordingly to Chamberlain. The heavily fortified Maginot Line was indeed impressive, but it ended at the Belgian border, leaving over one hundred and fifty miles thinly defended. Reitz's view was that the Germans would go through the forces there 'like a knife through butter'. Unhappily, Hore-Belisha's optimism obscured from his colleagues the true seriousness of the situation, the thinness of the line, the lack of equipment and inadequate air power. Hore-Belisha fell on 4 January 1940, more as a result of his acute disagreements with his senior military advisers on personal rather than policy issues, but his successor Oliver Stanley was not notably more dynamic. The British tank and armoured position was especially alarming, but the response to Eden's concerns was not energetic. Complacency reigned.

Churchill's experience exactly mirrored Eden's. Although he had much on his hands at the Admiralty, what he saw in France dismayed him. There were only eight British divisions there, and the proportion of fighting troops to the total number of British troops in France was alarmingly low; in Britain, munitions production was lower than it had been in 1915; he was not impressed by the senior commanders, and although he admired Lord Gort, the former Chief of the Imperial General Staff and now commanding the British Expeditionary Force, and his successor as CIGS General Sir Edmund Ironside, he had his doubts even about them. But his endeavours to expand his Admiralty sphere were resented and rejected. It was a period of acute frustration for him also, but at least he had a sphere of military activity denied to Eden.

In this eerie period, the one success of the Government was Churchill, completely in his element. His speeches both in the Commons and on the radio breathed the true martial spirit so lacking in his colleagues. If his statistics of submarine sinkings were distinctly on the optimistic side, they were certainly good for morale; and the successful attack on the pocket battleship *Admiral Graf Spee*, forced to scuttle after the Battle of the River Plate on 27 December after the joint action of the cruisers *Achilles*, *Exeter* and *Ajax*, was a brilliant naval feat. Churchill also had the unique facility to put forward reverses as unfortunate but inevitable events to be seen in the context of overall success.

Opinion polls were very crude, but before the war they had shown Eden notably more favoured for Prime Minister than Churchill;* now the latter's prominence and strong public personality reversed this situation outside Westminster and Whitehall. Inside Government, he was still regarded with suspicion and dislike. Thus, when he urged that Eden become War Secretary to replace Hore-Belisha, the suggestion was not accepted. Hore-Belisha went, but Eden remained at the Dominions Office. Chamberlain

---

*One held in April 1939 by the British Institute of Public Opinion gave Eden 38 per cent of the votes to succeed Chamberlain; Halifax and Churchill, the closest challengers, received 7 per cent each.

would not hear of Amery or Duff Cooper joining the Government; Cranborne had been brought back, but Chamberlain could hardly bring himself to speak to him. As Churchill remarked to Eden, 'If it were not for Hitler neither of us would be here.' It was grimly true.

Thus, as Churchill's star rose dramatically, that of Eden, if not declining, made little progress. He was, as always, a competent minister, skilfully developing Dominion involvement and co-operation and dealing ingeniously and successfully with the problems caused by Irish neutrality, particularly those which arose over the thousands of young Irishmen who at once volunteered for the British forces.* But although it was an important position, it was insignificant compared with a post in the War Cabinet, and Eden chafed impatiently.

It was this impatience that took him to Cairo in February 1940, ostensibly to meet the Australian and New Zealand forces due there – but in reality to see the position for himself. It turned out to have been a very important decision. He met, for the first time, General Sir Archibald Wavell, the British Commander-in-Chief, Middle East, whom he liked and admired at once. As in the case of Charles de Gaulle, of whom no one outside a very limited circle had heard in early 1940, this was destined to be a judgement that Churchill did not share. Eden was delighted by the Anzacs and an Indian Army brigade, but more doubtful about young King Farouk of Egypt – which was to be fully justified by events – although he found him strongly anti-Mussolini. There were ominous reports of further Italian reinforcements in Libya. Eden went to Palestine to see Australian camps and was exhilarated by the experience.

Eden obtained a deep personal enjoyment from the company of soldiers, at every level. As Charles Mott-Radclyffe wrote of a later occasion in Egypt:

I have never seen any Inspecting VIP, military or civilian, who displayed in the same degree the unerring touch that Eden had with troops. Normally inspections are regarded as hell and as soon as they are over everyone breathes a sigh of relief in the hope that there will not be another for a long time, and while the inspection is taking place it is always a nightmare, from the Commanding Officer downwards, to wait to hear what the VIP is going to say. Eden was completely relaxed and in his element. There was flash-back to the First War in which he had served, with distinction, in the 60th Rifles and due to this, no doubt, he felt doubly at ease with any Green Jacket unit. He talked to every man in the front and rear rank of my Company. He had his hair cut in the Corporals' mess. His subsequent address to the troops, assembled in a semi-circle in the sand, was a masterpiece.... When

* De Valera was worried about the obvious implications of large numbers of ·young Irishmen in manifestly British uniforms on leave in a neutral country. The problem was resolved by providing them with civilian clothes before they returned home for leave.

he finally departed my Company Sergeant Major asked me whether I could arrange for a second Inspection on his return. This, so far as I know, is a unique tribute.

For his part, Eden was deeply moved by the sight of all the young Commonwealth men coming so far from home to support and fight for Britain and, speaking in Liverpool after his return on 19 February, he gave expression to his admiration for these men who,

though separated by thousands of miles of ocean ... might very well have been excused had they failed to appreciate the extent of the peril that pressed in the first instance upon us, but which they saw clearly from the first. They understood the issue, and it is this clear perception, the vision of the men beyond the seas who see truly, that should give us courage now.

But he returned to a dismal mood. With the spectacular exception of Churchill, everything was continuing as though Britain was at peace. There was no urgency, no decisiveness, no sense of the shortage of time. The Russian invasion of Finland had seemed to cause more outrage than the Nazi savagery in Poland; it was still indeed All Quiet on the Western Front; rearmament was proceeding, but without the energy and priority it should have received. As Eden had seen for himself in Britain, France and the Middle East, the general condition of the British and French forces was alarmingly weak. He longed more than ever to lay his hands on the War Office, and for a truly National Government, not a Conservative one of old men for whom he had absolutely no feeling of personal friendship or political trust.

In these circumstances he was increasingly drawn towards his former *bête noire* Winston Churchill. Always modest about his own speaking abilities, he was amazed by the sensitive oratory that Churchill was deploying, his prodigious work and his intrepid spirit. All his former reservations now vanished. There were to be many disagreements, and even on occasion hard words, but their destinies had merged. Eden pressed for the creation of the post of Minister of Defence to be given to Churchill; Churchill continued to press the claims of Eden for the War Office. But, although Halifax was responsive, the Prime Minister was not. Churchill was at least in the forefront of affairs, but Eden was not. As he later wrote:

I was only on the fringes. I enjoyed my work with the Dominion High Commissioners and with their Governments, but my position in the Cabinet was highly anomalous, not to say humiliating. Two years before, I had been a principal figure in the Cabinet, now I was back again, not because my former colleagues wanted me to join them, but because the country had judged me to be right and them wrong in the controversy over my resignation. I was there on condition that I took no effective part in anything outside the work of my department.*

* Avon, *The Reckoning*, p. 91.

In fact, as his diaries and letters reveal, he did not at all enjoy the work of his department. As Saville Garner, one of his officials, wrote, 'his restless energy could not be tamed to endure the futile inactivity of this strange period'. The general conflict of this war at first alarmed and then enraged him. When Hoare became Air Secretary, Churchill told Eden that he was 'saddened and disgusted. He had not been consulted, only informed.... Winston maintained that there would be more chances, many more, on this rough voyage and sought to hearten himself in this strain, and no doubt me too. But he was worried and depressed, which is not wonderful' (diary, 1 April). Eden was also worried and depressed, his mood not lightened by the persistent gloom and defeatism of the American Ambassador, Joseph Kennedy; and he was certainly not encouraging to Sumner Welles' attempts to arrange an armistice, if not the end of the war. Hitler and Stalin held not only all the cards, but the territory. The brave Finns had been defeated after inflicting terrible casualties on the Russians, who had now seized all the Baltic states. Poland was as irretrievably gone as Czechoslovakia, and Hitler could now transfer his forces to the Western Front, where Allied lethargy reigned. On 9 April the Nazis attacked Norway, Chamberlain having just declared – in a speech which ended him – that Hitler had 'missed the bus'.

There was a considerable irony that the subsequent disastrous Norwegian campaign could well have redounded to Churchill's discredit, but the national mood had changed, as had that of the House of Commons. In one of the most brilliant and memorable debates in modern times on 7 and 8 May the pent-up anxiety and humiliation of the House of Commons boiled up into censure that was best expressed in Amery's famous Cromwellian declaration, which he applied to the Chamberlain Government: 'You have sat here too long for any good you have been doing. Depart, I say, and let us have done with you! In the name of God, go!' But Roger Keyes – dressed in full uniform as Admiral of the Fleet – Duff Cooper and Lloyd George were hardly less effective. Chamberlain, very unwisely, appealed to his friends for their support. Churchill wound up courageously in an angry House, supporting the Government. In the dramatic vote, 41 Conservatives and supporters voted against the Government, and 60 abstained, giving the Government a majority of 81 as opposed to its nominal majority of 213.

Winston rang me up about 9.30 and said that he wanted to see me as soon as possible; while shaving he rehearsed to me the events of the previous evening. He thought that Neville would not be able to bring in Labour and that a national Government must be found. Later I lunched alone with him and Kingsley [Wood], when they told me that Neville had decided to go. The future was discussed. Kingsley thought that W should succeed and urged that if asked he should make plain his willingness. Meeting had been arranged for 4.30. Some talk with Oliver [Stanley] and K at intervals during day. Dined with Winston when he told me he thought it plain N.C. would advise King to send for him. Edward [Halifax] did not wish to succeed. Parliamentary position too difficult. W had made it plain he hoped N.C. would stay, would lead H of C and continue as chairman of party. W would be Minister of Defence as well as P.M. W quiet and calm. He wishes me to take War [Office]. I told him I would obey orders and serve or not and where he thought I could best help. Position will be very difficult one for state of army is inglorious, and it will not be easy to maintain harmony with W. (Diary, 9 May)

Subsequently Eden expanded this account from his recollections. At the luncheon meeting Kingsley Wood had shocked Eden by warning Churchill that Chamberlain wanted Halifax to succeed him, and said to him, 'Don't agree, and don't say anything.' Eden's shock was because Wood had been so blatant and so sycophantic a Chamberlain supporter,* not because he disagreed with the advice, which indeed he endorsed. Others, including Bracken and Beaverbrook, have claimed that they gave Churchill the same advice.

At the meeting with Halifax and Churchill that afternoon Chamberlain said that Labour must enter the Government, but when Clement Attlee and Arthur Greenwood joined them they said that the reaction of their Party, then holding its Conference in Bournemouth, would almost certainly be against serving under him. After they had left, Churchill maintained an uncharacteristic silence, upon which Halifax said that as a peer it would be impossible for him to be Prime Minister at such a time; and that 'I thought Winston was a better choice. Winston did *not* demur. Was very kind and polite but showed that he thought this right solution.'† Churchill returned to work at the Admiralty. He realized that the tide was with him, but when he dined with Eden Chamberlain remained Prime Minister.

In the early hours of the morning of Friday 10 May the full fury of the German blitzkrieg fell upon neutral Holland and Belgium. At six in the morning Hoare, Stanley and Churchill urgently conferred, and Eden was telephoned at 7.40 for an immediate Cabinet. For a while it seemed that the crisis had persuaded Chamberlain that he could not leave at such a time, but Kingsley Wood had told him this was impossible, as indeed it was. The news from Holland, Belgium and France was awful, and, as Chamberlain informed the Cabinet at a second meeting later in the morning, Labour was not prepared to serve under him. But there were still delays and hesitations, and it was only later that day that Chamberlain

* Cadogan's description of Kingsley Wood as 'a chicken-hearted little mutton-head' (Dilks (ed.), *The Diaries of Sir Alexander Cadogan, 1938–45*, p. 272) deserves to be remembered. Eden did not disagree with this assessment.

† *Ibid.*, p. 280.

resigned; the King, who had personally favoured Halifax, sent for Church-ill. The Labour leaders went to Admiralty House to express their agreement to serve. Churchill drew up his first list of ministers to serve in the War Cabinet. He would become Minister of Defence. He chivalrously retained Chamberlain* as Lord President and Halifax as Foreign Secretary; Attlee became Lord Privy Seal and Greenwood Minister without Portfolio; another Labour MP, A. V. Alexander, became First Lord of the Admiralty; Churchill's old friend Sir Archibald Sinclair, the Liberal leader, became Secretary of State for Air; Eden became Secretary of State for War, as he and Churchill had both desired, but was not a member of the War Cabinet. Neither had desired that their opportunity would be in the most desperate circumstances in British history, fated to become even more desperate in the following weeks.

Even Cadogan wrote, 'I'm not at *all* sure of W.S.C.,' and in Downing Street John Colville was writing despairingly of the prospect of Churchill as Prime Minister. Both quickly realized how terribly wrong they had been – and admitted it frankly – but the hostility to Churchill in Westmins-ter and Whitehall was intense, and that to Eden only marginally less so. Churchill and Eden took Office not only at a grim time, but surrounded by doubters and enemies, and with very few friends and admirers.

The new ministers were sworn in at Buckingham Palace. For some reason that the Clerk of the Council explained but Eden could not understand, he had to take the Oath before Chamberlain. Eden noted: 'N.C. looked ill and clearly was hating it all. He said he was staying in the Government with a heavy heart; he was depressed that at such a critical time we should be considering questions of personalities.' Eden for his part thought it extraordinary that Chamberlain should be obsessed by personalities at such a time.

All Churchill offered to his new ministers in his first meeting with them – and then, memorably, to the nation – was 'blood, toil, tears and sweat'. He was, by his relentless energy and total dedication to the prosecution of the war, and by his matchless oratory, to establish a position nationally and internationally unparalleled by any British Prime Minister. He could be, and frequently was, intolerable and inconsiderate of other people. Errors were made. Defeats were suffered. France and virtually the whole of Europe were to fall under the Nazi yoke. The margin of Britain's survival was to be frighteningly narrow. The war was to engulf huge areas and large numbers; it was to last for another five years, in which so many millions

---

* Chamberlain only retained his post until the end of September, and died of cancer in November. Until October he retained the Leadership of the Conservative Party which Churchill, mindful of Lloyd George's fate, then secured for himself.

were to perish, and countless others to mourn. It was to be a terrible period in which the words Total War had an especially complete meaning. For a long time nothing went right. But the beacon of liberty blazed in Britain. It was indeed this nation's finest hour, as it was Churchill's. And beside him marched Anthony Eden.

One did not have to be a pessimist or a defeatist to recognize how bad the situation was. When Eden entered the War Office to be met by the CIGS, Ironside, whose name belied his resolution at this level, it was to be greeted with unrelieved bad news. 'The years that the locust hath eaten' had eaten away the triumphant British Army of 1918. The British Expeditionary Force under Lord Gort was under heavy pressure on the left Allied flank; the full power of the German armour and air power was falling on the French and the Belgians. What amazed everyone, including Churchill, was the speed of the German advance, heralding a new era in military thinking and action.

Churchill moved swiftly to establish close relations between Ministers and their military advisers, determined that there was going to be no repetition of the division and mutual mistrust of the Great War. Major-General Hastings Ismay – universally known as 'Pug' – at once took a leading role as the Prime Minister's representative at Chiefs of Staff Meetings 'and generally to act as my Staff Officer through whom I am accustomed to pass the bulk of my communications to the three fighting departments'.* Ismay initially regarded Eden as a charming lightweight, an opinion he came to change totally.

Eden's relations with his Permanent Under-Secretary, P. J. Grigg, were not good. Grigg had a high esteem of himself, and had the unpleasant habit of denigrating his political masters, Hore-Belisha, Stanley and now Eden. The latter's account of his time at the War Office makes no reference to Grigg at all; as the papers of Colville and others demonstrate, Grigg was consistently disloyal to Eden. Grigg's appointment in 1942 as Secretary of State for War had Eden's approval, although he was doubtful about it; these doubts were to be abundantly justified.

Eden himself looked at the deteriorating situation with bleak dismay. The position in France was complicated, but from Holland and Belgium came reports of the effectiveness of paratroops, and their demoralizing impact. Eden at once grasped the importance of meeting this menace, and two days after he became War Secretary he broadcast to the nation.

Since the war began, the Government have received countless inquiries from all over the Kingdom from men of all ages who are for one reason or another not at

---

* Martin Gilbert, *Finest Hour: Winston S. Churchill, 1939–1941*, p. 323.

present engaged in military service, and who wish to do something for the defence of their country. Well, now is your opportunity.

Eden explained that all men between the ages of seventeen and sixty-five would be eligible. They would be given uniforms and would be armed, but would receive no pay. They would serve for the duration of the war. They would be called the Local Defence Volunteers.

The response was immediate, huge, and embarrassing in the sense that there was an acute shortage of uniforms and weapons for the Army, let alone the LDV. While Eden was very attached to the title, the Minister of Supply, Herbert Morrison, thought it uninspiring and suggested 'Civic Guard'. Churchill himself came up with the title of 'Home Guard', which Eden strongly resisted – a fact he does not mention in his memoirs. On 22 July he wrote in his diary, 'we discussed LDV. He [Churchill] was still determined to change name to Home Guard. I told him that neither officers nor men wanted the change, but he insisted.' If the idea itself – which was Eden's – was inspired, so was Churchill's change of title. The Home Guard throughout the war took over from the armed forces and police a wide range of duties, and although at the outset it seemed comical for men to parade without uniforms or weapons, it was all very serious, and the remarkable enthusiasm with which men volunteered – particularly after the fall of France – was evidence enough of the spirit of the country that Churchill evoked. Over a million and a half men were to serve in the Home Guard; by September 1940 its men released over 9,000 soldiers for Army duties.

As Secretary of State Eden had inherited a situation in France which was militarily and politically bad, and which rapidly got worse. On the ground and in the air the Germans were dominant; Eden's diaries and his accounts of War Cabinet meetings and discussions with his military advisers and with Churchill consist entirely of reports of bad news. The French were disintegrating under the fierce and apparently unstoppable German onslaught. At one point Ironside gloomily remarked to Eden that 'This is the end of the British Empire', and even Churchill's resilience and optimism often gave way to something more than deep concern.

The position of the BEF had become grave. Eden urged the immediate evacuation of those British troops encircled at the Hook of Holland, to which Churchill agreed. On 19 May the War Cabinet, on Eden's advice, again supported by Churchill, decided to order Gort to move his forces to the south-west to join with the French, but Churchill was now contemplating the possibility of evacuating the BEF if French resistance continued to crumble. This it showed every indication of doing. Churchill had flown to Paris on 16 May to see the new Prime Minister Paul Reynaud and the French ministers and military commander, only to find, in his own words, 'Utter dejection ... written on every face.' The Germans were now advancing rapidly on Boulogne and Calais, the former being evacuated on the night of 23/24 May. On the 17th General Bernard Montgomery, commanding the 3rd Division, was ordered to retire south through Brussels. While these desperate decisions were being discussed, another evacuation – from Norway – also occupied the attention of ministers, while the consistent imbalance in the air was a haunting and constant concern.

One particular problem was that of communications with Gort, but on the evening of 22 May Lord Munster, who was Gort's ADC, on his instructions telephoned Eden to tell him how grave the BEF position was. Eden telegraphed to Gort giving him latitude to withdraw to the Channel ports if the attacks on his communications forced him to do so. On the 25th Gort, in a decisive action, moved north towards Dunkirk. In the general blur of events in these desperate days, with imprecise information, bad liaison with the French and the accompanying confusion of battle, the supreme significance of this decision could not be seen at the time. But Eden followed it up with emphatic orders that the Channel ports must be held at all costs.

The only remaining British regular infantry in Britain was sent at once to Calais under the command of Brigadier Claude Nicholson, the brother of the Conservative MP for Farnham, Godfrey Nicholson, who had voted against the Chamberlain Government on 8 May. The main German assault on Calais began on 24 May, and on the following morning the Navy told Eden that if the British garrison, now driven into the inner town but resisting heroically, was to be withdrawn it must be done at once. Eden and Ironside went to see Churchill. In what both Eden and Churchill considered one of the hardest decisions of the war, they agreed that Nicholson must be ordered to fight on. It was a decision even more poignant for Eden as battalions of the Sixtieth Rifles and the Rifle Brigade, with many officers and men he knew personally and had served with, were involved. Churchill recorded that he felt 'physically sick' at having to take such a decision. Eden's anguish was even more personal. But it had to be done.

The epic defence of Calais could have only one ending, as two German armoured divisions were needed to end the fierce British resistance, but it bought precious time, and involved the diversion of more troops, tanks and aircraft than the German commanders had intended or wished. If there had been no Calais, there would very probably have been no Dunkirk. The move towards the Channel ports and the defence of Calais were the decisive turning-points in the salvation of the British Army – and much else besides.

*　　*　　*

Eden's orders to Gort, approved by Churchill, were intended as the prelude not to evacuation, but to the redeployment by sea of the BEF, free of the possibility of encirclement. But on the night of 27/28 May the Belgian Army surrendered, and General Harold Alexander was ordered to effect the evacuation of the British and French forces now converging on Dunkirk. Gort, brave soldier but clearly not of sufficient calibre, was ordered home, and Ironside offered to stand down as CIGS, to Eden's immense relief; Ironside was replaced by General Sir John Dill, one of the finest of modern British commanders, with whom Eden developed a close and warm friendship. Unhappily he never gained Churchill's confidence; 'he [Dill] strikes me as being very tired, disheartened, and over-impressed with the might of Germany,' Churchill minuted to Eden on 10 July. Eden considered this grossly unfair, as indeed it was, and stood by Dill. Few Chiefs have taken over at such a calamitous moment.

Operation Dynamo, as the Dunkirk evacuation was codenamed, turned out to be crucial to Britain's salvation, but at the time it caused intense concern and apprehension in London. Eden always believed that the Germans, in their concentration upon destroying the French, and unexpectedly tied down at Calais, failed to realize their opportunity until it was too late. He saw at the time, as did Churchill, that the BEF, hemmed in around Dunkirk, now faced calamity and the nation the greatest military disaster in British history.

Those were terrible days, and Churchill sought the advice of the Chiefs of Staff whether it would be possible to continue the war if France were defeated and Italy, as appeared very probable, entered the war. Their reply was that so long as the RAF and the Navy maintained their strength, and the morale of the armed forces and the civilian population remained high, it was possible. The fact that even Churchill was asking such questions emphasizes the gravity of the position. Halifax was actually proposing that Mussolini should be approached as a possible mediator for a peace settlement with Hitler, which even Chamberlain initially opposed, although not as vehemently as Churchill, Eden and Attlee. Indeed, this was a fevered Cabinet, at which Halifax offered to resign. Meanwhile Gort was saying that he did not 'rate very highly' the chances of saving the BEF, a pessimism which doomed him in turn. Churchill had to tell the House of Commons that it should prepare itself for 'hard and heavy tidings'. But when, after an exhausting War Cabinet still debating the possible peace negotiations, Churchill saw the other senior ministers of all parties he found them resolute, even passionate, for fighting on, and they pledged him their full support. This was, politically, another turning-point.

Following urgent and somewhat dramatic personal representations from Lord Munster and Churchill's nephew Johnny, who came straight from the beaches, an appeal was issued for ships of all sizes to proceed at once to Dunkirk. The response was immediate, and the most astonishing flotilla in history set off from the English coast into the Dunkirk inferno. Virtually anything that floated and was propelled crossed the Channel. Churchill's task was to persuade the French that this did not mean the British were abandoning them, but the defeatist mood in Paris was now palpable.

Two hundred and twenty-two warships and 665 other British ships took part in the Dunkirk evacuation, in which six destroyers and twenty-four other ships were sunk. The final total of those that got away to England was some 335,000 British and French soldiers. If this was a triumph of its kind, Churchill rightly warned the immensely relieved Commons that 'Wars are not won by evacuations.' He ended his speech with the immortal peroration, 'We shall fight on the beaches, we shall fight on the landing grounds, we shall fight in the fields and in the streets, we shall fight in the hills; we shall never surrender.' That was indeed the mood – but with what were the British to fight?

Eden was very close to Churchill throughout these terrible days, indeed closer than any other member of the War Cabinet. His close friend and member of the Eden Group, Ronald Cartland, had been among those killed; there had been only a handful of survivors at Calais; Nicholson was one, but he was to die later as a prisoner of war. If the bulk of the BEF had been saved, many had been lost, including many officers and NCOs. Virtually none of its precious equipment had reached Britain. Vast quantities of guns – including all the 25-pounders – tanks, vehicles, rifles, shells and ammunition, representing almost all the matériel the British Army possessed, had been left behind. Although the Germans had received some unpleasant surprises from the BEF and the RAF, the latter had lost precious aircraft and even more precious pilots in the fierce air battles over the beaches. These losses prompted the decision that further sacrifice of the slender squadrons over France could not be countenanced. This decision was to prove another turning-point. At the time it evoked further charges of betrayal, but few knew how thinly fortified Britain was, even in the air. Churchill and Eden did. As in the case of Calais, a decision had to be made. It cost the lives and liberty of many people, but it was right.

As Eden discovered when he toured the camps hurriedly established to quarter the army, the men were exhilarated and resolute; he wrote, 'their temper was that of victors'. But, as he said in a broadcast on 2 June, 'Brave hearts alone cannot stand up against steel. We need more planes, more tanks, more guns.' Looking at the charts he had had prepared for him on the walls of his office, he could see at a glance how crippling and frightening were the deficiencies. Like Churchill, in public he radiated confidence; in private, he was sombre and tense. There was much to be sombre and tense about.

On 11 June he, Churchill and Dill flew to Briare, on the Loire, to see Prime Minister Reynaud, the aged Marshal Pétain and General Weygand in a last desperate venture to bolster the French. Both Churchill and Eden have described that dismal encounter vividly, at which they had their first real meeting with Charles de Gaulle, now Under-Secretary for Defence. They flew back to London without escort, in considerable peril, with, as Eden wrote, 'only sorrow and a sense of vacancy'. The utter unreality of those days bore down on everyone. The inconceivable and the impossible were actually happening. The French were collapsing, the Germans were triumphant everywhere, the remaining British troops in France were in dire jeopardy and themselves would have to be evacuated before too long. The only gleams of solace in the darkness were the control of the sea by the Navy and the evidence that the RAF was a match for the Luftwaffe in equal combat. But in spite of feverish work, urged on by Beaverbrook as Minister for Aircraft Production, the numbers of aircraft and pilots meant that the RAF would not for some time be equal numerically.

No one who was alive then can forget the combination of one of the loveliest of English summers, the relentless procession of terrible news and the spirit of unity, amounting almost to exaltation, among the people. It was a terrifying time, and yet unforgettable. The Home Guard may have had no uniforms or weapons, but they took to heart Churchill's admonition that 'you can always take one with you', and at least they had petrol and explosives, for which Eden, very mindful of his own experience, urged expert advice and training. As Churchill wisely appreciated, the British could take bad news, but they needed inspiration. They got both.

But the remaining British forces in France were not the only ones in jeopardy. In the Middle East, Eden was convinced that the Italians would come in as soon as France fell; no one knew how the French forces in the area would behave, and his visit to Cairo and his meetings with Wavell had deeply impressed upon him how serious the situation was there. If the Suez Canal went, so did the war. But Churchill, with his eyes, naturally enough, fixed upon the immediate situation, pressed vehemently for eight battalions to be brought back at once to defend Britain. Wavell refused, and Eden backed him up. Churchill accused the War Office 'of a feeble and weary Departmentalism', to which Eden angrily replied that his department was always the whipping boy for failure; he stood by Wavell, pointing out that he was moving troops from India to the Middle East, which could release regular British units. This was Eden's first experience of Churchill's fierce authoritarianism and angry minutes, often followed by heated and lengthy War Cabinet arguments, but he responded in kind, and held his ground. It was as well he did, for after the fall of France the opportunistic Mussolini did indeed enter the war, and the Middle East became another front and the Mediterranean another battlefield. All talk of bringing British troops home abruptly ended.

France sued for armistice – and Britain stood alone. Except in the air and at sea, the nation was virtually defenceless. General Thorne, charged with the defence of Kent, Sussex and Surrey against a German invasion, reported to Eden that he had not a single anti-tank gun; nor, of course, did he have any tanks.

The conduct of the war so far had revealed grievous weaknesses at all levels in the Army, particularly in the higher echelons, and Eden had no doubt that sweeping changes must be made, and at once, to remove those who had clearly failed and to promote those who had given clear evidence not only of courage but of intelligence and leadership.

Eden had been very impressed by the performance of General Alan Brooke in France, and commended him to Churchill to command the Home Forces in the place of Ironside, who had been briefly in command, his career now definitely at an end, albeit very honourably. General Claude Auchinleck, whom Eden had also come to admire, succeeded Brooke.* Churchill accepted this advice, and found Brooke considerably more congenial to his temperament than Dill or Wavell. With Ironside and Gort out of the way, and with other changes at all levels on which Eden insisted, he believed that he was creating a command structure that was worthy of the Army. The creation of the Commandos was also a joint decision. In what Brendan Bracken – now close to Churchill at Downing Street and, on Churchill's insistence and to the King's dismay (and others'), appointed a Privy Councillor – described as 'a whizzing crisis', such decisions had to be made rapidly. No doubt, errors were made and there were injustices to individuals, but the situation required the most drastic action. Eden made a point of seeing the departing and incoming commanders personally; Churchill told him that a letter would do, but Eden insisted on a personal interview with each, to explain the reasons for promotion and dismissal. The latter meetings, obviously, were the more painful, but only one man – whose name Eden refused to disclose then or later – took it badly. Eden

---

* Ironside was the prototype for John Buchan's 'Richard Hannay', and Churchill was so impressed by his service and voluntary retirement as CIGS that he made him a field marshal and a peer in 1941. Gort, whose immense personal courage was demonstrated by his Victoria Cross, Distinguished Service Order with two bars, and Military Cross, became Governor first of Gibraltar and then of Malta. He was High Commissioner in Palestine in 1944–6, when it was discovered he had cancer. Gort was aged fifty-four in 1940, and Ironside sixty.

had considerable sympathy for them, feeling acutely how difficult it is for a British commander with few resources at the beginning of a war to achieve much, but he had discerned those who had succeeded and those who had not.

His selection of Brooke was to be particularly important. Churchill's preference was for dashing and risk-taking commanders, the Mountbatten, Roger Keyes, Freyberg and Orde Wingate type; Eden went for more thoughtful and serious senior officers who had shared his experiences as a young officer in France, and was more attracted to men like Dill, Wavell and Brooke. But there is a danger in oversimplifying this. Churchill was to develop complete trust in 'Pug' Ismay and in Alan Brooke, who was to succeed Dill as CIGS in 1941, while Eden was to conclude sadly that he had perhaps overrated Auchinleck and that Wavell's chance had come too late in life.

Where they completely agreed was that the Army was encumbered with officers who were too old, too lazy or incapable of grasping the new technical and military realities. They had to go, and they did. The effect on the morale of ambitious and enthusiastic young officers was dramatic.

Eden had been a notably reluctant supporter of the decision of the War Cabinet on 16 June to permit Reynaud to make inquiries from the Germans about armistice terms provided he ordered the French fleet into British ports. He was in a minority of one, and the fact that the French fleet largely remained technically neutral, but under the control of the Pétain–Laval-dominated Vichy regime that was permitted to rule unoccupied France, fully justified his opposition. Nor was he particularly impressed by Churchill's dramatic offer of Anglo–French union, which in any event came too late. But the possibility of the French fleet, especially in the Mediterranean, engaging in hostilities against Britain was even more chilling than the French Army doing the same in North Africa or the Middle East. With France defeated and divided and with loyalties so actively split, Eden looked with increasing interest and admiration to de Gaulle, who had reached London to raise the banner of the Free French.

This was not simply *realpolitik*. Eden's admiration for soldiers was one element, and de Gaulle's combination of being a brave but thinking soldier was in itself attractive to him. But de Gaulle was also an exceptionally cultivated man, a political soldier with a contempt for most politicians, solitary and sensitive, and a fugitive under sentence of death. At a time when he was assumed to be of little account and was regarded by Churchill as a pestilential nuisance, Eden befriended him and held him in high regard. Eden's almost perfect French, his love of France, and his record attracted de Gaulle at once, but it was Eden's warmth that was decisive, when so many in London were cold towards him. A remarkable, and lifelong, friendship was thus created: 'de Gaulle is full of sweet reasonableness when A.E. sees him,' Oliver Harvey was to recount in 1941. What has been underestimated is how similar they were in experience and in temperament. It was thus, also, with the leader of the Free Polish Government in London, General Sikorski, another foreign soldier–politician widely regarded as impossible to deal with. In him, also, although to a lesser extent than with de Gaulle, Eden found much in common.

Eden worked tirelessly. The task of reorganization of the BEF and other units rescued from France was itself formidable, but it was undertaken remarkably quickly. In addition to these divisions there were fourteen divisions of the Territorial Army, a second armoured division and four tank brigades in process of formation; unfortunately, they had no tanks. The 1st Canadian Division had arrived, mercifully fully equipped. But, in the whole of Britain there were less than five hundred tanks – mostly light and obsolete – and less than five hundred guns, principally light. All that Eden could report was that, having retrieved eighty thousand precious rifles from France, every man in the Regular Army had at least a personal weapon. The Home Guard still had virtually nothing. 'We have a million men waiting for rifles,' Churchill told Roosevelt on 15 August. As Eden urged, matériel production must be placed on an absolute priority basis, as Beaverbrook was ruthlessly doing for the RAF – and making innumerable enemies in the process. Weapons must be purchased at once from the United States. The Army must be re-equipped. 'Never has a great nation been so naked before her foes,' Churchill later wrote. None knew this better than his Secretary of State for War, yet after the departure of Ironside, although there was realism there was never defeatism at the War Office.

Eden, and Britain, were fortunate in the fact that Arthur Purvis was responsible for arms purchase in the United States. The most urgent need was for basic arms. In one shipment alone Purvis sent ten million rounds of rifle ammunition, fifty thousand rifles and a hundred 75-millimetre guns; they were desperately needed, and much more was required if the expected German invasion was to be effectively resisted.

Indeed, there was a shortage of everything, but of all the three services the Army in Britain was the worst equipped for the storms to come. As late as 30 September Churchill told Eden that No. 7 Commando at Felixstowe had no Bren guns, no anti-tank rifles, only a few Tommy guns, and no ammunition. 'I am sorry to be insistent upon these small points,' Churchill minuted, 'but they have an alarming aspect.' Eden knew full well how alarming it was. As Churchill later wrote of Eden's role in 1940:

He played a fine part as Secretary of State for War during this terrific year, and his conduct of Army affairs brought us very close together. We thought alike, even without consultation, on a very great number of practical issues as they arose from day to day.

Eden's new feelings for Churchill were demonstrated in the relatively few personal notes that passed between them during this grim period. Thus, on 19 May, after one of Churchill's finest broadcasts:*

My dear Winston
You have never done anything as good or as great. Thank you, & Thank God for you.
Yours,
Anthony

And, on 30 November, Churchill's birthday:

Very few men in all history have had to bear such a burden as you have carried in the last six months. It is really wonderful that at the end of it you are fitter and more vigorous, and better able than ever to guide and inspire us all.

To which Churchill replied: 'Thank you so much dear Anthony, I am truly grateful for your help and kindness. Winston.'

Britain now braced herself for a German invasion, with a fine spirit and high morale, but with only a relative handful of fighter aircraft and pilots and the precious radar chain between her precarious survival and cataclysmic subjugation. But at least she now had the crucial foundations for her Army. That this had been plucked from the burning was the greatest single service rendered to his country by Anthony Eden.

Although the situation at home was grim, and the arrival of ships carrying precious munitions from the United States was awaited on each occasion with acute anxiety, Eden's concerns also lay in the Middle East. The attitude of the Vichy French forces was difficult to anticipate, but they would certainly not be involved in any operations against the Italians. Malta was now highly vulnerable, and was essential not only for maintaining British naval strength in the Mediterranean but for protecting the shipping routes to and from the Suez Canal. The Canal itself was under threat, as was the Sudan. The Italians had over a quarter of a million men in Abyssinia alone, substantial forces in Libya, and a fleet that was modern and large. They also had Albania, and an invasion of Greece seemed very likely. Eden was reasonably confident of Turkish neutrality, but elsewhere

---

* It ended: 'Today is Trinity Sunday. Centuries ago words were written to be a call and a spur to the faithful servants of Truth and Justice: "Arm yourselves, and be ye men of valour, and be in readiness for the conflict; for it is better for us to perish in battle than to look upon the outrage of our nation and our altar. As the Will of God is in Heaven, even so let it be." '

the situation was deeply unpromising. One decisive moment had occurred on 3 July, when the Royal Navy destroyed three French warships at Mers-el-Kebir near Oran, killing over 1,250 French sailors, having failed to obtain satisfactory assurances about the ships' use and deployment. This very necessary action removed one threat, but inflamed French feeling, thereby adding another complication to an already perilous situation. An Anglo–Free French assault on Dakar (Operation 'Menace') in September turned into a fiasco when the Vichy French forces fought back, and on the 25th Eden supported Attlee and others who urged that the operation be called off, as it was. This was another dispiriting reverse, even more so for de Gaulle than for the British. Torn by divided loyalties, the French were to remain a consistent source of difficulty and bewilderment to the British, not least in North Africa and the Middle East. This was another factor that no one had anticipated.

The Middle East was the only area in which the British Army, having been driven out of Europe, could attack for the foreseeable future, but all Wavell had were one very incomplete armoured division, two incomplete infantry divisions and another capable only of policing duties. As Eden well knew, he lacked tanks, vehicles, anti-tank weapons and artillery, while the air position, so crucial in that area, was inadequate; ammunition was meagre – but so was everything.

Eden and Dill had a high regard for Wavell; unhappily, Churchill did not. He minuted Eden on 13 August:

I am favourably impressed with General Wavell in many ways, but I do not feel in him that sense of mental rigour and resolve to overcome obstacles which is indispensable to successful war. I find, instead, tame acceptance of a variety of local circumstances in different theatres, which is leading to a lamentable lack of concentration upon the decisive point.

Eden considered this grossly unfair, and made plain his complete confidence in Wavell, as he had in Dill. What Churchill did accept was that Wavell must be reinforced, and in another brave decision he authorized Eden's request for an armoured division with 154 precious tanks to be sent from Britain. Churchill wanted them to sail through the Mediterranean; the Navy refused. With an ill grace, Churchill accepted that they must take the long route round the Cape, but when a British convoy reached Malta without incident, he renewed his criticisms of his service advisers.

As Jock Colville later wrote of Churchill at this time, 'Never notably considerate, except to those in pain or trouble, he was more than normally inconsiderate and demanding during the last months of 1940.' Mrs Churchill courageously wrote to her husband to warn him of the bad effect he was having upon those around him, even upon those who admired him most.* What Eden, with his sensitiveness, appreciated was that Churchill was carrying an almost unbearable personal load, and that his variable moods required different approaches; he became skilled at this art, but it was one that Dill and Wavell never mastered, although Ismay did. Indeed, Churchill's criticisms of Wavell's inactivity became so heated that Eden and Dill threatened resignation, and meant it. Churchill calmed down. Wavell was brought home to meet Churchill personally and to explain his needs, but although Eden thought Wavell's exposition 'masterly', and he won substantial increases in men and supplies, Churchill's doubts remained. When he lectured Wavell on his dispositions, Eden noted with exasperation, 'P.M. most anxious to move this battalion here and that battalion there'. Wavell told Eden that if this situation were to continue he had better find another Commander-in-Chief. Eden was able to mollify him, Churchill muttering that Wavell 'would make a good chairman of a Tory Association' (which, from him, was abuse on a fairly formidable scale), and Wavell did not help his cause by an abrupt manner which owed more to shyness than to lack of intelligence. There was talk of replacing him by Auchinleck, but Eden resisted this. Wavell returned to his post, with the promise of reinforcements from Britain, India, and Australia and New Zealand.

That Churchill thought no less of Eden as a result of these differences was demonstrated when he contemplated changes in the Government. Neither Eden nor Sinclair were in the War Cabinet, and Churchill now wanted to bring both in, as well as Ernest Bevin, the Minister of Labour and National Service, and to put Beaverbrook in charge of Supply. He was dissatisfied with Halifax as Foreign Secretary, but Eden, whom Churchill had in mind as a replacement, wanted to stay where he was. As Eden noted in his diary, 'Winston seemed relieved.'

All this, it must be emphasized, took place in the context of the Battle of Britain and of what was thought to be the imminent invasion of Britain. Eden had rented a small house near Dover, but, although perhaps ideal as a vantage point for the invasion, it had its disadvantages in other respects; he rented a house at Frensham in Surrey for Beatrice and the boys. While the battle raged above, and the bombing of London began in earnest, Eden's constant preoccupation and concern was now to equip his forces. The Atlantic lifeline became crucial. The margin was very narrow.

Eden's battles with Churchill over supplies to the Middle East were often heated. After one such argument Eden noted that Churchill had called him in privately; 'He told me that I ought not to be so violent with him, for he was only trying to help me. I told him that he was for ever

---

* Colville, *The Fringes of Power*, p. 280.

nagging at the Army and was unjust to it. He retorted that he was far harder on the Navy, which I did not accept.'

Churchill remained discontented with his Government, and was anxious to promote Eden, in spite of these differences. After discussion of possibilities, Eden wrote to Churchill on 30 September to say that 'I am in your hands, and will take any office that you consider will lighten your burden – or none. If you leave the matter to my personal choice I am content to stay here.' On the next day, after another long conversation, Eden reiterated his desire to remain at the War Office but conceded that he was prepared to become Lord President, 'To assist the Prime Minister in the general conduct of the war', if that was what Churchill wished: 'You know that all I want to do is to help you.'

The proposed changes – necessitated by Chamberlain's retirement – foundered on Halifax's refusal to leave the Foreign Office; Halifax also advised the appointment of Sir John Anderson as Lord President, as he had 'that sort of orderly mind which Neville had – and which I don't think Anthony has'. This was hardly a recommendation likely to appeal to Churchill, but he moved Anderson to Chamberlain's post, Morrison becoming Home Secretary and Beaverbrook Minister of Supply. Stafford Cripps had been sent on an 'exploratory mission' to Moscow which had developed into his appointment as Ambassador there; Ernest Bevin entered the War Cabinet (with Eden's strong support) and Kingsley Wood became Chancellor of the Exchequer. As Eden was still not in the War Cabinet it appeared to some that he had been by-passed, but Churchill told him that 'the succession must be his' and that he would not make 'Lloyd George's mistake of carrying on after the war'. What was agreed at the beginning of October, with the Battle of Britain won and the invasion increasingly unlikely, was that Eden should stay at the War Office for the time being and should go to the Middle East to see the situation for himself.

Eden kept a detailed diary of this visit, from which he has quoted extracts in his own memoirs. Those that he did not quote contained highly disparaging comments on the Malta defences, on the Governor, General Sir William Dobbie, and on his wife ('A strait-laced intolerant old Plymouth Sister if there was one. I am sure that she regards all the Maltese as condemned to hell fire, and they return the compliment'); Dobbie's days in his post were consequently numbered. Nor was Eden always impressed by the officers he met. 'All the men I saw certainly seemed fit and cheerful, but in some battalions officers appeared to be only a moderate lot. Manchesters, a territorial battalion, the weakest in this respect. The company commanders too old and too sedentary. We must give the good youngster his chance and make it for him.' He found difficulties with Freyberg, the New Zealanders' commander: 'Truth is that F, tho' a very brave man, is angular and prickly and, worst of all, wholly lacking in sense of humour.'

It was a hectic trip, including visits to forces in Trans-Jordan commanded by the British officer John Glubb and to King Abdullah; he held a major counsel of war with Smuts in Khartoum, in addition to visiting as many British and Commonwealth units as possible. It was obvious that the air situation remained bad, and Eden constantly cabled for urgent priority on this. What he could not entrust even to the cypher were Wavell's plans for a major offensive against the Italians. As this was unknown in London, more difficulties arose, particularly when the Italians invaded Greece at the end of October, following the German–Italian invasion of Rumania earlier in the month. The Balkans began to smoulder again.

This new front aroused Churchill's ardour. Crete was to be occupied, and forces diverted to assist the Greeks. Eden and Wavell strongly resisted this, and Eden asked to return to London 'to give Cabinet the picture here, which they have not got, details of certain projects we have in mind, and, above all, try to stop folly of diverting men, aeroplanes and material from here to Greece'. 'Egypt is vital, Greece is not,' he wrote on 2 November. 'We are barely strong enough in Egypt as it is; weakness in air specially dangerous.' But Churchill refused him permission to come home, and Eden could not tell him of the details of Wavell's plans. Eden was one of the very few who knew that the British had broken the secrets of the German Enigma cypher, and although the vital and brilliant unit at Bletchley was in its early days, the British were already receiving information of unique importance. British satisfaction at this *coup*, one of the most jealously guarded of all secrets throughout the war and long after, was shadowed by the possibility that the Germans might have broken the British codes. In fact they had not, but Eden's caution was fully justified.

On 3 November, using his personal cypher, Eden told Churchill: 'Entirely for your own information Wavell is having plans prepared to strike blow against Italians in Western Desert at the earliest possible moment.... It is of this plan that I wish to speak to you on my return.'* At the time, Churchill found Eden's messages and policies incomprehensible. Eden noted on 2 November:

Tirade from Winston. This includes such assertions that Athens was more important than both Khartoum and Kenya etc. Accused us of favouring safety first tactics, etc.... The weakness of our policy is that we never adhere to the plans

---

* Carlton, *Anthony Eden*, p. 168, describes this telegram as 'unequivocal' and has made something of a mystery of it. What Eden could not do was to reveal any details; as he wrote in his memoirs, he could not cable 'proclaiming our plans'. Also, his cable referred to Wavell 'having plans prepared', when in fact they were completed. It is ironical that this calculated and obvious deception has deceived historians as well.

we make. If we had ever thought to help Greece we should long since have laid our plans accordingly. Instead of which we took a deliberate decision not to do so, and then go back on it and seek to improvise out of air, at the expense of air here.

Eden also wondered whether the Italian attack on Greece was a deliberate diversionary tactic to draw British forces away from Egypt, the Canal and the Sudan. 'What is melancholy', he wrote on 4 November, 'is that we once again enter here the peril of grave risk to a vital artery and these new commitments have an uncanny habit of growing despite all promises that they will not. I feel that I am learning quite a lot about the art of waging war!'

Eden concurred that Crete should be occupied, and only agreed with great reluctance to send three air squadrons to Greece and an additional battalion to Crete. All he could secure from London was a promise to make up these deficiencies. The Greeks resisted the Italian invasion with conspicuous success, and even advanced into Albania, but they were still calling for assistance.

The Commons had changed its hours so that Members could get home before the blackout and the bombing. There was little effective answer to night bombing at that stage, and as London and other cities burned Churchill was desperate for some military success to proclaim. This was entirely natural, but Eden and Dill refused to put pressure on Wavell. Even after Wavell was triumphantly successful Churchill was querulous and critical, and when Eden described his judgement as 'ungenerous', he also noted (12 December) 'Our talk was less cordial than usual.'

The attack was launched against the Italians in Libya on 9 December and provided the first, precious and warming British victory of the war. The British and Commonwealth forces achieved complete surprise and immediate superiority. Bardia fell on 5 January, Tobruk on the 22nd, and Benghazi on 6 February. Italian casualties were heavy, large numbers were taken prisoner, and vast amounts of equipment were captured. British fatal casualties were 133. In the south the victory was no less complete, and in May 1941 Haile Selassie re-entered Addis Ababa in triumph. Eden's faith in Wavell had been abundantly justified. If he had only had more air power and armoured vehicles the Italian defeat would have been a total rout, and North Africa would have been at his mercy. But he had to operate with what he had.

Eden's reputation with Churchill soared, and he even suggested that Eden should take command in the Middle East, reminding him that Wellington had done so 'straight from Parliament'. Eden was amused by Churchill's characteristic imagination, but 'I declined very firmly.'

* * *

At this moment, after seven exhausting months in what he always described as 'the job I liked best', Eden's fortunes again changed.

Lord Lothian, although regarded by both Churchill and Eden as a 'Municheer' and appeasement supporter, had turned out to be the best British Ambassador in Washington in memory. He and Arthur Purvis – who had developed a close relationship with General George Marshall, then generally unknown in Europe – had achieved marvels in obtaining equipment from the United States and in fostering, with Churchill, mounting American support for the British cause. But, a devout Christian Scientist, Lothian refused medical attention for a relatively trivial ailment, from which he died on 12 December.

Churchill, long eager to get rid of Halifax from the inner circle and to bring Eden in, seized his opportunity. His first thought was Lloyd George, as Halifax was deeply reluctant to go to Washington – his wife was even more hostile. Then Halifax suggested Eden, who adamantly refused. Churchill had his way, although Halifax writhed. Eden urged that Oliver Lyttelton should be his successor at the War Office, although the job went to Margesson. Thus Anthony Eden returned to the Foreign Office, with considerable doubts and regrets, but, as Churchill later wrote, 'like a man going home'.

[7]

The Politics of War, 1941–4

Even in peacetime, the exact role of the Secretary of State for Foreign Affairs lacks precision, and its importance and achievement depend upon the experience, capacity and political status of the occupant and his relations with his colleagues – especially the Prime Minister – and with Parliament and public opinion.

Too often, a British Foreign Secretary is the victim rather than the initiator of events, and such diplomatic skills as he has tend to be employed more in reducing damage than in real creativity. In the nineteenth century, when British political and military power was so strong, utterly unexpected events in India, South Africa or the Levant could, and did, gravely disrupt the tranquillity of governments and precipitate wholly unplanned consequences. So could the actions of subordinates and administrators. The annexation of the Transvaal in 1877 was a classic example; others were Disraeli's purchase of Suez Canal shares two years previously, and Gladstone's intervention in Egypt in 1882. With a huge colonial empire and inadequate communications much depended on local initiative, often with unexpected results. Even in the first half of the twentieth century, the sheer vastness of British possessions around the world, despite better communications, still gave considerable authority and responsibility to ambassadors and to senior officials down to district level, while the armed forces, particularly the Army, jealously preserved their autonomy. And, inevitably, standards of competence and commitment varied greatly in the public service.

To be Foreign Secretary amid the buffeting winds of war, especially in the circumstances of 1941–5, provided countless additional complications. Eden had become War Secretary at one of the most cataclysmic moments in British military history. He had now become Foreign Secretary again in the context of unrelieved disaster. The reputation of Britain may have been high, but her actual power, economic as well as military, was negligible. It was another example, as he later caustically remarked, of his fabled 'good fortune'. With Europe under German domination, Britain under sustained air and sea attack, the Balkans threatened, with an ever-increasing military and political commitment in North Africa and the Middle East, with dissident – and usually difficult – governments-in-exile in London, and the anti-submarine Battle of the Atlantic gravely in doubt, the room for the exercise of diplomatic skills by the Foreign Secretary was indeed gravely constrained.

Anthony Eden certainly had the experience and skills essential for the post, and that indefinable sensitive understanding for foreign affairs that so impressed all those who worked with and for him. He also had a feeling for war itself, and could relate and combine military and political factors. His public standing was immensely high, and his relations with Churchill were now close, even intimate. Churchill and Eden had developed great affection for each other, admiration for the other's physical and moral courage, and grave doubts about the other's judgement. Colville recorded in his diary on 9 July 1941 Churchill saying of Eden, 'He would equally well charge a battery or go to the stake for his principles – even though the principles might be wrongly conceived and he might charge the battery from the wrong angle'* – words which Eden could have used with equal (perhaps even greater) justice of Churchill himself. Many storms were to occur. There was to be much mutual exasperation and vehement disagreement. The cold analyst may assess whether one or the other was right on this or that issue. But these were not cold times, and neither Churchill nor Eden were cold men. They were fervent patriots, resolved to win the war. Neither was concerned for his own safety. Each was passionate and had, quite reasonably, a good conceit of himself. At no point, in spite of sharp disagreements, did either lose his faith in the other, nor did anything weaken their late-burgeoned and close friendship. A curious telepathy emerged, and as neither could fully explain it themselves the biographer and historian cannot do so. But it existed and developed.

In the Commons, however, Eden was more highly regarded on the Opposition than on the Conservative benches. Shortly after he had taken over the Foreign Office again he dined with Richard Law on 2 January 'and we had some political talk afterwards. He talked much of the Tory party and my duty to lead it,' Eden wrote in his diary. 'I told him that I had little sympathy with it or men who composed it.'

This was to be a regular refrain. Matters were not improved when James Stuart succeeded Margesson as Chief Whip, and Eden was constantly urging Churchill to 'clean out the Whips' Office', which remained full of Municheers. He felt, rightly, that the Conservative Party tolerated Churchill and himself only because it had no choice, and the one feature of the war that consistently pleased him was the blessed absence of party politics. He had already come to like and admire Ernest Bevin's robust common sense, often amounting to wisdom, his patriotism and application. Sir

* Colville, *The Fringes of Power*, p. 412.

Stafford Cripps, Ambassador in Moscow and then Cabinet colleague, had his deficiencies, but lack of ability and a keen intelligence were not among them. Attlee, whom Eden had always liked, steadily grew in his estimation, and he had many friends among the Liberals. Although his old foe Beaverbrook could be on occasions an impossible colleague, he had drive and fervour, and in his day was the best company in London, rivalled only by Bracken, for whom Eden's pre-war antipathy had vanished, and Churchill himself. It was a Cabinet that worked immensely hard, but it had a core of personal unity and friendship that made it unique. All his colleagues regularly cursed the Prime Minister for his moods, his temper, his unfair admonitory minutes, his complete lack of consideration for others, and the terrible hours he kept and imposed on others. But working under him at such a time was an experience so exhilarating and exciting that these foibles and weaknesses were accepted, although not always willingly or cheerfully.

To work under Churchill required a formidable stamina, which Eden had, but he was to push it to its limits. Those who foolishly thought his health frail and his nerves brittle found him in the early hours of the morning with Churchill, cigar in hand and with a drink at his side – after which he would be up early for work. For four and a half years he was a Foreign Secretary who travelled widely, a member of the War Cabinet and the Defence Committee, and for nearly three years Leader of the House of Commons. It was a burden equalled only by Churchill himself, whose own health nearly broke under the pressure; not until 1944 did Eden begin to flag.

At the Foreign Office Cadogan still reigned, to Eden's relief and pleasure. When Cadogan's diaries were published in 1971 there was considerable surprise, shared by Eden, at the tartness of some of his comments on Eden, but when Cadogan re-read them he wrote:

I see that I sometimes wrote rather sharply about Anthony. I don't think any Secretary of State I served excelled him in finesse, or as a negotiator, or in knowledge of foreign affairs. When something had to be done, Anthony would long to do it. That quality was perhaps carried to a fault; but on the whole it was a good fault for a Foreign Secretary. No one worked harder. And then to take on the Leadership of the House!*

Then, the physical circumstances of working in a city under almost constant nightly attack were unprecedented. The move of Beatrice and the boys to Frensham had not been a success, but in the late summer of 1941 they found Binderton House near Chichester in Sussex, of which Eden bought the lease, and where he found and made his first garden. But there

---

* Dilks (ed.), *The Diaries of Sir Alexander Cadogan, 1938–45*, p. 345.

was not much time for Binderton. Eden moved into a flat in the Foreign Office and his separation from his wife became more marked than ever. The Eden marriage, in severe difficulties for so long, was to become another casualty of the war. Simon joined the Royal Air Force at the first opportunity, and was to be one of those sent to Canada for his training, first as a pilot and then as a navigator. Eden was proud of the son he loved so much, but he missed him deeply.

Although Eden's personal relations with Churchill were excellent, Churchill had taken into his hands every aspect of strategy, considering foreign policy in war to be an adjunct of the great military struggle. Eden fully accepted this fact. Churchill's eagerness to bring in the United States met with considerable success. The passage of the Lend Lease Act was a triumph for Roosevelt and himself, and early in 1941 Roosevelt sent Harry Hopkins, a former Secretary of Commerce and now special adviser to the President and a true confidant, to Britain. Roosevelt's defeated Republican opponent, Wendell Wilkie, was also dispatched. Upon these two very different men Churchill lavished all his charm and persuasiveness, with outstanding effect. Eden was also closely involved, and characteristically preferred Hopkins' quiet impressiveness and capacity for listening, rather than Wilkie's brashness, although of the latter's goodwill and enthusiasm for the British cause there could be no doubt. Thus were the foundations laid for Churchill's famous shipboard meeting with Roosevelt off Newfoundland in August 1941 and for the Atlantic Charter, about which Eden was conspicuously unenthusiastic, high-sounding rhetoric not being one of his favourite exercises. But it was significant that Churchill left his Foreign Secretary behind. All-powerful, impregnable, at times dictatorial, Churchill ran everything, and that initially included foreign affairs.

One of Eden's first acts was to ask for the return as his Principal Private Secretary of Oliver Harvey, languishing in the Ministry of Information, where Duff Cooper had proved a disastrous failure as Minister. Harvey at once noted Eden's resentment at Churchill's 'monopolistic tendencies' and wrote on 8 October: 'AE groans to me at the inactivity, at the lack of results of work at the F.O., and longs again for the Army or the W.O. "I like excitement." He loved the Army and is as much an amateur strategist (a better one, I think) as the P.M. himself.'

Eden was the one politician that Harvey admired, although even he became irritated by Eden's volatile temperament and sensitivity to criticism. What he underestimated was the sheer physical and mental strain that Eden endured. Harvey, like others, considered that Eden was 'always attracted by the idea of a trip'; it was true that Eden always relished the prospect of going to wherever there was trouble to see for himself what was happening – an admirable tendency, which paid many dividends –

but wartime travelling was dangerous and uncomfortable. As David Dilks has noted, while he was Foreign Secretary Eden 'travelled once to Ankara, twice to Washington and Quebec, thrice to Athens and Moscow and four times to Cairo, in addition to attending the conferences at Tehran, Yalta, San Francisco and Potsdam'.* That he achieved this while earning high esteem as Foreign Secretary and proving a highly successful and respected Leader of the House of Commons was an extraordinary achievement in itself, but it was one for which a heavy price had to be paid. As before and after, he drove himself, and others, too hard, and the occasional exasperation of Cadogan and Harvey must be seen in this context. When Churchill and Eden left Office in 1945 Harvey wrote, 'I'm afraid Winston and A.E. had latterly become quite exhausted.' This was true; the cause of that exhaustion was their service to their nation and to the highly precarious cause which they had inherited in May 1940.

As 1941 opened, the Germans, after nine months of almost total success, had good cause for complaint against, and contempt for, their Italian allies, who had been thrown back into Albania by the Greeks, had been routed by Wavell in Libya, and were rapidly losing Abyssinia. The Fleet Air Arm had found half the Italian fleet at Taranto on 11 November 1940 and put it decisively out of action. Much of what was left was destroyed swiftly and devastatingly by the Navy off Cape Matapan on 28 March 1941. Reviewing the situation, the Germans realized that they must undertake a decisive Balkans campaign of their own and build up their military strength in North Africa, General Erwin Rommel being dispatched specifically for the latter purpose.

British policy in the area was to consolidate the North African position, give at least some support to the Greeks, and bring Turkey into the war. Yugoslavia, under the temporizing Prince Regent Paul, was to be stiffened and dissuaded from its timorous and appeasing attitude to the Germans. This was the purpose. It failed on every single count.

Eden's pleasure at returning to the Foreign Office was perhaps less than that at being in the War Cabinet, and after his experience at the War Office he was eager for further involvement in the military sphere. Cadogan noted critically that 'He is always jumping about the room, itching to "to do something". He has to be humoured, but the best one can do is to restrain him.'† If this was somewhat severe criticism, it had a strong element of truth in it.

The Greek situation was not, on close inspection, at all promising. The death of the dictatorial but resolute General Metaxas on 9 January, and his

---

* Dilks (ed.), *The Diaries of Sir Alexander Cadogan, 1938–45*, p. 345.
† *Ibid*, p. 376.

replacement by the nervous and haunted shadow of Alexander Koryzis – 'whose pallid complexion did not suggest a constitution equal to the onerous task'* – in itself created some demoralization and political disarray, while the Greek forces under General Papagos were dangerously stretched, ill equipped and notably lacking in serious air power. Against the Italians this had not mattered, but if the Germans intervened it was clear that a very different situation would emerge. The Greek requests for British assistance and involvement became stronger. With the Germans menacingly building up their forces in Bulgaria, and both Greeks and Turks apprehensive, the issue of whether to provide greater British support grew more pressing.

In the consequent débâcle, personal factors played a large part. Wavell was the one British commander who had achieved a victory in the war, and having destroyed eleven Italian divisions and taken 130,000 prisoners his reputation was at its height, particularly with Churchill. As Eden and Dill had been Wavell's champions, their reputations were proportionately raised.

Eden was equally concerned with involving Turkey on the British side, but the Turks were significantly cautious and apprehensive of German power, and the Bulgarian situation put the Greeks into the front line. Also, there was a formal British commitment to Greece of 13 April 1939. The Defence Committee agreed in principle to assist the Greeks, and informed Wavell that 'assistance to Greece must take priority over any advance in the Western Desert'; the War Cabinet decided to send Eden and Dill to the area. What then occurred was, and remains, one of the most controversial episodes in Eden's entire career.

The tragic odyssey, which was to last for two months, began badly with a nightmare journey in appalling weather during which Eden's Sunderland flying boat was nearly lost, reaching Gibraltar with very little fuel left. So bad were the conditions that the party, having left London on 12 February, did not reach Cairo until the 19th. When Wavell met Eden he commented, 'You have been a long time coming,' and told him that he had begun to concentrate forces for dispatch to Greece. This was entirely in line with Churchill's instructions to Eden, whose principal directive was to send speedy help to Greece and to involve Yugoslavia and Turkey if that were possible. But Prince Paul, a contemporary from Oxford days, would not even see Eden. For this he was to be much reviled, but the fact was that Yugoslavia had no armour and no air force.

That the priority was now to assist Greece was agreed by all. The North African situation seemed secure – on that Churchill sought, and received, assurances from Wavell – and there was also in the minds of Churchill and

* Mott-Radclyffe, *Foreign Body in the Eye*, p. 59.

Eden a special feeling for the Greeks that was something different to *realpolitik* and military strategy. As Eden wrote on his arrival in Cairo, 'to stand idly by and see Germany win a victory over Greece, probably a bloodless one at that, seems the worst of all courses'. The British Ambassador in Athens, Sir Michael Palairet, vehemently took the same view, Dill became persuaded, and General Sir Henry Maitland ('Jumbo') Wilson was given the command. The British party then went to Athens to discuss the matter further. Papagos proposed to withdraw three divisions from Macedonia and Thrace to the so-called Aliakhmon Line in the north. This meant the abandonment of territory, but a concentrated defence on a good position. The British would supply three and a half divisions, an armoured brigade and aircraft. Thus it was decided. Papagos later denied that it had been so positive, but Wavell and Eden had no doubts.

Eden then went to Ankara, where he found increased Turkish nervousness, particularly about German air power, and polite reluctance to become involved. On his return to Athens he found that Papagos had not even begun his withdrawal to the Aliakhmon Line, and was also giving alarming signs of irresolution, even defeatism. London was now becoming concern. Churchill telegraphed to Eden:

We must liberate the Greeks from feeling bound to reject the German ultimatum. If on their own they resolve to fight we must, to some extent, share their ordeal. But rapid German advance will probably prevent any appreciable British imperial forces from being engaged. Loss of Greece and Balkans by no means a major catastrophe for us provided Turkey remains honestly neutral.... We are advised from many quarters that an ignominious ejection from Greece would do us more harm in Spain and Vichy than the fact of submission of Balkans, which with our scanty forces alone we have never been expected to prevent.

Another cable emphasized the point that opinion in London had altered: 'Do not feel yourselves obligated to a Greek enterprise if in your hearts you feel it will only be another Norwegian fiasco; if no good plan can be made, please say so.' Ismay has written of the Chiefs of Staff: 'left to themselves, they would have advised its abandonment, but they were not as yet prepared to disregard the advice of the men on the spot, who included one of their own number, in the person of Dill.'* Churchill confirmed this view, but Palairet passionately protested that 'We should be pilloried by the Greeks and the world in general on going back on our word.' Eden confirmed the unanimous opinion of his military advisers. 'We are all agreed', he reported to Churchill, 'that the course advocated should be followed and help given to Greece.' As Ismay subsequently wrote, 'That settled it.'

* Lord Ismay, *Memoirs*, p. 197.

What had really 'settled it' was Wavell's assurance, with which Dill concurred, that the Northern African situation was secure. As Churchill had written to Wavell on 6 January, 'It is quite clear to me that supporting Greece must have priority after the Western flank of Egypt has been made secure.' That assurance proved – with terrible consequences – to be entirely misconceived.

Large numbers of British, Australian and New Zealand troops and aircraft were being committed under circumstances that looked to the Chiefs of Staff and Churchill increasingly worrying. But the military commanders on the spot, although realistic, were unanimous that the right decision had been taken, and the War Cabinet had before it on 7 March Eden's emphatic recommendation:

Collapse of Greece without further effort on our part to save her by intervention on land, after the Libyan victories had, as all the world knows, made forces available, would be the greatest calamity. Yugoslavia would then certainly be lost; nor can we feel confident that even Turkey would have the strength to remain steadfast if the Germans and Italians were established in Greece without effort on our part to resist them.

This was a political judgement, and an accurate one. Those in London who, like Ismay, were becoming deeply concerned by the military commitment and prospects had to accept that they were dealing with the unanimous recommendation of the Foreign Secretary, the CIGS, and the local commanders, who had all proved so right over the Libya campaign. Also, Smuts, whom Eden saw in Cairo, shared London's military apprehensions but saw no honourable or reasonable way out of the British commitment. Churchill had cabled to Eden on 24 February: 'while being under no illusions, we all send you the order "Full Steam Ahead",' but although the mood had definitely changed in London the War Cabinet took Eden's advice and formally assumed responsibility for it.

Eden remained in Cairo, with forays to Cyprus and Greece, in a grimly disintegrating situation. Prince Paul, desperately trying to prevent the invasion of his country, would not see him or respond to British urgings. Even after he was ousted by a less pliant regime on 27 March, with the full approval and involvement of the British, the fact of German military superiority made the position in Yugoslavia and in Greece still precarious. Papagos had new and more ambitious plans, and Dill failed to persuade Belgrade to make decisive dispositions. London was now convinced through the work of the Bletchley cryptographers that Hitler had decided to attack Russia, but would divert sufficient forces to deal with Yugoslavia and Greece. The Russians, although thoroughly alarmed by German ambitions in the Balkans, would not believe the first part of the British information.

Eden travelled indefatigably in the area; he visited the British troops in northern Greece; and he continued to put pressure on the Yugoslavs to co-operate closely with the Greeks. But the storm was about to break.

It began when Rommel counter-attacked, with devastating success. Suddenly, Cairo and the Suez Canal seemed threatened again, and Tobruk imperilled. On 6 April the Germans invaded Yugoslavia and, in a campaign even more brutal and effective than that in France, secured surrender within eleven days. Then it was the turn of Greece. Within two weeks it was crushingly defeated. By 21 April Wavell was urgently seeking permission to evacuate the surviving British forces. By the time Eden reached London on 10 April the British position in the eastern Mediterranean was precarious, and was soon to become even worse. There was a pro-Nazi *coup* in Iraq, which – it was resolved – had to be suppressed, thereby adding to Wavell's commitments. In the North Atlantic the *Bismarck* and *Prinz Eugen* put to sea and sank HMS *Hood*. A significant number of those British forces that could be evacuated from Greece were sent to Crete, obviously the next German target, and the pro-German Vichy forces in Syria now sought to intervene. So grim was the position that Eden wrote to Churchill on 26 May:

My dear Winston,

This is a bad day; but tomorrow – Baghdad will be entered, *Bismarck* sunk [it was]. On some date the war will be won, and you will have done more than any man in history to win it.

Yours,
Anthony

Churchill did not hold Eden accountable for the Greek disaster. But when Crete fell after ferocious fighting and heavy losses on both sides and Wavell's June counter-attack against Rommel completely failed, Churchill finally lost confidence in the Commander-in-Chief. Even Eden admitted that 'some of his recent reactions seem to indicate that he is flagging' and accepted that Wavell should be replaced by Auchinleck. Wavell became Commander-in-Chief in India.

Eden never considered that his ill-fated Greek expedition had been a mistake, and he was always fiercely defensive about the decision to aid Greece. Where he had good cause for complaint was that at no stage did the military commanders express any concern about the position in North Africa. The clear assumption throughout was that this was secure, so that *additional* forces were available for Greece. When this turned out to be manifestly not the case, all Churchill's doubts about Wavell and Dill were confirmed. Eden can be legitimately criticized for the vehemence of his advice to the War Cabinet, but he did not then fully appreciate how grave were the doubts in London. He was certainly right to do all he could to bring in the Yugoslavs and the Turks, and, although Cadogan was probably right to rate the possible success so low as to be hardly worth the time and effort, in those circumstances it was very much worth the attempt.

It is even doubtful whether, as Eden and others have claimed, Hitler's Balkan campaign seriously delayed the attack on Russia, and thereby justified the British actions. But it must be emphasized that the British 1939 commitment to support Greece if attacked was a fact, and could only have been dishonoured at a heavy price in British prestige, particularly among the neutral states, most of all in America. It was also the case that the Germans suffered heavily for their gains, not immediately but as the Partisan war developed in the Balkans. It was to be among the ugliest of conflicts, cruel, internecine as well as anti-German, in which the roll of barbarities is long indeed. But the fact that when the British returned they were greeted as friends and true allies emphasizes that Eden's endeavours had not been wholly in vain. War is not all calculation.

That Eden had not lost Churchill's confidence was shown in many ways, public and private, but criticisms were strongly expressed in the House of Commons and in the press, especially after the fall of Crete, and Eden admitted that he had 'lost enough tail feathers' when Churchill seriously considered sending him to the Middle East in a permanent capacity. In the event, Oliver Lyttelton temporarily became Minister of State in the Middle East and Eden mused on the very wise advice of Lord Tyrrell that he should never go abroad again without sufficient force and authority, advice which Cadogan strongly endorsed. When military disaster strikes, as Churchill remembered so well over Gallipoli, a political scapegoat can swiftly be found, and, for a while, until other events superimposed themselves, Eden's reputation definitely fell.

The debate in the House of Commons was in itself a near disaster, and Eden was acutely sensitive to the bleak atmosphere – 'cold' he described it in his diary – that greeted him. His was not a good speech, and he sat down in complete silence, Duff Cooper later commenting waspishly that it was the best speech made against the Government. Fortunately, Churchill's speech was one of his very best, and the vote was 447 to 3, but Eden's position was not good. He could have echoed Churchill's subsequent comment on Gallipoli: 'I was ruined for the time being in 1915 over the Dardanelles ... through my trying to carry out a major and combined operation of war from a subordinate position. Men are ill-advised to try such ventures.' Eden was not ruined by this episode, but might well have been – however unfairly – had he not received Churchill's total endorsement and support.

* * *

The Soviet interest in the Balkans, which had gone as far as a treaty of friendship with Yugoslavia, had been one positive aspect of events, and Eden's good relations with Ivan Maisky, the Soviet Ambassador in London, maintained a reasonable contact. The British now knew with certainty of the proposed German invasion of Russia, but Stalin remained impervious to all warnings. Eden was awakened at Chequers on the morning of 22 June by Churchill's valet, who said to him, 'The Prime Minister's compliments and the German armies have invaded Russia.' He then handed to him a silver salver on which reposed a large cigar. New and immense problems – political, economic and military – now arose, but Eden recognized the symbol: Hitler had made his first major blunder, and the Prime Minister was jubilant. After the miseries of the previous months, this good fortune was indeed opportune, not least for the Foreign Secretary.

Churchill, jovially remarking that if Hitler invaded Hell he would make a favourable reference to the Devil, swiftly announced British military support for Russia while stopping short of full collaboration, a point that Eden made to Maisky and to the House of Commons. The British had baulked at the Russians' demands for recognition of their seizure of the Baltic states, and generally relations had been at best formal during the period when the Russians had been watching the conflict and benefiting from it. There were also the unpleasant reports of Russian atrocities in eastern Poland, which proved only too true; and Russian appeals for military equipment simply could not be fulfilled. But the important point was that Russia was now in the war, and must be kept in it. Here was an opportunity for real diplomacy.

Churchill's reputation in the Soviet Union was irredeemably tarnished by his passionate and practical support for the White Russians in the post-1918 civil war when he was Secretary of State for War, and his consistent denunciations of 'the foul baboonery of Bolshevism' were not forgotten. But the Russians had been impressed by the resolution of the British, and now needed all the help they could get. In these circumstances, past disagreements assumed a lesser importance, as they also did for Churchill. If it was a loveless liaison, the important thing was that a liaison there had to be. Although the British were doing very badly in the Battle of the Atlantic, the monthly secret reports of tonnage sunk chilling the War Cabinet, and matters were bad in North Africa, the chances of an invasion of Britain had definitely receded and the tide of the air battle was slowly beginning to turn. If British cities were still being heavily bombed, and the RAF had not yet mastered the technique of effective night-fighting, German cities also were under attack from Bomber Command, German submarines were being sunk, and convoys were getting through. The British situation, although deeply worrying, was no longer desperate. That of the Russians was.

Cripps – who was in London at the time of the German invasion – told the Cabinet that the prevailing view in diplomatic circles in Moscow was that the Russians could hold out for only three or four weeks; Dill told Eden that his estimate was longer, but he, also, was speaking in terms of weeks. As the German forces poured into Russia and advanced with amazing speed, it seemed that they were right. The effects of Stalin's pre-war military purges, and of his refusal to believe firm information of German intentions were now harshly exposed. The German tide seemed inexorable.

It was now that Eden's good relations with the Russians became so vitally important. His first task was to restore relations between the Russians and the Free Poles in London, led by General Sikorski, whom Eden so liked and respected. The Russians had large numbers of Polish prisoners of war, whom the British wanted released along with Polish political prisoners; the Soviet–German treaties of 1939 had to be abrogated; and normal relations between the Polish and Soviet Governments established. If these things were done, Poland would join in the common battle. The Russian–Polish agreement was signed on 30 July. As the Russians realized, they were the weaker party, and had little choice. The release of the imprisoned Polish was to add a formidable, and formidably bitter, number of soldiers and airmen to the Allied cause.

German influence in Iran became another area for Anglo-Soviet action and co-operation. Diplomatic pressure having failed, it was resolved to invade Iran, the Russians from the north and the British from the south. The Shah was deposed – to be replaced by his son – and the German agents taken prisoner, fortunately bloodlessly. If it was not an ideal solution, it preserved the only rail link for supplies to the Soviet Union and guaranteed British oil resources. Eden feared serious friction with the Russian forces, but although there were strains the common need was paramount. If some eyebrows were raised about the moral aspects of the military invasion of a neutral country, Moscow had no doubts; nor did Churchill or Eden.

But, as the Russian position became even more sombre, what was to become a wearyingly familiar litany arose from Stalin. He wanted more and more munitions, and he demanded that the British launch an immediate Second Front in Europe or in the Balkans to draw off German forces. If these were not forthcoming, the Soviet Union would be defeated. As was also to become so familiar, appeals were accompanied by threats and by the active encouragement of a Second Front Now propaganda campaign in Britain that attracted much support, not only in the Labour and Communist Parties and among their sympathizers. Beaverbrook and his newspapers joined in the campaign, with the *Daily Mirror*, rapidly developing into the most popular and influential newspaper of all, and the Communist *Daily Worker*. As the gravity of the Russian position became obvious to anyone who could read a map, and stories of Russian valour and German brutality were reported, this became a serious domestic political factor.

The reality was that the British were in no position whatever to invade Europe or recapture the Balkans, nor even to launch a diversionary attack of such strength in either area to change significantly the balance of forces in Russia. Beaverbrook and Ismay went to Moscow to talk about supplies where they were joined by Averell Harriman, another of Roosevelt's trusted advisers. With the excellent new Ambassador in London, John G. Winant, Hopkins in Washington, Harriman active in Moscow, and American naval forces in the Atlantic so co-operative, the American interest in the war mocked her neutrality. But the Russian demands grew as their position continued to deteriorate, the Germans besieging Leningrad and advancing on Moscow. Cripps was proving difficult, obsessed with post-war settlements, in which Churchill was wholly uninterested. After considerable discussion, it was agreed that Eden should be sent to Moscow, or elsewhere in the Soviet Union if Moscow was invaded. Eden's tentative offer of sending some British troops to the Caucasus had now become impossible to fulfil, as Auchinleck's attack, eagerly anticipated by Churchill, had floundered in November, and the commander of the Eighth Army was relieved of his command. These were gloomy circumstances under which to visit Stalin, but it was eventually agreed that Eden must go if relations were to be put on a better basis than recriminations and demands, fomented deliberately by Soviet propaganda in Britain.

Eden took with him Cadogan, Harvey, and Frank Roberts of the Central Department. The trip began badly, when Eden fell ill on the railway journey to Invergordon, and gastric influenza, among the most miserable and debilitating of afflictions, was diagnosed. In this mood, he was summoned to the telephone to speak to the Prime Minister, a summons he responded to with reluctance and annoyance. Churchill's Prime Ministerial vice – which Eden was to emulate – of telephoning his Ministers at any time that suited him, frequently on quite trivial matters, exasperated less intense colleagues than Eden.

But this was not trivial. The Japanese had attacked Pearl Harbor and were moving rapidly on British possessions in the Far East. The United States and Japan were at war, and the British declaration had followed. Another massive front had been opened.

While Eden was absorbing this information from a highly excited Churchill, the Prime Minister merrily told him that he was off to America to see Roosevelt; Eden asked when? Churchill replied, 'Next Thursday.'

Eden vehemently remonstrated. This would mean that the Prime Minister and the Foreign Secretary would be abroad simultaneously, and the cancellation of his visit to Russia was unthinkable. Cadogan and Harvey entirely shared Eden's dismay, and, having failed with Churchill, they telephoned Attlee – who entirely agreed with them – and Winant, who also favoured delay. 'Really the P.M. is a lunatic,' Harvey wrote in his diary; 'he gets in such a state of excitement that the wildest schemes seem reasonable. I hope to goodness we can defeat this one. AE believes the Cabinet and finally the King will restrain him, but the Cabinet are a poor lot for stopping anything.'* And so it proved. There were more calls and pleadings, but Churchill had secured the agreement of the War Cabinet, and that was that. Eden accordingly embarked on HMS *Kent* for the long and bleak trip, physically ill and in the worst of tempers. It was not improved when, on the 10th, he received the news that the two British capital ships *Prince of Wales* and *Repulse* had been sunk by air attack by the Japanese and that the American naval losses in Pearl Harbor had been severe. Eden thought that this provided another reason for Churchill to stay in London for the time being; Churchill did not. The only gleams of light were reports that the Russian winter had broken, and that the Germans were definitely held outside Moscow. But then came another message from Churchill to say that aircraft were being diverted from the Middle East to Malaya and that the proposed offer of ten squadrons to the Russians was cancelled. This confirmed Eden's fear that Churchill, to enthuse the Americans, would divert essential forces from the Middle to the Far East, and so effect a bleak opening to Eden's discussions with Stalin.

The *Kent* arrived off Murmansk on 12 December in a thick fog. Maisky, who had virtually locked himself in his cabin during the voyage, now emerged to go ashore to find out what transport was available, returning with the choice of flying in hazardous conditions or making a sixty-hour journey in an armoured train. The British opted for the train. Then there was a remarkable episode when Maisky asked for a private discussion in Eden's cabin, and produced a black bag that contained large packages of rouble notes. He was aware, he said, of controversies between Britain and Russia over exchange rates, and this money was placed unreservedly at the disposal of their guests. Eden later wrote,

I was agape at so much wealth and asked Maisky to thank Mr Stalin for the hospitable thought which had prompted this action. I assured him, however, that we could meet our expenses without having to put him to this trouble and that

---

* Harvey (ed.), *The Diplomatic Diaries of Oliver Harvey*, Vol. 1, p. 70.

we should not have need for the currency. The Ambassador seemed downcast at my reply but, when I persisted in it, replaced the roubles and relocked his bag.*

Eden was noticeably modest about his capacities as a writer, and until *Another World* was published in the last year of his life there was a general opinion that, in the Churchill comment on Attlee, he had much to be modest about. But his diaries reveal what a good, natural descriptive writer he was. This is his diary for 13 December:

Russian delegation, Admiral, General, etc. came aboard about noon, I still feeling far from well. After luncheon we left the *Kent* in half-light and whirling snowstorm, a most eerie proceeding. 'Pipe' says captain to chilled mariners, who do their manful best and we clamber down the side to the bowels of a warm and greasy tug. So, farewell England. A few minutes and we are alongside and step ashore to a most picturesque scene. Still this uncanny half-light. A line of soldiers in their sheepskin uniforms making a smear of ochre, decked out by the flags of the two nations, over-bright, rather cheap and new, as the only splash of colour, behind them log huts, unfinished shacks, a few idle spectators who as black smudges brace the scuds of snow. The bands strike up. We salute, and the usual ceremonies take place. The men look very young. The effect of the whole scene is surprisingly beautiful.

Soon we are packed into cars and off for sixteen mile drive to Murmansk. Soviet troops mount guard at intervals along the half-dark route. No better testimony to Soviet manpower.

As we topped the hill above Murmansk, the clouds lifted and the harbour looked most beautiful in its semi-circle of hills and half-lights. The colour of a pale pearl grey and of a fairy texture. Quite indescribable and unpaintable, the air crisp and fresh. This Arctic scenery has a beauty which is the exact antithesis of the Christmas card of tradition. Soft, melting half-tones. Nothing brittle or garish.

The train itself was remarkable for the contrast between, on the one hand, the luxurious comfort provided for the passengers – 'All plush and silk curtains and tassels, just like a nineteenth-century drawing room', Harvey noted – the gargantuan meals and lavish supplies of caviar and alcohol, and, on the other hand, the predicament of the troops with their anti-aircraft guns in open trucks, enduring the intense cold. On 15 December the party arrived in Moscow late in the evening.

Eden's first meeting with Stalin on the next evening was recorded by him as 'friendly'. This was of short duration. Stalin was obsessed with frontiers and his post-war possessions. As the Germans were within twenty miles of Moscow, this avariciousness was extraordinary, and a weird discussion took place about the division of the spoils. On the next day, in Eden's

* Avon, *The Reckoning*, p. 287.

words, 'Stalin began to show his claws.' He insisted on recognition of the 1941 frontiers, giving Russia all the Baltic states and half of Poland. When Eden said that he had no authority to promise this, Stalin said that it looked as though the Atlantic Charter was anti-Soviet. Another meeting on the next day was equally abortive. Eden held his ground, and Stalin's comments became more cutting. Eden proposed a tripartite meeting to include the Americans, which Stalin almost contemptuously rejected, and Eden spoke of returning to London as soon as possible. The atmosphere was now thoroughly bad. In the justified belief that their rooms were fitted with microphones, Eden put on a pretty show of storming up and down, denouncing the Russians and regretting that he had ever come to Moscow, Cripps and Cadogan providing an approving chorus. Shortly afterwards Maisky rang to say that Eden's request to go to the Front, hitherto ignored, had been met by Stalin. Accompanied by General Archibald Nye, Eden made the journey on the 19th. It was a grim experience, which included meeting some German prisoners, young, cold and ill clad for the bitter temperatures. 'They looked pleasant enough boys,' Eden noted sadly, 'and I felt very sorry for them. God knows what their fate will be, but I can guess. Hitler's victims.'

Back in Moscow, Molotov, under orders, was obdurate that without concession on the 1941 borders no agreement was possible, and London reported total Cabinet agreement with Eden's firm line. It was a complete impasse, but when Eden next saw Stalin something had happened. The border issue remained, but there was now – for the first time – talk about improved Anglo-Soviet relations, and a good discussion about the grave military situation in the Far East. Suddenly, Stalin asked if Eden and his party could dine with him. The time was fixed for 10.00 p.m. It was then nearly nine, and the rest of the British team had begun a notably frugal meal, from which they were extricated to go to the Kremlin. Eden told them that Stalin had produced a communiqué in amiable general terms that said nothing about the frontiers.

There then followed an amazing evening and morning that the British never forgot. In a city where there was widespread malnutrition and acute shortages of everything, even milk, and with the German guns clearly audible, the British were extravagantly plied with much excellent food and a vast quantity of alcohol. General Timoshenko, the hero of the defence of Moscow, was drunk before he arrived and became even more drunk. There was much drinking of toasts – Harvey claimed he counted thirty-six – with one by Eden after midnight in honour of Stalin's birthday. Timoshenko kept making increasingly incoherent speeches and proposing toasts. There was then much talk of past events – Stalin blaming Molotov for the Soviet–Nazi Pact! – more alcohol, an interminable Russian military propaganda film, and no rescue for the British until five in the morning. All the British were struck by the contrast between this luxury and hedonism with what was happening outside, and by the sycophancy and fear with which the Russians showed to Stalin.

Although the British were exhausted – Eden sleeping until three the following afternoon – the mission had ended on a far more cordial note than could have been expected. Eden saw Stalin again before he left, and once more the atmosphere was good.

Both Cadogan and Harvey were derisive about Eden's concern over the publicity for the visit, both judging that it was the result of his jealousy of the publicity given to Churchill's visit to Roosevelt and to Beaverbrook's to Russia. In fact Eden's anxiety was due not to 'vanity' but to a real concern that the Russians could not see the Moscow discussions as inferior in importance to Churchill's in Washington. Also, something had to be shown to the Second Front Now movement that the Government was closely in touch with the Soviet Union, although the subject had not even been raised at the Moscow meetings!

Although Eden had stuck firmly to his position in Moscow, it was clear that the 1941 frontier issue would have to be addressed if the Allies were to have full collaboration from the Russians, now more urgent than ever with the disastrous situation in the Far East. But, as Harvey noted, 'As between Russia on one side, who thinks she is doing all the fighting against the Germans, and America, who thinks she can dictate the peace on the other, poor HMG are going to have a difficult time. We shall be in trouble with both.'* This was precisely the position. But when Eden cabled his views to Churchill in Washington he received a shocked response. Churchill took the noble aspirations of the Atlantic Charter with a seriousness that Eden did not share. Also, Churchill, all his endeavours to bring the United States into the war now in fruition, and legitimately exultant at his achievement in persuading Roosevelt to give American priority to the European War, saw no reason for any concessions whatever to what he still called 'the Bolshies'. Cripps, who had been relieved as Ambassador, reported that Stalin had refused to see him for a farewell meeting, and that all the old suspicions were reviving.

Churchill, brimming with confidence on his return from Washington, found a less pleasing situation at home. Auchinleck's new offensive had been repelled and Rommel was on the rampage again; Eden's faith in Auchinleck was greatly diminished. The news from the Far East was unrelievedly bad, with the fall of Singapore and the tame surrender of a large army perhaps the single most dispiriting episode of the entire war.

* Harvey (ed.), *The Diplomatic Diaries of Oliver Harvey*, Vol. 1, p. 85.

Churchill's decision to send out Duff Cooper as his special representative – accompanied by his wife, which occasioned particular criticism and resentment* – had not received Eden's support, as he was becoming uneasy about Churchill's enthusiasm for ministers of areas. Duff Cooper's involvement in the Far East had been brief and, absolutely through no fault of his own, inglorious, but this method of handling things was becoming chaotic.

The widespread unease in Whitehall and in the press was reflected in Parliament, where criticism of the Government and the Prime Minister rose to such a level that Churchill demanded a vote of confidence. On 12 February, to cap everything, the German warships, *Scharnhorst* and *Gneisenau*, escaped from Brest and passed through the English Channel with only one forlorn attack from heroically flown biplane Swordfish aircraft to inconvenience them.

Discontent with the Government, especially with Churchill, now became acute. But when Erskine Hill, the Chairman of the 1922 Committee, sought Eden's involvement in an anti-Churchill move, Eden refused to have anything to do with it. What he did urge upon Churchill, in a series of private meetings and long discussions,† was the urgent need to reconstruct the Government, particularly the War Cabinet. Pushed on by Jim Thomas and Cranborne, he put himself forward, although not with great enthusiasm, as Leader of the Commons, and found himself once again the victim of intense intrigue from the Whips' Office, organized by Stuart. In the event, the post went to Cripps; the one Eden would have really liked, Defence, was obviously denied so long as Churchill remained. And although there was now concern about Churchill's physical as well as his political health, Eden would not push his claims. It was a grim period; in retrospect, Eden thought it the most grim of all. Militarily, everything was continuing to go wrong everywhere, and confidence in British commanders was low. The Germans were preparing for a massive offensive in Russia, the Japanese were advancing and conquering everywhere in the Far East, Rommel was dominant in North Africa, and everywhere the Allies seemed to be not only defeated but humiliated.

---

*The Duff Coopers had sent their son to the United States in June 1940. This had, rightly, been ill received.

† Fortunately, Eden kept a war diary, but it is not complete and has many gaps at times of high activity. Churchill did not, and although the documentation of the Churchill Government is formidable, much business of real importance was conducted over the telephone or in private meetings that were not recorded. This applied especially to Churchill's relations with Eden. The latter kept a full record of what he considered particularly important discussions when he had the time to do so, and these are often far more revealing than minutes and submissions. As they saw each other so often, their correspondence is meagre, and their long telephone conversations are lost for ever.

Eden wrote in his diary on 21 January 1942 that he, Beaverbrook and the First Lord of the Admiralty A. V. Alexander had discussed the situation over drinks after a late Defence Committee.* 'Winston was tired & depressed, for him,' Eden recorded.

His cold is heavy on him. He was inclined to be fatalistic about the House, maintained that bulk of Tories hated him, that he had done all he could & would be only too happy to yield to another, that Malaya, Australian Govt's intransigence & 'nagging' in House was more than any man could be expected to endure. I urged reforms in Whips' Office & organization of pro-Govt speakers. Max backed me in latter citing example of last war. But Winston would not be interested arguing that Ll G was young & therefore right to ensure against future, but that he was 67.

On 9 February Churchill told Eden in strict confidence that his doctor was becoming worried about his heart and disliked his plan to visit India. 'W did not look well and yet did himself as well as ever at luncheon,' Eden wrote. Beaverbrook's capriciousness was only one of his problems, although a major one. After a long and difficult meeting with Churchill on 18 February about ministers, Churchill ended by saying that 'I should be leader, long eulogy of me. Finally made it clear he would like to be out of govt & go to U.S.A.' On the 20th, in another long and intimate talk, it was agreed that Margesson must go and be replaced as Secretary of State for War by P. J. Grigg. 'I urged on Winston that he must clean out the Whips' Office. They were inefficient & nursed grievances about the past instead of being active for the future.'

This problem came up again on 27 February when Bracken came to see Eden:

He was much troubled by Winston's health tho' his account of it was confused. It seems that [Doctor] Williams fears that the heart will affect his circulation & perhaps even his speech, that there may be something in the nature of a 'blackout' temporarily on occasion. All this sounds very alarming & more like a stroke. Anyway B maintained that Winston must give up more work or he would not be able to carry on. He was most depressed now, sat with his head in his hand, talked of lasting only a few weeks, etc. Only way out was to get him to shed greater part of his Defence duties & only person to whom he might shed them was me. He had not sufficient confidence in anybody else. Could I consider Deputy Min of Defence with F.O. perhaps appointing a Deputy F.S.? I said that physically I had

* The drinking habits of Churchill have been grotesquely exaggerated. Indeed, he seemed to gain a perverse enjoyment from encouraging these legends, and they certainly did him no harm with the British public. Both he and Eden unashamedly enjoyed good food and wine throughout their lives, but for both of them work came first, and dominated pleasure. No two men worked harder for the moments of the latter. Both were Cavaliers rather than Roundheads, but neither had any time for those who drank to excess.

no doubt I could combine the two but reminded B that (a) Attlee would object (b) we had all been saying for weeks past that no such appointment was necessary. But B was resolute to put suggestion to Winston and I did not discourage him, for I think that I could help. All the same I hardly think that Winston will readily agree.

The secret of this major crisis was very well kept, as it had to be. The military news everywhere was bad, the Russian pressure for the Second Front and munitions was constant and fierce, and at this point Beaverbrook announced his departure from the Government in order to advocate that cause. On 4 March, to Eden's dismay, Churchill was talking freely of his impossible difficulties with the Labour ministers – notably Cripps – and reverting to a purely Conservative Government. 'He had a strange hankering after party politics again,' Eden gloomily wrote, and in a series of telephone calls urged him to think again. By 9 March, when the question arose of Cripps going on a special mission to India, Eden was relieved to find Churchill talking of Cripps' 'loyalty & integrity. I supported him strongly in this belief. On the other hand he criticized Attlee freely for his small-mindedness & perpetual hunt for [Labour] party places.... I suggested that Attlee should lead the House instead of me, since I had already more than a full day's work, but he would not hear of it. If I would not do it, he would.'

Eden's role as a pacifier at this critical time was crucial. Churchill's intense depression from time to time was a part of his character that those who knew him best understood, and in the spring of 1942 there was good cause for depression. Also, the effects of gross overwork played their part. Eden and Bracken were the two people outside his family who were closest to him at this time, Cherwell being regarded as a scientific genius but not a politician; and of all the Conservatives Eden was closest to the Labour ministers. He was therefore the unifier and vital link, without whom the Government might well have disintegrated. The fact that this did not happen was principally Eden's work, but it took place while he had a very full load at the Foreign Office and in the Commons. He wrote on 10 March: 'Feeling rather wretched after bad night with the "old pain" as Beatrice calls it. Strongly urged by her to slacken off or a breakdown certain. Made my statement in House on Hong Kong massacres [by the Japanese]. A gruesome task.'

It was now definitely decided that Cripps would go to India to see the position and report back and that Eden would be temporary Leader of the House. Cadogan was not the only one who regarded this as madness, especially as everyone knew that Eden would be a conscientious Leader, as he was. It was another burden, on so many others, but it demonstrated again how indispensable he had become. 'To bed tired, but a bad night with pain until after two. It is disheartening,' he wrote on 14 March. Weekends at Binderton, although much enjoyed, particularly when Nicholas was there, were too few. Although Eden never referred to these matters in his memoirs, he called his chapter on this period 'A Low Ebb', as indeed it was.

Eden's role as pacifier was not confined to the internal workings of the Government.

The entry of the United States into the war caused, and continued to cause, as many difficulties as it brought benefits. At that point, American suspicions of the Soviet Union were deep: as Eden wrote in a memorandum for the War Cabinet, 'Soviet policy is amoral: United States policy is exaggeratedly moral, at least where non-American interests are concerned.' Here again his relatively good relations with Stalin helped, and his friendship with Winant became stronger. The future of the Baltic states and Poland, and the question of post-war frontiers, provoked strong disagreements, and an uneasy compromise. Eden was even more alarmed by American plans – brought over by General Marshall and Hopkins – for the Second Front in 1943, with a smaller operation in Europe in the autumn of 1942. With Malta under desperate siege, the Germans advancing again in Russia, and little prospect of success in North Africa, Eden thought the proposals at best dangerous and at worst insane. Dining with Law on 7 April Eden commented that the War Cabinet was not working, that the Defence Committee met irregularly, and that 'There is no day to day direction of war except by Chiefs of Staff & Winston. I would not object to this if it gave results, but it doesn't.' Churchill, as he reflected, 'wants to move all the pieces himself'. But at least Churchill had emerged from his dark depression, 'striding about his room in vest and drawers with cigar in his mouth, whisky and soda at his side', and agreeing with Eden about the perils of a too early Second Front.

When Molotov arrived in London on 20 May he did so, as Eden wrote, 'in an uncompromising mood'. For reasons that puzzled Eden, after intense and often severe negotiations, Molotov accepted Eden's proposed Soviet–Polish Treaty, that made no mention of frontiers and did not approximate to the Soviet 'minimum conditions'. As Eden rightly surmised, the principal immediate Soviet interest was the Second Front, and when Molotov went to Washington he achieved a communiqué expressing 'full agreement ... with regard to the urgent tasks of creating a second front in Europe in 1942'. This was a tribute to Molotov's wiliness and American naivety. The British were not consulted, and felt that they had no choice but to accept the wording, accompanied with strong warnings about its hopeless unfeasibility. 'It is a tough job to make progress with these people [the Russians],'

Eden wrote on 1 May. 'They always ask for more.' Winant fully shared Eden's views about his Government, but reported that he could make no progress with the President or his Under-Secretary of State Sumner Welles. Eden was dismayed when Churchill, 'struggling with his bath towel, like a Roman Emperor in his toga', told him he proposed to replace Halifax and make Beaverbrook the Washington Ambassador! Eden prevented this, but could not prevent the Russians going home in triumph, convinced that they now had full support for a 1942 Second Front.

The sheer impossibility of this was demonstrated by Rommel's new offensive, in which he forced the surrender of Tobruk, effecting another major British reverse. Churchill was in Washington with Roosevelt when this disaster occurred, and on his return the Government had to face a censure motion in the Commons, which it survived – only twenty-five Members voting in favour of the motion – more as a result of the disunity and incompetence of its opponents than of real confidence in its capacity. Cripps made a mess of the organization, choosing Lyttelton, now returned to the Government, and inexperienced in the ways of the Commons, to open the debate. The talk of having Eden as the permanent Leader now became stronger.

What was not known was that Churchill, shortly before his departure to the United States, had written to the King:

In the case of my death on this journey I am about to undertake, I avail myself of Your Majesty's gracious permission to advise that you should entrust the formation of a new Government to Mr Anthony Eden, the Secretary of State for Foreign Affairs, who is in my mind the outstanding Minister in the largest political party in the House of Commons and in the National Government over which I have the honour to preside, and who, I am sure, will be found capable of conducting Your Majesty's affairs with the resolution, experience and capacity which these grievous times require.

This remarkable tribute testified to the intimacy of the relations between the two, and to Churchill's increasing confidence in Eden's judgement. The 'pacifier' was also the only senior minister apart from Bevin who could really stand up to him and persuade him out of dangerous courses. When Churchill brooded on going out personally to Egypt in the aftermath of Auchinleck's fiasco, Eden talked him out of it, arguing that he would be in the way. ' "You mean like a great blue-bottle buzzing over a huge cowpat!" said Winston. I said this was just what I did mean!'

A subject on which Eden's advice was more doubtful was whether the British should encourage and support Germans opposed to Hitler, principally in the Army. Eden was as sceptical about these as he had been about the alleged purpose of the bizarre flight to Britain of Rudolph Hess, not least because the political record of the German Army officers in the past had been notably unheroic. Also, if rumours of British interest in peace-feelers from dissident Germans reached the Russians, now under heavy pressure again, their already considerable suspicions of British good intentions might be disastrously fortified. Eden's opinion – confirmed by the War Cabinet – was that it must be made abundantly plain that 'if any section of the German people really wished to see a return to a German state based on respect for law and the rights of the individual, they must understand that no one would believe them until they had taken active steps to rid themselves of their present regime'. With the German forces triumphant everywhere, it was indeed difficult to believe that these flicker-ings of unorganized dissent could be treated seriously. The perils of even appearing to want to parley with an alternative German Government seemed to Churchill and Eden far to outweigh any possible advantages. For this Eden was subsequently much criticized – although never by Churchill – but the evidence from British secret intelligence was not encouraging. As Eden anticipated, it was not until the turn of the military tide in 1944 that the opposition in the German Army to Hitler assumed serious proportions.

Eden subsequently remarked that the most difficult aspect of working with Churchill was that although so many of his ideas, often coming at unexpected hours and without warning, were, if not wrong, at least in need of caution, others were marvellously sound, and he was always concerned not to discourage Churchill's amazing intellectual fertility and eagerness for action. 'It was never my job to be the wet flannel, the constant No-Man.' This difficulty also often confronted Alan Brooke and Ismay, but Churchill's meteoric temperament meant that he needed around him men he trusted. To his great credit he realized this as well, but it did not make for an easy life for anyone in the very small inner circle. Thus, having reluctantly abandoned the plan for an instant visit to Egypt, Churchill suddenly, within two days, leapt at the suggestion from the new Ambassa-dor to Moscow, Sir Archibald Clark Kerr, that he should go to Russia to see Stalin. Eden advised that he should, if he received a definite invitation from Stalin and 'of course subject to the doctor's all clear'. This also put a new complexion on the Egypt visit. It was agreed that he could combine the two, and go to Cairo with only Brooke and Cadogan. Eden shared Churchill's deep concern with the Middle East Command, but it was also vital to persuade Stalin of the impossibility of the Second Front.

By this point the only American senior officer who was committed to the European venture was General Marshall, but Roosevelt had now become convinced of its futility in the teeth of British resistance. The new plan was for an American landing in North Africa, code-named first

'Gymnast' and then 'Torch', to the west of Rommel's forces. As this part of North Africa was occupied by the French under Vichy administration, de Gaulle became more of a problem: he objected to deals with the Vichy leaders and was himself disliked by Churchill and Roosevelt, but his prestige among the Free French meant that he could not be ignored. But, for the time being, Churchill could offer Stalin something. Eden ensured that Beaverbrook's wish to go with Churchill was unfulfilled.

In Egypt, Churchill replaced Auchinleck with Alexander and appointed General W. H. E. 'Strafer' Gott to command the Eighth Army. Almost immediately Gott's aircraft was shot down and he was killed; on Brooke's direct recommendation Montgomery was appointed. The British had at last found their winning combination in North Africa. In Moscow, Churchill, after several severe exchanges with Stalin, was able to stand firm on the 1942 Second Front, his case buttressed not only by the promise of Torch but by the terrible losses suffered by the British in their convoys to Russia. It was considered by all involved that the Russians demonstrated little appreciation of the ordeals of the British naval and merchant seamen, but it was difficult even for Stalin to claim that the British were making no effort. Churchill's visit ended, as had Eden's, with late-night revelling and toasts, but it was Eden who was becoming the more seriously outraged at Soviet attitudes, ingratitude and imperious demands and threats. But, as with the Americans, compromises had to be made if the flimsy Alliance were to hold. And, as the torrid year of 1942 entered its third quarter, it seemed very flimsy indeed.

As Eden subsequently realized, although he did not at the time – in spite of complaints and outbursts, typically on quite trivial matters while remaining calm on the big ones – he was severely overburdened. His biography is not a history of the war, but of his role in it, and the circumstances of his life. This was a life of almost unremitting work, with blessed intervals at Binderton or snatched dinner parties with friends, and too much time was also occupied with necessary political functions and public speeches, as well as attendance in the Commons, now sitting in the Lords after the destruction of their Chamber and after a hapless interlude in Church House, the Lords sitting in the Robing Chamber. The only consolation here was that, because of the bombing and blackout, the Commons met at reasonable hours; but Members were as demanding as ever, and notably querulous about the lack of success. Eden's success in the House of Commons was even more remarkable given his solitariness. Oliver Harvey noted, rightly on 24 July:

I wish A.E. would see more of his colleagues. He ought to keep constant touch with Bobbety, Cripps, Lyttelton. For the four together could do more than one alone in influencing the P.M. As it is, the P.M. is apt to go into a huddle with A.E. ... and tho' I think A.E. can do more with him than anyone, it still isn't much. The relation of P.M. to A.E. is father to son and heir, but the others are left out in the cold and there is risk of A.E. himself becoming isolated from his own age group of colleagues.... His relations with the press are close and good. But for his colleagues and the H. of C. he has an invincible distaste.*

As Eden realized, MPs were under great pressure themselves from constituents and a critical press, but their complaints and questions were a severe additional load. Whether it was a strength of democracy or not, the fact was that the parliamentary institutions continued to function as before, as Eden's diary reveals:

14 August
A day in the constituency. B heroically came with me.

Cannot pretend we enjoyed it much. Crowded journey both ways. Luncheon of people very smugly middle class. Kind but patronizing!

Forty minute wait for return train at station and an hour late at Paddington. Gossiped to some soldiers standing in the corridor. That was the best part of the day.

6 September
Long talk with B about our future plans. I am bothered about money. There is no security in politics, and I feel that for boys' sake and my own old age I ought to take something that will last a few years and at least allow me to put up my private income, which at present I am over-spending at £1,000 a year or more. Moreover I do not really feel confidence in myself as No. 1 at home, and it looks as if, *faute de mieux*, I might drift that way. Beatrice saw the force of all this, but argued that I had gone too far to turn back now, tho' she admitted India was only possibility. Truth is I feel too tired to tackle these post-war problems. I am desperately in need of a change and I do not know enough of economics.

8 October
Simon had breakfast with us and left during the day for Oxford and his air training. It is sad to see him go, and he is so very young. Not yet eighteen.

The Allied Commander-in-Chief for Torch was General Dwight D. Eisenhower, and his Chief of Staff was Brigadier-General Walter Bedell Smith. Eden at once liked both, and had complete confidence in them. Although Eisenhower had felt strongly that the British opposition to a European landing – Operation Sledgehammer – had been wrong, and was himself initially hostile to Torch, he and Bedell Smith warmly returned that confidence. Eisenhower's appointment was an inspiration, and he had in addition to his military qualities a quite exceptional grasp of the importance of good public relations and of being on good terms with the press. In this he shared Eden's good fortune in being handsome and

* Harvey (ed.), *The Diplomatic Diaries of Oliver Harvey*, Vol. 1, pp. 143–4.

photogenic, and within a very short time he had become the most famous of all the Allied Commanders, only later rivalled by Montgomery, who likewise realized the importance of a good press. Eisenhower's hot temper was another characteristic he shared with Eden, but nothing, not even the events of 1956, was to damage their friendship and co-operation. It was at this time that Eden also met for the first time John Foster Dulles, who brought a plan from the Norwegian Foreign Minister, Trygve Lie, which Dulles himself disliked, for the smaller European states to become British satellites. Eden also disliked it, but when Dulles proposed larger national blocs in Europe arising out of the confederation of equals, Eden was negative. It was not a good beginning.

Those who disliked Eden later said that it was his habit of calling people 'My dear' that irritated Dulles, as it did others. Since Churchill constantly called his friends 'dear' without causing any known offence at all, this is an odd explanation. What was much more important was that Eden wrote immediately after their meeting that he considered Dulles' views 'uninstructed' and that the Americans 'know little of Europe'. This was undeniably true, but with large numbers of American troops arriving in Britain and with the United States now assuming an increasingly dominant role there were certain to be difficulties.

Suddenly, the military position began to go right. On 23 October Montgomery successfully attacked El Alamein. The American landings in French North Africa began on 8 November and, despite meeting resistance in some places, were successful. In retaliation, Hitler seized Vichy France, and on 26 November the French fleet was scuttled at Toulon. Both General Giraud and Admiral Darlan had asked for the supreme command, and, with the Americans established, agreed between themselves to divide the control of the French Resistance in North Africa. De Gaulle was prepared to work with Giraud, who had been consistently anti-Vichy, but not with the Pétainist Darlan, whom the Americans favoured. Nor did the prospect appeal to Eden, who felt strongly that de Gaulle's position as leader of the Free French must be protected. Matters were not improved by Churchill, under Roosevelt's influence, who, in what Eden described in his diary as 'a shouting match' on the telephone lasting over half an hour, to Eden's fury announced that he preferred Darlan to de Gaulle. The argument was taken to the War Cabinet. Eden pointed out that Darlan took his authority from Pétain, and that the Allies were 'dealing with turncoats and black-mailers' and it was astounding that they were in effect establishing a Vichy Government, led by a charlatan. Churchill, eager to keep Roosevelt happy, was not persuaded.

The political vacuum in North Africa was filled by the appointments of Harold Macmillan as Minister of State in Algiers (while retaining his post as Under-Secretary for the Colonies) and of Robert Murphy, a career diplomat, as Roosevelt's personal representative at Eisenhower's head-quarters. They faced an awesome political task, but it was improved when Darlan, to Eden's ill-disguised relief, was assassinated on 24 December. Even so, the dilemma was not resolved.

Eden's acceptance in November of the Leadership of the House of Commons was further evidence of his indispensability and of his close, if often heated, relationship with Churchill. But to assume another burden was, as Cadogan emphasized, a major mistake. He was as conscientious and diligent a Leader as had been expected, and made a great success of the job, being popular and respected, and having a gentle touch. But this additional work, as Eden later wrote, 'meant a ruthless burning of the candle at both ends for the best part of three years, for which excess there is always a price to be paid'.

In mid-January 1943 Roosevelt and Churchill met at Casablanca for two weeks, an occasion described by Macmillan as 'a mixture between a cruise, a summer school, and a conference'. Eden, who disliked unstructured and unprepared ventures of this nature, did not attend, but had to deal with a deeply suspicious and unco-operative de Gaulle in London, who required much persuading by Eden to accede to Churchill's invitation to travel to Casablanca. As the two leaders had appointed Giraud to command in French North Africa this was hardly surprising, and it was at considerable cost to his own feelings that de Gaulle consented to pose for a photograph shaking hands with Giraud. What was more important even than this truce was that the British persuaded the Americans that the Mediterranean should be the main sphere for the present, with the object of knock-ing Italy out of the war, and that the cross-Channel invasion of Europe should be postponed again. Politically the central – and perhaps unfortu-nate – feature of the Conference was Roosevelt's description of the Allied purpose as 'unconditional surrender'. The War Cabinet agreed to this phrase on the proviso that it applied to Italy as well as to Germany and Japan.

Immediately after Casablanca Churchill flew to Turkey, against Eden's strong advice. As Eden had anticipated, nothing was achieved, and when Churchill returned he went down with a severe cold that developed into pneumonia. Before this, Churchill, who had already told Eden that his Leadership of the Commons was 'febrile' and that he resented his oppo-sition to his Turkish trip, was caustically critical of the Foreign Office. Eden himself was not only very tired, but was enduring the agonizing experience of seeing his sister Marjorie die of cancer, his misery not reduced by Lady Eden's insistence on coming with Tim. 'She was tough and "spiky" all evening,' Eden wrote. The funeral took place on 12 February at Warwick. 'Funerals always strike me as barbaric,' he noted. 'Poor Marjorie. As B said she was the one member of my family who was consistently kind to me from my childhood onwards thro' the years. She has played a part in every phase, marriage, constituency, & against Mamma. I wish she could have been spared to go back to her sunshine after the war.' In these circumstances, Eden took Churchill's strictures ill, particularly when he said, looking hard at Eden, 'I bear no rancour.' Then Speaker Fitzroy died, and the urgent task of finding a new Speaker acceptable to the House fell on Eden.

There was a dangerous feeling in Britain that, as a result of the North African successes and substantial Russian advances, with the Battle of the Atlantic almost won and the Blitz over, the war was as good as won. Although Churchill warned that 'This is the end of the beginning,' more interest was being shown in the report published by Sir William Beveridge in December with far-reaching proposals for major social reform after the war whose financial assumptions were, to put it mildly, dubious, but which attracted considerable support. Churchill was impressed by the weaknesses rather than the theme, and the Conservatives misjudged the national reaction. Eden made a point of meeting Beveridge to discuss matters, and came away with the impression 'that the old man didn't seem to know much about his report'. But when it was debated in the Commons on 22–23 March the chief speakers were Anderson and Kingsley Wood, who demonstrated such lack of enthusiasm, even interest, that 119 Labour and Liberal MPs voted against the Government.

Not unreasonably, as Foreign Secretary, Eden was concerned about the post-war international situation, although he knew how far the war was from being won in Europe and the Far East. The phrase 'the United Nations' at that time referred solely to Britain, Free France and the United States; but, although the League had clearly failed, the principles behind it deserved to be preserved, this time with the full involvement of all the victorious Powers. Eden submitted a paper to the War Cabinet on these lines, and made overtures to test Soviet reactions.

Churchill's illness prevented Eden from going to Washington, at Roosevelt's personal invitation, until 12 March. His discussions with the Americans were not as hopeful as he had expected, and he found Roosevelt's cheerful post-war division of Europe 'alarming in their charming fecklessness'. As Churchill was discovering, to his anger, Roosevelt's enthusiasm for self-determination and freedom extended to the British Empire, notably – but not exclusively – India. Although Eden was less of an Imperialist than Churchill, he could not accept these sweeping attitudes, particularly when the Japanese were on the Indian borders, the Indian

Army was a crucial and dedicated military factor, and Gandhi was raising the banner of Indian independence again.

Eden's increasing mistrust of Roosevelt and the Americans was not a perverse personal reaction. The American economic domination over Britain after 1942 was immense, and bound to increase. It was accompanied by, on the one hand, a moralizing condemnation of Imperialism that especially enraged Churchill, and on the other by a calculated determination to ensure post-war domination. Oil provided the most serious element of difference, the Americans resolving to increase their position in Iran to the exclusion of the British and, in effect, to expropriate Saudi Arabia. Thus, while denouncing one form of Imperialism they ruthlessly pursued another. These events caused the strongest and fiercest of all the Anglo-American disputes, and the fact that in the Middle East avariciousness was not backed by a clear US foreign policy made the situation even worse. Eden's resentment at these brazen power-politics by a close ally in an area vital to Britain left a deep, and enduring, mark, with what were to be momentous consequences.*

Characteristically, more agreeable were visits to American military units, and most agreeable of all was an invitation to speak in Maryland, in Annapolis, prompted by the Baltimore–Eden connection, when Eden was able to put forward his vision of a truly effective United Nations. On this, on his return to Washington, there were further conversations with Roosevelt which were more positive, and a sombre one with Hopkins on the progress of 'Tube Alloys' – the atomic bomb. They had a convivial dinner together. Eden thought no more about this until he read a full account of it in Hopkins' biography by Robert Sherwood. 'Diplomacy is never off the record,' he commented ruefully. No harm was done, but it is a lesson for all in politics or diplomacy to take to heart. Fortunately perhaps, it is usually ignored, or political life would be impossible.

When Beatrice and Eden had spoken about the future and India in the previous autumn they were contemplating the Viceroyalty, it being generally agreed that Lord Linlithgow should come home and be replaced. Eden was far more keen on the idea than his memoirs reveal, although his interest in the post can be detected by a careful reading.

Churchill at first would not hear of the idea, although Eden had some powerful advocates. But after dinner on 12 April he startled Eden by revealing that he had completely changed his mind. Eden wrote in his diary:

---

* For the best study of this aspect of the Alliance, see Gabriel Kolko, *The Politics of War, 1943–45.*

He was positively enthusiastic. Said what a calamity it would be to win the war & lose India that he was convinced that only I could save India. That I was his chief lieutenant & only really intimate friend and that tho' he would hate to lose me etc. etc. In short Winston's imagination has clearly caught fire, encouraged no doubt by the difficulty of finding anybody else & the fun of reconstructing his Govt which he proceeded to do straight away! I managed to head off the suggestion of Max to W'ton & Edward home so that Max is to lead the House of Lords. 'Oh Boy, O Boy!' Bobbety is to succeed me. Brendan came in during the later stages of all this, to which I have given faint justice for all were most kind throughout & not so crude.

Eden was immensely attracted. Here was a position of real power and influence at a critical moment. But there was the fact that, whatever Churchill might promise about membership of the War Cabinet and about the succession being assured, Eden realistically saw that in practice both would be impossible. This was also, and very strongly, the view of the King. His Private Secretary Sir Alexander Hardinge telephoned Eden to say that 'I must stay here to have some influence on Winston,' and the King wrote directly to Churchill about the prospect of losing 'your Second-in-Command'. The King also spoke to Eden personally on the same lines on 8 May. If it was not a royal veto, it was very close to one. When Attlee heard of it, he was equally adamant that it was impossible at such a time. Leo Amery, Secretary of State for Burma, on the other hand, urged the appointment strongly, and Eden was torn between his desire to accept it and the knowledge that such a major reconstruction had several national disadvantages. Similar problems affected the other possibility, Lyttelton, who was proving an invaluable member of the Government, although never destined to find the Commons an easy or congenial audience. Even on 8 June Churchill still favoured Eden as 'the only appointment that could redeem the situation'. But by the following day he, and Eden, accepted that neither Eden nor Lyttelton could be spared, and Wavell was appointed Viceroy and Auchinleck succeeded him as Commander-in-Chief.

Thus the glittering vision of the Viceroyalty had to be reluctantly abandoned. It was significant that Eden was so attracted by the opportunity of 'a *real* job'. But instead of the dilemmas and perils of the Indian subcontinent he had to return to those closer home.

Had Eden gone to India, the first result would almost certainly have been the removal of de Gaulle as leader of the Free French. Churchill, in Washington again, found American feeling running strongly against the Algiers-based French Committee of National Liberation and de Gaulle as its chairman, and, given his own antipathy to this prickly and often uncongenial genius, was very sympathetic to this attitude. What they grossly underestimated was de Gaulle's position in France, where the Resistance was growing and where de Gaulle's name was synonymous with Free France.

Eden was urgently summoned by Churchill to fly to Algiers, where he had gone after Washington. There was talk of a special mission of the two to tell Stalin that the Second Front had been postponed again, until 1944, but thankfully this was abandoned. The problem of the Free French dominated everything, even the question of what was to be done after the imminent Allied invasion of Sicily. Eden saved de Gaulle, but the hostility of Roosevelt and Churchill was as strong as ever. Eventually, the command of the French forces was divided, 'a partition like that between Octavius Caesar and Mark Antony', as Eden later wrote. But the situation had again been saved by the pacifier.

The complex, and often ferocious, relationship between Churchill and de Gaulle merits – and has received – special treatment of its own,* and some of the disputes now appear petty and even incomprehensible in the context of the world war, but at the time they assumed large proportions, and took up an inordinate amount of Eden's time. He considered it worthwhile, a view that we can now strongly endorse. On 12 July, to take one example, Eden noted that after dinner with the Churchills, with Henry Stimson, the US Secretary for War, and Winant present,

we had a fierce but friendly argument about French in Cabinet room until after 2 a.m. I told W again all I felt. He maintained that De Gaulle could not be allowed to dominate Cttee & he must see how things worked out before recognition [of the Committee] was accorded. Admitted that if we broke on this I should have much popular support, but warned that he would fight vigorously, to the death. I told him I wasn't contemplating resignation! ... Then we discussed Tory party & both agreed how little we liked it & how little it liked us. On which harmonious note we parted.

But on the next day Churchill called him to the Annexe (the Prime Minister's wartime headquarters) to tell him sombrely that 'we might be coming to a break'. Then, on the 19th, he climbed down and agreed to telegraph Roosevelt on the emollient lines Eden had proposed. Again, characteristically, they stayed up late together chatting with suitable refreshment. 'All this [the French problem] was wedged in of course with much talk on the progress of the war and future plans,' Eden noted. 'Winston was in very good form and could not have been more friendly.'

The genial ending to this issue was partly the result of the successful Allied invasion of Italy on 10 July and the dramatic resignation of Mussolini. Churchill considered that these developments, and the planning for

* See in particular François Kersuady, *Churchill and de Gaulle*.

the cross-Channel invasion of France in the following year (Operation Overlord) required another Anglo-American conference, and Quebec was the agreed choice. Eden was not present at the principal meetings, and concentrated on attempting to get American recognition of the French Committee. But American hostility to de Gaulle was insuperable. An agreement to differ was all Eden could achieve. The real item was how to arrange another meeting with the Russians, and at what level it should be.

In Eden's most private papers there is this contemporary account, written immediately after it had occurred, of a strange episode during the Quebec Conference. Eden had enjoyed a brief few days' fishing and swimming with his Private Secretary, Nicholas Lawford, when they received an urgent message to dine with Churchill in a special cabin put at his disposal. Eden's account, only part of which he later published, runs:

Read some documents & then Charles Wilson* came in. He spoke to me apart about W. He is worried, says that he appears to be unduly depressed by troubles that are not immediate and to be unable to throw them off. 'For instance he keeps bothering as to whether we shall have to fight Russia after Germany is finished, an event he will not anyway live to see (meaning fight against R). Incidentally the doctor warned of the indiscretion of speaking in this way about Russia in front of strangers who were only too likely to repeat it.

When W arrived I admit that he confirmed C.W.'s diagnosis. He did not look at all well and was a bad colour. He said to me that he felt the need for a longer change. I urged him to take it. He was very sweet, said it had been absolutely right to bring me out, fussed about the party on our 'Clipper'. 'I just don't know what I should do if I lost you all. I'd have to cut my throat. It isn't just love, though there is much of that in it, but that you are my war machine. Brookie Portal you & Dickie [Mountbatten]. I simply couldn't replace you.'

Then we had some talk on politics. All this while W was splashing about in his bath, most of time by the light of one candle, the lights having fused.

He also confirmed his doctor about Russia, warned me over & over again, said G & I had been the great restraints upon R. We were committed to destroy both. R would then be immensely powerful. All this was mainly my business; it might be that I should still see many years of war, perhaps all my life. I admitted that all this might be true but argued that only possible basis for a policy was to try to get on terms with Russia. In view of past history suspicion only too easily bred suspicion. I thought it a good sign that Joe wanted a three-power commission set up in Italy.

Eden returned to London, while Churchill went on to Washington. It had been agreed that the next stage would be a Foreign Ministers' meeting

* Churchill's doctor, subsequently Lord Moran.

with the Russians, but whereas Eden wanted the meeting in London, Roosevelt was keen for Moscow, and persuaded Churchill. Eden was exasperated at what he considered this 'subservience' to the Americans. When Cordell Hull, despite his age, agreed to go, Eden had to accept that it was to be Moscow, yet again.

Although this meeting was to be held, again, on Russian soil, Eden was determined that it should be properly and professionally prepared, and that the British side should have a clear idea of what their objectives were. Whether they could achieve them would be another matter, but Eden had had enough of ill-prepared top-level chats. It was at this point that Ismay realized how much he had underestimated Eden.

Eden and his party travelled to Moscow by way of Cairo and Tehran, where Hull joined them. They reached Moscow with an agreed agenda, with each government having established its dominant priority. As Churchill had just returned to Stalin a singularly offensive message about the Arctic convoys, it was difficult to anticipate their reception, but in fact it was warm and friendly. The crisis at Stalingrad had ended, admittedly at dreadful cost, in a decisive defeat for the Germans, and the Russians were engaged in preparing a substantial counter-attack. As Eden noted, although 'the impression of drab dreariness persists' in the Moscow streets, his hosts looked markedly better than they had on his last visit. Stalin's resentment at the return of his message provided a difficult beginning, which Eden was able to resolve by saying that he had instructions to discuss the matter further. The atmosphere relaxed.

Eden had briefed himself in great detail on the military aspects of the position, on the convoy situation and on the logistics for Overlord. Stalin reciprocated with information about the Soviet situation, and admitted that the Allied advance up Italy, although slow, was holding down significant numbers of German troops. Their discussions were notably friendly and deeply informed. When Hull complained of the slowness of the progress, this being his first experience of direct negotiations with Molotov, Eden spoke to Stalin directly. As Eden later recorded, Stalin said,

'What do you want?' I replied: 'Decisions on the subjects we have been discussing for more than a week.' Stalin nodded and said he would talk to Molotov.

I became hopeful, but the next two days were as abortive as their predecessors and when we had finished I had to tell Hull that evidently I had failed. However, on the afternoon of October 30th the atmosphere appeared suddenly to change. Molotov became brisk and businesslike, he was always a superb workman, as skilful at disentangling as at stalling. In an hour or two we had reached conclusions on all the ten days' discussions.*

* Avon, *The Reckoning*, p. 415.

Preparations and diplomatic skill had their rewards. Stalin accepted the new date for Overlord – June 1944 – and there was full agreement on the Arctic convoy situation. He also agreed to send a Soviet mission to work with the Yugoslav Partisans and with the existing and active British mission helping them. An Inter-Allied Advisory Council would deal with Italy, and a joint European Advisory Commission would plan for the armistice with Germany and its enforcement; on American insistence there was a special declaration which was the genesis of the involvement of both in the post-war United Nations. By tacit agreement, the issues of Polish–Soviet relations and the Polish frontiers were not dealt with.

The Conference ended in the now traditional feasts and toasts. One of Eden's most important achievements had been to persuade Stalin to attend a meeting at Tehran with Churchill and Roosevelt, and the Moscow discussions ended in an atmosphere that had not seemed possible a few days before.

In London, even the deeply sceptical Cadogan was impressed by all Eden had achieved, and Ismay and the whole British delegation realized that it had been very much a personal triumph. Although Eden considered Stalin's reluctance to look him in the eyes, even when shaking hands, and his whole demeanour to be 'creepy and sinister', and disliked the Soviet system more on every visit, there was a core of mutual regard between these two very different men. Ismay considered that Eden's handling of Stalin was 'masterly', and Eden for his part always had a high opinion of Stalin's acute intelligence and exceptional skills as a negotiator. Although he does not even imply this in his own account, it was clear to the British and American teams that the Russians considered Eden to be an exceptional professional: they also liked and trusted him. What Ismay called his 'pretty wit, and transparent integrity', and his known war and political record, now made him a highly favoured emissary and comrade-in-arms. Moreover, although the Russians had turned the tide, there remained much to be done, and they desperately needed the Alliance still. But the general opinion that no one except Eden could have masterminded the most successful of all wartime Allied conferences was absolutely right. As Eden later wrote, 'It was the high tide, if not of good, at least of tolerable, relations between us.' But the achievement was to be swiftly undermined.

Back in Cairo, Eden once again attempted to persuade the Turks to join the Allies. He was now able to speak with confidence of the inevitability of Allied victory. He found the Turkish Foreign Minister and his Chief Secretary strangely hard of hearing. 'No one can be so deaf as a Turk who does not wish to be persuaded,' Eden ruefully commented after three days 'of ding-dong argument'. The Turks remained neutral.

In Greece, as in Yugoslavia, there was civil war between hostile factions as well as resistance to the Germans, and Communist influence there was considerably more troubling than in Yugoslavia. For the time being, it was decided on Eden's insistence that the King must declare that he would not return until invited to do so and that British assistance must concentrate on the non-Communist elements. But, in the prevailing military situation, there was little more that could be done. Eden's fears about the post-war shape of Europe mounted, but there were severe limitations to wartime diplomacy, as the British hand became weaker and that of the Soviet Union stronger. It was on the battlefields, in the air and on the oceans that the fate of post-war Europe was being decided.

The Anglo-American bombing offensive against Germany, after a bad beginning in which many serious losses had been suffered, was now virtually a nightly event, inflicting cruel damage which was to become even worse. The first one-thousand-bomber raid had been in May 1942 on Cologne, and with the American involvement these huge armadas became regular. The policy of area bombing had been created by Cherwell and approved by the War Cabinet, and was put into devastating effect by Air Chief Marshal Sir Arthur Harris. Churchill's views on the campaign were, and remained, ambivalent. Eden developed a warm regard for 'Bomber' Harris, and when he and Bomber Command received scant recognition for their dedication and sacrifice after the war Eden went out of his way to keep in touch with him, considering that he had been scurvily treated, both by Churchill and by the post-war Labour Government. Eden's only serious disagreement with him was in 1944 when he opposed the bombing of French railways and roads, fearful of heavy French civilian casualties and alienation of the French: in the event his fears were not realized, as by that stage the bombing had become remarkably accurate.

Eden's reputation, fully merited, of not being a fair-weather friend was seen most significantly in his relations with de Gaulle and Harris. Neither was ever to forget it.

Eden returned briefly to London to report to the House of Commons on the Moscow talks and to find British euphoria about the Soviet Union at new heights, with Churchill very affable and complimentary. This was just as well, for in addition to the rows about de Gaulle Eden had strongly and successfully opposed the plan to seize the Azores from neutral Portugal. The plan, which Churchill had strongly favoured, was abandoned after, as Eden noted in his diary, 'Something of a shouting match going on for an hour or more'; and then:

W & I had long chat about other things after meeting alone. As I said good night he said he was sorry if he had been obstreperous at the meeting but he felt that

S[alazar] was intolerable. I replied that I had been obstreperous too. 'Oh, you, you were bloody!' On which note we said 'good night'!! (2 August)

He [Churchill] was very apologetic afterwards & said he would end by killing us all by these late hours, which may well be true. Bed 1.30 a.m. (28 September)

I feel that the call of rest & Binderton grows stronger. Jim [Thomas] says that MPS are very flattering about my leadership of House. No doubt shall stumble down soon. (30 September)

As Eden's diaries and letters demonstrate, whether he was in London, Quebec or Moscow, he longed for Binderton and the English countryside. His workload at the Foreign Office, in the House of Commons and in the Cabinet – which he chaired in Churchill's absence ('felt rather scared, but everyone very kind') – and on his international missions was too severe. He began to suffer severe migraines again, fainted once, and complained about 'the dazzles' when he became dizzy. A lamentable doctor, whom Eden consulted for too long, advised an operation on his tonsils, which Eden rejected as impossible. It was also a peculiarly ridiculous diagnosis of severe overwork.

Then it was back to the Middle East, and Tehran, with the Big Three.

Although the Polish question had not been discussed in Moscow, it was to be one of the principal items at Tehran, and as the Russians advanced westwards their political approach hardened. Roosevelt and Churchill had been in Cairo in military and other discussions with Chiang Kai-shek for three days before Eden arrived on 24 November. Churchill had travelled in the battle-cruiser *Renown*, accompanied by his second daughter Sarah. He had a heavy cold when he embarked, and was troubled by his necessary inoculations. He was not particularly interested in the Chinese discussions ('lengthy, complicated, and minor' as he described them) but was keen to obtain increased American involvement in Mediterranean actions to speed the German defeat. Roosevelt would not agree, and was proposing a single Supreme Commander for all operations against Germany, which was unacceptable to the British. They held their ground, but it was clear that they were being gradually pushed into a minor role. Tehran was a very different meeting to that in Moscow, with even Churchill complaining about the lack of businesslike working, and both he and Eden – especially Eden – concerned about American lack of interest in the post-war European situation and their enthusiasm for Chiang Kai-shek. On both issues the British had to do a holding operation. It was an ominous occasion.

Eden and Churchill flew to Tehran on the 27th, very early. 'W had lost his voice, I think from too much talk last night, and was sorry for himself until he had a stiff whisky and soda, at 8.45 a.m.,' Eden noted. 'He appeared on aerodrome as Air Commodore in khaki drill and amazed me by translation into blue before we reached Tehran. His travelling wardrobe must be prodigious.' Eden was driven to the British Embassy on his own, surrounded by cavalry and with much pomp; at its entrance they had to stop until a donkey and its owner had been removed, Eden pondering on how easy a target for assassination he was. When he arrived he found an indignant Churchill, who had been sent a circuitous way, and took it ill that his Foreign Secretary had been cast in the role of decoy.

Unhappily, Eden's role throughout Tehran was essentially peripheral. The bulk of the discussions was on future military operations, but what was worrying to Eden was the manner with which Roosevelt so easily responded to Stalin's skills and macabre jokes. Also Churchill, manifestly unwell, was not as strong or as well prepared as he should have been. When he proposed for southern Germany 'a Danubian confederation' this was the first Eden had heard of it. He considered that Churchill and Roosevelt were more impressed by, and subservient to, Stalin than was necessary. He was also depressed by their casual attitude to the details of the Polish frontiers, as though it were a minor matter. In contrast to Moscow, it was an ill-prepared, amateur (on the Allied side), convivial gathering that only reinforced Eden's deep dislike of this manner of conducting serious diplomatic and political business. Cadogan noted that Eden was 'rather in despair about this hazy conference', and with very good cause. The road to Yalta had been opened.

Eden's concern for Poland increased when he came to appreciate Roosevelt's complete indifference to the matter. The discussions on the Polish frontiers became increasingly academic on the American side, and, when the Russians realized this, harder on the Soviet. 'I began to fear greatly for the Poles,' Eden subsequently wrote. Again, no progress was made with the Turks. Also, Roosevelt took an entirely different view to Eden over the role of the King of Greece after a meeting with the latter, and complained strongly to Churchill that Eden was trying to deprive him of his crown. As the State Department had agreed with Eden, he was very indignant, and the Conference which Eden had done so much to initiate ended bleakly. Stalin had won every point, and Roosevelt had conceded every one. Eden's optimism about good relations with the Russians faded; so did his respect for Roosevelt, and his dislike for ill-prepared casual meetings of this kind was augmented. 'Being fresh to it', Cadogan wrote, 'I am rather appalled at the haphazard, amateurish surroundings of the President. How *do* these people carry on?'*

---

* Dilks (ed.), *The Diaries of Sir Alexander Cadogan, 1938–45*, p. 586.

The whole venture nearly ended in complete disaster when Churchill's cold developed into pneumonia in Tunisia and he became seriously ill. Eden by this stage had returned to London, where he had to deal with the highly emotional issue of which side the British ought to be supporting among the Yugoslav Partisans. It was the worst time for Churchill to be so seriously unwell, and it was not until the middle of January 1944 that he was allowed to leave his convalescence at Marrakesh for Gibraltar, to return to Britain in HMS *King George V*.

Eden subsequently believed – and historians have tended to support him – that it was from this point that Allied co-operation began to disintegrate. At Tehran the Russians, on the pretext of an alleged German plot to assassinate Roosevelt, had moved the American party into the compound of the Soviet Embassy, where the staff were all members of the Soviet secret police, and in which it can be reasonably assumed listening devices had been installed. But it seemed to Eden that Roosevelt and even Hopkins had been drawn into the Soviet compound in another sense, with Churchill dangerously in compliance. Also, as the British and Americans prepared for Overlord, they had become badly bogged down in Italy, while the Russian movement westward was inexorable. Both in Greece and in Yugoslavia the fight for post-war supremacy was becoming increasingly bitter, with active Soviet involvement and influence. 'I confess to growing apprehension that Russia has vast aims,' Eden wrote in March 1944, 'and that these may include the domination of Eastern Europe and even the Mediterranean and the "communizing" of much that remains.' The new hard attitude of Moscow towards the Free Polish Government was significant, and ominous. When the Russian forces crossed the Polish frontiers in the spring of 1944 the balance had definitely changed.

One of Churchill's principal features was his intense reluctance to interest himself in post-war problems, at home or abroad, with the result that the sole British strategy was reduced to simply winning the war. The single most important piece of legislation during the war was Butler's 1944 Education Act, a remarkable achievement personally, but also a fine example of what can be done in a coalition with personal and political goodwill. It is very doubtful that Churchill ever grasped its essentials, let alone its details, but at least he was not hostile to it. In foreign affairs, however, this obsession with military immediacy had its severe limitations. Eden could do little about the Allied pledge on unconditional surrender, not least because the Russians were fiercely committed to it, but when the Commonwealth Prime Ministers met in London in May they gave full support to Eden's provisional proposals, based on a Foreign Office paper, for a future world organization to build upon the experience of the League. The paper ended, 'Its name might well be "United Nations", which is now a phrase to which we are all accustomed.' Churchill's interest was limited to a proposal for regional councils, which the Prime Ministers rejected, and Eden's view prevailed. Cadogan was sent to the preparatory meeting of what was to become the United Nations, at Dumbarton Oaks in Washington, with instructions on these lines. It was an illuminating example of the different approaches of the two men.

Both, also, were now noticeably tired. 'A. can't bear his double burden any longer,' Cadogan wrote on 21 March. 'Everyone's exhausted.' Eden himself noted in his diary after another long day, 'Some talk with Brendan Bracken when House rose. He is convinced that I should give up Foreign Office. I am so weary I hardly care so that I am released from one.' This uncharacteristically ungrammatical entry gives its own message. On 3 February he exploded in his diary against Bracken and Beaverbrook and their 'gangster politics.... I would as soon go to Satan for advice on any serious issue & I like Max as I like Satan! Cunning is the quality that Max admires most.' On 10 February Churchill said to him that his burdens were clearly too heavy; 'I cordially agreed & said I was quite ready for any modification but he didn't follow this up. He couldn't have been sweeter.' But the plan to move Eden from the Foreign Office and replace him by Cranborne never really made much progress, not least because Cranborne was very doubtful about how he would get on with Churchill, a doubt shared by others, including the Prime Minister. On 5 April Churchill urged Eden to see a doctor and meanwhile to take some leave. 'He could not have been kinder. "You are my right arm; we must take care of you" – & much more to the same effect.'

This was exactly the problem. Eden was not only Foreign Secretary and Leader of the Commons, but he was also in effect Deputy Prime Minister, Deputy Leader of the Conservative Party, and chief confidant, regarded by Churchill as being available at all hours and for all matters. When they disagreed, as they often did, the emotional strain on Eden was greater than on Churchill. Eden's admiration and affection for the old man were undimmed, but he often questioned his judgement on foreign affairs, as he did Roosevelt's. It was this that principally persuaded him to remain as Foreign Secretary, but his responsibilities were now so wide that Cadogan and the Foreign Office felt that they received a disproportionately small amount of his time. In fact, he was as meticulous as ever in his handling of paperwork but Cadogan's often expressed exasperation at seeing so little of his Foreign Secretary is very understandable. Yet this was not Eden's fault.

With both the Dominion Prime Ministers' Conference and Overlord imminent, and with the interminable difficulties with de Gaulle, and the Russian alliance coming under increasing strain, this was hardly the moment to bring in a new Foreign Secretary. So Eden persevered, taking two weeks' so-called leave at Binderton, returning to London certainly better, but plunged at once back into his many rigorous and severely taxing responsibilities.

The principal difficulty was that diplomacy was totally dependent upon the military situation. Until the middle of 1944 the British Empire had more forces engaged with the enemy than any other belligerent; after that the balance changed, and changed dramatically in Europe. Particularly in the case of de Gaulle, Eden remained the pacifier, but so far as the Russians were concerned the Moscow Conference had been the high point. Thereafter it had been a catalogue of unpleasantness.

The Allied invasion of Europe began on 6 June, but, although initially successful, it ran into difficulties and severe delays that aroused much anxiety until the decisive breakthrough that was to sweep the Allies to the German borders. But another cause of anxiety was the arrival of the V-1 pilotless flying bomb, one of which landed very close to Binderton and blasted in most of its windows. The Cabinet had reports of the development of another weapon, the V-2 rocket. Much now depended on the skill of the RAF in finding the sites or the speed of the Allied advance in capturing them.

The consequent strain was manifested in the Government. Eden wrote in his diary on 6 July:

After dinner a really ghastly Defence Cttee nominally on Far Eastern strategy. W hadn't read the paper and was perhaps rather tight. Anyway we opened with a reference from W to American criticism of Monty for over-caution which W appeared to endorse. This brought explosion from CIGS [Brooke]. 'If you would keep your confidence in your generals for even a few days I think we should do better.' W asked for explanation – 'When have I ever failed to support my generals etc?' CIGS – 'I have listened to you for two days on end undermining Cabinet's confidence in Alexander until I felt I could stand no more. You asked me questions I gave you answers. You didn't accept them & telegraphed to Alexander who gave the same answers,' & more in the same vein. W protested vehemently. He was clearly deeply hurt on his most sensitive spot, his knowledge of strategy & his relations with his generals. I tried to pour oil.

As the Allies advanced, news came of the attempt on Hitler's life and the failed *coup* organized by a group of German officers. This information arrived while a Cabinet was taking place. 'Ernie B[evin] at once said that it was Nazi stunt to popularize H. Brendan said it was Goebbels' work. I said it was hard to tell so far, but I didn't think so.' Eden was right that 'there had been some real trouble in Germany,' and the plot only narrowly failed. Later there was criticism that the Allies had given insufficient encouragement and assistance to the plotters, and that if they had the war could have ended in 1944. This was not Eden's view, then or later, but he was one of the few leading Allied figures who detected the seriousness of the attempt, while wondering, as did many others, why it had not been made much earlier. He concluded that it had been precipitated only by German military defeats in the field on all major fronts. On this, controversy continues to this day.

These new developments prompted Churchill to see Roosevelt again in Quebec early in September. Eden joined them for four days, and was struck by how drawn and ill Roosevelt looked. He found that his presence was not really required at all, and there was much 'hanging about', and a memorable row with Churchill when Eden was scathing about the Henry Morgenthau Plan (to 'pastoralize' Germany after the war) which Churchill and Roosevelt had initiated, 'so was rather peevish & fear must have hurt W's feelings'. Ismay was so fed up with Churchill that he had offered to resign, and Churchill's ill humour led him – for the first and only time – to criticize Eden personally in the presence of foreign representatives. The strain was evident on everyone. The only solid achievement in Eden's eyes, apart from killing off the Morgenthau Plan, was that the Americans, at long last, accepted the French Committee as the *de facto* civil authority, paving the way for its recognition in October as the French Provisional Government.

Years later, Eden was asked how he could explain the prolonged hostility to de Gaulle on the part of Roosevelt and Churchill, and replied, simply, 'I can't.' In June Churchill wrote to Eden of de Gaulle: 'Remember that there is not a scrap of generosity about this man, who only wishes to pose as a saviour of France in this operation without a single French soldier at his back'; on 15 September Eden recorded that 'Winston did however go so far as to say that he would rather have a de Gaulle France than a Communist France, a distinct advance!' Eden considered that de Gaulle's fatal error was to believe that the only way to deal with Churchill was to make the stiffest possible demands in the stiffest possible manner, which was the last way to deal with him. But although Eden constantly urged de Gaulle to take a warmer and more sympathetic, indeed seductive, approach, he was unsuccessful. Eden himself had many of the aspects of a prima donna, albeit one with a sense of humour, but in this respect he was hardly in the same category as Roosevelt, Churchill and de Gaulle, lacking their supreme self-confidence, which amounted often to arrogance. This was essentially the problem. But, as Eden had always emphasized, when the French Resistance took de Gaulle as its leader he *had* to lead the Provisional Government. How so obvious a fact had eluded the American and British leaders for so long, and had caused so much acrimony, baffled him. Yet the pacifier had, belatedly, succeeded again.

But now, the Soviet darkness was falling over Eastern Europe, particularly Poland, as the Russians continued to advance. The agony of Warsaw, destined to last sixty-three days at the cost of 200,000 dead, began in August when its people rose against the Germans. The British could give little help; the Russians gave none. The Balkans were in turmoil still, with the situation in Greece especially worrying. The British liberation of Greece had, ironically, made the position even worse. The Germans having left, the Communist and other warring factions could turn upon each other, and did. It was to try to clear up these increasing differences that Churchill decided to go to Moscow again in October, taking Eden with him.

This meeting was indicative of the changed atmosphere and the new realities. As Harvey noted of the Russians: 'All very friendly, but unmovable.' Tito had left British protection, to British dismay, and had flown to Moscow, and there were other difficulties over Poland and the Balkans. Stalin conceded that Greece was primarily a British concern, and after hard negotiation there was agreement on Churchill's percentage proposals* for influence in the Balkan countries, which the Russians were to ignore. The talks over Poland were even worse; Stalin was implacable. Churchill's success in persuading the Russians to receive members of the London Poles was marred by his clear desire that the latter should make significant concessions to the Soviet Lublin Committee on borders and on forming a joint government, a desire which Eden did not share. His experience of meeting the puppet Lublin Poles was sobering: 'They seemed creepy to me,' Eden recorded. They turned out to be much worse than that.

As usual, Russian hospitality was immense, and Stalin and Churchill got on excellently. But the military and political realities had changed. Also, although the Americans and British had definitely changed the Far East war, there was – literally – a very long way to go, and the assurance of Soviet involvement in the war against Japan after the European war had ended was considered crucial. This, of course, gave an additional and very powerful bargaining advantage to the Russians, as they well knew. They certainly did not agree with Eden's admiration for the saying of John Quincy Adams that 'The more of pure moral principle that is carried into the policy of a Government, the wiser and more profound will that policy be.'†

Churchill and Eden returned by way of Cairo, Churchill to travel

---

* These were: Rumania – Russia 90 per cent, others 10 per cent; Greece – Britain 90 per cent, Russia 10 per cent; Yugoslavia – 50 per cent and 50 per cent; Hungary – 50 per cent and 50 per cent; Bulgaria – Russia 75 per cent, others 25 per cent.

† Quoted approvingly by Eden on 28 March 1944 in a speech to the Free Church Federal Council.

immediately to London and Eden to visit the British forces in Italy. But Eden received an urgent message to go to Athens, where the situation had become confused and critical. Eden was alarmed by what he found, and called for an economic expert to deal with the roaring inflation and lack of supplies. His personal reception was ecstatic, and he was awarded the freedom of Athens, but the general situation caused him immense concern. Matters were not improved by the arrival of Harold Macmillan and Alexander. Macmillan had achieved a considerable reputation for his work as Resident Minister in the Mediterranean, but Eden had never liked him. Indeed he was highly critical of Macmillan; the latter had achieved a position of enormous influence and power in the area, which Eden probably resented. None the less, it was the judgement of them both that if the British military and naval forces had not been present there would have been a Communist takeover already; but the situation was, to say the least, hazardous, and urgent remedial action had to be taken. The situation was temporarily stabilized, but Eden's fears of imminent civil war proved abundantly justified.

What was probably less justified was the enthusiasm for foreign travel, to which both Churchill and Eden were prone. Almost as soon as Eden returned to London he found plans for himself and Churchill to go to Paris to accompany de Gaulle at the head of the march on Armistice Day up the Champs-Élysées. It was a highly emotional occasion. 'Not for one moment did Winston stop crying,' Eden recorded (with some exaggeration), 'and he could have filled buckets by the time he received the Freedom of Paris.' With them marched Duff Cooper, the new Ambassador to France, whose love of the country and admiration for de Gaulle outweighed Eden's reservations on his other enthusiasms, particularly his obsession with establishing a formal Anglo-French Alliance and a Western European defence union, which would obviously be seen by the Russians as directed against them. But he was to prove a fine and popular Ambassador, and his views were closer to Eden's than to Churchill's.

Although Eden could feel more satisfaction in being with de Gaulle than Churchill could, this came after a visit in bad weather to British forces in northern Italy. Eden went down with a throat infection, and then had to deal with King George of Greece. The Polish borders issue still preoccupied him, but the constant travelling and consequent tiredness did not help, particularly with a House of Commons – especially a Labour Party – which failed to realize the menace posed by the Greek Communists and the need to resist them. Eden, in one of his most successful speeches, dealt effectively with this in the Commons on 20 December, but found opposition in the Cabinet and strong doubts on Churchill's part about his proposal to create a Regency.

The proposed Regent, Archbishop Damaskinos, was anathema to Churchill, who told Eden that he was 'both a Quisling and a Communist'. But sentiment in Britain and the United States saw the Greek Communists as noble freedom fighters, and matters became more complex when a message from Churchill to General Scobie in Athens ('Do not ... hesitate to act as if you were in conquered city where a local rebellion is in progress. . . . We have to hold and dominate Athens. It would be a great thing for you to succeed in this without bloodshed if possible, but also with bloodshed if necessary') was communicated in error to Washington, and promptly leaked to the American press. Churchill robustly told the Commons that 'Democracy is no harlot to be picked up in the street by a man with a tommy-gun.' Eden, on 8 December, meeting an Amendment regretting British intervention, and again on the 20th, emphasized to the House that British purposes were a cease-fire, the restoration of order, and humanitarian aid to a starving people. To Eden's dismay, Churchill's decision was that they should both go to Athens, where they arrived on Christmas Day. This bold stroke unexpectedly paid off, and Churchill's doubts about the Regency under Damaskinos were removed. The King was reluctantly persuaded to agree to the appointment and to the commitment Eden had long sought that he would not return unless summoned by a free and fair expression of national sentiment. A truce was signed with the Communists. The British would continue to give the Government its strong military support. Eden's solution had been accepted, and on 19 January was overwhelmingly confirmed in the House of Commons.

There was a certain neatness that Eden had been able to involve himself again positively in the affairs of Greece. But the task he had assumed in December 1940 was not yet complete.

[8]

Rejection and Return, 1945–51

Nineteen forty-five, destined to be the saddest year in Eden's life, opened with his feeling the effects of five years' unremitting work amid a darkening international political situation. The German counter-offensive in the Ardennes had taken everyone, and particularly the Americans, by surprise, and was an uncomfortable reminder of German military skill and ruthlessness. Although this desperate venture was to prove as unavailing as the great German offensive of March 1918, of which Eden had such vivid memories, at the time it caused considerable alarm and, coming soon after the Arnhem débâcle, further jolted the Allies' complacency.

As Eden noted in his diary, Britain was now conspicuously war-weary, and he himself was becoming increasingly alarmed at what he considered to be Churchill's near-infatuation with Stalin. Over them both loomed the shadow of the meeting with Roosevelt and Stalin at Yalta on 4 February, but, whereas Churchill looked forward to it eagerly, Eden did not. He disliked and distrusted meetings that had not been carefully prepared, and he did not share Churchill's almost brotherly feelings for Stalin. Indeed, he had developed very hostile views about the Soviet leader and his brutal ambitions, while Churchill – and Mrs Churchill to an even greater degree – took a more favourable view. Eden recorded on 4 January:

A heavy morning's work, the most important item being a talk with Alex C[adogan] about a meeting of the three great men. I am much worried that the whole business will be chaotic & nothing worthwhile settled, Stalin being the only one of the three who has a clear view of what he wants & is a tough negotiator. P.M. is all emotion in these matters, F.D.R. vague & jealous of others.

On the next day Churchill called him after returning from Paris to say that

the battle still sways & its outcome is yet uncertain. He thinks Americans have lost 100,000 men.* Russian attitude towards Poles bad & I am still anxious, as I told W, about meeting of big three. There is still no preparation, no agenda, & no agreement as to how long meeting will last. There is much work to be done & I

---

* Fortunately a gross exaggeration.

doubt if they will get down to it. Therefore I urged preliminary meeting of three Foreign Secs. W was doubtful & said we should do better all together.

Eden's gloom was increased when Stalin on that day announced that the Soviet Union recognized only the Communist Lublin Committee as the provisional Polish Government. Churchill decided against a meeting of the Foreign Ministers. 'What a horror the world is,' Eden noted on the 6th. 'War & the threat of future wars.'

Terrible Cabinet. ... Whole thing lasted 4+ hours. Really quite intolerable. I was in pretty b—y temper in first half for everyone started taking a hand at drafting messages for me [over Greece], including Bevin. W rambles so that everything takes many times longer to decide than is necessary. (Diary, 12 January)

Eden was very tired, more than he realized, and he was also unwell, with internal pains. He travelled with Churchill to the Crimea by way of Malta (in separate aircraft) where there was a fruitless meeting with the Americans, Roosevelt arriving on an American cruiser. But the visit had one pleasant incident:

Alex[ander] and I went for a walk late in evening which did me good. Talked to one or two soldiers on the way who seemed very cheerful. Nothing gives me more comfort than when a soldier's face lights up with pleasure when he recognizes me. I suppose this is vanity, but I hope not entirely. The truth is that I like our people & to be with them. (Diary, 29 January)

Eden noted in his diary that Roosevelt

gives the impression of fading powers. ... Impossible to get even near business. I spoke pretty sharply to Harry [Hopkins] about it, when he came in later, pointing out that we were going into a decisive conference and had so far neither agreed what we would discuss nor how to handle matters with a Bear who would certainly know his mind.

Yalta was even worse. The Foreign Secretaries met each morning, and Eden concentrated upon persuading Stalin personally to withdraw their troops from Iran and strongly opposed his proposal to dismember Germany after her defeat; in both arguments Eden was successful. But Poland was his chief concern, and although he pressed successfully for a provisional government including both the Lublin and London Poles, no agreement was possible on the key issues of the Polish western frontier and free Polish elections. 'The essential thing for us', he wrote to Churchill, 'is that there should be an independent Poland. The danger is that Poland will now be insulated from the outside world and to all intents and purposes run by the Russians behind a Lublin screen.' This is exactly what happened. Roosevelt and his new Secretary of State, Edward R. Stettinius, were consistently and conspicuously unhelpful, and the Russians absolutely refused to permit any Western involvement in or even observation of Polish elections as outlined in a document Roosevelt produced entitled 'Declaration on Liberated Europe' that promised 'the right of all peoples to choose the form of government under which they will live'. Churchill later wrote defensively that this was 'the best I could get'.* Eden told Colville that 'the Americans had been very weak. The President looked old and ill, had lost his powers of concentration and had been a hopelessly incompetent chairman'.†

The reality of Yalta was that Stalin's military and political positions were now immensely strong, and his advancing forces, with the British and Americans temporarily halted, gave him great and improving geographical, military and political advantages which he exploited ruthlessly. To ensure eventual Russian involvement in the war against Japan, Churchill, to Eden's dismay, agreed to terms in the Far East that effectively ignored the Chinese and were detrimental to British interests. As Eden glumly noted, both Churchill and the evidently sick Roosevelt seemed mesmerized by Stalin, particularly Roosevelt, who made no serious attempt to use his own military power in Europe to counter that of the Russians. All Eden's apprehensions about Yalta were abundantly justified. Ill prepared, ill thought out and feebly conducted by Roosevelt and Churchill, Yalta was a disaster for the Western Allies and especially for the Poles. 'President vague and loose and ineffective,' Eden wrote. 'W understanding that business was flagging made desperate efforts and too long speeches to get things going again. Stalin's attitude to small countries struck me as grim, not to say sinister.' It was a spheres-of-influence meeting at which the Russians gained almost everything they wanted, and Roosevelt and Churchill conceded almost everything they asked. Some brands were plucked from the burning, but not many.

One issue subsequently received widespread and emotional publicity. The Russians pressed hard for the repatriation of all Soviet citizens who had served with the German forces; they were to face charges of treachery and treason, and their fate was all too obvious. In the context of the time, and having regard to the barbarities that the Germans had inflicted on the Russian people, neither Roosevelt nor Churchill saw any reason to reject this demand which would involve the handing over to the Russians of a large number of their citizens who had surrendered to the Allies, principally to the British.

* 'He is trying to persuade himself that all is well, but in his heart I think he is worried about Poland, and not convinced of the strength of our moral position,' Colville wrote of Churchill (*The Fringes of Power*, p. 565).
† *Ibid.*, p. 560.

The repatriation order was formally signed by Eden on behalf of the British Government at Yalta. A strong critic of Eden's action – which was in fact the decision of the War Cabinet – has written that 'This was no cynical policy of *realpolitik*. Eden and his advisers were not postponing an inevitable confrontation: they sincerely believed in Stalin's goodwill. Eden himself felt for Stalin strong affection and admiration.'* Every single statement in this passage is incorrect. Eden certainly did not believe in Stalin's 'goodwill', and his feelings for him were not those of 'affection and admiration'. It was indeed a reluctant response to *realpolitik*, and had to be part of the bargaining process, including Greece. Even Cadogan, who hated the Russians, wrote that he was 'reluctantly driven to the conclusion that we shall have to hand these men back to the Soviet [Union], if the latter demand it'. Demand it they did. As Eden minuted,

To refuse the Soviet Government's request for the return of their own men would lead to serious trouble with them. We have no right whatever to do this and they would not understand our humanitarian motives. They would know that we were treating them differently from the other Allied Governments on this question and this would arouse their gravest suspicions.

There was the additional factor that as the Russians advanced they were liberating a considerable number of British troops in German prisoner-of-war camps, and Eden was concerned that they should be well treated and repatriated as soon as possible at the end of the war. It was not as easy a decision as has subsequently been alleged, but the Russians held all the cards. Also, it should be recalled that neither the British nor the French were to treat considerately those of their nationals who had served, or collaborated with, the Nazis; these included the son of Leo Amery, executed after the war in Britain for his involvement on the German side. War is Hell.

Eden hated Yalta. 'I take the gloomiest view of Russian behaviour everywhere,' he wrote in his diary. 'Altogether our foreign policy seems a sad wreck and we may have to cast about afresh.' What was even worse was that he had to defend in the House of Commons a conference he had never wanted, and whose conclusions – rejected by the Free Polish Government in London – he disliked intensely. The consolation, that the terms might well have been even worse if he had not been there, was a meagre one.

If it was unrealistic for Conservatives, who included Lord Dunglass, to denounce the Polish provisions of Yalta, it was very understandable. What notably irritated Eden was that so many of the Conservatives who opposed Yalta – twenty-five voted against the Government, others abstained – had

* Nikolai Tolstoy, *Victims of Yalta*, pp. 76–7.

been prominent supporters of pre-war appeasement and of Munich. As Harold Nicolson noted, 'Winston is as amused as I am that the warmongers of the Munich period have now become the appeasers, while the appeasers have become the warmongers.' Eden was not amused at all. His warnings had gone unheeded, and Roosevelt and Churchill had walked into Stalin's lair without real preparation or thought, with predictable consequences.

What made the situation even worse was that when Yalta was debated in the Commons Churchill praised Eden lavishly as 'second to none among the Foreign Secretaries of the Grand Alliance' and thanked him for the 'aid and comfort he has been to me in all our difficulties'. Eden had to wind up the two-day debate, which had demonstrated very considerable Conservative disgust at the treatment of Poland, with which Eden was in much sympathy. His approach to this difficult task was conciliatory and understanding, arguing that politics was the art of the possible, and that 'If any life is to be restored to Europe, if it is to be saved from anarchy and chaos, it can only be done by the three Powers working together.' What he could not publicly say, which was the truth, was that there were now only two Powers, and that the weakness and naivety of Roosevelt had meant that in practice there was only one. Nor could he say that one positive aspect had been that Greece was agreed to be in the Western sphere of influence and that Czechoslovakia would have free elections.

It must also be remembered that the world war was far from over, and that the Americans and British were desperately eager for Russian involvement in the war against Japan when that in Europe had ended. Meanwhile, the Russian armies surged forward in Europe, while those of America and Britain were paralysed by their involvement in reversing the Ardennes setback, by bad weather and by problems with lines of communication. As Eden had forecast, it had been the worst possible time and place to hold a major meeting. The shadows of Yalta hang over us to this day.

On Eden's return there were difficulties with Churchill over Rumania and Yugoslavia, and he now had to plan for the negotiations over the United Nations Charter, which meant a long and wearying journey to San Francisco as the British representative and signatory. He felt almost continuously unwell and tired, and was deeply depressed about the European situation, particularly Eisenhower's refusal to take Prague, which he could easily have done, and which Eden urged on the Americans. The death of his old governess 'Doodles' was another break with the past. There was a meeting in Glasgow which he fulfilled in spite of a sore throat and vile weather, and was startled to find a packed hall and the singing of 'Will ye no' come back again' at the end, 'which caught me completely unprepared for; I was half off the platform & didn't know what it was, never having heard it before. . . . Long journey back with throat still painful. Snatches of sleep.'

By the middle of March, the Western forces had renewed their advance in Europe, Germany was clearly facing utter defeat, and the Labour members of the great Coalition were becoming restive about its continuation.

Meeting of W[ar] C[abinet] only at the beginning. W spoke of danger of our breaking up before the war was over. Labour men didn't respond much then E.B. complained that W had accused them of going back on nationalization. This he showed he resented. W said he hadn't meant to infer that & instanced incident as showing our growing difficulties. I said my conviction was unchanged that if country could express itself we should go on as we were until end of Jap war. W agreed. H[erbert] M[orrison] said real difficulty was in domestic legislation where our differing views on State & private enterprise were causing delay & difficulty. But even that isn't quite true because if we once made up our minds to go on together we could work out a programme, compromising no doubt on that, but it would be a programme. (Diary, 22 March)

To Eden's deep regret, this marked the beginning of the end of the Coalition. He was saddened by this, but he was to part from his former colleagues with much goodwill, particularly with Bevin. They were an unlikely pair, but it often happens that men so opposite in background and temperament work well together. Attlee's affection and respect for Eden were likewise entirely returned.

Eden did not relish the prospect of going to San Francisco, but the final stages of preparing and agreeing on the United Nations Charter were clearly of prime importance, and it was a task in which he believed. Cranborne had become violently anti-Soviet, did not want Eden to go (nor did he wish to go himself), and threatened resignation if there were any more concessions to the Russians. Eden had no illusions whatever about the Soviet Union. 'The Russians are behaving so abominably in every respect that I hope you will not mind my suggesting that it might be well that you should cut down your personal messages to Marshal Stalin to a minimum,' he minuted to Churchill on 24 March, on which Churchill noted, 'I quite agree. W.S.C.' But this deteriorating situation made it more important than ever that Eden and Cranborne should both go, which the latter reluctantly conceded, particularly as the British delegation included Attlee and Halifax. Also, with his personal experience of where the League had gone wrong, Eden had taken a close personal interest in all the complex negotiations that eventually resulted in the Charter and in the veto for the Five Powers on the Security Council.

As it happened, the timing was better than he had anticipated. Roosevelt died suddenly on 12 April. This was a thunderclap event, especially as he was succeeded by the almost unknown Vice-President, Harry Truman, whom there was a tendency in London as well as in Washington to dismiss as a limited nonentity. Churchill had thought of flying to Roosevelt's funeral, but matters in Europe were such that he felt he could not; instead, Eden represented Britain at the funeral and met Truman afterwards. He came to a quick and positive view of the new President, describing him as 'honest and friendly', and liking his integrity and humility in his unexpected new position. In this appreciation of one of the most remarkable of all modern American Presidents, Eden was ahead of his time, but there was no question about Truman's lack of international experience, as he himself openly admitted. What few realized was that this former Midwestern senator and failed businessman was a self-taught historian and scholar with considerable knowledge of the world, who had served with distinction on the Western Front in 1918, and had a deep understanding of European affairs. His political record showed that he lacked neither courage nor application. Eden glimpsed at least some of this, and reported accordingly. As he telegraphed to Churchill: 'In general, I was struck by the President's air of quiet confidence in himself. He said at one point in our talk, "I am keen to make decisions, and whether they prove right or wrong I am going to take them." ' He also appreciated that Truman was a warm friend and admirer of Britain and her Prime Minister, and was certainly no isolationist.

Although Eden's optimism for the nascent United Nations was guarded, it was genuine. The key lesson of the League, as he emphasized at San Francisco, was that success lay only in Great-Power harmony, and it was imperative that the Great Powers be in it, unlike the League. Alas, the wartime alliance was only too obviously unravelling, but he kept this reality to himself and to private discussions with an obdurate Molotov. He minded deeply that his presence in San Francisco meant he could not be in Britain when the European war ended on 7 May, and when the unspeakable nightmare that had ravaged the Continent and its peoples was at last over. Eden particularly wanted to be with Churchill at his hour of triumph; instead he had to be content with a celebratory dinner. The end of the European war meant that he had to return home with Attlee, and he arrived in London on 17 May to be plunged into election talk, the end of the Coalition and the unwelcome return to party politics. He also felt unaccountably unwell, which he put down to the exhaustion of his travels. But his spirits were low, as others noticed.

Eden was now convinced that Labour would leave the Coalition, and on 21 May Churchill, and later Colville, telephoned to confirm that Churchill's offer to Labour to continue together until after the defeat of Japan had been definitely rejected. 'I never thought there was much chance of it,' Eden noted, 'tho' I much want it & Max & others have always wanted to break up the coalition early. W had strong impression from Attlee twice that he would recommend acceptance, but I think that this was only Attlee's timidity in an interview.' On 23 May it was officially announced that the Coalition was ended, and that polling day for the general election would be on 5 July, although, because of the services' vote, the result would not be declared until the 26th. Eden favoured an earlier rather than a later general election; subsequently Churchill and he discussed whether the result would have been different: Eden had no doubt on the matter.

Dinner with Winston & Clemmie. A pleasant party. W was tired & Clemmie not impressed with his list of ministers so there was some bickering. Later, & most unfortunately, Brendan came in & began to talk of Bretton Woods & impossibility of his accepting B[oard] of T[rade] unless he knew our attitudes to that. Earlier he had criticized list. This brought explosion from W in which Brendan soon joined. In fact they were soon shouting at each other. In vain I called 'oh do be quiet, you two': they had a grand old row. James [Stuart] & I went out after a while & when we came back, half an hour later, row seemed at exactly same stage. Then Brendan flounced out having refused B of T. Max was sent for. More talk; no result. I eventually saw Max alone at 3 a.m. He also professed not to wish to serve. I had told W earlier that only he would be sorry if neither appeared in the list. I loathe these scenes. They are a hideous waste of time & after my father's rages, these storms only bore me.
  Result – No progress at all & no appointments made. (Diary, 24 May)

There was much subsequent trouble about the list of ministers, wearily recorded by Eden, in clear irritation, in his diary over the next few days. The Americans now proposed that there should be a meeting at Potsdam between Stalin and Truman, which Churchill would be invited to join later. Churchill did not like this at all, nor did Eden, whose mistrust of the Americans was growing, as he foresaw more appeasement concessions to the Russians; the Americans, he wrote in his diary, 'would gladly give Russia all Europe – except perhaps us – so that America might not be embroiled. All the errors & illusions of Neville C, substituting Russia for Germany. Pain during night again woke me up. It comes at different times but it always comes.'

There were also long discussions with Wavell, Simon and Churchill over Indian policy ('Simon hostile in true snake style, for he had informed me at No 10 that Wavell was a foolish, woolly-headed old man,' Eden wrote with bitterness), but the doctors had now belatedly diagnosed that he had a duodenal ulcer and ordered treatment and rest at Binderton. He had been in such pain that the diagnosis came as a relief, and he was thankful to turn his back on domestic politics. 'Felt in pretty wretched form for some reason or other. Bob [Dixon] came down for lunch. Inflicted my cares on him. My dislike of much that Tory Party stands for or pretends to stand for' (diary, 23 June).

Meanwhile, Eden received increasingly ominous news of the condition of his mother from Tim. It would be painful to recapitulate the acute and often bitter difficulties that her children had experienced with her. Several have been related in this narrative. Others could have been. Whatever affection Anthony Eden had ever had for her had long vanished, although he always understood how terribly she had suffered from the deaths of Jack and Nicholas. But this could never make him forget her crucial role in the loss of Windlestone. Lady Eden was not only grossly irresponsible about money, requiring constant rescue operations, principally by her two sons, who could ill afford these repeated depredations; she was also markedly ungrateful, and even vicious, on occasion. She informed the press how she was badly treated by her children. She still had repeated recourse to local moneylenders, despite their punitive interest rates, never kept a bank account, and had consistently sold or pawned furniture, jewellery and pictures that were not hers to dispose of. After her death Eden saw his and Nicholas's silver christening cups and 'some very good old spoons and forks' from Windlestone in London in the window of a Victoria Street pawnbroker. This was a not inappropriate valediction.

These difficulties had gone on for so long that the brothers had become resigned to their mother's embarrassing and lamentable activities, and by paying local creditors had done their best to reduce the very real possibility of major scandals. It was upon Tim that the main burden had fallen, and he had coped valiantly. He reported to his brother on 2 February about the situation at Park House:

The place is filthy & squalid. She herself is dirty & clearly no longer able to look after herself. . . . She potters about all day, talking aloud to herself, or cursing the people who come & help her. Physically she is quite well, but thin and very bent. She is not fed properly – only mismanagement again. But she herself seems oblivious of it all, always living in hopes of servants who do not materialize or, if they come, do not stay.

On 15 June Tim wrote to warn his brother that their mother had had a slight stroke, but that her general condition was very poor: 'She isn't too unhappy, knows herself it is the end – sings periodically.' The end was mercifully short and painless, as Tim reported to Anthony on the 19th:

It is not only the sadness of death, but the atmosphere of dirt & muck (meta-phorically) that one feels in the background. All those horrid people who battened on Mama & from whom she borrowed money sneaking about – not that I see them, but I smell them! – you know what I mean. 'Where the carcase is, there

will the vultures be gathered together' – and then much unctuousness & gush –
'One of God's angels', and all that tripe!...

Yes, we are the only two now left – Those happy days at Windles seem to
belong to another world. .... She is in her wedding-dress, as she wished, & looks
very peaceful.

Tim telephoned him not to come to the funeral. Eden was in any event
too ill to go, but he had little inclination to do so. Yet, for all the many
and acute difficulties their mother had caused to Tim, Marjorie and himself,
Eden was saddened by another break with the past, especially as Doodles
had also just died. But far worse now befell him.

In the uneasy lull between polling day and the actual declaration of the
results of the general election Eden's already low spirits were plunged into
profound worry about his elder son, Simon.

Simon had become one of the great joys of Eden's life. Eden always had
a natural affinity with children – as he had with animals – and although he
often deplored Simon's rebelliousness and independence he also admired
them. They had become very close, and much enjoyed each other's company during their long walks and talks. Simon had inherited his father's
sensitivity and courage, although not his shyness, which gave him an
extrovert quality that Eden lacked, and which made him happy in any
company. Simon revered his father, and truly loved him; these strong
emotions were returned, so much so that Beatrice once remarked that they
were more like brothers than father and son.

Simon's ambitions to become a pilot in the RAF had not matured. He
wrote to his father of his time in training in Canada:

From the start I knew I should never be much good. I couldn't judge the height
when landing and although my methods of getting the aeroplane down on the
deck were safe, the style was not up to air force standard. In due course I did my
first solo, a very irregular sort of affair and after that things were more fun. I
learned aerobatics and the greatest thrill of all flying – the art of hedge-hopping,
not dangerous if careful and gives an exaggerated sense of speed beyond any scenic
railway. .... [But] the powers that be decided that my career as a pilot was finished.
I was not disappointed. I knew it was only a matter of time and I had enjoyed it
immensely while it had lasted.

His enjoyment of Canada was marred only by the interest of the press in
the son of the British Foreign Secretary, and he returned to England as a
qualified navigator before being posted to India, to which he and his crew
flew in February 1945.

Simon wrote what he called an 'account written in starts and snatches,
in aeroplanes, in various hangars and messes in the world, and is scrappy

as a result'; this was in fact a journal. He wrote of the long flight to India, of his three fellow crew-members, 'Jonny the wireless operator, a tall easy-going creature born in South Africa but living in Bournemouth; Duggie the bomb aimer (a co-pilot as he likes to be called), Lancashire bred. Ken the pilot lives in Grantham and educated at Oxford.'

Simon was deeply shocked by what he and his crew discovered when they reached Karachi, which he described as 'this acreage of misery' compared with the luxurious British cantonments. The latter he contemptuously referred to as 'the India of poets, romantics, and Hollywood. ... Here the rulers can live in complacent contemplation of themselves as being the master race – here they eat cheaply, for they pay for food not with rupees but with the souls, characters, and hopes of their neighbours.' The lavish bookshops he found were a cover for pornography: 'This is what they consider fit dishes to tempt the European customer. A delightfully disgracefully frank insight into the Indian's opinion of their white rulers.' Simon's detailed notes on Karachi reveal a far more thoughtful, and at times severe, nature than his friendly and easy-going manner often implied to his friends.

From Comilla, his new interim base in India, which had to be described circumspectly to his father as 'a few acres of dusty sand surrounded by a few moth-eaten trees with a river going through', he wrote to Eden on 15 April that 'It certainly seems rather a nerve the way these Right Wing creatures [in Britain] want to fight Russia when they didn't want to fight Germany. ... Perhaps if you asked these gentlemen nicely they might also be able to pick a quarrel with the U.S.A. and China!' After he reached Burma there was an ominous sentence: 'The weather here has broken, it's started to rain, the Monsoon deluge will be here any moment, and I don't think I shall like flying through them.'

The war in Europe was moving to its inevitable and brutal conclusion, but that in Burma continued to be fiercely contested. Few sagas in the annals of the British armed forces compare with their performance in this bitter, bloody, cruelly forgotten war. Superbly led by General Sir William Slim, they recovered from total defeat and humiliation to brilliant victory fighting under physical conditions and across a harsh terrain that very few of the young British soldiers and airmen had ever conceived of, let alone experienced. It was a war in which all the European rules had to be changed, and in which the army had to be fed, armed and sustained from the air.

The valour of the British and American flight crews who maintained these supplies had become legendary long before Simon reached Akyab, the main supply base in Burma, in late April. He and his crew were quickly in action as the Army prepared for its successful drive towards and beyond

Rangoon, with the ultimate objective of destroying the Japanese forces. Nothing was easy, on the ground or in the air. Looking down on one ferry flight, Simon saw Mount Poppa near Meiktila, 'a hot, snake-infested mountain covered with thick undergrowth. The Japs were forced from this loathsome place by a campaign conducted by the army under conditions of squalor, privation, discomfort, under which no modern allied army has ever been so ill-fortuned as to fight.' For their part, the soldiers on the ground knew only too well that the price of supplying them from the air had been a terribly high one in men and machines. Their lives depended on the supply-dropping Dakotas, and they knew it.

Simon was also greatly impressed by the ground crews, toiling in blistering heat and humidity to keep the aircraft in the best condition possible under the worst possible circumstances. He wrote to his father:

It is these jobs behind the scenes that the public forget; they have no glamour, these oil-stained mechanics. They fight with spanner, not with sword, gun, or pistol. Yet they can win or lose their battles with consequences as disastrous as an army that loses in the field. Working, toiling, fighting in the heat of the tropics are men who come from all roads of life; some married, some single, rich and poor, all mixed together and miles from home. There were few things to keep these men amused, yet they laugh because they must. If they cease to be amused they cease to live.

Simon found himself as much at home in this strange environment as his father had in France thirty years before.

The weather was in many respects an even more perilous enemy for the air ferry than the Japanese ground fire and air force, the latter now severely punished by the RAF. Simon recorded a particularly bad, but far from typical, flight in May in the pre-monsoon squalls and storms:

We flew along towering banks of cloud trying to find a gap. Those clouds, with savage up and down currents of air meant destruction to any Dakota that tried to force its way through. Gently we nosed our way along till we saw a gap. We tried it, we got through the first barrier, and on to the next. This time the gaps were not so obliging. We descended to try our luck underneath. The mist and rain enveloped us in a blinding shroud; we flew by instruments and instinct, peering out through the windscreen wipers, trying inadequately to deal with the torrential water that hammered its ceaseless tattoo on the aircraft. The currents of air caused the plane to bump, pitch, and jolt, [and] it was blown we could only guess where. The normal air navigation, as used over Europe, is useless over the hills and valleys of Asia. In squalls like these you guess and keep your fingers crossed.

The time came when we judged ourselves over the Irrawaddy and its fertile valley. Slowly we went down; we must find the river to check up our position on the map. Eyes were really strained this time. The pilot opened the throttle time and time again as the shadow of a hill crept below our wings, dangerous, sombre, forbidding. Then again we would go down and once we saw a green hill top half a mile off our port wing, and the summit was above us. We were in a valley. God alone knew what valley. We never stayed to find out; we went up again to try later. This game continued for ten minutes that seemed like an eternity, then the weather cleared and the Irrawaddy lay before us, glimmering in the sun, a friendly symbol of safety.

The danger was not over, nor had the storms passed; in these circumstances Simon's navigation, under the conditions he described, was remarkable. The load was parachuted to the marked reception zone, but the flight back was equally bad:

The Dakota started to climb. There was no cargo on board. We were trying to find our way in the clear air above the cloud. Five thousand feet, still dirty and grey. No change at ten thousand or at twelve. We thought they were too high for us and we should have to fly beneath them again. But at sixteen thousand we suddenly entered the sunlight. The plane was cold, everything you touched was chilled; we sat,

At this point Simon's narrative abruptly ends.

Throughout the war a telegram was the most dreaded of all missives, and remained so for members of that generation always thereafter. On 27 June Eden received a 'Strictly Personal' cable from Air Marshal Park to tell him that Simon's aircraft had disappeared on its return from a supply mission on the 23rd. The period of waiting for further news was agonizing for Simon's parents, as Eden's diary reveals:

6 July
Lovely sunshine. Better night. Woke about 6 a.m. Wonderful morning. Decided to take Nicholas to round mile walk. The sunshine on the valley towards Chichester was indescribably beautiful. A pale milky hazy blue which yet had a transparent quality such as you sometimes see on that early blue Chinese porcelain. As I came in through the garden and lay in bed afterwards I couldn't help thinking of the best son any father ever had. I didn't deserve his companionship, but he who enjoyed life so much?

7 July
B & I talked a great deal about S. We agreed that he had been very happy here last year and was a grand mixer with all & sundry. His school years were not happy. . . . B thinks that he would never have taken kindly to any form of discipline.

13 July
Said goodbye to B in morning. Both of us pretty wretched . . . Work at boxes after dinner. Found in them letter from Group Captain which was most pessimistic yet. Utterly miserable all the evening, the agony of it seems to get worse.

On 14 July he wrote to Beatrice.

Darlingest Beatrice,

This is just a word to say how sad I am to leave you alone at this time, how much I miss you and what hell I know it to be for you just now.

I have often told you, though you probably never thought I really meant it, how immensely proud of & happy I was with the two wonderful boys you have given me. I think that they have been happy too. Certainly no two boys have ever had a more wonderful mother, nor any man a more wonderful wife.

It was always fun when we four were together; we may be again.

> Bless you, my darling,
> ever your devoted
> A

Don't be cross with me for writing this; it is just true & I had to say it!

Hope still remained that the aircraft had been forced to land in friendly territory and that the crew were safe. This had happened before, and communications in Burma were so bad that crews had not been heard of for weeks, yet had survived. Mountbatten cabled that 'While offering you and Beatrice all my sympathy in your anxiety, I think you should know that there have been numerous cases of crews bailing out safely or having forced landings and taking anything up to two weeks to get back to civilization.' But the officer commanding the squadron, Wing Commander Davy, reported to Eden that at the time of its disappearance the plane was being flown by Simon's regular pilot Kenneth Roe, and that the weather on 23 June had been particularly bad; he made it clear that the possibilities of the crew having survived were small, and 'I do not wish to raise false hopes.' He added that Simon had just been recommended for a commission.'

The news that Simon was missing brought to the Edens a remarkable quantity of letters and messages of concern, many from complete strangers who were sharing, or had shared, a similar experience. De Gaulle, Haile Selassie, Weizmann and J. R. Clynes were among those who wrote, as well as ambassadors, Foreign Office officials, colleagues and friends. Mrs Churchill wrote from Hendaye (10 July):

... I pray that this sorrow will not cause a set-back in your recovery. You are badly missed & needed. Your Broad Cast was so calm & fine & steady & perhaps your enforced rest may have helped to give it serenity and perspective.

Winston grieves over the unpleasant and uncertain future. But he is rested & is painting the lovely bay of St Jean de Luz with the Pyrenees behind. They look like scenery & not like real country. I do hate mountains!

> Your affectionate
> Clemmie

From Attlee (9 July):

My dear Anthony,

I was so sorry to hear that your boy is missing. I hope you will soon have good news. It is most distressing that you should have this anxiety when you have so many public cares.

Please, don't trouble to answer this.

> Yours ever,
> Clem

An especially touching letter came from Eden's Labour opponent in Warwick and Leamington, Donald Chesworth, who was also an RAF navigator and had trained with Simon in Canada. All the letters radiated hope that good news would soon come.

The Edens characteristically realized that the families of the other crew members were enduring their own agony. As soon as any information was received, Eden ensured that they were immediately informed, but there was very little except optimism on the basis of other remarkable survivals in the Burma jungle. Mr Roe wrote in reply to them on 22 July:

My wife & I are deeply indebted to you for your very kind letter.

To learn of your son's admiration for our boy fills us with pride, & I feel I must say that Ken cherished the honour of Simon's companionship, & always spoke so highly of him.

In these anxious days we send to you & Mrs Eden our sincere sympathy, & we find some consolation in the knowledge that everything possible is being done to locate them.

On the same day that this brave letter was written the Dakota had been found by a Gurkha patrol near Sumsen village. It had crashed into high ground in particularly atrocious weather, and was burnt out; the pay book of the pilot was the only identification of the crew. Thus did hope end for the Roe, Eden, Loder and Hyne families, whose sons had been lost within weeks of the ending of the war.

For the Edens it was a crushing blow. Among the many letters and telegrams they received was one from de Gaulle: 'C'est avec beaucoup d'émotion que j'ai réçu confirmation de la mort héroïque de votre fils. Veuillez croire combien je m'associe à votre peine.' Eden treasured his son's letters, read his diaries when they were returned to him, and was surprised to find also the draft of a novel in Simon's hand. Ill, exhausted and unhappy as he already was, the agony of waiting for news of Simon's fate for a month, and then the final news of his death, combined to make this an especially dark and wretched period of Eden's life. He found that he did not particularly care much about politics, his Office or his own future. Too many of his hopes for that future were buried at Sumsen.

There was to be a melancholy footnote. On 18 September the Director of Personnel Services at the Air Ministry wrote to Eden to inform him that

Simon 'has been appointed to a commission in the Royal Air Force as a Pilot Officer on probation with effect from 9th June 1945. His number is now recorded as 199961.'

It is not unusual for a child to be closer to one parent than to another. Simon was very much Anthony Eden's son, whereas Nicholas was nearer in temperament and affection to Beatrice. While Anthony loved Nicholas, it was Simon who commanded his greater feelings, with whom he felt very close, and whose companionship he had always enjoyed. To Robert Carr – who was himself to suffer the same tragedy – he said in 1950 that no one who had never experienced it could ever understand what the loss of a beloved son could mean. He rarely spoke of the matter thereafter, but the hurt of this special loss was never repaired.

Had some sleep until 5.30 a.m. as a result of good dope. Took Nipper for a turn in garden soon after 6 a.m. Downs looked lovely in sunrise, the sweep of them is so still at this hour and I so utterly wretched that I am ashamed. It seems a selfish thing to write but it is Simon's companionship above all else that I shall miss. We understood each other so perfectly and we knew each other as I knew no other man. He was the best friend I had in the world. (Diary, 3 June)

Eden wrote to Tim on 29 July from Binderton:

I confess to you that I have not yet summoned up the courage to tell Nicholas; the poor boy is white and worried as it is. But I will soon, and I will then give him your letter. Nicholas has been an immense comfort these days, for I took him to the 'count' [at Warwick and Leamington] & it all helps to make one forget. Dickie Mountbatten has been immensely kind and flew to Simon's squadron before joining us in Berlin. He brought further details and a diary & a book he [Simon] was writing. I feel that I now know all that there is to know, & try to pretend that this makes a difference. ... The garden is a joy. I read & prune & forget politics.

On the 14th he had written to Tim that 'I confess to you that I did not know one could be so wretched. In these last years Simon has been such a companion. It was a joy to be with him, and I just don't know how to face life without the thought of his home-coming & the joy that this would bring. Poor Beatrice is amazingly brave, but very white & miserable.'

What Eden did not tell even Tim was that Simon's death was to prove to be the final blow to his marriage. It had been under such strain for so long that it was probably ended by this stage, and the prolonged wartime separations had made the situation impossible for both, although deep affection and respect always remained. Simon's death brought Anthony and Beatrice together in their grief, but Nicholas, although young, saw and felt the tension and unhappiness between his parents, which the unity of sadness at Simon's death could not reduce.

Of all the tragedies that Eden endured in his life, the most acute were the deaths of his brother, Nicholas, in 1916 and of Simon. But the loss of a beloved younger brother, however hard to bear, was not as sharp or distressing as that of a son with whom Eden had felt especially close, and for whom he had had such high ambitions. As was written above the Windlestone Chapel, 'The grass withereth, the flowers fadeth.'

This anguish had coincided with the general election. In retrospect, it can be seen that the Conservatives were set for defeat in 1945, but it did not seem so at the time, and there were very few in any Party who foresaw the result. Certainly, Eden did not, but from his sick-bed in Binderton he observed the campaign with mounting distaste, describing it to Robert Bruce Lockhart as 'the dirtiest and cheapest' he had ever experienced. Eden's mood was reflected in his diary for 6 June:

A grim morning of wind & pouring rain, which continued unabated all day. Depressing. Wrote to Nick from whom I had a very sweet letter. Bob [Dixon] brought me down quite a fanmail of letters of sympathy from friend & foe (political!) alike. Oliver L & Stafford C wrote particularly pleasant letters to receive.

Read my Gibbon & thought about politics a good deal. I am afraid that I am not really much use as a party man. I dislike our extreme right more than somewhat & I seem for ever to be seeing the other feller's point of view. In other words I am not a political warrior like Winston but only a civil servant. All the same I am not sure that's fair for I care deeply for our people. They are good, decent, generous people, the best in the world. That's why I like to talk to them, but not at public meetings. That is why I liked the War Office because I had the chance to see men & talk to them from time to time and I would like to feel that these men were working with me, that they liked me & that together we could build a better England. But how to do this thro' the sordid medium of Tory* party politics & how else to do it? Perhaps I could make something of the C[onservative] party if I had it.

Of all Eden's writings, speeches and letters, this gives perhaps the best self-portrait, true in every respect. Allowance must be made for the fact that he was ill and always hated elections, but this passage is absolute self-truth.

Although Beatrice, carrying the flag in Warwick and Leamington, sent back reassuring messages from that front, Arthur Mann told him the Conservatives were losing. Eden was made extremely uneasy by the aggressive tone struck by Churchill in his broadcasts, as though the war were still continuing, but with Attlee and Professor Laski – the Labour Party

---

* This word was subsequently excised from the diary. I have retained it, as it represented Eden's true feelings when he made the original entry.

Chairman – cast as minor Hitlers and Himmlers. Churchill's brand of politics had never lacked robustness, but in 1945 he seemed strangely out of touch with the new mood, and was certainly misled – as were so many others – by the triumphal nature of his reception wherever he went. With the war still raging in the Far East, with every indication that it would be long and bloody, and with all the problems of ravaged post-war Europe unresolved, it was the worst possible time for a general election. Churchill's own belligerent and party-partisan approach in his radio broadcasts was unhelpful, and at times embarrassing to those who admired and loved him.

In these circumstances it was decided that Eden, however ill, must do the major Conservative broadcast. Eden had become exasperated by his own doctor ('he is the most undecided man I know'; 'I have no faith in doctors') and Churchill sent Moran down, who ordered a month's complete rest and treatment, permitting only the broadcast.* Eden recorded on the 10th: 'Had a talk of more than half an hour with Winston on 'phone. [Leslie] Rowan told me that he had been very depressed & asked me to speak. He still sounded it, and was particularly gloomy about Russia, repeating over & over again that position was more dangerous than 1939.' It was an appeal that he could not refuse.

Eden took much trouble over this broadcast – to the intense annoyance of Cadogan – bearing in mind the priceless advice he had received from an American master of the medium who had told him to choose one listener and to speak to him or her directly and personally. Norman Carmichael was staying at Binderton, so Eden chose as his one listener Sergeant Harrop, whose life he had saved in 1916; he also thought of the dead Reg Park and of Norman Carmichael and the nights they had spent at Plugstreet in 1916 planning the post-war world, which had turned out so differently.

Thus, an ill and sad Anthony Eden recorded his talk at Binderton. It was much the best broadcast Eden had ever done, with a sincerity and sensitivity that, far more than the content, made an immense impression. Bruce Lockhart was so impressed that he considered that if it had been made at the beginning of the campaign it would have had a decisive influence on the result. This is very questionable, despite the real importance of radio in the 1945 election, but Eden's broadcast further raised his reputation, and there were glowing messages from Warwick and Leamington. But as Eden and others were soon to realize, Warwick and Leamington was not a representative constituency. 'Poor Beatrice,' he wrote on 28 June. 'It is hell for her tackling constituency in all this. It is not much better lying here.'

*   *   *

* 'I made a mistake allowing that old man to butt in,' Eden wrote on 5 July. 'He is solely concerned with W, & would quite cheerfully sacrifice me!'

Meanwhile, Eden was dealing at a distance with his more important Foreign Office tasks, the greatest of which were the increasing problems with the Russians. There were also difficulties with Churchill and the Americans, and Eden wrote in his diary on 5 July: 'Am beginning seriously to doubt whether I can take on F.O. work again. It is not work itself, which I could handle, but racket with Winston at all hours.' So the negotiations over Poland and other matters continued, with Eden increasingly angry with Churchill's obsession with Stalin and admiration of him: 'He kept repeating', Eden wrote in his diary of Churchill's comments on Stalin, 'I like that man.' This was not an opinion that Eden shared. 'I am deeply concerned', he wrote to Churchill, 'at the pattern of Russian policy, which becomes clearer as they become more brazen every day.' Eden, justly cynical about Soviet objectives, kept pointing out the implications of what Stalin was demanding, but Churchill ignored him and his advice. Eden was deeply troubled about Stalin and his proposals; Churchill was more relaxed, and confident of victory at the election, whereas Eden, infuriated with Churchill, wrote in his diary: 'Depressed and cannot help an unworthy hope that we may lose, or rather have lost, this election. If it were not for the immediate European situation I am sure it would be better thus, but that is a big "if", I admit.'

The Russians were in no mood to make any serious concessions. They were now hard on the Turks, making territorial and facility demands that amounted to an ultimatum. But the real clash between Eden on the one side and Churchill and Truman on the other was over Eden's pledge for genuinely free elections in Poland. Eden regarded the Soviet proposal of voting for a list of candidates prepared by the puppet Communist Government as 'a farce'; Churchill and Truman were keen to do positive business with Stalin, and in any event had to face the realities of the situation. Eden was also a realist, but he felt strongly that the West should not let the Russians get away with this without at least a fight. He was also despondent about the American domination of Western diplomacy. A senior Foreign Office official, Sargent, told him at Binderton that he found the Americans 'deplorably weak; I said that we couldn't allow them to dictate our foreign policy and if they were wrong we would have to show independence' (diary, 3 July). The Americans even refused to join with the British in supporting the Turks' resistance to the Soviet demands; when they later agreed to do so, the Russians immediately backed down.

The discussions over the new Polish frontiers showed the Russians at their most implacable, and the Americans at their weakest. As over the Polish elections, Eden was absolutely right to press for the borders to be further to the east and not to absorb territory to the west that was German in tradition and language, but the Russians were determined to seize and

The Edens, 1906: left to right, Timothy, Marjorie, Lady Eden, Nicholas, Jack, Sir William Eden, Anthony

Anthony Eden, Etonian

Anthony Eden, aged fifteen

Right: Aldershot, 1915
Far right: Military
Cross, 1917

France 1917: Sergeant
Tom Dale front left;
'Tiger' Pratt extreme
right

5 November 1923

MP, 1928

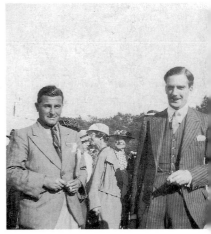

With his Agent at a
Conservative Garden Party,
Warwick, 1926

Post-resignation, 1938: Beatrice and Anthony Eden with Lucy and Stanley Baldwin

Eden and Neville Chamberlain, 1937

29 August 1939: Winston Churchill and Anthony Eden, out of Office, walking to the House of Commons

Noon, 1940

With Nasser and Sir Ralph Stevenson, Cairo, 22 February 1955

Happiness in Uxbridge: Eden campaigning, 1955

Harold Macmillan and
Anthony Eden

Suez: British paratroops advance

With Wiltshire friends in retirement

With Clarissa, in the garden she created at Alvediston

hold as much territory as possible. Again, Eden felt that Churchill and Truman acquiesced much too easily in this deliberate policy of aggrandizement, which now spread far beyond Europe; but he made little progress. He was still unwell and tired more easily than usual; he looked strained and much older than his forty-eight years. Cadogan attended a Cabinet on 10 June and noted that 'P.M. looks rather pale, and indulged in a long monologue in a depressed monotone – all about the menace of Russia sprawling over Europe. Quite obvious, but nothing to be done about it.'* Eden took the view that there was indeed much that could be done about it if the Americans would awake from their fatuous delusions about the Russians, but this was impossible to achieve so long as the Prime Minister, if only up to a point, shared them. It was a deeply depressing period.

As the Potsdam Conference was to open between the casting of votes in the general election on 5 July and the declaration of the result, Churchill invited Attlee to accompany Eden and himself, which mystified the Russians greatly and aroused the impertinent intervention of Professor Laski, which Attlee totally ignored.

In the short time before Potsdam, the Polish pass had been sold, to Eden's disgust, and to the fury of the Poles in London. When the Free Polish Ambassador Raczynski told Cadogan that the matter had been settled in a manner unworthy of Great Powers, Eden could only agree '[Eden] getting restive and insists on putting a finger in the pie,' Cadogan wrote on 4 July. 'If he's out of action, he ought to remain so. .... It's hard enough when *no one* is in charge of F[oreign] A[ffairs], but it becomes impossible when *two* are.'† There was much justice in this exasperated comment, but Churchill was the boss, and Foreign Office opinion as represented by Cadogan supported him.

Churchill, Eden and Attlee flew to Potsdam on 15 July, where the physical damage shocked Eden. But what was even worse for Eden's mood were the reluctance of the Prime Minister to undertake much work, Truman's breezy and businesslike, but manifestly inexperienced, approach, and Stalin's absolute intransigence. Eden wrote on 17 July:

W was very bad. He had read no brief & was confused & woolly & verbose about new Council of Foreign Ministers. We had an anti-Chinese tirade from him. Americans not a little exasperated. .... Alec & I & Bob have never seen W. worse. Dined alone with him & again urged him not to give up our few cards without return. But he is again under Stalin's spell. He kept repeating 'I like that man' & I am full of admiration of Stalin's handling of him. I told him I was, hoping that would move him. It did a little!

*Dilks (ed.), *The Diaries of Sir Alexander Cadogan, 1938–45*, p. 752.
† *Ibid.*, pp. 758–9.

'The P.M., since he left London, has refused to do any work or read anything,' Cadogan wrote to his wife. 'That is probably quite right, but then he can't have it both ways: if he knows nothing about the subject under discussion, he should keep quiet, or ask that his Foreign Secretary be heard. Instead of that, he butts in on every occasion and talks the most irrelevant rubbish, and risks giving away our case at every point.'* Dealing with Molotov – 'a most able but ruthless automaton', as Eden noted – did not reduce Eden's lack of professional and political satisfaction with Potsdam.

There was one crucial incident, when Truman told Churchill that the atomic bomb had been tested satisfactorily at Alamagordo. This test explosion had been spectacular, the power generated being awesome, but there were serious doubts whether a bomb would actually work under wartime conditions, and the Americans also could not assess its effectiveness as a weapon. Truman took Churchill and Eden into his confidence, and at a key meeting on 22 July it was agreed that one atomic bomb should be dropped on Japan if she did not accept unconditional surrender; whether it would actually explode, or, if it did, what damage it would achieve, were unknown.

Discussions then followed as to whether Stalin should be told. Eden believed he should, and Churchill agreed. But when Stalin was told by Truman he merely replied, 'Thank you', and did not appear surprised. At the time Eden thought that perhaps Stalin thought it was just another big bomb; he later realized that Stalin's sources of information rendered it no surprise at all.

Eden thankfully left Potsdam on 25 July to return to Britain for the election results, not nearly as optimistic as Churchill, but certainly not prepared for what actually happened. His diary tells the story:

25 July
We had a meeting in morning, uneventful. After it was over Molotov, surrounded by Vyshinski, Sobolev etc expressed his good wishes in the warmest terms saying that they all hoped for my success, and much more besides. I must be a very bad Foreign Secretary & give way too often that they should want me back! Americans also very warm in their good wishes, to an extent which was almost embarrassing in Attlee's presence. . . .

Good flight, during much of which I slept. Nick met me at aerodrome. Lovely to see him. We drove together to Ditchley through lovely country in which we revelled. Found Ronnie [Tree] & Jim [Thomas] at D, latter on his way to Hereford.

Late in evening Gibbs [Conservative agent in Warwick] rang up to say he had seen boxes & that they were better than he had expected. He was in great spirits.

---

* Dilks (ed.), *The Diaries of Sir Alexander Cadogan, 1938–45*, p. 765.

Thought of ringing up W to report but Ronnie warned that this might not be typical. So I didn't.

26 July
N & I left Ditchley soon after 9 a.m. & were at Warwick about ten. We had a pretty long wait when we got there, count taking more time than expected. Tables were remarkably even, all but two showing 2 to 1 in my favour over Labour.* Liked my Labour opponent & young R.A.F. Sergeant with him. Declaration to small crowd in rain about noon. ... Rumour had it that we were doing badly elsewhere so stopped at C[onservative] club where gloomiest reports were confirmed. ... Rang up Winston & said what I could. He confirmed that Labour must have majority & urged me to hurry back. Said I must complete tour. To Kenilworth & Stratford, very large crowd at latter & best demonstration of all. ... Completed tour in pouring rain & dreary drive back [to London]. W told me on arrival that he had already resigned, quite rightly.

Dinner with only family present. Inevitably mournful enough though all tried to put brave face on it.

It was not at all a happy occasion. Churchill had taken the overwhelming defeat personally, and could not understand how the cheering crowds that had greeted him everywhere could have been so unrepresentative; they might actually have voted against him. In his own constituency he had not been officially opposed by either Labour or Liberal – an act of political generosity unfortunately unthinkable today – but an unknown Independent, whose programme advocated one hour's work a day and 'a philosophic community', had polled over ten thousand votes. By the time Eden arrived to dine with the Churchills in the Annexe for the last time, Churchill had already advised the King to send for Attlee. He told Eden that he had offered Eden's services to provide continuity at Potsdam, but that Labour had not been enthusiastic.

It took some time for the enormity of the Conservative defeat to sink in. Labour had won 393 seats; even with the Ulster Unionists, the Conservatives could only muster 197, with 15 National Liberals; the official Liberals had only 12 seats. If it was not quite such an electoral holocaust as in 1905 or at the Labour downfall in 1931, these were hardly consolations. Bracken, Macmillan, Leo Amery, the Party Chairman Ralph Assheton, Duncan Sandys and Randolph Churchill were among the long list of the defeated.

Eden left Churchill's dinner to see Attlee at the latter's request, and said that while he was available to return to Potsdam with him, he would not be hurt if he was not invited. 'He seemed relieved,' Eden wrote in his diary. The entry continued:

* Eden's majority was 17,634.

Returned to W & reported this. Then Bob [Dixon] came with me across to F.O. He tells me that my successor may be Dalton. This would be very bad; it should be Bevin.

Thus ends this staggering day. Before campaign opened I thought Labour would quite likely win & Bobbety & I both expressed that view at San Francisco. But I never expected such a landslide as this. Nor do I think it need have been. We fought the campaign badly. Beaverbrook was no help. It was foolish to try to win on W's personality alone instead of on a programme. Modern electorate is too intelligent for that, & they didn't like being talked down to. Finally, while there is much gratitude to W as war leader there is not the same enthusiasm for him as P.M. of the peace. And who shall say that the British people were wrong in this?

We should, I think, have probably been beaten anyway, but Labour majority should have been smaller.

On 27 July Churchill held his farewell Cabinet. Eden wrote in his diary of the final meeting:

It was a pretty grim affair, with people like Simon present. After it was over I was on my way to front door when W. called me back & we had half an hour alone. He was pretty wretched, poor old boy. Said he didn't feel any more reconciled this morning, on the contrary it hurts more, like a wound which becomes more painful after the first shock. He couldn't help feeling his treatment had been scurvy. 'Thirty years of my life have been passed in this room. I shall never sit in it again. You will, but I shall not,' with more to the same effect. I replied as best I could that his place in history could have gained nothing by anything he might have achieved in this room in the post-war years. That place was secure anyway. This he accepted and at length we parted. I couldn't help reflecting as I walked down the passage on all that the experience of these war years in that Cabinet Room has meant to me. I cannot believe I can ever know anything like it again. . . .

After supper [with Nicholas and Richard Law] went in to see W at latter's request. Found [Ralph] Assheton there and there was talk of peerages & who was to have the chance to stand again. Annoyed to find worst by-election proposed for Dick Law & young [Peter] Thorneycroft at bottom of list for later attempts. Exploded. Told A in front of W that if he & his friends continued to regard our party as close corporation for extreme right it had no future. This treatment was typical. Remained glowering all the evening, thought it necessary.

To lose Office is always a painful experience, but to do so in the circumstances Eden experienced in 1945 was especially so. On the 28th he took his leave of the King and gave up the Seals of his Office, noting, 'I was regretful at parting.' Eden wrote in his diary:

Left for Palace soon after 10 a.m. to give up seals. Lascelles had suggested night before that I don't go but have interview next week. Didn't like this tho' there was little time this morning. King told me that Attlee had proposed Dalton as my successor but that he had demurred strongly, saying F.O. now most important post in govt, & suggesting Bevin. I agreed that last was best man they had available.

Found [John] Simon waiting for me when I came out. He asked me to drive him away. He haunts me these days. At this moment Bevin arrived & asked for talk so that I sent J.S. off in my car.

Told E.B. at his request something of the problems. After this we spoke of election. He was critical of W's tour. Said he went to most of places afterwards. It had done us harm, especially in London. ... He said that he had asked for Treasury & that only at 5 p.m. previous evening had he been told he was to take F.O.

A morning of tearing up papers etc, save for a break when N & I went to National Gallery. First time he had been.

Jim [Thomas] joined us at luncheon & we motored home together, for the last time in F.O. car.

Churchill had asked the King to be permitted to recommend Eden as a Knight of the Garter, but he had refused the honour himself (making the characteristic comment that as the British people had given him the Order of the Boot he could hardly accept the Order of the Garter from his Sovereign); when Eden was told this by the King he said that in these circumstances he could not accept the honour, which the King entirely understood, and admired.

After six years of virtually unceasing activity and responsibility, there was now suddenly nothing in particular to do. Simon was dead, Beatrice was away, Parliament had not yet assembled, and Eden felt not only tired but drained; those most potent of all political stimulants, excitement and interest, had gone, and he felt, in his own word, 'flat'.

W. and I dined at 8.30 alone at penthouse at Claridge's. He deplored my having been ill and said that as a result he had no one to consult, that if I had been at his side he would not have made mistakes in broadcasts, which is not true though very generous, because each must say what he thinks. But we agreed that there was anyway a strong leftward undertow. We spoke of Hendaye where he will go, and he urged me to join him. Finally I left him alone at midnight. It was a staggering change of fortune from a week ago when at his nod came running secretaries to Chiefs of Staff and behind this was real power. Of course he feels the blow heavily and his pride is hurt. But maybe it is for the best for his reputation in history. (Diary, 1 August)

On 2 August Eden took the Oath of Allegiance in the Commons, and saw colleagues: 'They were reasonable except Osbert Peake who was silly I thought, & suggested Sam Hoare for the Shadow Cabinet. There is no hope for the Tory party unless we can clear these disastrous old men out, & some of the middle-aged ones too!'

The first major surprise was the abrupt ending of the war against Japan on 14 August, after the atomic bombs had devastated Hiroshima and Nagasaki. Churchill gave a dinner for colleagues and friends at Claridge's, after which Attlee curtly broadcast to the nation. Churchill had not been asked to say anything. 'We went home. Journey's end,' was Eden's subsequent laconic comment.

There was after this – to Eden – a surprising example of his personal popularity when he was invited on VJ evening to a reception at Admiralty House. Oliver Lyttelton drove him in his car, but Eden was recognized by the rejoicing crowd in the Mall and received an immense ovation; Lyttelton's car was thronged in an enthusiastic and friendly, but damaging, manner. When they eventually reached Admiralty House, Lyttelton muttered some dark observations about the perils of kindness to friends. The First Lord, A. V. Alexander, observing the scene, asked what the tumult was about. 'Oh, they're just cheering Anthony,' he was told. Years later Lyttelton recalled this episode as one of the most remarkable spontaneous and sincere demonstrations of affection and regard for a politician that he had ever experienced.

'My own future was now all uncertain, but I was too saddened by my son's death to care,' Eden later wrote. This is completely confirmed by his diaries and letters at the time. He was considerably attracted by the possibility of becoming the first Secretary-General of the United Nations, and, although he did not actively promote his candidature, he would certainly have accepted had it been offered to him. There was at first no objection from the Russians, and none from the Americans, but the Labour Government was opposed, less from any personal hostility to Eden than as a result of the tacit agreement that the occupant of this post should not be a national of any of the Permanent Members of the Security Council. Eden later came to believe that his chances had been quashed by Labour purely on partisan political grounds, but this would have been highly unlikely, as Attlee and Bevin held him in such personal high regard, and the political benefits of removing from British politics the Deputy Leader of the Opposition, and one of the most widely popular men in public life, would have been very attractive to them. For this reason alone it could hardly have been possible. There were discussions with Edward Bridges, who told Eden that ministers thought he was 'not available'; Lascelles said that the King 'would consider himself very lonely if I were to do any such thing & that he would want to warn against. . . . Bridges added that nothing would therefore happen unless I made a move. He mentioned that he thought others would be likely to take King's view too' (diary, 21 December). Winant pressed him to put himself forward: 'If UNO was not made to work by someone with statesmanship – & there was none of this at its disposal at present – it must fail & result would be another war & atom bomb. He may well be right' (26 December). But Churchill telephoned on several occasions, urging Eden not to accept.

Although Eden was told confidentially that the Russians 'were said to be not unwilling', they had no intention – then or later – of agreeing to the appointment of a strong, experienced and independent-minded Secretary-General, especially one who had fought them so hard over their expansionist policies in Europe and the Balkans. They liked and admired Eden, but it was obvious to them that he was no friend of the Soviet Union and its regime. As the Secretary-General is appointed by the General Assembly on the recommendation of the Security Council – which means in effect that the latter is the appointing body – Eden's chances of the necessary unanimous recommendation by the five Permanent Members cannot have been high. But Eden was very definitely and positively attracted, which gives a clear view of his mood at the time as he surveyed his future. In the event, Norwegian Foreign Minister, Trygve Lie, was elected, the Russians believing, on his past form, that he would be pliant to their pressures and influence. They were to be proved wrong, but it was an unhappy appointment from every point of view. Eden would have been incomparably better, but in both national and international political terms it was not possible.

Grey day, but no rain & was able to work in garden. Did so nearly all day, mostly at dahlia bed which is now tidy for weekend.

I confess that I enjoy this life and feel no restlessness for any other. If I could get a directorship or two that made it financially possible, I should be quite happy. Nicko [Henderson] sent me the photographs of our days at Potsdam; they made me thankful that I was out of it all and I felt no urge to go back. Above all, fond as I am of Winston, I do not feel I have the strength to undertake life & work with him again; it is too much of a strain & struggle. (Diary, 31 August)

Another diary entry reads: 'A relief to be home [Binderton] again. I find it even harder to leave the garden for London.'

Anthony Eden was physically and emotionally worn out. He had no political Office, and little expectation of another. Of his immediate family there remained only Tim and his surviving son, Nicholas. His marriage, always tenuous, now sadly existed only in formal terms. The Secretary-Generalship of the United Nations had been taken away from him. In political terms, years of futile Opposition loomed before him; in personal, apart from Nicholas, the prospects were meagre. There was little money or solace. It had been a long march, with some rewards but many wounds on the journey. He was lonely, unwell and depressed. Everywhere looked bleak. He was only forty-eight, one of the most admired public figures of his time, nationally and internationally, and yet solitary, bruised and despondent. His parents, Windlestone, his brothers Jack and Nicholas, and his sister Marjorie had all gone. The loss of Simon was the most acutely felt of all. Beatrice was fading out of his life. What was there left?

But these despairs were hidden from others. Anthony Eden braced himself for new challenges, without enthusiasm but with resolution. The public façade was never broken.

As Tim had written of Sir William Eden: 'So this remarkable figure stalked through life, with his head in the air and a superb assurance, but with sorrow and disillusionment in his heart.'

The condition of the Conservative Party on the morrow of its shattering defeat was indeed forlorn. Not only had it suffered an overwhelming reverse at the polls, losing some of its most conspicuous personalities in the process, but it had virtually no organization at local and national level and its finances were dismal. Labour, in contrast, had its trade union organizations and funds, and many constituency organizations had been maintained and improved during the war, while most Conservative ones had been permitted to fade, and in many cases had almost disappeared. Michael Astor, elected for East Surrey, was not the only Conservative candidate who was selected single-handed by the Association Chairman (whom he cordially loathed),* and much of the pre-war laxity engendered by easy elections and assured victories had made too many Conservative Associations dormant. It had become part of Tory legend that whereas Conservatives were abroad fighting the war, the Socialists were in protected occupations toiling for domestic political victory. Like many myths, it had some basis in fact, but the reality was that the Conservative Party had gone into the 1945 election supremely over-confident and with no policies, believing that the magic of Churchill's name and record, and the relative obscurity of the Labour leaders, would be more than sufficient. The party was ill-prepared, amateurish and arrogant.

But the Conservatives' problems were much deeper than those of finance and organization, serious though these were. Labour had had a programme: the Conservatives only had Churchill, now seen to be a very dubious asset. The war had caused fundamental changes in attitudes and expectations – especially the latter – to which Labour had responded, and the Conservatives had not. Of the principal Conservative leaders only Eden had recognized this, but if he and Butler had sensed this before disaster struck, there were now many, especially among the Party's new young recruits,

* Michael Astor, *Tribal Feeling*.

who realized that the task was now to rebuild the Conservative Party, and to give it a philosophy and policies that were identifiably Conservative and yet positive and attractive in a very different political environment to the pre-war one.

The organization problem was resolved very swiftly when Lord Woolton, who had been entirely non-partisan as a supremely successful Minister of Food, offered his services to Churchill and joined the Party. Churchill was deeply touched, and knowing Woolton's extraordinary talents as an organizer as well as his national prominence and popularity, gave him the organizational role of Chairman of the Party in succession to Assheton. Woolton flung himself into his new task with a gusto that wrought what seemed to be miracles but were in reality the result of hard work and enthusiasm. Woolton was not an easy colleague and was wholly uninterested in policy formation; the relationship between him and Butler was noticeably tense, but as a Party Chairman for raising funds and enthusiasm he was incomparable.

The real difficulties were more complex. The first, although it was heresy to utter it, was the leadership itself. Mrs Churchill had not been the only person who had wished that Churchill had retired at the height of his glory as a national leader. But there were many others who had wanted him to lead in 1945, believing that he would be the talisman of Victory, but who now took a very different view. The Party pressures upon Churchill to retire were not in fact very substantial, and he, deeply hurt and stung by his defeat, after reflection and rest was in no mood to go. He declared robustly that his health was excellent and that he still had a role to play. Ever sanguine, he did not give the Labour Government a long expectation of life. He had surrendered Office with much reluctance and surprise, and burned to resume it again. Throughout the next five years there were constant mutterings about his leadership, but so long as he wanted it, it was his.

The difficulty was that he was understandably tired after his Herculean work over the past six years, and eager for warmer climes and relaxation. He had also contracted, for a huge sum that would guarantee a wealth and security for himself and his family which they had never previously enjoyed, to write his war memoirs, and the contract schedule was tight. With typical military style and organization he put together a formidable team of researchers and assistants. But it was none the less to be a mammoth personal commitment of time and energy for a Leader of the Opposition, and one that was keenly resented by a considerable number of his colleagues, who were more concerned about their precarious political future than with reading about the glorious past. Yet however strongly they felt in private, in public Churchill was unchallengeable and unassailable, repeatedly

315

lauded and proclaimed by Woolton as the Party's greatest asset, far above the fray.

This was the problem. It was all very well having a Titanic leader who made the occasional grand parliamentary appearance and major speech in the country or abroad, but the day-to-day business of parliamentary Opposition had still to be properly organized and new policies prepared and expounded. Churchill was notably uninterested in the latter, always favouring the broad-brush approach, with as few commitments as possible, and he made it clear that he did not wish to be much involved in policy activities; nor was he.

Winterton, who was a far shrewder political observer than he was given credit for, subsequently – after a warm tribute to Churchill's role as a world statesman in Opposition – put his finger on the problem when he wrote:

The quality of Mr Churchill's speeches was of great benefit to the Conservatives in opposition, but the leader of a party in opposition needs to have other qualities than that of the gift of oratory; he should learn to endure boredom without showing how hard the ordeal is, and he should watch and wait in the chamber itself or be at hand in his room for instant recall by the Chief Whip during dull, ordinary debates. For no one can tell when a situation may arise which he alone, with his authority, can handle satisfactorily. . . . For reasons with which one can sympathize, Mr Churchill, unlike most of his predecessors, was not a regular attendant.*

This situation left a classic political vacuum, and it was one that only Eden could attempt to fill. It was not of course then known – and indeed is not generally known until now – how close he had been to leaving politics completely, and he did not at all relish the prospect of being the Leader of the Opposition without the title. He was understandably gloomy about the continuation of the long reign of the Crown Prince.

Nor was Opposition a sphere in which he had any interest; it is very significant that his memoirs virtually ignore this period of his career. He did not accept the dictum of Lord Randolph Churchill that 'the job of an Opposition is to oppose, and not to support, the Government'. He disliked the prospect of denouncing former colleagues and friends whom he liked and respected, and he would not do it. He believed deeply in the importance of maintaining continuity in foreign policy and in national unity. He might disagree with the Labour Government – and he could already see areas of considerable disagreement, particularly over nationalization – but he was not prepared to hate it as so many Conservatives were. The task which Churchill's absentee leadership now thrust upon him was unwanted and unwelcome. Eden was tired, too; he was also still very unwell, and it was

---

* Lord Winterton, *Orders of the Day*, p. 317.

from every angle a bleak period of his life. Also, like Churchill, he had other things to do outside politics, in particular to repair his own poor financial fortunes if Binderton was to be saved. He calculated that he had been overspending by some £1,000 a year since 1940, and he joined the Board of the Westminster Bank, and then those of Rio Tinto and the Phoenix Assurance Company; he found that he enjoyed the work enormously, telling Nicholas that he had never realized how enjoyable business was. His financial rewards were considerably less than Churchill's from his memoirs, but with no other salary beyond that of a Member of Parliament, and only a modest return on his investments, they were very necessary.

The *Daily Express* – and in this appraisal one detects the influence, if not the pen, of Beaverbrook himself – portrayed Eden thus:

Assets – wide popularity, well-recognized sincerity; long parliamentary and ministerial experience and attractive, if not particularly forceful, style of speech; a ready and acute, if not particularly dominating mind. *Liabilities* – Health showing signs of strain at the end of the war, lack of experience in Home and Empire affairs and in Opposition – the latter weakness shared by all his colleagues.

There was also the sad alienation from Beatrice, which was now very serious and virtually irreparable, and the continuing pain of the loss of Simon, which affected the Edens much more deeply than either publicly demonstrated. But, terrible though the blow had been to Beatrice, Eden felt Simon's death with special grief. His appetite for politics was very small.

But, as the principal avenue for escape had been closed, he had little choice, as his friends repeatedly pressed upon him, Jim Thomas being among the most insistent. He was Churchill's heir; his reputation both nationally and internationally was remarkable; his following among rank-and-file Conservatives was perhaps even greater than Churchill's; he was the hero and hope of the idealistic young Conservatives now flocking to the colours after the great defeat. These were the arguments that his friends used and pressed upon him in long discussions and letters. Above all, they said, do not let the Old Gang take over. The future lay with progressive liberal Conservatism, which only he could lead. I have no doubt that it was this particular argument that was the most persuasive of all. In a small rented house in Wilton Street, Eden gathered together young men of promise who had been recommended to him and who could build the New Conservatism, known as 'Anthony's Show'. From this moment of decision, however uneasily and reluctantly taken, there could be no turning back.

The manner in which Churchill ran the Opposition was conspicuously haphazard. The idea of 'shadow' ministers and a 'shadow' Cabinet with allocated subjects had not yet dawned, and Churchill's front-bench team was expected to turn itself to any task or issue that arose. Churchill liked to keep the great occasions for himself, but, although he asked Eden to watch foreign affairs for him, Eden also found himself asking questions and making speeches on a very wide range of subjects. Churchill gave regular lunches for his front-bench team at the Savoy, which were very jolly occasions, but there was a conspicuous absence of coherent thinking or even tactics. Brendan Bracken, who had been re-elected to the Commons, not at all convincingly, for Bournemouth, was given the job of opposing the nationalization of gas, which he undertook with much gusto, at one point reducing the minister responsible, Hugh Gaitskell, to tears. Butler was always thoughtful and effective, the two Olivers, Lyttelton and Stanley, much enjoyed discomfiting ministers over a broad range, and among the younger men Quintin Hogg, Peter Thorneycroft and Selwyn Lloyd were conspicuously eager and able; Harry Crookshank was a particularly good gadfly, and the return to the Commons of Harold Macmillan (for Bromley) was a particularly welcome reinforcement. There was no shortage of talent and experience; what was lacking was any strategy, or even a philosophy. What was the Conservative Party *for*? As Eden, Butler and others realized at once, blood-and-thunder Churchillian anti-Socialism was not enough.

The Conservatives' position was made more difficult by the fact that, although the Attlee Government faced a grim situation domestically and abroad, and embarked upon a highly ambitious and conspicuously ill-prepared nationalization and centralization programme, it had in men like Attlee himself, Bevin, Stafford Cripps, Dalton and Hartley Shawcross ministers of real quality, with a new generation of younger men in Office that included Hugh Gaitskell, Douglas Jay, Harold Wilson, Kenneth Younger, James Callaghan and John Freeman. Also, to general surprise, former back-bench rebels, notably Emanuel Shinwell and Aneurin Bevan, blossomed into capable, if controversial, ministers, while Herbert Morrison was a superb Leader of the House.

In addition to this ministerial talent, the Labour Government gave every impression of knowing where it was going; even at the height of its difficulties over the economy Labour did not lose a single by-election between 1945 and 1950, as Eden had reason to know, for he spoke in every single by-election campaign, noting ruefully that all he could record was a relentless string of defeats. Inevitably, Tory morale in the Commons became very variable, and the Whips warned both Churchill and Eden early in 1946 that they must be more regular attenders. Churchill took little notice, and Eden had his other interests, but he tried to respond, although without enthusiasm. At one point in February 1948, Macmillan was so worried about the conduct of the Opposition and its continuing inadequacy that he suggested a small Opposition 'War Cabinet' consisting of Churchill, Eden, Salisbury, Woolton and Stuart. Churchill was not impressed. 'I propose to continue the present system as long as I am in charge,' he wrote to Macmillan, sending a copy to Eden: 'I do not think things are going badly.' The trouble was that they were not going so well.

Where Eden felt he could make a positive contribution was in foreign policy, although on this Churchill often demanded precedence. Eden not only liked Bevin personally, but, as has been shown, he had strong views on the need for non-partisan continuity on these matters, especially as Bevin quickly grasped that the wartime amity with the Soviet Union was now only a memory. The disappearance of Czechoslovakia into the Soviet orbit was a major blow, and the Russian pressures on Berlin brought war very close in 1947, saved only by Western defiance and the celebrated airlift. Bevin also became very interested in European defence and Western European unity, and recognized that British power was so limited that American assistance was necessary, as in Greece and Turkey. In Palestine he was faced with a particularly difficult and emotive problem, ended only after much bloodshed and bitterness by the British withdrawal and the establishment of the State of Israel. He can be fairly criticized for certain aspects of his conduct of foreign affairs, but his achievements were notable and difficulties severe, as Eden well knew and recognized.

Among Bevin's problems were his back-bench colleagues, of whom a number remained infatuated with the Soviet Union and vehemently opposed measures such as the continuation of military National Service and any actions or statements remotely critical of the Soviet Union or in approval of the United States. In these circumstances Eden frequently had to come to Bevin's assistance, in the House of Commons and outside, although he sometimes deliberately criticized the Foreign Secretary to ease his embarrassment. The Labour jibe against Bevin, 'Hasn't Anthony Eden got fat?', and Oliver Lyttelton's taunt that Labour foreign policy demonstrated 'The Importance of Being Anthony', were uncomfortable for both men, but the truth was that on the great issues of Western unity, strong defence and close links with the Americans Bevin and Eden were in total agreement.

On one particular issue Eden was able to render a notable service to his country and Western Europe. On 5 June 1947, General Marshall made a major speech in which he proposed a programme of American aid for war-ravaged Europe. Bevin was nonplussed how to react, and called in Eden for his advice. Eden later recorded:

Ernie began, as he wd. sometimes do, to inveigh against his job. 'This is the 'ell of an office' he wd say & this time went on to complain about the difficulty of understanding what his allies were really at. Presuming that Ernie was referring to Marshall's speech I said 'Why not send for Lew Douglas & ask him about the speech?' to which E. replied 'I 'ave, 'e's just left 'ere & he doesn't know more than I do.'

After more weary sighing from him, I suggested that the best thing to do was to take Marshall's remarks literally & go banco on them. E. nodded. Probably he had come to the same conclusion himself and was with characteristic shrewdness just getting confirmation.

Eden left Bevin not sure how his message had been received, but on the following day in a speech in London, which Eden attended, Bevin indeed 'went banco' on the American proposal. 'What I most remember', Eden noted, 'is that as he [Bevin] did so he looked across at me & gave me the broadest wink I have ever seen.' What became famous as the Marshall Plan was to prove to be the salvation of Western Europe. Without it, the economic and physical reconstruction of Germany would have been impossible; so too, probably, would have been the maintenance of its still very fragile democracy. The British were now paying the heavy price of victory, and, although the Attlee Government was doing its best to help Europe, the fact was that Britain was now a major debtor nation with her own severe economic difficulties. The Marshall Plan was to be, literally, a life-saver, while the Brussels Pact of March 1948 provided for military, economic and cultural co-operation, in itself a substantial advance, which led to full American and Canadian involvement in the new North Atlantic Treaty Organization (NATO). These were momentous decisions, which Eden advocated and warmly supported on behalf of the Opposition.

His relations with Churchill were good, but somewhat spasmodic. Churchill had rendered a great international service in April 1946 when, at Fulton, Missouri, in the presence of Truman, he had warned his American audience that 'an iron curtain' had fallen over Europe. He was fiercely denounced in the Labour Party for thus denigrating the benign Soviet Union, but events rapidly proved how right he was. The Truman Doctrine brought the United States to involvement in Greek affairs and so ensured the defeat of the Communists; the East–West tensions and mounting mutual hostility made the sessions of the United Nations Security Council the stage of much recrimination and bitterness. Although Eden was by nature a pacifier and conciliator, he made it very plain that the Soviet Union under Stalin was a menace to the West, which must unite to resist it.

But Eden did not share Churchill's enthusiasm for the United Europe Movement, which led to the formation of the Council of Europe in Strasbourg in 1949. European unity was an admirable concept, but the vision of a federated Europe – in Churchill's phrase, 'A United States of

Europe' – did not attract Eden at all. In his view, Britain was a sovereign nation with huge colonial responsibilities, and was not, and never had been in modern times, a European nation. As he consistently argued in public and in private, the national destiny did not lie in Europe; Britain should certainly encourage and support Western unity and military strength, but she should never become involved in any supra-national entity. Like Churchill, he believed in the concept of the unity of the English-Speaking Peoples, and always felt particularly happy in Canada, Australia and New Zealand, which he revisited in 1949. Again, his instinctive prejudices against Europe were shared by Bevin* and by his successor, Herbert Morrison – who was to prove a most lamentable appointment. The divergence of views on European unity between Eden and Churchill never became a rift, but the difference in attitude was emphasized by the fact that Eden never even joined the United Europe Movement and was uninterested in the proceedings of the Council of Europe, whose actual powers were in reality negligible. What Eden underestimated was the importance of this forum as a meeting-place between former enemies and the creation of personal friendships that were to revolutionize Western Europe politically, as the Marshall Plan gradually did economically. This was a gap in Eden's comprehension that was never to be filled.

The decision of the Government, which had appointed Mountbatten as Viceroy, to grant India independence put Eden into a particular difficulty. All Churchill's instincts and memories led him to deplore this wanton sacrifice, as he saw it, of the greatest asset of the King–Emperor. He recalled how his almost solitary campaign against the granting of limited Dominion Status in the early 1930s had nearly destroyed his career. He had no time for a policy of 'scuttle', and forecast slaughter and misery if the Raj was dismantled. He never forgave Mountbatten for his advice and the speed with which he acted. The proposed partition of India into two states, Hindu and Moslem (the latter to be called Pakistan), was particularly loathsome to him. As Eden noted on one occasion, 'the old Bengal Lancer is very much alive and kicking'.

Eden fully shared Churchill's concerns, but was more realistic. Once the Labour Government had made up its mind and had come to terms with Nehru and Jinnah, there was little that the Opposition could do to change the policy, and to turn it into a Party issue could jeopardize Indian and Pakistani goodwill towards Britain and the Commonwealth. Eden's public acceptance of the decision was regarded as somewhat grudging, which it was, but his instinct proved to be right; in 1949 he had good discussions

---

* Bevin was in effect dismissed by Attlee early in 1951, for his own good; he died shortly afterwards.

with Nehru in Delhi, and was invited to address the Indian Parliament as an honoured guest, which would hardly have been possible if he had denounced independence *à outrance*, as Churchill had originally wanted. But Eden could not pretend to be happy about the matter, nor by the manner in which Mountbatten had conducted the withdrawal and the partition. Perhaps this was unfair to Mountbatten, yet in spite of their wartime associations and Mountbatten's kindness to him over Simon, Eden had never really liked him; now, although he did not share Churchill's new disgust, he thoroughly distrusted Mountbatten's judgement and style.

To some extent, Eden and Mountbatten had much in common, the great difference being the latter's great wealth. Each was unfairly handsome and photogenic, had style, had notable physical courage amounting to recklessness, and had always taken what is now called a high profile; neither was averse to publicity. Each in his own way, Eden in politics and Mountbatten in naval and military matters, were the stars of their generation. But it was not jealousy that affected Eden's view of Mountbatten, but the latter's judgement and integrity, and he did not feel that Mountbatten was fitted for a key political role. This mutual coolness was to have important consequences.

By 1947 Eden's marriage had ended. Matters had been wrong for a long time, and Eden had written in his diary on 15 June 1945 that 'B left at 10 a.m. & left me very sad. We had some good talks while she was here [at Binderton] and I hope all will be well. She is very restless, which is a change for her & due to war.' But it was deeper than that, and even deeper than Beatrice's detestation of the life of politics, Simon's death or the fact that they were chronically short of money. Nor were their infidelities a particular source of difficulty or recrimination. They had deep affection for each other, and were devoted parents, but the lack of common interests – quite apart from politics – when added to the strains of constant separations and tensions when they were together had made Beatrice yearn for another kind of life, with a different partner – and there was no shortage of suitors. Tragically, she was to choose the wrong one. Eden greatly blamed himself for the rift, but others – and, significantly, the Beckett family – took a different and more sympathetic view, knowing Beatrice so well. They had married too young, after too short an acquaintanceship, and not only came from different circles but had totally different attitudes, temperaments and interests. Matters had begun to go wrong very early; what was remarkable was that the marriage lasted so long, and how strong their mutual affection remained. But to a woman as warm and sensual as Beatrice, affection was not enough. Even if Simon had not been killed, it is improbable that the Edens' marriage would have survived, but it was certainly the final cataclysmic event. Beatrice, indeed restless and dissatisfied, sought a change.

Beatrice had now found, or thought she had found, happiness with another man, who declared that he wanted to marry her. Eden was doubtful whether the man, an eminent American, was indeed serious, and went to America to see her. In spite of everything, their devotion to each other and to Nicholas remained intensely strong. Eden urged her to reconsider, but received this wonderful letter, which he kept for the rest of his life.

Darling,

This is just to bring you birthday wishes – if a little late!

I think that I'm very happy in this fantastic country. I think there must be some pioneer (or buccaneering) blood in these elderly veins!

I'm afraid I won't change my mind now – but I do really hope you'll find happiness, peace, & contentment. I'm sure you will before too long.

Anyway, many, many and Happier returns of the Day & all possible blessings to you always.

B

It is very sad to record that Eden's doubts about Beatrice's paramour proved to be only too well founded, but he accepted her final decision, with much sadness and self-reproach. She asked for a divorce, to which he very reluctantly acquiesced; it became effective in 1950. But, on 7 June 1951 he wrote to Nicholas:

I dined with W[inston] on the way here, & stayed the night.

He mentioned that your Mummie had dined with him in New York, & that she had been very much moved when he spoke of me, & the work I was trying to do; but he admitted that he didn't think her dislike of politics was any less.

He had not told me before because there was no change about politics, but I was much touched at what he told me of your Mummie's feelings towards me. W. didn't pretend that they could overcome her aversion to politics. But you know that I am very fond of your Mummie.

I don't suppose she has said anything to you to show that her dislike of politics is any less, or that she would consider returning home?

Nicholas, who was devoted to both his parents, could only report sadly to his father that there was no hope whatever of his mother's return to England. She had left him with her final, lovely, letter, which Eden treasured.

And so the divorce went through, at Beatrice's insistence. She was not to find happiness, or another marriage, and was to die, too young, in 1957. Eden's biographer can only record, with some awe, the tenacity of the bonds between him and his wife. In 1950, on an official Opposition visit to Canada, he flew specially to New York to see her, and was greeted with affection and kindness. Eden was to find the happiness that eluded poor Beatrice – as she had sincerely wished for him – and he was deeply sad that she was not as fortunate as he. It had been an ill-starred marriage, in whose failure both had an equal responsibility, but neither could ever forget the happiness they had enjoyed together and their gratitude to each other for it. Their parting was gentle and sad.

This event did not make politics more agreeable.

Butler subsequently gave an admirable summary of the task that faced him and his colleagues as they surveyed the situation at the end of 1945. It was

> our need to convince a broad spectrum of the electorate, whose minds were scarred by inter-war memories and myths, that we had an alternative policy to Socialism which was viable, efficient and humane, which would release and reward enterprise and initiative but without abandoning social justice or reverting to mass unemployment. Until the progressive features of our thought had been fully exposed to public view, no one (to adapt Charles II's epigrammatic cynicism) was going to kill Attlee in order to make Churchill king. It was by no means easy to persuade Churchill of this.*

This was to prove a major part of the problem. If Churchill could possibly be politically categorized, he was firmly on the liberal wing of the Whig Party, and he was also fearful of positive commitments that he might not be able to fulfil in Office. This was understandable and honourable, but from the Party point of view hopeless. In particular, by-election candidates and the younger men and women who were seeking constituencies badgered Woolton and Central Office for policies on which they could campaign positively; this came out particularly strongly at the 1946 Party Conference, and led directly to the establishment of a special Industrial Policy Committee of the Opposition front bench, chaired by Butler. Churchill was lacking in enthusiasm, but told Eden that it would probably not do any great harm.

Eden's view was completely different. He remembered Noel Skelton's phrase, 'a property-owning democracy', which he himself used to great effect. But he was not simply referring to home ownership. As Robert Carr, who was to be his Parliamentary Private Secretary for four years, has written:

> Eden saw the improvement of industrial relations as a most urgent problem in tackling which the starting point had to be the establishment of a greater sense of partnership within industry through the deliberate promotion of share ownership

---

* Butler, *The Art of the Possible*, p. 132.

by employees, employee participation and profit sharing. All this he saw as an integral and central element in the development of his wider concept of a property-owning democracy.*

The manner in which the Party operated has been amusingly and wisely related by John Ramsden in his history of the Research Department.† But, while due credit has been given to Woolton at Central Office and Butler at the Research Department, Eden's role has tended to be underestimated. The fact was that he was not only Churchill's deputy but, in Churchill's frequent absences and on account of Churchill's indifference to policy formulation, the key figure. Although he and Butler were never really close to each other and, outside politics, they had little in common, on policy matters they were very close; when Eden was looking around for someone to assist him in speech research and preparation he was given one of Butler's ablest recruits, Reginald Maudling. Ursula Branston became another regular in the team, as did a new MP and friend, Toby Low.

Maudling was a delight to work with, and Eden quickly realized that he had one of the best political minds he had encountered. Maudling's task was to write economic briefs for the front bench, which were notable for their knowledge and phrasing, and he concealed his industriousness so well that he developed a reputation, which was wholly unfounded, for being lazy and self-indulgent. The fact was that his mind was so sharp and his dispatch of work so rapid that he could indulge himself in excellent lunches and fragrant cigars, seeing no point whatever in sitting behind a desk if there was nothing to do. He fitted in very well with the other members of the team that the Director, David Clarke, and Butler built up at the Research Department. The Conservative Political Centre, reborn at 11 Wilton Street under the leadership of Cuthbert Alport, always known as 'Cub', was planned as an intellectual challenger to the Labour Fabian Society and aimed to draw into the Party those who not only sought an intellectual basis for their politics but who could make a positive contribution to its development. Eden set particular store by this aspect of the Party's revival.

Eden would never have described himself as an intellectual, but he was an exceptionally cultivated and well-read politician with many friends in the world of scholarship, and his new work in the City opened to him other areas of interest from which he learned much. The Labour obsession with nationalizing almost everything, and massively increasing the power of the central government, worried him deeply, but it was undeniably popular. The Conservatives had to provide an alternative that was sensible practically, had political appeal, and could be sold to a reluctant Churchill and

* *The Times*, 8 January 1986.
† *The Making of Conservative Party Policy.*

to a Party which still contained a depressing number of reactionaries in Parliament and outside.

The Butler–Clarke team brought into politics a number of exceptionally able young men, including Michael Fraser, Peter Goldman, Maudling, Enoch Powell and Iain Macleod, and the acceptance of Swinton's offer of part of his Yorkshire castle as a residential college for the Party created an opportunity that became an institution for Party debate and argument, the making of new friendships, and much conviviality. Under the leadership of Reginald Northam, and then Clarke, Swinton College was able to replace the pre-war country house political weekends, and its importance and value were incalculable. Its passing in the frugal 1970s after Swinton's death was much to be lamented, as was the incorporation of the Research Department from its happy home in Queen Anne Street into the gloomy and gossip-ridden portals of Central Office in Smith Square.

What is difficult to convey is how enjoyable this period was for everyone involved. Given virtually a free hand by the Leader, they were in the business of rebuilding the Tory Party – indeed, building a new Tory Party out of the ashes of the old. There was an exhilaration in those days, and an enthusiasm and sense of purpose upon which all involved look back with real nostalgia.

The kind of Conservatism they were attempting to create was to be both a response and a reaction to Socialism but to present a positive and intellectually firmly based alternative. Eden, who detested the pre-war Tory Party (and much of the post-war one), championed this new radicalism enthusiastically and set out to lead it from the front. No one else apart from Churchill could do this, and Eden also relished the opportunity to leave foreign affairs for a period and to plunge into new waters, himself quite clear as to the right direction to be pursued. Oliver Stanley's witticism that the Party had become all Eton and Magdalene – pronounced Eden and Maudling – had much truth in it. Sadly, Stanley himself was not destined to live to serve in a Conservative Government; his relatively early death was described by Bracken as one of the greatest blows suffered by the Tory Party.

So radical was the new thinking that there was now serious talk of even changing the Party's name, the Young Turks arguing persuasively that the very word 'Conservative' was a liability, notably with Conservative-inclined Liberals, whom they were eager to win over with their new programmes and outlook and to bring into an anti-Socialist electoral pact. Eden was particularly keen on the latter aspect, which sometimes required his personal intervention to persuade Conservative Associations not to put up their own candidates but to support the Liberal in return for reciprocal arrangements by the Liberals. This was not always easy to manage, but in those days – before the introduction of the sweeping reforms put forward by Maxwell Fyfe for Party reorganization – Associations were notably more meek and responsive to leadership-guidance than they later became. Most difficulties were eventually resolved, although on occasion it was necessary to invoke the personal intervention of Churchill himself.

The proposal to change the Party's name led to some long and sometimes heated meetings and lengthy correspondence. There were those who favoured the Constitutional Party; others advocated the New Democratic Party; others simply wanted to call it the Unionist Party. But it was not only the reactionaries who were troubled; traditionalists, looking back to the Party of Peel and Disraeli, disliked the idea of making so comprehensive a switch from the past, and so the notion gradually faded away.

In his annual speech to the Warwick and Leamington Conservative Association in the summer of 1946, Eden made his first major speech on the philosophy of Conservatism and the future course of the Party:

We recognize that there is, indeed, much to be put right. Our social and economic structure needs to be continually amended and improved if it is to be kept up to date. But it must, we believe, be based upon firm foundations, which take account of our national character, if it is to be strong and enduring. The growth of modern industrial society, the steady spread of Marxist materialism, led inevitably to the development of a society where the emphasis is increasingly upon quantity.

The final development of this process must be the reduction of our society to a single, drab, dull monotone. We are fundamentally opposed to such a conception. We believe in emphasizing quality. We believe that the strength and the greatness of this country depend on the quality of our institutions, the quality of our industrial processes and, above all, upon the quality of our individual citizens. It is our intention to develop such qualities to the full, and this, to my mind, can only be done in a society where there is maximum of freedom for the development of the individual, and where effort and quality are accorded their due reward.

... We must, as a party, at all times base our approach to the problems of government and statecraft upon realism, upon practical requirements. We must not be tempted by the doctrinaire approach of our Socialist opponents to fall ourselves into the pit of doctrinaire anti-Socialism. All prejudices are equally fatal to good government ... It is wrong to oppose nationalization on grounds of prejudice as it is to support nationalization from blind subservience to a theory. ...

As this twentieth century develops it becomes ever more apparent that the problem of the relation of the individual to the state is the most urgent and vexatious problem of politics. It is not a problem to which one can give a single answer. It is as foolish to say that the state should have no authority over individual lives as it is to say that the individual has no right to freedom from the state.

In October the Conservative Conference was held at Blackpool, and, apart from Churchill's, Eden's was the principal speech. It was a long and detailed one, but the key passage, and the most quoted, was:

There is one principle that will unite all the solutions that we shall seek and propound. There is one principle underlying our approach to all these problems, a principle on which we stand in fundamental opposition to Socialism. The objective of Socialism is state ownership of all the means of production, distribution, and exchange. Our objective is a nation-wide property-owning democracy. These objectives are fundamentally opposed. Whereas the Socialist purpose is the concentration of ownership in the hands of the state, ours is the distribution of ownership over the widest practicable number of individuals. ... Man should be master of his environment, not its slave. That is what freedom means. It is precisely in the conception of ownership that man achieves mastery over his environment. Upon the institution of property depends the fulfilment of individual personality and the maintenance of individual liberty. ... It is essential that the worker in industry should have the status of an individual and not of a mere cog in a soulless machine. To substitute the state for the private employer as boss won't give the worker that status. He will never have it under Socialism. Nor will he achieve it in the economy of the twentieth century under a system of free enterprise unless we are prepared to foster and encourage schemes for the distribution of capital ownership over a wide area, and for giving men and women a closer interest and share in the purpose and operation of the industry that employs them.

One of the principal frustrations in working with Eden on a speech was his habit of cutting out any phrase that could be dramatic or memorable, but he luckily did not do it with 'property-owning democracy', which was seized upon eagerly by the Conference and the press; and his themes of the individual and incentive and the relationship between the individual and the state have become central to all post-1945 Conservative political thought. Eden recognized, as did Butler, that the state has, and must have, a beneficent role, but that if it intruded too far and became too dominant not only was efficiency at stake, but basic human liberties; industrial co-partnership between employer and employee was as vital as home ownership. To this theme he returned again and again, with great effect. Those Conservatives who wanted to go back to complete laissez-faire policies were discomfited, and were – if only temporarily – silenced.

The story of how the Industrial Charter was developed under Butler's chairmanship belongs more to Butler's biography than to Eden's, but Eden was a strong supporter of the work of his Industrial Policy Committee, and the eventual Industrial Charter was considered, amended and approved by the Conservative front-bench team under Eden's chairmanship.

The Charter was on exactly the lines he had pronounced at Blackpool, and its themes were increased incentive, co-partnership, contracts of service, equal pay for equal work, the reduction of taxation and controls, the shrinking of the Civil Service and a pragmatic approach to denationalization. These themes formed the core of the work of the Conservative Government in the 1950s. Churchill was not overwhelmingly enthusiastic or even much interested in the Charter (Eden doubted if he had even read it) and, as Butler has written, 'his ultimate imprimatur was not so much obtained as divined'. Butler and his team had gone to great trouble to seek opinion in the country and in Parliament and to explain their salient concerns and proposals – in itself a model of Party consultation at all levels that should have set a precedent, but did not. The Beaverbrook press, characteristically, saw the proposals as diluted Socialism, but the general reaction was very positive and even enthusiastic. The Charter was published on 12 May, and on the 17th Eden addressed an audience of over 20,000 at Cardiff Castle, describing it as 'a sincere and sober attempt to place the issue fairly before the country and to propound remedies for our present and growing ills. Its purpose is to bring government, capital and labour together in a common partnership in pursuit of a common objective. ... We hold out to the people a prospect of true freedom and fuller achievement.'

This was the first of many speeches that he made that summer and autumn to give publicity and support to the Charter. So successful had been the operation, and so positive the response, that there was now a call for more Charters, which duly appeared on agriculture, Imperial policy, on Wales and on Scotland; there was even a 'women's charter'. If none had the public impact of the Industrial Charter they demonstrated that the Conservatives were thinking their way through the post-war problems and producing fresh proposals, while the Labour Government remorselessly ran out of time, energy and ideas. The Conservative Party's *The Right Road for Britain* in 1949 was a comprehensive blueprint for reform at home and abroad that had huge sales and much attention. Labour condescension began to turn to alarm when the more perceptive realized how far their opponents had gone from their 1945 position; the combination of a revivified Conservatism and mounting disillusionment with Labour as it tried to deal with a deteriorating economic and industrial situation without success was a formidable one. Aneurin Bevan's introduction of the National Health Service was the one truly popular measure achieved by Labour, and its grudging acceptance by the Conservatives was a major political error. But by-elections obstinately showed how strong Labour support remained.

This was a difficult period in Eden's life. The sadness of his parting from Beatrice may have played its part in the relentless activity of his life. Being Leader of the Opposition in all but name was often frustrating, and, although he tried to curtail his speeches on foreign affairs and to concentrate on domestic issues, it was inevitable that he could not abandon the former altogether. He enjoyed his work in the City, but his membership of several boards was not honorific and involved much hard work. He spoke often, travelled in the country a great deal, and put forward his doctrine of the Three Unities in foreign policy – unity with the Commonwealth and Empire, unity with Western Europe and unity with the United States, which he claimed were 'not disparate, not incompatible, but complementary'. The trouble was that, by giving each the same importance and balance, no particular priority was given to any, and it was well known to those around him that his commitment to unity with Western Europe was at best half-hearted.

On his return from a world tour in 1949 the strain of carrying his several responsibilities was demonstrated when he collapsed while addressing a meeting of the United Nations Association. It turned out only to be a fainting fit, but it was a warning that he would have been wise to heed. However, apart from an appendix operation in 1948, his health was good; his ulcer had completely healed, and his energy and zest were impressive.

Above all, he had shown that his interests were not confined to foreign affairs, and that he could give clear and thoughtful leadership to the Conservative Party during its revival. His personal popularity inside and outside the Party had risen even higher.

Political commentators, while recognizing this, found it difficult to explain. As the *Liverpool Post* mused:

The explanation of this popularity is hard to discover. He is not an exciting speaker; he is not an originator of lively phrases or new ideas. . . . But he is the born unifier. He is a master of producing the greatest measure of agreement from apparently incompatible elements. Here lies his secret. He is the man of common opinions but uncommon abilities, that a hundred years ago was Bagehot's description of the successful political leader.

A profile in the *Observer* also concentrated on the phenomenon:

How has it come about that Eden is one of the figures that is held to be representative of the country? Why is he one of the few men who can get a hearing from all classes of the community? There is no simple answer to such questions, but it seems probable that Anthony Eden's reputation is based even more on what he is than on what he has done.

The figure of Anthony Eden is essentially a likeable one; it is also one to respect. To achieve fame and remain modest; to have authority and remain gentle; to contend for power without becoming coarsened and cunning – these are major virtues, as rare in private life as in politics. Perhaps it is these qualities that have gained for Capt. Eden, the Foreign Secretary who resigned, that special place in the regard of his countrymen which makes him one of the leading figures of our day.

What was manifest about Anthony Eden was that although he was a Conservative, with an imaginative and sensitive conception of what the Conservative Party should be, he was never a partisan. It was this that gave him a following that was probably larger outside the Party than it was within, and the respect felt for him was a vital element in attracting people who were not natural Conservatives to vote Conservative. But, although he was invariably the darling of the Party Conference, and of all Ladies' meetings, there were others who felt that he and Butler were taking the Party down a perilously neo-Socialist road, that he lacked combativeness and missed opportunities for assailing the Government; that he was, like Churchill, not really a Conservative at all; and that his courtesy towards the Labour Party was no way to treat such rabid Marxists, Socialists and destroyers of the British Nation and Empire. His appeal to the idealistic young was enormous. In 1945 he had been elected Chancellor of Birmingham University, and none could have had a more devoted and zealous Chancellor. If this was another burden, it was one which was immensely pleasurable for everyone, and his devotion to Birmingham was fully returned. As the extent of his papers on the university demonstrate, he was not a titular Chancellor.

Despite Eden's occasional irritation at Churchill's frequent absences and the consequent additional work put upon him, their relationship remained warm. When in January 1949, Eden celebrated twenty-five years in Parliament, Churchill, without Eden asking him, sent a glowing personal message to the celebrations in Warwick and Leamington.

I send my hearty congratulations to your Member on the completion of his first twenty-five years in Parliament. Warwick and Leamington has won national distinction by their choice and their steadfastness.

Anthony and I have been colleagues and comrades, heart and hand, in some of the most formidable events of war and we now work together to win for our country the prosperity and progress which are her due.

Winston S. Churchill

After a visit to Chartwell in June 1950, Eden wrote:

My dear Winston,

Thank you so much for my delightful visit to Chartwell. I always enjoy the days I spend there so much. But this time seemed so particularly kindly & memorable for me.

It is never easy to express gratitude adequately, particularly, I think, if one feels it deeply. So that I have never been able to tell you, as I would, how much I valued the strength & loyalty of the friendship you have shown me in these difficult months. I shall never forget it; & it will always give me heart and courage in the years ahead. Example can be an inspiration, & I must just try to be in some sense worthy of the confidence you have shown in me. . . .

Yours ever,
Anthony

Another example of Eden's integrity came in 1949 when the electoral boundaries were redrawn, gravely to his disadvantage. A new constituency was created, Stratford and South Warwickshire, that included most of the rural areas of the old Warwick and Leamington seat, which were solidly Conservative, and left him with the predominantly industrial area. He could, with no dishonour, have moved to the new constituency, which was eager to have him as its Member, but his commitment was such that he stuck to Warwick and Leamington, with all the attendant risks. This conspicuous example of loyalty was recognized and admired, and has never been forgotten. One can think of too many career politicians who would have taken a very different decision. It was exactly this kind of action that made Eden not only admired but loved. He brought honour and dignity, kindness and loyalty to the often grubby trade of politics.

Although they had not recaptured a single seat from Labour since 1945, the Conservatives went into the general election of February 1950 with high expectations of victory. They had a new programme and many young and excellent candidates – probably the best the Party has ever fielded – who included Macleod, Maudling, Powell, Edward Heath, Robert Carr, Angus Maude and Richard Fort.* The disadvantage of Churchill's age was matched by his high prestige and by the relative youth of his team. Woolton had little interest in policies, but, with the great assistance of the Maxwell Fyfe reforms, which were directly responsible for bringing in candidates with modest financial means, he had brought back enthusiasm to the Associations, had rebuilt the organization and its finances, and had wrought wonders. The Tory Party by 1950 bore hardly any resemblance to what it had been in 1945.

Eden again played a leading part in the campaign, although he had to devote more time to Warwick and Leamington in the new circumstances, and his approach was national rather than partisan. This time, Churchill was persuaded to take the same line, although not wholly with success as the pace of the campaign quickened. But the actual result was a deep disappointment. After an unforgettable night and morning on 23/24 February, when the Labour victories in the cities were wiped out by Conservative gains elsewhere and the Liberals underwent slaughter, the final

---

* Now, alas, forgotten. He was one of the ablest of them all, but was tragically killed in a car accident.

count gave Labour victory by 8 seats. Eden's own majority was 8,814, and fully justified his loyalty to his old constituency.

The new Conservative MPs entered the Commons with enthusiasm and a determination to harass the Government into defeat. These tactics were brutal, and included the eager exploitation of every procedural device to achieve long and late sittings to exhaust ministers and their supporters. It certainly did that, but it is not a period on which the believers in moderate courses can look with much satisfaction. Eden himself, although he had to play a full part in the House, had his doubts, but the mood in the parliamentary Party and outside was of the 'one last push' variety, and many were eager to make their names as soon as possible in Opposition so that they would be rewarded when Office came.

These methods aroused a degree of bitterness and rancour between the parties that was certainly not Eden's style. When Bevin stood aloof from the imaginative proposal by the French Foreign Minister, Robert Schuman, for European co-operation on iron and steel, Eden's own reactions were more sympathetic to Bevin than those of several of his colleagues, Heath making his maiden speech in support of the plan. But although Eden was compelled to criticize Bevin under strong Party pressure, it was conspicuously muted. The European Coal and Steel Community was established within a year, without Britain. Thus, at the outset of the process which was to lead to the formation of the European Economic Community, Eden was determined that Britain should not be involved. The 'Three Unities' meant close links with Western Europe, especially military, but they did not mean involvement. Even Eden's strongest admirers must lament this.

Where he was on infinitely stronger ground was in giving full Conservative support to the Government when North Korea invaded South Korea on 25 June. In a moment of folly the Soviet Union had withdrawn from the UN Security Council when the United States had refused to accept the representation of the victorious Communists in the cruel Chinese civil war and would only recognize that of the defeated Chiang Kai-shek, whose forces had been driven off the Chinese mainland and had found refuge in Formosa and its offshore islands. Although Eden had criticized the Government's somewhat swift official recognition of the Communists as the true Chinese Government, he was a realist; but he also knew of the anger and bitterness in the United States against the Truman administration for 'losing' China, of whom one of the most vehement critics was a hitherto obscure lawyer, John Foster Dulles.

The North Korean invasion was so massive, and so unexpected, that the South Koreans and American units were swept aside. American reinforcements rushed from Japan, and the United States forces found it impossible to hold their ground and were forced into a desperate enclave in the south. The Truman administration and American opinion had no doubt that this act of war must be defeated, on which Churchill and Eden entirely agreed. To the dismay of their left-wingers, the Labour Government gave full support to the Americans and pledged British forces. This commitment was greatly facilitated by the fact that, in Russia's absence from the Security Council, the Americans had made it into a UN operation, with the Western forces serving under the UN flag. The Korean War, with the UN forces commanded by General MacArthur, was a particularly terrible and bloody affair; and it assumed new perils when, after a brilliant counter-stroke by MacArthur, the Chinese intervened in force on the North Korean side, arousing real apprehensions in London about a full-scale war with China in which British forces would be involved. However, the situation stabilized after much bloodshed, and armistice talks opened in July 1951. Eden had no doubt whatsoever that the American and British reaction had been absolutely right, but he also believed that the war must be contained.

In July 1950, Eden visited Canada, a country in which he felt particularly happy; he then went to the United States, where he never felt as comfortable, but where he was greeted with much warmth and press attention as a true friend of America. It gave him the opportunity of spelling out, publicly and privately, the strength of British support for the United States over Korea, and of delivering some hints about the perils of the conflict spreading. As always on his trips abroad, he refused to say anything critical of the Labour Government and stressed those factors – the NATO alliance and Korea in particular – on which the British were united.

Eden had particularly noticed, and had stayed to listen to, a speech on industrial relations by Robert Carr, one of the new Conservative intake in the Commons; he had liked what he heard, and asked Carr to accompany him as his unofficial Parliamentary Secretary. Carr had seen Eden only as a remote, great man; he – and particularly his wife Joan – had been alarmed by an invitation to Binderton with their five-year-old son, David. As they drove up the drive they saw a shaking in the shrubbery, and their host emerged, in rather old and tattered gardening clothes, brandishing secateurs. They found him a wonderful host, and he took at once to David, treating him as an adult and marching off with him on long exploratory walks, the little boy stalking beside him and giving his views on various matters, to Eden's pleasure and genuine interest. As he watched this amusing and oddly touching pair striding off in deep and animated discussion, Carr realized what a wonderful father Eden must have been and what the loss of Simon had meant to him. Eden's sure touch with children and young people was wholly unfeigned and natural; so it was with animals, with which he had always found an instinctive rapport. His love of the countryside was also very evident. 'You have to realize', he told Carr, 'that I am really just a peasant at heart.'

Being closely involved with Eden had its different experiences for the Carrs. When Eden discovered, after one of their ferocious games of tennis, that Robert Carr was a Wimbledon umpire, he asked whether it might be possible for him to get him a ticket for the Centre Court; he could easily have obtained one in the Royal Box, but he simply wanted to watch the tennis incognito. Carr had two tickets as an umpire, and Eden sat with Joan Carr in obscure seats. The ruse totally failed, and a large section of the crowd devoted more attention to Eden and his beautiful lady companion than they did to the matches he was trying to watch. It was then that Joan Carr realized that Eden had, after Churchill, the most famous face in Britain. Eden was neither pleased nor flattered, but irritated, by all this attention when all he wanted to do was to watch good tennis, and profit thereby.

On the Canadian trip Carr saw the other Eden. The transatlantic flight in the pre-jet days was very long, and Eden arrived in their hotel tired and taut, insisting on immediate work. He found fault with everything prepared for him: his draft speeches and briefing papers, over which the Research Department and the British High Commission had taken immense trouble. As he went through the documents his anger rose, until Carr told him that he could not and would not take any more of this abuse and petulance, and was going to bed; he immediately did so, fuming against this impossible man. As he lay seething, the door opened and a deeply contrite Eden looked in. He apologized profusely, and added, 'Don't forget that I am just a bloody prima donna.' From that moment, all was well, and a lifelong friendship established. But it was a fact that Eden could be impossible and needed to be stood up to – as Cadogan always did – or calmed, at which Bob Dixon was the master. Carr realized from this experience that Eden was considerably more tense and sensitive, and more volatile in temperament, than he had expected, a man who needed careful and sympathetic – but strong – treatment to obtain the best from him. But he had also seen the qualities of the man – the countryman, sportsman, scholar and warm friend – that others, who only saw 'the bloody prima donna', never appreciated or understood. Carr also realized, which others did not, that Eden's alleged vanity was nothing of the sort, but was the apparent manifestation of a man who lived on his nerves, was very solitary and shy, and – to Carr's considerable surprise – lacked real self-confidence.

'Politically things are going well for us in the country,' Eden reported to Nicholas on 2 February 1951, 'but I think we made a mistake to divide the House on Defence this week. I tried to persuade W. of this before the event, but in vain. As a result we suffered our worst defeat & gave Bevan an opportunity he used very well. However, W. rang me up the next day & frankly admitted he had been wrong & I right – so perhaps better luck next time.'

Acute divisions existed between the British and Americans over the conduct of the Korean War and within the Government over rearmament, with Gaitskell, now Chancellor of the Exchequer, and Bevan already showing clear signs of incompatibility and even hostility. But in the defence debates Bevan unexpectedly emerged as a strong supporter of the rearmament programme which Attlee had announced in a major speech in Lewisham on 28 January, and which Eden believed the Conservatives should strongly endorse, regardless of the critical position in the Commons. Again, opposition for opposition's sake had no attractions for him on issues of national importance. Unquestionably, he was right.

To Eden's genuine regret and sadness, which he eloquently expressed, Ernest Bevin was compelled to resign as Foreign Secretary on 9 March. He had been ill for a long time, and his frequent absences commented upon, but he had struggled on until Attlee, somewhat brusquely, removed him; within five weeks he was dead. His successor, to universal astonishment which Eden fully shared, was Morrison. It was to prove one of Attlee's greatest mistakes, but it put Eden in a very difficult position in the House of Commons, which would not have mattered to a different man.

Eden had admired Bevin and, with some differences of emphasis on occasion, had given him full Conservative support on all major issues; although Bevin was no parliamentary orator he clearly knew what he was talking about. Morrison was an acute embarrassment; as was cruelly remarked, 'Ernie could not pronounce the names of the places right, but at least he knew where they were.' Eden liked Morrison personally, and thought him an excellent, if slippery, Leader of the House, which he certainly had been. At the Foreign Office and at the Dispatch Box he was a disaster, not only mispronouncing the names of countries and places but clearly floundering. There is dispute over whether Bevan had wanted the job, but he could be forgiven for watching with contempt the performance of his enemy.

Eden, ever remembering Baldwin's injunction about condescension, did his best to treat Morrison seriously. He was, after all, the British Foreign Secretary, and the Conservatives supported the main thrust of the Government's policies in Western Europe and Korea; they certainly were not in the business of giving any implicit encouragement to Morrison's left-wing foes on the Labour benches. But Morrison was so bad, and the House of Commons so increasingly derisive of his hapless appearances, that Eden found the balance very difficult to keep. The fact that he did keep it was admirable, although not perceived so favourably by the Conservative back benches who scented the downfall of the Labour Government and were eager to precipitate it. Eden played his part in matters outside foreign affairs, but without zest. To Nicholas he wrote on 25 February, 'I am slaving at articles & speeches as usual,' and on 11 March:

It is impossible to tell how long this govt. will go on. Might be six months or longer or less. But the whole tone becomes daily more bitter – I can't pretend that I enjoy it at all. I find I need my City activities more than ever to keep me sane, if not solvent. Also, dear Binderton. . . .

All together I am weary of the endless publicity of political life too – & feel I'd love to escape to a combination of the City & Binderton. But I suppose that there is no life in which one is more a prisoner than politics.

Ten days later the Government's majority fell to three. 'We are not having a very easy time with Mr C., who becomes very deaf & not a little impatient!' Eden lamented to Nicholas, who had just become a captain. Eden was delighted, but added, 'All the same I expect that you will be sad at leaving your platoon. The best part of the army is dealing with men, not paper. However, one cannot have everything & promotion brings its penalties.'

The departure of Bevin and the fatal illness of Cripps, combined with the resignations after Gaitskell's first (and only) Budget of Aneurin Bevan, Harold Wilson and John Freeman, were hard blows to the Labour Government, now harried unmercifully by an exultant Conservative Opposition. Then, in May 1951, the mercurial Prime Minister of Iran, Dr Mussadeq, nationalized the Anglo-Iranian Oil Company and its refinery at Abadan. The Conservatives and the British press were outraged at this cynical abrogation of international agreements, but, while Eden shared their alarm and anger, he saw the difficulties of the military action which Churchill favoured and for which the Party called. Privately, Eden agreed with Labour that the wisest course was to handle the matter calmly and not get into precipitate action in the volatile Middle East. He also knew that the Truman administration considered Mussadeq to be a barrier against Communism who should be supported; there were powerful American oil interests who saw the matter in the same light, for less ideological reasons. But the Government was now open again to Churchillian charges of 'scuttle', and Morrison's feeble performances in the Commons made matters considerably worse.

The combination of illness and exhaustion now meant that the Government's majority fell on major occasions to one, and on other issues it was regularly defeated. It was an impossible situation, and this sour and bitter Parliament was dissolved on 5 October. Again, Eden was the principal

Conservative spokesman after Churchill, but he concentrated much more on domestic than on international affairs, notably on housing. The Conservative Conference of 1950 had, most unusually, got out of control on this issue when a young Conservative, Harmar Nicholls, proposed a Party pledge to build 300,000 houses a year, a dramatic figure seemingly plucked out of thin air, to the dismay of the Party leaders on the platform. Butler has described what then happened:

Lord Woolton, who was sitting beside me as the figure began to be picked up by representatives with the mounting excitement one customarily associates with an auction, whispered 'Could we build 300,000?' I replied, 'The question is should we? And the answer is: it will make it that much more difficult to restore the economy. But if you want to know if it's technically feasible, ask David Clarke.' So the Director of the Research Department was consulted behind the scenes and opined (correctly) that the thing could be done, and Lord Woolton stepped forward to the front of the platform to declare in beaming surrender, 'This is magnificent.' And so, in a sense, it was. Both the promise and the achievement were magnificent politically; economically, however, they placed a severe inflationary strain upon our resources which contributed to the difficulties of 1954–5.*

On housing, the Conservatives, almost by mistake, had picked a political winner, as they were to do again in the late 1970s, but they could also capitalize on a government that had given the nation a surfeit of nationalization, controls, rationing and austerity. What they underestimated was the ability of Labour, and particularly Morrison, to play on fears about Churchill's capacity to be a peacetime Prime Minister in a dangerous world; others produced the 'warmonger' accusation in even cruder form, and the spectre of unemployment on the 1930s' scale was duly resurrected. The Conservatives considered that they ran a positive campaign, and Labour a negative one, but the Conservatives were not tardy in their denunciations of the record of the Labour Government, and Churchill particularly relished the alliterative felicity of Bevan and Abadan.

But the 'warmonger' charge worried Churchill and Eden, and they inserted into the Conservative Manifesto at the last moment a proposal to introduce an Excess Profits Levy to counter any profiteering in military contracts. The great irony of this was that it was very close in substance to Neville Chamberlain's National Defence Contribution of 1937 which Churchill had himself denounced – with many others – and which Chamberlain had had to withdraw. Butler, who had to telephone to the Research Department this new section of the Manifesto, so late was it, assumed that Churchill had forgotten this episode; that is highly unlikely. What had impressed Eden, and then Churchill, was that the Americans

---

*Butler, The Art of the Possible, p. 155.

had introduced punitive legislation on these lines, with what appeared to be success. It is very doubtful whether it was, as Eden and Churchill had hoped and intended, a politically successful response to the 'Whose Finger on the Trigger?' Labour campaign that ended on election day with a notorious issue of the *Daily Mirror*.

Nor was it easy to counter the Labour myth that Attlee, single-handedly, had prevented Truman from using atomic weapons over Korea. Eden suspected – rightly – that this was indeed a total myth, but he could not be sure, and the portrayal of Attlee in this heroic role, although carried to absurdity, formed an important part of the Labour counter-attack.

It very nearly succeeded, but after another agonizing election night and morning, the Conservatives were returned with a majority of 26 over Labour, and 16 overall. If it had not been a triumphant victory, it was victory none the less, and Winston Churchill returned to Downing Street and Anthony Eden to the Foreign Office.

PART THREE

Afternoon

[9]

Heir Apparent, 1951–5

When Winston Churchill formed his second Government in October 1951, although everyone knew that it must be his last, there were few indications of how long either would survive. Labour had only narrowly lost the election in terms of parliamentary seats, and its very high national vote demonstrated its strong following in the country. The new ministers were immediately confronted with substantial and complex problems at home and abroad that would have been daunting enough even if the Government had a large majority. Churchill himself, his point having been made, spoke of handing over to Eden within a year, and Mrs Churchill left no one in any doubt about her total lack of enthusiasm for 'the second innings'.

Churchill's desire to have around him at the top men whom he knew gave his Government a distinct air of *déjà vu*. Eden's return to the Foreign Office was greeted with general satisfaction and, in the Office itself, with undisguised pleasure. But this was the only positive feature of Churchill's nostalgia. He brought into the Cabinet Cherwell and Ismay, and for a few months even took himself the post of Minister of Defence as in the old days, until he realized it was impossible, and brought the hapless Alexander from being a notably successful Governor-General of Canada to become a notably unsuccessful Minister of Defence. As Colville, himself reluctantly recruited back into the Private Office at Number 10, has written, 'Auld Lang Syne was ringing out along the Whitehall corridors.'

The key new appointments were Butler as Chancellor of the Exchequer, Maxwell Fyfe to the Home Office, and Macmillan to Housing, where he was to make his name as a dynamic and successful domestic minister. Churchill himself said that what Britain needed was several years of quiet and steady administration, and his appointment of Sir Walter Monckton as Minister of Labour and National Service was significant; Monckton, an eminent barrister and adviser to King Edward VIII during the Abdication crisis and subsequently to the Nizam of Hyderabad, was a very late entrant to politics, succeeding Oliver Stanley at the age of sixty, but already famous as a conciliator and friend of all. His job was, as he explained to his Parliamentary Private Secretary, purely to keep the peace with the trade unions. At this he was superbly successful, but at a certain cost. As the

343

new Secretary of State for the Colonies, Oliver Lyttelton was to achieve spectacular success, particularly in Malaya and in Kenya, where his mixture of firmness and willingness to negotiate for the future brought peace out of conflict. Far less successful was Churchill's innovation, in Woolton and Lord Leathers, of Overlord ministers covering several departments, a characteristically dramatic announcement that puzzled observers, and ministers even more.

Another unexpected appointment was that of Selwyn Lloyd as Eden's Minister of State. Lloyd was a competent lawyer who had specialized in economic and legal matters in the House since his election in 1945, and by his own frank admission knew nothing about foreign affairs, understood no foreign languages, had never travelled abroad except as a soldier during the war and actively disliked foreigners. These were hailed by Churchill, who knew nothing about Lloyd, as positive virtues, and a very bewildered Lloyd presented himself at the Foreign Office for duty, to find Eden already at work holding an office meeting on Iran in the Secretary of State's room. Lloyd was to prove himself an able subordinate, but his lack of experience and his awe of Eden were to prove to be liabilities. He was grossly overpromoted and out of his sphere. Eden had had little to do with Lloyd's appointment, and indeed hardly knew him. This contrasted with the appointment of Anthony Nutting as Under-Secretary, on which Eden had insisted, as he did on that of Robert Carr as his PPS.

Eden had developed extravagant hopes for Nutting as a future Foreign Secretary, and Nutting had become his protégé. Unhappily, this often happens in politics as in other areas of human concerns. Eden saw in Nutting – ardent, intelligent, articulate and enthusiastic – something of himself, and something of Simon. He enjoyed the company of Nutting and his wife at a time when he was lonely, and came to think highly of Nutting, whose knowledge of the Middle East was certainly impressive. Eden was not alone in his high estimation of him.

The salaries of MPs being still low, Robert Carr had to continue his work in industry, but Eden actively encouraged this, as he still felt that he knew less of this part of Britain than he felt he should, and wanted Carr not only to be his 'eyes and ears' in the Commons but also his links with industry and commerce. There were those who considered that Eden should have chosen an older and more experienced man and one who could give more time to Parliament, but Eden had already developed a strong affection, trust and regard for Carr – one of the founders of the One Nation Group of Conservative MPs – which were reciprocated in full. Carr had already proved that he could stand up to Eden and was not frightened of him; although he could not travel with his Secretary of State as a result of the

Government's small majority, his influence and help were wholly beneficial, and they were to be close friends for the rest of Eden's life.

One early feature of Eden's return to the Foreign Office was quickly noted at Downing Street. In his case the wartime relationship was *not* to be resumed. Eden's position in the Party and Government was now such that Churchill needed him more than he needed Churchill. He was obviously the heir and, after the Prime Minister, the best-known and most respected member of the Government nationally and internationally. Eden knew that Churchill's interests did not lie in domestic affairs, and while Eden's respect and admiration for Churchill remained strong, he was determined to be màster of foreign affairs. Churchill, believing that the old relationship would continue, was at first puzzled and then hurt; Colville was not the only survivor of the wartime Government who noticed a new tension between the two men, which was to increase steadily. It was a tension not reduced by the fact that Eden expected – and had good reason to expect – that he would succeed Churchill as Prime Minister in a matter of months. Churchill was seventy-seven, had suffered two minor strokes, was becoming very deaf, and, in Oliver Lyttelton's somewhat unkind words, had the tired look of a trawler captain who had reached harbour after a buffeting. No one expected that he would stay as Prime Minister for four and a half years.

While other ministers grappled with severe problems at home, Eden addressed himself with energy and enthusiasm to the international situation. The years of Opposition had refreshed him, and his health, in spite of some mysterious internal malady that no one could diagnose, seemed good. The celebrated 'bloody prima donna' temperament was still there, but after Morrison the Foreign Office was delighted to be back under the leadership of a professional, as was the House of Commons, where Eden's authority became absolute and remarkable.

I had personal experience of this early in 1952 when, a schoolboy, I paid my first visit to the Galleries of the House of Commons, to find the House in uproar. The Chamber was full, and the Labour Opposition in full cry against the Government; ministers at the Dispatch Box were having an unhappy afternoon until Eden's turn came. At once the tumult ceased, Eden was listened to in silence and with evident respect, and Emanuel Shinwell eventually rose to thank Eden 'for the first sign of good manners we have had from the Treasury Bench all afternoon'. When Eden's appearance and question period ended, the uproar broke out again.

Brooding over his wartime and previous experience while in Opposition Eden had become convinced that success lay only in setting clear objectives, in detailed preparation, and in caution. While Churchill hankered after

345

top-Power summits without agenda or preparation, Eden's experience told him that these exercises were at best futile and at worst perilous. In his first speech as Foreign Secretary he said that the road to peace lay in 'preparation, conference and agreement; starting from small issues, and working to the great'.

There was no shortage of issues small and great confronting him. Western Europe, still devastated by war, was in political disarray, and in Berlin the situation remained bitter and menacing. The Korean armistice was precarious and tense. In Indo-China the French were experiencing severe difficulties and heavy losses in their war against the Viet Minh; the Iranian situation remained bad; Egyptian nationalism was making the position of King Farouk and the British forces in the Canal Zone increasingly difficult, while in Cyprus there were signs of the revival of the Greek Cypriot call for *enosis*.

Although Britain was still a major world Power geographically and militarily, she could not compare with the United States or the Soviet Union, and had become a major debtor nation. When Eden compared the situation with that of 1937, or even of the war years, he commented that although the work-load of the Secretary of State had dramatically increased, the actual power of Britain to affect events had proportionately declined.

As has been recorded, Lloyd's first sight of Eden at work was at an office meeting on Iran. Here, ominously, Eden was at odds with the Truman administration, which persisted in seeing Mussadeq as a bastion against Communism and continued to finance him to protect American oil interests. Britain also had substantial oil interests involved, but Eden did not believe that the way forward was to buttress Mussadeq, whom he regarded as a megalomaniac whose word – as had been proved – was worthless. He recognized that forcible military intervention, what Churchill described as 'a splutter of musketry', was impossible. What he did urge upon the Americans, with eventual success, was a drastic reduction of all aid to Mussadeq and a 'holding' policy. He appointed a small but very experienced team to work on the subject exclusively, while trying to persuade the Americans that their assessment was wrong and that Western interests were at hazard so long as Mussadeq was in power. The Americans took some persuading on this, and did not change their attitude until the Eisenhower administration. Eden also had difficulties with the Anglo-Iranian Oil Company officials which tried his patience and temper sorely. His policy was to play it along, that 'no agreement would be better than a bad one', and certain clandestine steps were taken to hasten Mussadeq's downfall.

What only a handful of people knew was that Eden sold his Anglo-Iranian shares, then at their nadir. Colville was one of the few who knew of this, and was horrified, as was Churchill. There is no obligation whatever on Ministers to sell shares on taking Office, although they must resign from all other employment, but Eden considered that his ownership of a substantial holding in the company could be interpreted as an interest which no Foreign Secretary dealing with the future of the company should own. On this, a matter of honour, he would not budge, and the shares were sold, at an appalling loss which he could not afford, and which doomed Binderton. Had he held on to the shares he could have become rich for the first time in his life, but he was not that kind of man. Churchill was both moved and deeply impressed. This secret has been kept until now.*

But the immediate problems were rather closer to home.

The Pleven Plan of October 1950 had initiated negotiations for the formation of a European Army in which all national forces, including those of a rearmed West Germany, would be wholly integrated. There would be a European Minister of Defence responsible to a European Assembly, a European Defence Council of Ministers, and a single European Defence Budget. In Opposition some Conservatives had been enthusiastic about the proposal, as they were over the Schuman Plan for a European Coal and Steel Community. Churchill's own speeches in support of a United States of Europe, and even – at Strasbourg on 11 August 1950 – in support of the principle of a European Army, had given great encouragement to a number of senior Conservatives who had taken an active role in building up the Council of Europe and encouraging European expectations that a Conservative Government would take a positive lead in European co-operation and integration.

Eden's objections to the European Army were both political and practical. He did not at this stage want a British commitment on the Continent of Europe on this scale, and had a suspicion of a permanent involvement of this nature. As a soldier, he could see all the practical difficulties of what Churchill described as 'a sludgy amalgam'. His position, and that of the Cabinet – although with some unease – was that Britain should encourage France and Germany to form the European Defence Community (EDC) and support the Schuman Plan, but that Britain should not participate in them, and should instead persuade the Truman administration that they should both help from without rather than participate from within.

* I am very grateful to Sir John Colville for giving me details of this episode.

The Mediterranean and the Middle East

USSR

BLACK SEA

ALBANIA

Thessalonika

Istanbul

Ankara

GREECE

TURKEY

SICILY

Athens

MALTA

Alep

RHODES

SY

CRETE

CYPRUS

Beirut

LEBANON

Damas

MEDITERRANEAN SEA

Haifa

ISRAEL

Amm

Benghazi

Tobruk

Alexandria

Port Fuad

Jerusalem

Dead S

Port Said

Gaza

JORD

Suez
Canal

Gaza Strip

Negec

Cairo

Suez

SINAI

Eilat

Gulf of
Suez

Straits of
Tiran

Sharm-el-Sheikh

RED S

LIBYA

EGYPT

R. Nile

Aswan

SUDAN

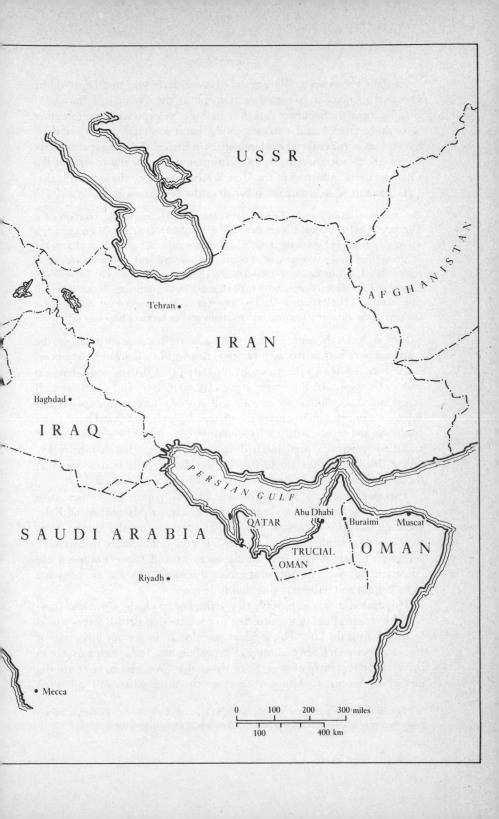

USSR

AFGHANISTAN

Tehran •

IRAN

Baghdad •

IRAQ

PERSIAN GULF

SAUDI ARABIA

Abu Dhabi

QATAR

Buraimi

Muscat

TRUCIAL
OMAN

OMAN

Riyadh •

• Mecca

0   100   200   300 miles

100   400 km

At the Cabinet on 22 November, Maxwell Fyfe said that he would be expected to make a favourable statement to the Council of Europe at Strasbourg on the Schuman Plan, but doubts were expressed about whether it would be ratified, and it was suggested that it was viewed with suspicion by workers in the coal and steel industries in Britain. Eden was particularly strong about 'surrendering to any European authority the control of the Coal and Steel Industries of the United Kingdom'. But the statement that Fyfe was authorized to make on behalf of the Government was that

the initiative taken by the French Government concerning the creation of a European Coal and Steel Community and a European Defence Community is a major step towards European unity. They welcome the Schuman Plan as a means of strengthening the economy of Western Europe and look forward to its early realization. It is our desire to establish the closest possible association with the European Continental Community at all stages in its development. If the Schuman Plan is ratified His Majesty's Government will set up a permanent delegation at the seat of the authority to enter into relations and to transact business with it.

Fyfe spoke on these instructions at Strasbourg and, not surprisingly, the reactions were enthusiastic and positive. But within a few hours, at a press conference in Rome, Eden categorically stated that Britain would have no part in the proposed European Army. Although Fyfe had given no such commitment, the difference in tone and attitude between his speech and Eden's abrupt statement caused the British delegation at Strasbourg much confusion and embarrassment; Fyfe considered that he had been let down;* and the French were particularly dismayed, and suspected that the reality of the British commitment to Europe was flimsy. The trouble was that these suspicions were well merited so far as Eden was concerned.

This was a bad start, and was profoundly disappointing to Conservative enthusiasts for Europe, who in the Cabinet included Macmillan and Fyfe; some of Churchill's glowing Opposition speeches on the subject were recalled and quoted. The fact was that Eden did not consider Britain to be a European nation. She had a duty to assist and foster European co-operation, but not to be part of it except through NATO. He was prepared to be helpful and understanding, but little more.

This approach was impossible to sustain, and gradually Eden was compelled by the realities of the situation to concede that British forces would be linked with the EDC. The incident revealed an important difference of emphasis between Eden and some of his colleagues. In his first message to British representatives abroad, Eden wrote that 'We wish to cultivate the idea of an Atlantic Community based on the three pillars of the United

---

* For the strange sequel to this episode, see p. 614. In July 1969 Mr Ben Pimlott, at Eden's request, prepared a detailed account, which I have found especially valuable.

States, United Kingdom (including the Commonwealth) and Continental Europe,' the priorities themselves being significant. When Macmillan submitted a paper in January suggesting that Britain might join a European confederation or union similar to the Commonwealth, and with its full support, Eden firmly rejected this possibility in Cabinet on 12 March. Maxwell Fyfe and Macmillan subsequently regretted that they had not pressed the matter further, but, after all, Eden was the Foreign Secretary, and they had other very heavy responsibilities of their own. They also recognized that Eden was not prepared to have anyone, even the Prime Minister, interfering in foreign policy.

It must be emphasized that these were indeed early days for European economic co-operation, and there were many in the Conservative Party who entirely shared Eden's suspicion of European entanglements and his belief in the benefits of the Empire and Commonwealth trading arrangements; Labour was wholly isolationist on this matter, as was Sir Ivone Kirkpatrick, who became Permanent Under-Secretary at the Foreign Office at the beginning of 1953.

For several months Eden fought tenaciously to make the Anglo-European link a simple guarantee without any treaty obligations, and he was determined that Britain would not delegate her independence and freedom of action to any supra-national European organization. He was very willing to end the Allied occupation of Germany and grant sovereignty to the new German Federal Republic, but he would go no further than a treaty of mutual security between Britain and the EDC members. His actions may have been realistic, but he gave the clear impression of deep scepticism about Britain's role in Europe, which he made clear when he received an honorary degree at Columbia University in January 1952. Britain's real interests, he said, lay far from Europe, and any suggestion that Britain should join a federation of European states was 'something which we know, in our bones, we cannot do'. It was not to be wondered at that statements such as this were a considerable blow to Britain's friends in Europe, and a particular disappointment to Robert Schuman, the visionary French Foreign Minister. Eden simply did not share that vision; indeed, it does not go too far to say that he was repelled by it. The French drew their conclusions, and the opposition to the EDC in the French Assembly and outside it began to gather force.

Eden's moods were always variable, and on several occasions during his career he had been close to leaving politics. Now there occurred another, when the Secretary-Generalship of NATO was discussed. Eden recorded on 4 March:

Not much refreshed after a bad night.

Morning with documents. Sleep after luncheon. Then Bob Dixon arrived to announce that France had refused Stikker [of the Netherlands] & insisted upon an Englishman. After much discussion offered myself. They refused to take it seriously though I would greatly enjoy the work & would give so much to be on my own.

... Still tempted by NATO.

This was only a passing whim, although by no means a frivolous one. Ismay was persuaded to take the post, which he conducted with brilliant and memorable success. Eden resumed on what he called 'my treadmill'.

Eden's attitude to European unity – from outside, not inside – would have been better justified if his relations with the United States had been more sympathetic. Here, there was a serious lacuna in his international wisdom and understanding. Unlike Churchill and Macmillan, themselves each half-American, Eden never felt at home in the United States, although he always did in Canada, and he tended to be excessively critical of American policies and purposes and had – with good cause, it must be conceded – serious doubts about American capacities in international affairs. He had to work with them, and did so; he had many American friends and admirers; but there was something lacking, an absence of warmth and respect which was noted and resented. Matters were not helped by the fact that Eden and Dean Acheson fell out seriously over Iran and Korea, where in both cases Eden urged greater flexibility and caution. When the British view prevailed at the United Nations on Korea, Acheson launched into a diatribe against Lloyd and Eden for their disloyalty, and added 'one day you will find that it never pays to win victories over your friends'.

Lloyd concluded that the rapturous reception given to Eden at the UN on his return to the international stage had occasioned some jealousy. This was doubly unfortunate, as, although Acheson's period as Secretary of State was coming to an end, he liked and respected Eden, and Eden him. As Macmillan shrewdly noted, they were both aristocrats, looked remarkably alike physically, and had much in common temperamentally. Each had physical and moral courage, strong opinions strongly expressed, a disdain for the pettiness of politics, and exceptional intelligence and experience. This should have been a close and positive relationship, but it was not, and matters were not improved by the fact that in his dealings with the Americans throughout his last period as Foreign Secretary Eden was consistently right. Acheson found this difficult to forgive.

But the root cause of Eden's reserve towards both Europe and the United States was that, although he realized intellectually that Britain was a poor country which was grossly overstretched as a major colonial power and must face harsh realities, he could not accept that she had become a satellite of the United States or had suddenly become, after generations of isolation and the power of the Empire, a European continental offshore island. He realized – few better – how circumscribed British power was, but at heart he did not accept the implication of Britain as an inferior nation, devoid of influence or even power. He also looked to the future, when the parlous British economic restrictions might be lifted. He could be described as the last of the Liberal Imperialists. If some American and European politicians – particularly the former – felt that Eden, behind his veneer, was contemptuous and suspicious of their amateurishness and inexperience, these suspicions were not wholly misplaced.

Eden saw his job, as he reiterated again and again in public and in private, as being to protect and further *British* interests, not those of other countries. In this sense he was a nationalist – but a nationalist with a unique internationalist sense.

He certainly saw no value to British interests in becoming enbroiled in a war with China. He entirely agreed with the Americans and Churchill that if the North Koreans broke the armistice and invaded the South again there should be a strong Allied response, including the bombing of airfields in Manchuria, which had been agreed by the Labour Government. But Britain would not support a naval blockade of China, and when the Americans bombed power stations on the Yalu River close to the China border in June, although Eden defended the Americans publicly, his private reactions were censorious. In Indo-China he supported the French, but there was to be question of intervention. The Americans, who saw the Communist peril everywhere, chafed at his caution and at his refusal to commit Britain further than was absolutely necessary.

Differences with the Americans in the Middle East were not confined to Iran.

The situation in Egypt caused Eden as much concern as any of the issues that mounted upon his desk and tested his intellect and energy. This was a job, he remarked, that had killed Bevin and destroyed Morrison, and now he understood why. Wartime diplomacy had, in comparison, been relatively easy; this was a nightmare in which the principal players were constantly changing. French and Italian Governments came and went with alarming rapidity, making continuity virtually impossible; Truman's announcement that he would not run again in 1952 had made the American situation very unpredictable in a presidential election year. As Acheson could well testify, the McCarthyite poison was at its most virulent, John Foster Dulles eagerly joining in the squalid onslaught on the administration and its alleged pro-Communist sympathies in company with a hitherto obscure (to Britain) senator from California, Richard M. Nixon. Eden may have had his difficulties with Acheson, but the more he heard about Dulles, and the possibility that he might become Secretary of State if the Republicans won, the less he relished the prospect.

The rising tide of Egyptian nationalism had led to the unilateral abrogation of the 1936 Anglo-Egyptian treaty and the 1899 Condominium establishing dual control over the Sudan, and there were now demands for British evacuation of the Suez Canal Zone and the Sudan. On the latter, in spite of American pressure, Eden was emphatic; the principle of self-determination for the Sudanese was to him a resigning issue, and on this he was fortunate. While anti-British riots in Cairo became so grave that the possibility of committing British troops was seriously considered and while the situation in the Zone became more dangerous and tense, a military *coup* in July removed King Farouk, to universal rejoicing, and brought in a military junta headed by General Mohammed Neguib. Eden went out of his way to be conciliatory to the new regime, and was rewarded by the abandonment of Egypt's claim to the Sudan, which a year later opted for independence.

The reasonable attitude of the new Egyptian regime encouraged Eden to transfer the headquarters of the Middle East command from Egypt to Cyprus and to begin discussions about the withdrawal of British forces from the Canal Zone. He had no doubt that their position was untenable, and unnecessary in modern conditions. Churchill was dismayed, as was a small but very vocal minority of Conservative MPs led by Captain Waterhouse and including Julian Amery, determined to resist this abandonment of British territory and interests. The negotiations, and the bitterness within the Conservative Party, were to last for two years. On 8 April, Colville recorded that Eden 'is rather discredited in the P.M.'s eyes at present' (over Egypt), but the fact was that the Government, and Churchill himself, were also discredited, as disastrous London County Council elections demonstrated. There was much discontent with Churchill on the Conservative benches, as the Chief Whip, Patrick Buchan-Hepburn, bravely told him: and Colville wrote on 30 May that 'Mrs Churchill does not think he will last long as Prime Minister.'

In the midst of all this, Eden flew to Belgrade to see Tito to discuss the claims of Italy and Yugoslavia to Trieste, which had been under Anglo-American occupation since the war. Eden was the first major Western politician to visit Tito since his break from the Soviet Union, and although no immediate resolution was achieved, Eden was authorized to present Tito with a formal invitation to visit London early in 1953, not to everyone's pleasure. By October 1954 the Trieste dispute, which had caused tension and bloodshed since 1945, was peacefully resolved. Many a Foreign Secretary would have been satisfied with one such achievement in his term of office; to Eden it was one of many in his extraordinary period. What had been a major international problem ceased to be one, and with some very well-applied flattery and pomp and circumstance Tito was welcomed in London, and Anglo-Yugoslav relations dramatically and beneficially transformed. The Yugoslav émigrés and many Conservatives were angered by the invitation and by the recognition given by the British Government to a man they loathed, but others recognized that it was an act of great imagination which, almost magically, removed the Trieste issue from the international agenda.

All this was being done in the context of continuing poor health, which manifested itself in a sharp attack of jaundice, whose real cause was not suspected.

Motored down to Winston at Chartwell late in evening. He was alone.

General talk. Nothing very new on international scene. He appeared to expect me to ask for more work on home front. Would I like to take on chairmanship of Home Affairs [Committee] in place of Woolton who had too much. I said I couldn't do this without abandoning F.O. for which I was not prepared. He agreed.

All most friendly. He complained of 'my old brain' not working as it used to do. Yet later was looking forward to working with Eisenhower after November. . . .

I didn't think W looked well, & he is doing very little work. I told him of my concern about economic & financial outlook & that we must take some important decisions within the next five or six weeks. Our export trade was not getting the necessary priorities. (Diary, 4 June)

Churchill did not raise the matter of his retirement, nor did Eden, and all talk of Churchill leaving after a year had mysteriously ended. He was certainly not the dynamic Churchill of old, but he enjoyed being Prime Minister with a young and beautiful Queen,* and the prospect of working with Eisenhower if the latter won the Republican nomination and the November presidential election was exhilarating for him. But Eden would have been wise to have considered more seriously the offer to go into more domestic concerns. He was so deeply involved in so much at the Foreign Office that it was probably impossible, and now that he had taken on so much any successor – and none appeared obvious – would have had

* King George VI had died on 6 February.

considerable difficulty. In any event, Churchill stayed in Downing Street, Eden at the Foreign Office.

Eden lamented his illness and his appalling colour in lighthearted letters to Nicholas, now ADC to the Governor-General of Canada, but in the early summer he had a more difficult letter to write to his son.

Anthony Eden had first met Clarissa Churchill, the daughter of John Churchill and the famously lovely Lady Gwendelene, and niece of Winston, at Cranborne, when she was sixteen, where she 'was struck by his bottle green tweed jacket and tweed *pinstriped* trousers'. To her he was only the glamorous but remote Foreign Secretary, while to him she was only Churchill's very attractive, intelligent and shy niece. But in 1947 they sat together at a dinner party in London where, to Clarissa Churchill's chagrin, Eden was monopolized by a very eager and voluble lady on his right, and they did not exchange a word until the end of the meal when Eden abjectly apologized and asked if she might dine with him one evening. She agreed, but it was only slowly that casual friendship and pleasure in each other's company developed into something stronger.

Although Eden was now deeply in love, he hesitated. He was worried by Nicholas's possible reactions, knowing his devotion to his mother. He was uncomfortable at the prospect of marrying again after his previous unhappiness, and was nervous at the prospect 'at my great age', as he wrote to Nicholas; and he knew that to marry someone so much younger who was also the niece of the Prime Minister would inevitably arouse hostile comment. Although Clarissa Churchill did not share Beatrice's loathing of politics, it was not a world that attracted her. Also, even in 1952, Church and press hostility to divorce remained very strong, as Princess Margaret was to experience three years later when she wished to marry Group Captain Peter Townsend, when Eden was Prime Minister. But these doubts and apprehensions were swept aside. Eden insisted that the proposed marriage should be kept strictly secret for six months, until August 'when everyone would be away'. As a result, the Churchills were not told until a short time before the event. Churchill, with his warm sense of family and his devotion to Eden, in spite of all difficulties, was delighted, and at once insisted that he should be the principal witness at what had to be a Registry Office ceremony and that the wedding reception should be at Number 10. Lady Churchill, therefore, had to return specially from a holiday in Capri so that she could organize the reception. Churchill, who had sadly seen the marriages of two of his children end and whose own marriage had had its stormy moments, much disliked divorce but had come to accept it. He had been specially sympathetic to Eden in his sadness, as had Mrs Churchill. He warmly welcomed the new attachment, and gave it his unreserved blessing. So did Nicholas, to Eden's great relief and gratitude.

The only shadows came from certain elements in the Churches,* notably the *Church Times*, though its censures were denounced not only by national newspapers (notably the *Manchester Guardian*) but by individuals – including several clergymen – who wrote to Eden to deplore these criticisms and to wish him and his bride well. Some of these letters were very moving, particularly from those who had experienced an unhappy first marriage and a happy second one. To take one example out of many, a lady wrote from Australia, outraged by the comments of the Dean of Sydney, who had compared Eden to the Duke of Windsor:

May you both find perfect happiness, health, love and companionship in your new partnership. As a fellow human my wish is truly sincere as, one similarly placed through a broken marriage, I could appreciate now the beauty of a true affinity.

This was indeed the majority view, and the marriage took place on 14 August, amidst much rejoicing, and the hopes of the kind lady from Sydney were entirely fulfilled.

What was *not* fulfilled was Eden's attempt to minimize publicity by having the wedding in August. In fact, in the press's classic 'silly season', and with journalists and editors desperate for stories to fill their papers, the Edens got far more attention than they would at any other time. It was a very good, if minor, example of Eden's innocence in these matters, and another corrective to the myth of his 'vanity'. He had genuinely wanted, and had planned, a very private occasion. What he and his bride got was massive national and international publicity. Clarissa, at least, saw the funny side of it.

Their honeymoon was spent in Portugal, but Churchill took the opportunity of Eden's absence from the Foreign Office to invite Truman to join with him in a joint message to Mussadeq to warn him of the consequences of his actions if he continued on a course inimical to Western interests. This was something of a *coup*, as until this point the Americans had refused to be involved in any joint action or declaration, Acheson still convinced that if Mussadeq fell something much worse would succeed him. (In December Eden was told that the Export–Import Bank proposed a further

---

* Robert Carr asked Mark Chapman-Walker, Director of Publicity at Conservative Central Office, about Party reactions. Chapman-Walker wrote to Eden on 15 August: 'I have spoken to a very large number of constituency officials from all over the country and have also received a report from our own Public Opinion Research Department, and all the evidence obtained indicates the immense public approval of your marriage.... I am afraid this all sounds very pompous but I really want you to know that there is absolutely nothing to worry about.'

loan to Mussadeq: 'Hoped I wouldn't mind! Had to telegraph W[ashington]. Also sent for Jimmy Dunn to tell him exactly how much I did mind.') But although Churchill had consulted the Foreign Office he did not tell the Foreign Secretary, to the latter's great indignation. It was not so much the content of the message but the fact that the Prime Minister was interfering without consultation in a highly sensitive area that so enraged Eden. The latter had right on his side, but the incident did not improve relations between the two men.

The year ended on a bad note politically.

Impossible Cabinet in afternoon on Egypt – which was not on Agenda.

Lord Chancellor [Viscount Simonds] passed me sympathetic note when my exasperation was at its height – that all Cabinet was with me.

I think this was true. W had no alternative policy whatever; just moaned. I asked him point blank at one time what his plan was. Did he want to march on Cairo? This brought a denial, but nothing more constructive. (Diary, 22 December)

At the end of the year the Edens visited Tim at his home in the New Forest. This was not a success, as Eden was saddened to see many of the Windlestone treasures in an unfitting context, but he wrote on 29 December:

Raining & cold.

Clarissa says this is the right way to run F.O. Lie in bed, direct office by telephone & read Delacroix!

Very good too.

Churchill's eagerness to pay another visit to the United States to bid farewell to Truman and greet President Eisenhower was so strong that although Eden – and the new Ambassador to Washington, Sir Roger Makins – doubted whether Eisenhower was equally enthusiastic, Eden did not consider that it would do any harm. The Churchill party, which did not include Eden, sailed on the *Queen Mary* on 30 December and, after a holiday in Jamaica, was back in London on 14 January. As Churchill had quietly reneged on his promise to stay for only a year, the problem of when he would go was now seriously exercising his colleagues. Eden recorded on 23 January:

C & I dined with Harry Crookshank & his old mother in Pont Street.

When we were left alone Harry spoke of the future. I told him how little I knew of W's plans. He said that he was convinced that W was an increasing liability to us, that if he had not been leading us at the General Election we should have had another sixty seats, & that more than half the party deeply resented his association with Beaverbrook....

Harry also said that no one could tell when a General Election might have to come, merely thro' casualties. It could be next year. Therefore W should go at the Coronation.* There was historical precedent for it.

I said that I didn't think that W would much like the precedent.† Harry said some of them must consider how to make their views known to W but he hadn't wished to make any move without consulting me.

All Eden could say, which he did repeatedly, was that he could be no party to any move by his colleagues to persuade Churchill to retire, as he was the obvious successor, and certainly could not treat an old friend and colleague in this manner. If others felt – as he did – that Churchill's fading powers made a change desirable, they should make their representations, but that he could have no part in them.

These plans were to be swiftly, and cruelly, overtaken by events. Eden and Butler flew to Washington on 4 March; as they were about to leave Eden's Principal Private Secretary Evelyn Shuckburgh told Eden that Stalin had suffered a stroke, and the indications were that it would be fatal – as it was. The removal of this evil but massive world figure was obviously a major political event, but at that stage it was impossible to calculate who would succeed him or what, if any, changes would occur in Soviet policy. The successor was Malenkov, about whom very little was known in the West.

Churchill had not been at all favourably impressed by Dulles, and Eden himself had been so concerned by all he heard and knew of him that he had privately urged Eisenhower not to appoint him Secretary of State when the future President had been given a farewell dinner as the outgoing Supreme Commander of NATO in London the previous summer. But Eisenhower had come to respect and like Dulles, and the pressures upon him to appoint him from within the Republican Party and his own entourage had been overwhelming. Eden was disconcerted, as he was also by the appointment of Winthrop Aldrich – announced without consultation with the British‡ – as US Ambassador to London in succession to Walter Gifford. Eden never developed a real rapport with Aldrich, whose interests often appeared to be more in society than in politics, but he had got on excellently well with Gifford.

Dulles, however, went out of his way to be friendly and helpful. On Egypt, Eden noted, 'He was very friendly but still rather vague in ideas &

---

* Arranged for 2 June.

† Namely, the resignation of Baldwin in 1937 and the succession of Neville Chamberlain to coincide with the Coronation of King George VI.

‡ This was entirely an oversight. Eisenhower had told Dulles to inform Eden, but he had forgotten to do so (see S. Ambrose, *Eisenhower The President*, p. 50).

found Winston's messages tiresome.... He promised me as much time as I wanted while I was here, & I think he meant it.'

Bad telegram from London refusing to accept any of our joint proposals about Egypt. It had clearly been sent by W without consultation with anyone. It included a message to Ike which we all thought – Rab & I and Roger [Makins] – both foolish and bad tempered. (Diary, 8 March)

Despite this, Eden made good progress with Eisenhower and Dulles, his purpose being to obtain an American guarantee of freedom of passage in the Suez Canal when and if there was an Anglo-Egyptian agreement on the Zone Base. Eisenhower agreed, while emphasizing his concern 'of offending Egyptians by the appearance of joint action. Whole talk was very friendly.' Unhappily, not only did the Egyptians object, but the Americans backed down.

Most importantly, the American administration now realized the threat posed by Mussadeq. In October 1952 he had broken off relations with Britain, and now appealed to Eisenhower for more American aid. But Eisenhower had come to the conclusion that the British were right, and refused to provide aid or to purchase Iranian oil. He had also decided to use the CIA, headed by Dulles' brother Allen, in conjunction with British Intelligence, to restore the Shah to power – Operation 'Ajax'. When Mussadeq dissolved Parliament in July 1953 and ruled by decree the Shah fled Tehran and the Russians announced that they would aid Iran; Ajax was put into operation. By 22 August the Shah was back and Mussadeq under arrest. It had been a brilliant, although very expensive, exercise, portrayed as a spontaneous uprising by the Iranian Army and people against Mussadeq's dictatorial and ruinous rule. It had indeed been both, but the organization of his downfall had been anything but spontaneous. It was also a superbly concealed operation, and was to remain so for a long time.

This account is in defiance of chronology, but it stemmed from Eden's visit to Washington and was a complete vindication of his warnings about Iran falling into the Soviet sphere, in defiance of the Truman administration's persistence in seeing Mussadeq as anti-Communist and worthy of support. The British lost their monopoly, retaining only 40 per cent of Iranian oil, but that was much better than nothing; an American consortium also got 40 per cent, and Eisenhower at once allocated aid to Iran of $85 million.

This episode is perhaps not for the pure in heart and soul, but it is what happened, and a major problem for the West, and particularly for Britain, had been resolved.

*　　*　　*

Eden's heavy burden of work and travelling were thought responsible for his feeling so unwell throughout 1952, but this was not noticed in public until the Tito visit in March 1953, when many observers – including this one – were alarmed by his appearance and colour, on which Tito himself commented with concern. It was ascribed to the effects of his jaundice, but his ministerial colleague, Charles Hill, had already, with his doctor's eye, appreciated that Eden was seriously ill. He was certainly notably testy:

An exasperating day. No time to prepare my statement for House, the Treasury part of which was melancholy bromide.

Had hoped to escape greater part of Cabinet to do this. But when I arrived found Winston was still in bed dictating reply to one P.Q. [Parliamentary Question] so had to preside. When he eventually did arrive we had of course to hear it, causing further delay, before we got down to business. Had in the end to protest that my statement mattered at least as much as his P.Q. Fear that as a result of all this my statement carried too many clichés – Couldn't say anything on economic side. Anyway, House was distinctly unpleasant. (Diary, 17 March)

As this statement, on his Washington visit, had also to be sandwiched between a luncheon at Buckingham Palace given by the Queen in honour of Tito and an official dinner, it was not surprising that Eden was infuriated and certainly not at his best in the House. But neither he, nor anyone else, realized how ill he was.

The Tito visit was in itself exhausting, although politically it was outstandingly successful, and acknowledged – albeit grudgingly in some quarters – to be a notable personal achievement for Eden. But the interminable difficulties with Churchill rumbled on, as his diary entries show:

2 *April*
William [Strang] & Bob Dixon came over [to 1 Carlton Gardens] and we discussed once again question of my meeting with Molotov. We all agreed that events were moving fast enough & that a meeting would endanger EDC, encourage French to hang back & generally cause confusion at this time. If matters dragged this would be another question.

Winston arrived about 11.30. I explained to him our thought & he accepted it completely. William was there. He added on his own account that the situation had changed markedly in the last few days. He also agreed some suggestion about restraint of use of aircraft in Buraimi.

X ray at luncheon time. Depressing. Apparent gall-bladder trouble. Said I wanted to see [Sir Horace] Evans.

W rang me up in evening & said he had drafts resulting from morning talks but was very tired. Could they wait until tomorrow? I said 'certainly they could'.

3 *April*
I was taken aback by W ringing in the morning & saying somewhat challengingly 'So you have given up the idea of seeing Molotov. I don't like that at all.' He had

entirely forgotten yesterday's conversation – went over it again with him carefully & he appeared to agree & begin to recollect. However his telegram to Ike when it arrived showed that he hadn't really understood our reasons for not asking for early meeting or alarming Ike with report that we were doing so now.

... Spoke to Miss Portal (W's Sec) so that he should understand before he rang me up. When he did ring up it was evident he still did not, but he gave up idea of sending message himself.

The diary also noted: 'Evans came at 10 a.m. I liked him, but his account was gloomy.'

Evans' preliminary investigation indicated that Eden's persistent ill health was the result of gallstones, and that an operation on the gall bladder would be necessary. Eden recorded in his diary on 4 April:

Fine early morning, followed by April showers. Up in good time to be at X ray place at 9.30. Four photographs taken, but apparently they didn't satisfy. Then a number more. Evans, who impresses me, [and the other doctors] got together & gave their verdict which was certainly emphatic. They would not let me go on my journey & advised immediate operation. So there we are. Evelyn [Shuckburgh] met me at doctors & motored me back. Told C[lemmie] & W. Stayed up for luncheon. Then tired & to bed reading Delacroix.

Evans' diagnosis had proved absolutely correct, but Eden wrote cheerfully enough to Nicholas on the 8th that 'I have to go into a nursing home for a tiresome operation, not dangerous, for my gall bladder! Isn't it stupid? But they all say I shall be the better for it.' 'All is well otherwise,' he wrote to Nicholas again on 10 April, 'except that W gets daily older & is apt to ring up & waste a great deal of time. Between ourselves the outside world has little idea how difficult all that becomes. Please make me retire before I am 80!' There was no premonition of disaster.

What then happened was a decisive and tragic turning-point in the fortunes of Anthony Eden and in modern history.

The operation took place on 12 April in the London Clinic, and was conducted by a surgeon very experienced in such operations, which are relatively simple and normally wholly successful. This one was not. Eden was later told that 'the knife slipped'; what certainly happened was that his biliary duct was accidentally cut. He had a high fever and lost much blood; his body was being poisoned and he was rapidly losing strength. When he recovered from the anaesthetic he was given the grim news that another operation was urgently essential; what he was not told, until much later, was that it was necessary to save his life. 'Isn't it Hell?' he jotted a note to Nicholas: 'I must say that I dread it.'

The eminent surgeon, who had been gratified to have had such an eminent patient, was now plunged into personal and professional dismay and remorse, his normal ebullience and self-confidence shattered, but this was little consolation. The second operation was a desperate affair to attempt to repair the havoc of the first. Eden bled extensively and frighteningly, and very nearly died. He was subsequently told that his life had been saved by the energy and skill of a junior surgeon and his team, and that it had been a very close thing. But if they had saved his life – just – the original damage was irreparable. The body poisons that pass through the bile duct to be expelled from the body would now seep into his system, causing high fevers and, eventually, death. The professional prognosis was awful, although Eden himself did not realize how bad it really was. Although very weak, he was relieved that the second operation was over, and was for a short time very optimistic. Robert Carr came to the Clinic to read him 'Saki' short stories, at Eden's request, and, although Eden looked desperately ill, he was cheerful and optimistic.

This was not the opinion of his doctors. But then Eden's luck changed. By pure chance the major American specialist in this problem, Dr Richard Cattell, was visiting London at this time to lecture, and Evans brought him immediately into the case. Eden's duct was blocked and he had jaundice again. Cattell at once realized that he could not recover unless he had a third operation to repair the duct with a particular procedure he had pioneered and perfected in Boston, which involved the insertion of a tube in the biliary duct. He judged Eden's condition as so serious that he advised that the operation be undertaken in Boston, where he had his staff and facilities, to which Evans agreed.

Lord Moran, however, thought that the operation could just as well be done in London, and Churchill, who had no idea how serious the operation was nor how desperate Eden's condition, did not want his Foreign Secretary to be removed so far. Evans and Cattell went to 10 Downing Street to see Churchill in the Cabinet room, where they made their case at some length; Churchill also reacted at some length, at one point saying that King George VI had been operated on during the war on a kitchen table in Buckingham Palace and had made a complete recovery; the doctors patiently explained to him that this had been for appendicitis and that Eden's condition was infinitely more complex and critical. Churchill eventually agreed with an ill grace. Cattell later recorded that, although this meeting had been in the early evening, and lasted for a considerable time, neither he nor Evans were offered any refreshment of any kind; when Eden learned this he realized how dismayed Churchill had been, and how much he resented the doctors' advice.

When Eden had told him of the original operation, Churchill had written to him:

Foreign Secretary

As I fear you will be away for five or six weeks it will be necessary for me to take over officially from you. Happily we are fully agreed in outlook, and I will look after your foreign policy as well as your political interests. These latter seem to be in a very healthy condition judging by today's NEWS CHRONICLE gallup poll.

Now, it was clear that Eden was going to be away for a long time, and the moment that Churchill, with deep reluctance, accepted what Evans and Cattell told him, he responded characteristically by offering the Edens the full use of Chequers while Eden gathered his strength for the journey to Boston.

Churchill also realized that such operations were very expensive and it would constitute a heavy burden on Eden's limited finances. While he judged it improper that the taxpayer should meet the cost of the Foreign Secretary's operation abroad, he gave orders – not a request – that Party funds should be used. Eden protested, but the Party Treasurer, Christopher Holland-Martin, whole-heartedly agreed, and made the necessary arrangements. As there were stringent Treasury rules on exchange control and payments abroad Eden's private office had to enter into complex negotiations with the Treasury on his behalf. At length, these tedious vexations were resolved, but there was much correspondence and many meetings about how much Clarissa Eden would be allowed each day in dollars, and other trivialities that seem astonishing today but tell us much about the economic condition of Britain in 1953 and Treasury mentality. In marked contrast, when the Canadian Government heard of the true gravity of Eden's condition, it offered to fly him across the Atlantic in a specially equipped aircraft, and the Lahey Clinic – Cattell's centre – said that it was very willing to undertake the operation without any charge, a most kind and generous offer that was politely declined; there were many individuals on both sides of the Atlantic who wanted to pay the full costs themselves, in itself a remarkable tribute to Eden's popularity and standing. These were declined with gratitude, but the Canadian offer was accepted.

Churchill took on the Foreign Office with much satisfaction – too much for Eden's taste – ostensibly assisted by Salisbury. Without consultation with the latter or with Eden, now resting at Chequers, he made a major speech in the House of Commons on 11 May on foreign affairs in which, after a graceful tribute to Eden, he conducted a superb survey of the world scene before he came to the post-Stalin situation in the Soviet Union, which he regarded with great optimism. Then, in complete defiance of what he knew were Eden's views, he said:

I must make it plain that, in spite of all the uncertainties and confusion in which world affairs are plunged, I believe that a conference on the highest level should take place between the leading Powers without long delay. This conference should not be overhung by a ponderous or rigid agenda, or led into mazes and jungles of technical details, zealously contested by hoards of experts and officials drawn up in vast, cumbrous array. The conference should be confined to the smallest number of Powers and persons possible. It should meet with a measure of informality and a still greater measure of privacy and seclusion. It might well be that no hard-faced agreements would be reached, but there might be a general feeling among those gathered together that they might do something better than tear the human race, including themselves, into bits.... At the worst the participants in the meeting would have established more intimate contacts. At the best we might have a generation of peace.

It was magnificent theatre, and magnificent politics – in domestic terms. Churchill had exactly caught the mood of optimism, almost amounting to euphoria, that had swept Britain following the death of Stalin. A summit! 'A generation of peace!' The Commons was ecstatic, and Churchill had a marvellous press. Eden was furious, and Salisbury was so angry that he threatened to resign, and meant it until Eden, on the telephone from Chequers, talked him out of so drastic a step at such a time. Eden himself was so weak and ill that there was little he could do except protest, which he did very vigorously in the circumstances, but he noted how popular the speech had been, and reckoned that neither the new Russian leaders nor Eisenhower would have anything to do with the proposal – in which he was right. Everything Churchill now suggested – a top-level summit of the mighty few, with no agenda and no preparation – Eden had objected to throughout his diplomatic life, and he reflected with some bitterness that it was exactly this prime ministerial approach to foreign affairs that had led to his break with Chamberlain.

Eden always believed that Churchill's 11 May speech was a major disaster, and he wrote in his diary on 27 November 1954:

It must be long in history since any one speech did so much damage to its own side. In Italy, as de Gasperi openly stated to Winston, & I believe elsewhere, it lost de Gasperi the election, i.e. his gamble for an increased majority. In Germany, Adenauer was exasperated. Worst of all it probably cost us EDC in France. At any rate, the whole summer was lost in wrangling. The speech was made without any consultation with the Cabinet, & I fear that the *Economist* is only too right in saying this week that it was playing party politics. Nutting fought all he could against it. I, of course, never saw it at all, but W is not to blame for this for I was much too ill. He knew well though what I should have thought of it.

But Eden's first priority was to gain in strength after his close brush with death before his operation in Boston early in June. Cattell knew very well how difficult his task would be. When Colville asked him the pro-portion of patients who survived such an operation, made a partial recovery, and made a full recovery, the percentages were indeed sombre.

Eden's operation took eight hours, and was a grim ordeal. Cattell and his team did a brilliant job of patching Eden up, but even their superb surgery and his strong constitution could not fully repair the deadly damage already inflicted upon him. They saved his life, but the cost had been severe.

As much has been made of Eden's health after 1953 – usually erroneously – the facts must be set out. Cattell's surgery ensured that Eden's circulation was restored to normal, but there was always the possibility of attacks of cholangitis, whose characteristic was an intensely high fever. Eden suffered the first of these attacks, as will be related, in October 1956, after three years in which he had recovered completely from his operation. Sir Horace Evans prescribed mild sulphur drugs if a fever occurred. Evans and Eden's new doctor, whom Evans recommended, have testified in confidential documents I have seen, that this was not uncommon treatment at that time, and there was no question of abuse of any other drug, including alcohol and other hypnotics. His general health in all other respects was good, and apart from the October 1956 fevers, which recurred a few months later and again subsequently, although at long intervals, he was rarely seriously unwell; after 1957 he was accepted for life insurance on favourable terms after a rigorous medical examination. What was the case, however, was that for a man who had suffered two duodenal ulcers, was highly tense and worked far too hard for his own good, the new weakness created by the 1953 events provided the peril that it could unexpectedly flare up again, and that the use of drugs, however mild, and sedatives, if on an irregular basis, presented its own problems. But the fact was, as both his medical records and his political and physical activity testify, he made an astonishing recovery, and it is wholly incorrect to ascribe subsequent events to his health which, until October 1956, was excellent. He did, after all, live until his eightieth year.

It is absurd to portray Eden as being from this point a sick man, dependent upon drugs and stimulants. He was not. Nineteen fifty-four was to be perhaps the most active and demanding year of his life, and there were no traces of excessive fatigue, fevers or illness. But the melancholy fact is that he had incurred an internal weakness of great unpredictability as a result of a human error on the operating table, which even Dr Cattell's brilliant surgery could not fully repair. Eden's courage, and his refusal to let this calamitous reverse depress him or reduce his activities, were admirable, but there was to be no complete recovery of his health. Of all the ill fortunes Eden suffered in his life, this was the cruellest of all.

Nor was it only a medical misfortune. The Edens had flown to North America immediately after the Queen's Coronation, which Clarissa Eden had attended but her husband could not. They had been seen off at the airport by the Churchills. Although Churchill had assumed responsibility for the Foreign Office with much pleasure – Selwyn Lloyd as Minister of State being invited to Cabinet meetings – this additional burden was in itself severe, and on top of this were the preparations for the Coronation, the great day itself, and the subsequent meetings with Commonwealth leaders who had attended. His own health had already been causing concern to his doctor, Lord Moran, although Churchill – now a Knight of the Garter, and Sir Winston – felt well, and was in excellent form. But on the evening of 23 June, after being the host at a Downing Street dinner for the Italian Prime Minister, de Gasperi, at which he had spoken at his best, he found that he could not get out of his chair and his speech had become very slurred. The assumption by some was that the Prime Minister had drunk too much, although those who knew him best were considerably more concerned. Moran was summoned, but was not at home, and came next morning in response to an urgent summons.

Churchill had suffered a stroke. As so often in these cases, it was impossible to make an immediate medical judgement of its gravity. It appeared to Moran and to Dr Russell Brain, the top specialist in these matters, that the stroke had been relatively mild, but the appearance of the patient was not good.

What then happened remains a matter of considerable controversy. The doctors prepared a somewhat vague bulletin which stated that Churchill had suffered 'a disturbance of the cerebral circulation' and that they had advised the abandonment of the Bermuda meeting with the Americans and French and at least a month's rest. The politicians, however, saw the political perils of even this reference to what had actually happened, knowing full well that the British press was well equipped with excellent medical advisers who would immediately see the implications of this phrase.

Salisbury and Butler, the senior Cabinet members in Eden's absence, were in a very difficult position. No one could know for certain how serious would be the effects of Churchill's stroke – he conducted a Cabinet on the morning after, and Macmillan was among those who noticed nothing wrong except that Churchill looked very white and, unusually, said little. Eden, the heir apparent, was incapacitated. A situation in which the Prime Minister and Foreign Secretary were palpably out of action would be bound to have a severe impact upon national and international perceptions of the capacity of the British Government. Thus, the eventual bulletin announced that 'The Prime Minister has had no respite for a long time from his very arduous duties and is in need of a complete rest. We have therefore advised him to abandon his journey to Bermuda and lighten his duties for at least a month.' Moran considered this bulletin to be 'a gamble' that Churchill would recover, and for several days it looked as though it would be a gamble that would fail, as Churchill's paralysis increased. But in political terms it was wholly successful. Very few knew the truth, and kept it firmly to themselves. Colville took what he later called 'immediate defensive action' by writing personally to Camrose, Beaverbrook and Bracken, who came at once to Chartwell where they 'paced the lawn in earnest conversation'.* They achieved the all but incredible, and in peacetime possibly unique, success of gagging Fleet Street, something they would have done for nobody but Churchill. Not a word of the Prime Minister's stroke was published until he himself casually mentioned it in a speech in the House of Commons a year later.

As an exercise in political deception of Parliament and the public it was masterly; whether it was justifiable on any other terms is more questionable.

The key factor in taking this action was Eden's absence. Churchill did not consider that Butler was ready for the premiership, which added to his own determination to carry on as long as possible. But if Eden had been there, it is more than probable that Lady Churchill's insistence that he must retire would have carried the day.† It is also certain that many ministers, including the Chief Whip, would have pressed for honourable retirement and Eden's immediate succession, promised for so long. But in the circumstances this was impossible, and so the deception was maintained throughout the summer. When Eden returned Churchill had made – or appeared to have made – a remarkable recovery, and the chance was gone.

The first the Edens had known of the situation was by a personal and confidential letter to Clarissa Eden from Colville, written from Chartwell on 26 June, which also said that there was agreement between advisers, Salisbury and Butler, that if, as appeared likely, Churchill had to resign, the advice to the Queen would be for a 'caretaker' government nominally headed by Salisbury, who would not take the title of Prime Minister, until Eden was fit. Jim Thomas reported to Eden on the 29th after a visit to Chartwell that 'active life is over' for Churchill, but by 4 July Colville was writing to Clarissa Eden of a remarkable improvement in Churchill's condition, adding that the possibility of the 'caretaker' government had receded. As Churchill continued with his astonishing improvement, the familiar vagueness descended over his plans. Thomas and Robert Carr were sure that he would go in October, and they and Toby Low seriously

---

* Colville, *The Fringes of Power*, p. 669.

† Lord Moran, *Winston Churchill, The Struggle for Survival*, p. 415. Butler makes no reference in his memoirs to the false bulletin. It has been alleged that Butler saw his own interest in maintaining Churchill in the premiership, but this can be wholly discounted. He and Salisbury – not a man to be involved in Machiavellian manoeuvres – were dealing with a real and immediate problem of the Government's public standing.

discussed whether Eden should return to the Foreign Office. Their collective and individual advice to him was that he should not, but should become Deputy Prime Minister and Leader of the House, so that he could be much more visible to Members of Parliament and would be spared the gruelling pressures of the Foreign Office and foreign travel. Churchill, however, was unenthusiastic, but he wrote to Eden on 30 August about proposed government changes – including the abolition of the 'Overlords' – saying that 'there could be no change at the Foreign Office unless it was your wish to take up the leadership of the House of Commons as Deputy Prime Minister. My own future depends for the moment upon my health.'

From Thomas there came a tragi-comic account of playing croquet at Chartwell, under the stern orders of Montgomery. 'Uncle [Churchill] said he felt so much better for it but at times he looked dreadful. Very cosy & sweet to me but it was a bit macabre.' In contrast, Shuckburgh had become convinced by Colville's reports that Churchill was 'mentally determined' to stay on. This was indeed the situation, and sheer willpower seemed to conquer his incapacities; but, again, no firm decision was to be taken until October and the Party Conference at Margate.

Of all the 'ifs' in Eden's life this remains the most tantalizing of all. Of course, it would have been best for him if Churchill had retired in 1945 or even 1952, his political point made, but had Eden's operation succeeded in April 1953 he would almost certainly have become Prime Minister in June or July. He would have been in full health, at the height of all his powers, with a completely united Cabinet and Party, and with an Opposition in tatters. But one error by a surgeon had destroyed all this. Fate can be very cruel, and seldom more so than it was to Anthony Eden in 1953. He had lost his health and the premiership as a direct result of a medical mistake.

Eden himself, so unwell and so far away, had not at first appreciated how serious Churchill's condition was. This was not deliberate deception, as the doctors themselves were unsure about how matters would develop, but his wife had received enough information to make him realize that something very serious had happened. Not surprisingly, although still feeling weak after his three operations – and looking it – and although recognizing that he was in no condition to assume the premiership immediately, he was impatient for information and eager to return to Britain as soon as his doctors would permit.

The Edens returned to London in late July, and his officials and friends were struck by his gaunt pallor and by his eagerness to know how things stood. But he could not, and would not, raise the matter directly with Churchill, with whom he and his wife lunched on 27 July at Chequers.

Churchill himself was in a variable mood, one day talking of an autumn resignation when Eden was fully fit, and then on others musing on the great tasks lying ahead of him. No one – least of all his successor – could bring himself to tell the Prime Minister that this time he really must go. Instead, the fiction was preserved that all Churchill needed was rest and that he was at work, when the reality was totally different. Thus, for three months, Britain had neither an effective Prime Minister nor a Foreign Secretary. It is not to be wondered at that Eden was fretful and frustrated; however, he had no choice but to accept that he must recover his health, and went with Clarissa on a Mediterranean cruise as the guests of the Navy in HMS *Surprise*.

An added source of frustration was Churchill's revival of his grand summit dream. Churchill's hopes that Eisenhower would be willing to respond were false, the new President describing them in private as 'completely fatuous'; Churchill persevered in public and in private to urge his summit, but without response, as Eden had expected.

The Edens' cruise in *Surprise* was originally intended for a month, at Churchill's invitation, but difficulties arose when Mountbatten characteristically wanted the ship for the second half of September. Jim Thomas, now Lord Cilcennin, interceded strongly, and the Edens had their voyage, marred by poor weather and by the need for Clarissa Eden to have a painful wisdom tooth operation in Malta. Nor could they keep entirely away from events at home. As Eden noted in his diary on 2 September: 'Many letters about politics on arrival at Athens. Bobbety [Salisbury] & Harold [Macmillan] urge earlier return. Troublesome. I don't want to. I cannot feel it to [be] really necessary, though this may be due to my lack of enthusiasm for politics which remains constant.'* Carr, Thomas and Salisbury kept him informed about the Churchill situation, which was best summed up by Cilcennin after a visit to Chequers that 'nothing has been decided'.

The Edens returned to London with Nicholas on 30 September, and were met at the airport by Salisbury and Nutting; Eden was still wholly in the dark about what was to happen, if anything. He felt considerably

---

* It was at Athens that there was an unfortunate episode. The Greek Prime Minister Field-Marshal Papagos expressed a wish to see Eden, who told Sir Charles Peake, the British Ambassador, that he would only do so on the clear understanding that no serious business was to be discussed, and certainly not Cyprus. What was intended as a courtesy call almost immediately changed when Papagos raised Cyprus. Eden refused to discuss it, and was very annoyed by this breach of the understanding of the meeting. He was even more annoyed when in 1959 he read Peake's report to London which ascribed remarks to him on Cyprus which he had never made. But 'It was then, however, too late to take up the matter with Peake, who was dead' (note by Eden, 1962).

better, but his appearance was not good and demonstrated to many for the first time how grave had been the crisis.

Talk with W. this morning for over an hour, having first seen Sir Horace who seemed well pleased.

Made it clear to W that I was ready to serve in any capacity, but he made it evident he wanted me to stay on at F.O. Asked him about plans & he said he wanted to try himself out, first in Margate & then in the House. Have some doubts as to how that will go physically. Some talk of international situation & he seemed to accept conclusion that latest Soviet answer showed little desire for talks at any level (but he admitted he hadn't read it!). We also spoke of Bobbety's desire for younger men in govt. & I told him this was [a] widespread complaint. He made no comment, but clearly doesn't want any changes now.

Bobbety & I & Rab dined with W in evening. Long talk, almost entirely on Foreign Affairs. It was difficult at times. W didn't like my lack of enthusiasm for May 11th speech. He kept emphasizing its popularity to which I replied that I was not contesting that. Later Bobbety pulled him up very sharp – even angrily – when the former thought his loyalty to W had been impugned. I had to make it clear that I did not regard four power talks at the highest level as a panacea. He maintained that in the war it was only the Stalin Roosevelt Churchill meetings that had made our Foreign Secretaries' work possible. I said this was not so, nor was it true that to meet without agenda was the best method with Russians. I believed they liked to have an agenda which they could chew over well in advance. Our most productive meeting with them had been with [Cordell] Hull at Moscow in 1943 before Teheran when we had used just these methods about Second Front, creation of UNO, Austria etc. This had led to Teheran meeting. Anyway the important question was 'what next?' On this W appeared to have no ideas. A depressing evening. (Diary, 1 October)

Churchill remained tenacious about his summit, to be held preferably in the Azores, and had approached Eisenhower, who, in Eden's diary note, 'returned a dusty answer'. Eden wanted to invite Dulles and the French Foreign Minister Georges Bidault to London for talks, but Churchill procrastinated for an entire day before giving grudging acquiescence, by which time Dulles had left for his Canadian eyrie for an undisturbed holiday. Eden's exasperation was intense, and Salisbury continued to make strong resignation noises in response to signs that the policy of 11 May might be continued.

And so to Margate, where, on 10 October, Churchill made the concluding speech of the Party Conference. His family, friends and those few colleagues who knew of his real condition were intensely nervous on his behalf, but it was a triumph. There was characteristic slyness when, deriding public opinion polls, he remarked that 'It is not a good thing always to be feeling your pulse and taking your temperature; although one has to do this sometimes, you do not want to make a habit of it. I have heard it said that a Government should keep its ear to the ground but they should also remember that this is not a very dignified attitude!' There would be no election this year, or next. He moved easily, and apparently effortlessly, over the whole range of government actions and achievements, from housing to red meat, finances to denationalization. When he came at last to international affairs he opened with a glowing tribute to Eden, which was ecstatically received, but his survey concentrated upon the need for a period of calm and the involvement of West German forces in NATO.

When he referred to the 11 May speech ('This humble, modest plan announced as the policy of Her Majesty's Government raised a considerable stir all over the place and though we have not yet been able to persuade our trusted allies to adopt it in the form I suggested no one can say that it is dead'), he defended the principle of meetings between heads of state, which was a statement acceptable to Eden and Salisbury (in the latter case, only just) and fell short of the 11 May optimism.

But the key sentences came at the end:

One word personally about myself. If I stay on for the time being bearing the burden at my age it is not because of love for power or office.

I have had an ample share of both. If I stay it is because I have a feeling that I may through things that have happened have an influence on what I care about above all else, the building of a sure and lasting peace.

Let us then go forward together with courage and composure, with resolution and good faith to the end which all desire.

The manner and content of the speech, and the fervour of the response of the audience, meant that an early retirement on grounds of incapacity was no longer an argument available to those who wanted him to go. On 3 November he spoke with wit and force in the debate on the Address in the Commons, and on foreign affairs at the Lord Mayor's Banquet at the Guildhall on 9 November, where he said nothing about summits. The differences in attitude between Churchill and Eden on this matter remained, and rankled, but the public appearance was one of complete unity and amity. All talk of Churchill retiring faded away, and Eden resumed his place as Foreign Secretary.

It has been suggested by some who knew both men that the relationship between Churchill and Eden never really recovered from this time. Like all such sweeping statements it exaggerates, but there is some truth in it. Eden's private references to Churchill, particularly in his letters to Nicholas, remain affectionate but increasingly despairing and critical. It was not pleasant to be working with a rapidly ageing and obstinate Prime Minister who had enjoyed his brief time as acting Foreign Secretary and still saw himself as a major international figure. So he was, but Eisenhower was right when he wrote with sadness that 'Winston is trying to relive the days of World War II. Much as I hold Winston in my personal affection and much as I admire him for his past accomplishments and leadership, I wish that he would turn over leadership of the British Conservation [*sic*] to younger men.' This emotion exactly mirrored Eden's. A harder and more different man than he would have drawn together colleagues, MPs, and friends in the press into a grouping which sincerely believed that the long and marvellous saga of Churchill's great and unique career should not end in bathos and embarrassment, and push both in private and in public for a graceful retirement. The Conservative Party, although it revered Churchill, had never fully taken him to its heart, and there would have been little trouble from that source. An overt Churchill Must Go campaign was unthinkable; but if Eden had given the word, a covert campaign, conducted with sensitivity, might well have succeeded. But it was not in Eden's nature to behave like this.

There were those who wished then, and later, that it had been in his nature; and his failure to act in that way was thought to reveal a fatal lack of political toughness – 'unChurchillian' in fact, a charge that ignored Churchill's scrupulous loyalty to Neville Chamberlain. This undoubtedly did his reputation harm in inner Conservative political circles, where references to 'poor Anthony' became more frequent. It was also believed by some that Churchill was clinging on because he had lost confidence in Eden as his successor. Eden knew of these whisperings; they did not improve his temper nor lessen his frustration, but he would not act out of character to intrigue to bring down his friend and leader. If this was carrying loyalty and friendship too far, his biographer would not have had it otherwise.

But the relationship was now grimly similar to that between Rosebery and Gladstone in 1892–4. In that case the Foreign Secretary, virtually agreed by all to be the successor, a tense and keenly intelligent man with an enormous popular following, had to endure serving under a legendary personality now far past his prime whom old age had made both deaf and obstinate, but who hung on to the premiership almost out of habit, partly out of personal vanity, and who constantly interfered in foreign policy matters. When Gladstone was eventually forced out by his own Cabinet and Rosebery took his place it was, as Churchill himself had written of this episode, to an inheritance that was 'bleak, precarious [and] wasting'. The analogy is not totally exact, but it is close enough to merit comment.*

---

* See my biography of Rosebery, published in 1963. The comparison occurred to me at the time, but not the remote possibility that I would one day be Eden's biographer.

Rosebery always keenly disliked his relationship with Gladstone being described as 'filial', and so did Eden deeply resent his relationship with Churchill being described in similar terms – and with good cause. But both had the misfortune to spend a key period of their political careers under the shadow of men who had towered over the political scene for decades, and who stayed on too long. Eden would not have been human if he did not feel exasperated by his situation, but it did not show in public, and he would have nothing to do with cabals. For a brief while early in October he seriously considered insisting on leaving the Foreign Office and taking another Cabinet post, but Churchill had little difficulty in talking him out of this. To his old Oxford acquaintance, Chips Channon, 'He was affectionate, but in a sudden burst of nerves revealed to me that he is on bad terms with Winston. "I get all the knocks; I don't think I can stand it much longer," he suddenly said. We talked for some time and I have the feeling that he was fed up and almost hysterical.'*

Such outbursts in private were, as has often been emphasized, a feature of Eden's personality, fierce but short in duration, and far less common than has often been claimed. This one was absolutely understandable, and his moods were not improved by the fact that the failure of his first operation had not only damaged his health – how badly was not yet apparent – but had almost certainly cost him the premiership that year. The moods came and went, he accepted the situation, albeit with much impatience, and returned to his work with a vigour which in his physical condition was probably unwise. The Churchill reign continued.

Eden was still far from well when he accompanied Churchill to Bermuda for the postponed conference on 1 December. It was characterized by Churchill talking warmly about the prospects of closer relations with the Russians, and Eisenhower and Bidault taking a very different and indeed aggressive line. Indeed, so coarse was Eisenhower's language, and his threats of the use of atomic weapons in the Far East and Indo-China in certain eventualities, that even Churchill became concerned. Eden was appalled by the prospect, particularly when Eisenhower made it clear that he considered atomic weapons to be merely another weapon, which the United States felt free to use. Compared to a difference of this magnitude, discussions with the French on the EDC were not of great significance.

But the meeting had had one major benefit in alerting Eden to the magnitude of the gulf in attitudes between the British and Americans. The American approach to all matters under discussion was crude. If the French did not ratify the EDC the United States would be forced into 'an agonizing

---

* Rhodes James, Chips, The Diaries of Sir Henry Channon, p. 470.

reappraisal' of American policy towards Europe, including NATO; the Russians only understood one language; Communism in South-East Asia must not only be resisted but defeated, if needs be by war and atomic weapons. Dulles did agree to attend a Foreign Ministers' conference in Berlin in January, but Eden left Bermuda deeply troubled – and with good reason.

To Clarissa he wrote:

Conference is very hard going now, & I am sad & tired, not so much about details as about this poor world & what I fear lies ahead.

But more of this when we meet.

Meanwhile all devotion
                    from A.

P.S. I am well, & the President delighted with my appearance which he said so much better than reports.... W hears nothing at the conferences, which doesn't reduce my problems.

I still like Ike.

Nineteen fifty-three had been a year Eden wanted to forget, as he wryly noted, but at least he had survived – more narrowly than all but a few realized. He looked frail, and his appearance deeply worried his colleagues, some of whom continued to urge him to step down from the Foreign Office and take a less onerous home department which would give him a stronger domestic experience and position. It was good advice, but Eden's lack of self-confidence outside his own field was the true cause of his refusal, and not, as some averred, his concern for status. He also felt that, as times were dangerous, and much needed to be done in foreign affairs, only he could undertake these tasks. In this he was proved to be absolutely right.

The Berlin Conference of the Foreign Ministers of Britain, the United States, France and the Soviet Union lasted from 25 January to 19 February. Eden boldly proposed free all-German elections for a representative reunified German Government with whom a peace treaty could then be negotiated. He knew that even in the post-Stalin climate Molotov could never agree to this, but his real purpose was to make the British position clear: that the British Government had made a positive proposal towards German reunification, which had been rebuffed by the Soviet Union. He also hoped to encourage the French to ratify the EDC. There was no progress on an Austrian peace treaty either, but the fact that a real and serious dialogue had taken place represented a significant advance. Most important of all, it was agreed to hold another Foreign Ministers' meeting in April in Geneva to discuss Korea and Indo-China.

The French position in Indo-China had now come under intolerable strain, and in these circumstances Eden had decided that Western support for what was clearly a losing – if not lost – cause was futile as well as dangerous. Dulles' obsession with Communist China and his fear of it spreading its power throughout Indo-China and South-East Asia was genuine and deep, and it was with the greatest difficulty that Eden persuaded him that the Chinese should be represented at Geneva. What really worried Eden, and with very good cause, was that as the French position deteriorated the Americans might intervene militarily and seek British support. This was a fearful prospect, and one Eden was determined to defeat.

The danger increased when it became clear that the position of the large French garrison at Dien Bien Phu was growing desperate. The purpose of this bold but inept initiative had been to draw the Viet Minh into open battle by creating a Verdun-like fortress which they would have to attack. Attack they did, with massive numbers and using considerable military skill. The battle of Dien Bien Phu had a particular savagery, and heavy casualties resulted. Gradually the perimeter was reduced, and the French urgently asked for American air support. The Americans then proposed to Britain that they should issue a joint warning against Chinese intervention, backed by the threat of military action against China if they did and by actual intervention in the Indo-China conflict.

There is no question that Dulles and the American Government were immensely serious. Admiral Arthur W. Radford, Chairman of the Joint Chiefs of Staff, and Vice-President Nixon were strongly in favour of American air strikes to assist the beleaguered garrison at Dien Bien Phu, and the matter was put to a secret meeting of leading members of Congress on 3 April. Radford frankly said that this action would provide a very real possibility of war with China and that if the air action failed ground troops might well have to be brought in to help the French. It was Senator Lyndon Johnson, the Democrat majority leader, who raised the question of where the British stood, and it became clear that the only intervention that the congressional leaders could recommend would be one on Korean lines in concert with Britain and the Commonwealth countries, particularly Australia and New Zealand. There were also serious doubts whether the American public, heartily relieved by the armistice in Korea, and rather less troubled by the Chinese offshore islands than their Government, would be at all enthusiastic about intervention in what many perceived as a French colonial war.

Dulles' own attitude was graphically demonstrated in a press conference he gave on 13 April in London – where he had flown on 10 April to urge co-operation on the British:

What would you regard as a reasonably satisfactory settlement of the Indo-China situation?

Dulles: The removal by the Chinese Communists of their apparent desire to extend the political system of Communism to South-East Asia.

That means a complete withdrawal of the Communists from Indo-China?

Dulles: That is what I would regard as a satisfactory solution.

Is there any compromise that might be offered if that is not entirely satisfactory with the Communists?

Dulles: I had not thought of any.*

Dulles attempted to put the maximum pressure on the British both in London and later at a NATO Council meeting in Paris, when he asked Eden for British support for American air action to save Dien Bien Phu. 'I am fairly hardened to crises,' Eden later wrote, 'but I went to bed that night a troubled man.' He had not dismissed the idea of a South-East Asia Defence organization on the NATO model, which Dulles had proposed in London, although he had doubts about its feasibility, but he was not prepared to consider internationalizing and expanding the Indo-China conflict into a major war, whose possibilities were incalculable. When Radford did not discount the use of atomic weapons, his alarm increased.

As the Americans knew that congressional support for intervention hinged on the British response, Eden's role was crucial. He flew back to London to inform Churchill and the Cabinet of what was being planned, and received their complete support for absolute refusal to become involved in any way. Although Dulles was told this on 25 April he called a meeting in Washington for all British Commonwealth, French and some South-East Asian ambassadors to discuss united action in Indo-China, to be known as Operation Vulture. Eden was again in Paris when he heard of this by cable from Makins, and immediately returned to London to see Churchill at Chequers. They were of like mind on the matter, and Eden cabled Makins in very firm terms to forbid him to attend the meeting. Makins told Dulles very diplomatically about his instructions. Dulles was upset and angered. He considered, quite unfairly, that the fact that Eden had not rejected the idea of a defence organization in South-East Asia had constituted a pledge to support joint action to help the French, whereas Eden had consistently made it clear that this was out of the question. Dien Bien Phu fell on 7 May.†

The Geneva Conference opened on 26 April. Dulles was reluctant to go, and was still angry at the British response – particularly with Eden – and made a point of refusing to shake hands with Chou En-lai, the Chinese

---

* Leonard Mosley, *Dulles*, p. 355.

† For the best account in English, see Bernard B. Fall, *Hell in a Very Small Place.*

Deputy Prime Minister. It was a very public snub, and it wounded Chou En-lai deeply. Much was to flow from that rejection of a handshake, but Dulles was not rational on the subject of China and of what had happened since the revolution.

The Americans played little part in Geneva, but Eden took the lead. He was helped by the fact that the French were now demoralized by their dreadful losses and by the heavy cost of a war they clearly were not winning, and the French Government headed by Pierre Mendès-France came into Office pledged to seek as quick and as honourable a settlement as possible. Also, Eden found Molotov unexpectedly reasonable. In these circumstances Eden was able to secure unanimous agreement for an armistice. But, as in the case of Korea, difficulties arose over the composition of the supervisory commission, and these dragged on for weeks.

This was Anthony Eden at his best, and in his element. Alarmed by the tone of the opening speeches ('Foster was not, I thought, effective, mainly because unlike Berlin we have no obviously reasonable proposition to put before the world. Chou En-lai tough & uncompromising,' he wrote in his diary for 28 April). On the 29th he used his role of President of the Conference to take decisive action.

Foster droned on and little S. Korean seemed in no hurry to do anything.

I said we should either agree upon proposition we could put before the world (i.e. Free elections & international supervision) as we had done in Berlin & stand by it, or bring general discussion to an end as soon as possible & get down to business. This kind of discussion could do us no good at all. Everybody agreed with me except Foster & S. Korean. Latter seemed mainly interested in speech he is thinking of making next Monday. Eventually we agreed to set up small committee to draft our proposals.... Molotov unpleasant but not particularly effective.

On 3 May Dulles left. 'I went to see Foster off. It was meant as a gesture but I don't think it did much good. Americans are sore, mainly I suspect because they know they have made a mess of this Conference.' But Dulles had left behind Walter Bedell Smith, the American Under-Secretary of State, whom Eden liked and trusted. On 4 May Churchill telephoned to say that he wanted to invite Smith to Chequers for the weekend: 'I said this would arouse the wildest speculation & we must stay on the job. When I returned & made a guarded reference to possibility of Bedell visiting London Bidault said at once that if this happened he would be off!' But Smith sincerely tried to bridge the Anglo-American divide, and Eden was very willing to go as far in his direction as possible, 'maybe too far', he noted. And on 5 May he wrote: 'An unexpectedly relaxed evening with Molotov who was in helpful mood. Maybe a deliberate exercise in dividing us from Americans. But I hardly think so. Anyway it was enjoyable and may have been useful.' One of the key issues was to persuade the Conference to accept the principle of separate treatment for Laos and Cambodia, which 'We must if we are to save them,' Eden wrote.

Old international conferences are as exciting to read about as old speeches and although this one was no exception it was to prove of historic importance, and tested Eden's political and diplomatic skills, and his patience, very considerably. But he proved equal to the intellectual and physical strains, which was all the more remarkable because he was simultaneously involved in the final delicate negotiations over the Suez Canal Base and Iran and the normal work of the Foreign Office, principally conducted from Geneva. The Chinese, worked on by Molotov, began to thaw, and Eden's famous charm and courtesy had a considerable impact upon them, in contrast to Dulles' behaviour. Early in June they suddenly made important concessions that opened the way for separate armistices for Laos and Cambodia and the division of Vietnam. After weeks of exhausting negotiation, Eden suddenly saw the way forward.

Meanwhile, relations with Churchill were not good. Eden still believed strongly that under current conditions, military, economic and political, the large British base in the Suez Canal Zone, which was under constant pressure, was insupportable, and he was pressing for completion of the treaty of withdrawal. As he argued in Cabinet and with Churchill, in the era of nuclear weapons and jet aircraft, and given the state of the British economy, the presence of very large numbers of British forces in the area made no strategic or economic sense. Churchill, ever the instinctive Imperialist, and highly sensitive to charges of 'scuttle' and 'appeasement', remained deeply unhappy. So was the Suez Group. This clandestine body organized its operations with rare skill; among its members was Julian Amery, son-in-law of Macmillan and holder of a name famous in Empire matters. Their numbers were not large, and they perhaps overplayed their hand, but they had a sizeable number of Conservatives in sympathy with them, as well as elements in the Conservative press. Churchill was among those who were sympathetic, and the dispute with Eden caused him genuine distress and concern, particularly as Eden had virtually the complete support of the Cabinet.

Churchill was also unhappy about the deterioration in Anglo-American relations. The threat of direct American intervention in Indo-China still overshadowed Eden's valiant efforts in Geneva, but in the American press, Congress and State Department these were not only ill appreciated but were being heavily and frequently censured. Thus Eden was in the extraordinary and uncomfortable position of being denounced in Britain for being an appeaser of dictators in Egypt and in the United States for being an appeaser of Communist dictatorships in South-East Asia. There was at that time little gratitude in the United States for the fact that Eden, virtually single-handedly, had kept America out of a war in Indo-China that could easily have escalated into a major and appalling confrontation between the nuclear powers. Nor was there much gratitude in the Conservative Party for his plans to face the realities of world politics in the Middle East. *Punch*, which under the editorship of Malcolm Muggeridge had taken a deep and mystifying hostility to everything Eden did, depicted him as another Neville Chamberlain, a charge that especially enraged Eden, for obvious reasons.

Also, Churchill still clung obstinately to his dream of a last great summit of the Powers as the culmination of his great career, while Eden remained at best unenthusiastic and usually very hostile. He was now more protective than ever of his position as Foreign Secretary, and any attempt by Churchill to involve himself met with strong resistance. There were now more rows and disputes than at any time in their long relationship, and, although these were often followed by warm reconciliations, the general atmosphere was painful.

And behind such disagreements on policy, there lay the still unresolved matter of when Churchill would go, which was making the Cabinet restive and unhappy, and Eden, who was again grossly overworking, increasingly frustrated. This was the personal context in which he had to work in 1954, which he did with a skill and resilience that astonished all who knew how close he had been to death only twelve months before.

On 24 June Churchill and Eden and their official party flew to the United States for the long-planned meeting with Eisenhower, the importance of which was now greater than ever.

To everyone's surprise, Eisenhower at once agreed in principle to meet the Russians, to Churchill's delight and Eden's mortification and Dulles' dismay. They also agreed on the need to rearm West Germany in spite of the vehement objections in Britain and France, but when Churchill waxed eloquent in favour of supporting the Americans in their military support of anti-Communist rebels in Guatemala Eden again found himself in strong disagreement. This, inevitably, caused more tension between the two.

What Eden did achieve was to extract from a very reluctant Dulles agreement to the partition of Vietnam under the proposed, but still incomplete, agreements at Geneva. In return for this the British agreed to set up a study group to prepare for Dulles' cherished 'Asian NATO', which was eventually to become the South-East Asia Treaty Organization (SEATO). Also, crucial to the Anglo-Egyptian negotiations, the Americans endorsed the principle of international freedom of traffic through the Suez Canal.

After a brief, and virtually courtesy, visit to Canada, the party set sail on the *Queen Elizabeth* on 1 July. It would have been far better had they flown home, for on the voyage frictions, disagreements and arguments broke out again. Churchill now wanted to go to Moscow early in August to ask for Austrian independence, and told Eden he would definitely retire in September, probably on the 21st. Churchill prepared a telegram to Molotov inviting himself to Moscow; Eden argued that he disliked the idea in any event, but that such a major step could not possibly be taken without Cabinet approval; Churchill said that if the Cabinet did not approve he would resign; Colville argued that this would give the new Government an anti-Russian appearance from the beginning; so the telegram went to the Cabinet. Both men were aggrieved by this compromise, and there was then what Colville called 'a blood row' between them over the entry of China into the United Nations. 'Eden got red in the face with anger and there was a disagreeable scene. They both went to bed in a combination of sorrow and anger, the P.M. saying that Anthony was totally incapable of differentiating great points and small points (a criticism that has an element of truth in it).'* In reality, in this instance Eden had grasped the big point, while Churchill, obsessed with keeping in with the Americans and more than sympathetic to their continuing veto of Communist China's entry into the world organization, took the small view. On the next day there was a great reconciliation, but Eden foresaw major difficulties when the Cabinet considered Churchill's Moscow plans, and in this he was right.

At the Cabinet on 7 July Salisbury led the charge against the Russian visit, threatening resignation, and Macmillan took the unusual step of calling upon Lady Churchill to warn her of the seriousness of the situation, which she raised in her characteristically forthright way at lunch, to her husband's indignation. The fact was that, knowing the Cabinet would raise strong objections to his visit, he had tried to act independently, and had been found out. Also, he now realized that Salisbury's resignation on such a matter would be highly damaging to the Government and to him personally. Crookshank joined with Salisbury, and, although Eden did not threaten to resign on the matter, his hostility to the project was made very plain. Churchill was again muttering of resigning himself, but the Russians then conveniently called for a Foreign Ministers' meeting to discuss European security, a way out that the Cabinet accepted with relief. Churchill had been in the wrong throughout, and Eden in the right, but one still wonders if the storm would have happened at all had it not been for the five days' unfortunate relaxation at sea.

*   *   *

* Colville, *The Fringes of Power*, p. 699.

The visit had had the major advantage of enabling Eden to persuade Dulles to return to Geneva; getting the Americans to participate in the final stages proved more difficult, but he eventually succeeded after a somewhat fraught series of meetings in Geneva and Paris. Eden then personally prepared the final draft agreements, and had his reward for months of arduous work and brilliant political diplomacy when success was achieved on 21 July. A ceasefire was to take place throughout Indo-China; Vietnam was to be divided at the seventeenth parallel; although Korean reunification had not been achieved, there was at least agreement by both sides on non-interference in the internal affairs of the other. There was no agreement on a multilateral guarantee of the agreement, and the Americans would not endorse it; they only took note, but they did undertake not to use force to disturb it. A bitter and terrible war that had lasted for eight years had been ended, and it had been proved possible to do sensible political business to reduce grave international tensions. What was not known at the time, and not for many years later, was how Anthony Eden had prevented the eruption of a super-Power conflict in South-East Asia that could well have involved atomic weapons.

None the less, there was a general perception of what he had achieved, against very formidable odds. His strategy and tactics were models to be followed by anyone with serious interest in the diplomatic arts. He had a clear idea of his objectives, of which he never lost sight, and yet he was flexible; he worked immensely hard and drove his staff hard, yet found time for relaxed working meals with delegates, where his persuasion could be at its most effective; his temper and impatience were strictly reserved for off-stage occasions – in public, and at private meetings, he was invariably courteous and patient. He coaxed, he flattered, he steered the Conference firmly without appearing to do so, and gained all his purposes in an atmosphere of genuine goodwill. The Chinese in particular were greatly impressed by him, and Molotov became, as Eden noted with amusement, 'almost genial'. The Americans, and certain sections of the British press, were churlish and unimpressed, but others recognized one of the most remarkable diplomatic achievements of the post-war world. The hope that matters of such bloody controversy could be resolved peacefully soared as a direct result of this triumph – for such it was.

But in the House of Commons, although there was widespread admiration for what Eden had done – Churchill paid generous and public tribute by defying House of Commons rules in referring directly to 'Anthony Eden' instead of the conventional 'My Right Honourable Friend' – the Suez revolt remained ugly. Churchill, however, had now changed his view. In his discussions with Eisenhower, and reading papers submitted by the

Ministry of Defence, he had come to the conclusion that the development of the hydrogen bomb had changed everything. To Colville he said that 'the difference between the hydrogen bomb and the atomic bomb is greater than that between the atomic bomb and the bow-and-arrow', a somewhat typical exaggeration and over-dramatization but, as always, perceptive. Another factor was the entry of Greece and Turkey into NATO which in Eden's view, as Churchill conceded, had significantly changed the strategic balance. Neguib had behaved very reasonably over Sudanese independence – as it transpired, too much for his own good – and attacks on the British base had become only very occasional and notably feeble. What was not sufficiently appreciated in London was the significance of the fall of Neguib in February 1954 and his replacement by Colonel Nasser as Premier; this was only temporary, but Nasser and his allies bided their time, and in October Neguib was definitely deposed. But by this time the Anglo-Egyptian agreements had been signed. Reports from Cairo on Nasser, although critical, were far from hostile, and he made an excellent impression on Nutting – who signed the agreement on behalf of the British Government – and on Selwyn Lloyd. Churchill, having changed his mind, now put his formidable influence into supporting Eden; this was vital as Eden had to face what could well have been an extremely unpleasant meeting of the back-bench 1922 Committee. As it was, it was not at all pleasant, and a close friend has told me that he has seldom seen a man more nervous than Eden was when he was sitting in the Commons corridor waiting to be invited into the room to meet his bitter critics – and bitter they certainly were. But Eden won over the majority.

The British insistence on the right of re-entry into the Zone in case of emergency had remained the principal obstacle to an agreement, but in July the United States, under heavy British and domestic pressure, undertook to support the principle of freedom of navigation through the Canal, and the Egyptians agreed not only to the reactivation of the British Zone in emergency circumstances but also endorsed the Constantinople Convention of 1888 guaranteeing freedom of navigation. The British would evacuate their forces within twenty months, but the base would be maintained by British civilians for another seven years. It seemed a classic compromise between the demands of Egyptian nationalism, the rights of the shareholders of the Suez Canal Company (which would continue to run the Canal but with a much greater proportion of dues going to Egypt), and long-term Western strategic interests. Commending the treaty to the House of Commons on 29 July Eden was utterly convincing and very impressive. The Suez Group was effectively isolated, and Eden's soaring reputation rose further. To his increasing number of admirers on both sides of the Commons he now seemed capable of achieving anything.

Nor was this all. On 5 August it was possible to announce that an international oil consortium, in which Britain retained almost half the shares, would produce and market Iranian oil, with a fixed-sum compensation for the Anglo-Iranian Oil Company. This was a complete vindication for Eden's policy of playing the matter long and, as in the case of the Canal Zone, reaching a solution that was in the interests of both Iran and the West, without any colonial or exploitative content. It was another masterpiece of skill and sensitivity. The fall of Mussadeq may have been engineered by British and American agents – as it was – but a clumsy handling of the critical issue of Iranian oil would assuredly have provoked the return of those passions that had brought him to prominence in the first place. Had it been left solely to the Americans, that is what would have happened. Unhappily, neither in Iran nor in Indo-China were subsequent American administrations able or willing to learn the lessons that Eden had taught them of what realistic diplomacy is about.

In December, looking back on this amazing year, Eden wrote in his diary:

It is a strange thing about this year that though many people have written about the problems we have, we hope, solved: Western European Union, Egypt, Indo-China, Persia, [Saudi] Arabia (Buraimi) very few have given much credit to Persia which was, I believe, the toughest of all. Three senior officials have helped me in turn – Makins, Dixon & Caccia. All excellent.

There was first the problem of getting the Americans to see eye to eye with us. This meant curing the Mussadeq mania & was never accomplished until the new administration. Americans were incurably convinced that Mussadeq was [the] only barrier against Communism. Then there was the question whether to act before relations were broken or to wait. That was the most difficult decision of all. I called in one or two from outside.... Mercifully we decided to wait. Then there were all the problems of the Company.... Harold Caccia did a grand job there.

Eden may have driven the Foreign Office, and particularly his Private Office, very hard – in some individual cases much too hard, with distressing results – but this series of successes against the odds sent Foreign Office morale higher even than at the height of Bevin's reign, while the reputation of the Government rose with that of the Foreign Secretary. No one, of course, knew that Eden had impoverished himself by his sale of his Anglo-Iranian shares, except Churchill and a very few others.

Meanwhile, what of the succession?

Colville recorded in his diary:

The Cabinet went away for the recess, some of them glum, some of them bewildered. Winston retired to Chartwell where I spent much of August with him.

As the days went by he became less reconciled to giving up office and adumbrated all sorts of reasons why he should not. Never had a P.M. been treated like this, that he was to be hounded from his place merely because his second-in-command wanted the job. And what was there in the argument that the new regime needed a year to take over before an election? On the contrary there was little for a new Government to offer and as an election drew near it would be a target for abuse by half the country. Eden had far better start an entirely new deal after a General Election. It looks like a terrible and painful struggle.*

Eden recorded in his diary for 27 August:

Rab & Harold asked to see me at 11.

Rab said that he had been much embarrassed, that he had a double loyalty to W & to me & had told W so. He was convinced that W was determined to stay. Neither pretended that this was nationally desirable. The issue was what to do. Rab clearly wanted me to consider whether I could take over Home front & leadership of the House. This he urged would make me P.M. in everything but name. Harold did not conceal his concern at attempting to carry on with W as he now is. Nor did I. The reshuffle was merely a device to enable him to carry on longer while doing even less. He would then do nothing except interfere with F.O. This might have disastrous results. We all agreed that it was essential to have a meeting of a number of colleagues soon.

We were all pretty gloomy but friendly. A disagreeable feature of this whole business is that in the reshuffle I am sure we will find W actuated by animus against Bobbety, Harry Crookshank & perhaps Lord Chancellor.

After long talk with Harold & Rab walked across to see W.

Interview opened stiffly. He paid various compliments about F.O. documents since my return. I did not respond. Eventually we got to the point. He asked me what I thought of the position. I said 'I have your letter, you have mine, what more is there to say?'

He then launched out into a long rigmarole as to how he felt better (he didn't look it & his argument was often confused – for instance when later he discussed whether I should stay at F.O. or lead the House he gave the arguments for one in support for the other). He also argued that this was a bad time for him to go; not possible for the new administration to make its mark in the last year. This was Woolton's view too. Unfortunate I had been ill when he had his stroke last year. Now better wait until he fell ill again, or nearer the election when he would give me all the help he could.

I said I had explained what I thought many times. If I was not fit to stand on my own feet now & choose an administration now, I should probably be less so a year from now. The Govt was not functioning well & this was putting a heavy strain on all his senior Ministers. These were able men but there was no co-ordination.

Of course he didn't like this & said he had never missed a day since his illness. I said that wasn't the point. There was no co-ordination on home front & Cabinets

* Colville, *The Fringes of Power*, p. 703.

dragged on far too long. There was much argument about this which got us nowhere. I said that I would have been glad of the chance to take over a year ago, but it meant less to me now, & would mean less still next year if I were still there. I added that I envied Oliver [Lyttelton]* & would like to do as he had done. He replied that the Party would never forgive me if I did, that they were counting on me, etc. I was young. It would all be mine before sixty. Why was I in such a hurry? Anyway if I felt like it he would be ready for me to take over Leadership of House and home front. I showed no enthusiasm and felt none.

He said there was another alternative, that I might lead a rebellion of five or six Ministers. But that would be very grave. I said of course it would & he knew perfectly well that I was the last person to want to do this after our many years of work together.

Then there was some emotion, after which I said I would like to talk it all over with political colleagues together. He didn't like this much, but eventually agreed as long as it was a discussion of reconstruction and not of his resignation (it wasn't put like that, but that is what it amounted to).

The situation was indeed desperate, and extraordinary.

The tension between the two men was demonstrated by a letter to Eden from Churchill in early September:

I am sorry you are not happy about Home Affairs. I must admit I have had a rather trying time myself during the last fifteen months. During the first part of these I was much troubled by your absence through illness and the uncertainty about whether & when you wd be able to return.

Since this has happily occurred, I have been distressed by the continuous pressure of some of yr friends who want me to retire in yr favour. I have tried to discharge the duty to wh I was appointed by the Crown & Parliament. I am glad to say I have not missed a single day's control of affairs in spite of a temporary loss of physical mobility. Now I have good reports from my doctors....

So, the door was closed again. 'It is unbelievable,' Clarissa wrote in her diary, but there was nothing she or her husband or the Cabinet could do about it, short of an act of gross disloyalty and intrigue, with which Eden would never associate himself – as the Churchill camp well knew, and as the Neville Chamberlain camp had known in 1938–9.

And at this point another international crisis occurred.

On 8 September agreement had been reached in Manila to establish SEATO, but on 30 August the French Assembly – on a procedural motion – had failed to ratify the EDC. Eden was dismayed, but saw no point, as he put it, of placing the French 'like a naughty child in the corner'. None the less, this was a crisis that had to be resolved, on which he pondered at

---

*Oliver Lyttelton, to Eden's great regret, had announced his retirement from the Government and politics to go to the Lords and return to the City. He took the title of Viscount Chandos.

home at Rose Bower, Broad Chalke, and came up with another initiative. The more he thought about the difficulty, the more he became convinced that the answer – if it could be achieved – would be to bring West Germany into NATO and make the 1948 Brussels Treaty a mutual defence pact. This would remove many domestic objections to Britain's membership of the EDC and increased military contribution in Europe. If it was an inspiration – and it was – it was based on much experience and much thought. In the course of six months he had moved from establishing a ceasefire in Indo-China and preventing a major war in South-East Asia, to a resolution of the Iranian problem and a settlement with Egypt; now he moved back to European reconstruction. And all this in the middle of the confusion and embarrassment over the succession.

Eden's two concerns were graphically portrayed in his diary for 1 September:

A strenuous day in London. Saw Rab in morning. He was no more confident about the reconstruction, but thought we ought to try & urged home front upon me. He didn't think it would last long, but we have heard that so often.

Saw W at 12 and had general talk about what to do. He wants to send message to Adenauer; no harm in that. He lunched with us. C[larissa] had done very well with oysters and grouse. Cabinet presented no problems though very rambling. As a result was late for Krishna [Menon] & had to see him twice. Also ... the press, to whom I gave rather a rambling discourse.

Am sure an 8 Power meeting makes more sense than NATO, & London must take a hand.

Patrick [Buchan-Hepburn] came to dinner, still anxious I should take over home front.

Late drive to cottage.

On 5 September, at Rose Bower:

Lovely sunny day. Made the most of it. Read & gardened & painted an indifferent water colour of C's favourite view.

Had a thought that it might do good if I did a tour of the six capitals before our conference.

This was to prove another inspiration. The Conference – to include the United States and Canada in addition to the European NATO members – was to be in London on 28 September, and Eden was already preparing not only his strategy and tactics but the dramatic proposal that was going to transform the situation. Meanwhile, as his diary shows, the problems at home rumbled on:

10 September
W came to luncheon with Clemmie. He was in very poor shape & claimed of dizziness caused by reading in the car. They were very late & hadn't seen Makins, his only appointment of the day.

Had further talk with Patrick & Harold. They were gloomy at the prospects of the Party if W remained & a little inclined to complain, perhaps rightly, that I had made things too easy for him. I am quite clear that Ministry of Defence gambit is impossible & told them so. They were keen to press for departure on birthday.* I don't think we can succeed, but no harm in trying.

11 September
Woke up at seven, finished my box & wrote to W & Harold. W will not like the letter but I had to tell him that no scheme of reconstruction so far devised was any good if the Govt was to function & we were to have best chance of winning next election. Both Harold & Patrick were insistent that I should write this because W is now merely fiddling with names of juniors & all the old men in Cabinet are still to stay. But it isn't easy for an 80 year old to sack a 70 year old.

C came to see me off. Also all six Ambassadors; quite a party.

In Brussels, Spaak was enthusiastic and helpful; in Berlin, so was Adenauer, who agreed to membership of NATO and limitations on West German rearmament to allay French apprehensions. In Paris, Eden had considerable difficulty on this score with Mendès-France and his colleagues, but after two days of intensive discussions he was able to persuade them of the merits of his case and the strength of the safeguards. Once again, unhappily, the Americans provided the greatest difficulty, and Dulles' sudden arrival in Bonn was an alarming and unwelcome intrusion, fortunately with no ill effects. Dulles needed considerable persuasion that Eden's plan was a step towards, and not away from, all-European integration in the long run, but first Eden had to listen to further mutterings about the possibility of the withdrawal of all American assistance from Western Europe if divisive policies continued to be pursued that could prevent Dulles' dream of a revivified, democratic and united Europe, free of all Communist influence. It was a remarkable feat that Eden was able to persuade both him and the French, with totally different fears, that what he was proposing was in their national interests as well as in the interests of NATO. And then, at the Foreign Ministers' meeting in London, chaired by Eden, he dramatically announced on 30 September that Britain would maintain four divisions in Europe and the tactical air force virtually in perpetuity. What had proved difficult was Churchill's quite unexpected opposition, which emerged at a decisive meeting at Downing Street on 28 September, when Eden's paper seeking Cabinet authority for the undertaking was discussed. What the Cabinet Minutes do not emphasize sufficiently was that Churchill was, in Eden's account, 'very difficult, considerably to my surprise', but Salisbury and Swinton strongly supported Eden, and no one else said anything; Churchill's objections were tacitly overruled. This unprecedented commitment to permanent British military presence on the Continent, 'given

* Churchill's eightieth birthday, 30 November.

to prevent a war and not win a war' as Eden put it to the Conservative Party Conference on 6 October, convinced the French of British sincerity.

Eden gained all his objectives. The Allied occupation regime in West Germany was ended, she became a full member of NATO, and a Western European Union was established in Paris. For someone often depicted as 'anti-European' because of his doubts on full economic integration, this was the greatest single service that a British Foreign Minister has rendered to the reunification of Europe and to the ending of the wounds of war. As he willingly acknowledged, he built on Bevin's foundations, but his own support for Bevin had been vital in that earlier period.

This new triumph was universally admired and praised, even Dulles being warmly generous. Eden was awarded the Wateler Peace Prize by the Carnegie Foundation, the *Daily Mail* named him 'Politician of the Year', and the Queen renewed the offer of the Garter made by her father in 1945. This time, as Churchill had already accepted the high honour, Eden did so as well, it being conferred on him at Windsor on 20 October, amid widespread enthusiasm and much pleasure, his political opponents going out of their way to express their sincere congratulations.

But the succession matter dragged on.

Then over to talk to W at his request. It took time but amounted to very little. He seemed inclined to [the] view I couldn't leave F.O. at present reshuffle. I said I wasn't eager to do so. But if I stayed there until a week or so before General Election I wouldn't have chance to make any impression home front. Silence on this. (Diary, 22 September)

It would have been very difficult for Eden to have left the Foreign Office at this stage, for although the decisions of the London Conference were finalized in Paris on 23 October, there were highly sensitive areas – notably on nuclear matters – that required further work and negotiation with the Americans, Dulles again coming over to Paris in December to work out an agreed formula for the use of nuclear weapons in certain circumstances. This could have caused considerable difficulties, but Dulles was now in a helpful mood, and in circumstances of great secrecy the two – with Lester Pearson, the Canadian Foreign Secretary – agreed on a formula 'evolved mainly by Foster, which met our needs admirably. Later when F & I saw Mendès he took it without a word: so did Scandinavians. . . . Foster dined with me at Embassy. Useful discussion of all our problems in a helpful spirit.'

As this remarkable year in Eden's life drew to a close a member of his very hard-pressed Private Office, Andrew Stark, said to him that 'this has been an *annus mirabilis*'. So it had been. More had been achieved in twelve months to resolve critical issues than in the entire post-war period; a major war in Indo-China, and possibly a world war, had been averted; the position of Western Europe had been immensely strengthened; West Germany had been brought in from the post-war cold; the Iranian situation had been stabilized; relations with the Soviet Union were markedly better; the key decision to withdraw from Egypt had been taken; and, by the end of 1954, relations with Dulles had significantly improved. It was indeed appropriate that it was the year in which he had received the Garter.

What had particularly amazed those who worked closest to Eden was his extraordinary mental and physical energy. To have such ideas and inspirations was remarkable enough; for someone who so recently had been very sick, and who had looked so dreadful at the end of 1953, it was a tribute to his physical resilience and his determination. Nicholas Eden has told me of how his father was exhausted after a set of tennis that summer, but within a quarter of an hour was back on the court 'knocking hell out of me'. Much the same happened in the international diplomatic sphere; disappointments were to be regarded as mere setbacks; opportunities were to be seized; unremitting hard work was the response to problems; the human factor was never to be ignored in negotiation.

But seeing the matter in retrospect, the pace of that year, with its constant travelling and very long days and short nights, was an extremely fierce one, which certainly reduced some Foreign Office officials to complete exhaustion. Colville had a glimpse of this when there was a trivial incident over a diplomatic bag from the United States intended for him at Downing Street but sent in error to a Foreign Office official of the same name at a distant Embassy. When Colville raised the matter of the missing bag, which contained especially sensitive material, with a senior Foreign Office official he was advised to write a strong letter of complaint which could be formally noted for Office purposes and responded to with an official apology. Colville did as he was advised, and was astounded to receive back from a member of Eden's staff a virulent, five-page letter in the man's own handwriting. Colville tore the letter up and the matter ended, but Colville then realized the intense strain under which Eden's staff were working.

It often happens in Office that the burdens are heavier on the staff than on the leader. The latter, after all, has the exhilaration of leadership, the publicity and the glamour of achievement (though it carries with it the odium of failure) which can take one through strain and weariness in a way denied to the staff. Eden was a far more thoughtful and considerate minister than he has often been given credit for, and his staff enjoyed being on a winning team. But if they felt the strain, which they did, it had similar effects on Eden, and although there was no recurrence of illness or fever in 1954 he was often desperately tired and tense; for a man who had only just recovered from three major operations a price would have to be paid. 'A walk in p.m. [at Rose Bower] which I found sadly tiring,' he wrote on 28 December.

The only shadow on this year of triumph remained that of the succession. As 1954 drew to an end the National Union of Railwaymen made strong demands and threatened a national strike, on which the Cabinet was divided. Eden's attention had been elsewhere for so long that the event came as a surprise to him, but he took a robust view that the NUR should be confronted and the British Rail management supported. Churchill was not so sure, the normal pacifier, Monckton, referring to the Prime Minister in private as 'The Ancient Mariner'. But this matter, requiring a firm response by a united Cabinet, merely emphasized how bad the situation had become.

Just when it seemed that even Churchill thought it might be a convenient time to go he produced a triumph that again changed his mind. On his eightieth birthday on 30 November he received the unprecedented tribute of both Houses of Parliament in Westminster Hall, a wonderful occasion to which he responded with an unforgettably characteristic speech of wit and fire. The puckish humour, the calculated asides, the perfectly modulated control of voice, and that incomparable moral sturdiness made him look, and sound, years younger than his true age. Tributes poured in upon him and Lady Churchill from throughout the world as well as from their fellow countrymen. Even to someone as egotistical as Churchill this volume of gratitude and praise genuinely surprised and moved him. Also, he was enjoying an Indian Summer in the House of Commons, often embroiled in controversy, but scoring regularly off his critics, to universal pleasure. As he now did very little real work he could concentrate on these occasions, and he was enjoying himself. Macmillan, Crookshank and others were pressing him hard on Eden's behalf, but the old man could see no good reason why he should retire while things were going so well, particularly on the economic front, where Butler's strategy of controlled deregulation and the reduction of taxes was proving popular and successful, assisted by a significant change in the world balance of trade that favoured Britain. For the first time since the war the British people found themselves moving out of the prolonged period of austerity, and were greatly relishing the experience. Unemployment was falling, prosperity was rising; hated controls and rationing were being abolished; the Macmillan housing programme was proceeding at great pace, although at high cost.

In contrast, the Labour Party was in deep disarray, the Bevanite faction pursuing its purposes with a vigour that often degenerated into venom and vendetta. For those within it, the Government seemed to be without real leadership or purpose; to outsiders it seemed impressive and self-confident, while Labour looked divided, dispirited and without real policies. Eden's successes abroad made people proud to be British again. There was new hope in the air. Why, then, Churchill mused, should he retire when everything was going so well?

Additionally, there was what Eden described as Churchill's 'lunatic obsession' for his beloved summit, which he was determined to resist. It was an unhappy time, as Eden recorded on 21 December:

Felt far from well all day, & temperature in evening but determined to have my talk with W after dinner. Mentioned to Bobbety on telephone that I was going & he told me there was something I should know. He would come round & see me.

He did, and told me that Fred W[oolton] had told him in H of L that afternoon that W had asked him & James [Stuart] & Rab to stay behind after Cabinet. He had then raised & discussed with them possible Spring election (without a word to me). Fred had also said to Bobbety that of course no one would dream of wanting a March election except to get rid of W.

Rab had been against it. James had kept silent. Evidently a preparatory lobbying. Interesting, considering he [Churchill] has consistently refused a meeting with me present. He never mentioned this talk when I saw him later, nor admitted prior consultation except with Rab night before.

Set out for No. 10 at 9.30. Found Clemmie there with W. She was charming & worried at my colour. W said he supposed I had been living too well in Paris. Then when Clemmie had gone after a long pause he said 'What do you want to see me about?' in his most aggressive tone.

I said that he had had my letter and said he would be ready to discuss it. And slowly the argument began. At first he would have nothing. All was as well as possible. There was no hurry for an election or for him to hand over, the end of June or July would do very well. Laboriously I explained first that the new administration should have a chance to establish itself with the public. This gave us none. Second that it would place me in a much stronger position if I could take over in a month when an election was possible. Then, if my authority or mandate was challenged I would have the option either to fight it out in Parliament or to say very well let the country judge, & go to the country. This I could not do in July.

He wasn't much interested in this but when I had made it quite clear that I was not interested either in taking over at the end of June he eventually agreed to meeting at 3 pm with the people I chose. But it was all most grudging. There was much rather cruel 'divide et impera'. For instance, he asked me how I got on with Harold. I said 'very well, why?' He replied 'Oh, he is very ambitious.' I laughed.*

22 December

Meeting of Ministers at 3 pm on lines I had asked for last night. Not a pleasant business. Rab had told me yesterday evening on telephone how unsatisfactory

---

* In 1965 Eden noted that 'This was the only occasion I recall when Winston warned me about a colleague.'

whole position was, that Cabinet I had missed had taken no decision, etc., etc. All of which did not prevent him coming out with a mass of technical arguments against an election in March. Harold eventually debunked all this by saying that if there were an emergency he could presumably overcome these difficulties, to which Rab somewhat naively replied 'Yes'.

After a certain amount of further desultory conversation & explanation of value of an option to a new Govt, W rounded on me and said it was clear we wanted him out. Nobody contradicted him. Earlier he had said that I had made no difficulty about end of July last year. I replied that he had first said Queen's return if not sooner. End of July had been an afterthought.

At the end W said menacingly that he would think over what his colleagues had said & let them know his decision. Whatever it was he hoped it would not affect their present relationship with him. Nobody quailed. James [Stuart] said afterwards to me that it had been painful but absolutely necessary. He had to be told he could not pursue a course of 'such utter selfishness'.

Later Bobbety & Harold repaired to my room at F.O. We gloomily surveyed the scene. It was clear to us that Rab would give no help. I said that I had said my say & they agreed that no more could be expected of me. Therefore they would try to hold a meeting without W or me of the remaining colleagues [still in London] before Christmas. Bobbety charged himself with this task & later Rab assured him that he would attend and only wished to be helpful. What the result of all this may be I cannot tell except that the old man feels bitterly towards me, but this I cannot help. The colleagues are unanimous about drawling Cabinets, the failure to take decisions, the general atmosphere of '*après moi le déluge*' & someone had to give a heave.

Christmas at Rose Bower was interrupted by telephone calls from Monckton, seeking Eden's help in standing against surrender to the railwaymen. 'I asked whether W was trying to go back on Cabinet decisions. He said that he was. I said then course was clear. He only had to say that he W could not himself do that & suggest calling of a Cabinet. I was ready to come up.' Macmillan also called to say that Churchill was trying 'to bully Walter to go to Chequers'.

It was a sad and unsatisfying end to the *annus mirabilis*.

[10]

Prime Minister

Nineteen fifty-five had opened still without any clear indication of what Churchill had in mind about his retirement plans. Churchill himself, in spite of strong hints from colleagues, family and friends, still saw no reason why he should go, and the very thought of leaving office depressed him profoundly. Although fading he still had the capacity to rise to great occasions, as he was to demonstrate again in one of the finest speeches of his extraordinary career on 1 March; his boredom with most of the areas of government did not include international affairs, least of all his cherished summit. He had been understandably elated by his reception on his eightieth birthday, remained in excellent form at Questions in the Commons, and believed with much passion and sincerity that he had one more great service to perform before he retired. Eden's palpable lack of enthusiasm for an ill-prepared summit irritated him, and continued to cast a shadow between them. There is something both moving and pathetic about the dream of this wonderful old man to end his glorious career as mediator, honest broker or go-between to bring together the nuclear powers. The fact that none of the others wanted it served as a stimulant rather than a depressant. It was wholly unrealistic, yet one can admire the ambition.

The truth was this. He could still make a great speech, as was proved in the Defence debate on 1 March. Indeed, none could rival his oratory or his ability to inspire. But he was aging month by month and was reluctant to read any papers except the newspapers or to give his mind to anything that he did not find diverting. More and more time was given to bezique and ever less to public business.

The preparations of an answer to a Parliamentary question might consume a whole morning; facts would be demanded from Government departments and not arouse any interest when they arrived: it was becoming an effort even to sign letters and a positive condescension to read Foreign Office telegrams. And yet on some days the old gleam would be there, wit and good humour would bubble and sparkle, wisdom would roll out in telling sentences, and still, occasionally, the sparkle of genius could be seen in a decision, a letter or a phrase.*

* Colville, *The Fringes of Power*, pp. 706–7.

Not surprisingly, Eden chafed. He could not and would not remove Churchill, and his standards of conduct made the fomentation of a whispering campaign or back-bench revolt unthinkable. He would not even be faintly disloyal or surreptitious in his dealings with political journalists, since that he rightly despised. His own programme as Foreign Secretary was formidable and his application as strong as ever, particularly over Formosa and the offshore islands, which he confessed was one of the most difficult issues he had ever had to deal with. The crucial first SEATO meeting in Bangkok was due for mid-February, and the Commonwealth Prime Ministers' Conference from 31 January to 8 February. The decision of Britain to develop its own hydrogen bomb had its international as well as domestic implications.

The year opened with the rail dispute undecided, and with Churchill still clinging to office. The combination increased the tension between him and Eden, and at this time it seemed difficult for them to agree on anything. Eden recorded on 6 January:

Motored up to Cabinet. Met at 11.30. Explained to us that we didn't yet know what Robertson proposed to say at meeting this afternoon. No certainty either that NUR would even now accept. Considerable evidence of communist desire for row. R.A.B. told me when he joined W and I at luncheon later of this evidence & that he would rather have row now than later.

W & I had rather a sharp altercation at Cabinet. He attacked me for having been bellicose from the start & added 'You'll get your strike alright.' I countered that he had chucked the reins on the horse's neck & said I agreed with *Times* and *M. Guardian*'s leaders this morning.

C & I lunched with W and Clemmie. Argument continued more mildly there. He said I was a Tory, that my City experience had done me no good & had imbued me too much with rights of private property. I said I had been brought up to believe this was a liberal principle. Clemmie agreed. There was much talking at luncheon about the handing over, Clemmie talking [to] C about showing her kitchen etc. Rab told me in the late afternoon that he would like it to be Commonwealth Conference, but that Easter was more probable.

The threatened rail strike was called off on the following day, but the tensions remained, especially over Churchill's obsession with his final summit, now encouraged by Mendès-France, and the consequent vagueness over plans. On 13 January, Eden had a long discussion with Harry Crookshank, in which he reiterated that late June or early July for the change was unacceptable, and that 'Easter was not good, but just acceptable since, if we were driven to it, May election was conceivable. Best was after Comm. Conf. because this would spare me long absence. Harry agreed, tho' he added that best days for change were already past. He said he would tell others.' On the 17th, Eden, after a considerable amount of work and preparation, delivered a radio broadcast; he commented: 'Not a word from W, though I sent him successive copies of broadcast. Nor have I heard anything from him for days. He is either ill, or in the worst of tempers!'

The situation was embarrassing for everyone. On 1 February Eden wrote:

After consultation with Rab, Harold and Bobbety all of whom agreed situation must be chased up, I asked to see W this afternoon at 3 p.m. All was quiet & smooth. After discussion of my plans I asked for his. At my suggestion he sent for calendar. He admitted he could not carry on & after discussion said I could base my plans on his departure during last week of session after Easter. I told Rab who confirmed later that W had spoken to him in similar terms.

Churchill, once the most resolute of men, had become irresolute. He had few real plans, although many dreams and hopes, particularly in international affairs; these were admirable, but too many of them defied the hard practicalities with which ministers and especially Eden had to deal.

Perhaps the saddest aspect of all was that Churchill could not understand why Eden was so tense. Churchill's egotism and sense of destiny had been his greatest strengths, although others regarded them with distaste, but in old age they ceased to be virtues. As Colville wrote in his diary: 'The thought of abandoning office grows more abhorrent as the time comes nearer. I doubt if he realizes what trouble is in store for him from his Cabinet colleagues if he stays on.' But he did stay on. Promises had been made, and broken; clear hints had been dropped, and then forgotten. Even if Eden had possessed saintly tolerance – which he never claimed as one of his qualities – the situation would have strained any successor's patience to breaking-point. To someone of Eden's temperament the waiting was intolerable; that he tolerated it, at least in public, was a remarkable achievement of enforced self-control.

But the difficulties had not been resolved, and in the midst of heavy Foreign Office work Eden had to cope with Churchill's continuing evasiveness. On 7 February Eden noted: 'Earlier had talk with W. He still maintains plans as described to me, but wants to send message to Ike which does not fit in with line we have all agreed.' But on the 10th Churchill rang to say that he wanted to see him and Butler to agree on the date of the Budget and the timing of his departure, which was to be on 5 April; this meeting was held on 14 February.

Butler later came to believe that there was a possibility that he might have succeeded Churchill. It is clear that he came to this thought because he was invited with Eden to see Churchill, whereas the reason for his presence was simply to co-ordinate the dates of the Budget statement and

Churchill's resignation. As Salisbury wrote to Eden some time afterwards, when he heard of Butler's incorrect interpretation of his presence, 'There was no question of who was to succeed Winston. The only problem was the timing.'

This was to prove to be a very real problem, but meanwhile the work of the Foreign Secretary had to continue, with concerns over the situation in the Far East over Formosa and the Chinese offshore islands, where British and American perceptions continued to differ, and over the Middle East. In the latter the Iraqis had proposed to strengthen and expand the Arab League by including Turkey, with the involvement of the United States and Britain. The possibility of what Eden described as 'a NATO for the Middle East' involving not only Iraq and Turkey but also Iran, Pakistan and Jordan, with strong Western support, was profoundly alluring and exciting. It would strengthen Western interests and act as a major inhibiting resistance to Soviet infiltration and influence. It would also put pressure upon Nasser, and give new security to Israel. The Baghdad Pact opened the real possibility of a political and military non-colonialist alliance sympathetic to the West and protective of its interests, specifically oil and the Suez Canal.

To achieve this would be another outstanding diplomatic and political *coup*, perhaps the most important of Eden's period at the Foreign Office; but the obstacle was Nasser, backed in his hostility by the Soviet Union. But although Eden knew there was little possibility of persuading Egypt to join the pact, he took the opportunity of his journey to Bangkok for the first SEATO conference (which began with his departure from London on 19 February) to stop at Cairo and to see Nasser personally.

What happened at this famous meeting has entered Egyptian and anti-Eden mythology. By the Nasser account, much embellished by others, Eden treated him as 'a prince dealing with vagabonds' and demonstrated traditional colonialist and condescending arrogance, which Nasser's biographer, Heykal, ascribed to Eden's desire to impress Clarissa Eden.* For Eden to have behaved in such a manner would have been so grossly out of character that one should regard this version with scepticism, but it is also strongly denied by others who were present. What was perhaps unfortunate was that the dinner meeting was held at the British Embassy, which Nasser hated for its past associations.

The British version is that the meeting was cordial, but that Nasser considered the Baghdad Pact a barrier between Arab states and the West, rather than a form of improving relations between them. Clarissa wrote of Nasser in her diary: 'Great impression of health and strength – terrifically

---

* She was not even present at the meeting, but joined them later at dinner.

broad and booming.... A. came up very late, having had a good talk with Nasser except regarding the Turco-Iraq Pact, upon which he was very bitter.' Nasser professed strong sympathies with the West – which his listeners had good cause to doubt. The only jarring moment was before the talks, when, just as Nasser and Eden positioned themselves to be photographed standing together, Nasser unexpectedly, and quite deliberately, seized Eden's hand and would not let go until the photographs were taken. Eden was not the only person who pondered on how well this would look in the eyes of the Suez Group, or in Sudan, Iraq or Israel. He reported to London that 'No doubt jealousy plays a part [in Nasser's hostility to the Pact] and a frustrated desire to lead the Arab world.' He was undoubtedly right on the second point, but Nasser's ambitions were not to be frustrated for long.

No one present on the British side believed that Eden handled the meeting badly; he had greeted Nasser in Arabic, they conversed amicably, and Eden went to considerable trouble to emphasize the positive features of recent Anglo-Egyptian relations. Nor was he condescending, let alone rude, as some Egyptian versions have averred. But there is no doubt that something went wrong, and the cause was mutual suspicion. Eden suspected the genuineness of Nasser's professed devotion to the West, and Nasser suspected that one result of the Baghdad Pact would be to put Arab pressure on him. Both these suspicions were justified, but Nasser clearly regarded Eden as the personification of all he disliked in the British; and Eden, for his part, distrusted Nasser. Also, each seriously underestimated the other, with disastrous consequences.

None the less, although Eden had not expected Nasser to embrace the pact, he still believed – and was to do so for some time – that judicious British and American attitudes and assistance could at least preserve Egyptian neutrality and inhibit Russian influence. Nor was Nasser's opinion of Eden as hostile as he later alleged. In April 1976 Dr John Laffin wrote to Eden: 'I have been looking up my notes on an interview with Nasser in April 1956. He said, "I respect only two Englishmen – Eden because he is honest and intelligent, Churchill because he is dishonest and cunning. One is a gentleman, the other a rogue."'

Eden flew to Bangkok by way of Pakistan, where his reception was notably friendly, and had a 'wholly delightful' stay with Nehru in Delhi; all went well in Iraq, and on his return to London Eden had no difficulty in persuading the Cabinet that Britain should join the pact. The Labour Party, although concerned about Israel, did not oppose it, and later in the year Pakistan and Iran joined, 'giving the pact a frontier stretching from the Mediterranean to the Himalayas', as Eden described it.

Although it was to prove a very flimsy frontier, and with several large and crucial gaps, it was an excellent example of Eden's seizure of an opportunity, and its formation could well have been a major turning-point in the history of the Middle East. But it was not to be. This was his one apparent diplomatic triumph – for as such it was generally perceived at the time – which was to destroy all its participants.

The timing of this meeting was very important – and very unfortunate. The Egyptians had expected a warming of relations with Turkey, but when the Turkish Prime Minister Menderes visited Baghdad in January to sign the mutual defence pact there was an outburst of orchestrated rage against the Iraqis from Cairo, and an attempt by Nasser was hurriedly made, which failed totally, to persuade the Prime Ministers of the Arab states to condemn Iraq and the Baghdad Pact. The Iraqi Prime Minister Nuri refused to attend the meeting, and Syria and Lebanon were hostile. Only Saudi Arabia, with its implacable hostility to Israel, demonstrated any interest.

From Nasser's point of view this was a major diplomatic humiliation in the Arab world; on 28 February he received a military one. Goaded beyond endurance by Egyptian-inspired fedayeen raids, the Israelis launched a major counter-offensive in the Gaza Strip. It was a punitive expedition that was well prepared and conducted with ruthlessness as well as skill. The Egyptian forces were utterly defeated, and although the real cause was bad leadership and training, it was convenient to put the blame on inferior equipment. As the Western powers retained their policy of arms equality, Nasser looked elsewhere. In the Soviet Union he found ready sympathizers. His needs would be met technically by Czechoslovakia in return for cotton and rice; when this was eventually announced by Nasser on 27 September it was accompanied by charges that the British had not been able to meet his requests, that the American conditions would have imperilled Egyptian independence, and that the West was in any event supplying Israel clandestinely with arms.

Nasser, perhaps by mistake, had moved into the Soviet sphere. The Russians noted with interest and appreciation how the language of Radio Cairo and the strictly controlled Egyptian press echoed the vehement denunciations of Western Imperialism which Nasser uttered wherever he went. Western Intelligence knew about the Czech arms deal long before it was publicly announced – as did the Israelis.

These events, and not the meeting with Eden, provided the spark that lit the fuse for the explosion in July 1956.

* * *

This long, arduous but important trip had taken Eden away from Britain when the principal topic of political discussion was the timing of Churchill's departure, and Robert Carr and others had kept him closely informed of developments on that front. They were not sanguine, and Eden could not be blamed for being distracted by these concerns on his travels; when he returned he found that Churchill had again backed away from his commitment.

The major international event had been the sudden and, to the British, wholly unexpected downfall of the Soviet leader Malenkov, and his replacement by the duumvirate of Bulganin and Khrushchev on 8 February. The British Ambassador in Moscow, Sir William Hayter, reported to London that 'None of us could believe our ears when we heard it announced.' Bulganin was clearly a dignified figurehead, and when Eden asked for an assessment of Khrushchev Hayter reported that his 'personality, and the over-simplified, heavy-handed line he takes on foreign affairs, coupled with his total ignorance of them, are not encouraging. He is not the mad dictator type; indeed he is a sane and perhaps even good-natured character, a kind of un-neurotic Göring.' But Hayter also recalled a lunch when Khrushchev had suddenly moved from geniality to belligerence, declaiming that world peace could only be achieved by world Communism. What could not be realized at this very early stage was that Khrushchev's arrival was to transform Soviet attitudes towards the Middle East, where they had previously been relatively passive. Hayter divined, rightly, that a dominant objective of the new regime was to get the United States out of Europe; it was several months before it became clear that another one was to force the British out of the Middle East. The more the Russians looked at the Egyptian situation in particular, the more interested they became. Nasser willingly accepted invitations to visit Russia, Poland, Hungary and Bulgaria, where he was treated with much respect and attention. He was one of the principal stars at the Non-Aligned Nations' Conference in Bandung in April, where his cordiality to the Chinese aroused fierce reactions from Dulles. This was all noted in London.

But the new situation in Moscow also greatly intrigued Churchill. A new situation had arisen! Would the new Soviet leaders be interested in Four-Power talks at the top level? As will be seen, when Bulganin responded positively in March, Churchill's excitement was great, and he again proposed to delay his retirement.

Colville has described the next episode in this melancholy saga:

On Friday, March 11th, I set off with Winston for Chequers in a Rolls Royce he contemplated buying. On the way we went to the Zoo to see his lion, Rota, and his leopard, Sheba. Shortly after we had reached Chequers, and had settled down to bezique, there arrived a minute from Anthony Eden covering a telegram from Makins in Washington which described various manoeuvres suggested by the Americans for inducing the French to ratify the [1954] London–Paris agreements.... These included a suggestion that Eisenhower should go to Paris on May 8th 1955, the tenth anniversary of v.e. Day, and solemnly ratify the agreements in company with President Coty, Adenauer and Sir Winston Churchill. W did not take in the implications at once. Lord Beaverbrook came to dinner (the first time for many months) and it was not until he was gone that W re-read the telegram and the somewhat discouraging and disparaging minute which accompanied it. Of course, he said to me, this meant all bets were off: he would stay, and, with Eisenhower, meet the Russians. I pointed out that no suggestion of meeting the Russians was made, but he brushed this aside because he saw a chance of escape from his increasingly unpalatable timetable.*

The matter was in fact rather more complicated than this summary, but the essence is absolutely correct. Eden was at Dorneywood, the very new official residence of the Foreign Secretary, which the Edens detested and seldom used. He was grappling with the very sensitive issues involved – not least the possibilities of causing German offence by the choice of ve Day – and did not want the Russians involved. Nor did he want a Heads of Government meeting at this point, but one of Foreign Ministers. 'I think we should certainly say that our aim is still a top-level meeting of the Heads of Governments,' Churchill minuted to Eden on 14 March: 'If Eisenhower is still resolute against it, as I understand that Aldrich says, he should be made to say so. That would be a relief to me on personal grounds.' Eden was worried that ratification might be interpreted as interference in French domestic politics, and would certainly involve a sharp Soviet reaction.

The unhappy tension between the two men is only too clear from their exchanges.

Churchill to Eden, 12 March
... It is the first time President Eisenhower has responded to my appeals beginning on May 11 1953, and has shown willingness to visit Europe in person and after securing ratification of the London and Paris agreements, to quote Lay plans for a meeting with the Soviets in a sustained effort to reduce tensions and the risk of War, unquote. This proposal of a meeting of Heads of Governments which he could attend himself must be regarded as creating a new situation which will affect our personal plans and time-tables.

... 2. It also complicated the question of a May election to which I gather you are inclining. Your proposed last sentence in your paragraph 7 might be dangerous as it seems to suggest that the Party politics of a snap Election to take advantage of Socialist disunity would be allowed to weigh against a meeting of the Heads of

* Colville, *The Fringes of Power*, pp. 705–6.

Government which would give a chance to the world of warding off its mortal peril. The British national reaction to this would not be favourable. . . .

. . . 4. The magnitude of the Washington advance towards a Top Level Meeting is the dominant fact before us now and our reply must not underrate it or fail to encourage its development.

Eden to Churchill, 12 March
Prime Minister,
1. I have your message of to-day.
2. I was not aware that anything I had done in my public life would justify the suggestion that I was putting Party before country or self before either.

Churchill to Eden, 12 March
Your paragraph 2. Nothing in my minute suggested or was intended to suggest that you were putting Party before country or self before either. What I meant, and mean, is that the last sentence of paragraph 7 of your minute would be taken to imply a snap Election in May. This would in any case rouse a Party struggle of intense bitterness. That our treatment of the Eisenhower/Dulles proposal was in any way associated with our electoral schemes, and this became known, as it well might, would certainly be made the grounds for a Socialist charge that we had discouraged a Top Level approach to the international problem for reasons connected with our Party tactics. That is why I deemed the sentence dangerous in this context.

I am distressed that you should have read a personal implication, which I utterly repudiate, into a discussion of policy. There are enough difficulties already without misunderstanding between you and me after all these years.

The situation was lamentable, and at the end of the next Cabinet Eden raised the personal issue, and, in Colville's vivid account, 'W., in the face of silent and embarrassed colleagues, said coldly that this was not a matter on which he required guidance or on which Cabinet discussion was usual.'* In fact the Cabinet was wholly in sympathy with Eden, particularly as they knew that Churchill was ardently pursuing a chimera. Colville's account continues:

The ensuing days were painful. W. began to form a cold hatred of Eden who, he repeatedly said, had done more to thwart him and prevent him from pursuing the policy he thought right than anyone else. But he also admitted to me on several occasions that the prospect of giving everything up, after nearly sixty years in public life, was a terrible wrench. He saw no reason why he should go: he was only doing it for Anthony. He sought to persuade his intimate friends, and himself, that he was being hounded from office.†

* Colville, *The Fringes of Power*, p. 706.
† Colville, *ibid.*, p. 706. This is what Colville wrote at the time, and while he felt that he could not correct the entry for publication, he has emphasized to me that 'hatred' was far too strong a description of Churchill's attitude towards Eden at this time, but his diaries do demonstrate vividly the tension between the two men.

Then, on 27 March, Churchill learnt that Bulganin was again speaking favourably of Four-Power talks, even though Eisenhower had rejected them; he concluded that, with two serious national strikes and the Budget looming, and the date of the election still undecided, he could not possibly go at such a time. On the morning of the 29th he sent Butler to tell Eden that in these circumstances the timetable must be changed again. As the Churchills were due to dine with the Edens that very evening at what was supposed to be a farewell dinner, Eden would have been justified in having one of his notorious outbursts. But Colville had wisely sent word to Eden's Private Secretary that 'amiability must be the watchword', and Eden sensibly kept quiet. On the following day Churchill called in Eden and Butler to tell them, at long last, that the timetable would be unchanged, saying to Colville that, 'I have been altered and affected by Anthony's amiable manner.'

The culmination of this extraordinary story at least had some style. Churchill declared that 'no two men have ever changed guard more smoothly'. Those who knew what had actually happened were not sure whether he was being heavily ironical, mischievous or tactful. It was certainly at variance with the facts since 1952, but the final act was played well by all concerned.

On 4 April the Churchills entertained the Queen and the Duke of Edinburgh to dinner at Downing Street, of which there are several accounts, some very moving, others very irreverent and funny. A London newspaper strike prevented any national coverage of the end of Churchill's official career which took place on the following day.

On the morning of 6 April Eden kissed hands as Prime Minister. With television still a rarity, it was somewhat eerie to have the long-awaited affair conducted thus, as though at dead of night. There could also be no press attention given to the warm tributes in the House of Commons that afternoon to Churchill, nor to the welcome given to Eden by both sides of the House. In his charming congratulatory speech Attlee quoted the advice given to Melbourne by a secretary when he was hesitating whether to accept the Sovereign's invitation: 'Why, damn it all, such a position was never held by any Greek or Roman, and if it only lasts three months it will be worthwhile to have been Prime Minister of England.' In his reply, Eden good-humouredly observed that Melbourne's period of office as Prime Minister had been considerably longer than that – six years in fact – and Emrys Hughes asked, amid laughter, about the relationship between Caesar (Churchill) and Anthony. It was a happy and civilized House of Commons occasion that emphasized the genuine affection and regard felt for the new Prime Minister, not least on the Labour benches.

* * *

Thus Anthony Eden had at long last reached the premiership. He seemed to be outstandingly qualified, after over thirty years in the House of Commons, a widely popular and respected public figure, one of the best – perhaps the best, as Macmillan and many others believed – parliamentarian of his time, and a major figure in international diplomacy. His record spoke for itself, and his critics seemed puny in comparison. His courage, charm and unrivalled political experience had ensured him the succession without demur. Although the British press was perforce silent, the foreign press, especially in the United States and France, gave him an exceptionally enthusiastic welcome. If the immediate circumstances of his accession had been painful, and if the political situation at home and abroad was uncertain, few Prime Ministers of modern times have reached Downing Street with more goodwill and widespread respect.

Eden was determined from the moment he entered Downing Street that there must be an early general election. The Labour divisions were manifest, the Conservative Party was in good heart, and all the political indications were very promising. To delay until the autumn or even later might not only be to miss a golden opportunity, but would deny the electorate a chance to give an immediate vote of approval to the new Government. This was the reasoning, on which all the Party advisers agreed. But there was no certainty of victory, and it was a brave decision.

It would have been difficult, after this decision was taken, to have had a major restructuring of the Government, and the only significant changes were the appointments of Macmillan to the Foreign Office, Selwyn Lloyd to Defence, the Earl of Home to Commonwealth Relations, and Reginald Maudling to Minister of Supply, with some other minor adjustments lower down.

This can now be seen to have been a major, and significant, mistake. There would obviously have had to be a new Foreign Secretary appointed at once, but the opportunity should have been taken for a major recon-struction, to make it very definitely an Eden rather than a Churchill Government. Woolton, the Chancellor of the Duchy of Lancaster, who certainly wanted to go and told Eden so, was persuaded to stay, and other opportunities were missed to replace ageing or unsuccessful ministers and to bring on younger MPs who had made their mark on the back benches. The result was disappointment among the latter, and a general – if discreetly muted – surprise within the Party that so little had been done. There was then the expectation that the major reshuffle would follow the general election. When this did not happen, discontent, concern and criticism were further augmented. Psychologically, as well as politically, it had been a serious error, from which the false legend of 'indecision' began, and which was to prove so corroding to Eden's position.

Those closest to Eden knew of his lack of self-confidence outside his only real sphere of knowledge and experience, foreign affairs. When he considered how he was to conduct his premiership, he looked back to Baldwin: 'I thought Baldwin's method of frequent consultation *alone* with each of his principal colleagues was good and I followed it ... we saved the Cabinet some extra stress of business that way.'* In fact, it had been a bad method, which had caused much difficulty and misunderstanding, but Eden was over-reacting to the Churchill method of interminable and inconclusive Cabinets and substantial paperwork. This was understandable, but it was an error. Collective decision-making has its defects, but there are many advantages; at the outset of his premiership Eden elected for the Baldwin technique. To ministers long used to another, this was a surprise and a disappointment. Eden informed ministers that he was always available to each one of them in private whenever they wished to see him, but it takes a very confident and senior minister to avail himself regularly of such an offer.

There were strong personal factors. Like Churchill, he wanted to have around him men he knew and trusted, and as the Government had proved to be generally successful it would have been a poor reward to end the careers of those who had been involved in that success. Also, Eden's frequent absences abroad since 1951, and his concentration on foreign affairs, meant that he was heavily dependent upon the advice of the Chief Whip, Patrick Buchan-Hepburn. But the mistake was less to have a reconstruction in April than not to have one after the election. And from this error much difficulty arose. As one Cabinet colleague later remarked, with truth: 'Anthony never built a Cabinet in his own mould. He inherited one, and then tinkered with it.'

Buchan-Hepburn was a man of considerable charm and ability, but it was generally considered in the House of Commons that he was an uneven judge of character and lacked strength, which in a Chief Whip are grievous limitations. A new team had to be created at Number 10. As Jock Colville had decided to leave the public service, it was necessary to find a new Private Secretary for the Prime Minister. There was general agreement that he should not be a Foreign Office official, but should come from the Home Civil Service. The first choice had had a wholly innocent peripheral connection at Cambridge with Donald Maclean and his circle, and Whitehall nerves were so taut on that matter that he had to be rejected – going on to a career of much distinction in another sphere of the Civil Service – and Frederick Bishop was appointed, to Eden's satisfaction and pleasure. Being head of Eden's Private Office was never a bed of roses, but Bishop's

* Avon, *Full Circle*, pp. 269–70. My italics.

dedication, tact and skills came to be deeply appreciated and valued. In Norman Brook, Eden had as Secretary to the Cabinet a wise, experienced and totally loyal public servant, with Burke Trend as his Deputy.

As his Press Officer, Eden surprisingly chose William Clark, the diplomatic correspondent of the *Observer*, a journalist of great charm and good humour, of unswerving honesty, with a strong internationalist outlook, particularly for developing countries, with which he had great sympathy. It was a curious appointment, not destined to be successful, but Clark's job, no more than Bishop's, was not an easy one.

Robert Carr remained as Eden's admirable and devoted Parliamentary Private Secretary, now joined by Robert Allan, who after a notable career in the Navy had attracted Eden's attention. Carr and Allan were exceptionally nice and able young men, in whom Eden had total confidence and trust, but with all the wisdom of hindsight it might have been better to team Carr with an older and more experienced fellow PPS, of a hardened and cynical disposition. But this was not the type of politician who had any attraction to Eden; he preferred to have close to him those whom he liked and trusted.

The trouble was that Eden's frequent, and often prolonged, absences from the Commons since 1951, either for health reasons or travelling abroad, meant that he had little personal knowledge of present or potential colleagues – especially the latter – except through experience of the former in Cabinet or the Government, and his only really close political friends remained Bobbety Salisbury and Jim Cilcennin. The fact that he was not, and never had been, a convivial House of Commons man proved another disability. When he looked at the Conservative benches he saw in the main the faces of complete strangers. The great Lord Salisbury, whose vagueness was famous, was said not to recognize even his own Cabinet members, and Arthur Balfour studiously never read newspapers, but these were different times. The majority of Conservative Members had hardly ever met Eden, except in the most perfunctory manner at best, and only saw him from afar. Many of them sensed – and not only in the Suez Group – that he did not particularly want to know them better. From the beginning, he was an aloof and distant Prime Minister, ironically more in the Neville Chamberlain than in the Stanley Baldwin tradition. What was in truth a mixture of shyness and reserve was ascribed to vanity and self-esteem, two vices that he conspicuously lacked. Also, his dislike of wearing spectacles meant that he often genuinely did not recognize people, and thereby some oversensitive egotists were offended.

Macmillan, in total contrast, was, like Churchill, very much a House of Commons man, revelling in the gossip, banter and companionship of the smoking room and attentive to new Members – to all of which Butler in turn was as indifferent as Eden. These differences in approach and attitude to the Parliamentary Party were destined to assume great importance.

The general election of May 1955 was subsequently regarded as immensely dull, and was depicted by the *Annual Register* as 'a humdrum affair'; there was much talk of electoral apathy, and concern about the significance (or otherwise) of the new political medium of television. This was not the experience of those involved in the fray, and there was a bad moment for the Conservatives early in the campaign when Gallup recorded that the Party's percentage lead of some 4 points had mysteriously disappeared. Public meetings – as I recall vividly – were not only lively but in many cases singularly bad-tempered. Eden had taken a keen interest in the various drafts of the Conservative Manifesto, which he amended significantly. It was he who added the words: 'In these last few months for the first time since 1939 no war is being waged anywhere on the earth's surface. No impartial observer at home or abroad will deny our country's part in this patient and fruitful diplomacy.' A reference to 'hangovers from the past' became 'relics of the past'. The original title, 'Together for Peace and Prosperity', was considered by Macmillan to be 'rather banal' and he suggested instead 'For Peace and Progress'. Eden and Woolton agreed, and the title became, 'United for Peace and Progress'. It was also on Eden's insistence that it refused to make easy and specific promises, and, in his own radio and television broadcasts, at which he was especially skilled and took professional advice, while he emphasized Conservative achievements and Labour disunity, he deliberately put himself forward as being less a Party politician than a responsible statesman in office. The Bulganin offer for the summit was accepted, Eisenhower and Dulles agreeing to attend out of a genuine desire to assist Eden, and the signing of the Austrian Treaty was certainly convenient. Attlee, with the Bevan schism barely concealable, had a difficult task, which he conducted with characteristic dignity, but in hardly an inspirational manner. The Conservative posters had a photograph of Eden with the words, 'Working for Peace' – again his idea – to which Labour responded with one of Attlee captioned, somewhat limply, 'You Can Trust Mr Attlee'.

The style of the Conservative campaign was based not only on Eden's strong personal views but on his memories of 1945 and his perceptions of the mood in 1955. It was principally for these reasons, and Eden's understandable desire to emphasize that a new chapter had opened, that Churchill was virtually ignored in the Conservative strategy and campaign. He had expected to play a more public and significant role, and, although he realized why he was being virtually excluded, he was genuinely hurt at his minimal role as an ordinary Conservative candidate. This was as understandable as the decision itself, but the matter could have been handled better, and more consideration given to the feelings and public respect enjoyed by this astonishing man. Many Conservatives felt less enthusiasm for Eden as a result of this, although in fact it was a collective decision. Moreover, Churchill himself seemed to many to behave unreasonably and to expect too large a role. In order to mollify him, it was agreed that he should do a television broadcast. The studio was booked, and all arrangements made, but then he cancelled it for reasons that were not made clear; this occasioned much irritation.

Eden's own progress around the country was a brilliant success – particularly in Scotland and the West Midlands – which aroused in some memories of Churchill's tour in 1945, but this time the genuine respect with which he was usually greeted was to be reflected in votes, and his final television performance on 21 May was outstandingly moderate, responsible and appealing.

Peter Tapsell, who had attracted notice at the Research Department through his speech-writing skills, was deputed by Woolton to assist Eden and to accompany the Prime Minister throughout the campaign. He, and Chloe Otto, also of the Research Department, constituted the entire team. Until Eden received a death threat, they had virtually no security; even after this it was minimal. The back-up support from London was also small, and subsequently Tapsell was amazed to recall how amateurish the whole thing had been. On occasions, while Eden was actually speaking, Chloe Otto would be typing out the next pages while Tapsell rushed them to Eden on stage. It was, as he has recalled, an entirely 'one-man show' and 'we made speeches and even policies on the hoof'. It was all immensely wearying; however, Eden's irascibility and rages at minor mishaps did not affect his calmness on the big occasion, not what Tapsell later admiringly called his 'hypnotic charm' with audiences. At the Rag Market in Birmingham a vast gathering estimated at some ten thousand listened almost reverently; it was an open meeting, not a Conservative one, and everywhere Eden went there were cheering and smiling crowds.

As always, Eden was impossible to write speeches for. When Shinwell made a wild and inaccurate speech on National Service, Tapsell lovingly prepared a devastating response: Eden refused to touch it, as he liked Shinwell and thought he had been an excellent Defence Minister. In this, as in his whole campaign, he refused to act out of character. When, at one open-air meeting in London he was asked a question, long forgotten, Eden replied with heat that he would rather lose the election than give a pledge he could not fulfil; he was so patently sincere that it made an immense impression.

This was indeed the story of the 1955 campaign, almost a personal and deliberately low-key one, admiringly received. Conservative candidates, even those with uneasy memories of 1945, found that the mention of Eden's name invariably brought applause. But the burden put upon Eden in the last of the old-fashioned general election campaigns – with no daily press conferences, little television, and with Attlee, driven hazardously by his wife, jotting his speeches on small pieces of paper as he went from meeting to meeting – was excessive, and his occasional explosions of anger at some minor defect wholly understandable. By the end of it his 'campaign team' – himself, his wife, Chloe Otto and Tapsell – were exhausted, but exhilarated.

But when the votes were counted, the Conservatives – who in the last days were expecting a really large majority – were disappointed. On a voters' turnout of 76.8 per cent, it transpired that the Labour vote had fallen by 1.5 million, but that the Conservative vote had also fallen from 13.7 million to 13.3. This gave the Conservatives and their allies 345 seats as opposed to Labour's 277, the Liberals 6, and Sinn Fein 2 – a healthy majority, but not as healthy as had been expected in the last days of the campaign. Still, it was more than sufficient, and for a Party in government to win re-election in peacetime with an increased majority had not been achieved since 1900. Eden's determination to go for a quick election had been abundantly justified, and his own personal authority and popularity greatly enhanced.

It was unfortunate that, the victory won, no steps were taken to complete the reorganization of the Government, but it was immediately faced with a locomotive drivers' strike and another in the docks, which necessitated the declaration of a state of emergency before both were brought to an end, after much industrial and economic damage had been done. Throughout, Eden was concerned to keep the dialogue between employers and unions going, and representatives of the TUC and the Federation of British Industries were invited to Downing Street. He fully shared the dislike of both sides for legislation to curb unions' powers – a clear legacy from Baldwin and the 1920s – and his attitude throughout was firm but conciliatory. What he did achieve was the acceptance of a twenty-one-day 'cooling off' period between a decision to strike and actual action. Although this was not contained in legislation, its general acceptance seemed at the time to be at least one step forward.

Eden's dominant concerns and interests, however, remained in foreign affairs. The six principal European powers of the European Coal and Steel Community met early in June at Messina, in Italy, and they agreed to begin work on the establishment of 'a common European market, free from all tariff barriers'. Although Britain sent a representative, there was a very large difference between the approaches of Eden and Macmillan. Eden was extremely dubious about this proposed Common Market, bearing particularly in mind the special position of the Commonwealth countries: so was Butler. Macmillan, while he recognized the strength of feeling against full British membership of the proposed European Common Market, urged a much more positive approach, in which Britain should take a lead. There was no meeting of minds on the matter, and relations between the two, never notably warm, cooled appreciably. Eden began to realize the disadvantages of having a strong Foreign Secretary with a mind of his own.

A clear difference was now also opening between the perceptions of Eden and Macmillan about the Egyptian situation. Eden was now so concerned about Nasser's virulent anti-West propaganda and actions that he proposed an international military force to protect the Suez Canal in the event of war between Egypt and Israel. The British decision to permit the French to use Cyprus as a refuelling stop for the Mystère fighters being delivered to the Israelis was the cause of Nasser's dramatic public announcement on 27 September that he had secured a substantial amount of modern military equipment, including jet aircraft, from Czechoslovakia. This clear evidence of Soviet involvement was a deeply serious event. Eden told the Cabinet on 4 October that 'our interests in the Middle East oil, and our experience in the area is greater than [the United States']', and that Britain must not be restricted over-much by reluctance to act without full American support. He made enquiries of the British Ambassador Humphrey Trevelyan in Cairo about Nasser's position; Trevelyan reported that Nasser's position and popularity were greater than ever because of the Czech arms deal and the announcement of keen Russian interest in financing Nasser's most cherished project, the Aswan High Dam. Macmillan's view, as he told the Cabinet on 20 October, was that although the Russians 'had clearly embarked on a deliberate policy of opening up another front in the Cold War' there was no need for despondency. Eden argued that the best counter would be for the West to finance the Dam. On this there was no disagreement, but Eden's gradually increasing hostility to, and apprehensions of, Nasser were not wholly shared by the Foreign Office or the Foreign Secretary, who urged caution; Macmillan told Eden that he did 'not propose to pursue' the Prime Minister's idea of an international force for the Canal. The differences were of degree, but they were significant. It was probably at this point that Eden became convinced that he would have to find another Foreign Secretary, a thought that had occurred to him more than once during the summer.

But Macmillan was not the only senior minister with whom Eden was having difficulties. Although it is a generalization, it is fair to say that British Prime Ministers tend to fall into one of two categories – the Olympian and the Interferer. From almost the day he entered Downing Street, Eden was the latter. Even if he had had real experience in domestic matters this constant interference, usually in the form of telephone calls at inconvenient times, would have been irritating to busy ministers, who had got used to the latter-day Churchillian Olympian method of conducting business. Perhaps some had become rather too relaxed under this genial regime and needed sharpening up, but Eden's methods aroused the maximum annoyance, creating an atmosphere of tension that was not helpful. Those who had only heard reports of Eden's famous temper now experienced it personally, and disliked it. He also seemed excessively concerned about the press, seizing upon some report or allegation and at once demanding, often in peremptory terms, an immediate explanation. Clarissa Eden's fierce and loving protectiveness of her husband, and her burning faith in him, were admirable and were admired, but this also had its disadvantages.

One of the great pleasures of working with Churchill was that, although he hated criticism, he could listen to it, and his private entourage was not frightened of him. Eden, to everybody's surprise, proved not to have this quality as Prime Minister, and he generated a nervousness and self-doubt that at first seemed a mere nuisance, but which over the months became corroding. When even so relaxed and calm a man as Home became exasperated by the daily telephone calls, too often at very early or very late hours, the reactions of others less urbane may be gauged. Some put this down to ill health and overwork; others began to believe that he simply did not have the temperament to be a successful Prime Minister; others, more shrewdly, guessed that the basic cause was his lack of self-confidence in any area except foreign affairs. Even at this very early stage, Eden's lack of practical experience in domestic politics was becoming clear to his colleagues.

It would be wrong to exaggerate this unease at Eden's methods of working, but what is striking is that it began so early, and pervaded Whitehall and Westminster so soon. Those ministers who had initially welcomed prime ministerial energy after the comparative lassitude of the last period of Churchill's reign now entertained doubts. What they did notice was that his weekends at Rose Bower or Chequers had an almost magical effect on his nerves, temper and judgement. 'A sweetly full of Wiltshire rest and zest,' as Clarissa Eden wrote in her diary. It was a pity that they were not there more often, and for longer.

On the matter of handling the press, Eden was a complete innocent, and

Clark's abilities were matched by deficiencies that included garrulousness and indiscretions which found their way back to Downing Street. He was in fact immensely loyal – although at times this was doubted by some at Number 10 – but it was not the best of appointments to a very sensitive post. It was significant that Eden was genuinely astonished, and even shocked, to learn that in the Churchill regime a small group met regularly to decide which confidential documents should be leaked to the press, and specifically to which newspapers and reporters. One political correspondent in particular was at first bewildered, and then enraged, when his sources of information suddenly dried up, and became notably hostile to the Eden Government as a result. For reasons that I do not comprehend, the Berry family, and particularly Lady Pamela Berry, the wife of the owner of the *Daily Telegraph*, turned against Eden so strongly that Eden began to feel that there was a deliberate vendetta against him; Malcolm Muggeridge was cruel and unrelenting in *Punch*; Randolph Churchill in the *Evening Standard* rarely lost an opportunity of pouring scorn and worse upon Eden personally in his column. From a very early stage the Eden Government received a bad press.

There was one incident that was very small in itself, but that said much. Clarissa remarked to the Chequers administrator that she did not particularly like seeing the family washing of a tenant fluttering on a clothes line that was clearly visible from Chequers and by the distinguished international guests visiting the Prime Minister. On being told of this, the tenant promptly rang up the press, with the result that a horde of reporters descended, and the cartoonists had a marvellous time. Clarissa was consumed with remorse that a polite request had caused all this turmoil, and was very worried that it might cause her husband more public odium. Eden dismissed it for the absurd triviality that it was, but, magnified out of all proportion, it gave a bad impression at a difficult time, and certainly did not raise the Edens' estimation of Fleet Street, particularly when reporters eagerly asked other tenants about Lady Eden's allegedly imperious methods, without receiving any evidence, to their disappointment.

Eden was resolved to force a stiff and strong pace on his ministers, as he had always done in Office, and one is reminded of Cadogan's lament that Eden 'always wanted *to do* something'. A goad can be a useful device, but when used to excess has its disadvantages.

There was also the problem for a Party leader that there were certain aspects of politics that Eden keenly disliked, particularly people seeking Honours, or requesting an opportunity to give him their views. A good – and not at all untypical – example of this occurred in March 1956 when the retiring Chairman of the National Union, Mrs Evelyn Emmet, wrote to him to remind him, meaningly, that she had worked for the Party for twenty-five years and that 'There are some things I would like to say, if you can spare me half an hour of your valuable time.' Mrs Emmet, MP for East Grinstead, was far from being one of Eden's favourite colleagues, and he viewed the prospect of a meeting with her with much distaste. 'The Prime Minister cannot see Mrs Emmet in the near future and he does not particularly want to do so at all,' Philip de Zulueta of the Prime Minister's Private Office minuted. 'What would the Chief Whip advise? I think that the Prime Minister will have to write to Mrs Emmet anyway, but the terms of his reply will depend on what the Chief Whip says.' Heath replied that 'I believe she has some inkling of your views about her and, as she is not without influence, it might be quite a good thing to give you her view of the Party as she has seen it as Chairman of the National Union for the past year. Perhaps you could spare her a few minutes in two or three weeks' time?' On this wise minute Eden bleakly noted 'Yes, A.E.' His letter to her notably lacked enthusiasm, and, pleading 'an unusually heavy burden of work at the moment', postponed the unwelcome occasion for a month, and then reduced it to a hurried fifteen minutes. It was all understandable, but in political terms very unwise.

There was another side to Eden the Prime Minister, and the man.

Ten Downing Street is a home as well as the Prime Minister's office, and the Edens were unusual in that they both loved the house, for which many Prime Ministers and their wives have developed a considerable dislike. Clarissa Eden was particularly interested in restoring the State Rooms, which had been grievously redecorated in the 1930s, and she found Sir John Soane's original plans and wallpaper; but her husband, exhorting his colleagues on spending cuts, found it difficult to press this proposal. What nobody realized was that Downing Street was in a terrible structural condition, and had to be virtually rebuilt between 1960 and 1963. The later changes were more controversial. Many who knew 'the old Number 10' felt that it had lost its unique character through the changes. Clarissa Eden thought it 'the loveliest house in London' and for the first time in her life had staff to assist her. Her standards of hospitality were as high as her husband's, and much higher than those of the Government's official hospitality organization. At one of her dinners she heard Dulles say to his neighbour, with vivid memories of many British official dinners, 'I bet you five pounds I can tell you exactly what every course is going to be.' It was with great satisfaction that she saw him lose his bet; she had brought in a private caterer.

She very much liked the garden, especially because it had such potential, and at the height of the Suez Crisis was to gain some relaxation by planting roses and lilies. She also saw to it that not all the guests were politicians or visiting statesmen and that old friends were remembered. Those first months were supremely happy; Clarissa Eden was the youngest Prime Minister's wife in memory, and her influence was strong, while Eden himself looked years younger than the gaunt and haggard man of 1953–4. With the youthful Robert Carr, the whole atmosphere was one of youth and excitement, in very marked contrast with the last Churchill years. All prospects looked fair.

In 1955, Charles Mott-Radclyffe, Conservative MP for Windsor, had lost his wife, and was deeply saddened and low in spirits. During a division at the House of Commons, Eden went over to him and asked, 'How are you sleeping?', to which Mott-Radclyffe replied, 'Not very well.' A few days later he received an invitation to lunch at Downing Street. He accepted, assuming that it was an official occasion to which he had been kindly invited. When he arrived at Number 10 he was greeted by the butler, who apologized for the fact that the Prime Minister was detained, but he had been instructed to show the guest to the drawing-room and to offer him a drink. Shortly afterwards, Mott-Radclyffe was joined by the Edens, and he suddenly realized that he was the only guest. Eden had gone to great trouble to choose his best wines for the lunch, and Mott-Radclyffe was overwhelmed by the care and thoughtfulness that they had put into the occasion. After a delicious lunch and excellent talk, Eden had to excuse himself to return to work, and asked Mott-Radclyffe when he had to return to the House. When he said not until later, Eden said, 'Then, you must go into the drawing-room, have a good sleep, and the butler will wake you up with a cup of tea when it is time for you to have to leave.' Mott-Radclyffe did so, and never forgot this example of Eden's sensitive understanding of his unhappiness and the great trouble to which the Prime Minister and his wife had gone to try to cheer him up.

This was not at all untypical. What some of his friends and staff have called, rather oddly, Eden's 'feminine side', by which they meant his propensity to take political matters too personally and his over-sensitivity to criticism, had its very positive aspects. He had always been an admirable host, and Clarissa Eden's touch was sure. If he had few real friends in politics, they were staunch and tried. There was nothing artificial or contrived in his kindness and charm, least of all with children. If he seemed to live on his nerves, and often appeared fraught and tense, he did have the capacity to relax, and Rose Bower was his haven and the Wiltshire countryside his joy. As Clarissa once wrote, on their return to Rose Bower after a heavy week: 'We are very happy to be at the Bower – roses, sweet peas – lobster, strawberries & cream, Mersault – complete peace and enclosure from the world.' Eden had found total happiness in his marriage, the only disappointment being that their great desire to have a child was destined not to be fulfilled. Clarissa's miscarriage in 1954 was a keenly felt tragedy, but their devotion to each other was intense and Eden had a personal contentment he had never before experienced.

His health remained good, and it seemed that Cattell's surgery had put him into the small percentage who made a complete recovery from that operation. There were some bad days and nights, but no fevers, and his judgement or capacity for work were in no way affected. His appetite for the latter, however, was perhaps excessive. But it was not in his nature to run at a medium pace when so much needed to be done, and his determination to succeed at his job was intense – in retrospect, too intense.

Some selection of Eden's personal minutes in 1955 on matters other than foreign affairs have their interest.

Minister of Defence, 6 June
On my recent extended travels throughout the country, I have noticed with some concern what appears to be the steady encroachment of the military authorities on what remains of our agricultural land. Aerodromes as well as Army establishments seem still to be going up everywhere. Is my impression correct? And when can we hope to see an end to the business?

I feel sure that you are keeping a vigilant eye on all this. Of course it is always tempting to sprawl and the Service Departments are quite good at it. But with all our balance of payments difficulties looming ahead, every acre that can grow food is of value to us.

To the Chancellor of the Exchequer, 7 July
... I have read the minutes of the Economic Policy Committee with much interest. I do not agree with all that was said about the advantages of increasing prices to the consumer. I quite understand that this, taken individually and in isolation, helps to 'mop up purchasing power'. But is it realistic to suppose that increases in the cost of necessities such as coal and bread will not lead to demands for further wage increases, not all of which can be resisted? Such wage increases push up our costs and reduce our competitive power. We cannot afford to be priced out of the export market. Surely our policy should aim at keeping the cost of living stable?

To the same, 13 July (on The Remuneration of Ministers)
... I am a little concerned at the comparison you make between the remuneration we receive as Ministers and the salaries of professional posts of various kinds, for after all Ministerial Office is not a career.... If people are going to wish to stay in Office because of the money they get there, apart from the attractions of political life, they are going to be more difficult than ever to remove, and removed some of them must be, as I know you agree....

To the Minister of Labour, 29 July
Lord Nuffield came to see me, and authorized me to pass on to you, that after a lifetime in the motor car industry he believed that the secret ballot would solve industrial difficulties. In his view the men would most of them prefer it. He

415

reminded me that, during the 1926 strike, in 46 establishments which he controlled not one man came out.

I expressed my view that the secret ballot, although useful on certain cases, would not cure unofficial strikes. He said that he was speaking not only of a secret ballot before a strike but also of a secret ballot in elections of union officials.

He emphasized that the Electrical Trades Union was in a dangerous situation being Communist led and pointed to them as an example of a union which would be much better if its officials were elected by secret ballot.

But Walter Monckton, the Minister of Labour, was not convinced, and, most regrettably, the matter was dropped for nearly thirty years, to the profound disadvantage of British industry and the trade union movement itself. Eden was definitely interested, and a more confident and experienced Prime Minister might well have overriden Monckton's characteristic irresolution and caution about doing anything that might possibly evoke trade union hostility, but Eden accepted Monckton's judgement, and a great opportunity slipped by.

Eden was worried by the economy, the increase in inflation and imports, a poor export record and the heavy burden of defence expenditure. Ideally, he would have liked to end military conscription completely and revert to all-volunteer professional armed forces, but this was resisted strongly by the Chiefs of Staff, who pointed out, with reason, that only if the Government agreed to further drastic cuts in its commitments in Europe, Cyprus, the Middle East and in the African and Caribbean colonies could this be possible. What Eden did achieve was a reduction in the numbers of those conscripted to 100,000 a year, and he looked forward to abolishing it altogether; this was to be achieved by his successor.

On the economy he wanted more tax cuts, greater incentives for industry and savers, and the raising of reserves; he agreed with Butler's belief that there would have to be a credit squeeze. He spelt out his concerns in a particularly long minute to Butler on 17 August which, with qualifications, echoed Butler's own concerns and proposed remedies, including the ending of the bread subsidy – which was to cause notable uproar, but was unquestionably right. On 30 August he minuted to Butler that 'we must put the battle against inflation before anything else. . . . If we . . . could take a series of steps aimed at reducing the cost of living we should have a right to speak to [both sides of industry] and the Nation will back us up. Can we work these out?' But Butler was moving rapidly in the direction of increasing purchase tax and a comprehensive credit squeeze; Eden's judgement was to prove more sound, but again he did not press his concerns too strongly on his Chancellor. It would have been better if he had. As he wrote to Butler on 3 September, 'if our plans were thought to be partial either in the political or economic sense, the nation would lose confidence in us, and we should deserve this'. Butler would have been wise to heed this advice, but the strain of four years at the Treasury and the loss of his wife was exerting its toll, far more than he or Eden fully realized at the time. Eden's concern, minutes and frequent telephone calls irritated him mightily. One of Rab Butler's most attractive qualities – unless one was on the receiving end – was his sardonic and often malicious wit, which was usually at the expense of his colleagues. The trouble was that these sallies often got to the ears of their victims, who were displeased, and Butler thereby had acquired a reputation for disloyalty. My own view was that he simply could not resist a witticism, and that few of them – if any – were carefully prepared. They just bubbled out, to the delight of those closest to him; but they had an unfortunate habit of being gleefully repeated in Whitehall, and came to the attention of those who had been mocked. If they laughed at all, it was with much uneasiness; most did not laugh. On a more serious plane, Eden was uncomfortable about what Butler was now proposing.

Eden's minutes continued to cover a very wide range of issues.

To the Home Secretary, 13 October
I have seen several reports and some complaints of light sentences on drivers who are found drunk in charge of a car. Am I right in thinking that they do get off too lightly? If so, is this due to the law or leniency on the part of the magistrates? If the law is at fault, I feel sure that Parliament would be willing to strengthen it.

The Home Office responded that the law was adequate, but that a circular of advice would be sent to magistrates. The results were negligible; public tolerance of drunken driving was destined to continue, on the 'There but for the grace of God go I' principle.

Eden's resistance to Churchill's great summit of the Four Powers had been less on substance than on form, and from the beginning of his Government he was resolved upon further improvement of East–West relations. The most notable tangible sign of this was the Soviet agreement to the independence and reunification of Austria and the withdrawal of their forces, on which Eden had been patiently negotiating for years. As this was the first instance – and, at the time of writing, the only one – of the Russians voluntarily withdrawing from a territory they had occupied by force, Eden was particularly eager to capitalize on the apparent new mood in the Kremlin. Eisenhower and Dulles remained sceptical, but they were willing to help Eden at the beginning of his premiership, and also saw the opportunity of building upon the new advances. The Russians had initiated the proposal on 26 May, proposing Vienna, but the Western Powers asked for Geneva as a more suitable site, to which the Russians agreed. The meetings were opened by Eisenhower personally, who made an offer of reciprocal military information to reduce the possibility of serious misunderstandings; Eden proposed a security pact between the Powers and a reunited Germany. The latter once again met with a firm rejection by Bulganin, but the discussions were characterized by what the *Annual Register* has called 'a uniform amiability'.

In his report to the House of Commons on 27 July, Eden was also able to announce that Bulganin and Khrushchev had accepted his invitation to visit Britain in the following spring. All comments were highly favourable, and the passage of the Austrian State Treaty Bill was also marked by warm praise for Eden and Macmillan. Parliament rose for the Summer Recess with the Conservatives in good heart, and the Government's standing high, despite denunciation by the *Economist* of the Government's programme as 'stodgy'. The newspaper, rail and dock strikes had all ended, and the state of emergency was ended. Abroad, the outlook seemed exceptionally bright. At home, few knew of Butler's growing concern about the economy, which was to prompt him to ask for the recall of Parliament in September; this Eden at first supported, then strongly resisted.

But the problems were mounting. One subject that concerned ministers was the arrival in Britain of an increasing number of West Indian immigrants, which by 1955 numbered some 50,000. Churchill had been particularly alarmed by this development, as was Salisbury, who warned the Cabinet of the effect on 'the racial character of the English people' if unrestricted immigration were permitted to continue unchecked; percipiently, he warned of the possibility of massive immigration from the Indian subcontinent, which in 1955 was virtually non-existent. The problem was that under the then concept and law of United Kingdom citizenship and British passport holders, most Commonwealth citizens had the legal right to settle in Britain, and both Lennox-Boyd and Home were concerned by the political effects in the Commonwealth of legislation that would clearly be discriminatory against black and coloured Commonwealth citizens, while the Whips reported that Private Members' Bills hostile to immigration introduced by Cyril Osborne, MP for Louth, had been decisively voted down by Conservatives.

The matter was referred to a Cabinet committee chaired by Kilmuir, the Lord Chancellor (formerly Sir David Maxwell Fyfe); it was to be more than six years before the Conservative Government faced up to this problem – which by 1961 had become considerably worse – and then only timidly, for which it was denounced as 'racist' by Gaitskell and the Labour Opposition. Eden's own preference was for limiting entry for five years only, and this was one option referred to the Kilmuir committee, whose labours in the end produced nothing of value. The matter continued to drift, with momentous consequences. To be fair, these were very difficult to foresee in 1955. Lloyd George reported that the West Indians were in the main law-abiding, employed, and did not make any 'undue' demands on National Assistance; the only real problem they presented, in which they were not alone, was in housing. This 'influx' must also be seen in the context of an unemployment figure of less than 1 per cent and a labour demand for unskilled workers which was filled by the new immigrants. It is too easy to be wise after the event.

Meanwhile, the Cyprus situation deteriorated. Archbishop Makarios may well have been an exceptionally devious and bad man, but the indications were that real control had passed to the Communists and to EOKA (National Organization for the Cyprus Struggle), which was characterized by fanatical ruthlessness and led with considerable skill and brutality. All British attempts at tripartite negotiation foundered on Greek and Turkish obduracy – especially the former – although Eden, Macmillan and Lennox-Boyd tried hard throughout the summer and early autumn for a reasonable settlement. By the end of September, it was decided to strengthen British forces in the island and to send Field-Marshal Sir John Harding as Governor. All attempts at mediation having failed, a state of emergency was declared on 26 November. British casualties began to mount, and the atmosphere became acrid. Three NATO nations were in bitter dispute, and British troops were being killed and injured. The British offered a substantial measure of self-government and economic aid, but Makarios and the Greek Government obstinately and arrogantly stood out for complete self-determination and *enosis* (union with Greece) on a majority vote, which the Turks would not contemplate. Passions rose, blood was shed, and in the middle of this dismal tragedy stood The Poor Bloody British Infantryman.

That first summer of the Eden Government also included one decision that was to have considerable long-term results.

The campaign for the abolition of the death penalty for murder had been active for several years, but the proposal had been consistently voted down in the Commons, although with gradually diminishing majorities. Sadly, it had become politicized, so that with only a few exceptions Labour was for abolition, the Conservatives for retention: it was a highly emotive issue among Conservative Party activists, and invariably retention was strongly and enthusiastically endorsed by the Party Conference. But there were already indications that among the new Conservative MPs there was a significant number who were for abolition, at least for a trial period, and their concerns were greatly heightened by the case of Mrs Ruth Ellis.

Ruth Ellis was a sad, brittle but attractive woman who had, under great provocation and not long after a miscarriage, shot and killed her former lover, David Blakely, who had deserted her. No one else was involved, and it was a classic case of a crime of passion by a distraught young woman. Murder is murder, and there was no question of her guilt; what few expected was that she would actually be executed.

It was a long-standing convention that the decision whether to advise the Royal Prerogative of Mercy or to let the law take its course was exclusively the duty and the responsibility of the Home Secretary, who in 1955 was Gwilym Lloyd George. It was a task that no one in public life envied him, but as he alone had full access to all the details of each case it was accepted that it must be an individual judgement.

The Ellis case evoked exceptionally intense press and public interest, to the point when, most unusually in capital cases, it was discussed by the Cabinet; when it was pointed out that public opinion was aroused to an unusual degree, Lloyd George responded that such opinion by itself was 'an unreliable basis for a policy'. To considerable surprise, Lloyd George could find no redeeming features, and refused to make a recommendation for mercy.

Eden makes no reference whatever to this matter in his memoirs, and there is nothing in his papers about the case. He accepted that the decision was the responsibility of the Home Secretary, in whom he had full confidence, but there are indications that he was troubled about it – and with good cause. Even many hardened supporters of the death penalty were appalled, and its opponents raised a storm of frenzied protest inside and outside Parliament. They could not save Ruth Ellis, who was hanged on 13 July, but the cause of abolition had made a considerable advance; indeed it was her execution that made many previous unthinking supporters of the death penalty reconsider the matter, and it can be seen as a major turning-point in public attitudes towards the death penalty. In immediate political terms, Lloyd George's decision did the Government no good at all, and the personal position of Lloyd George never fully recovered in the House of Commons. As the events of the following spring and summer demonstrated, a major shift in public and parliamentary opinion was the result of a decision that was manifestly the wrong one.

Ruth Ellis' execution also coincided with the publication of a book by Michael Eddowes on Timothy Evans, hanged in 1950 for the murder of his child. The case had aroused little attention at the time, but in 1953 it was discovered that Evans had shared the same house as the palpably insane pathological mass-murderer Christie, who had been the principal witness against Evans; at his own trial Christie said that he had murdered Mrs Evans, among many others. As the *Economist* wrote of the book, 'If Evans had not been hanged, but sentenced to life imprisonment, he would be a free man today, for, once the facts in the Christie case were known, no Home Secretary could have kept him in prison.'

These matters added to the burdens of Government, and put new strains on the cohesion of the Conservative Parliamentary Party at a very early stage of the new Parliament.

Another problem was how to handle the defection to the Soviet Union in 1951 of the Foreign Office officials Donald Maclean and Guy Burgess. The Australian Royal Commission investigating Soviet operations in Australia had produced more damaging information, and the Labour MP, Marcus Lipton, named their colleague, Kim Philby, under the protection of parliamentary privilege, as 'the Third Man' who had tipped them off that they were under investigation. Nothing had been found against Philby, but he had left the Foreign Service and had become a journalist specializing in Middle East matters. The defection had been under the Labour Government, and Eden was anxious not to imply that the then Foreign Secretary, Morrison, was in any way responsible. None the less, there was genuine public concern, and Eden proposed to Attlee that an all-party conference of Privy Councillors should examine security procedures to prevent any repetition. Attlee entirely agreed, and the debate early in November, opened by Macmillan and closed by Eden, was of a high level. When Eden raised the question of 'How far are we to go in pursuit of greater security at the cost of the essential liberties of the British people?' and invoked the spectre of McCarthyism, he received considerable praise and support, there being no division. It was only several years later that it was known that Philby had indeed been 'the Third Man', and Lipton's apology to the House for his allegation was formally expunged from the record. At the time, the speeches of Macmillan and Eden were widely praised; what is strange is that Eden makes no reference whatever to the matter in his memoirs. The feeling at the time was that the Government, and Eden in particular, had handled it sensitively and admirably – as indeed they had, given the information at their disposal.

The history of this episode has not yet run its course, but it forms no part of a biography of Anthony Eden.

The first serious setback to the Government's position concerned the economy, a crucial area in which, as with foreign affairs, the Churchill Government had seemed to excel. Butler's achievements since 1951, and his uniquely urbane style and self-confidence, were very considerable, but the death of his devoted wife Sydney in December 1954 from cancer had been a terrible blow: 'the domestic shock was not at once fully apparent but gained increasing force during the year,' as he subsequently wrote. If his pre-election Budget had been a success, his revising one in October, concentrating on profits and restoring purchase taxes reduced in April, was a political disaster. It gave Gaitskell, actively seeking the Labour leadership, his great opportunity, which he seized eagerly and superbly; Butler fought back with equal verve, destroying the hapless Morrison, who had ineptly moved a motion of censure, with a speech of merciless effectiveness that settled the Labour leadership there and then. But Eden, coming to Butler's support at the end of the rowdy debate, made an ineffective speech. Shouting above the hubbub of a post-dinner Commons, with the Opposition out for blood, was not his style, nor was the economy his subject, and although the Conservatives loyally cheered him on, it was with unease. He himself was as unhappy about his own performance as he was with the alarmingly rapid decline of the Government's fortunes. The retirement of Attlee at the beginning of December and the easy victory of Gaitskell over Bevan and Morrison for the Labour leadership was another indication that matters were unlikely to become any easier.

Gaitskell became leader of the Labour Party at the worst possible moment for Eden and a nervous Conservative Party. The emergence of a younger man as Leader of the Opposition is never welcome to an incumbent Prime Minister already under pressure; even less welcome was one who had been Chancellor of the Exchequer and had made a formidable reputation in Opposition both in the House of Commons and in his Party, in which he had definitely emerged as the spokesman of moderate anti-Bevanite Socialism. Highly intelligent, articulate, responsible, and in personality the complete antithesis of Bevan's jibe about 'a desiccated calculating machine', Gaitskell posed a challenge to Eden from the moment of his election as Leader. Conservatives hoped that the animosity between him and the Labour left would continue, but were unsure even about this. A week after Gaitskell's election, the Conservative candidate for Torquay, Frederic Bennett, was re-elected with a fall of 9.4 per cent in the Conservative share of the poll, which in those days was regarded as near-cataclysmic. Conservatives had become unused to such reverses, and the reaction was disproportionately strong.

The feeling that a significant restructuring of the Government was essential was shared by the press, the Conservative Party and the Prime Minister himself. If it had been done in the long Summer Recess it would have been far better, but the personal and political issues Eden faced were not easy. To have replaced Butler before the hapless autumn Budget would have looked like base ingratitude to a recently bereaved colleague, to one of the unquestioned successes of the Churchill Government, and a major contributor, as many considered, to the May election triumph. Macmillan had hardly settled into the Foreign Office; Crookshank, as Leader of the

House, retained his attractive dominance over the Commons; Monckton was universally popular; Buchan-Hepburn was considered the outstanding Chief Whip of his generation, and Lloyd George an excellent Home Secretary. By December, none of these judgements held true. Eden had hoped that he could make his changes carefully, and in his own time, but by December the shrill calls for change had become accompanied by severe and unfair criticisms of his weakness and lack of resolution. Thus when the changes did come at the end of 1955 they gave the unhappy impression of being a hurried response to Party and press clamour, whereas in truth they reflected the experiences of the previous six months.

As early as September Eden had confided his concerns to Butler, the latter recording in his diary at the time that

The P.M. is an artist far more able and resolute than the newspapers give him credit for. He had, he said, sedulously attempted to avoid interference with the Foreign Office. Having been there so long he found it difficult to work with so strong a character as Harold Macmillan.... Anthony said that he had never had the idea that I should go to the Foreign Office since I would be under him and that he would not like. He fancied Selwyn [Lloyd] for the F.O. and said he would be the best subordinate.*

But the shuffle itself was maladroit. While it was not the wide-ranging reconstruction many believed necessary, several of the changes proved unfortunate. To move Butler was probably inevitable, and in his own interests as well as those of the Government, but his replacement by Macmillan was to prove a profound error. The causes lay deep in long-standing personal antipathy, but the short-term causes were that Eden had found it impossible to stop his eyes wandering often and critically towards the Foreign Secretary. He had appointed a strong, energetic and ambitious man who enjoyed his job and was demonstrating clear signs of developing his own views and policies. Eden, ironically enough, was in the same difficulties as Prime Minister towards his Foreign Secretary as Neville Chamberlain had been with him. Why Eden had appointed Macmillan in the first place remains a mystery; but by September he believed that he had made a mistake, and Butler's retirement to lead the House of Commons as Lord Privy Seal seemed to provide an excellent opportunity of rectifying the error while mollifying Macmillan by giving him the Treasury.

But, far from being mollified, Macmillan was greatly angered by what he considered to be an unmerited demotion after only nine months from a post he had long coveted, while Butler quickly regretted accepting a post without any departmental element, which he later considered the

* Butler, *The Art of the Possible*, pp. 180–1.

greatest blunder of his career. Eden had also lost an outstanding departmental minister, who revelled in ideas and legislative skills, which were wasted in his new post. Crookshank and Woolton retired, but a truly strange selection was that of Walter Monckton for Defence. Monckton had little experience in this area, nor much interest in it. He was exhausted after his long period at Labour, and his real ambition – never fulfilled – was to be Lord Chief Justice. He was accordingly a tired and disappointed man, who took up his new responsibilities without enthusiasm. Eden had great affection for him, was grateful to him for his advice and assistance, and wanted him beside him in the Cabinet. This was very understandable, but to give Monckton a post which he did not want and in which he was not interested was a major mistake – how major was to become apparent in due course. But Eden also believed that the period of appeasing the unions, at great immediate benefit but at heavy long-term cost, must end, and a stronger man was needed. His eyes had been on the exceptional Iain Macleod for some time, and it was he who took Monckton's place. Also, the appointment of Heath as Chief Whip (Buchan-Hepburn becoming Minister of Works) and the entry of Home into the full Cabinet were admirable.

A very fortunate survivor of the changes was Nutting, whose conduct as Minister of State at the United Nations General Assembly in the early winter had been such as to cause acute embarrassment and serious discussion about his immediate recall. Eden knew that Nutting's marriage was under serious strain, and for a senior minister to be recalled before the end of the Assembly would only increase the rumours that were widespread in New York and bring the matter under intense press scrutiny. It may have been this factor that also prevented Eden from dropping him from the Government in the reshuffle, but although his papers on this unfortunate episode are very complete, they do not give the answer; my estimate is that the cause was loyalty to a friend in personal difficulties. It was to prove very singularly misplaced and ill rewarded, and did not even save Nutting's marriage, which foundered shortly afterwards. Macmillan, who had been understandably outraged by Nutting's conduct as a minister on duty, went from the Foreign Office, and Nutting stayed. These were to prove grievous errors, for which Eden paid very dearly.

Eden's appointment of Selwyn Lloyd to replace Macmillan occasioned considerable surprise, but brought to the Foreign Office a colleague whom he had hardly known in 1951 but whom he had come to trust and respect. The trouble was that Lloyd's experience in Parliament and foreign affairs did not approximate to Macmillan's, and the suspicion was freely expressed that Eden, intent on being his own Foreign Secretary, had appointed a tame nonentity rather than tolerate a politician of his own rank in the Party and the House of Commons. This was harsh on Lloyd, and took no account of the tense relationship between Eden and Macmillan, but it did contain the truth. Therein lay the fundamental difficulty of Lloyd's position. He was liked in the House of Commons, but not extravagantly so. His Dispatch Box manner was somewhat wooden, and he gave the impression – wrongly, as it happened – of being devoid of humour and political sensitivity. Abroad, his appointment caused puzzlement. Lloyd himself confessed to having misgivings 'about a Minister with only eight months' experience in the Cabinet taking over the very senior post of Foreign Secretary', and he was not alone.

The House of Commons and the press had become used to strong Foreign Secretaries, Morrison being generally regarded as a melancholy aberration between Bevin and Eden, and Macmillan appearing to take the dominant role that was expected. Lloyd, derided by a rising young political journalist, Bernard Levin, as 'Hoylake Urban District Council', did not seem to fit the mould. He sounded legalistic, unfamiliar with the scale of the problems confronting him and out of his depth. Again, there was at least some truth in these apprehensions. But the fact was that Eden had found Lloyd to be a diligent deputy whom he liked and had confidence in, and this was what he wanted and needed rather than a putative challenger whom he distrusted. No one, least of all the profoundly disgruntled Macmillan, could conceive what momentous results would flow from this decision.

The reshuffle was poorly received by the Party and the press, and personal criticism of the Prime Minister increased in normally loyal newspapers, notably the *Daily Mail* and the *Daily Telegraph*, especially the latter, which carried a virulent article by Donald McLachlan entitled, 'The Firm Smack of Government'. This said that one of Eden's speaking characteristics was to clench his right fist and punch it into his open left hand – but stopping at the last moment. The implications were clear, and Eden responded with what Butler has called 'a pained and pungent oath'. Eden wrote in his diary for 3 January 1956:

Torrents of abuse these days in press. *D[aily] T[elegraph]* has of course encouraged Tory discontent, because nobody knows the personal vendetta that lies behind it. But on the whole I think that the enemy is overplaying his hand.

7 January
Y[orkshire] P[ost] has a very helpful article as *Express* had yesterday, but this is about the lot. Otherwise plenty of attack. Personally I think overdone.... Clark rings up to say *People* are to carry story that I am resigning in June & begging for denial, which I reluctantly gave.

This was a dreadful mistake, as both Eden and Clark soon realized. What was intended to be simply a denial of a specific newspaper story that was pure and inaccurate speculation appeared to take the form of an official statement that only made matters much worse. Butler, asked at London Airport as he was leaving for a much needed holiday whether Eden was 'the best Prime Minister we have got', naturally replied 'Yes', which was widely misquoted as 'he is the best Prime Minister we have got', words which ricocheted round the world as a feline disparagement of Eden.* When Butler realized what had happened, as Eden noted, 'Rab from airport & Oliver [Chandos] from his home rang up to complain about press. I promised them I was quite unconcerned. *D.T.* had really made the mischief.'

Eden was genuinely angered by his bad press, but instead of ignoring the matter, as he should have done, he embarked on a counter-attack, devoting a speech at Bradford on 18 January to an unwise denunciation of 'cantankerous newspapers' and pledging that the Government and he ('If God wills') would serve their full term. His Conservative audience cheered him warmly, but even in Bradford there was uneasiness about what seemed to be serious overreaction to the press. It is indeed difficult to quarrel with this estimate. It was an unpromising beginning to 1956.

From these domestic tribulations Eden travelled to the United States on the *Queen Elizabeth* on 25 January, with the Middle East situation at the top of his agenda. The new Soviet presence in the area was a particular concern, and the potential cause of a major Israel–Egypt arms race. But while the Americans shared this concern, they were not prepared to offer more than moral support for the Baghdad Pact; as Eden noted, they seemed more impressed by Egyptian and Saudi hostility to it than by its membership and potential. The Americans also, for the first time, expressed doubts, principally on economic grounds, about Eden's enthusiasm for Anglo–American support for the World Bank to build the Aswan High Dam. Lloyd considered the talks 'rather disappointing', the only high spot being Eden's speech to a joint meeting of the US Congress, which contained the passage:

Brought to a halt in Europe, Soviet expansion now feels its way south and probes in other lands. There is nothing particularly new in this. You can read it all in Russian imperialist history. But the emphasis has changed, and the symbol and method, too.

This is a struggle for men's minds, once expressed in these regions in conflicting faiths, but now in rival ideologies. From the Kremlin streams forth into the lands of what we call the Middle East, and into all Asia, a mixture of blandishment and threat, offers of arms and menaces to individuals, all couched in terms of fierce hostility for Western ideals.

* 'I do not think it did Anthony any good,' Butler later wrote. 'It did not do me any good either.'

The Americans were polite and friendly, but in reality little had been achieved.

Meanwhile at home the Government had run into severe difficulties over the death penalty issue. The new House of Commons took a different view from the old, and against Lloyd George's advice voted by 293 to 262 on a free vote on 16 February to suspend the death penalty for an experimental period of five years, forty-eight Conservatives voting with the majority. Not only the Ruth Ellis case had caused this change of view. On 24 January Lloyd George had announced free pardons and compensation for three men wrongly convicted of grievous bodily harm against a policeman; as was pointed out by the opponents of the death penalty, if the policeman had died from his injuries it was virtually certain that at least one of the innocent men would have been hanged.

The Government, itself divided on the matter, and now knowing that it did not have a majority in the Commons on this issue of conscience, then decided to give time for the passage of a Private Member's Bill introduced by Sydney Silverman, a highly vocal but, in the Tory Party, not a widely esteemed Labour MP. Eden contended that the Government could not introduce a Bill itself which its chief spokesman had advised against, and promised that it would again be on a free vote at all stages. Silverman's Bill was carried on Second Reading on 12 March by 286 to 262, and then went to full Committee on the Floor of the House, with results that will be described.

This compromise particularly distressed Conservative activists and supporters outside Westminster, who were overwhelmingly and stridently in favour of the death penalty; but to confuse matters further, all opinion polls demonstrated a majority in favour of abolition. It was not until the autumn of the year, after the Silverman Bill had been rejected by the Lords, that the Government took the lead with a modified Bill that limited the death penalty to specific forms of murder; it was carried through Parliament. It would have saved much time, division within the Government and Party, and accusations of weakness and irresolution hurled at the administration by both sides of the argument, if this had been done earlier.

In January and February the British Government had made great efforts to produce a Cyprus settlement, again with no success. Although the British now had clear evidence from captured documents of Makarios' complicity in the EOKA terrorist campaign, Lennox-Boyd and Harding persevered until it was obviously impossible. The decision was then taken to arrest and deport Makarios, together with the Bishop of Kyrenia and two other implicated priests, to the Seychelles on 9 March, to jam broadcasts from

Athens, and to increase the activities of British forces. These actions may have been justified, but the response was strong both in Cyprus and in the House of Commons. That beautiful island became the scene of bitter inter-communal brutality and anti-British campaigns by EOKA, which had no compunction in using school children in its operations. Harding himself narrowly escaped an assassination attempt, and executions of EOKA terrorists inflamed the situation even further. All British offers of new constitutions, even one that would have given them the overwhelming preponderance in a National Assembly, met with total Greek-Cypriot opposition. When Lennox-Boyd in the House of Commons said that partition could be 'among the eventual options' under self-determination he was roundly denounced by the Labour Party and much abused in Athens. He was to be proved absolutely right, although under very different circumstances. Fanatical Greek-Cypriot bigotry, supported from Greece, drove Cyprus down a road that the Eden Government, to its credit, attempted to prevent. In wanting everything, the Greek-Cypriots destroyed everything, with disastrous results for themselves and Cyprus. In the meanwhile, British troops were killed and injured, Greek and Turkish Cypriots died and suffered, and all British attempts at compromise met the solid rock of utter intransigence.

One of the most important factors in life, politics and war, to which historians tend to devote too little attention, is sheer luck, good or ill; Napoleon's faith in lucky generals contained much wisdom. The last Churchill Government, for all its qualities, had been blessed with much good fortune, from the ending of the Korean War to the dramatic shift in the international trade balance, for which it had very little responsibility, but which made its task considerably easier. Its members could claim with justification that they had worked for, and deserved, their good fortune, but it had certainly been a very lucky Government. But almost from its inception, the Eden Government seemed cursed by bad luck, as if a malevolent being had determined that if anything could go wrong, it would. Butler had stumbled badly over the economy and the world balance of trade had turned against Britain; Lloyd George was in serious difficulties on the home front, not only over capital punishment; Cyprus was becoming grim; even the long-forgotten IRA re-emerged with daring and successful raids on Army arms depots. The conduct of American affairs was erratic, particularly in the Middle East, where the new Soviet involvement caused Eden mounting concern.

A hostile press now blamed him personally for every new shift in ill fortune throughout the world; his response was to work even harder to change the tide, but at times it seemed inexorable.

This sequence of misfortune since the early autumn of 1955 had further increased the burdens of the premiership, coming as they did after five intensive years of hard work and severe illness. Now, another blow fell.

Jordan, and King Hussein personally, occupied a particular place in Eden's interests and concerns in his endeavour to strengthen the Baghdad Pact, to the point where his eagerness to attain Jordanian membership of the Pact pushed Britain into offering further commitments to Jordan that were so comprehensive that towards the end of 1955 the Chiefs of Staff were instructed to prepare plans for military action against Israel – including seaborne invasion – if Israel attacked Jordan. The Chiefs, in presenting their tentative plans, concluded that Jordan's Arab Legion, commanded by General Sir John Glubb, universally known as 'Glubb Pasha' and almost as celebrated in Britain and the Middle East as T. E. Lawrence had once been, was not an impressive military force. The British offered tangible military assistance and equipment to Jordan to counter Saudi money and influence, which were sedulously undermining the position of the Hashemite monarchy in Iraq and had ambitions for change in the Hashemite monarchy in Jordan. At Macmillan's suggestion, the Chief of the Imperial General Staff, Field-Marshal Sir Gerald Templer, flew to Amman to discuss not only supplies of equipment but a new Anglo-Jordanian Pact as soon as Jordan joined the Baghdad Pact; Eden considered that it would be unwise to press Hussein too hard on this, as the King was now coming under intense pressure in Amman from hostile elements loudly encouraged by Radio Cairo and financed by both Egyptian and Saudi forces. So bad was the situation in Jordan itself, and the Legion so stretched, that the British made preliminary measures to hold forces available in Cyprus to go to Hussein's assistance if required, and a clear warning was conveyed to Nasser about his policy of inciting the people of Jordan to civil war and to attacks on her British ally. Saudi Arabia was also told that in the event of a Saudi attack on Jordan – which now looked probable – Britain would fulfil the obligations of the 1948 Treaty. This worked. The Saudis hurriedly drew back their forces from the Jordanian frontier, but increased their subversive activities within Jordan.

Nasser assured the British Ambassador in Cairo, Sir Humphrey Trevelyan, that propaganda against Jordan and Britain would be stopped; in fact, there was no lessening of it, there were more attacks on Iraq, and then an actual increase in virulence against Hussein and Glubb.

Those who at the time and later saw Nasser as a genial, if misguided, Third World leader of an anti-colonialist crusade, concerned only for the liberty and well-being of his people, made, and some continued to make, a grave error. Egypt's internal problems were acute, even desperate, but

Nasser's lavish assistance from the Saudis and the Russians did not go to the poverty-stricken fellahin but was devoted to weapons, to the armed forces on whose total loyalty his very life depended, and to deliberate subversion of the two Hashemite Kingdoms by every means he could command. As he ceaselessly reiterated, the destruction of Israel was the overriding purpose not only of Egypt but of the Arab world, of which he was the self-proclaimed spokesman. His incessant radio propaganda was coarse, but very effective, against the infidel colonialists who still tried to be the Arabs' masters through the treacherous Arab puppets they had created and now sustained. In this there was a subtle and clever admixture of truths and untruths, of nationalism and religion, and of exhorting the oppressed to rise against their oppressors. The combination was a deadly one.

But Eden, in spite of Nasser's activities and the Czech arms deal, had not entirely lost hope. In October 1955 he had prepared for Trevelyan a Note for delivery to Nasser criticizing his conduct strongly, with the result that 'our relationship has deteriorated. The continued vituperation against us in the Egyptian Press and radio has led us to doubt the value of Nasser's assurance. . . . In particular, public opinion in Britain will not tolerate the supply of arms to a country which daily denounces us and which seeks supplies from the East.' Britain was determined to defend her position in the Middle East in face of the Soviet threat to the area: 'In this position we are entitled to ask Egypt where she stands. If Nasser wishes to continue to denounce Britain and oppose British policy in every way, let him say so. If not, let him make determined efforts to carry out the promise he made to me, and he will find me more than willing to meet him halfway.' As evidence of this, Britain was very keen to assist, with the United States and the World Bank, Nasser's most cherished grandiose new project, the Aswan High Dam, in which the Russians were now showing such a keen and positive interest.

There was no deception in this. Eden was pressing the Americans hard to support the dam for political reasons to counter Soviet involvement and as a demonstration of Western goodwill. As he said to Clarissa and to others, 'If the Russians get the contract we have lost Africa.'

But Trevelyan considered this Note 'inopportune', and, on reflection, Eden agreed with him that it should not be delivered 'for the time being'. This may have been a mistake, but it could hardly have made any difference.

Then, on 1 March, without any prior warning, Hussein peremptorily ordered the immediate dismissal of Glubb and his principal officers. Nasser was particularly satisfied, speciously congratulating Selwyn Lloyd, who had the misfortune to be in Cairo when the news broke, on a British action to improve Anglo-Egyptian relations.

As Eden suspected, and this was confirmed by a conversation he had with Glubb on his return to Britain, personal as well as political factors had been involved in Hussein's sudden decision. Eden also knew from the Chiefs of Staff report that Hussein's complaints about the standards of the Legion had some justification, although these were not Glubb's fault. Eden considered that Hussein had made a terrible mistake and, by becoming – very temporarily – a Nasser hero, had got himself into a very dangerous position. Hussein had certainly been influenced by his ADC, Colonel Ali Abu Nuwar, whom he shortly made Chief of Staff, but who later was found in his true colours and had to flee to Egypt for his safety.

The initial reaction of Eden was one of great anger, although it was not quite as violent as Nutting later claimed,* at this humiliation to a loyal servant and to the British position in the Middle East made without warning by a close ally. Although the British thought that Nasser was not directly involved in Glubb's downfall, it was clear that his allies within the Jordanian Government and Army had been, and it looked – and indeed was – a notable victory for his all-pervasive influence in Arab affairs. It was certainly seen as such throughout the Middle East and in the Western press.

But, after an initial flurry of fierce telegrams from London to Amman that remain sensitive, calmer views gradually prevailed. Glubb had himself behaved admirably when he discussed the situation with Eden at Chequers on 4 March, emphasizing to Eden that allowance must be given not only to the severe difficulties of the young King but to the natural feelings towards an older man, a famous foreigner, holding such a position. It was deeply in the interests of the West to help Hussein and to repair the damage. This was also the view of the British Ambassador in Amman, C. B. Duke, and although indignation continued in London, Nasser made the British point by offering to Hussein to make up all lost British aid – if that happened – while the Russians also offered lavish financial and military assistance. Hussein was now very concerned indeed about his position, with good reason, and was anxious to restore Anglo-Jordanian amity. Eden

* Nutting, in his account (*No End of a Lesson*, p. 29), gives a vivid description of keeping Eden up half the night on 1 March, trying to persuade him to modify his indignation against Hussein for Glubb's dismissal. In fact, Eden had striven to avoid any break with Hussein, 'even at the cost of a disastrous Parliamentary debate', as Eden noted in 1970. Eden had no recollection whatever of this discussion with Nutting, and the record of Glubb's visit to luncheon at Chequers on Sunday 4 March discloses that afterwards Nutting, who avers he was not there, was present at a meeting attended by Salisbury, Monckton, the Chiefs of the Imperial General Staff and the Air Staff, and Sir Ivone Kirkpatrick, Permanent Under-Secretary at the Foreign Office. Shuckburgh's note records: '*With the exception of Mr Nutting* [my italics], these stayed to dinner and the meeting continued afterwards. Sir Walter and Lady Monckton stayed the night.'

urged a meeting between him and King Feisal to establish partnership and co-operation with Britain; this took place, and the Glubb crisis itself evaporated.

If Eden had initially overreacted to Glubb's dismissal, as the tone of his telegram to Amman clearly demonstrates he had, so had the British press and the House of Commons. At the very time that Eden was restoring the situation, and, in the absence of Lloyd, carrying the Foreign Office as well as his other responsibilities, the Labour Opposition demanded a debate in the Commons on 7 March. As Eden later wrote, 'I had no time to prepare the speech I must make, and it is always difficult to say nothing convincingly.'* Clarissa Eden wrote in her diary on 7 March: 'The events in Jordan have shattered A. He is fighting very bad fatigue which is sapping his powers of thought. To-night's winding up of the debate was a shambles.'

In retrospect, many considered that Eden should have opened, rather than closed, the debate, but the pressures of time, which made an opening almost impossible for him, and his fame as the master of the wind-up speech were such that no one questioned the decision. Yet Eden was tired, he could not describe how delicate discussions were progressing, and the House was in a noisy mood. Eden later privately described his speech as 'disastrous', and in his memoirs as 'one of the worst in my career'. What was worst of all was that he lost his temper, a very rare event in public for him, and amid derisive taunts of 'What's your policy?' he petulantly shouted, 'Really, the House *must* listen to the Prime Minister.' The Conservatives were upset, the Opposition exultant, and he sat down amid howls of 'Resign!' and an embarrassed and feeble cheer from his supporters. I certainly never heard him make so bad a speech before or after.

But it is never easy, particularly in a rowdy House, to make a diplomatic speech, and Eden was acutely aware that he must say nothing to affect the gradual warming of relations with Hussein or to harm Hussein's fragile position. In his own words, 'It was an occasion for doing nothing.' This was absolutely right, but the national humiliation of Glubb's dismissal followed by the personal humiliation in Parliament of the Prime Minister seemed, at the time, to be more important than in fact they were. We can now see that Eden was totally right. It would have been easy to denounce Hussein or announce the ending of British aid to Jordan; it could only have made Hussein's position worse, and could conceivably have driven him into the Egyptian and Soviet camp, not by desire but by *force majeure*. That this did not happen was a notable achievement by Eden, but not an easy one.

---

* Avon, *Full Circle*, p. 352.

Selwyn Lloyd returned with a notably bleak view of Nasser. As he later wrote:

I thought that he had deteriorated since our meeting three years before. He smiled a great deal more, for no apparent reason. He had lost the simplicity which I had rather liked in 1953. He did not exactly condescend, but he gave the impression that he thought he had better cards in his hand, or, to put it another way, with the Base agreement in his pocket and Communist arms in the hands of his troops, he could do more harm to us than we could do to him.*

These views were set out in his report to the Cabinet on 21 March, when Lloyd said that he was satisfied that Nasser was not willing to work with the West in securing peace in the Middle East; that he was aiming at leadership of the Arab world; and that Britain could not establish friendly relations with Egypt so long as it was ruled by Nasser. This being the case, the purpose of British policy should be to counter and isolate Nasser by strengthening the Baghdad Pact, assisting Britain's other friends in the area, and, with the United States, putting economic pressure on Egypt, including the withdrawal from the Aswan Dam project. This statement made a considerable impression on the Cabinet, but Eden was more cautious, particularly over the Aswan Dam.

But Nutting is correct in one matter in his account. Eden's opinion of Nasser's ambitions, character and methods had declined precipitately further, and it was at this time that he began to compare Nasser with Mussolini in his private comments. The dismissal of Glubb marked another milestone on the road to Suez.

On 18 April, Bulganin and Khrushchev arrived at Portsmouth. Eden had known that the invitation carried considerable political risks, but also great potential advantages in further reducing East–West tensions and improving mutual understanding, not least in the Middle East, in which the Russians were now taking such an active interest, as they had not done under Stalin. He considered the risks worthwhile, and took particular care to warn the security services against any activities that could embarrass his guests or the British Government. On this point he was emphatic, and he received a categorical assurance.

The actual discussions went well. It was obvious that Bulganin, whose courtesy and bearing were impressive, had no real power, whereas the mercurial Khrushchev was the man to watch. His sensational repudiation of Stalin had led some to believe that he was likely to be less assertive of

* Selwyn Lloyd, *Suez*, pp. 47–8.

Soviet policies outside Russia, a delusion that was to be swiftly dashed by experience of this cruel, cunning but not wholly unattractive villain. Eden had no delusions about Khrushchev, but he considered that he was a man with whom one could do business, and who certainly had a very clear understanding of *realpolitik*. Eden was above all eager that the Geneva agreements should stick, and that the co-chairmen should work together effectively to calm down the still heated situation in South-East Asia by their respective influences on the United States and China. He also wanted to give the Russians a clear and unambiguous warning about the crucial nature of Middle East oil to the West, and that there should be no misunderstandings about the British withdrawal from the Suez Canal Zone. On both these points he found the Russians perfectly reasonable.

But the visit was not generally popular. Émigré organizations and the Jewish community were hostile, and Khrushchev had an unamiable tendency to react violently to any criticism. The spectacle of one man by the side of the road shaking his fist at his car sent him off into a paroxysm of rage, and a dinner party with the Labour leadership at the House of Commons broke up in some disorder when George Brown, quite rightly but without tact, challenged Khrushchev's version of recent history; Gaitskell went to the Russian Embassy on the following morning to apologize, but the general feeling was that Brown had been right and that Gaitskell's apology had been unnecessarily servile. This incident certainly did not assist Eden in his task, and he was understandably angry that Brown had raised the temperature which he was trying to lower. Press comment tended to be at best unenthusiastic about the nation's visitors, with the expected exception of left-wing journals.

Eden later wrote that these were the longest discussions between two powers in which he had ever taken part, and there was no lack of topics. Only when Eden, referring to Middle East oil, said that Britain would be prepared, if need be, to fight for it did Khrushchev's notorious temper flare. Lloyd later wondered whether there had been a failure in translation that had wounded Russian pride at such a simple and clear remark – for there was no shortage of blunt speaking on the Russians' part, whether Khrushchev was acting, or whether it was something he did not want to hear. What is not in doubt is that the point was taken, and Eden was able to calm him down.

The visit, mercifully, had its moments of high comedy. At the Harwell research station, Khrushchev was asked bluntly when the Soviet Union was going to have free trade unions, and when the visitors reached Oxford the university and city turned out in force. The windows of the booksellers were filled with biographies of Stalin, and a huge crowd of undergraduates and Oxford citizens linked arms and sang 'Poor Old Joe', to the genial mystification of Bulganin and Khrushchev and the barely concealed hilarity of Selwyn Lloyd, desperately endeavouring to keep a straight face. Amid fireworks and good-natured barracking and heckling, the party left Oxford for Chequers, the Russian visitors considerably impressed by the size of the crowds, although Lloyd suspected that they thought them organized, on the Soviet model. Still, no harm had been done. It is a reflection upon changed times that security was minimal, and it is inconceivable today that a head of state (or his equivalent) could be so openly exposed to large crowds under such circumstances. But it was a world in which the British Prime Minister drove openly with his wife to and from a virtually unprotected cottage, accompanied only by a detective.

This was not the only moment of comedy, as William Deedes has related:

Bulganin and Khrushchev paid a state visit to London. For reasons which escape me, the Home Secretary, Gwilym Lloyd George, and his minions, Lord Mancroft and myself, were either not properly advised of this appointment or forgot it altogether. The Home Office of those days was not at all the jolly 'welcome on the mat' place it is today. So when B & K arrived at the entrance they were shunted by the doorkeepers into a small, unattractive chamber on the immediate left of the entrance, reserved for unwelcome visitors, aliens and so forth, and told to cool their heels. This was unfortunate, but only the start of much greater misfortunes. Lord Mancroft was the first of us to reach the beleaguered Russian leaders. In course of this operation, someone in the crowd outside the Home Office shouted 'Boo'. A policeman on duty in the Home Office muttered: 'Hear, hear! But I mustn't say so.' Lord Mancroft thought this droll, and passed it on attributably to a representative in the press. Adding injury to insult, it appeared in print. The Prime Minister was enraged. Lord Mancroft was summoned to Number Ten for a wigging. He now tells me, though I had forgotten this detail, that he came to me for tea and sympathy before going to the Prime Minister. I appear to have advised him that the Prime Minister was very apt to get excited over such trifling matters, and that on no account should Mancroft offer his resignation. Eden was. Mancroft didn't.

For important visitors to be publicly disparaged by a minister was hardly 'trifling', and Eden was entitled to be angry. Much was at stake, and whereas insults to the visitors from Labour politicians could be borne with some equanimity, this was a bit much. In the event Eden calmed down, Mancroft remained, but it was unhelpful at a tricky moment.

Far worse now occurred.

When the visit ended an agreed communiqué was issued, which said remarkably little, but Eden made a broadcast on the evening of 27 April, the day of the Russian leaders' departure, in which he admitted little progress on some subjects – notably Germany, again – but agreement that both parties wanted a settlement of the Arab–Israeli dispute and greatly improved trade between Britain and the Soviet Union. Announcing this on television and radio, Eden said that no doubt those who had wanted 'a revolutionary agreement' would be disappointed, but it could mark 'the beginning of a beginning'.

Meanwhile, rumours had been appearing in the press about the mysterious disappearance of a British naval frogman, Commander Lionel Crabb RNVR.

Eden had been well informed about the keen interest of Naval Intelligence on both sides in the warships of the other, and not only in what could be seen and assessed above the surface or from agents operating in each other's naval shipyards and design teams. The Royal Navy knew that Russian frogmen had been examining their ships' hulls underwater when they had been on an official visit to Leningrad in the previous October, and were anxious in return to inspect the Russian cruiser *Ordjonikidze* and her accompanying destroyers when they docked at Portsmouth with the Russian leaders. The British were particularly interested in two features of this ship below the waterline, and it was because he was fully aware of this that Eden issued very firm and quite unambiguous orders that this temptation must be resisted.

It was not until 29 April that the Admiralty, the press hot on the trail, issued a statement that Crabb 'did not return from a test dive which took place in connection with trials of certain underwater apparatus in Stokes Bay, in the Portsmouth area, about a week ago'. On 4 May the Government received a formal Note from Moscow pointing out that a frogman had been seen floating near the Russian warships in Portsmouth Harbour, and asked for an explanation.

In 1970, having consulted his papers, Eden dictated this memorandum for his biographer:

Though this sad event took place on Thursday April 19th the Ministers knew nothing about it until May 3rd, when the First Lord of the Admiralty (Lord Cilcennin) and the F.O. were informed. My recollection, and that of Mr Bishop, is that Lord Cilcennin came across to me from the Foreign Office on the following day. I then asked Sir Norman Brook, who was Secretary of the Cabinet, to prepare a short report for me on the incident. This was submitted to me on May 8th. On May 9th I addressed a personal minute to Sir Edward Bridges asking him to enquire into the circumstances under which the operation had been mounted and miscarried. This was the more necessary since I had issued a minute before the arrival of the Russians forbidding any such activity.

This report was submitted to me on May 18th and after examination and consideration, was discussed at a meeting between the Foreign Secretary, the Minister of Defence, the First Lord of the Admiralty and myself.

At that meeting, having decided what disciplinary action should be taken in relation to that particular incident, we decided to ask Bridges to look further into the question of Ministerial responsibility for, and inter-departmental co-ordination of certain types of covert operation.

I did not at any time take any part in the enquiries myself, still less did I cross-examine any witnesses, as suggested in an article which appeared in the Colour Supplement of the *Sunday Times* in the winter of 1969/70.

Eden had good cause to be very angry indeed that his specific orders had been so blatantly ignored. As sometimes happens, the decision had been taken at a relatively low level, and Cilcennin and his senior officers and officials, and the heads of British Intelligence, were completely exonerated of responsibility. What Eden's intense enquiries did reveal was that Crabb had indeed been attempting to survey the hulls of the Russian cruiser and her attendant destroyers, and it had to be assumed that he had been discovered and killed.

Eden acted swiftly and firmly to take control. Instead of permitting the junior Navy Minister in the Commons to answer the barrage of Questions now being tabled by Labour Members, he stated himself on 9 May that what had been done had been done without the Government's authority or knowledge, that appropriate disciplinary measures were being taken, and that it would not be in the public interest to disclose the circumstances under which Crabb had disappeared. On the same day the British Government conveyed to the Russians a Note that fully acknowledged that Crabb had indeed approached the Russian warships without permission, and apologized completely. There is good reason to believe that the Russians were not particularly distressed by the incident – which they had obviously anticipated – and were not disposed to embarrass the British Government after a visit that had resulted in some remarkably positive reporting about Britain in the Russian newspapers.

Gaitskell would have been wise to have taken the same course, but to the dismay of many on his own side, anxious to make his reputation as a hard-hitting Opposition Leader, he initiated, in Opposition time, a full debate on the matter on 10 May. In fact, as so often happens, the collective view of the House of Commons was that the matter was over, and that, outside certain newspapers, there was fading public interest in it.

Eden chose to wind up the debate, which caused some nervousness on the Conservative benches after the Glubb debate fiasco, but he was proved entirely justified. He was at his most calmly authoritative, and was listened to with quiet respect. He would say no more on the subject. He had done, and was doing, his best to improve Anglo-Soviet relations. The Government had had no responsibility for this event. He deplored the debate, and sat down amid warm approval from his side and virtual silence from the other. The Labour lack of zest for Gaitskell's action was seen when the Government had a majority of 87, 30 above its average figure. Gaitskell had rescued the Government from what was potentially an acute embarrassment, while the style and manner of Eden's response and speech completely restored his House of Commons position.

But the Government did not enjoy a quiet summer. Eden had no doubt that it was right to permit time and free votes on the Death Penalty (Abolition) Bill, but by doing so had put Lloyd George in a highly uncomfortable personal position and also exposed those Conservatives who supported the Bill to very heavy, and often almost hysterical, difficulties in their constituency associations. The fervour and intolerance of these views were very strong, and there was widespread criticism of the Government for having let the matter get out of its control and allowing such 'Socialist' legislation. Also, as it had been agreed to have the Committee Stage on the Floor of the House and not in Standing Committee, much other business suffered. In the long and heated debates and votes, the Bill received some odd amendments, including one to retain the death penalty for murder committed by a person serving a sentence of life imprisonment, while rejecting one to retain it for the murder of policemen; on Report stage the amendment was defeated, thereby increasing the confusion and ill feeling. The third reading was carried on 28 June, to the fury of its opponents in the House and among Conservative supporters outside – the latter being the more serious. It was rejected by the Lords, but the subject would not go away.

As all reports from the constituencies indicated, there was much rank-and-file discontent with the Government. The dismissal of Glubb was seen as a national humiliation about which the Government had done nothing; the visit of the Russian leaders had not pleased the Party at large; and feeling in favour of the death penalty was running very high indeed, so that it took a brave Conservative MP to be on the other side. These, also, blamed the Government for putting them in this predicament, and accused it of not giving a lead. Again, there was much talk of indecision at the top.

By-elections may be a poor guide, but they matter to politicians, far more than most are prepared to acknowledge. The Torquay by-election had upset the Conservatives, although to modern eyes a majority of over 10,000 hardly seems sufficient cause for panic: but on 7 June the Government nearly lost Tonbridge, the general election majority of 10,196 reduced to 1,602 in a straight fight with Labour. The cause was Conservative abstention, and local factors were partly blamed. But a major factor was expressed in a letter to *The Times* by a Conservative lady, a Mrs Beryl Platts, who wrote that although she was not a Tonbridge voter she would have abstained in order to jolt the Party towards doing its duty to the middle classes. Her letter, which received considerable attention, ended:

The Conservative agents who describe that result as due to apathy delude themselves. It is a wonderfully encouraging gesture from a class which, after all, refuses to be exterminated. For – and let the Conservative headquarters be under no misapprehension about this – if we refuse to vote and thereby admit the Socialists to power, we allow a period of Socialist legislation which can later be revoked. If we permit the Conservatives to frame Socialist measures in their ill-considered bid for left-wing support, we are saddled with such measures for ever. Which is the greater evil?

The formation of the Middle Class Alliance and the Peoples' League for the Defence of Freedom were also seen as portents of increased Conservative disaffection with the Government and the Prime Minister, but opinion polls disclosed that although the Government was clearly losing ground, Eden's personal rating remained high, and it was then noted that in Tonbridge the Labour vote had also fallen, although not as precipitously as the Conservative. The problem lay within the Conservative ranks, not in any public surge towards Labour.

On 1 June Eden, speaking in Norwich, strongly defended the British position on Cyprus, which was needed as a war base for the defence of British interests. 'No Cyprus, no certain facilities to protect our supply of oil. No oil, unemployment and hunger in Britain. It is as simple as that.' This was the language the disgruntled Conservatives wanted to hear.

Eden conducted so much of his business as Prime Minister in private meetings with individual ministers or on the telephone, to which his colleagues felt he was inordinately attached, that his personal minutes to ministers give us a less accurate record than in the case of Churchill Governments, when so much was committed to paper, at Churchill's insistence, and to the pleasure of historians. Those that there were, however, do give us the flavour of Eden's premiership. Some examples can be given:

To the Minister of Agriculture, Fisheries and Food, on food prices, 1 January 1956
This is surely a policy of despair for the cost of living. The spiral is to be encouraged so that the State should pay less to the farmers. I could never agree to that.

To the President of the Board of Trade on the gelatine and glue industry, 7 January
I am not at all satisfied with the reply which it is proposed that I should send. I really do not understand what is going on. ... It is very sad that we should have to think of knocking this little industry about for the sake of some possible advantage in Europe. European producers are knocking us about quite enough as it is.

To the Minister of Defence on absence of hot weather accommodation in Aden, 3 March
This necessity must have been obvious long ago, and we should have been warned of this.... The more the planners, the worse the plans.

To the Chancellor of the Exchequer on defence expenditure, 24 March
We ought to establish first what are the right things to do: it is at a later stage that we should consider how much of it we can afford. This has always been considered to be the right method of dealing with the problem of defence expenditure.

To the same, on the White Paper on the Economic Implications of Full Employment, 24 March
Your White Paper seems to have attracted quite a lot of attention. There is no harm in that provided that it is read aright. Some of the press, however, seem to have been too easily led to interpret what was intended as informative background as a statement of policy.

To the Minister of Agriculture, Fisheries and Food, 28 May
Can you explain to me why, if we have such a large surplus of milk, we cannot make more butter and cheese, instead of pouring the milk down the gutter?

To the same, on the proposal to increase sugar prices, 15 October
At a time when stability of prices and wage claims are uppermost in our thoughts ... I should be grateful if you would explain these mysteries to me.

These are, obviously, only a small selection. Throughout the year Eden was dominated by the international situation, especially in the Middle East.

To the Foreign Secretary, 30 April
Middle East. On the Middle East generally, we should pursue our attempt to reach agreement with the United States on a common policy.

[11]

Suez – The First Phase

By July 1956 Anthony Eden had been Prime Minister for fifteen months, and the first five months of the year had been especially gruelling. His own personal position had improved from its low point at the beginning of the year, and his failure in the Glubb debate had been largely forgotten, although not by him. His concerns about the Middle East remained strong, and the reality of the new Russian presence and influence in the area was a constant refrain in his conversation and minutes, but he believed that one benefit of Khrushchev's and Bulganin's visit was that they had no doubts about the vital nature of British oil interests, and, in spite of the Crabb episode, Anglo-Soviet relations were cordial. Macmillan's first Budget, with its concentration on encouraging savers, had gone well;* Butler was developing into a highly successful Leader of the House of Commons; and Heath was already proving himself an exceptionally able Chief Whip. By-elections had not been at all good, but they had not been completely disastrous, and John Morrison reported a reasonably good mood in the 1922 Committee.

The Commonwealth Prime Ministers' Conference – which lasted from 28 June to 6 July – had been another burden, with much discussion about Britain's role as a nuclear power and its implications for Commonwealth relations, as well as alarm about possible British involvement with the proposed European Economic Community. Macmillan produced an ingenious alternative, a European Free Trade Area, that attracted Eden but not all his colleagues. Macmillan found the discussions with the Commonwealth Prime Ministers notably ill informed and prejudiced, but at least something had been achieved. Eden, who believed deeply in the Commonwealth and was equally suspicious of supra-national European organizations, always enjoyed these meetings, but this year they were specially difficult and lengthy, and were, as always, accompanied by

* Macmillan's speech introducing it was one of the best – and certainly the most enjoyable to hear – Budget speeches of modern times. When he announced the introduction of Premium Bonds he said, 'You cannot call it gambling, as you cannot lose.' (Harold Wilson unwisely called it 'a squalid raffle': it was a very popular innovation.) When he quoted from Dickens he mournfully looked around him and asked: 'But who reads Dickens nowadays? – apart from the Russians!'

official receptions, meals and speeches. As he admitted, and his staff knew, he was tired and in urgent need of a good holiday.

One of the many advantages of Eden's marriage was that Clarissa Eden believed in holidays, and knew better than anyone, with the possible exception of his doctor Horace Evans, how important they were for her husband. Happy weekends in the cottage were invaluable, but did not constitute a real holiday, which Eden had not had since he became Prime Minister – indeed, not since his 1953 convalescent voyage. As Eden later wrote:

When the July days came our thoughts turned to holiday plans. The year before they had not worked out, but this time my wife and I had firm hopes of three weeks' rest in August. We both longed above all things for hot sunshine and seas in which to bathe. The Governor of Malta, Sir Robert Laycock, had most kindly found for us one of the loveliest villas in the island, by the sea. We began to count the days.*

These hopes existed under sombre shadows. By the early summer the British evacuation of the Suez Canal Zone was virtually complete, but relations with the Nasser regime remained at best cold and formal, as the stream of abuse against the West and its Middle East friends and Israel continued without respite from Radio Cairo. Those Conservatives who had seen the Zone Agreement as a classic act of appeasement of a dictator, and one which had not worked, remained vociferous in their condemnations, supported by a significant element in the British press. The arrival of the Russians in Egyptian affairs may have been given more importance than in fact it warranted, but in the House of Commons and outside in the Conservative Party there was mounting concern, sometimes openly expressed, but also conveyed discreetly through the Whips or the Party organization to Downing Street. Eden was fully aware of these emotions, as he was of the volatility throughout the Middle East, for which Nasser was very largely responsible.

This was clearly shown in Eden's minutes. 'I entirely agree with you and the Secretary of State for War that we should not accelerate our withdrawal from the Canal Zone,' he wrote to Monckton on 19 January, and, again to Monckton, on 10 March:

We have just got to get it into these people's heads [the British Ambassador in Baghdad and representative in Bahrein] that the situation in the Persian Gulf may become highly dangerous at any moment.

We cannot allow the oil to be endangered. Therefore a plan must be worked out without further delay as to what reinforcements are necessary and where they

* Avon, *Full Circle*, p. 419.

can be put. Meetings at intervals of over a fortnight as Bahrein suggests are not going to get us anywhere. Both the political and military difficulties have got to be overcome.

We have the resources. We must take the necessary measures to make them available. This is apart from the question of showing the flag in the Gulf, etc., about which I understand that action is being taken. I know that you are fully alive to this. We must make sure that others are. I will give you all backing in my power.

To Lloyd he minuted on 18 March that 'We have no present interest in bringing Egypt and Sudan together or in pressing on with the [Aswan High] Dam.' On 12 April he urged Monckton 'to continue our "trickle" [of arms] to Israel', particularly anti-tank and anti-aircraft weapons, although on 8 June he was pondering, 'In considering economies, I have been wondering whether we could perhaps wind up our base in Egypt altogether.'

Eden's greatest concern was over the Israeli–Jordanian situation. His nightmare was a war between the two nations, in which Britain would be legally and morally bound to support Jordan, but at dreadful political cost in both Britain and the United States, especially with an American presidential campaign looming. British public opinion would be difficult to anticipate accurately, but King Hussein's popularity in the West had definitely fallen as a result of the dismissal of Glubb, and sentiment in favour of Israel was not limited to the Jewish community. Also, if a conflagration did break out, how could it be contained? These were sobering matters on which to reflect, and British influence and energies were concentrated upon avoiding such a disaster and in building up the Baghdad Pact.

In fact the Israeli Government was less concerned about an open conflict with Jordan than with the ominous situation in the south, the continued banning of its shipping through the Suez Canal, the impasse in the Straits of Tiran, and the entirely new element in the arrival in Egypt of sophisticated Russian aircraft with their pilots and advisers. The Israeli Air Force was at that time a very modest military element, as the Prime Minister David Ben-Gurion and the Israeli commanders knew only too well. They had turned to the French, who were receptive, but a modern air force cannot be created swiftly by the mere acquisition of new aircraft. Thus it was the arrival of the Russian and Czech pilots in Egypt, rather than the aircraft, that caused such consternation in Tel Aviv.

Air power had played a relatively minor role in the 1948 Arab–Israeli war, which goes far to explain why the Israelis had been so surprisingly negligent in this area, while building up a formidable citizens' Army, originally planned to deter the Arab Legion but now facing a major new threat on the Sinai border. In the largely arid Middle East, air power is absolutely crucial, as the North African campaigns in the war had demonstrated so clearly and brutally. In that terrain, there are very few hiding places, and the finest of armies cannot survive if control of the air is lost. Opinion in Israeli military circles was hardening in favour of a pre-emptive strike against Egypt, but this would be impossible without at least parity in the air. Thus the Israelis began to talk seriously to the French; the latter, obsessed with the Algerian war and the active encouragement and assistance given to the nationalists by Nasser, at once agreed that they had much in common. The Franco-Israeli conversations, whose ultimate purpose was the toppling of Nasser, were pursued in great secrecy. The British were not involved, and, because of their other concerns in the area, could not be involved.

Another new factor was the variable approach of the Americans, and particularly Dulles. Eisenhower, while convalescing from an operation for ileitis, had formally handed day-to-day control of affairs to Vice-President Nixon, but the reality was, as Nixon later said, 'Dulles was really the general at that point.' Dulles' over-frank and boastful claims for his 'brinkmanship' had aroused much public criticism, and his position as Secretary of State seemed in such jeopardy that Eisenhower had to issue a public statement of confidence. But the fact was that Dulles was very definitely in charge at this moment.

He, also, had lost patience and faith in Nasser. Nasser had lied to him about the Eastern-bloc arms supplies, and had ignored his strong request not to go to the Bandung Non-Aligned Conference, where he had spent much time with Dulles' arch-enemies, the Chinese; now he was being armed by the Russians. *Al Ahram*, edited by Nasser's close friend, Mohammed Heykal, built up the tension. The American Ambassador to Cairo, H. A. Byroade, who had worked hard to improve US–Egyptian relations, now had an unfortunate altercation with Nasser after a labour expert on his staff was badly beaten up when allegedly suspected of being a spy. Dulles sent a letter about the Czech arms deal that amounted to a virtual ultimatum about the continuation of American goodwill, which Nasser contemptuously ignored. These events amounted to a humiliation for the United States, joyfully reported on Radio Cairo and in *Al Ahram*. The position of the Egyptian Ambassador in Washington, Dr Ahmed Hussein, who, like Byroade, believed in good and positive relations between the two countries, became as difficult as that of Byroade in Cairo. The ability of Nasser to make powerful enemies from a position of considerable military and economic weakness was indeed considerable, but every snub and rebuff to the West further heightened his popularity and position not only in Egypt but virtually throughout the Arab world. There was much bluff in all this — although it is still an open question whether this was deliberate or whether Nasser really believed he had little to fear from outside forces — but there was now acute division in the Middle East between those who believed that Nasser was a saviour and those who regarded him as a perilous menace. There was no doubt on the latter point in Tel Aviv, Baghdad, Paris or London, but the real, and crucial, blow came in Washington.

The Aswan Dam, built by the British, had been the most beneficent engineering and economic project in Egypt since the Suez Canal, the purpose being to control the waters of the Nile and so avoid the arbitrary floods which swept down each year and which, although bringing the precious water and silt, came only briefly and violently. For years plans existed for another dam higher up the Nile, an even greater project in terms of scale and cost. It was built up into the project that would be the salvation of Egypt, providing not only the life-giving water throughout the year but abundant cheap electricity, and no opportunity was missed by the Nasser administration of creating expectations far beyond what were actually feasible. If this constituted brilliant public relations, giving excessive hopes for a glittering future, it was also politically cynical, as not only Western but Egyptian engineers had grave technical doubts about the value of the dam — doubts which have been fully justified. But to express such reservations in Egypt was treasonable, and the arguments over the High Dam had nothing whatever to do with its technical merits, cost, environmental implications or effectiveness; it had everything to do with politics, and the survival of the Nasser regime.

The World Bank, at Egypt's request, had undertaken feasibility studies which concluded that the dam was technically sound and within the capacity of the Egyptian economy, given reasonable foreign financing arrangements. Nasser informed the Americans that he preferred Western financing to Russian, and, urged on by Dulles and Eden, the Bank's President Eugene Black seemed to have reached a high measure of agreement with Nasser by the end of January 1956, although the Egyptian President remained suspicious about British and American conditions, which in fact were standard loan conditions, but which were seen by Nasser as unreasonable and which he wished to see changed. There was a clear opportunity at the beginning of February 1956 for the matter to be resolved definitely, and very much in Egypt's interests. Nasser, convinced he could improve the terms, refused to settle, and insisted on changes. Dulles' vision of linking the dam with a comprehensive Arab–Israeli settlement, on which he sent Robert B. Anderson on a secret mission early in 1956, had foundered on hostility both in Israel and in Egypt; thus, when Nasser submitted his case for amendments, the mood in Washington and London had changed.

Nasser had staked much of his internal prestige on the High Dam, and had certainly learned enough from other dictators to judge the importance of symbols, and of the value of offering glowing prospects to allay current discontents, of which there were many in Egypt. The withdrawal of the British may have been popular politically, but financially it was a heavy blow to the precarious Egyptian economy. While the Egyptian armed services seemed to prosper, the lot of the poor did not improve at all, and the mercurial nature of the Cairo mob was a constant cause of worry to the Egyptian leadership. Nasser and his ministers had many enemies, who were watching him closely, and who included officers in the Army who deeply resented the treatment of Nasser's predecessor, General Neguib. If there was a certain element of paranoia in Nasser's entourage it has to be conceded that they had much to be paranoiac about. There was also the factor, which was gravely underestimated in the West, that there was little enthusiasm either for Communism or for the arrival of Russian and Eastern-bloc military equipment, or for advisers who spoke little English or Arabic and whose training manuals were in incomprehensible Russian or Czech. Communism as a creed and a political force was greatly feared by the Egyptian governing and commercial classes, whether pro- or anti-Nasser.

But Byroade had now fallen out with Dulles, and his keen understanding of the situation – matched only by that of Harold Caccia, the senior Foreign Office official responsible for Middle Eastern affairs – was now coolly received by Dulles. Furthermore, his new Assistant Secretary of State was Herbert Hoover, the son of the former President, who knew a great deal about the engineering and technical aspects of dams; he was also notoriously suspicious of the British, and considered that the High Dam was not only technically unfeasible and even undesirable, but that the wily British – and particularly Eden – wanted the dam to be built by them principally at American expense for purely British political interests in the Middle East. The belief that the British wanted the contract solely for themselves, although Hoover and George Humphrey, the Secretary of the Treasury, believed it fervently, was incorrect; the rest of their assessment was right. Eden and Dulles recognized clearly that this was a political dam – a Western dam. It would be funded from the West, and as it would take ten years to build it would give the West a major stake in the Egyptian economy, keep out the Russians, and greatly assist in reducing West–Egyptian tensions. That was its purpose, but Humphrey and Hoover saw it in other terms.

Eden had been very enthusiastic indeed about the dam. In November 1955, Eisenhower had telegraphed 'details of very disturbing information we have just received about the likelihood of an Egyptian–Russian deal over the Aswan Dam. If the Russians were to succeed in this, they would, of course, be ruthless with the Sudan and abuse their control of the Nile waters. The outlook for Africa would then be grim indeed.' Eden responded that Britain would join the Western consortium as 'I am convinced that on our joint success in excluding the Russians from this contract may depend the future of Africa.' On 15 December he telegraphed to Eisenhower that 'it is a political rather than a commercial matter.... We must surely press home and clinch the agreement now we have got so far.' British information was that the Saudis, the Russians, the Egyptians and the Syrians were working together: 'If we don't want to see the whole Middle East fall into Communist hands,' Eden cabled Eisenhower on 16 January, 'we must first back the friends of the West in Jordan and Iraq. This we are trying to do.' On 5 March he warned Eisenhower about Egyptian and Soviet collaboration to destroy the Baghdad Pact, which he again urged the United States to join: 'a policy of appeasement will bring us nothing in Egypt. Our best chance is to show that it pays to be our friends.' This was to be a constant theme, to which Eisenhower was not unsympathetic. But Eden's urgings for a common line were not successful, although Eisenhower wrote to him on 5 April that 'we sd not be acquiescent in any measure which wd give the Bear's claws a grip on production or transportation of oil which is so vital to the defence and economy of the Western world'. Eden assured him that he would tell the Russians that any interference with Western oil supplies 'will create a most dangerous state of tensions, since the British are not the kind of people to let themselves be quietly strangled'. With this Eisenhower entirely agreed, but then he fell ill, and was out of action at the critical time.

In Washington, Eugene Black was prepared for the World Bank to advance $200 million provided that the United States provided another $130 million and the British $80 million. The British agreed at once, which deepened Humphrey's suspicions. Hoover and Humphrey – the only member of the administration who could match Dulles' power – turned decisively against the dam, and Humphrey was adroit at manipulating congressional opinion. This was not too difficult. The pro-Israel politicians were warned of the consequences of supporting the economy of a country dedicated to the destruction of Israel; Southern senators and congressmen were given dark warnings of the impact on the price of cotton of a fertile Nile Valley; Nasser's notorious Czech arms deal alarmed the forces of anti-Communism in American politics and the press.

But it was only gradually that Dulles turned. If he had not been so constantly rebuffed by Nasser and had not become so personally hostile towards him, it might have been possible for him to have used his position with Eisenhower to resist these pressures, but his heart was not in the matter. He saw the great advantages of a strong Western influence in Egypt, but he also now had enough experience of Nasser's trickery and dissimulation to make him not unsympathetic to the complaints that now poured in upon him. Outside of some officials in the State Department and the World Bank, the dam had few American friends.

Also – and this was critical – enthusiasm for the dam had notably declined on the other side of the Atlantic since the beginning of the year, and it was Selwyn Lloyd's view, conveyed to Makins, that it should 'wither on the vine'. In his account in *Full Circle*, Eden spelt out the reasons why the British came to this new judgement – the raising of the Egyptian demands and conditions, their heavy expenditure on Soviet-bloc arms, Egyptian machinations in other Middle East countries, the constant anti-West and particularly anti-British propaganda from Radio Cairo, and manifestly greater Soviet influence. But whereas Lloyd had become positively hostile towards any dealings with Nasser, Eden took the view that the dam matter could continue, and that 'There was no need to hurry.' Although Eden's own support for the dam had notably waned by July, he saw no need for any precipitate action.

This was the situation when the Egyptians informed Dulles that their Ambassador would return to Washington in July, and that he was instructed not to insist on their previous conditions. This put Dulles into a quandary.

Several accounts of what then happened have been seriously inaccurate – not least Selwyn Lloyd's – and it is necessary to describe these crucial developments.

Anglo-American discussions on financing the dam had continued throughout June. Three options were considered: either to withdraw the Western offer, or to reaffirm it, or to leave it open linked to some proposal such as a conference of Nile Valley states or further negotiations on the terms. No decision was taken, the British view still being that it ought to 'languish'.

On 13 July Makins discussed the matter with Dulles, who told him that he had spoken to Eisenhower about it that morning and would discuss it again with him on the following week (the 13th being a Friday). Dulles said that his own opinion was hardening against proceeding with the offer, which he was sure the Egyptian Ambassador would raise directly with him in the following week. His reasons were the opposition to the dam in Congress, the Egyptian economic situation and his doubts whether Western aid would improve relations with Egypt. The congressional situation clearly worried Dulles, who told Makins that Congress was now trying to run foreign policy. This was confirmed on the Monday, 16 July, when the Senate Appropriations Committee reported on the Mutual Assistance Bill with a rider that none of its funds were to be spent on the dam without specific congressional approval.

On that day, London commented on Makins' report of his discussion of the 13th with Dulles, and suggested that the Egyptians should be told that their lavish spending plans raised questions about their ability to handle the dam project, and on the next day, the 17th, Makins was instructed to propose this to Dulles and to tell him that the British were not in favour of withdrawing from the project, and wanted to hold out the hope of giving further aid to Egypt. London also hoped that there would be further exchanges before a decision was taken. One can clearly see the hand of Eden in this particular telegram.

On the 18th Dulles told Makins he would be seeing the Egyptian Ambassador on the next day, at 4.00 p.m., and would like to discuss the line to be taken in the morning. Makins reported to London that he had the clear impression that Dulles intended to withdraw the American offer — which would automatically end the World Bank's involvement — but had not yet decided on the manner in which he should tell the Egyptians of this, nor whether he should keep the door open for other forms of aid, as the British had suggested. London replied that this approach 'would suit us very well', a significant difference from the previous message to Makins.

At their meeting on the morning of the 19th, Dulles told Makins that personally he would like to play the matter longer, as London wished, but after seeing Eisenhower he had come to the conclusion that the congressional situation did not allow this, and it was quite possible, given its mood, that it would forbid any aid at all to Egypt. Makins said that the attitudes of the two governments were much in line, although his Government would still prefer to let the matter rest where it was. Dulles agreed, but said that the decision had been taken by the President, and that the United States Government took full responsibility for it.

Makins' telegram to London crossed the one from London on the same day, which had been sent at the close of business in the Foreign Office. Thus, for several vital hours, Makins had in effect been without instructions beyond the telegram on the 17th. This dilatoriness did not imply any feverish concern by Eden and Lloyd, who were fully informed by Makins of what Dulles was likely to do, and the reasons for it. If they had been concerned, there could have been direct and immediate contact at Foreign Minister or even Prime Minister-to-President level. It was very reasonable to assume in Washington that London was not particularly troubled about the matter, which was exactly the case.

The American records show that Dulles' advice to Eisenhower against the dam had been rather stronger on the 13th than he had implied to Makins on the same day, but he was frank with Makins, whose report to

London was, as always, completely accurate. At no stage did London urge Makins to talk Dulles out of his decision or to impress upon him any particularly strong British views. Eden subsequently wrote that 'We were informed but not consulted and so had no prior opportunity for criticism or comment.... We were sorry that the matter was carried through so abruptly, because it gave our two countries no chance to concert either timing or methods....'* In fact there had been perfectly sufficient time for London to give any 'criticism or comment' – six days, in fact – and Lloyd's version that 'Makins ... was informed one hour before the meeting. I had had no idea that there was going to be this abrupt withdrawal' is equally wrong.† London's attitude made Dulles draw the obvious – and right – conclusion that the British were indifferent. Dulles' conduct of American foreign policy can be legitimately criticized on many counts, but not on this one. Subsequent complaints by Eden and Lloyd about Dulles' handling of the matter are only justified in the unfortunate manner with which Dulles handled his meeting with Ambassador Hussein on the 19th; but they have no justification whatever in claiming that they were ill informed about what the Americans had decided. Eden was on firm ground in his account in recording his preference for playing the matter long, but a preference is not a particularly strong line to take in such a situation.

Thus, at 4 p.m. on the afternoon of the 19th, Ambassador Hussein duly called on Dulles at the State Department with a letter from Nasser which in effect met all the American and World Bank conditions. But he opened the discussion with a foolish joke that if the West did not finance the dam the Russians would. As it happened, this disastrous gaffe had no effect on the decision that had already been taken, but it enabled Dulles to work up a fine demonstration of indignation about his treatment by Nasser before informing Hussein curtly that a communiqué had already been issued to the American and world press announcing American withdrawal from the project. This meeting may be fairly adjudged to stand high in the catalogue of the most unfortunately handled diplomatic exchanges of modern times.

Interestingly, Dulles then doubted whether he had made the right decision, confiding his concerns to senior State Department officials. But the deed had been done, and the view in London was that any differences between the British and American Governments on the issue were those of nuance between outright refusal and implied refusal. Thus, at the Cabinet on the 20th, with minimal discussion, it was agreed that Britain would follow the American line, and on instructions Harold Caccia saw the Egyptian Ambassador in London that afternoon to convey the British

* Avon, *Full Circle*, p. 422.
† Lloyd, *Suez*, p. 71.

decision, emphasizing that it had been taken entirely on economic grounds, that Britain wanted good relations with Egypt, and that the decision did not mean that she was not interested in the future development of the Nile Valley. The decision was the same, but the manner in which it was conveyed was a very marked improvement on Dulles'. Nasser may well have planned what then happened, but it was the manner of the American decision that gave him the opportunity to describe this as a deliberate humiliation to himself and his country. There was little he could do to strike back at the Americans, but the British were another matter.

The fact that this was indeed a political dam was graphically demonstrated by an incident which, like others in this account, has not been previously published.

The Board of Trade had made an independent study of the project and had come to the conclusion that even if the Americans and the World Bank withdrew, it could be financed and undertaken by a West European consortium. The senior officials had gone further, and had in effect drawn one together. When the American decision was announced, the Permanent Secretary, Sir Frank Lee, put the matter before the President of the Board of Trade, Peter Thorneycroft. Thorneycroft was so impressed by the detail of the work undertaken by his Department and the strength of the consortium that he considered he should see the Prime Minister personally about it, which he did in a private discussion in Downing Street.

Although Thorneycroft had known Eden for a long time in Parliament and in Government he had never previously personally experienced one of Eden's famous rages. He now did. Eden described the proposal as – among other things – 'a monstrous suggestion', and worked himself up into a fury that amazed Thorneycroft, who had thought that his officials had produced a solution to the problem that ensured Western involvement at no significant government expense. He was left in no doubt that he had intruded into an area in which he and his Department had no place whatever and that the Aswan Dam project was definitely dead. None of his Cabinet colleagues knew of this. It was to prove a very significant instance of Eden's methods of conducting his office.

As Nasser well knew, the British claim that they had taken their decision purely on economic grounds – in itself seen as an insult to the Egyptian economy and capacities – was specious and inaccurate. This had been a political decision, designed to put Nasser in his place, an expression of Western hostility to his policies, propaganda and attitudes. The fact that the decision was bound to push Nasser further into the Soviet orbit was remarkably ill-appreciated in London, and this had been the true cause of Dulles' unease about whether he had, after all, done the right thing. What was also underestimated was the Western assessment of Nasser's own volatile, conspiratorial and theatrical personality. Eden had already mentally classified him as another Mussolini – vain, megalomaniac, with vaulting ambitions and grandiose ventures in whose dreams of fame and glory his unfortunate people were cast not only as his admiring audience but as docile participants and, if need be, victims. It was not as bad an assessment as many have alleged, and there are certain very striking features in common between the two men, but Eden never asked himself the key question: 'In such circumstances, what would Mussolini have done?'

No one, in Washington, London or Paris, remotely anticipated what Nasser's response would be.

It is very probable – as Heykal has stated – that Nasser had anticipated this rebuff. Several years later he told Erskine Childers that 'I was sure that Mr Dulles would not help us by financing the Aswan Dam. . . . I was surprised by the insulting attitude with which the refusal was declared. Not by the refusal itself.'* There were many in Washington and London who believed and hoped that it might destroy Nasser's position and lead to a more congenial Egyptian leadership. But any examination of Nasser's character and political record should have led to the conclusion that he was certain to react violently. Lloyd, in a discussion in the Cabinet on 17 July, had agreed to circulate a memorandum on how the withdrawal of the Western offer should be put to the Egyptians, but throughout there was no sense of urgency in London or any appreciation of what, if any, reaction there would be apart from more abuse from Radio Cairo and *Al Ahram*. There was also no sense of possible reactions in Washington, apart from Dulles, where the decision was generally applauded.

If Nasser had anticipated the Western rejection, he had not anticipated its manner. What is not beyond doubt is that he had made contingency plans, and that what then happened was not on a sudden impulse. Foreign ownership of the Canal had been an Egyptian grievance for generations, and plans had certainly been made for taking over the Canal when the concession ended in 1968. On 23 July it was decided that these plans would have to be drastically brought forward. As Nasser later said:

Of course, we had studied the military situation of Britain, the economic situation of Britain – we had studied every aspect before the declaration of the nationalization. It was clear to us that Britain would not be ready to have any military movement before three or four months. We studied the deployment of the British troops, and, of course, there were British troops in Libya, British troops in Germany. We thought at that time that it would be possible to reach a sort of a settlement during these three months.†

* Anthony Moncrieff (ed.), *Suez Ten Years Later*, pp. 42, 43.
† *Ibid.*, p. 44.

On 24 July Nasser denounced the United States in violent terms in a speech opening a new pipeline near Cairo. This had been expected. But two evenings later, before a vast crowd in Alexandria, he concentrated upon Britain, and when he used the words 'de Lesseps', this was the prepared code for the seizure of the property of the Suez Canal Company by force, the nationalization of the company, and the proclamation of military law in the Canal Zone, to be put into immediate effect, as it was. The humiliation and anger at the American–British treachery were thus brilliantly converted into a spirit almost of exaltation among the immediate crowd and the vast listening audience beside radios throughout the Arab world. The Western Imperialists had struck at the future of the Egyptian people; they had struck at Arab nationalism; the friends of the hated Israel were bent on the ruination of a poor but brave people. Very well, they shall learn that those people would take back into their possession what was rightfully theirs, and would no longer be slaves in their own country.

It was superb oratory, but, more importantly, careful plans could now be implemented. The great international waterway, on which Nasser had given firm guarantees on 10 June, was within hours under Egyptian military control.

The Suez crisis had begun.

Eden was the host at an official dinner at Downing Street on the evening of 26 July in honour of King Feisal of Iraq when the news of Nasser's speech and actions was received. The reactions of the Iraqis were very similar to those of the British, and Nuri told Selwyn Lloyd that the British 'should hit Nasser hard and quickly'. Another guest at this celebrated dinner was Hugh Gaitskell, whose own diary account reads:

He [Eden] thought perhaps they ought to take it to the Security Council. . . . I said 'Supposing Nasser doesn't take any notice?' whereupon Selwyn [Lloyd] said 'Well, I suppose in that case the old-fashioned ultimatum will be necessary.' I said that I thought they ought to act quickly, whatever they did, and that as far as Great Britain was concerned, public opinion would almost certainly be behind them. But I also added that they must get America into line.*

Eden was calm, and gave instructions to summon the Chiefs of Staff, the American Chargé d'Affaires, A. B. Foster, and the French Ambassador, Jean Chauvel, for immediate consultations after the dinner. Reports by those who were not there that the occasion broke up in confusion and alarm are emphatically not confirmed by those who were present. There

* Philip Williams, *Hugh Gaitskell*, p. 419. Most remarkably, neither Eden nor Selwyn Lloyd in their accounts even refer to Gaitskell's presence at this dinner, let alone his comments.

was a particularly comic moment when, the Iraqis having left, Salisbury told Kilmuir that none of them could leave the room until the Lord Chancellor had done so.

The meeting was attended by three of the Chiefs of Staff – Marshal of the Royal Air Force Sir William Dickson (Chairman), Lord Mountbatten, First Sea Lord, and Sir Gerald Templer, Chief of the Imperial General Staff – the American and French representatives, and those Cabinet Ministers who had been present at the dinner, Eden, Salisbury, Kilmuir, Home and Selwyn Lloyd. It was agreed to concert common action with the United States and France, and ministers postponed further decisions until a Cabinet to be summoned for the following morning. The Chiefs of Staff were instructed to prepare an assessment of the military options, and a draft statement to be made by Eden on the following morning in the House of Commons was agreed. Reports were still coming in from Cairo from the British Embassy, but the general situation was only too grimly clear.

The most vivid account is by William Clark:

It was a deeply humiliating meeting. In effect, the Prime Minister said that there had been an act of aggression against us and, while asking the Foreign Office to look into our legal remedies, he wished to respond forcefully and immediately. What could the Chiefs of Staff recommend? Their answer was ill prepared but perfectly clear: we could do nothing immediately. It was suddenly obvious that Britain was armed to participate in a nuclear armageddon with the Soviet Union or in small colonial guerilla wars ... but had no capacity for this kind of emergency.*

On the following morning, if ministers had had any doubts as to the response of the British press and Parliament to Nasser's action they were swiftly removed. Without serious exception the action was condemned, often in terms so vehement and warlike as to be alarming, but the message was very clear and very emphatic.

A Conservative MP, Nigel Nicolson, whose political career was to be destroyed by the Suez crisis, has admirably described the mood:

It was not so much what he [Nasser] did, as his method of doing it, which united this country against him. It was a dictator's typical gesture of defiance, a *quid pro quo* for his disappointment in failing to tempt the American and British Governments to invest in his project for an Aswan Dam, a highwayman's exploitation of the geographical accident that the isthmus of Suez lay in Egyptian territory. All this, and much more, was said by spokesmen of all political parties during the first days of August. It was an act of robbery which the British nation, and most of their western allies, were not prepared to accept with a mere protest.†

* Quoted on p. 405 of Leonard Mosley, *Dulles*. Although Clark was very reticent about his time at Downing Street, he confirmed to me the complete accuracy of this quotation.

† Nigel Nicolson, *People and Parliament*, p. 108.

In France the reaction was even more virulent. Thousands of Frenchmen had shares in the Canal Company, and in addition to the practical implications the French Government and people had had enough of defeat and humiliation, and Nasser's involvement in the Algerian war had made him even more hated in France than in Britain. Prime Minister Guy Mollet and Foreign Minister Christian Pineau shared these emotions entirely; Nasser must be brought down, and force would be needed. They took that position from the beginning, and from it they never wavered, supported by every shade of political opinion in France, from de Gaulle in retirement to the Communist Party. They were untroubled about how it might be done; it was to be a war of revenge, for the very salvation of metropolitan France.

The British press is not invariably an accurate reflection of the popular mood, but on this occasion it was, and the House of Commons instinctively reflected British anger with equal acuteness. It was difficult indeed to find a newspaper, commentator or Member of Parliament which did not condemn the Egyptian action and call for action to repeal it. Even the *Daily Herald*, no friend of the Government, declared that 'No British Government can resign itself to Colonel Nasser's being in control of a vital British Commonwealth life-line.'

This upsurge of feeling was indeed astonishing, and it certainly astonished Nasser. 'I was surprised by the reaction of Britain,' he later said. 'I was waiting for reaction from Britain. I was surprised by the *amount* of the reaction of Britain.'

The House of Commons met in an angry mood. Although the sitting did not begin until 11.00 a.m. the building was surprisingly full long before this, and I vividly recall the strong emotions of MPs of all Parties.*

This was reflected at 11.00 a.m. Eden's statement was short, calm and moderate. The action of the Egyptian Government affected the rights and interests of many nations, and consultations were taking place with the other Governments immediately concerned. Gaitskell, to warm cheers fom Conservative Members, who looked to me considerably disappointed by Eden's somewhat prosaic and cautious statement, went further by denouncing the action as 'high-handed and totally unjustified', and there were even warmer cheers for the Labour MP, Reginald Paget, who remarked that 'this

---

* I had been appointed a junior Clerk of the House of Commons in October 1955, and my immediate superior was the Clerk of Public Bills, Sir Robert Dent. Dent was a firm believer that the best way of learning about the House of Commons was to attend its proceedings, so, in addition to my duties in the Office and as a junior Clerk on Standing Committees and recording divisions, I had a regular place in the special galleries. I attended all the Suez debates and Question Times, and if my own experiences intrude into this narrative occasionally it is because I was there.

weekend technique was precisely what we had got used to in Hitler's day'
and made pointed references to the perils of appeasing dictators. Eden was
not pressed further in the House, and went to chair an immediate Cabinet
meeting. The House dispersed after the brief exchange, and there were
serious and, in some cases, anguished discussions in the Lobbies and
corridors; if there were any voices raised in defence of the Egyptian action,
I did not hear them. The mood was one of outrage at an act of international
piracy which could obviously have the most grievous consequences for
Britain and the West. There was a certain complacency among the members
of the Suez Group, which, although unlovely, was certainly very understandable.

It has often been claimed, notably by those who have endeavoured to
portray Eden as a weak and indecisive man, that personal political pressures
forced him into his course. 'Nobody can fully understand the Suez crisis',
Nigel Nicolson has written, 'unless he takes into account [Conservative]
growing unease that Britain's position in the world, and the reputation of
the Conservative Government at home, were being whittled down through
lack of strong leadership.'* Although Nicolson was to be an opponent of
the Government's policy – if somewhat belatedly, although courageously –
he is never unsympathetic to Eden in his account, but this particular charge
is wholly wrong.

Butler subsequently put his finger with great accuracy on where Eden
differed from many of his new supporters:

I admired his courage, his gallantry, his wartime record and his Foreign Office
achievements. He seemed thoroughly in character in standing up for British rights
in the Middle East and I supported him.... These were deep-seated emotions
affecting liberal-minded people, but they coalesced only too easily with less
generous sentiments: the residues of illiberal resentment at the loss of Empire, the
rise of coloured nationalism, the transfer of world leadership to the United States.
It was these sentiments that made the Suez venture so popular, not least among
the supporters of the embarrassed Labour party.†

Such attitudes were wholly alien to Eden's record and personality, and
at no point in his long career had he been anything but unsympathetic to
extreme right-wing Conservative Imperialism now once again typified by
the Suez Group and its adherents in the Party outside Westminster. He
did not remotely belong to the same political school as the MP Captain
Charles Waterhouse or the Jingo sections of the British press, and he had
no reason to feel any gratitude to, or respect for, these elements, who had
worked so sedulously to portray him as weak and ineffectual. He was
certainly not prepared to court them; to have their ringing endorsement

---

* Nicolson, *People and Parliament*, p. 114.
† Butler, *The Art of the Possible*, pp. 188–9.

and support, usually couched in blood-curdling terms that would have made even Joseph Chamberlain uneasy, was not particularly welcome.

Eden saw the seriousness of Nasser's actions immediately, and at once took charge. He led, rather than followed, Cabinet and Party feeling; what subsequently happened was his responsibility, from which he never shrank. To allege or imply that he was blown along by popular and political emotion on a course which otherwise he would not have taken is to mistake completely his own character and to misunderstand what really happened.

But it would be equally wrong to claim that *no* personal factors were involved. Eden had seriously jeopardized his domestic political position and reputation over the Base withdrawal, and he had shown an understanding of the realities of Egyptian nationalist feeling that was wholly opposite to the 'colonialist' attitude of which he was accused by Nasser. His relations with Neguib had been good, and he had tried to establish the same relationship with Nasser. With good reason he considered that he was entitled to some degree of reciprocal understanding for his even-handedness in Middle Eastern affairs, and he had consistently emphasized that the Baghdad Pact, far from being anti-Egyptian, would be strengthened with Egyptian participation. And now Nasser had done this.

As his life and career had shown, Anthony Eden was a warm-blooded, sensitive and emotional man, with strong feelings on men and events. He put great store on high standards of conduct, good manners, personal relationships, friendship and integrity. He had a detestation of dishonest and dishonourable politicians, which was why he always had so much time for men like Churchill, Bevin, de Gaulle, Bracken, Salisbury and 'Bomber' Harris. If to personalize one's politics is a deficiency, it is one that Eden has shared with most statesmen. A cold cynic like Talleyrand has his place, but Eden was of a totally different type, as his entire life demonstrated.

Thus, in Eden's eyes, what Nasser had done was a callous betrayal of his solemn pledges and agreements, which was despicable in itself, and he was clearly a man without integrity or reason. He now posed a grievous threat to British and Western interests that was intolerable. As all close to him quickly realized, Eden was now consumed with a real personal hatred of Nasser and all he represented. As he wrote in the foreword to *Full Circle*, 'the lessons of the 'thirties and their application to the 'fifties ... are the themes of my memoirs'. Like the French, from the outset of the Suez Canal crisis he was determined to destroy this new Mussolini. How this was to be achieved was a more complex matter, but this was his objective.

As the meeting with the Chiefs of Staff had made clear on 26 July, there was no possibility whatever of taking immediate military action to recover the Canal and thereby to deliver a mortal blow to Nasser. Such action could only have been attempted by a paratroop landing which, as the Germans had discovered at terrible cost in Crete, is one of the most perilous operations of war if unsupported. Also, even if the French and British had pooled all their airborne forces, these amounted to less than a division; and, even if they landed without great loss and established their position, they could be supported only from the air. It was an impossible option, and it was never considered.

Mountbatten, who was of course present at this meeting, later sedulously spread the legend (among others) that he had told Eden that the fleet at Malta could sail within a few hours and pick up marine commandos at Cyprus, who could occupy Port Said within three or four days and capture the first twenty-five miles of the Canal, covered by aircraft from aircraft carriers. The actual records show that Mountbatten thought that while 12,000 marines *could* take the Causeway, the problems of maintaining their position thereafter would be very great, and he wrote: 'I recommend that unilateral action by the Royal Navy and the Royal Marines should *not* be taken.'*

It often happens that people come to believe in their own fictions, and Mountbatten astonished Eden on 13 June 1976 by 'reminding' him that he had told him on the evening of 26 July that he could arrange to seize the first twenty-five miles of the Canal within three days. Mountbatten kept reiterating 'You *must* remember' when Eden said that this was the first he had heard of it, and it was not something he was likely to have forgotten. Immediately after the discussion Eden telephoned Templer, who confirmed that he had no recollection of this plan, but would check at once with Dickson and Air Chief Marshal Sir Dermot Boyle, Chief of the Air Staff; they immediately and completely denied Mountbatten's story. The records are wholly on their side.†

Why did Mountbatten subsequently deliberately falsify his position, especially as he must have known that it would eventually be revealed? Part of the answer may lie in the word 'eventually', because at the time all records were kept secret for fifty years. But, as his biographer has written of Mountbatten, with commendable candour: 'The truth, in his hands, was swiftly converted from what it was to what it should have been. He sought to rewrite history with a cavalier indifference to the facts to magnify his own achievements.'‡

*　　*　　*

* Philip Ziegler, *Mountbatten*, p. 538; my italics.

† Memorandum by Eden, 13 June 1976, of a discussion at the Provost's Lodge, Eton. The memorandum also contains this passage: 'At one point of the discussion he [Mountbatten] added that he had only disagreed with our later policy in respect of the Canal because of the loss of life it must entail.'

‡ Ziegler, *Mountbatten*, p. 701.

It is now necessary to move from the memoirs and recollections of those involved to an account of what actually happened. There are discrepancies between them on several occasions, and even the most accurate omit much, while the versions of others read very strangely when compared with the records of what they actually did and said. This is, accordingly, the first authentic account from the British sources of the unfolding crisis.

On 27 July, the Cabinet met immediately after the exchange in the House, at 11.20 a.m.; also present were Heath, Aubrey Jones (Minister of Fuel and Power), Templer, Mountbatten and Boyle.* Eden opened by informing the Cabinet of the meeting with the American Chargé and the French Ambassador the previous evening.

He had told them that Her Majesty's Government would take a most serious view of this situation and that any failure on the part of the Western Powers to take the necessary steps to regain control over the Canal would have disastrous consequences for the economic life of the Western Powers and for their standing and influence in the Middle East. Our first aim must be to reach a common understanding on this matter with the French, as our partners in the Canal enterprise and with the United States Government.

The legal situation had to be faced:

The Cabinet agreed that we should be on weak ground in basing our resistance on the narrow argument that Colonel Nasser had acted illegally. The Suez Canal Company was registered as an Egyptian company under Egyptian law; and Colonel Nasser had indicated that he intended to compensate the shareholders at ruling market prices. From a narrow legal point of view, his action amounted to no more than a decision to buy out the shareholders. Our case must be presented on wider international grounds. Our argument must be that the Canal was an important international asset and facility, and that Egypt could not be allowed to exploit it for a purely internal purpose. The Egyptians had not the technical ability to manage it effectively; and their recent behaviour gave no confidence that they would recognize their international obligations in respect of it. It was a piece of Egyptian property but an international asset of the highest importance and should be managed as an international trust.

The Cabinet agreed that for these reasons every effort must be made to restore effective international control over the Canal. It was evident that the Egyptians would not yield to economic pressures alone. They must be subjected to the maximum political pressure which could only be applied by the maritime and trading nations whose interests were most directly affected. And, in the last resort,

---

*Lloyd (*Suez*, p. 83) gives a summary of this Cabinet, which has at least one major inaccuracy when he states that it was 'quickly agreed' that the nationalization was 'a breach of international law'; he also fails to give the attendance accurately. Other accounts are likewise either incomplete or misleading.

this political pressure must be backed by the threat – and, if need be, the use of force.

At this point, it is necessary to pause to consider certain crucial features of this decision.

In the first place, the assessment and conclusions were agreed unanimously by a full Cabinet, whose only major absentee was Butler, who was unwell, and which was attended by the Secretary of State for Defence, Monckton, and by the Chiefs of Staff; the presence of Mountbatten becomes significant in the light of later events.

Secondly, it had been recognized at the outset that, technically and legally speaking, Nasser had been within his rights. What was intolerable was that a power that was no friend of the West now controlled the Canal.

Thirdly, the Cabinet assumed – quite wrongly – that the Egyptians did not have the technical competence to run the Canal.

Fourthly, while political pressure would be applied in the first instance, it would be accompanied by the threat 'and, if need be, the use of force'.

Aubrey Jones then spelt out the grim statistics. The oil passing through the Canal represented two-thirds (60 million tons) of the fuel supplies of Western Europe; in 1955, 14,666 ships had passed through it, one-third of them British, and three-quarters belonging to NATO countries; Britain's total oil reserves were only six weeks.

The Cabinet then turned to the Chiefs of Staff for their initial assessment of the military situation. It was as follows.

Egypt had three infantry and one armoured divisions, and about five hundred tanks; two-thirds of this force was in the Sinai; there were between six hundred and eight hundred Soviet and Eastern-bloc technicians attached to the Egyptian forces, but it was not known whether they would be involved 'in active operations'.

A military operation against Egypt, including consequential responsibilities for keeping the Canal in operation and controlling the area, would require the equivalent of three divisions. The necessary forces would be made available for this purpose; but, as a great quantity of vehicles and other heavy armoured equipment would have to be transported to the area by sea, the necessary preparations for mounting the operation would take several weeks. It would be necessary, moreover, to requisition ships and, possibly, to direct labour.

The Chiefs were more optimistic about the air and naval situation:

While the military plan was being worked out, preparations would be made to build up a ring of bomber forces at points around Egypt. Fighter squadrons would also be sent to Cyprus.... The size of the air force needed would depend on the type of bombing to be carried out.

The Cabinet agreed that:

In preparing any plan for military operations account must be taken of the possible effects on our Arab allies in the Middle East and the Persian Gulf if force were used against Egypt. It was important that the operations should be so planned as to reduce to the minimum the risk that other Arab States would be drawn into supporting Egypt.

Consideration should be given to the possibility of cutting the oil pipeline from the Canal to Cairo which was vital to the economic life of Egypt's capital.

The possibility of referring the dispute to the Security Council, following Gaitskell's remarks, was considered, but Eden took the view that it would 'invite a Soviet veto', as did others.

The record of this crucial Cabinet continues:

The Prime Minister said that against this background the Cabinet must decide what our policy must be. He fully agreed that the question was not a legal issue, but must be treated as a matter of widest international importance. It must now be our aim to place the Suez Canal under the control of the Powers interested in international shipping and trade by means of a new international Commission on which Egypt would be given suitable representation. Colonel Nasser's action had presented us with an opportunity to find a lasting settlement of this problem, and we should not hesitate to take advantage of it. . . .

The fundamental question before the Cabinet, however, was whether they were prepared in the last resort to pursue their objective by the threat or even the use of force, and whether they were ready, in default of assistance from the United States and France, to take military action alone.

The Cabinet agreed that our essential interests in this must, if necessary, be safeguarded by military action and that the necessary preparations to this end must be made. Failure to hold the Suez Canal would lead inevitably to the loss one by one of all our interests and assets in the Middle East and, even if we had to act alone, we could not stop short of using force to protect our position if all other methods of protecting it proved unavailing.

The Cabinet then dealt with a number of consequential matters, involving the blocking of Egyptian sterling balances in London and the protection of British citizens in Egypt. Exports of military equipment to Egypt were banned.

The final conclusions were clear enough:

The Cabinet –

(1) Agreed that HMG should seek to secure, by the use of force if necessary, the reversal of the Egyptian Government's action to nationalize the Suez Canal Company.

(2) Invited the Prime Minister to send a personal message to the President of the United States asking him to send a representative to London to discuss the situation with representatives of the Governments of the United Kingdom and France.

(3) Appointed a Committee of Ministers consisting of:

Prime Minister (in the Chair)
Lord President
Chancellor of the Exchequer
Foreign Secretary
Commonwealth Secretary
Minister of Defence ·

to formulate further plans for putting our policy into effect.*

(4) Instructed the Chiefs of Staff to prepare a plan and timetable for military operations against Egypt should they prove unavoidable.

This was the genesis of the Egypt Committee, whose secretary was Norman Brook. The Egypt Committee acted 'as a kind of inner Cabinet and was also responsible for supervising the military operations and plans'. A sub-committee of the Economic Policy Committee was set up to deal with the effects of the emergency on the economy, and a Defence (Transitional) Committee of the Permanent Secretaries of the Departments concerned, under the chairmanship of Norman Brook, and other departmental committees were established. Within hours of Nasser's action, a new Whitehall structure had been created.

That afternoon Eden informed Eisenhower of the position of the British Government:

... We are all agreed [here] that we cannot afford to allow Nasser to seize control of the Canal in this way, in defiance of international agreements. If we take a firm stand over this now, we shall have the support of all the maritime Powers. If we do not, our influence and yours throughout the Middle East will, we are convinced, be finally destroyed.

2. The immediate threat is to the oil supplies to Western Europe, a great part of which flows through the Canal. We have reserves in the United Kingdom which would last us for six weeks; and the countries of Western Europe have stocks, rather smaller as we believe, on which they could draw for a time. We are, however, at once considering means of limiting current consumption so as to conserve our supplies. If the Canal were closed we should have to ask you to help us by reducing the amount which you draw from the pipeline terminals in the Eastern Mediterranean and possibly by sending us supplementary supplies for a time from your side of the world.

3. It is, however, the outlook for the longer term which is more threatening. The Canal is an international asset and facility, which is vital to the free world. The maritime Powers cannot afford to allow Egypt to expropriate it and to exploit it by using the revenues for her own internal purposes irrespective of the interests of the Canal and of the Canal users. Apart from the Egyptians' complete lack of technical qualifications, their past behaviour gives no confidence that they can be trusted to manage it with any sense of international obligation. Nor are they

---

* Eden, Salisbury, Macmillan, Lloyd, Home and Monckton.

capable of providing the capital which will soon be needed to widen and deepen it so that it may be capable of handling the increased volume of traffic which it must carry in the years to come. We should, I am convinced, take this opportunity to put its management on a firm and lasting basis as an international trust.

4. We should not allow ourselves to become involved in legal quibbles about the rights of the Egyptian Government to nationalize what is technically an Egyptian company, or in financial arguments about their capacity to pay the compensation which they have offered. I feel sure that we should take issue with Nasser on the broader international grounds summarized in the preceding paragraph.

5. As we see it we are unlikely to attain our objective by economic pressures alone. I gather that Egypt is not due to receive any further aid from you. No large payments from her sterling balances here are due before January. We ought in the first instance to bring the maximum political pressure to bear on Egypt. For this, apart from our own action, we should invoke the support of all the interested Powers. My colleagues and I are convinced that we must be ready, in the last resort, to use force to bring Nasser to his senses. For our part we are prepared to do so. I have this morning instructed our Chiefs of Staff to prepare a military plan accordingly.

6. However, the first step must be for you and us and France to exchange views, align our policies and concert together how we can best bring the maximum pressure to bear on the Egyptian Government. . . .

Eden concluded by proposing an immediate tripartite meeting 'at a high level' either in London or in Washington.

Eisenhower responded to Eden, on 28 July, informing him of Robert Murphy's dispatch to London. 'While we agree with much that you have to say, we rather think there are one or two additional thoughts that you and we might profitably consider. . . . We are of the earnest opinion that the maximum number of maritime nations affected by the Nasser action should be consulted quickly in the hope of obtaining an agreed basis of understanding. DE'

This was to be the first of many exchanges between the two leaders, and demonstrated at the very outset a fundamental misunderstanding. American attitudes of affection and admiration for British courage and decency – although not universal – were strong throughout the war and in the post-war period, but even among those most admiring of Britain this did not extend to British Imperialism. *Life* magazine in 1942, in its 'Open Letter to the People of England', wrote that 'One thing we are sure we are not fighting for is to hold the British Empire together. We didn't like to put the matter so bluntly, but we don't want you to have any illusions.' For once, an editorial faithfully reflected both official and popular sentiment. Its causes lay deep in the American experience and history (and in the manner in which that history is taught in American schools), and it is curious that Churchill of all men should have found it incomprehensible. Thus 'self-determination' was as crucial to Roosevelt as it had been to Woodrow Wilson; for Churchill, it related wholly to the German-enslaved peoples of Europe; for the Americans it was a global principle. Sumner Welles was the classic personification of this view, but so was every American President from Roosevelt to Eisenhower. There was an obsession with 'federal' solutions on the American model. But, above all, there was a conviction that the war had been fought for a great principle; in Eisenhower's own description, it had been a Crusade.

The British post-war withdrawal from India, Burma, Malaya and Palestine had, accordingly, been warmly approved in Washington. The Middle East as a whole was more complex, as American interests were directly involved, and in Libya there had been in effect a pragmatic Anglo-American approach, as in Iran.

The inconsistency lay in the fact that American concern about combating Communism in such a sensitive area was often in competition with its insistence on the movement by the British and French towards colonial independence. Egypt had almost become a touchstone of this ambivalence. The 1954 Canal Zone agreement had been seen by the Americans as a major achievement, to be applauded and approved. As Dulles told the National Security Council on 1 November 1956:

For many years now the United States has been walking a tightrope between the effort to maintain our old and valued relations with our British and French allies on the one hand, and on the other trying to assure ourselves of the friendship and understanding of the newly independent countries who have escaped from colonialism.

But Eisenhower's views were far more definite. He had been very impressed by the American preparations for the independence of the Philippines; he certainly did not accept what he called Churchill's 'almost childlike faith' that the answer to all problems was Anglo-American partnership; as has rightly been written, 'He believed that the United States was the natural leader of the newly independent countries of the postwar era.'*

Dulles, on the other hand, was obsessed by the perils of Communism, the protection of American oil and other interests in the Middle East, the need for maintaining Britain and France as the United States' key allies in Europe, and his slowly developing but now strong personal antipathy to Nasser. It was this confusion of priorities and objectives in Dulles' mind that made him an almost impossible man for the British to do business

---

* W. Roger Louis, *American Anti-Colonialism and the Dissolution of the British Empire.*

with, but it also made him a very dangerous man to do business with, for his confusion did not reflect the clarity of the President's ideas. Eisenhower was deeply cautious, while Dulles' language was too often that of a risk-taker; Eisenhower was determined to keep America out of conflict, and his anti-colonialism was fundamental and genuine. Dulles, for all his faults, recognized the immense complexity of the Middle East situation, its real dangers, and the need in an area where America was weak to bolster Western influence and power; Eisenhower did not. And Eisenhower, not Dulles, ran American foreign policy.

This complicated dichotomy in American attitudes lies at the heart of subsequent events. Now, we can see it clearly: at the time it was not clear at all.

An additional complication was that Eisenhower, who was recovering from his operation for ileitis, had just been renominated as Republican candidate for the presidential election in November, although the Convention would not be until August. The only serious doubt about his re-election was his health, but he had made a strong recovery from his heart attack and operation, and was emphatically the candidate. Eisenhower, both at the time and subsequently, became very angry whenever it was hinted that his approach to the Middle East was at all affected by domestic political considerations, and the evidence – both private and public – strongly supports him. But although Eisenhower's belief that the United States should be the champion of colonial peoples working towards independence – even though, as he wrote on 3 August, 'we frequently find ourselves victims of the tyrannies of the weak' – was sincere and strong, his reputation as a peacemaker was important to him personally and to his presidency. His Vice-President, Richard Nixon, who later considered the American attitude in the Suez crisis to have been a serious mistake, judged that domestic political factors did have a significant effect on Eisenhower's approach, and that if there had not been a presidential election different policies would have been pursued. This, of course, is conjecture; what is incontestable is that Eisenhower's claims that the election had *no* effect on his attitude can be viewed with scepticism. Yet it certainly was not paramount; he was too big a man for that. But the looming election was not irrelevant to his thoughts. And this should have been better appreciated in London than it was.

At this point, in London, an important misunderstanding occurred.

Hugh Gaitskell's own sympathies, and even more those of his wife Dora, were strongly with Israel, which made him personally anti-Nasser. These were sincere emotions on which the Israeli Ambassador in London sedulously, and justifiably, played. Also, there was a long and honourable close relationship between the Labour Party and Israel, particularly with the ruling Israeli Labour Party, and strong British Labour sympathy with, and support for, Israel in its beleaguered position. The Labour Party had its Arabist supporters, but they were exceptional, and of these few had any sympathy for Nasser and his military regime. Gaitskell was outraged by Nasser's nationalization and military occupation of the Canal, which he rightly saw as inspired by hostility against Israel as well as the West. Given the choice between an unscrupulous military regime in Cairo that was dedicated to the destruction of Israel, and a Socialist democracy in Israel, he saw no choice at all. Also, far from being the 'desiccated calculating machine' of Bevan's imagination, Gaitskell was a man of much warmth, intensity and patriotism, qualities which were consistently underrated by the Conservatives, including Eden.

When Gaitskell asked for a private and confidential discussion, Eden willingly agreed. During this meeting, Eden emphasized that the Government had no immediate plans for military force, although this could not be ruled out if other alternatives were fruitless. With this, Gaitskell was wholly satisfied, but what he told those closest to him was that the Government 'had no intention whatever of using armed force'.* This is not what Eden had told him, and I very much doubt whether Gaitskell had misunderstood what Eden had said. The fact is that he did not demur.

Gaitskell's attitude was echoed by Bevan, who wrote an article in *Tribune* that was immensely displeasing to the slowly marshalling anti-war faction in the Labour Party which had been dismayed by Gaitskell's approach. Bevan, who fully shared Gaitskell's sympathy with Israel and his dislike of Nasser, never took a high moral line over the crisis, and in the early stages, while preserving his position, was not at all unsympathetic to Eden's policy. Under intense pressure from his Bevanite former allies, notably Barbara Castle, he qualified his stance, but he never went as far as they did. He liked and admired Eden, and loathed Nasser, and wanted the latter brought down. In this, he was far closer to Labour opinion than people like Castle, Douglas Jay or Christopher Mayhew, or those other Labour MPs who could reliably be counted upon to support any cause contrary to British interests and in those of Britain's enemies. There were several fellow travellers of this ilk, and Bevan despised them heartily. So did Richard Crossman, a passionate Zionist who was unfortunately abroad throughout August; and so did Alfred Robens, and Gaitskell himself. Thus, apart from some mutterings from the more disagreeable portions of the Labour Party, there appeared to be a remarkable unity on the Opposition front bench in support of the Government.

---

* Douglas Jay, *Change and Fortune*, p. 253.

On the afternoon of 30 July the Shadow Cabinet met, and, in Gaitskell's contemporary account, 'there was some anxiety about our going too far in a bellicose direction and it was felt important that we should stress exactly what our attitude was to nationalization, as contrasted with the breaking of international agreements or concessions'. Gaitskell, with James Griffiths, saw Eden that evening at his request, to stress that the Labour view was that 'force would be appropriate in self-defence or, at any rate, in circumstances which could be properly justified before the United Nations'. Gaitskell also proposed that Israel should receive more arms from the West, with which, Gaitskell thought, Eden privately agreed. Eden told Gaitskell that he favoured international control of the Canal, and when Gaitskell asked if, in the event of Nasser not accepting this, the British would use force, Eden replied, 'Well, I don't want to take that hurdle yet. I have already made it plain, I may say, that I doubted whether we could support force merely on those grounds.'*

During the afternoon of 30 July, the first substantive paper to the Egypt Committee was circulated by Macmillan, urging that British shipowners should pay their Canal dues directly to the Suez Canal Company in London, that Britain should place controls over Egyptian sterling, thereby putting her out of the transferable account area, and that she should persuade the United States and France to take comparable action. When the Committee held its first meeting that day at 7.00 p.m. Macmillan's paper was accepted.

On the following morning the tempo quickened when the Egypt Committee agreed to jam Egyptian broadcasts to Cyprus and was informed by the Chiefs of Staff that it would be necessary to call up between ten and twelve thousand reservists; that an artillery regiment should be posted to Cyprus; and that British troops in Libya could be concentrated on the Egyptian border. Also, two additional fighter squadrons could be sent to Cyprus. 'Such preliminary steps might provoke Egypt or the Soviet Union to raise the issue in the Security Council. On the other hand, they would help to avert, in this country, the criticism that the Government were inactive. Moreover, the execution of the military plans might be delayed

---

* Williams, *Hugh Gaitskell*, pp. 419–20. Williams, quite wrongly in my judgement, inserted the word 'only' in the sentence 'force would be appropriate in self-defence' between 'appropriate' and 'in self-defence', which very seriously distorts the original diary entry. Williams and I had a considerable exchange of public correspondence in the *Listener* in 1979 over Gaitskell's role in the Suez crisis. I was, and remain, very critical of his account, and although I both liked and admired Gaitskell, who was consistently very kind to me, I remain critical. This deliberate change in a diary entry seems to me extraordinary for a serious historian, but his early death in 1985 was a profound loss to modern British political historiography, and one which I greatly lamented.

if certain preliminary preparations were not put in hand at once.' The Chiefs were instructed to submit

a list of preparations which could be put in hand forthwith and would have the effect of bringing the operations forward. Ministers could then consider which, if any, of these measures were likely to disturb public opinion or to provoke other countries to raise the matter in the Security Council. . . . Militarily, it would be to our advantage if the Egyptian armoured division now astride the Canal could be induced to move east of the Canal. A demonstration by Israel might achieve this. But such a move would tend to range the other Arab states on the side of Egypt; and it was an essential aim of our policy to isolate Egypt from the other Arab countries. For this reason the French should be strongly discouraged from pursuing their proposal to reinforce Israel with Mystère aircraft.

Other preparatory plans were made; three aircraft carriers were to be made ready to proceed to the Mediterranean; a cruiser and four destroyers of the Home Fleet were to be put at four hours' notice, but there was not to be a general suspension of summer leave in the Home Fleet.

Meanwhile, there had been a somewhat casual discussion in Washington between Eisenhower, Hoover and the Deputy Under-Secretary of State, Robert Murphy; Dulles was in Peru attending the inauguration of the new President, but there seemed no need to recall him. Murphy was instructed to fly to London 'to see what it's all about', and Eden also told the Egypt Committee that Eisenhower was thinking on the lines of a conference of the affected maritime powers; this was not greeted with any enthusiasm; more to the taste of ministers was Eden's message to the Australian and New Zealand Governments, also to be transmitted to Canada and South Africa, informing them 'of the determination of Her Majesty's Government to carry the issue of the Suez Canal to a final conclusion . . . [including] our readiness to have recourse to military measures in the last resort'.

What was being overlooked in London, or severely underestimated, was the American dimension. Dulles was not alone in his suspicion that, as in 1914 and 1939, the British would start a conflict 'on the calculation that we would be bound to come in', and Eisenhower had been more disturbed by Eden's telegram than Murphy seems to have realized. At a meeting on 31 July with Dulles, Hoover, Humphrey, the CIA head Allen Dulles and the Chief of Naval Operations these doubts were forcibly expressed. The President thought the British attitude 'unwise' and the United States could not support military action without congressional approval, which was very unlikely to be given, particularly in an election year, and would probably require a special recall. Admiral Burke wanted to support the British, and John Foster Dulles said that 'Nasser must be made to disgorge his theft.' But the President was emphatic: a conference of maritime powers and international pressure was one thing, a Middle East war was entirely another; to support the British in such a war 'might well array the world from Dakar to the Philippine Islands against us.' Dulles was instructed to proceed immediately to London.

The principal cause of this sudden urgency in Washington was the reports from Murphy, who had seen Lloyd and Pineau on the evening of 29 July and on the morning of the 30th. There was also a meeting of the Egypt Committee that morning, which demonstrated how far apart the British and the Americans already were, and the different directions in which they were moving.

At this meeting it was agreed that if there *were* to be a conference of maritime powers, as the Americans urged, the British purpose

should be to limit the function of the conference to the approval of a declaration of policy ... [which] would form the basis of a Note to the Egyptian Government which we would be prepared, if necessary, to despatch on our own responsibility, and which would be a virtual ultimatum. If Colonel Nasser refused to accept it, military operations could then proceed.

There was no talk at this vital meeting of using force 'as a last resort'; indeed, the record bluntly states:

While our ultimate purpose was to place the Canal under international control, our immediate was to bring about the downfall of the present Egyptian Government. This might perhaps be achieved by less elaborate operations than those required to secure physical possession of the Canal itself. On the other hand, it was argued that our case before world opinion was based on the need to secure international control over the Canal.

In addition to the regular membership, this meeting was also attended by Butler, Mountbatten, Antony Head (Minister for War), Templer, Boyle and Harold Watkinson (Minister of Transport and Civil Aviation). It was agreed to enter into naval staff talks with the French 'without commitment on either side'; forces in Cyprus and Libya should be increased, which would require calling up between 20,000 and 25,000 Class A Reservists; twenty-four Valiant bombers were to be deployed in Malta, Tripolitania, Aden and Bahrein; fifty Canberras and two Hunter squadrons were to be sent to Cyprus; all airfields were to be well stocked with bombs. There was one change of thought. While Eden remained concerned about the possibility of Israel taking advantage of the situation by attacking Egypt, he had changed his mind about dissuading the French from sending more Mystères, and would consult the Iraqi Prime Minister Nuri; if his response was 'not unfavourable, further supplies of aircraft to Israel might be considered'.

This meeting marked another escalation in the British commitment. While Selwyn Lloyd, always the lawyer, and his Foreign Officer advisers fretted about proving Nasser's action to be illegal, most of the Egypt Committee – especially Macmillan – were concentrating upon what really mattered, namely the downfall of Nasser and the rapid deployment of British and French forces to achieve this.

Murphy had lunch with Eden and Lloyd at Downing Street after this meeting. While Murphy emphasized that the purpose of his visit was to discover British intentions and that he was not empowered to reach decisions, he reiterated Eisenhower's desire for the maritime conference, wisely not adding that this was simply a device to calm down the situation. Eden said that if the American Government could not take action themselves 'we would hope that they would keep a watchful eye on the Soviet Union and would restrain Israel'.

But Murphy's arguments made some impression upon Eden, and at the second Egypt Committee that day he moved away from his morning position, and said that 'such a conference would help to occupy the necessary interval before we should be in a position to take other action'. But the Anglo-French attitude was well summarized by Lloyd; there would be a resolution, a Note to the Egyptians, and 'In the event of an unsatisfactory reply, action would follow.' In other words, the ultimatum policy remained, and the sole purpose of the conference would be to order Nasser to repeal the nationalization order. The Anglo-American gulf became wider.

Eden informed the committee that the French had offered a division and a parachute brigade

for military operations against the Egyptians.... It was understood that the French contribution would be ready for action in about thirty days. It was understood that the French were anxious to participate in any military action to re-establish their traditional position in the Middle East. In view of the large share which the French at present held in the Suez Canal Company it would be difficult to exclude them altogether from any subsequent international arrangements for the control of the Canal.

Macmillan, who had emerged as the warlike fire-eater in the Cabinet, then raised the matter of the problems that would arise after the military occupation 'of the Canal Zone and of part of Egypt, while the international organization for control of the Canal and a new regime in Egypt were being established', and he and Salisbury were asked to examine this. Somewhat incongruously, but interestingly, Thorneycroft expressed concern about 'inflammatory articles in the Press, e.g. on the prospects of the use of force'. Head announced that the Chiefs of Staff 'were examining plans for operations short of a full-scale amphibious assault which might be undertaken initially as a means of overturning the present regime in Egypt'.

Lloyd's account of this meeting, which marked a critical point, has at least the merit – the only one – of being succinct: 'We then had another meeting of the Egypt Committee.... There was a long discussion of the forthcoming conference and various other matters. The call-up notices for the reservists were delayed for twenty-four hours.'* And that is all!

That evening, Murphy dined with Macmillan at 11 Downing Street. Although Murphy in his account gets the date wrong, and says that Barbour, the American Minister, was present, when in fact it was the Chargé, Foster, the key other figures present were Macmillan and Lord Alexander. There is no doubt at all that Macmillan, in his own words, 'succeeded in thoroughly alarming Murphy'. His message was that the British were fully prepared to put the matter to the test by the use of force, the French would participate, and it might start in August. Murphy concluded that Macmillan was saying that the matter could *only* be resolved by force, and that its use was imminent. Macmillan has always denied this, and recorded in his diary: 'We must keep the Americans really frightened. They *must* not be allowed any illusion. Then they will help us to get what we want without the necessity for force.' But the records of the Egypt Committee, which Macmillan had just attended, hardly justify this assessment; Macmillan was, as one of his colleagues has said, 'highly belligerent', and although Murphy later wrote that he thought the Anglo–French attitude 'not justified', he went after this fatal dinner immediately to the American Embassy to report the conversation to Eisenhower.

The President had already been very concerned by Eden's cable, and Murphy's report shocked him. The fact was that the British were in no position to launch an immediate operation, although Murphy was not as wildly far off the truth as Lloyd and others have claimed. But, whether there was a misunderstanding of what Macmillan said – and I doubt that there was – the reality was the reaction of Eisenhower. As already mentioned, he ordered Dulles to fly to London immediately; he then wrote this letter for Dulles to hand personally to the British Prime Minister. It is one of the key Suez documents, and must be given in full:

Dear Anthony,

From the moment that Nasser announced nationalization of the Suez Canal Company, my thoughts have been constantly with you. Grave problems are placed before both our governments, although for each of us they naturally differ in type and character. Until this morning, I was happy to feel that we were approaching decisions as to applicable procedures somewhat along parallel lines, even though there were, as would be expected, important differences as to detail. But early this

* Lloyd, *Suez*, p. 91.

471

morning I received the message, communicated to me through Murphy from you and Harold Macmillan, telling me on a most secret basis of your decision to employ force without delay or attempting any intermediate and less drastic steps.

We recognize the transcendent worth of the Canal to the free world and the possibility that eventually the use of force might become necessary in order to protect international rights. But we have been hopeful that through a Conference in which would be represented the signatories to the Convention of 1888, as well as other maritime nations, there would be brought about such pressures on the Egyptian Government that the efficient operation of the Canal could be assured for the future.

For my part, I cannot over-emphasize the strength of my conviction that some such method must be attempted before action such as you contemplate should be undertaken. If unfortunately the situation can finally be resolved only by drastic means, there should be no grounds for belief anywhere that corrective measures were undertaken merely to protect national or individual investors, or the legal rights of a sovereign nation were ruthlessly flouted. A conference, at the very least, should have a great education effort throughout the world. Public opinion here, and I am convinced, in most of the world, would be outraged should there be a failure to make such efforts. Moreover, initial military successes might be easy, but the eventual price might become far too heavy.

I have given you my own personal conviction, as well as that of my associates, as to the unwisdom even of contemplating the use of military force at this moment. Assuming, however, that the whole situation continued to deteriorate to the point where such action would seem the only recourse, there are certain political facts to remember. As you realize, employment of United States forces is possible only through positive action on the part of the Congress, which is now adjourned but can be reconvened on my call for special reasons. If those reasons should involve the issue of employing United States military strength abroad, there would have to be a showing that every peaceful means of resolving the difficulty had previously been exhausted. Without such a showing, there would be a reaction that could very seriously affect our peoples' feeling toward our Western Allies. I do not want to exaggerate, but I assure you that this could grow to such an intensity as to have the most far-reaching consequences.

I realize that the messages from both you and Harold stressed that the decision taken was already approved by the government and was firm and irrevocable. But I personally feel sure that the American reaction would be severe and that great areas of the world would share that reaction. On the other hand, I believe we can marshall that opinion in support of a reasonable and conciliatory, but absolutely firm, position. So I hope that you will consent to reviewing this matter once more in its broadest aspects. It is for this reason that I have asked Foster to leave this afternoon to meet with your people tomorrow in London.

I have given you here only a few highlights in the chain of reasoning that compels us to conclude that the step you contemplate should not be undertaken until every peaceful means of protecting the rights and the livelihood of great portions of the world had been thoroughly explored and exhausted. Should these means fail, and I think it is erroneous to assume in advance that they needs must fail, then world opinion would understand how earnestly all of us had attempted to be just, fair and considerate, but that we simply could not accept a situation that would in the long run prove disastrous to the prosperity and living standards of every nation whose economy depends directly or indirectly upon East–West shipping.

With warm personal regard – and with earnest assurance of my continuing respect and friendship.

As ever,
D.E.

Eden's interpretation of this letter was that 'The President did not rule out the use of force.'* This is technically true, but the whole tenor of the letter was in the opposite direction, and was confirmed by Dulles, who added his own comment on Eisenhower's letter, writing to Eden that it 'refers not to the going through the motions of having an intermediate conference but to the use of intermediate steps as a genuine and sincere effort to settle the problem and avoid the use of force'. This, as has been revealed, was very definitely not the view of Eden and the Egypt Committee, but although Eisenhower may have seriously misinterpreted the British position of *immediate* military action, Murphy's report had been a remarkably accurate portrayal of the Government's mood, almost embarrassingly supported by a popular press baying for war, which had prompted Thorneycroft's justifiable intervention at the Egypt Committee. Indeed, the mood in Britain and France was for war, as soon as possible; when Dulles went to Downing Street to see Eden he was enthusiastically cheered, the crowd believing that the old wartime relationship still existed, and that the Americans were strongly behind them in recovering the Canal by force and bringing down Nasser. Dulles was genuinely moved by this reception, and mentioned it often; it served to augment his personal ambivalence, with tragic consequences.

The British were not enthusiastic about the American proposal for a conference of the signatories of the 1888 Convention with certain additions, notably the United States and the Soviet Union. But Eden and Lloyd were encouraged by Dulles' general reactions, and knew that any early military action was out of the question. If the twenty-two nations to be invited could put real pressure on Egypt, it might be worthwhile; if not, they had at least tried. Their forebodings were not reduced when Nasser again raised the rhetoric by denouncing the Conference as 'Imperialistic', and stating that Egypt would not attend; the Americans were told that if Egypt did not have its way there would be 'great disturbance' in the area. Exhilarated

* Avon, *Full Circle*, p. 436.

by the ecstatic popular support for his *coup*, and wholly underestimating the extent of the anger in London and Paris, Nasser was now in a malignantly gloating mood. He failed to realize that not only was all this being closely monitored but that a considerable number of key individuals now took his bombast with deadly seriousness. When he decreed the Canal to be 'The Arabs' Canal' and its nationalization the beginning of the creation of a vast Arab Empire and the complete destruction of Israel he was believed, and not least in Tel Aviv. Nasser never thought that the British and French would actually use force; he and his commanders should have been prepared, both mentally and practically, for the possibility, but they were not. So, Nasser enjoyed his triumph, Radio Cairo poured out its vitriol, wholly unaware that there were men in London, Paris and Tel Aviv who were in real earnest in their plans for his destruction. Hubris is usually accompanied by folly; this was yet another example.

Although Eden and Dulles were uncomfortable with each other, they, in Lloyd's words, 'treated each other with exemplary courtesy, whatever they thought. Perhaps that was part of the trouble.'* The real trouble was that while Dulles was ambivalent, Eisenhower was not.

Eden and Eisenhower, in sharp contrast with several other participants in the Suez crisis, had one thing in common – complete consistency. Eden was determined from the outset to bring Nasser down, preferably peacefully, but he clearly recognized that this almost certainly involved the use of force. His lead in the Egypt Committee was consistently to this end. To him, if Nasser succeeded, the position of Britain and the West in the Middle East would be destroyed irretrievably. Nasser and his regime were the enemy, and must be defeated; if this could be done by political pressure buttressed by military force, so much the better; if not, then that force would have to be used. This was his position.

For his part, Eisenhower, once he realized from Murphy that the British were serious, was implacably opposed to the use of force to resolve the Canal issue. He did not share Dulles' personal hostility to Nasser; as he remarked to Dulles on 31 July, 'it was wrong to give undue stress to Nasser himself. He felt Nasser embodies the emotional demands of the people of the area for independence and for "slapping the white man down".' He also considered that 'Nasser was within his rights' and that 'the power of eminent domain within its own territory could scarcely be doubted'. He was – rightly – dismissive of British claims that the Egyptians were incapable of running the Canal.

Eisenhower did not think that the nationalization of the Canal was worth a war. The British and the French thought that it was, particularly the

---

* Lloyd, *Suez*, p. 100.

latter; Dulles hovered in the middle, inconsistent throughout, breathing hot and cold bewilderingly. 'We assumed that the American attitude ... was one of prudence rather than divergence,' Eden later wrote. The trouble was that there was divergence within the United States administration. If Dulles had been as emphatic as Eisenhower, much misunderstanding would have been avoided. The go-between became the menace to understanding.

Dulles was definitely surprised by the intensity of the British feeling, especially when he stayed briefly with Salisbury at Hatfield. In his private conversation with Eden – there were only the two present – Eden left him in no doubt of his resolve, and when he asked whether, in the event of an Anglo-French military operation against Egypt, they could rely on the moral support of the United States Dulles assured him that he could always count on the moral support and sympathy of the United States. He also told Eden that he did not want to know anything of their military plans. There is no reason whatever to disbelieve Eden's immediately recorded version of this vital discussion, and for a time Dulles soared in his estimation. If Dulles had said that the President would not have it, nor would the American Congress, this might not have changed British and French determination to bring the matter to a head, militarily if need be, but it would have represented the truth of the situation, and Eisenhower's later anger would have been more fairly directed against his ambiguous emissary than against Eden.

The Americans were also uneasy about the Panama Canal, on which they had a lease in perpetuity with Panama, and which they regarded as an American and not an international waterway, thereby in a totally different category to Suez; but however satisfactorily they regarded their legal case, the principle of arbitrary unilateral seizures of canals was not one they wished to encourage. This was another real element in the American ambivalence as personified by Dulles, who saw, and warmly approved of, Eden's speech on 2 August. As Dulles repeatedly emphasized, Nasser, by whatever means, must 'disgorge' the Suez Canal. It was a memorable phrase.

No possible blame can be attached to Makins,* whose objective reports on initial American reactions were very accurate. The fact was that, with a divided US administration, and the matter having been raised to the highest political level, the role of Foreign Office and State Department officials had already been gravely reduced, and was to be reduced even further. Hoover definitely had the ear of President Eisenhower, and in

---

*Makins had been appointed Joint Permanent Secretary to the Treasury, and his successor was to be Caccia. Makins was on leave in September, and returned to Britain to assume his new responsibilities in October. Caccia, as will be related, did not arrive in Washington until November.

London Sir Ivone Kirkpatrick was to be a strong and consistent supporter of the Government and of Eden personally. Partly because of security, but principally because leaders like dealing directly with leaders (or deceiving them), the Foreign Office and the State Department as official units were largely ignored; in consequence even high officials in London and Washington knew very little about what was going on. This often happens in major crises, and it was certainly not the habit of Eisenhower or Dulles to confide in career diplomats on major issues. If Eden had had a more experienced, self-confident and popular Foreign Secretary it is possible that the decision-making circle in the Foreign Office might have been discreetly enlarged, to the advantage of the Government as a whole. But, on both sides of the Atlantic, the dialogue was confined to the top echelons. Makins in Washington and Sir Gladwyn Jebb in Paris knew very little of what was happening. This would not have been serious had not Dulles, as his biographer writes, 'insisted on sustaining a tortured ambiguity. He thought the seizure [of the Canal] was legal, but he frowned upon it as bad international practice and so would not give it full countenance.'* In fact, Dulles went much further, and his personal loathing of Nasser was manifest in his discussions with the British. He was definitly *not* His Master's Voice.

Much has been made of Eisenhower's concern with his image of the Peacemaker President and his hostility to Imperialism, but although these undoubtedly played an important part in his reactions, the real difference was one of perceptions. Eden saw Nasser's action as, in his own words, 'a thumb on our windpipe' of vital significance to Britain, the Commonwealth and Western Europe. As Hoover never tired of emphasizing, American interests in the Canal were not great or direct, and both he and Humphrey were deeply suspicious of ill-defined 'British oil interests' in the Middle East. They suspected a British trap; Eisenhower, on the basis of Murphy's report of the Macmillan dinner, foresaw a Middle East war of horrifying dimensions involving, directly or indirectly, three of the closest allies of the United States – Britain, France and Israel. His initial relaxed reaction to the nationalization had been transformed into energetic concern to prevent a conflict at almost any cost. No doubt, his motives were mixed, and he was an infinitely more shrewd – and on occasion ruthless – politician than he was given credit for at the time. The British in London, in spite of all Makins told them of the reality, genuinely believed that Dulles ran American foreign policy, with a somewhat lazy and uninvolved President somewhere in the background, who would, if it came to the crunch, support his old wartime allies and friends. They seriously under-estimated Eisenhower's strength and resolution, and also his personal

* Townsend Hoopes, *The Devil and John Foster Dulles*, p. 349.

vanity and hot temper. Eisenhower was used to getting his own way, and, for all his charm, was authoritarian. He took the Truman view that the President of the United States' word and authority amounted to a military order, and were not subject to negotiation or question. And this also applied to America's allies. But if Eden misjudged Eisenhower, the President misjudged Eden, the French and the Israelis. The faults were not all on one side.

Cross-Purposes

The British Government was not at all attracted by the American insistence on a conference, especially as it would include the Soviet Union, and at a hurriedly convened meeting of the Egypt Committee at the House of Commons at 3.30 p.m. on 1 August this was declared to be unacceptable. None the less, the Americans were adamant that all possible steps should be taken to mobilize international opinion against Nasser; furthermore, the Conference must be well prepared. The British eventually agreed with considerable reluctance, urging that the Conference should be as brief as possible and should issue a strong communiqué 'as the price of United States co-operation', as the minute of a full Cabinet called at the House of Commons early that evening records. Ministers suspected, rightly, that the real American purpose was to introduce a delaying tactic to calm things down, but felt they had no choice.

On this day the Chiefs of Staff submitted their outline plan for 'Action Against Egypt'. All thought, if any had existed, of a rapid *coup de main* had gone; this was to be a deliberate and major operation, carefully mounted. 'We wish to emphasize that the parachutists and assault forces must not be committed to operations inadequately trained. We consider that time must be allowed in the programme for adequate rehearsal for amphibious and airborne assault forces.'

The concept of operations is based on poising a ring of forces within striking range of Egypt. When this is sufficiently far advanced, an ultimatum will be issued, failing acceptance of which a maritime blockade and air action will be instituted and – if this is still necessary – an assault will be made on the northern end of the canal and a threat posed to Alexandria. The assault forces which could be mounted are so slender that it would be necessary to mount and maintain a sufficiently heavy scale of air attack to ensure that a landing would not encounter serious opposition. For the same reason it would be highly desirable to supplement the sea-borne assault with the maximum parachute drop which is feasible within the aircraft and airfield capacities. Subsequent operations would probably involve occupying the entire Canal and possibly restoring law and order in Egypt. We do not plan to become involved in the permanent occupation of Egypt....

If air action is instituted, the initial aim would be to neutralize the Egyptian air force.

478

On timing:

All that is possible to say at this stage is that:

(a) With or without requisitioning, personnel moves would be completed within 28 days.

(b) Moves of freight and vehicles could be completed in five to six weeks from the date that requisitioning is authorized.

The Chiefs also asked permission for high-level aerial photography.

This was indeed a cautious approach, involving a slow build-up, but as it was now clear that there could be no military action until the Conference had been completed, the proposals of the Chiefs were approved by the Egypt Committee in principle on 2 August, which also approved requisitioning of merchant ships. It was at this meeting that Macmillan raised the possibility of involving Israel. 'It would be helpful if Egypt were faced with the possibility of a war on two fronts'; Lloyd and the Chiefs were asked to consider this.

Meanwhile, Kilmuir, the law officers and the Legal Adviser to the Foreign Office had produced a paper, circulated on 1 August, which proved to their complete satisfaction that Egypt had broken international law, thereby totally reversing their original advice. Lloyd was delighted, and the paper certainly gave Eden effective ammunition for the speech he was preparing for the next day in the Commons, but close inspection raises many doubts:

1. The threat of force to keep British or French subjects working in the Canal is itself a breach of international law.

2. The fact that this threat has been made establishes that in the absence of this compulsion Egyptians would not be able to operate the Canal and so provide free passage in accordance with their obligations under the Convention.

3. The Convention was entered into on the basis of a company operated by Britain and France.

4. This Company has in the course of years acquired an international character which is confirmed by the history of the company and various agreements made by the company with the Egyptian Government.

5. Some years ago an eminent international lawyer gave an opinion to this effect which was seen by the Egyptian Government and not dissented from at the time.

6. To nationalize a company of such an international character is of itself a breach of international law.

One does not have to be a lawyer to recognize that this was very thin gruel, but at the time it did not seem to matter, and the paper was only very perfunctorily discussed. No one apart from Kilmuir and Lloyd was interested in the legal niceties; Nasser had seized by force a major international waterway of crucial importance to Britain and Western Europe. Only later was the flimsiness of the legal argument exposed, but at the time it was unquestioned in the Government and in the House of Commons; feelings were running too high.

The key problem, if one were being legalistic, was that the 1888 Convention said nothing about the ownership of the Canal, but referred only to 'a definite system destined to guarantee for all times and for all Powers, the use of the Suez Maritime Canal'. Nasser's 1954 undertaking to maintain the international character of the Canal had already been broken over Israeli ships, and his nationalization and physical military seizure of it were certainly a total violation of his undertaking, but was it, strictly speaking, a breach of international law? The best endeavours of Kilmuir, the law officers, Lloyd and the Foreign Office – and one can estimate how hard they tried – could produce only this. Eden, as he had been from the beginning, was not much interested in tortured arguments over legality, recalling the Rhineland débâcle. It was a political issue, involving immense national and Western interests, not an issue for the International Court of Justice, and he was refreshingly right.

Relations between Eden and Gaitskell were cool, but Eden readily agreed to another meeting on 2 August. Gaitskell's diary account, written weeks later, states that:

I pressed him once more about the use of force. There was not disagreement on the military precautions but I said, 'What is your attitude to be if Nasser refuses to accept the conclusions of the further conference?' As I recollect and so implied in what I subsequently wrote to him, he said, 'I only want to keep open the possibility of force in case Nasser does something else.' I must add, in fairness, that he claimed later that he had said that he only wanted to keep open the possibility of force *or* if Nasser did something else. But at any rate I certainly thought he said the first.*

On 2 August, Eden opened the first major debate on the crisis in the House of Commons with a speech of considerable moderation and calmness. He rehearsed the legal arguments, but his principal point was that Britain could not accept arrangements for the future which left the Canal in the unfettered control of a single power that could exploit its position at will; the closure to all Israeli ships demonstrated what could be done, with devastating consequences, to the West and Britain. He referred to discussions with the Americans and the French, and to precautionary military preparations, announcing the calling up of reservists. One of his most effective points, in a particularly effective speech, even more impressive because it was delivered in a low key to a packed and sympathetic House, was to point out that Nasser had endorsed the agreement between the

* Williams, *Hugh Gaitskell*, pp: 421–2.

British Government and the Suez Canal Company only six weeks before: 'These undertakings are now torn up, and one can have no confidence in the word of a man who does that.'

In marked contrast, Gaitskell delivered a speech of considerable passion, in which he denounced Nasser personally for his intention to destroy Israel, and for his subversion in Jordan and other Arab countries: 'It is all very familiar. It is exactly the same that we encountered from Mussolini and Hitler in those years before the war.' At the end, in a relatively brief passage, he advised great care in using force; it might be necessary in self-defence or as part of some collective defence measures, but nothing must be done that would involve Britain in being branded as the aggressor. Gaitskell would not even have introduced this last-minute qualification if he had not been persuaded by Douglas Jay and John Hynd. Jay has recorded that 'Gaitskell at first thought this unnecessary, and had unfortunately been induced by his sympathies with Israel, and a visit from the Israeli Ambassador, to include some words in his speech about Hitler and Mussolini. But he agreed to our suggestion.'[*]

Subsequently, Gaitskell's defenders and his biographer, Philip Williams, fastened upon this passage to acquit him of inconsistency, but the fact was that the speech was not only passionate but bellicose, and other speakers from both sides were quick to echo the comparison with the pre-war dictators. What is interesting is that it was not Eden but Gaitskell who first – apart from Reginald Paget – introduced the analogy with the 1930s dictators into the Commons debates, although it had been freely expressed in the press. Gaitskell had been the first to propose economic sanctions against Egypt, and it now seemed that he had gone considerably further – as, indeed, he had. He described Nasser's seizure of the Canal as 'part of the struggle for the mastery of the Middle East' and said that issues of prestige were also involved; if Britain failed to assert her rights she would lose not only her allies in the Middle East but her oil. As Paul Johnson, who regarded this speech as 'disastrous', has written: 'The tone of the speech – and this, rather than the references to the Charter, is what impressed the House and the Prime Minister – was one of restrained bellicosity.'[†]

The restraint was not very obvious at the time. Dealing with Nasser's claim that Canal revenues could finance the Aswan Dam, Gaitskell asked: 'How can he at one and the same time both keep the Canal going, spend the necessary money on the repairs, extensions and reconstruction, pay the compensation or service the compensation loan to the shareholders, and also

---

[*] Jay, *Change and Fortune*, p. 254.
[†] Paul Johnson, *The Suez War*, p. 51.

find money for the Aswan Dam?' Gaitskell also referred, with considerable passion, to Nasser's ambition to destroy Israel and create an Arab Empire; his sole object was to raise his prestige in the Middle East. It was strong meat, and one had to be there to appreciate how strong it was in its delivery. As Paul Johnson has fairly written, 'the Government cannot be blamed for assuming that the majority of the Labour Party supported its threats of force'.*

Throughout this account, I consistently endeavour to be fair to everyone involved, including Hugh Gaitskell, for whom, as I have said, I had warm feelings; it is, after all, not every Leader of the Opposition who reads the first book of a very young and junior Clerk of the House of Commons and then goes out of his way to congratulate the author in private and in public, and I loved the fire and spirit of Dora Gaitskell. But his claims subsequently that Eden had misled him do not hold up, and indeed it would be more accurate to state that Gaitskell – even from his own account – misled Eden as to Labour's resolve. I doubt very much whether this was deliberate. Gaitskell was himself torn between, on the one hand, his deep sympathies with Israel, his detestation of Nasser personally and of what he had done and was doing in the Middle East (as Philip Williams has rightly written, he 'never believed in the "Third World" right or wrong, or approved of ambitious military dictators when their skins were dark'), and, on the other hand, the elements in his own Party that were in some cases simply pro-Nasser and pro-Arab and instinctively anti-Imperialist, or in others pacifist. He gained support in the Shadow Cabinet against saying anything that could be judged 'unpatriotic and ... irresponsible'. His own feelings, as the record shows, were more robust. His hostility to Nasser was expressed with much fervour and eloquence; his qualifications were notably more *sotto voce*. It was in this way that he seriously misled Eden, the House of Commons, the press and public opinion. It is insufficient to state that 'Gaitskell's lapses in communication were a serious professional weakness.'†

The tone of Gaitskell's speech and those of other Labour MPs, notably Herbert Morrison, and the reception in the House gave ministers great satisfaction, but there was an unfortunate tendency to assume that this meant that the Opposition was fully behind the Government. One Member, at least, was not deceived. Churchill had been eyeing the Labour benches very carefully; when Heath asked his opinion he replied, 'It won't last.' I, also, had noted the ominous silence in some Labour parts of the House when Gaitskell launched into his vehement assault, but no Member, apart

---

* Johnson, *The Suez War*, p. 52.
† Williams, *Hugh Gaitskell*, p. 423.

from Christopher Mayhew in an intervention, expressed any doubts, and the House rose for the Summer Recess with the appearance of complete unity.

Understandably encouraged, Eden wrote to Eisenhower on 5 August:

In the light of our long friendship, I will not conceal from you that the present situation causes me the deepest concern. I was grateful to you for sending Foster over and for his help. It has enabled us to reach firm and rapid conclusions and to display to Nasser and to the world the spectacle of a united front between our two countries and the French. We have however gone to the very limits of the concessions which we can make.

I do not think that we disagree about our primary objective. As it seems to me, this is to undo what Nasser has done and to set up an international regime for the Canal. The purpose of this regime will be to ensure the freedom and security of transit through the Canal, without discrimination, and the efficiency and economy of its operation.

But this is not all. Nasser has embarked on a course which is unpleasantly familiar. His seizure of the Canal was undoubtedly designed to impress opinion not only in Egypt but in the Arab world and in all Africa too. By this assertion of his power he seeks to further his ambitions from Morocco to the Persian Gulf....

I have never thought Nasser a Hitler, he has no warlike people behind him. But the parallel with Mussolini is close. Neither of us can forget the lives and treasure he cost before he was finally dealt with.

The removal of Nasser and the installation in Egypt of a regime less hostile to the West, must therefore also rank high among our objectives....

You know us better than anyone, and so I need not tell you that our people here are neither excited nor eager to use force. They are, however, grimly determined that Nasser shall not get away with it this time because they are convinced that if he does their existence will be at his mercy. So am I.

It was one thing to call up the reserves – the proclamation was signed by the Queen on 2 August – and to talk of military action, whether in the early or 'last resort' tone, and very much another to plan and achieve it. Eden had no lack of suggestions from his colleagues. Salisbury, to Eden's surprise, was the first of the 'doubters'. He fully shared Eden's determination that international control of the Canal must be restored and had no objection to the preliminary military precautions, but he was very concerned to ensure that Britain was in the right morally and legally, and could present its case to the country and international opinion on a firm base, particularly by reference to the UN Security Council – on which he tended to agree with Gaitskell. But on 2 August he wrote apologetically:

My dear Anthony,

I felt today that we were all being very unhelpful with our ifs and ands over the United Nations etc. But, tiresome though all these things are – & short though the time is in which decisions have to be made – I really think we made some progress – & Bob Dixon, whom some of us had a word with since I saw you, has an idea about a form of reference to the UN which may turn out to have advantages over anything we have thought of yet. I of course entirely agree with what you said, that it is vitally important to know what are the views of Foster & Pineau about a reference to the UN before they leave tomorrow. When we know that, we can plan ahead, both over Parliament and other things.

I am afraid the burden on you must be very heavy. I only wish that I was of much use. But I believe that, as a result of tomorrow's Big Three meetings, things should sort themselves out a great deal, both over the UN and over what the Americans may be willing to do in other things.

I shall be in London and at your disposal at any time – if at all you want me.

> Yrs,
>
> Bobbety

In notable contrast, Macmillan pressed for military co-operation with Israel, but at the Egypt Committee on 3 August Lloyd obtained approval for urging the Israelis to take no action, including a proposed test mobilization, until after the Conference. But Macmillan submitted on 7 August an alternative plan. He proposed that the invasion should be from Libya, with a landing west of Alexandria to take it in reverse and seize the port facilities, from which 'we can seek out and destroy the Egyptian forces and Government'.

What worries me [he wrote] is that I feel that the direction on which the Chiefs of Staff have framed the plan is the wrong one. It is to occupy the Canal. The object of the exercise, if we have to embark upon it, is surely to bring about the fall of Nasser and create a government in Egypt which will work satisfactorily with ourselves and the other powers. All this seems to me to lead to the conclusion we ought to think very carefully again as to the whole character of the plan before it is finalized. . . .

Summary

(a) I think it is doubtful whether the purpose of the plan is the right one.

(b) I think it is doubtful whether sufficient force is being made available to make it effective.

(c) I think we should consider urgently the minimum that we can accept without the use of force, and yet secure our purpose.

(d) I hope that further thought will be given to the Israeli question.

On 3 August Macmillan chaired a special meeting attended by Salisbury, Gladwyn Jebb, Leslie Rowan and Foreign Office officials to consider the post-operation administration of Egypt. Again, Israeli participation was discussed:

It was pointed out that the disadvantages of Israeli participation did not outweigh the disadvantages of failing in the military enterprise; but the meeting was of the opinion that Israeli assistance should, if possible, stop short of active intervention. Israeli presence alone should tie down considerable Egyptian forces.

The meeting recognized that it would probably be difficult, perhaps impossible, to restrain the Israelis, who could in any case be expected to try to extract a price for meeting our wishes.

Agreed that occupation of the Canal would be temporary, and would end when a congenial Egyptian Government had been established, with an International Authority responsible for running the Canal.

Meanwhile, Eden's anxieties remained concerning the possibilities of an Israeli attack on Jordan and of the Anglo-French activities being seen as anti-Arab or, even worse, pro-Israel. Macmillan saw the extreme military usefulness of working closely with the Israelis; Eden saw the immense political problems, and on this their estimates sharply diverged. The instructions to Jebb stated that:

It is most important, from the point of view of public opinion, especially in the United States and in Asia, that the purpose of our action should appear to be confined to establishing the security of the international waterway across the Isthmus of Suez, and not as being complicated by political designs against the Egyptian regime. It follows that the leakage of a document appearing to define our objective in wider terms could be disastrous.

Selwyn Lloyd's version of these instructions* significantly makes no reference to this key passage, which could reasonably be described as giving advice on public relations that was less than frank about the general thrust of British policy.

This gulf between what was being said – international agreement for the running of the Canal – and what was actually being planned became even more evident at meetings of the Egypt Committee on 7 and 9 August.

On the 7th, Macmillan's paper was only briefly discussed, but while his proposals were not dismissed the majority conclusion supported 'the strong practical and political arguments in favour of an operation directed towards the Suez Canal'. Macmillan, clearly not part of the majority, then pressed for more air resources; the Chief of the Air Staff said that the limiting factor was not aircraft but the capacity of the available airfields. 'For political reasons, it was proposed that bombs should not be stored on the airfields until about a week before the operations were to begin. Sufficient airlift was being reserved for this purpose.'

On the 9th the Committee authorized Monckton to hold regular press conferences for service correspondents, and then turned to 'the inter-relation between the forthcoming international conference, the summoning

* Lloyd, *Suez*, pp. 107–8.

of Parliament, and the launching of any military operation'.* The minutes record:

They recognized that very difficult problems of timing were involved. Some diplomatic exchanges with the Egyptian Government would have to be carried through after the end of the Conference. It was difficult to estimate in advance how long a time these might occupy. Although we should be unwilling to allow them to be unduly protracted, we might be liable to lose the support of other Powers if we appeared to be unwilling to entertain any reasonable counter-proposals which the Egyptian Government might make. We needed, therefore, some room, in point of time, for diplomatic manoeuvre. On the other hand, a military operation, once it was mounted, could not easily be delayed for more than a few days. And, if force was to be applied with sufficient speed after a final Egyptian rejection of our reasonable demands, the preparatory movements must begin at a relatively early stage – some of them, indeed, before the end of the international conference.

Similar difficulties would arise in connection with the summoning of Parliament. There were obvious difficulties in convening Parliament before the final attitude of the Egyptian Government was known. On the other hand, if Parliament were sitting when the final rejection of our demands was made, they would expect to be told what further action the Government proposed to take. It would be highly embarrassing, to say the least, to have to invite Parliament to approve a proposal to launch a military operation against Egypt. If the issue were put to Parliament at that stage such division of opinion as there was in the country would tend to be accentuated. It would not be easy for the Government to proceed with their intentions on the basis of a relatively narrow majority in a division in the House of Commons. In both the two world wars, and in the Korean war also, the Government had then invited Parliament to endorse their action.

It should be noted at this point that these comparisons were highly inappropriate, and historically very questionable. In 1914 the only serious parliamentary opposition to British involvement in the war had come from small minorities in the Liberal and Labour Parties, and although relations between the governing Liberals and the Opposition Conservatives had been exceptionally bad, on this issue there was no disagreement; the intervention was also strongly supported by the Irish Nationalists. In 1939, the mood of the House of Commons was considerably more belligerent than that of the Government – and certainly much more than Chamberlain's – and it was the Commons as a whole that was clamouring for a declaration of war by the Government. In the case of Korea the only opposition to involvement came from fragments on the Labour left, and the Labour Government knew that it would receive overwhelming support

* Those present were Eden, Salisbury, Lloyd, Monckton, Macmillan, Home and Thorneycroft.

from the House of Commons. Even at this early stage it was becoming clear that it was doubtful whether such virtual unanimity would be forthcoming. Technically, the advice given to the Egypt Committee was right, although on historically somewhat flimsy grounds; politically, it was conspicuously at odds with the circumstances of 1914, 1939 and 1950.

These considerations [the record continues] seemed to point to the conclusion that any military action against Egypt should be launched in retaliation against some aggressive or provocative act by the Egyptians. Various possibilities under this head were discussed. The conclusion emerged that the Government might be compelled to take advantage of any provocative act by Egypt, even though it came at a time when the preparations for military operations were less well advanced than might have been desired.

Selwyn Lloyd was asked for a study 'of possible actions by the Egyptian Government which might justify forcible retaliation'; Norman Brook was asked to put forward a possible timetable 'from the opening of the forthcoming international conference to the launching of a military operation against Egypt'.

The keynote of the military planners was complete Anglo-French integration on the wartime and NATO model; British officers were to be in charge at all levels with French deputies. General Sir Charles Keightley, the Commander-in-Chief, had Vice-Admiral Barjot as his deputy, and the Task Force commanders and deputies were, for the Navy, Vice-Admiral Durnford-Slater and Rear-Admiral Lancelot; for the Army, Lieutenant-General Sir Hugh Stockwell and General Beaufre; and for the Air Force, Air Marshal Barnett and General Brohon. The difficulties that arose stemmed principally from personality clashes rather than national ones, and from political rather than purely military differences, significant though the latter became.

If the object of the operation was to destroy Nasser, the obvious place for landing was Alexandria, providing not only the best landing beaches but also the shortest route to Cairo. But, if the purpose was to seize the Canal, then the landing would have to be at, or near, Port Said, which was physically as well as militarily far less attractive, with shallow and shelving beaches, and a causeway that was twenty-five miles in length and very narrow in most places. Also, as the port and harbour facilities in Cyprus were so limited and shallow, the bulk of the invasion fleet would have to sail from Malta, over a thousand miles away from Port Said. Alexandria had the additional merit of being nearly two hundred miles closer to Malta. From the military point of view Alexandria had everything in its favour and Port Said very little.

In these circumstances, it was not surprising that Stockwell and Beaufre disliked the Port Said prospect, and the first plans envisaged the far more attractive military proposition of landing at Alexandria. This was originally code-named 'Hamilcar' until it was realized that the French spelt the word 'Amilcar', and the code-name was changed to 'Musketeer'. On 8 August the plans, which involved the Alexandria landing followed by a pitched battle with the Egyptians, and finally, on the eighth day, the occupation of the Canal, came before the Chiefs of Staff. For this operation, some 80,000 men would be required, with substantial sea and air support, and there could be no question of launching a force of this size until the middle of September. Among the military there remained a significant *coup de main* school, particularly among the French, but it was a minority, and the notion was never put forward as an alternative to Musketeer. As the plans developed, they changed. The Egyptian Air Force was to be destroyed by Royal Air Force bombing, after which the troops would land at or near Alexandria on 15 September under naval bombardment and with air drops; the great battle would take place between the sixth and fourteenth days. Some doubts do arise about whether Cairo would be entered. Stockwell later said that his plans did not envisage this, but, as will be seen, the possession of Cairo, directly or indirectly, became a major feature of the objectives, although the military plan itself was to be changed drastically.

Beaufre was later very critical of the British obsession with planning and of their methods, but the real difficulty lay in attitudes and experience. The British military psyche had rightly been dominated by what went wrong at Gallipoli and Arnhem, and what went right in the later stages of the North African campaign and the D-Day landings. While it was axiomatic to the British that Allied and Egyptian civilian casualties must be kept to an absolute minimum the French, with their experience of Algeria and Indo-China and their passionate hatred of Nasser, had few qualms on this score. Also, while many of the British planners worried about the absence of a clear political directive the French saw the situation very clearly – it was to destroy utterly the Egyptian Army and Air Force and remove Nasser. On this even the French Communists were in full agreement, and throughout there were never the doubts or opposition to military action that developed in Britain. The British thoroughness and application to detail were admirable, and demonstrated the value of the teaching of military history and the hard-won experience of two world wars. But as no plans existed for the invasion of Egypt everything had to be done virtually from scratch, and although everyone worked very hard in miserable subterranean offices in London hated by all, the fact was that this took time if the thing was to be done properly. One can be very sympathetic both to the British planners and to the impatient French.

But the preparations disclosed some very uncomfortable facts. On paper, Britain seemed to be still one of the world's great military powers, with 750,000 under arms, a powerful and admired navy, and one of the best air forces in existence. The fighting capacities of the British serviceman were known to all, and respected by all, not least by Eisenhower. It had been the declared aim of the Government to have forces available for limited wars outside Europe which, for a major colonial power as well as a NATO member, made much sense. The only trouble was that the capacity to do this on any serious scale was extremely limited, and was certainly not available for an operation such as Musketeer. Indeed, the more the planners looked at the material at their disposal, the more troubled many of them became.

With the exceptions of Korea, Malaya and Cyprus, the British had not been involved in a major conflict for ten years; virtually all of their equipment was of wartime and even pre-war vintage, and most of it had proved notably inferior to that of other armies even in the war. There was a dismal shortage of transport aircraft suitable for parachutists, and the principal carriers, the Hastings and Vickers Valettas – of which there were only five squadrons – were of venerable lineage. Even the new FLN self-loading rifle was deemed unsuitable for North African conditions and was replaced by the hand-loading No. 4 rifle. The list of British military weaknesses for mounting, transporting and launching such an operation was long indeed.*

The British Chiefs of Staff and their planning staffs were later accused of planning on the assumption that they were taking on Rommel and his panzers instead of the Egyptians, and preparing for a rerun of Overlord rather than merely landing in Egypt against weak opposition and a paltry enemy. There was truth in this, but both the British and the French remembered that the Egyptian soldier was not to be despised, and, fighting for his own country on his own soil, could be a formidable proposition; the British in particular could recall, as could the French, that neither had realized what a tough proposition the Turkish soldier could be in similar circumstances, and 46,000 British, Commonwealth and French soldiers had been killed at Gallipoli as a result of this error. If some of the British officers rated the Egyptian armed forces higher than in fact they were, this was undoubtedly an error on the right side. But it all meant delay. The politicians and the press of both countries might be calling for swift and decisive action, but the military planners knew that men's lives were at stake. It is a fair criticism that this led to excessive caution and, for some,

---

*Roy Fullick and Geoffrey Powell, *Suez: The Double War*, ch. 4, details the position excellently; indeed this is the best military analysis of Suez that has been published.

a magnification of the difficulties, but it had been implanted in everyone that bad planning, wishful thinking and underestimation of the enemy provided the perfect conditions for disaster, and too many – including Eden himself – had personal experience of the consequences of such miscalculations. Also, not only men's lives but careers were at stake. It was not a question of doubts about the morality of the operation that caused the delays, but the sheer practical problems of men, matériel and military logistics.

This is a political, and not a military, account of the Suez crisis, but obviously the two cannot be separated. *If*, as Head had claimed in the House of Commons, and the 1956 White Paper on Defence had averred, the British had been equipped and trained for such a limited war, matters would have been very different. The reality was that they were not.

The scale of the political and military problems – both domestic and international – was already becoming apparent. Home reported that of the major Commonwealth countries only Australia and New Zealand wholly took the British line, the Canadians were very lukewarm about any military action, and, although agreeing with British outrage at Nasser's action, their views faithfully reflected Dulles' ambiguities; Nehru was evidently sympathetic to Nasser, and his strong hostility to any action representing 'Imperialism' and 'colonialism' meant that little help could be expected from that quarter; the Pakistan Government, while more understanding of the British position, made it clear that it could not support any Anglo-French military action to recover the Canal.

At home, while the general mood seemed very supportive of the Government there were definitely second thoughts emerging in the newspapers and even in the Conservative Party, who now began to hope that the London Conference would clear the matter up on terms that could be sold to the British public as an honourable and fair settlement. In contrast, there were strong and large elements in the Party and press who were becoming impatient already, calling for action as soon as possible and beginning to talk again about 'indecision' at the top.

The Chiefs of Staff on 10 August presented Musketeer to the Egypt Committee. There were four options: the Port Said landing, the Alexandria assault, limited operations at Port Said with the main attack at Alexandria, or a feint at Alexandria and the main landing at Port Said. They made it clear that the last two could be discarded at once, and strongly recommended the full-scale seaborne assault on Alexandria after the destruction of the Egyptian Air Force. The Committee at once accepted the new proposals, which had been signed by Mountbatten, Templer and Air Chief Marshal Sir Ronald Ivelaw-Chapman on behalf of the chairman, Dickson.

The emphatic warning from the British Ambassador in Tripoli, that if British troops in Libya were used in operations against Egypt 'there would be violent reactions and British forces would have to be used to restore order in the country', apparently closed another of Macmillan's options. There was also considerable concern about the French, as their security 'was notoriously bad'; the chairman of the Joint Intelligence Committee was ordered to make a special visit to Paris to impress this upon the French, and the Chiefs were told to restrict information to the French; other arrangements to deal with political propaganda were announced.

The French deputy force commanders were complaining so vehemently about the lack of information given to them that they threatened to return to Paris *en masse*; at a hurriedly convened meeting at Chequers on the following day, 11 August, it was decided that they must be given full information, but that in the French Government only Mollet and Bourgès-Maunoury should be kept fully informed. This saved the joint planning group from a startlingly early collapse, but French suspicions that they were being increasingly used by the British as subordinates rather than equals were absolutely justified. After Eden's decision that the French deputy commanders must be brought completely into the planning process matters improved significantly, but from beginning to end Musketeer in its various forms was British led and British dominated.

These difficulties were compounded by those on the political front. On 7 August the doubts in the Labour Party had been made public for the first time in a letter to *The Times* by Douglas Jay and Denis Healey, written with Gaitskell's approval. Gaitskell was now becoming worried about hostile Labour reaction to his Commons speech, and the Healey–Jay letter reiterated, virtually word for word, his argument that force could only be used in self-defence, 'or in pursuance of our international obligations and the United Nations Charter', or if Nasser were to violate 'the far more important principle of the security and freedom of the canal.... But he has not yet done this ... a unilateral act of force would be a stupendous folly – unless and until Colonel Nasser resorts to force himself.' This was not quite the ringing denunciation of the use of force under any circumstances that has been claimed for it, and it can rightly be said to represent Gaitskell's own view that it was certainly not an option to be rejected. The Labour and Liberal Parties had, after all, raised no objection to the calling up of the reserves and other military measures announced by the Government. If, as Gaitskell later averred, Eden had deceived him in their conversations that force would not be used in *any* circumstances, why had he supported the military measures? Also, the Healey–Jay letter did not, as Jay has claimed, argue 'against any use of force', but specifically gave examples of when it would be justified. An impartial reader of this letter would have been justified in assuming that the differences between the Government and Opposition were marginal at this stage.

On 8 August Eden broadcast to the nation. In this he himself used publicly, for the first time, the analogy with the pre-war dictators, and said that 'Our quarrel is not with Egypt, still less with the Arab world; it is with Nasser. With dictators you always have to pay a higher price later on.' There was

no question of denying her [Egypt] a fair deal, or a just return. But if anyone is going to snatch and grab and try to pocket what really belongs to the world, the result will be impoverishment for all, and a refusal by some countries at least to lead their life at such a hazard. Meanwhile, we have too much at risk not to take precautions. We have done so. That is the meaning of the movements by land, sea and air of which you have heard in the last few days.

We do not seek a solution by force, but by the broadest possible international agreement. That is why we have called the conference. We shall do all we can to help its work, but this I must make plain. We cannot agree that an act of plunder which threatens the livelihood of many nations shall be allowed to succeed. And we must make sure that the life of the great trading nations of the world cannot, in the future, be strangled at any moment by some interruption to the free passage of the canal.

How this measured statement could be described by Jay as 'hysterical' and be interpreted by some Labour MPs as the prelude to an immediate invasion is difficult to comprehend, and Gaitskell certainly did not interpret it in this way. But he felt compelled by the pressure of his colleagues to break his holiday and return for a special Shadow Cabinet meeting on 12 August, and he saw Eden again on the 14th; their discussion seems to have been virtually identical with that on the 2nd, and Gaitskell was satisfied. The Shadow Cabinet's statement put 'particular emphasis' on the final part of Gaitskell's 2 August speech, but endorsed it, and Gaitskell returned to his holiday. If, as the *Economist* wrote on 18 August, 'The Labour leadership has extricated itself with some delicacy from the charge of being allied with the Government's more belligerent supporters,' it had not made the reversal which was later claimed for it or which Eden later believed it had made, when he wrote with much feeling that 'The [Labour] retreat then began amid a clatter of excuses.'*

Morrison had urged Eden to keep in close personal touch with Gaitskell, which Eden was very willing to do, but Gaitskell insisted on bringing colleagues, and his own manner did not help. Eden noted in his diary of the 14 August meeting:

* Avon, *Full Circle*, p. 445.

Gaitskell gave us a donnish lecture about the situation of inordinate length but of unremarkable quality. We listened with all the attention we cd command but suddenly Bobbety cd take no more & burst out with indignation that he and the Prime Minister, having spent all their lives in foreign policy, cd not see the purpose of this lecture. I had a feeling that Nye silently enjoyed this outburst. We plodded on.

The Suez crisis has spawned many myths, and two have proved the most enduring. The Conservative version – which, regrettably, Eden himself partly encouraged in his memoirs – is that Gaitskell was initially a fervent supporter of military action but was then forced to back down into all-out opposition by his Party's left wing and neo-Communist fellow travellers. The Labour myth is that Gaitskell was consistent throughout in denouncing the military option, a version that, equally, cannot be sustained. The *Economist* on 18 August commented with some tartness that 'most Labour members will now follow the official line which proclaims – with a slight stretch of the imagination – that what he [Gaitskell] is saying now is what he has been saying all the time'. In this sense there *had* been a step backwards from the fervour of the 2 August speech, described by Lord Stansgate as 'heady wine'; but it cannot be described as a total *volte-face*, as has often been claimed.

The other Labour myth, that Eden completely and deliberately deceived Gaitskell at their meetings on 2 and 14 August, can also be totally rejected, and although Eden's biographer may regret that he did not tell Gaitskell more, there are always some constraints – personal as well as political – in such discussions. If there was a misunderstanding, it was not as substantial as was later claimed by Gaitskell's friends, and certainly did not amount to deliberate and Machiavellian deception of him by Eden.

Gaitskell considered that he had totally set out his colleagues' concerns in his letter to Eden on 3 August, in which he emphasized that

While one or two members of our Party indicated in the debate that they would support force now, this is, I am pretty sure, not the general view.... If Nasser were to do something which led to his condemnation by the United Nations as an aggressor, then there is no doubt, I am sure, that we would be entirely in favour of forceful resistance. But I must repeat, what I said in my speech yesterday, that, up to the present, I cannot see that he has done anything which would justify this.

In his reply Eden could give no specific assurances about the use of force, on which Gaitskell reiterated his concerns, but he became convinced that the Government was only using the threat of force to bring Nasser into serious negotiation. This was not at all as major a misunderstanding of Eden's position as Gaitskell later believed, but he does seem to have underestimated Eden's absolute determination not to accept the Nasser *coup*.

Eden's broadcast was extremely effective, and it certainly reflected his clear view of the situation, but in retrospect it can be seen that his anxiety not to be seen as anti-Egyptian and 'colonialist' made the controversy too personalized. Also, if there had been any faint chance of Nasser attending the London Conference, or sending a representative, this broadcast effectively ended it. Butler was not the only senior minister who, while supporting Eden's determination to stand up for British rights and the sanctity of international agreements, and not at all indisposed to the use of force if all else failed, was uneasy at the Hitler and Mussolini comparisons. 'Nasser was not in politics for the good of our health,' he later wrote, 'but he was no Hitler, no incarnation of evil, no megalomaniac who had to be toppled before free men could rest easy in their beds.'* This analysis of Nasser's personality and purpose is very much open to question; if he was not a megalomaniac he was certainly very close to being one, and Butler's view of the Nasser regime as 'a popular movement not an imposed tyranny' is rather strange, but the important point is that this represented a very clear difference of perception between Butler and Eden.

Even more important than Butler's doubts were those of Walter Monckton. As he later wrote:

I was in favour of the tough line which the Prime Minister took in July when Nasser announced the nationalization of the canal and I must say that I was not fundamentally troubled by moral considerations throughout the period for which the crisis lasted. My anxieties began when I discovered the way in which it was proposed to carry out the enterprise.†

His wife, however, was firmly convinced that his doubts began earlier and that he was disturbed 'by the thought of violent action'. Unhappily for everyone, and not least for his own reputation, he kept these doubts to himself, except for one intervention in the Cabinet on 28 August; Eden had no reason to doubt the full support of his Minister of Defence, who was a key member of the Egypt Committee and attended all its meetings until October. His biographer has described Monckton's position as 'a loyal but irresolute member of the team',‡ which constituted very much the worst of all worlds. It was not until relatively late in the crisis that Eden had any clear indication of the doubts and uneasiness of his Minister of Defence. If ever personal and political loyalty were misplaced, this was the occasion.

At least one Cabinet member later considered that Eden was very ill served by his senior ministers – Macmillan, Butler and Monckton – recalling that Macmillan was excessively vehement about military action

* Butler, *The Art of the Possible*, p. 188.
† Lord Birkenhead, *Walter Monckton*, p. 307.
‡ *Ibid.*, p. 310.

from the very beginning, virtually regardless of the consequences or the methods; that Monckton was not only timid but did not share his lack of enthusiasm with his colleagues; and that Butler 'did nothing at all – he simply distanced himself and gave no opinion one way or the other. The rest of us were not only junior, but were overawed by Eden, not because he was the Prime Minister but because of his great reputation in these areas. And so we went along with what we thought was wholly agreed by our seniors.'

The performance of Mountbatten is even more difficult to comprehend. His own subsequent version of the *coup de main* proposal, as has already been demonstrated, is wholly inaccurate; according to versions he later sedulously circulated, and put out in his autobiographical television memoirs, he had been 'dead against' the operation from the beginning, which sits rather uneasily with his other claim for being the master-mind of the mythical *coup de main*. Also, like Monckton, he kept his doubts to himself. Cilcennin tended to share them, but he was due to retire on 2 September, and he persuaded Mountbatten not to send to Eden a draft memorandum on the political aspects; two subsequent letters of resignation by Mountbatten to Eden were drafted but, somewhat mysteriously, never sent, and, as the records clearly demonstrate, Mountbatten did not fight his corner as strongly as he later claimed. Indeed, he did not fight at all. What is unquestionable is that his patent lack of enthusiasm for a military resolution had a strong influence upon Monckton. 'Yet outwardly', as his official biographer writes, 'he remained a loyal public servant doing his duty and preparing for war.'* This is not an impressive position for a man in a key post.

This was the problem. Mountbatten's doubts, at least in private, developed into strong opposition, but the circle who knew of them was very small, and did not even include the admiral who was his first choice to be in charge of the operation, nor his own Naval Assistant. His two First Lords, Cilcennin and then Viscount Hailsham, knew and sympathized, but Mountbatten accepted the advice that the political decisions were for ministers, and that the Chiefs' responsibility was to carry out the Cabinet's orders. One can have some sympathy for Mountbatten's position but his case would be much more substantial if there had been a wider appreciation of his attitude and if Monckton had been a stronger minister. Mountbatten regarded Eden as 'a very old friend' – a highly exaggerated description – which makes his silence, so far as Eden and all members of the Egypt Committee except Monckton were concerned, even more deplorable.

* Ziegler, *Mountbatten*, p. 541.

495

His biographer makes as good a case as possible for Mountbatten, although clearly with some uneasiness. 'Even if he did not set out his opposition formally to Eden at an early stage,' Ziegler writes, 'he can have left no doubt in Downing Street about his views.'* The trouble was that until very late he did, and Downing Street had no knowledge in the crucial early period that one of the Chiefs of Staff held these views. One can appreciate Mountbatten's dilemma, but his conduct was certainly unheroic, and, far more importantly, seriously misled the Prime Minister and the Egypt Committee, virtually amounting to a dereliction of duty.

Mountbatten was not just a serving sailor who had risen to the top of his profession. He was the former Viceroy of India, a close relative of the Royal Family and a major public personality, with far greater public attention and influence than most ministers. His overt opposition to the military option, even as a last resort, and confined to the Egypt Committee, would probably not have stopped the military preparations, but it would surely have had a major impact. It is true that there would have been no shortage of willing volunteers to take his place as First Sea Lord, but if even the threat of resignation had been known, the consequences must have been considerable, and would have confronted ministers with alarming political repercussions when the first bellicosity in Parliament and press was beginning to fade.

But Mountbatten's views were *not* generally known; he attended all the vital meetings; he confined his views, so far as ministers were concerned, to the naval and military aspects of Musketeer.

If he remained silent out of friendship for Eden – on which both Eden and his present biographer were and are sceptical – it was a friendship singularly misplaced, not least because Eden knew of Mountbatten's strong opposition to Munich as a young officer. In the event, he did Eden the gravest disservice possible.

On 6 August there was a puzzling intervention by Churchill, who invited himself to Chequers. Eden had hoped for a strongly supportive attitude, but Churchill – who, the Edens thought, had sadly deteriorated mentally and physically – read out a paper he had prepared, whose principal feature was the need to involve the Israelis in a joint attack on Egypt. When Eden pressed him on this, Churchill admitted that he had got the idea from Macmillan. There was also some desultory historical reminiscence about Napoleon's invasion of Egypt. In his memoirs Eden dressed up the occasion more favourably, but at the time he was deeply disappointed and sad.

The domestic political difficulties now became even more apparent. On the morning of 14 August, as Eden reported to a meeting of the full

* Ziegler, *Mountbatten*, p. 547.

Cabinet, he had seen the Opposition leaders again; they had asked for the recall of Parliament if a crisis arose in the Recess

and had indicated their opposition to the use of force to impose on Egypt any conclusion reached by the forthcoming conference. They considered that any international action should be considered at a special session of the United Nations and that the new authority should be set up under that organization. They had, however, recognized that if any new incidents occurred, such as interference with ships using the Canal, a new situation would arise in which force might be justified.

This was an accurate account.

Concern was also being expressed in the Cabinet about the forthcoming Trades Union Conference and the changing mood of public opinion:

Though there had been initially a reaction in favour of taking firm action against Egypt, the public were now becoming increasingly impressed by the difficulties of such a course and its possible repercussions in other Middle East countries. It seemed possible that there would be insufficient public support for the use of force against Egypt unless some new incident occurred. It was therefore important to impress on the public that if Colonel Nasser were allowed to get away with his recent illegal action, the United Kingdom's position in the Middle East would be undermined, with serious consequences to trade and employment in this country.

Eden had asked the Australian Prime Minister, Robert Menzies, to attend this Cabinet. Menzies was robust in his view that

Colonel Nasser's action followed the pattern of all military dictators and this aspect should be emphasized. The Australian Government were united in their support of the stand taken by the United Kingdom, and he was taking steps to ensure that public opinion in Australia was fully aware of all the dangers. He believed that American opinion was now alive to the risks involved in the present situation.

Selwyn Lloyd intervened to tell the Cabinet – most of whose members had had no access to the workings of the Egypt Committee – that 'It was important to avoid giving the impression that the [London] conference had been called merely to endorse decisions already taken to employ force against Egypt.' But Eden was considerably more frank when he told his colleagues that military preparations were being completed, and, together with the French, 'there would be ample force to deal with Egypt. There would, however, be a difficult question of timing, since the United Kingdom forces could not be maintained in a state of readiness for any protracted period.'

The Cabinet agreed with Eden that Canal dues should not be paid to Egypt; American payments were principally responsible for between 30 and 35 per cent of the dues being received by the Egyptians. To say that this was a major irritant in Anglo-American relations is to underestimate the matter, and the Cabinet willingly approved Eden's proposals.

I have contrasted Eden's frankness with Lloyd's statement, as the latter certainly gave a false impression, whereas Eden's account of his meeting with Gaitskell and his account – admittedly brief – of military discussions with the French demonstrated that the military option was under active consideration. It would have been far better if the full Cabinet had been circulated with the records of the Egypt Committee in spite of the security risks – which surely could have been overcome – but not a single member of the Cabinet who was not on the Committee raised the point.

The only senior minister who, in my judgement, had legitimate cause for complaint on this score was Butler. Although it was true that he had no departmental responsibilities, he was a major personality in the Government, he was the Leader of the House of Commons, and he commanded a large and important following in the Conservative Party inside and outside the House of Commons. Although temporarily in eclipse after the sad end to his remarkable tenure of the Treasury, he was widely regarded as having stepped into Eden's shoes as Crown Prince. On the other hand, Butler was unwell and lonely, and certainly did not press for information. If he had done so it is indeed difficult to believe that Eden would have denied it to him; but Butler did not. This was unquestionably an error on his part – which he later freely admitted in conversation with me – but Eden was also to blame for not ensuring that Butler was kept completely informed at all stages, even though he never asked. In my only discussion with Eden about Suez this was the one aspect about which he was clearly uncomfortable.

But there was no question of Eden deliberately excluding Butler from the inner circle. The sheer accident that Butler was unwell had meant he was not present at the early meetings, and his lack of departmental responsibilities virtually automatically excluded him from the Egypt Committee. But Butler should have insisted on complete information, and, although he did not, Eden should have ensured that he received it.

Thus it was tacitly accepted that these grave matters should be handled by the Prime Minister's inner team, and for any student of Cabinet Government this may appear to be extraordinary, were it not for the fact that everyone believed that the wartime practice had worked so well – and confidence in Eden was so high. It was also unanimously considered that this was a wartime situation. No one except Monckton had any idea of the strength of his own reservations and those of Mountbatten; if Eden and the Cabinet had known at this stage it is doubtful whether their judgement would have been significantly different, but those Cabinet members who were uneasy about the changing public mood would have been given important evidence of unease at the heart of the operation. As it was, they were left in complete ignorance of this, and were misled – intentionally or not – by Lloyd's version of the London Conference. They had good cause to be subsequently outraged by Monckton's silence when they learned his real views. As Butler later wrote of Monckton, in a mainly sympathetic portrait, 'he had insufficient firmness of purpose'.* This is characteristically 'Butlerian', and, also characteristically, it says all that needs to be said.

The one minister who expressed concern about lack of information to the Cabinet was Duncan Sandys, to whom Eden wrote on 22 August:

In view of the point you raised with me, I feel I should explain to you, before the next meeting of the Cabinet, the limits within which the Cabinet can discuss the possibility of a military operation in the Eastern Mediterranean.

Up to now the Cabinet have considered this only as a hypothetical question, viz., should we be prepared to take this course in the last resort if all attempts to achieve a satisfactory settlement by other means had failed. If that situation should arise, the Cabinet as a whole will of course be asked to take the final decision, in the light of all the circumstances at the time. I have meanwhile arranged for the Cabinet to meet from time to time, since Parliament rose, so that my colleagues might be kept informed of the progress of the international Conference.

It would not, however, be possible for the Cabinet as a whole to discuss the plans for any military operations that might have to be undertaken. Knowledge of the details must, for obvious reasons of security, be confined within the narrowest possible circle. Such political guidance as the military authorities may need in the preparation of their plans must continue to be given by me, in consultation with a small number of my most senior Cabinet colleagues and, as necessary, such Departmental Ministers as may be directly concerned.

Although Sandys remained troubled, he felt he had made his point about 'the final decision'; Eden's papers record no other minister who had challenged the manner in which the crisis was being handled.

On 14 August Norman Brook submitted a provisional timetable to the Egypt Committee:

16th August	International Conference opens
23rd August	International Conference concluded
25th August	Dispatch of Note to Egyptian Government, calling on them to accept the majority recommendation of the Conference
27th August	Parliament meets (to endorse the conclusions of the Conference)
29th August	Counter-proposals received from Egyptian Government
5th September	Egyptian counter-proposals rejected
7th September (at earliest)	Assault force sails from United Kingdom
17th September	Preliminary air bombardment begins
20th September	Assault landing in Egypt

* Butler, *The Art of Memory*, p. 142.

The committee appears to have done no more than take note of this, and indeed Eden said that it was clear that 'once the military operation had been launched, it would be practically impossible to call it off unless Colonel Nasser's Government collapsed before any action took place. It would also be impracticable to maintain the necessary forces at a high state of readiness in the Eastern Mediterranean for more than a day or two. In the circumstances, it would be preferable to delay the final decision to launch any military operation until it was certain that such action was required.' This was a significant step backwards, and the first of many delays.

The first factor was that the British were beginning to hope that, with strong American assistance at the Conference and the United Nations, Nasser might back down, or have his prestige so lowered that his regime might fall. In Eden's view Dulles 'had implied that they [the United States] had implied that they recognized the possibility that force might be used in the last resort, since he had asked whether we would be ready to justify such action before the United Nations'. This was not Eisenhower's view at all, but Dulles told Eden, who reported to the Egypt Committee on 20 August, that he was troubled about divided opinion in Britain having spoken to Gaitskell; Dulles had cautioned against provoking Nasser, but had also said that although the United States would not take part in any military operation he had warned the Soviet Foreign Minister 'that the United States Government would not stand by if the United Kingdom and France were involved in a war, which suggested that in the event of hostilities the United States would at least provide material help'.

So, once again, the British and Americans were at cross-purposes, to an ominous extent.

The issue of American attitudes had a very practical aspect, as US equipment supplied to Britain under the Mutual Defence Aid Programme was under strict conditions for employment only in the context of NATO.

Eden's later comment on the performance of the Americans was understandably sour, but it is justified:

If the United States Government had approached this issue in the spirit of an ally, they would have done everything in their power, short of the use of force, to support the nations whose economic security depended upon the freedom of passage through the Suez Canal. They would have closely planned their policies with their allies and held stoutly to the decisions arrived at. They would have insisted on restoring international authority in order to insulate the canal from the politics of any one country. It is now clear that this was never the attitude of the United States Government. Rather did they try to gain time, coast along over difficulties as they arose and improvise policies, each following on the failure of its immediate predecessor. None of these was geared to the long-term purpose of serving a joint cause.... The old spoor of colonialism confused the trail.*

Dulles' own biographer is hardly less damning:

... during the critical three months following nationalization, Eisenhower and Dulles were not really on the same wavelength; Eisenhower was Olympian and categorical in his opposition to force; Dulles seemed more to share the Anglo-French anxiety that an unpredictable Nasser could not be trusted, and that force might thus be justified in the last resort. He conveyed this feeling to his allies with a prudent obliqueness, but he maddened them at critical junctures by suddenly shifting his stance to avoid the danger of a public difference with the President.†

Dulles had returned to London on 15 August to find the British and French alarmed by reports in Washington that at a meeting between him and Eisenhower and congressional leaders on the 12th they had said that the United States would accept an international body for the Canal that was merely advisory to the Egyptians. Of this meeting, Eden wrote in his diary:

Foster came over at 12.30 & he & Winthrop [Aldrich] & Selwyn had a good talk until luncheon. F seemed quite as firm as before & ready to table joint resolution himself. He also seemed not to exclude possibility of joint use of force. I gave him certain details of our plans, in part in order to show him where we stood. He seemed to like idea that first step following Egyptian refusal might be to pay our money elsewhere. Pineau seemed quite steady.

At lunch with Lloyd and Pineau, Dulles was left in no doubt that Britain and France were insistent upon an international authority with real operational control. Dulles was impressed, and in his opening speech when the Conference convened on the 16th proposed that the Canal be operated by an international body established by treaty and associated with the United Nations. He placed much emphasis on the 1888 Convention, which had been 'grievously assaulted'. The question was whether confidence in it could 'peacefully be repaired'; if not, 'we face a future of the utmost gravity'. The British and French were delighted, Eisenhower was not.

This was a decisive moment. On the following day, Krishna Menon introduced an Indian counter-proposal which was in fact the original American one, namely to set up an international advisory body of user interests, and to make Egypt 'a party to a solemn agreement which comes

---

* Avon, *Full Circle*, pp. 458–9.
† Hoopes, *The Devil and John Foster Dulles*, p. 351.

under the obligations of international law and of the Charter of the United Nations'. As Eisenhower made clear to Dulles on 19 August, this exactly mirrored his own views, but Dulles had already made his speech, and could not turn back; in any case, as he told Eisenhower, the advisory solution was absolutely unacceptable to the British and French. It would be a major concession to Nasser, and should be held in reserve only 'as a matter of last resort in order to obtain Egypt's concurrence'.

It was unfortunate that it had been Menon who had made the proposal. Menon was personally obnoxious, long-winded beyond patience, arrogant, and only neutralist in the sense that he was patently anti-Western and pro-Russian; he also offended Dulles by gratuitously saying that Nasser had acted not only legally but 'properly' in nationalizing the Canal. Dulles despised Menon personally (and in this he was far from being alone) and had no time for neutralists in the great crusade against the Communist peril; when the Russians – still remaining surprisingly quiet – intimated their support for the Indian proposal, this settled the matter for him. Eisenhower, in a remarkable abrogation of presidential responsibility, and wholly contrary to his own views, cabled to Dulles that 'I understand the box you are in', and assured him of his support and approval 'in whatever action you finally decide you must take'. British and French policies may have had their problems, but the American position was chaotic.

Dulles now persuaded four countries heavily dependent upon American aid – Turkey, Iran, Pakistan and Ethiopia – to sponsor a resolution on the lines of his speech. This was supported by eighteen nations, while four others – the Soviet Union, India, Indonesia and Ceylon – supported the Indian one. Dulles had also arranged that the New Zealand Foreign Minister, Thomas MacDonald, should suggest that a committee of 'assenting nations' present the proposal to Nasser. The Soviet Foreign Minister protested that this would be an ultimatum, but it was agreed.

Eden now wished, understandably enough, that the author of the eighteen-nation proposals should take them himself to Nasser, but Dulles refused. In Hoopes' devastating words:

Although he had invented, presented, argued for, and dragooned others into accepting what became the majority proposal, Dulles now wished to slip away from further responsibility. Caught between distasteful choices, his tactical sense prevailed. He cabled Eisenhower, saying, 'I think it is preferable that we should become less conspicuous,' and returned home.*

Thus the task of presenting the majority Conference proposals to Nasser was given to a team led by Menzies, which arrived in Cairo on 3 September.

* Hoopes, *The Devil and John Foster Dulles*, p. 355.

On the following day Menzies saw Nasser, and on the 5th formally presented the proposals. As Humphrey Trevelyan had clearly warned London from Cairo, there was no possibility of their acceptance. Eden and Lloyd have laid much emphasis on Eisenhower's specific rejection of the use of force in his press conference of 4 September as a major factor in Nasser's rejection of the eighteen powers' proposals, but while it made Menzies' mission even more difficult than it already was, Trevelyan had been absolutely correct in his estimation of Nasser's attitude, also demonstrated by the fact that Nasser had told his military commanders that the Franco-British military preparations were bluff. Menzies told him that this might well not be the case, but Nasser's self-confidence was very high. The Menzies Mission returned with nothing except a suggestion that an independent body should be established to consider the various views. Menzies may not have been the best person to lead the Mission, of which he wrote a very long personal account to Eden, and which he has described more briefly in his own memoirs,* but it was a hopeless venture. Perhaps not surprisingly, the accounts by Menzies and Nasser of their meetings and of each other vary very considerably; what is at least clear is that they developed a strong mutual detestation for each other, and the Egyptian press and Radio Cairo faithfully abused Menzies as 'the Australian mule'. Menzies told reporters at London Airport that 'Egypt will have nothing to do with any peaceful solution of the Canal problem which does not leave Egypt sole master of the Canal,' which was precisely the position.

But, while this farce was being played out, there had been further developments.

Military and political discussions in the Egypt Committee during the Conference had been, inevitably, limited; on 22 August Eden successfully resisted Monckton's request for aerial reconnaissance of Egypt 'at the crucial stage of the international conference', although this meant a further postponement of D-Day to 19 September. On the 24th he reported on his exchanges with Dulles; Head told the Committee that seventeen days would elapse between a decision to attack Egypt and landing, and was asked if this could be reduced.

At the 24 August meeting Salisbury passed Eden a note suggesting that the matter should be put to the UN.

... and if we get no response to the needs of the situation, saying that we have no option but to leave UNO, on the ground that it is clear that it is quite ineffective for the purpose for which it was created, the maintenance of justice & the sanctity of treaties. We must therefore resume our liberty of action.

* Robert Menzies, *Afternoon Light*.

My difficulty is that I feel we must act firmly, but that there are no possible means by which we can do so within the terms of the Charter to which we have solemnly adhered. It might even be that such a threat by us might bring UNO up to the jump. I fully realize that, from the p[oin]t of view of Br[itish] public opinion, it would be a pretty formidable step to take. S.

It would indeed! – as Salisbury realized when Eden explained the American hostility to referring the matter to the UN at present, although that did not mean totally ignoring the Security Council in the long run. Eden also recalled to Salisbury what had happened over Korea in 1950 when the Russians had made the fatal error of walking out of the Security Council, an error never repeated. Nor did Eden agree that the British and French were unable to use force within the Charter, and Salisbury withdrew his comments. But it demonstrated how even one of the cleverest and most experienced members of the Cabinet felt so much frustration.

On the 27th Macmillan circulated a paper on 'The Egypt Crisis and the British Economy', which estimated the cost of a war at £100 million, but that disruption of oil supplies would be the most serious possibility: 'If supplies from the Persian Gulf as well as through the Canal and pipelines were lost, the economic position of the UK and Europe would not be viable.' Speaking to this paper on the 27th, Macmillan told the committee that 'If the Egyptian challenge was not effectively met, our economy would be slowly strangled.' At this meeting Lloyd urged reference of the dispute to the Security Council, which was agreed to by the full Cabinet on the 28th.

This meeting was a full review of the situation. It was agreed that 'There could therefore be no doubt that, if Colonel Nasser's policy succeeded, our whole position in the Middle East would be undermined, our oil supplies would be in jeopardy, and the stability of our national economy would be gravely threatened.' But Monckton, while agreeing that if all other methods failed force would have to be used, expressed for the first time his serious doubts:

If, together with the French, we took military measures against Egypt, our action would be condemned by a substantial body of public opinion in countries overseas, including several of the independent countries of the Commonwealth. Within the United Kingdom itself opinion would be divided. Our vital interests in other parts of the Middle East would also be affected; we must, in particular, expect sabotage against oil installations in other Arab countries. Moreover, once we had sent military forces into Egypt, it would not be easy to extricate them; we might find ourselves saddled with a costly commitment. While, therefore, he was ready to agree that we must contrive to use force in the last resort, he hoped that we should first exhaust all other means of curbing Colonel Nasser's ambitions and, in particular, that we should let no opportunity pass of securing an agreement by settlement.

Salisbury also urged the achievement of British purposes by peaceful means, with recourse to the United Nations before any military action, but he reminded the Cabinet of the lessons of the 1930s about checking dictators at the outset. Kilmuir strongly agreed, although he was worried that 'the real issue [might] be eroded by ineffective international debate'. Butler argued that the national interest could only be secured if the Government had strong public and parliamentary support, which required that 'they had taken all practicable steps to secure a satisfactory settlement by peaceful means'. Eden summed up the Cabinet's feelings on these lines, but emphasized the dangers of delay that could alienate the French and encourage Nasser, while at the same time increasing the difficulties of any military operation: 'While, therefore, the possibilities of a peaceful settlement should be fully explored, this should not be allowed to weaken our resolution or to reduce the weight of our pressure on the Egyptian Government.' That afternoon the Egypt Committee approved Musketeer but also postponed D-Day by seven days.

On 27 August Eden had written warmly of Dulles to Eisenhower, and stressed the Soviet interest in instability in the Middle East: 'All this makes me more than ever sure that Nasser must not be allowed to get away with it this time. . . . It is certainly the most hazardous [crisis] that our country has known since 1940.' The reply was unexpected, and very unwelcome. Eisenhower wrote that he was now hopeful

that Nasser will give way without the need for any resort to force. . . .

I am afraid, Anthony, that from this point onward our views on the situation diverge. As to the use of force or the threat of force at this juncture, I continue to feel as I expressed myself in the letter Foster carried to you some weeks ago. Even now military preparations and civilian evacuation exposed to public view seem to be solidifying support for Nasser which has been shaky in many important quarters. I regard it as indispensable that if we are to proceed solidly together to the solution of this problem, public opinion in our several countries must be overwhelming in its support. I must tell you frankly that American public opinion flatly rejects the thought of using force, particularly when it does not seem that every possible peaceful means of protecting our vital interests has been exhausted without result. Moreover, I gravely doubt we could here secure Government authority even for the lesser support measures for which you might have to look to us.

I really do not see how a successful result could be achieved by forcible means. The use of force would, it seems to me, vastly increase the area of jeopardy.

On 6 September Eden sent to Eisenhower a very long and detailed reply, setting out the British hopes that the Menzies Mission would succeed, but that if it did not then the general position, unacceptable to the British, remained unchanged. 'There has never been any question of our suddenly or without further provocation resorting to arms while these processes were at work. In any event, as your own wide knowledge would confirm, we could not have done this without extensive preparation lasting several weeks.'

Again, Eden dwelt heavily upon the experience of the 1930s and, more recently, of standing up to the Russians over Berlin:

Similarly the seizure of the Canal is, we are convinced, the opening gambit in a planned campaign designed by Nasser to expel all Western influence and interests from Arab countries. He believes that if he can get away with this, and if he can successfully defy eighteen nations, his prestige in Arabia will be so great that he will be able to mount revolutions of young officers in Saudi Arabia, Jordan, Syria and Iraq. We know from our joint sources that he is already preparing a revolution in Iraq, which is the most stable and progressive. These new governments will in effect be Egyptian satellites if not Russian ones. They will have to place their united oil resources under the control of a united Arabia led by Egypt and under Russian influence. When that moment comes Nasser can deny oil to Western Europe and we here shall all be at his mercy. . . .

The difference which separates us today appears to be a difference of assessment of Nasser's plans and intentions and of the consequences in the Middle East of military action against him.

You may feel that even if we are right it would be better to wait until Nasser has unmistakably unveiled his intentions. But this was the argument which prevailed in 1936 and which we both rejected in 1948. Admittedly there are risks in the use of force against Egypt now. It is, however, clear that military intervention designed to reverse Nasser's revolutions in the whole Continent would be a much more costly and difficult undertaking. . . .

I agree with you that prolonged military operations, as well as the denial of Middle East oil would place an immense strain on the economy of Western Europe. I can assure you that we are conscious of the burdens and perils attending military intervention. But if our assessment is correct, and if the only alternative is to allow Nasser's plans quietly to develop until this country and all Western Europe are held to ransom by Egypt acting at Russia's behest it seems to us that our duty is plain.

We have many times led Europe in the fight for freedom. It would be an ignoble end to our long history if we tamely accepted to perish by degrees.

With this analysis Eisenhower found himself in total disagreement, as he made plain in another long letter on 9 September to Eden. He considered that 'you are making of Nasser a much more important figure than he is', and his view of the Middle East consequences of prolonged discussion 'a picture too dark and ... severely distorted'.

The use of military force against Egypt under present circumstances might have consequences even more serious than causing Arabs to support Nasser. It might cause a serious misunderstanding between our two countries because I must say frankly that there is yet no public opinion in this country which is prepared to support such a move, and the most significant public opinion that there is seems to think that the United Nations was formed to prevent this very thing.

It is for reasons such as these that we have viewed with some misgivings your preparations for mounting a military expedition against Egypt. We believe that Nasser may try to go before the United Nations claiming that these actions imply a rejection of the peaceful machinery of settling the dispute, and therefore may ask the United Nations to brand these operations as aggression.

At the same time, we do not want any capitulation to Nasser. We want to stand firmly with you to deflate the ambitious pretensions of Nasser and to assure permanent and effective use of the Suez waterway under the terms of the 1888 treaty.

It seems to Foster and to me that the result that you and I both want can best be assured by slower and less dramatic processes than military force. There are many areas of endeavour which are not yet fully explored because exploration takes time. . . .

Nasser thrives on drama. If we let some of the drama go out of the situation and concentrate upon the task of deflating him through slower but sure processes such as I describe, I believe the desired results can more probably be obtained.

On 4 September it was agreed to recall Parliament for a two-day debate on the 11th and 12th; it was also agreed to supply both Saudi Arabia and Israel with arms which they had requested; Hailsham reported that two Soviet submarines had left the Baltic manned by Egyptian officers and Russian crews. At full Cabinet on 6 September Eden fully reported Eisenhower's continued 'disquiet at the prospect that the United Kingdom and France might have it in mind to take military action before all the possibilities of securing a peaceful settlement had been finally exhausted'.

At this point the Chiefs of Staff and the military force commanders made a remarkable *volte-face*, which has never been fully explained. The Port Said option had been definitely abandoned, and all planning had been for the Alexandria landing. Now, on 7 September, in a paper circulated by Monckton on their behalf, with 'certain omissions' for which he took full responsibility, they had returned to the Port Said option. This had been the first, and rejected, proposal of the British Joint Planning Staff, and its unexpected resurrection caused Eden and the Egypt Committee understandable consternation.

It has frequently been alleged that this was a political decision made by Eden on grounds of national and international opinion,* whereas exactly the opposite was the case. Why it was done remains a mystery, since all the military factors that had led to the previous recommendation remained, except that the Port Said option had become militarily even less attractive. Beaufre was astonished, and he found Stockwell 'fulminating against the politicians', whereas the reality was that the politicians were fulminating against the military; this was especially true of Eden, who was intensely angry.

Keightley and the Chiefs declared themselves alarmed by the delays, and now envisaged a prolonged economic, naval and air action against Egypt until the Nasser Government capitulated, after which the land forces could enter Port Said without an assault landing. Even so, they envisaged 'some very bitter fighting. It would be a mistake to underestimate the courage of the Egyptian soldier, he has always fought resolutely; it is only his officers who had failed.' Monckton's paper had an additional point. 'It is therefore of the greatest importance that this invasion of Egypt is launched with our moral case unassailable and the start of the war clearly and definitely Nasser's responsibility and no one else's.'

The revised Musketeer caused Eden considerable concern, which he raised with the Chiefs of Staff on the 7th, as it seemed certain to result in extensive devastation and a much higher loss of Egyptian civilian lives than had been considered earlier; the plans also seemed to him to be dangerously inflexible. On the 10th Monckton circulated the new plan, which was chilling:

The opening phase is a sudden and intensive air attack on the Egyptian Air Force aimed at its complete neutralization.

At the conclusion of this phase, which should occupy only a few days, we would put over to the Egyptians that they were now unprotected from the air and helpless to resist whatever other pressure we might choose to exert.

If this did not produce a favourable reaction, the next phase would be a systematic and graded application of pressure by air attack on certain carefully selected economic and military targets, accompanied throughout by psychological warfare. The principal economic target would be the oil supply to Cairo. We would also hope to bring about the demoralization of the Egyptian Army.

The third phase would be the move into Port Said of a land force designed to restore order in the Canal Zone and to assist in the reopening of the Suez Canal.

* For example, Fullick and Powell, *Suez: The Double War*, pp. 55–6. But they did not, of course, have access to the papers of the Chiefs of Staff or the Egypt Committee. Their excellent book is of notable accuracy and fairness, marred only by an instinctive bias against 'the politicians' – fully shared by Beaufre – and in favour of the military for the changes in objectives, whereas the impetus for the latter in fact came from the military.

This was to prove a decisive turning-point. All Eden's military and political experience warned him against Musketeer Revise, and he argued against it with great vehemence, and, according to one of the Chiefs, with considerable rudeness and anger. Indeed, he had much to be angry about. For, with the troops, aircraft and ships mobilized, and after weeks of the most intensive planning that any officer involved could recall, which by contrast made the wartime exercises seem leisurely, the whole plan was to be totally changed. Why? Eden kept demanding, to which he simply got the reply that the Chiefs of Staff had changed their minds. If Monckton had been a different kind of Defence Minister he would have been asking the same questions, but even Head was acquiescent to the new advice.

Everything about Musketeer Revise was wrong, except that its sole purpose was to seize the Canal, which both politically and militarily made some sense. It meant that all the planning had been wasted, that it would all have to start again from the beginning, and that the original purpose had been lost. As Eden recognized – rightly – the French would be incensed, and the result could only be further delays, with the consequent reduction of real pressure upon Nasser.

But even Churchill at the height of his power would have hesitated to overrule his senior Defence Ministers and Chiefs of Staff and force commanders on a matter of such magnitude, and there was the personal factor that whereas Eden regarded Stockwell as 'prickly and temperamental' he liked and respected Keightley, who was the Commander-in-Chief and one of the principal authors – almost certainly *the* author – of Musketeer Revise. Thus, against all his inclinations and experience, and with great reluctance and unhappiness, Eden felt he had to accept the military advice. He was not to realize that the Chiefs of Staff were to let him down again.

The Egypt Committee accepted Musketeer Revise on 10 September; as one of the senior military planners remarked, without originality, it was 'back to the drawing board'. The committee also decided that, as 'The Egyptian Government would be incapable of running the Canal without the European pilots' they would no longer be advised to stay at their posts. Further economic pressures were discussed.

Now, over a month had elapsed since Nasser's action. Large numbers of British reservists had been recalled, merchant ships either requisitioned or marked down for requisition, the Mediterranean Fleet substantially augmented, huge quantities of stores, equipment and ammunition conveyed to places convenient for the main southern England ports, and anyone rising early could see columns of military vehicles now painted in an unfamiliar sand colour filling the roads. In Malta, Dom Mintoff, no friend of Britain, kept his Labour Party friends in Britain closely informed on the state of readiness there. Eden became so concerned about open press reports of movements that he made a personal appeal to newspaper owners and editors; but what could not be concealed was the mounting restiveness in the armed forces, especially among the reservists. They had returned to the colours with great enthusiasm, and regular units were pressing to be included in the operation, but as the weeks passed, and nothing appeared to be happening, the mood changed.

This was also very evident in the press and in the Conservative Party in Britain; in France, impatience had developed into intense frustration. The French wanted Nasser smashed militarily, as quickly as possible, and were not much troubled about the legal or moral niceties, a mood exactly reflected in Israel. While the British, pressured by the Americans and with increasing doubts within the Cabinet, hesitated, and appeared to the French to be dithering, exasperation grew in Paris. The unilateral abandonment of Musketeer for Musketeer Revise by the British was merely another source of grievance and worse to the French, but even before this they had begun to look elsewhere for more resolute and more ruthless allies.

'The first intimation that France was interested in coordinated action with Israel against Egypt reached us on September 1, 1956,' Moshe Dayan has written. 'Ben-Gurion was present, and he instructed me to reply that in principle we were prepared to cooperate. If what was required from us was only intelligence on Egypt's armed forces, this information would be furnished by the office of our military attaché. If the French had in mind the participation of the Israeli army in military action, the minister of defense was prepared to send me to Paris to discuss it.'* Although these were only 'exploratory talks' between Israeli and French military representatives, they marked a crucial new dimension in the crisis, and one which the British knew nothing about.

The position of the British Government had now become acutely difficult. At home, it was under increasing criticism both from those who wanted rapid military action and from those who wanted none at all. There was a distinct drop in morale in the armed forces, unpleasant accusations from the right wing of the Conservative Party and its press, disquieting noises from several Commonwealth countries, and discordant but certainly unhelpful warnings and proposals from the United States, where the presidential campaign was now being conducted in earnest.

But Dulles had thrown in another idea. While on a weekend break at his retreat on Lake Ontario he had brooded upon the Suez situation and returned with a proposal for a Suez Canal Users' Association (SCUA)

---

* Moshe Dayan, *The Story of My Life*, p. 151.

whereby the users would employ their own pilots, pay the Canal dues to SCUA, which would pass on to the Egyptians 'what they considered a fair share'. These proposals were handed to Makins on 4 September.

Eden was, understandably, astonished, asking Makins if Dulles was really serious; Makins replied that he was, but the more Eden looked at it the more attracted he was, particularly by the fact that Canal dues would go not to Nasser but to the Users' Association. If the United States were to participate fully – and it was, after all, an American plan – not only would Nasser's revenue be reduced so drastically from the Canal as to be minimal, but the reality of control would be removed from Egyptian hands. The Suez Canal Company would simply now be called the Suez Canal Users' Association! Although the French, still calling for action, were sceptical, Eden was very anxious to push this plan, despite the reservations of Lloyd and Macmillan, who saw it merely as a delaying device. Dulles certainly urged its merits very strongly upon Eisenhower and the French, whom he told that it had the full authority of the United States and would be pressed by them upon the Egyptians; if they refused, economic sanctions could be imposed.

It is very easy to see why Eden was so attracted. If Nasser had accepted, it would have been a virtually total climb-down and have made a mockery of nationalization. It was for this very reason that it was a ludicrous proposal. It repudiated the eighteen-nation proposals, with its emphasis upon agreement with Nasser, and it wholly ignored the crucial issues of sovereignty and jurisdiction. It had become a technical, not a political, problem, to be resolved by these means. Nasser was for once wholly justified when he pointed out that 'it is impossible to have two bodies to regulate navigation through the Canal', and he commented caustically on the likelihood of the British accepting a 'Port of London Users' Association' which would pay the British what it deemed appropriate.

On 11 September Lloyd informed a full Cabinet that the Menzies Mission had failed, but that although the United States was strongly opposed to military action and reference to the United Nations, it now favoured the Users' Association which he described.

Macmillan said that

it was unlikely that effective international control over the Canal could be secured without the use of force. He regarded the establishment of the users' organization as a step towards the ultimate use of force. It would not in itself provide a solution.... It should, however, serve to bring the issue to a head. This was of great importance from the point of view of the national economy. If we could achieve a quick and satisfactory settlement of the issue, confidence in sterling would be restored; but, if a settlement was long delayed, the cost and the uncertainty would undermine our financial position. He therefore hoped that Parliament could be persuaded to give the Government a mandate to take all necessary steps, including the use of force, to secure a satisfactory settlement of this problem.

But Monckton, showing his true colours for the first time, wholly disagreed; he saw the possibility that the Nasser regime could be overthrown by means short of war, and that 'Any premature recourse to force, especially without the support and approval of the United States, was likely to precipitate disorder throughout the Middle East and to alienate a substantial body of public opinion in this country and elsewhere throughout the world.' Kilmuir and Salisbury argued that if the Egyptians rejected the association proposal the use of force was not inconsistent with the UN Charter; Butler remarked that 'the Conservative Party in the House of Commons would be ready to support the use of force if they were satisfied that all practicable steps had been taken, without success, to secure a settlement by peaceful means'.

But, in spite of Monckton's intervention, the Cabinet agreed with Eden that 'every reasonable effort must be made' to restore international control by peaceful means, 'but that, if these should fail, we should be justified in the last resort in using force to restore the situation. It would be a difficult exercise of judgement to decide when the point had been reached when recourse must be made to more forceful measures.'

With this there was no disagreement.

There had been intense telegraphic communications between London and Washington, in which the precise form of words to be employed in the statements to be made in each capital was discussed and agreed. But although the State Department and the Foreign Office seemed to be clear about exactly what was to be said, Eisenhower held a press conference on the 11th at which he was asked if the United States would support Britain and France if they had to resort to force, to which he replied:

I don't know exactly what you mean by backing them [the British and French]. As you know, this country will not go to war ever while I am occupying my present post unless the Congress is called into session and Congress declares such a war. And the only exception to that would be in the case of unexpected and unwarranted attack on this nation, where self-defence itself would dictate some quick response while you call Congress into action.

The full text of this statement was not available in London until after the Cabinet meeting, and its full impact and importance were not immediately appreciated.

Eden subsequently – and, indeed, for the rest of his life – considered that his acceptance of SCUA was the greatest mistake of his career, for which he reproached himself greatly. He was certainly shaken when, on the morning of 12 September, Selwyn Lloyd, having seen what Eisenhower had said, came to tell him that he had changed his mind, that SCUA was unworkable and that the British should go to the Security Council; but it was too late. The Cabinet had endorsed SCUA, the House of Commons was reassembling, the debate was to open in a few hours. The exact phrasing had been agreed with Washington. Lloyd's doubts were too late for practical politics; time was pressing, and at long last it seemed that the Americans had grasped the situation.

But the fault did not lie with Eden. It was the American plan, and the exact agreed words between London and Washington were these:

I must make it clear that if the Egyptian Government should seek to interfere with the operation of the Association, or refuse to extend to it the essential minimum of co-operation, then that Government will once more be in breach of the Convention of 1888. In that event, Her Majesty's Government *and others concerned** will be free to take such further steps as seem to be required either through the United Nations, or by other means for the assertion of their rights.

This was the agreement; as the telegrams make plain, there was no doubt or ambiguity. These were the precise words to be used in Washington, London and Paris.

While ministers – especially the Egypt Committee – grappled with the increasingly complex situation, there were conflicting impressions of Opposition attitudes. Bevan had emerged as strong a denunciator of Nasser as Gaitskell, the latter recording after a Shadow Cabinet meeting that Bevan 'was in no doubt about Nasser being a thug ... [or] about the need for international control'.† But on 24 August Gaitskell had given Dulles the clear impression that half the country would not support the use of force and instead favoured international control, without describing how this might be achieved in the face of Nasser's intransigence. In an interview in the *Manchester Guardian* at the end of the month, Gaitskell said that 'Nasser is an ambitious military dictator.... But, so far, what he has done does *not* justify armed retaliation.' What he now proposed, somewhat oddly, was that the West should boycott the Canal if Nasser refused to negotiate on the London proposals, a line he had also taken with Dulles. What he had in mind was alternative pipelines and transport, and increased American supplies of oil to Western Europe, which ignored the immediacy of the problem, as well as the other implications of Nasser's success.

Gaitskell's position was complicated by the fact that his left, and the traditional pacifist element in his Party, had now strongly reacted against his own early line and that of Morrison, whereas Morrison was seeing Eden regularly to give him his strong support, which was echoed by the President

---

* My italics.
† Williams, *Hugh Gaitskell*, p. 426.

of the TUC General Council, Charles Geddes, and its international committee. Gaitskell was fully aware of the fact that they spoke for many trade unionists.

Gaitskell's biographer repeatedly claimed a complete consistency in Gaitskell's position. The reality, and it is no disparagement of Gaitskell at all to say so, is that he had to react to changing circumstances and to the changing balance of opinion within his Shadow Cabinet and his Parliamentary Party. It was only gradually that his own personal leadership began to emerge, but meanwhile he was an uneasy leader of a divided Labour Movement.

This changed mood was very clear when the House of Commons met on 12 September. The Labour Party had expected Eden to announce a reference to the Security Council following Nasser's rejection of the Menzies Mission; the Suez Group was hoping for the announcement of military action; what they got was the announcement of the Users' Association.

Up to this point, after Eden had given a calm review of the course of the crisis and the grave issue involved, he had received a quiet and serious hearing. The details of the Association, he said, had yet to be worked out, but he could give a broad outline:

The Users' Association will employ pilots, will undertake responsibility for co-ordination of traffic through the Canal, and, in general, will act as a voluntary association for the exercise of the rights of Suez Canal owners. The Egyptian authorities will be requested to co-operate in maintaining the maximum flow of traffic through the Canal.... But I must make it clear that if the Egyptian Government should seek to interfere—

Mr Harold Davies (Leek): Deliberate provocation.

The Prime Minister: —with the operations of the Association, or refuse to extend to it the essential minimum of co-operation, then that Government will once again be in breach of the 1888 Convention. (*Hon. Members*: Resign!) I must remind the House that what I am saying (*An Hon. Member*: What a peacemaker!) is the result of exchanges of views between three Governments. In that event Her Majesty's Government and others concerned will be free to take such further steps—

Mr S. O. Davies [Merthyr Tydfil]: What do you mean by that?

The Prime Minister: —as seem to be required—

Mr [S. O.] Davies: You are talking about war.

The Prime Minister: —either through the United Nations or by other means, for the assertion of their rights. (*Hon. Members*: Oh!)

Eden ended his speech to a thunderous Conservative ovation and Opposition tumult. Gaitskell, who had known nothing about the Users' Association beforehand, protested at the clear threat in Eden's speech, demanded a pledge not to use force contrary to the Charter, and called for more negotiation.

Eden's speech caused consternation in Washington, especially in the White House. How Eisenhower had failed to grasp the implications of Dulles' SCUA proposals is unfathomable, but he was appalled by the clear threat implied in Eden's speech. Dulles accordingly called an immediate press conference in which he dissociated the United States from every aspect of SCUA that had made it so attractive to the British; the most damaging remark was that, if opposed, American ships would not shoot their way through the Canal, a phrase of great vividness but quite irrelevant.

The most remarkable feature of this performance was that Dulles had faithfully read out the agreed statement, in exactly the terms used by Eden in the Commons; but it was in answer to supplementary questions that Dulles caused such chaos. 'We do not intend to shoot our way through. It may be we have the right to do it but we don't intend to do it as far as the United States is concerned. . . . I do not recall just exactly what Sir Anthony Eden said on this point. I did not get the impression that there was any undertaking or pledge given by him to shoot their way through the Canal.' As Eden later wrote, 'It would be hard to imagine a statement more likely to cause the maximum allied disunity and disarray.' Eisenhower later in his memoirs derided SCUA, and remarked that 'any thought of using force [was] almost ridiculous', but the fact was that he had endorsed the SCUA initiative, and then pulled back, leaving the British Prime Minister stranded. In the unhappily long saga of Anglo-American duplicity, this ranks very high.

What Dulles and Eisenhower had done was to wreck SCUA and put the British Government, in the middle of a major parliamentary debate, in a desperate position. Once again, Anglo-American unity was seen to be at best tenuous, and Eden's reaction to Dulles' performance was understandably sulphurous, a reaction in which he was joined by a substantial majority of the Conservative Party and press. Even a hostile commentator like Paul Johnson described it as a 'double-cross', and his biographer has nothing to say for Dulles at all except complete denigration. In Hoopes' words,

[Dulles] insisted on playing the leading role in formulating the 'international authority' and SCUA plans, and he ardently advocated their adoption by his allies; the readiness of those allies to accept and pursue the proposals rested heavily on the supposition that the United States was a serious party at interest; moreover, by any objective reckoning, neither plan was realizable without concerted Western pressure and probably not without resort to force. Yet Dulles showed no hesitancy in backing away from all such implications after his allies, at his urging, were publicly committed. He insisted, in short, on total control, but very limited responsibility.*

* Hoopes, *The Devil and John Foster Dulles*, p. 362.

Dulles' press conference had effectively wrecked his own SCUA, but Eden was now trapped by it. With perhaps excessive loyalty to the United States – almost saintly in the circumstances – William Clark was instructed by Eden to tell the press that SCUA was a British proposal, although slyly adding that it had 'a foster father'. The Commons debate resumed on the 13th with confusion on the Tory benches, and much passion on the Labour side. From the Conservatives, a former Attorney-General Sir Lionel Heald called for reference to the Security Council before a resort to force; Gaitskell demanded of Lloyd an assurance to this effect, which in view of the commitment to Dulles Lloyd could not give. When Eden wound up the debate, Gaitskell demanded whether the British would 'shoot their way through the Canal', to which Eden replied that if Egypt rejected SCUA the matter would be referred to the Security Council. The debate ended with votes which the Government won by majorities of 70 and 71. It had been, as Lloyd wrote with understatement, 'acrimonious'. The apparent consensus of early August had collapsed; so had British and French governmental confidence in the administration of the United States. If it had been, in the House of Commons terms, one of the worst days a modern British Government has had to endure, it also marked a new low point in Anglo-American relations.

Eden was optimistic enough to write to Churchill on 10 September that 'the Americans seem very firmly lined up with us on internationalism.... The BBC is exasperating me by leaning over backwards to be what they call neutral and to present both sides of the case, by which I suppose they mean our country's and the Dancing Major's.' But on 21 September he reported to Churchill that 'I am not very happy at the way things are developing here, but we are struggling hard to keep a firm and united front in these critical weeks, firm is even more important than united. Foster assures me that U.S. is as determined to deal with Nasser as we are – but I fear he has a mental caveat about November 6th [presidential election day]. We cannot accept that.'

If the British were angered, as they were, by American perfidy, for the French this further betrayal confirmed everything they had suspected about the Americans' resolution and good faith, and they were indignant with the British for having persuaded them to go along with this farce. Nasser rejected SCUA out of hand, and brought in pilots from Yugoslavia, Russia, Greece and East Germany to assist the Egyptians, who had succeeded in putting through as many ships a day as before nationalization. The British and French had been humiliated again.

There is a profound unreality about the further deliberations of the eighteen nations when they met again in Lancaster House on 19 September to discuss the corpse of SCUA, which Dulles insisted was still alive. But in his speech Dulles further bewildered the British and French by declaring:

We all want a world in which force is not used. True, but that is only one side of the coin. If you have a world in which force is not used, you have also got to have a world in which a just solution of problems of this sort can be achieved. I do not care how many words are written into the Charter of the United Nations about not using force; if in fact there is not a substitute for force, and some way of getting just solutions of some of these problems, inevitably the world will fall back again into anarchy and into chaos.

Dulles remained firmly against reference to the UN at the beginning, but under pressure wobbled again. In private discussions with Selwyn Lloyd he said it was 'imperative' that Nasser should lose, but that a war would make him a hero; there should be economic measures, such as refusing to buy Egyptian cotton, discouragement of tourism, switching purchases of oil and making use of Jewish bankers. Lloyd described this as a 'rather fatuous little homily', but SCUA was still technically breathing.

Difficulties did arise about what it was to be called. Lloyd's entertaining account should not be omitted from this sombre chronicle:

It had first been called CASU (Co-operative Association of Suez Canal Users). That turned out to be a dirty word in Portuguese. Various other combinations were tried. Almost all of them meant something revolting, usually in Turkish. Eventually SCUA survived all tests and the Suez Canal Users' Association came into being.*

Truly has it been often remarked that tragedy and farce are close companions.

By this stage, the Anglo-French position had become hapless. Dulles' performances had persuaded many – including Nasser – that the Americans were not in reality believers in their own idea, and Dulles' continued hostility to referring the matter to the Security Council exasperated Eden, who decided that the British and French must retrieve the initiative. So on 23 September the request was made. Macmillan was in America at this time attending a meeting of the International Monetary Fund. He found Eisenhower relaxed and anti-Nasser, preoccupied with his re-election campaign. But Dulles was indignant about the Security Council reference; the result was that the United States voted, not only for the British item on the agenda, but also for an Egyptian item that denounced the Anglo-French military precautions as a threat to international peace. There was the additional problem that the French, while agreeing to go along, considered the UN reference futile. Although Mollet contemplated the remote possibility of a peaceful settlement, Pineau gave Eden and Lloyd

* Lloyd, *Suez*, p. 145.

the clear impression when they met the French leaders in Paris on 26 September that there must be military action before the end of October and that the French were not interested in any other solution. Meanwhile, the Israelis were becoming incensed at continued murderous fedayeen raids from Jordan.

On top of this Dulles held another press conference on 2 October, the day Lloyd arrived in New York, in which he said that 'The United States cannot be expected to identify herself 100 per cent either with colonial powers or the powers uniquely concerned with the problem of getting independence as rapidly and as fully as possible.' These, and other comments, again seemed to concede the Egyptian claim that this was a purely 'colonial' problem. Next, when asked if scua's 'teeth' were being pulled, Dulles said that 'I know of no teeth: there were no teeth in it so far as I am aware.' Dulles apologized to Makins on the following morning, but Eden and Lloyd were incensed, Lloyd later remarking that it was just as well that he did not see Dulles until 5 October.

This was a bad meeting, Pineau also being present. Eisenhower, Dulles said, was against war and the use of force, but then he agreed that it was right to keep its 'potential' use in being; he also said, as Lloyd reported, that if attempts to secure a peaceful solution at the Security Council failed, then it would be 'permissible' to use force as an alternative.

The Security Council debates that began on 5 October followed a foreseeable pattern, and in the private sessions the Egyptian, Dr Fawzi, was studiously vague. Menon arrived with his own proposals, and absolutely no progress was being made. This did not prevent Eisenhower from telling the press that progress was 'most gratifying' and that 'there is a very real prayer of thanksgiving', whereas all that had been achieved was an inchoate agreement to use the Anglo-French Six Principles, which included respect for Egyptian sovereignty, free and open passage through the Canal, its insulation from the politics of one country, and provision for arbitration in any disputes, as a basis for negotiation. Dulles explained away the President's statement to Lloyd that no one should take election speeches too seriously! Not surprisingly, Fawzi quoted Eisenhower's words with much satisfaction, as did Radio Cairo, while the American press, briefed by the US Mission to the UN, was well informed about the rift between the Allies. When the resolution came for a vote, that part setting out the Six Principles was agreed to; that part calling on Egypt to conform to them was vetoed by the Russians.

The French considered that this justified all their scepticism about the UN; Lloyd believed that something had been achieved, and that the British had been seen to be negotiating in good faith. In London there was exasperation, and much caustic comment on the futility of international organizations, which was hardly fair on Dag Hammarskjöld, the UN Secretary-General, but it was a view widely shared in and out of the Government.

Meanwhile, the French, their cynicism about the UN and doubts about British resolution amply confirmed, had turned elsewhere.

[13]

Suez – The Crisis

The secret discussions between the French and the Israelis on how to remove Nasser were initiated by the French, now intensely frustrated with the British, as regards both purpose and timing. On both matters Ben-Gurion agreed with them, but the immediate Israeli concern was the steady increase in raids from across the Jordan border, which they were determined to respond to. This demonstrated how real was Eden's fear of a major Jordanian–Israeli conflict, as Ben-Gurion himself fully appreciated. The British were very serious about Jordan, and after an Israeli foray against an Arab Legion post, during which there was hard fighting and many casualties, the British response was a communication in such severe terms that Ben-Gurion became justifiably concerned. He did not share the general Israeli view that Eden was pro-Arabist and anti-Israel; he did appreciate the importance that Eden attached to British links with Jordan and Iraq. The stern British warning was heeded.

Ben-Gurion was not interested in invading Jordan, or in capturing the Suez Canal, the Gaza Strip or the Sinai Peninsula; what he was very interested in was control of the west coast of the Gulf of Aqaba and the Straits of Tiran, thereby making Eilat a major port to further his dream of the development of the Negev. Border raids from Jordan would be retaliated against, but so long as Jordan did not support Egypt militarily and allow the Iraqi army to use Jordanian territory, there would be no major action against Jordan.

The next stage of the Paris negotiations involved Foreign Minister Golda Meir, Transport Minister Moshe Carmel, the Director-General of the Defence Ministry Shimon Peres, and Dayan. Ben-Gurion was worried about the United States, and very suspicious about the British, and when the Israeli delegation met Pineau, Bourgès-Maunoury and other senior French representatives on 30 September it was made clear by Pineau that this was exactly the view of the French. Eden, Pineau told the Israelis, was in favour of military action, but others in Britain were not, preferring 'a policy of passively waiting for some miracle'.* There was the additional point that the French coalition Government was becoming tense and

* Dayan, *The Story of My Life*, p. 206.

fragile. Their military advisers were alarmed at the prospect of a winter campaign; ministers were apprehensive of the political consequences of further delay. It was made plain by the French to the Israelis that they wished to accelerate the matter.

Pineau then made a key point, which led to what can rightly be called the turning-point in the Suez saga, that under the 1954 Anglo-Egyptian Treaty the British had the right to return to the Canal Zone in an emergency 'so that war between Israel and Egypt could provide Britain with the juridical pretext to put her army back in the Canal Zone'. But Pineau also told the Israelis that if Britain drew back, as seemed to him very possible, the only alternative was a French–Israeli plan of military action.

The Israelis remained worried about Britain's close links with Jordan, and about the likely reactions of the Americans and the Soviet Union. The French believed, on their British information, that Dulles would be acquiescent, and that a relatively short campaign would preclude Soviet intervention, but they emphasized that these were judgements, not certainties. What worried them most was that they did not have suitable bombing aircraft, which the British did, and they proposed that the Israelis open the campaign, in the hope and expectation that the British would join in later. The Israelis, very reasonably, found this an unattractive proposition, not least because Ben-Gurion strongly doubted whether the French could or would act militarily with Israel without the British.

None the less, detailed military discussions were held. The Israelis' plan was that they themselves should be responsible for destroying Egyptian forces in the Sinai to the east of the Canal, while the French should eliminate the airfields west of it and seize the Canal itself. But when the French also spoke of taking Cairo, the Israelis were unenthusiastic. The Israeli purposes were to be strictly limited: in Dayan's words, 'We, too, would have wished to see Nasser replaced by a new regime in Egypt which would establish peaceful relations with Israel. But this was not an integral ingredient of our military objective, as it was for the French and British. In capturing Sinai, we would gain our objectives even if Nasser remained in power.'* This was indeed a fundamental difference of purpose, but Dayan was highly attracted by the opportunities offered by French–Israeli action even without the British. On their return to Israel, fortified also by French assurances on the delivery of new equipment, Dayan and his officers began to formulate their plans.

There was one particularly important moment. The Israelis, asked how long it would take them to reach the Canal, replied that it would be achieved within five to seven days: the French were incredulous, and, when later

* Dayan, *The Story of My Life*, p. 213.

informed of this, so were the British. Their assessment was at least two weeks. Much was to hinge upon this miscalculation.

The French – and in this they had Israeli support – also brought forward the possibility of creating a pretext for action, such as sending an Israeli ship to seek passage through the Canal and thereby courting a hostile Egyptian response. Ben-Gurion would have none of this, telling those around him that he was not interested in any contrived *casus belli* of this nature.

Ben-Gurion's apprehensions remained, particularly about the air aspect. If the French could not use Cyprus, they would have to operate from Israeli bases, and thus Israel itself would be subject to air attack. His judgement was now moving towards rejecting Israeli participation, but Dayan was vehemently in favour of the plan. Ben-Gurion pressed the French on the later stages of the campaign and after, to which the French had no answers, giving the Israelis the clear impression that they wanted action as soon as possible to recover the Canal, and would deal with the consequences later. Ben-Gurion's doubts were not assuaged. For Israel, defeat or even partial victory could have grave, and even fatal, results, and the stakes were terribly high. Eventually Ben-Gurion agreed that the talks on operational planning and equipment with the French could continue, but without the British involvement the project looked – and was – immensely hazardous, politically even more than militarily. The French returned to Paris on 5 October, with much agreement at the military level although much less at the political.

But another crucial step had been taken. Even Ben-Gurion had not said that the project was impossible or too perilous to contemplate seriously, and Dayan proceeded with his planning. Then, on 10 October, the Israelis launched their major attack on a Jordanian police fort, with a diversionary assault. Both were successful, but the Arab Legion fought back hard, and the British, presented with the spectre of the Anglo-Jordanian treaty, had reacted strongly. Thus, at this point, there was no British involvement in the developing Franco-Israeli plot.

The strain of the crisis was beginning to tell upon almost everyone closely involved, particularly upon the Prime Minister and all at Downing Street. Parliament had been in session for much of the year before Nasser seized the Canal, and ordinary Members of Parliament could thankfully disperse for rest early in August; but ministers and senior military and civil officials could not, although some drew a certain consolation that August proved to be an especially bleak, wet and miserable month. Eden had had an exhausting year of very varied fortune and tension, and, even if he had been in entirely good health, he deserved, and needed, some rest – this he was denied. It had been snatched away from him by the crisis, and furthermore he took upon himself a disproportionately heavy physical and emotional proportion of the burden.

Throughout his life Eden had always publicly dismissed his recurrent afflictions, and even in private maintained a fierce hostility to surrendering. Also, he had always had a remarkable capacity for resilience after illness, and an eagerness to return to normal working and activity, often before it was wise. But he had not realized fully how the failed 1953 operation had made him vulnerable. On 21 August there had been an ominous warning:

Felt rather wretched after a poor night. Awoke 3.30 onwards with pain. Had to take Pethidine in the end. Appropriately the doctors came. Kling* was more optimistic than Horace [Evans]. We are to try a slightly different [diet] regime. Agreed no final decision until a holiday had given me a chance to decide in good health.

A holiday, apart from a day or two snatched in Wiltshire, was out of the question. The 'final decision' related to the possibility of another operation or a drastic change of treatment if the abdominal pain returned. It did. On 7 September Eden wrote: 'A fair night. Sleep at least uninterrupted, but not long – 5 hours.' On this occasion he did not call the doctors, and successfully concealed his discomfort, but the heavy strain was beginning to have its effect. And it was after this bad night that he had had his vitally important meetings with the Chiefs of Staff, Monckton and Keightley about more changes to Musketeer Revise. Eden was not enthusiastic, but was eventually persuaded by Keightley in a private meeting between the two of them later in the day that it was essential.

To political strains, which were acute, with constant meetings and discussions, delayed meals and physical pressures, there were also personal worries. Clarissa Eden was unwell, and it was while he was visiting her at the beginning of October at University College Hospital on a Friday afternoon that Eden suddenly felt freezing cold, and began to shake uncontrollably with a violent fever. The doctors were summoned, and he was put to bed in a room close to his wife's. His temperature rose to 106 degrees until the fever responded to treatment. He was allowed to leave on the Monday, 'feeling much refreshed by my rest', as he later wrote. This was deceptive. As Eden was to learn, these violent fevers, which were the direct result of the 1953 operation, were short-lasting but, although they left him feeling surprisingly well after treatment, even exhilarated, they were profoundly weakening, and then caused bouts of lassitude, against which Eden fought irritably. Perhaps wrongly, the doctors considered that

* Dr Kling, an eminent American general practitioner.

he was well enough to carry on with his work, but a sinister bell had been sounded.

Eden warned the Egypt Committee on 1 October, and the full Cabinet on the 3rd, that there was no doubt about French impatience 'at the obstacles which were preventing the Western Powers from imposing a satisfactory settlement on the Egyptian Government'. There was increasing concern about unrest in the Navy by time-expired ratings and by Army reservists in Malta. And at the Cabinet on 3 October Eden said that 'There was indeed a risk that the Soviet Union might conclude a pact of mutual assistance with Egypt; if that happened, it would become much more hazardous to attempt a settlement of this dispute by force.' On 8 October Butler chaired a meeting of the Egypt Committee. There was a discussion on the Users' Association and its funding, but the principal topic was military operations. Nutting announced the plans for payment for local labour and supplies in those parts of Egypt 'occupied in the early phase of any military operations', and it was decided – on Macmillan's motion – that Egyptian currency should be obtained from the Sudan. Nutting's subsequent disclaimers of knowledge of what was being planned are emphatically destroyed by his contribution to this meeting. He evinced no sign of any reservations – indeed, he gave his colleagues the distinct impression of one thirsting for action. And Macmillan's ardour was undiminished.

The developing crisis at least meant that Eden could appoint a Secretary for Defence who actually believed in the operation. The full extent of Walter Monckton's private unhappiness and lack of enthusiasm had not been evident to the Prime Minister or his colleagues, but there had been warning signs in the Egypt Committee and full Cabinet which should have alerted them. On 24 September Monckton wrote to Eden to say that, on the grounds of health alone, he felt he could not continue, but there were other factors, principally differences with colleagues over the size and cost of the armed forces, and the handling of the Suez crisis. Monckton later believed that he should have resigned completely from the Government, but he accepted Eden's offer that he should stay in the Cabinet with the largely honorific post of Paymaster General, 'thus preserving the unity of the front', in Monckton's own words. In his letter to Eden on 1 October, Monckton wrote, 'I think it would do harm if I went altogether now, and as long as we do everything we can to get a satisfactory settlement by other means first, I have never excluded the use of force in the last resort.'

If it could be considered, as it was by several then and later, that Monckton's attitude throughout was somewhat muddled, he was genuinely torn by conflicting emotions of friendship, loyalty and modesty on the one hand and deep unease on the other. He felt that the great majority of his colleagues positively wanted a war; he positively did not, but he clung to the 'last resort' formula, without at any time truly specifying exactly what it was. It was, accordingly, with much relief that he left Defence, and the true causes were carefully and successfully concealed. Indeed, it hardly caused a ripple.

This event gave Eden the chance he had privately long sought to appoint Head, who as War Minister had been closely involved from the beginning and who was an enthusiast rather than a doubter. He also had youthful ardour and health and practical military experience, all of which Monckton had conspicuously lacked. One can only conjecture how matters would have been different if he had been in command from the outset.

Communications between Eden and Eisenhower had slowed down in September, but Eden was so encouraged by the discussion between Macmillan and the President that he wrote on 1 October enclosing a warning letter from Bulganin that 'small wars can turn into big wars'. Eden declared:

There is no doubt in our minds that Nasser, whether he likes it or not, is now effectively in Russian hands, just as Mussolini was in Hitler's. It would be as ineffective to show weakness to Nasser now in order to placate him as it was to show weakness to Mussolini. The only result was and would be to bring the two together.

No doubt your people will have told you of the accumulating evidence of Egyptian plots in Libya, Saudi Arabia and Iraq. At any moment any of these may be touched off unless we can prove to the Middle East that Nasser is losing. That is why we are so concerned to do everything we can to make the Users' Club an effective instrument. If your ships under the Panamanian and Liberian flags would follow the example of those under your flag that would greatly help.

I feel sure that anything which you can say or do to show firmness to Nasser at this time will help the peace by giving the Russians pause.

Eisenhower, in reply (11 October, a delay largely the result of his presidential campaigning), remarked that Bulganin's letter was 'rather forbidding', and wholly agreed that:

It is clear that the Soviets are playing hard to gain a dominant position in the Near East area, and it is likely they have developed quite a hold on Nasser. This problem will probably remain with us whatever may be the result of the talks in New York. I know that Foster is working there closely with Selwyn Lloyd, and I deeply deplore the suggestions of the press both here and abroad that you and we are at cross purposes.... I got a chance at this morning's press conference to say something on how much Britain and the British mean to U.S.   D.E.

There were at the same time other cables and letters between the two, chiefly relating to the German purchase of British tanks – which did not take place – and to a proposed announcement on the conversion of British bombers for American nuclear bombs, which Eisenhower refused on consideration of 'a number of sensitive issues, both in our domestic political situation and in our relations with other allies, which the proposed announcement might raise'. By 'domestic political situation' Eisenhower meant the presidential election; it would hardly look good for 'The Peace Candidate' to agree to such an announcement, but although there is no hard evidence to confirm this supposition, it is my clear interpretation of Eden's eagerness to make such an announcement that he wished to cause both the Russians and the Egyptians deep concern and to emphasize the strength and depth of the Anglo-American military alliance. If this was the purpose, it did not work. Eisenhower's letter was a masterpiece of its kind; while applauding all public evidence 'of keeping before the world the high degree of cooperation and mutual confidence in the United States–United Kingdom relations which is typified by our joint efforts in the military atomic field', he wished to hold in abeyance 'the proposal which was the subject of your letter with the understanding that we would continue our study of the question and that at a later date we might again examine the advisability of proceeding'. There was, accordingly, no announcement of the kind Eden had proposed.*

'In view of what you say,' Eden cabled on 28 October, a quite remarkable delay in response to such an important message, 'I accept that we should leave this in abeyance for the time being.' The curtness and delay in the reply speak volumes for Eden's disappointment and resentment at Eisenhower's reaction, but also for how their relationship had become so distant and cool.

At the Conservative Party Conference at Llandudno, there was considerable drama, and not only before the immediate audience and the television cameras. The debate on Suez was marked by two very different speeches, one of great courage against the prevailing temper and the Government's policies by William Yates, MP for The Wrekin, and one fervently – indeed, passionately – in favour of it by Nutting, which could only be described as highly belligerent and vehemently anti-Nasser.

This speech was to have been given by Salisbury, but he became suddenly unwell. Nutting later claimed that he had been instructed to make the speech at the direct order of Downing Street, and that when he spoke to Eden by telephone he was told, 'You will be making Bobbety

---

*Eden's proposed text was: 'The President of the United States of America and the Prime Minister of the United Kingdom announced today that a programme directed towards adapting certain Royal Air Force aircraft to carry United States atomic weapons is under way and is nearing completion. The programme has been undertaken under the provisions of the Atomic Energy Act of 1954 and provides for aircraft modifications and the training of loading and delivery crews.'

Salisbury's speech, which has been cleared by the Cabinet. He is sending it round by special messenger. Just get on the train and don't argue.' Eden had no recollection of such a conversation, and in any event Salisbury's speech had not been 'cleared' by the Cabinet. Nutting then claimed that he and his Private Secretary toned down Salisbury's draft, although it remained 'a very combative piece of prose'.*

Other accounts tell a very different story. Heath recalls Nutting saying to him gleefully, 'This is Nutting's speech and Nutting's day,' and that Nutting 'loved' making the speech and the great applause it received. This was certainly the clear impression not only of everyone there but of those who watched it on television, and Nutting's performance lacked nothing in fire and fervour. Anything less than an unhappy and reluctant man reading out someone else's speech would have been difficult to imagine.

Eden wrote in 1967:

I was not conscious of opposition on Nutting's part to the policies which the Government were pursuing until some date after the Party Conference, where he delivered Lord Salisbury's speech. I would hardly have asked him to make that speech had I any such premonition, for clearly it needed to be delivered by somebody who believed in it. Nor, as I recall, did the author [Nutting] show any reluctance to make this speech. On the contrary, he showed some reluctance to have it attributed to Lord Salisbury. Mr Edward Heath can confirm this.

Lennox-Boyd's account is contained in a memorandum to Nutting of 20 June 1967:

A copy of Lord Salisbury's speech was also given to Mr Alan Lennox-Boyd. He arrived in Llandudno earlier than Mr Nutting, for whom he left a message to contact him at whatever time he arrived however late. Mr Nutting called on him late in the evening and they discussed the speech. In this conversation he made no comments to Lord Boyd which made him think that Mr Nutting was anything but in agreement with the sentiments he was proposing to expound.

On Eden's return from the Conference on 14 October the French acting Foreign Minister, Albert Gazier, and General Maurice Challe, a deputy Chief of Staff of the French Air Force, came to see Eden at Chequers at Mollet's urgent request. Nutting was present, as Lloyd was still in New York. Challe set out The Plan. Israel would be encouraged to attack Egypt across the Sinai; the British and French would give them enough time to defeat the Egyptians and then demand that both sides withdraw from the Canal to allow the Anglo-French forces to occupy it. Eden was non-committal, and Lloyd, when informed of The Plan, initially hostile, but

* Nutting, *No End of a Lesson*, p. 82.

they decided that they must see Mollet and Pineau at once. So, although Lloyd had only just flown from New York, they flew to Paris on 16 October.

This meeting took place without officials present, not even the Ambassador Gladwyn Jebb, who was at the time deeply resentful at his exclusion. Mollet and Eden continued to prefer a peaceful settlement on satisfactory terms, which still emphatically included an effective international authority to control the Canal. As this was clearly not possible, and disillusionment with SCUA and the Americans was so strong, they turned to alternatives. The French thought that the Israelis would attack Egypt, but did not reveal to Eden and Lloyd the extent of their discussions with them. But when the question was directly put to Eden – if the Israelis did attack Egypt and the Canal was threatened, would the Anglo-French force intervene? – he replied that he thought the answer was 'Yes', but that he would have to consult the Cabinet.

Eden's caution over the Challe Plan had been genuine, but at some point – and on this his papers do not give the answer – he became converted to it. At the Cabinet on 18 October, however, the minutes do not confirm Lloyd's later account that Eden had told his colleagues the full story and sought, and received, their approval for The Plan. Nor is it at all likely that the minutes are incorrect, as The Plan itself was still remarkably vague.

The French, however, were convinced that Eden had agreed, and – no doubt with some exaggeration over Eden's enthusiasm – put The Plan to the Israelis. Dayan's account is accurate:

The first paragraph [of the proposal] stated that Britain and France would demand of both Egypt and Israel that they retire from the Canal area, and if one side refused, Anglo-French forces would intervene to ensure the smooth operation of the Canal. The purpose of this paragraph was to provide the legal, political, and moral justification for the invasion of Egypt by Britain and France. The second paragraph declared that the British would not go to the aid of Egypt if war broke out between her and Israel. But this was not the case as regards Jordan, with whom Britain had a valid defense treaty.*

The French strongly emphasized to the Israelis that Britain 'would join the campaign only if she could appear as an intermediary, as one who restored order'. Not surprisingly, Ben-Gurion's suspicions were not reduced, but he agreed to fly to Paris with Peres, Dayan, and the head of Dayan's bureau, Mordechai Bar-On. After an extremely long and difficult flight they arrived at the Villacoublay military airfield outside Paris on 22 October. The meeting-place was a villa at Sèvres, on the outskirts of the city, the home of an eminent French family, the Bonnier de la Chapelles. The French participants were Mollet, Pineau and Bourgès-Maunoury.

* Dayan, *The Story of My Life*, p. 174.

The discussions were long, somewhat confused and at times almost acrimonious. Ben-Gurion set forward a comprehensive solution of the entire Middle East question, involving *inter alia* the partition of Jordan, whereas the French were interested only in the immediate military problem. This, they insisted, was immediate indeed. There was no doubt about French resolve, but the longer the crisis continued the more difficult was Eden's position in Britain, while Nasser's links with the Russians grew daily stronger. The weather was bound to deteriorate, the Americans were involved in their presidential elections, and the Russians were experiencing severe difficulties in Eastern Europe. The Anglo-French forces could not be kept much longer in a state of readiness. Action would have to be taken soon, or not at all. Ben-Gurion, obsessed with his comprehensive solution, was not persuaded. Dayan was eager to be involved in any joint military operation against Egypt, and could see all the advantages; Ben-Gurion could see the perils. His concerns and his demands rose. The seventeen-hour flight had been exhausting for the Israelis, but Ben-Gurion, although far older than his compatriots, was fresh and alert. He wanted solid guarantees, and objectives wider than the destruction of Nasser.

Pineau reiterated The Plan:

Israel would start military operations against Egypt, which she was fully entitled to do:

Britain and France would then issue an ultimatum to Egypt and Israel demanding their withdrawal from the Canal area:

When Egypt refused, the Royal Air Force would destroy the Egyptian air force and airfields, and the Anglo-French force would seize the Canal.

At 7 p.m. Selwyn Lloyd arrived at Sèvres, somewhat shaken by having been narrowly involved in a serious car accident while being driven from Paris.

First, he met the French. Pineau told Lloyd that the Israelis had decided to attack the Egyptians, which they had every right to do, but they needed British and French air support. This certainly reflected Dayan's views, but not Ben-Gurion's.

Dayan's portrayal of Lloyd was bleak: 'Britain's foreign minister may well have been a friendly man, pleasant, charming, amiable. If so, he showed near-genius in concealing these virtues. His manner could not have been more antagonistic. His whole demeanour expressed distaste – for the place, the company, and the topic.'* This opinion was fully shared by the other participants, who rightly considered that Lloyd was wholly unconvinced by his mission, and was personally unattractive – 'a cold stick', as one has described him.

* Dayan, *The Story of My Life*, p. 180.

Lloyd's recollection was 'of a room of utterly exhausted people, mostly asleep. One young man [Bar-On] was snoring loudly in an armchair. Ben-Gurion himself looked far from well.... [He] seemed to be in a rather aggressive mood, indicating or implying that the Israelis had no reason to believe in anything that a British Minister might say.'

Lloyd had only one official with him, one of his Private Secretaries. Lloyd has given his account of what then happened, of which there is not – as yet – another British version available. A very detailed account was written by Bar-On at the time, but on Ben-Gurion's insistence, honoured by his successors, it has never been published nor made available to anyone outside a very limited circle. Ben-Gurion was a strange man, but he was a man of his word. He later assured Eden personally that, so far as the state of Israel was concerned, what happened at Sèvres was a secret, and would always remain so. And so, officially, it has remained.*

Lloyd spoke in a somewhat unattractive, hectoring manner familiar to those who knew him better than the Israelis. He intimated that agreement with the Egyptians over the Six Principles was close, but the problem was that it would strengthen Nasser, and what was now proposed was an Israeli attack, to reach the Canal within forty-eight hours, on which the British would, with the French, issue their ultimatum to both sides. If the Egyptians rejected it, the Anglo-French attack would be launched, the Canal seized and Nasser overthrown. Little of this attracted Ben-Gurion, but Dayan was enthusiastic. His account – verified by other sources – is that:

Selwyn Lloyd was not shocked. He did not even seem surprised at my plan. He simply urged that our military action not be a small-scale encounter but a 'real act of war', otherwise there would be no justification for the British ultimatum and Britain would appear in the eyes of the world as an aggressor. To this, Lloyd insisted, Britain could not agree, 'for she has friends, like the Scandinavian countries, who would not view with favour Britain's starting a war'. I did not dare glance at Ben-Gurion as Selwyn Lloyd uttered this highly original argument. I thought he would jump out of his skin. But he restrained his anger, though not his squirming, and all I heard was the scraping of his chair.†

The French were gloomy about the meeting, and Ben-Gurion very unimpressed about what he now called 'Dayan's plan'. But at meetings with the Israelis on the following day – Lloyd having flown back to London late at night – the discussions turned more to timing than to principle. Ben-Gurion remained very doubtful, and pessimistic; Dayan remained highly positive. When Dayan and Peres saw Pineau later in the day it had

---

* There are occasions when an historian, especially dealing with sensitive matters that are so relatively recent, has to use his discretion on his sources. This is one of them.

† Dayan, *The Story of My Life*, p. 181.

to be made clear what the position was. Pineau went to London to report to Eden; when he returned on the afternoon of 24 October Ben-Gurion had been persuaded by Dayan. The structure had been agreed, only the details remained to be settled.

Pineau reported that the British had agreed to advance the timetable and that their ultimatum would include the demand that British and French forces enter the Canal Zone, so that Egyptian rejection would be a certainty.

At 4.30 the British representatives, Donald Logan and Patrick Dean, arrived for the last act in the agreement. The meeting was long, and the Israelis adjourned at one point for their own discussions, Ben-Gurion being notably tense.

This was not a matter to be decided orally, or by a handshake among friends. Indeed, the atmosphere of mutual mistrust was not improved by the fact that the British had sent officials rather than ministers. Everyone insisted on a typed and signed agreement, especially Ben-Gurion. The Treaty (or Protocol, as the British termed it) of Sèvres was as follows:

On the afternoon of October 29th Israeli forces would launch a full-scale attack on the Egyptian forces.

On October 30th the British and French Governments would appeal to Egypt for an absolute cease fire, the withdrawal of forces to ten miles from the Canal, and acceptance of the temporary occupation of the key positions on the Canal by Anglo-French forces.

There would, simultaneously, be an appeal to the Government of Israel for an absolute cease fire and withdrawal of forces to ten miles east of the Canal.

If either of the two governments rejected the appeal, or failed to give its agreement within twelve hours, the Anglo-French forces would intervene; if the Egyptians refused, the Anglo-French forces would attack early on October 31st.

Israel agreed not to attack Jordan, but if Jordan attacked Israel the British would not go to Jordan's assistance, as the Anglo-Jordanian Treaty referred specifically to the defence of Jordan against Israeli (or other) attack.

Israeli forces would seize the western shore of the Gulf of Aqaba and ensure control of the Gulf of Tiran.

This is what happened. Lloyd subsequently claimed – falsely – that 'we had not asked Israel to take action. We had merely stated what would be our reaction if certain things happened.'* He also claimed that Logan and Dean had only signed the Sèvres document as 'a record of the discussion on which the three delegations would report'. Furthermore, it was agreed – which Lloyd also omits to mention – that there would be total official secrecy between the parties on what had been agreed, not only then but permanently.

* Lloyd, *Suez*, p. 186.

Dean reported to a special meeting at Downing Street at 11 p.m. on 24 October. In addition to Eden, those present were Butler, Macmillan, Head and Mountbatten. It was agreed that The Plan would be recommended to the full Cabinet on the following day. As always, Mountbatten willingly assented. Only when action actually began did he express his opposition, and then only feebly.

The sequel was even more remarkable. Eden was dismayed that any written documents existed, and ordered Dean and Logan to return to Paris on the 25th to destroy the record. They were left for several hours by themselves, inside locked doors, in the Quai d'Orsay while the request was being considered. They were eventually told by Pineau that the request had been refused, and that in any event a copy was already on its way to Israel. It did not require too much ingenuity to deduce that Pineau had been telephoning Tel Aviv. At Eden's insistence, the British copy of the 'Protocol' was sent from the Foreign Office to 10 Downing Street, and has not survived. The others have.

It is very difficult for his biographer to be precise about the factors that pushed Eden from an absolutely legitimate position to what was perilously close to being an illegitimate one. Those who were closest to his thinking – Brook, Kirkpatrick and Head – are dead, and although Macmillan wholeheartedly supported virtually any means of bringing Nasser down, Eden did not confide in him any more than he did in Butler, who was loyal, but doubtful and distant. Eden did not keep a diary at this time, and although his records are copious, they do not give the clue. We know that he was desperately worried about the almost daily evidence from Intelligence sources of Nasser's increasing links with the Russians: his concern about Middle East stability and Western interests if this continued were genuine, and fully merited; he was acutely aware of the increasing puzzlement and boredom of the armed forces, especially those in Cyprus and Malta, and sensitive to the derisory cartoons in *Punch* and other journals about 'The grand old Anthony Eden / He had ten thousand men / He marched them up to the top of the hill / And marched them down again'; he knew of the Conservative restlessness; the pressure from the French was constant.

All these factors are clear, and are understandable. To recall the reservists and call off the whole operation was never put forward once by a minister as a conceivable option, but Nasser's skilful refusal to do anything that would earn UN condemnation meant that no new *casus belli* existed. I must assume – and it is an assumption – that Eden felt he had exhausted the non-military routes to international control and the humiliation of Nasser, that time was rapidly passing, and that the new plan provided a way out of the dilemma that could be put forward to national and international opinion as a justifiable intervention to save the peace in the area. It was plainly, as he knew, a pretext for achieving the destruction of Nasser; but it was so obvious a pretext that one still wonders why he believed it would not be seen as such.

Also, despite Dulles' contradictory signals and Menzies' fierce loyalty, he must have known that American reactions were more likely to be hostile than otherwise, as would be those of the bulk of the Commonwealth. He could have had no illusions at this stage of the probable reaction of the Labour Opposition. But what he did believe, and on this there is no doubt whatever, is that he would have the strong support of a significant majority of the British people, who cared little for niceties and wanted Nasser toppled and 'our' Canal returned to its rightful owners. His almost mystical love-affair with his countrymen was never so graphically demonstrated. He believed that the servicemen were eager to attack – as indeed they were – and that the British, like the French, were fed up with humiliations from megalomaniac tinpot dictators. On this he was also right, although the majority was not to be as large as he believed it would be. And there was also his personal hatred for Nasser, which has often, and quite wrongly, been seen as the only motive for his actions.

Whatever the final factors that made him take the course of becoming involved in the French–Israeli plan, and I am sure they were a complex combination of many, once he took it he knew there could be no turning back, and he seemed to become relieved and relaxed once it had been decided. He was certainly not suffering from the delusions of a sick man, as some have claimed; the calculations were fairly precise, but no one – least of all Macmillan – had foreseen the one catastrophic weakness in this exercise of *realpolitik*, which was not military, but political and economic.

Eden had told the full Cabinet on the 18th in general terms of his conversations with the French; he added that there were some signs that the Israelis 'might be preparing to make some military move ... [and] while we continued to seek an agreed settlement of the Suez dispute in pursuance of the resolution of the Security Council, it was possible that the issue might be brought more rapidly to a head as a result of military action by Israel against Egypt'. Butler had been privately told by Lloyd what was probable, and he had given his support. This was, incidentally, the last Cabinet attended by Monckton as Minister of Defence. But at the next meeting, on the 23rd, Eden told his colleagues:

It now seemed unlikely that the Israelis would launch a full-scale attack against Egypt. The United Kingdom and French Governments were thus confronted with the choice between an early military operation or a relatively prolonged negotiation. If the second course were followed, neither we nor the French could hope to maintain our military preparations in their present state of readiness. . . .

The French Government were seriously concerned at this possibility and were disposed to favour earlier military action.... They would not, however, be in a position to take such action effectively unless we gave them facilities to operate from Cyprus, and it was possible that they might press us to grant those facilities.

There was then a discussion about possible Egyptian proposals, and Lloyd said that 'he would not exclude the possibility that we might be able to reach, by negotiation with the Egyptians, a settlement which would give us the substance of our demand for effective international supervision of the Canal [but] ... he saw no prospect of reaching such a settlement as would diminish Colonel Nasser's influence throughout the Middle East.'

The Prime Minister said that grave decisions would have to be taken by the Cabinet in the course of the next few days. For the present, however, the discussion could not be carried further until the attitude of the French Government was more clearly known.

At the Cabinet on 24 October Eden told his colleagues that 'the military operation which had been planned could not be held in readiness for many days longer', and he outlined the salient features of The Plan without revealing what had been agreed at Sèvres:

If a military operation had to be undertaken during the winter months, it would be similar in scope to that which had been planned for the summer and it would have the same objectives. The first objective would be to obtain control over the Suez Canal by landing an Anglo-French force after a preliminary air bombardment designed to eliminate the Egyptian Air Force and to weaken the power of resistance of the Egyptian Army. It could, however, be assumed that if such an operation were launched Israel would make a full-scale attack against Egypt; and this might have the effect of reducing the period of preliminary air bombardment. The second objective of the operation would be to secure the downfall of Colonel Nasser's regime in Egypt.

In response to concerned questions about whether this would unite the Arab world in support of Egypt, Eden replied that, although this was a serious risk, a far greater one was the extension of Nasser's power and influence:

It was known that he was already plotting *coups* in many of the other Arab countries; and we should never have a better pretext for intervention against him than we had now as a result of his seizure of the Suez Canal. If, however, a military operation were undertaken against Egypt, its effect in other Arab countries would be serious unless it led to the early collapse of Colonel Nasser's regime. Both for this reason, and also because of the international pressures which would develop against our continuance of the operation, it must be quick and successful.

But the Chiefs of Staff continued to be worried about what would happen after Musketeer Revise, and on the 25th submitted another paper to the Egypt Committee which set out their apprehensions of the military implications of having to take and occupy Cairo, and possibly Alexandria as well, requiring three or four full divisions. But the Chiefs, while spelling out the strategic and logistical problems, did not signify that they were insuperable. They would involve the removal of one infantry division from Germany, a large commitment of the strategic reserve to Egypt, the prolonged retention of some reservists, and the need to retain National Service at its present level.

In full Cabinet on the 25th, Eden unfolded The Plan.

It now appeared, however, that the Israelis were, after all, advancing their military preparations with a view to making an attack upon Egypt. They evidently felt that the ambitions of Colonel Nasser's Government threatened their continued existence as an independent State and that they could not afford to wait for others to curb his expansionist policies. The Cabinet must therefore consider the situation which was likely to arise if hostilities broke out between Israel and Egypt and must judge whether it would necessitate Anglo-French intervention in this area.

The French Government were strongly of the view that intervention would be justified in order to limit the hostilities and that for this purpose it would be right to launch the military operation against Egypt which had already been mounted. Indeed, it was possible that if we declined to join them they would take military action alone or in conjunction with Israel. In these circumstances the Prime Minister suggested that, if Israel launched a full-scale military operation against Egypt, the Governments of the United Kingdom and France should at once call on both parties to stop hostilities and to withdraw their forces to a distance of ten miles from the Canal; and that it should at the same time be made clear that, if one or both Governments failed to undertake within twelve hours to comply with these requirements, British and French forces would intervene in order to enforce compliance. Israel might well undertake to comply with such a demand. If Egypt also complied, Colonel Nasser's prestige would be fatally undermined. If she failed to comply, there would be ample justification for Anglo-French military action against Egypt in order to safeguard the Canal.

We must face the risk that we should be accused of collusion with Israel. But this charge was liable to be brought against us in any event; for it could now be assumed that, if an Anglo-French operation were undertaken against Egypt, we should be unable to prevent the Israelis from launching a parallel attack themselves; and it was preferable that we should be seen to be holding the balance between Israel and Egypt rather than appear to be accepting Israeli co-operation in an attack on Egypt alone.

Selwyn Lloyd strongly supported Eden, painting an alarming picture of increasing Egyptian and Russian penetration and influence. 'Our influence throughout the Middle East was gravely threatened. It was true that, from the point of view of opinion throughout the Arab States, Israel's intervention in our dispute with Egypt would be unfortunate. But there seemed to be little prospect of any other early opportunity for bringing this issue to a head.'

As so few members of the Cabinet had had any knowledge of what had been planned, Eden's explanation of what he proposed caused very considerable surprise, and to some astonishment. This was by no means negative, as several were deeply impressed by what seemed a brilliant device to bring down Nasser without incurring odium, and some were carried away by the cleverness involved. But voices were also raised against the proposal, several ministers being particularly concerned about American reactions and the position at the United Nations. Derick Heathcoat Amory was especially worried on this score, but, as Minister of Agriculture, he had little standing. This should have been the moment for a decisive intervention by Monckton, who was privately distressed by an alliance with 'the Jews', as he always called the Israelis, against Arabs, but, although he expressed concern, no such intervention was forthcoming. The majority view was with Eden to accept The Plan, although enough voices were raised in hesitation and doubt to have given him pause; but, of course, by now it was almost too late. Butler had given his assent; Salisbury, who might well have joined the doubters, was still unwell. If Butler had been a serious doubter, Iain Macleod might well have joined him. But the Cabinet

agreed in principle that, in the event of an Israeli attack on Egypt, the Government should join with the French Government in calling on the two belligerents to stop hostilities and withdraw their forces to a distance of ten miles from the Canal; and should warn both belligerents that, if either of them failed to undertake within twelve hours to comply with these requirements, British and French forces would intervene in order to force compliance.

As the Cabinet records emphasize, this was not the decision of a united Cabinet. The records do not give the names of ministers who argued that the operation 'might do lasting damage to Anglo-American relations. There was no prospect of securing the support or approval of the United States Government'; 'we should not appear to be holding the balance evenly between Israel and Egypt'; 'we could be charged with failure to comply with our obligations under the Tripartite Declaration'; 'in seeking to separate the two belligerents we should be purporting to undertake an international function without the specific authority of the United Nations.' These were solid and merited arguments, but at the end the operation was agreed to. What was particularly strange is that no one put his finger on the real weakness in The Plan, which was that if Egypt and Israel accepted the Anglo-French ultimatum there could be no political justification for continuing the operation. Macmillan, who was particularly captivated by the proposal, only realized this gradually; others do not seem to have grasped it at all.

One can only guess at why those Ministers who held such strong doubts did not carry them further. Although they knew nothing about Sèvres – and many did not know about it for several years – it was perfectly obvious that nothing was going to be done to stop the imminent Israeli attack and that this was a clear pretext for putting Musketeer Revise into operation. No one present* at this meeting could have been left in any doubt of what Eden, strongly backed by Lloyd, Macmillan, Kilmuir and Head, and with Butler's acquiescence, was proposing; he himself – without any elaboration – had raised the question of 'collusion' with Israel. Cabinet ministers did not know everything, but Eden's statement to them was abundantly clear and frank. None could possibly claim that he was deceived, or did not know what he was consenting to. Monckton later explained his inaction by saying that his resignation would have brought down the Government; Amory's modesty, his lack of experience in foreign affairs and relatively low position in the Cabinet seem to have inhibited him from going further than expressing strong and sincere reservations at the Cabinet table, although his unease became very clear later.

What they were now presented with was something quite new, which had never been envisaged – except by Macmillan, eager for co-operation with the Israelis from the outset – since the Canal had been nationalized. Eden himself had used the words 'pretext' and 'collusion'. His colleagues were realistic and practical politicians. But it was clearly one thing to use the threat of force 'as a last resort' to buttress diplomatic and political pressure and quite another actually to use it as part of what was plainly a conspiracy. It may well have been a justified conspiracy, but there was no doubting what it was.

One factor, as Monckton conceded, was that 'the ordinary man in the country was behind Eden'. If this factor affected Monckton, with no remaining political ambitions, its impact on others can be assessed. 'I have never been able to convince myself', Monckton wrote on 7 November, 'that armed intervention was right, but I have not been prepared to resign. I have lived on from day to day, and am still so living on, in the hope that

---

* These were Eden, Butler, Kilmuir, Lloyd George, Home, Monckton, Sandys, Heath-coat Amory, Macleod, Macmillan, Lloyd, James Stuart, Lennox-Boyd, Head, Thorney-croft, Eccles, Selkirk, Buchan-Hepburn and Heath. Monckton identified Eden, Salisbury, Macmillan, Head, Sandys, Kilmuir and Thorneycroft as the strongest advocates of the operation, to which list must be added Lloyd; but, as has been emphasized, Salisbury had had his moments as a doubter, as had Lloyd, although few knew of it.

I could within the Cabinet contribute towards a settlement as soon as possible.'*

Macleod later told Butler that, if the latter had resigned, he would have done so as well, but Butler, with whatever misgivings, had given his support to The Plan. Another factor was Macmillan's absolute confidence, after his talk with Eisenhower, about the American reactions. As he later wrote, 'we altogether failed to appreciate the force of the resentment which would be directed against us. For this I carry a heavy responsibility. I knew Eisenhower well ... and I thought I understood his character.... I believed that the Americans would issue a protest ... in public, but that they would in their hearts be glad to see the matter brought to a conclusion.'† But although Macmillan can justly be criticized for his role during the crisis, on this aspect the blame lay in continued American ambivalence, particularly on the part of Dulles. The signals from Washington had been, and were to continue to be, hopelessly and fatally mixed.

But the decision had been made, and had been ratified by the Cabinet. The doubters did not press their doubts to outright opposition in Cabinet, or to resignation, or even to the threat of resignation.

It was at this moment that a series of utterly unexpected events occurred in Eastern Europe.

Dulles' reiterated language about the 'liberation' of Eastern Europe had been faithfully and regularly broadcast by the Voice of America and Radio Free Europe, and it was widely believed that in the event of revolution the West would intervene. When it did happen, the Americans were not only taken by surprise, but had no plans at all to assist those they had been actively encouraging for years to rise against their Communist and Russian masters. As Eisenhower's own biographer has written: 'Liberation was a sham. Eisenhower had always known it. The Hungarians had yet to learn it.'‡

First, disturbances and riots in Poland, which the Government could not control, swept aside the Soviet-dominated regime and brought in Gomulka. On 22 October the Hungarians followed their example with massive demonstrations demanding the return of Imre Nagy, who had been removed by the Russians the year before. Although Nagy was restored on the same day, rioting continued, and the pent-up frustrations and hatred against the regime and the Russians boiled over into harsh fighting when the Russians sent in troops and tanks to restore order. Eisenhower adamantly refused all suggestions for assistance to the rebellion, and for a few days it

---

* Birkenhead, *Walter Monckton*, p. 310.
† Harold Macmillan, *Riding the Storm*, p. 157.
‡ Ambrose, *Eisenhower The President*, p. 355.

seemed that his caution had been justified, as the Russians, severely shaken by the vehemence of the Hungarian resistance, first exercised restraint and then withdrew. For a very short time it seemed that the Russian Empire had suffered a major, and perhaps mortal, blow.

This event, and his election campaign, may go far to explain why Eisenhower did not anticipate what might happen in the Middle East. His principal fear was that Israel, clearly preparing for something major, would attack Jordan to recover the West Bank and Jerusalem, while the British and French would take advantage of this situation to seize the Canal. United States Intelligence let him down badly. Heavy radio traffic between England and France was reported, which could not be decoded; the air reconnaissance reports disclosed major military activity in the Middle East, but the elaborate network of agents and other sources could give no definite information about what it all meant. When the Israelis ordered mobilization on the 28th, Eisenhower assumed that they were about to attack Jordan and sent strong warnings, particularly as Jordan, Egypt and Syria had joined in the Pact of Amman with an Egyptian commander-in-chief. It was only too late that the American administration realized what was actually happening, and considered they had been comprehensively double-crossed by their three closest allies within days of the presidential election and at a time when the Russians were in deep trouble in Europe. Eisenhower reached for the Tripartite Declaration; Pierson Dixon, now Permanent Representative at the UN, described it as 'ancient history and without current validity'.

Eisenhower did not, unlike many around him, particularly blame the British and French for maintaining tight security, but he had good cause for complaint about the quality of the advice and information he received from American sources. There is also the factor that he could not bring himself to believe that the British and French would do something that he regarded as foolish and dangerous, and he seriously overrated American influence on the Israelis. What then happened was a complete surprise to the President and his advisers. One of the many extraordinary features of the Suez story is how this can have been so, after all that had happened, with all the evidence and knowledge of the Anglo-French military build-up on Cyprus and in the Mediterranean, and the clarity of the declaration of the British and French of their determination to bring the matter to an issue if they failed to achieve their objectives by other means. The Americans had been deceived far less by their allies than they had deceived themselves. They did not see the matter in this light, but it was the truth.

On 29 October the Israelis launched Operation Kadesh against Egypt, the first phase being a parachute landing at the eastern end of the Mitla Pass, while behind them came the Israeli armour and infantry, with every Israeli aircraft that was serviceable in the air above the Sinai. Off Haifa, the French destroyer *Kersaint* attacked and immobilized an Egyptian destroyer that had attempted to bombard the port. The Israeli estimate of the operational capacity of the Egyptian Air Force – considerably lower than those of the British and French – proved to be accurate, although that of the Israeli Air Force was not outstandingly better. The Egyptian forces were often in well-prepared and well-defended positions and, provided the attack was frontal, gave a good account of themselves; it was only when they were by-passed and their retreat closed that they lost confidence. The Israelis advanced, having seized the initiative, but this was not as easy a battle as has sometimes been described, and Dayan and the Israeli commanders had many anxious moments during the 30th, although they were making progress. There were also failures in local command caused by over-eagerness, the most conspicuous being the attack on the Mitla Pass by Colonel Sharon, which cost the lives of thirty-eight men killed and 150 wounded. Also, the commander of the Seventh Armoured Brigade went into action twenty-four hours earlier than his orders required, with what could have been disastrous results; fortunately for the Israelis, although the Egyptians fought well, the quality of their command was not high, and the determination and initiative of the Israeli forces were better. But it was nothing like the easy walk to the Canal that has been often depicted. As Fullick and Powell have rightly remarked, 'the Israeli Army was by no means the flawless instrument which some of its propagandists have suggested';* nor was the Israeli Air Force, with only fourteen (out of thirty-seven) of its Mystères serviceable, its old Meteors, and often raw pilots. Throughout those long two days the intervention of the Royal Air Force assumed vital proportions, as Ben-Gurion had anticipated.

The British Cabinet met at 10 a.m. on 30 October. Eden informed his colleagues of the Israeli invasion and of the draft Notes to be sent to both Governments, that to the Egyptians to 'ask' that Anglo-French forces should be allowed 'to move temporarily into key positions at Port Said, Ismailia and Suez in order to guarantee freedom of transit through the Canal'; these were approved 'as a basis for the forthcoming consultation with French Ministers'. In reply to questions about American reactions, Lloyd said that Winthrop Aldrich had told him that his Government was proposing that the Security Council condemn Israel as an aggressor, but he would appeal to the Americans for their support for the Anglo-French operation. Although many ministers thought such an appeal unlikely to succeed, 'we should do our utmost to reduce the offence to American

---

* Fullick and Powell, *Suez: The Double War*, p. 95.

public opinion which was likely to be caused by our notes to Egypt and Israel. Our reserves of gold and dollars were still falling at a dangerously rapid rate; and, in view of the extent to which we might have to rely on American economic assistance, we could not afford to alienate the United States Government more than was absolutely necessary.' Meanwhile, the Egypt Committee approved cuts of 10 per cent in motor fuels to garages, but petrol rationing would take two months to implement.

The meeting with the French was, of course, a formality, and the Notes were handed to the representatives of Egypt and Israel shortly before Eden made his statement in the Commons at 4.30 p.m. Preliminary orders had already gone to Keightley, and British and French forces put on full alert.

At 1.28 p.m. London time on 30 October Eden sent Eisenhower a detailed message. After briefly reminding Eisenhower of the abortive debates in the Security Council, it continued:

Now this [the Israeli action] has happened. When we received news of the Israel mobilization we instructed our Ambassador in Tel Aviv to urge restraint. Soon afterwards he sought and obtained an assurance that Israel would not attack Jordan. This seems to me important since it means that Israel will not enlarge the area of conflict or involve us in virtue of the Anglo-Jordan Treaty. In recent months we have several times warned the Israeli Government both publicly and privately that if they attacked Jordan we would honour our obligations. But we feel under no obligation to come to the aid of Egypt. Apart from the feelings of public opinion here Nasser and his Press have relieved us of any such obligation by their attitude to the Tripartite Declaration.

Egypt has to a large extent brought this attack on herself by insisting that the state of war persists, by defying the Security Council and by declaring her intention to marshal the Arab States for the destruction of Israel....

We have earnestly deliberated what we should do in this serious situation. We cannot afford to see the Canal closed or to lose the shipping which is daily on passage through it. We have a responsibility for the people in these ships. We feel that decisive action should be taken at once to stop hostilities. We have agreed to go with you to the Security Council and instructions are being sent this moment.

There was little in this to which Eisenhower could reasonably object. But he was so alarmed already by what he had heard, by his discussion with the British Chargé d'Affaires, John Coulson, at the White House the previous evening and by Dixon adamantly maintaining that his government would not be involved in any UN action against Israel that, as he cabled Eden, he could now foresee the Security Council branding Israel an aggressor, Egypt appealing to the Soviet Union for help, 'and then the Middle East fat would really be in the fire. It is this latter possibility that has led us to insist that the West must ask for a United Nations examination and possibly intervention, for we may shortly find ourselves not only at odds concerning what we should do, but confronted with a *de facto* situation that would make all our present troubles look puny indeed.' But Eisenhower's appeal for concerting policies and removing any mis-understandings was immediately overtaken by Eden's second telegram of the day informing him of his imminent statement in the Commons, of which Lloyd had given Aldrich a copy:

We are asking for Port Said and Ismailia and Suez. As the Israelites appear to be very near to Suez the requirement affects them as well as the Egyptians. We are emphasizing of course that this is to be a temporary measure pending a settlement of all these problems.

As I told you in my previous message, we entirely agree that this should go to the Security Council. But as you know well, the Council cannot move quickly in a critical position and we have felt it right to act, as it were, as trustees to protect our own interests and nationals. You may say we should wait until we are asked to move by the Security Council. But, of course, there could never be agreement on such a request.

Either side may refuse; in which case we shall take the necessary measures to enforce the declaration.

Now you will wonder why apart from the Security Council we have acted so promptly. Of course my first instinct would have been to ask you to associate yourself and your country with the declaration. But I know the constitutional and other difficulties in which you are placed. I think there is a chance that both sides will accept. In any case it would help this result very much if you found it possible to support what we have done at least in general terms. We are well aware that no real settlement of Middle Eastern problems is possible except through the closest cooperation between our two countries. Our two Governments have tried with the best will in the world all sorts of public and private negotiations through the last two or three years and they have all failed. This seems an opportunity for a fresh start.

I can assure you that any action which we may have to take to follow up the declaration is not part of a harking back to the old colonial and occupational concepts. We are most anxious to avoid this impression. Nothing could have prevented this volcano from erupting somewhere, but when the dust settles there may well be a chance for our doing a really constructive piece of work together and thereby strengthening the weakest point in the line against Communism.

This, of course, was wholly different in tone and content to the previous cable. Aldrich was astounded and angry when Lloyd gave it to him shortly before Eden was to announce the ultimatum in the Commons; Lloyd had thereby made a dangerous enemy. Eisenhower heard of it from press reports. These blunders brought personal factors into the crisis, which were to assume vital and large proportions in the next few days. Eden's telegram to Eisenhower was sent three hours before his Commons state-ment, which should have given adequate time for the President to receive it before the public announcement, but it was very short notice indeed, and decyphering delays were later blamed for what happened. This explanation was regarded with great suspicion by the Americans, as by others.

On that crucial day, Eisenhower had been told by Ben-Gurion that there was no question of an Israeli cease-fire, and certainly not of a retreat. In the early afternoon, Dulles read to him the Anglo-French ultimatum taken from the Press Association teleprinter. Eisenhower was dismayed, but calm, and would not join in what has been described as 'an anti-British frenzy' in the White House and State Department. Yet he was appalled at what he considered the sheer ineptitude of the plan. His first reactions in reply to Eden's messages had been cautious, and by no means unsympathetic, but when he heard the ultimatum his reply was swift. For once, the message did not begin 'My dear Anthony', which was a sign in itself of his reactions.

Dear Mr Prime Minister,

I have just learned from the press of the 12 hour ultimatum which you and the French Government have delivered to the Government of Egypt requiring under threat of forceful intervention the temporary occupation by Anglo-French forces of key positions at Port Said, Ismailia and Suez in the Canal Zone.

I feel I must urgently express to you my deep concern at the prospect of this drastic action even at the very time when the matter is under consideration as it is today by the Security Council. It is my sincere belief that peaceful processes can and should prevail to secure a solution which will restore the armistice conditions as between Israel and Egypt, and also justly settle the controversy with Egypt about the Suez Canal.

Sincerely,
D.D.E.

Then, to British dismay, Eisenhower issued this singularly bleak — but by no means totally condemnatory — message to the press.

Eden subsequently, in private discussions, blamed himself for not having kept Eisenhower better informed, but it is indeed difficult to see how this could have been done without breaking the vow of secrecy with the French and Israelis, and Eden knew well that although Dulles might be variable, Eisenhower had been consistently hostile towards military action throughout, and would almost certainly have done everything in the power of the United States to prevent the operation being launched at all.* But it would

---

* Eden would have been wise to have taken closer note of a revealing letter Eisenhower had written to him in March 1953:

I once had a very wise commander who wd use a very simple illustration to point out to me the difference between 'command' & leadership. It goes:

'Put a piece of spaghetti on a platter. Take hold of one end & try to *push* it in a straight line across the plate. You get only a snarled up & knotty looking thing that resembles nothing on earth.

'Take hold of the other end & gently *lead* the piece of spaghetti across the plate. Simple!'

have been far better if Aldrich had not been treated in the way he was, and if Eisenhower had not learnt of the Anglo-French ultimatum from Press Association reports. When Eden later on 30 October sent Eisenhower a long cable of explanation it was too late. The British felt that they had been badly treated by the Americans throughout the crisis; the way in which the matter was handled by the British when the crisis broke made the Americans feel, with much intensity, that *they* had been badly treated. Personal relations between Eden and Lloyd and Winthrop Aldrich were not as good as they should have been, but after the way the US Ambassador was treated they deteriorated fatally.

But the principal reason for Eden not taking Eisenhower or Aldrich into some degree of confidence was the deadly assumption that the Americans would lament publicly and do nothing. No countries in the world were closer to the United States spiritually and historically than Britain, Israel and France. Macmillan, like Eden, was absolutely convinced that the Americans, on the eve of a presidential election, would tacitly support their allies against an avowed enemy of Israel and the West. In any event, what could the Americans do? It would be inconceivable for the Sixth Fleet to intervene to attack her NATO allies, and the American military and political presence in the area was a limited one. If the new British Ambassador – Caccia – had been in place in Washington, whither he was travelling *by sea*,* and if he had had the ear of the President, matters might have been better handled at the personal level, but this was not the situation.

Eden made his statement at 4.30 p.m. in the House of Commons. The immediate reactions were more of astonishment and confusion than of enthusiasm or anger, although each was evident in the subsequent exchanges. Gaitskell had had no prior knowledge – fifteen minutes' notice can hardly be described as such – and his first task, which he handled extremely competently, was to urge caution on the Labour Party until the situation was clearer, and to secure a brief debate later that evening.

In the debate Gaitskell's approach was to accept Eden's view that an attack by Israel on Egypt must be halted at once, but that Britain should propose in the Security Council an immediate Israeli withdrawal and prompt redress of her grievances. He also, more convincingly, probed about consultation with the United States and the Commonwealth and asked what the Government would do if it proved that the Israeli forces were too far from the Canal to threaten it. From the back benches Denis Healey made the first major speech denouncing the Government's ultimatum, and when Eden refused to give an assurance that the Council

---

* This was at Caccia's request, to which Eden had agreed to his subsequent regret.

would be consulted before any military action was taken, Labour divided the House. Although the Government had its usual majority − 270 to 218 − this had a major effect upon Eisenhower. 'I could not dream of committing this nation [to war] on such a vote,' he told an agitated Senator Knowland, who was pressing for a special session of Congress, which Eisenhower refused to call.* The news also had a considerable impact on Nasser and at the United Nations.

This had been a major misfortune for the Government, for which Eden must take the responsibility, and not the Party managers of the Commons' business. Gaitskell's response had not been at all unreasonable − in the view of many of his supporters it had been much too reasonable − and he had seemed to be giving the Government the benefit of the doubt until the situation was clearer. Eden knew that the matter was certain to be raised in the Security Council. He should have indicated that, although Britain could not necessarily feel bound to accept any decision contrary to her interests and those of Israel, this was clearly a situation that threatened international peace and security. This would, of course, have been somewhat duplicitous, but the assurance could have been sufficiently vague to have averted a vote that was, both nationally and internationally, highly damaging. It also raised tempers and tensions in the Commons to an alarming degree.

Meanwhile the situation at the United Nations had become chaotic.

At the Security Council on 30 October, the Secretary-General, Dag Hammarskjöld, reported on the Canadian General Burns' attempts on behalf of the UN to secure a cease-fire and announced the expulsion by Israel of a UN observer team on its line of advance. Then the Soviet Ambassador, Sobolev, read out an Associated Press report of the Anglo-French ultimatum, to which Dixon could only lamely reply that he was awaiting the full text of an important statement by Eden in the House of Commons. The Council adjourned until the afternoon, when Dixon − in the view of one who was there, 'obviously shaken'† − read it out. The US representative Cabot Lodge then introduced a resolution demanding Israeli withdrawal and stating that compliance with this would remove the basis for the Anglo-French ultimatum. This was promptly vetoed by the British and French, to general astonishment and American anger. Then, in a remarkable example of tactical quick thinking, the Russians submitted the American resolution again with an amendment removing the clause calling on all UN members to refrain from the threat or use of force. This, also, was vetoed by the British and French.

* Ambrose, *Eisenhower The President*, p. 361.
† Brian Urquhart, *Hammarskjöld*, p. 173.

Hammarskjöld was genuinely shocked by the ultimatum from the two nations he most admired, and told the Council that his position was impossible if major members were to behave in this manner. There was a flurry of speeches, in which the British and French joined in urging him not to resign. In private, Dixon angrily told Hammarskjöld that he was not 'playing fair', which drew a particularly sharp response. The Yugoslavs then produced another sensation, by invoking the so-called Uniting for Peace Resolution originally put through in the Soviet absence in the Korean crisis in 1950 by the United States and its allies – notably Britain – whereby in the event of disagreement and veto over 'a threat to the peace, breach of the peace, or act of aggression' the matter should be referred at once to the General Assembly, which in October was then in full session. The Americans – who almost certainly had put the Yugoslavs up to it – strongly supported the resolution, but although the British and French protested, procedural motions in the Council cannot be vetoed, and it was thus decided.

The Anglo-French veto not only paralysed the Security Council and enraged the Americans but on 1 November completely ended Gaitskell's caution; he denounced the action in his strongest and most impressive speech so far as 'an act of disastrous folly whose tragic consequences we shall regret for years' and pressed for assurances which ministers refused to give. Political passions were rising rapidly, and did so further when that evening the British bombing offensive against Egypt began.

The military results were to be devastating, but so were the political ones. There had been nothing in the Notes about bombing, and, although the British were meticulous in attacking only airfields and military targets, the simple fact that the Royal Air Force was bombing a country with which Britain was not at war and without any declaration of war, intending only 'to separate the belligerents', raised the political temperature to such a level that, after scenes unparalleled in modern experience, the Speaker wisely suspended the Commons for thirty minutes to let tempers cool. It was a brilliantly timed intervention, and had its effect, Bevan in particular calming Labour MPs by arguing that suspensions of the House could only be to the benefit of the Government. After the suspension Eden spoke to an Opposition Motion of No Confidence.

There could be no better example of Eden's hold upon the House of Commons than this speech. He opened in an atmosphere not far removed from frenzied hatred on the Labour benches, but he deployed the Government's case at first calmly, and then with mounting strength and eloquence until the Labour benches were almost silent and the Conservatives exultant. Eden sat down amid intense Conservative cheering and a remarkably subdued Opposition. Speaker Morrison, inspired throughout, then called Harold Davies, the Labour MP for Leek, a popular, likeable but notoriously verbose speaker with a high-pitched voice not congenial to the House. There was a roar of laughter, the House emptied, and, very briefly, the tension broke.

The British air offensive had not been without its difficulties, and the concern about inflicting civilian casualties had meant that the heaviest bombs dropped were only of 1,000 pounds, but the Egyptian Air Force had been eliminated, and the greatly feared MIGs and Ilyshins operated by Russian and Czech pilots had been hurriedly flown to Syrian and Saudi Arabian airfields. The British fighter-bombers on the morning of 1 November had complete control of the air, and were vexed only by the shortage of targets. French Corsairs sank an Egyptian torpedo boat, and the British carrier- and Cyprus-based aircraft destroyed all military targets they could find. In the Red Sea, the cruiser HMS *Newfoundland*, in an Anglo-French task force, encountered and sank an Egyptian frigate escorting a convoy in the direction of Sharm el-Sheikh; the Egyptians fought back bravely, but it was a brief and unequal contest. By the evening of 1 November the Egyptian position was desperate, but it was not until the next day that Radio Cairo was destroyed. London had been under the impression that it was in Cairo; in fact it was fifteen miles outside the city, in the desert, and totally vulnerable. For twenty-four vital hours Radio Cairo had the air informing the world, with horrific — and totally inaccurate — accounts of the barbarity of the British bombing of innocent civilians.

Having destroyed 260 Egyptian aircraft on the ground, for the loss of seven British and French aircraft (but only two French and one British naval pilots) the air war had been successfully accomplished in military terms, but at severe political cost. Even those in Britain who supported the Government were unhappy about this aspect, not least because it was unexpected; and, after the experiences of the Second World War, not many could accept that only military targets had been hit, although in fact this had been the case. The British could easily have bombed Cairo into panic, if not surrender, and Port Said and Alexandria as well. There was literally nothing to stop them from doing so, and a more ruthless foe would not have hesitated. But Eden's insistence throughout on the very minimum of civilian casualties prevented this course, and his biographer is glad that it was so. As a leading Israeli commented: 'Humanly, it was admirable: politically and militarily it was not. He wanted to win a war without inflicting any casualties. This is not possible.' One can too easily think of other political leaders who, with the enemy at his mercy, could have ended the matter within hours by concentrated bombing and slaughter. There was nothing to prevent the British inflicting aerial devastation upon the

Egyptian cities and exposing the bombastic hollowness of Nasser's claims and the ineptitude of his military judgement. The carnage would have been terrible. But Eden would have nothing to do with such notions. It was not even a temptation.

Everyone, including the Americans, expected the Anglo-French invasion to follow almost immediately, and the wholly unexpected announcement that Russian forces were pulling out of Hungary made American rage even greater. At the very moment when it appeared that Soviet colonialism in Eastern Europe had received a devastating blow, from which it might never recover – although Eisenhower did not share the euphoria of the Dulles brothers on this – here in Egypt was a classic example of the old colonialism. But Eisenhower himself kept remarkably calm, some would say too much so, although he was firm in his speeches and television appearances, and ordered an immediate embargo on US military sales to Israel, ignoring a clearly opportunistic appeal from Adlai Stevenson to do the reverse. This would have been the moment for the Americans to have made a decisive intervention to stop the operation; as they were to prove, they had the means to do so. UN resolutions are all very well, but there are other methods of imposing pressure. The fact that Dulles, long unwell, at this moment had to enter hospital for a major operation for cancer may have had some impact upon the mysterious blandness of Eisenhower's public statements, as compared with Lodge's sanctimonious censure at the UN. But although Dulles fumed at Allied perfidy, he remained ambivalent, half-hoping that the Egyptians would be crushed militarily and Nasser broken.

It is not difficult to see in Eisenhower the same divisions and mixed emotions. He was angry at not having been consulted or even warned adequately; he could see no point in the military operation, which he thought was itself being handled badly; but he was an honorary British citizen (which he ruefully thought might now be taken away from him), had a veneration for British fighting qualities, and fully shared Eden's and Dulles' opinion of Nasser. As he told General Alfred Gruenther, 'I believe that Eden and his associates have become convinced that this is the last straw and Britain simply *had* to react in the manner of the Victorian period,'* a shrewd but hardly censorious assessment.

The American pressure was to be applied in the Security Council. To an extent that is usually not understood, at the United Nations – and especially the Security Council – there develops among the national representatives and senior members of the Secretariat an atmosphere something akin to a global club in which, as in the House of Commons,

---

* Ambrose, *Eisenhower The President*, p. 365.

political differences and even strong words do not preclude personal friendships and alliances. It was not that the British Mission was disloyal to its government; the problem was that it did not know what was going on, and in Urquhart's words, 'while their public statements caused general indignation, their personal dilemma and obvious dismay evoked considerable sympathy'.* 'The effort of concealing these feelings', Dixon later wrote, 'and putting a plausible and confident face on the case was the severest moral and physical strain I have ever experienced.'† One of the most painful aspects of all was the complete breakdown of relations with the Americans and Canadians – the latter even angrier, if it were possible, than the former – but the strain with other Commonwealth delegations, with the exception of the Australians, was hardly less hurtful. The Russians could hardly credit their good fortune, and the spectacle of Sobolev leaping from the dock to become a chief prosecutor was only marginally less bearable than Lodge's assaults. The first-ever Emergency Special Session of the General Assembly met at 5.00 p.m. New York time (10 p.m. London time) on 1 November, and lasted, with a two-hour break, for nearly twelve hours, in an atmosphere of tension and drama that made a lasting impression on everyone present. At 4.20 a.m. New York time on 2 November the Assembly adopted a resolution calling for a cease-fire, the withdrawal of Israeli, French and British forces and the reopening of the Canal. The novelty was the proposal by Lester Pearson of Canada for a United Nations Force 'large enough to keep these borders at peace while a political settlement is being worked out ... a truly international peace and police force'.

The only United Nations Force in the brief history of the world organization‡ had been the one involved in the Korean fighting, which had been an entirely Western and American-led military operation only conducted under the UN flag as a result of the Russian absence from the Security Council. Although Hammarskjöld himself was initially highly sceptical of the practicality of creating such a force, seeing only too clearly the daunting political, military and logistical difficulties, the idea took hold – Dixon conceding, on instructions from London, and quoting directly from Eden's speech, that 'if the United Nations were willing to take over the physical task of maintaining peace in the area, no one would be better pleased than we'. Politically, both internationally and in Britain, a wholly unexpected and potentially lethal card had been put on the table.

*   *   *

---

* Urquhart, *Hammarskjöld*, p. 175.

† Piers Dixon, *Double Diploma*, p. 278.

‡ As previously related, the only League of Nations precedent was the force created for the Saar Plebiscite by Eden himself.

It was not only in New York that British representatives were having a hard time. Virtually identical telegrams had been sent to British High Commissions in Canada, India, Australia, New Zealand and South Africa explaining the British position to be conveyed to the respective Governments. Nehru reacted as hostilely as was expected, although the tone of his long reply was more regretful than condemnatory, ending with the words, 'I have set down my feelings freely and frankly for I think it is due to a friend that I should do so. Unless these wrong courses are halted the future appears to me to be dark indeed.' In London Mrs Pandit, while following her instructions faithfully, and leaving the British in no doubt about India's condemnation, succeeded in preserving civilized relations. From Australia, although Menzies reported much sympathy and support for the ultimatum, 'We are however distressed by what appears to be an open conflict in Security Council between United Kingdom and France on one hand and United States on other.' He ended:

My thoughts are with you. You must never entertain any doubts about British quality of this country. Having said that I should express hope that you would make it your personal business to do everything possible to secure some broad basis of agreement with United States having regard to fact that our common enemies would regard a serious cleavage in democratic ranks as one of their greatest successes in cold war.

Eden took this as an endorsement ('I cannot tell you how much your message has heartened me,' he cabled at 11.35 a.m. on 1 November), but said that 'The United States could not have agreed to what we proposed and we should have found ourselves involved in a long wrangle.'

From Ceylon came strong condemnation from S. W. R. D. Bandaranaike, expressing 'my sense of shock and perturbation' and urging immediate withdrawal. More serious was the message from New Zealand Prime Minister Sidney Holland. He reported on 1 November that his Government sent an assurance of 'our deepest sympathy for the United Kingdom in the situation now confronting her. It is our desire, as always, to be of the utmost assistance'; but he added that they were shocked by the Anglo-American breach in the Security Council and outside, and critical of the lack of Commonwealth consultation. The fact that the New Zealand warship *Royalist* might take part in active operations opened the real possibility of New Zealand becoming isolated and even charged as a fellow aggressor. Although Menzies and Holland – especially the former – were sympathetic to the British, the strength of the American reaction had clearly deeply disturbed them, and in both countries the Opposition parties were pressing hard on the matter of lack of prior consultation.

Although the British representatives in Washington and New York had the worst time of all, the Acting High Commissioner in Ottawa had a notably painful meeting with the Prime Minister Louis St Laurent, who 'spoke under obviously great emotion and indeed anger.... He said he had nothing good to say about Nasser but Canada could not accept the idea of using armed force to get rid of him.' St Laurent was personally affronted by the fact that, like Eisenhower, the first he knew of the British action was from press reports of Eden's Commons statement. The Pakistani reaction, in contrast, was surprisingly mild and not at all unsympathetic, but it pointedly drew attention to the impact not only upon the Commonwealth but upon Pakistan's membership of the Baghdad Pact. And from Baghdad itself the Crown Prince gave a clear warning of the effect of the action on Arab opinion, and complained that it 'has put the friends of Britain, among whom I count myself, in a critical position towards Arab and Iraqi opinion'. Sir Michael Wright, the British Ambassador in Baghdad, reported that he had done

my best on my existing instructions to explain the position to him, but he refused to be comforted. He said that if immediately, or within a day or two at most, action by Her Majesty's Government to compel Israel forces to withdraw from Egyptian territory could be achieved, position would be altered very much and perhaps decisively for the better. But failing this he doubted whether Iraq regime and government could hold the position much longer. A week was the very outside.

To this, Eden responded in a personal message to the Crown Prince, giving

the most categorical assurance that the sole purpose of the intervention of British forces is to put a stop to hostilities between Israel and Egypt and to safeguard the Canal. We believe that only the presence of our forces at key points can secure these results. All our information shows that Israel has inflicted decisive defeat on Egypt and that only the action we have taken has saved Egypt from further disasters. We hear that the Israeli forces intend to abide by our latest request not to advance further than ten miles from the Canal although the gates of Egypt [Cairo?] itself are now wide open to them. This at least is something gained and I hope it will soon be apparent to the world that our action was the only one which could have brought about this result. As soon as we have occupied the key points on the Canal, we shall ask the Israelis to withdraw from Egyptian territory.

Thus, for once, the United Nations was a faithful reflection of the anger, confusion and dismay with which nations usually friendly to Britain, and ministers on excellent and long-standing personal relations with Eden, reacted. With the exceptions of Australia, New Zealand and South Africa – and all three were qualified in their support – the British and French were utterly isolated. In the Arab world, as the Ambassadors reported, the

Libyans were enraged, whereas the Iraqis had been courteously horrified. In spite of a few personal supporters – notably the Belgian Foreign Minister and former Prime Minister Paul-Henri Spaak – Western European Governments found themselves, and their public opinion, increasingly drawn into the American camp.

Eden had told his Cabinet that the attack on Egypt must be 'quick and successful', but it could not be quick, as the sailing time from Malta for the main landing forces meant that, sailing on the 29th, they could not reach Port Said until 6 November, with the airborne landings on Port Said and Port Fuad on the 5th. Even at this very late hour, the force commanders were discussing, sometimes heatedly, further changes to Musketeer Revise, while the Israelis mopped up remaining resistance in the Sinai. British and French aircraft ranged freely in the Egyptian skies, while below them the Egyptians were carrying out the sinking of blockships in the Canal, and completely closing it. On Egyptian initiative, the Syrian oil pipeline, vital to the West, was blown up. Anti-British demonstrations convulsed Arab capitals. Paris was calling for greater speed, even the acceleration of the airborne assault, but the logistics of Musketeer Revise were inexorable, and the fleet sailed on across the Mediterranean, very impressive to behold, but very slow. Time now became the Government's worst enemy as the political situation abroad and at home moved against it.

By now, in Britain so all-pervading was the crisis that no one seemed capable of talking or thinking of anything else. Like Munich, it divided families and broke long friendships. Dinner parties became hazardous, and frequently broke up in acrimony. The universities, which had been dormant politically for the past five years, reacted as strongly as elsewhere. It was argued, then and later, that the universities and 'the intellectual community' were totally opposed to Suez. In reality, these elements were also deeply divided, and among those who publicly supported the Government were the doyen champion of the League and UN, Professor Gilbert Murray, Isaiah Berlin and the American Professor A. L. Goodhart; others, then less eminent than they were to become, were also strongly supportive. The more one looks at what actually happened the more one appreciates how fallacious are the generalizations. In any group, and almost in any family, the divisions were acute, and usually acrimonious, but what is important to emphasize is that a very substantial body of British opinion, intellectual as well as populist, strongly supported the Government and Eden. And it is this fact that makes the courage of those Conservatives, notably Edward Boyle and Nigel Nicolson, who took an opposite view all the more praiseworthy. As a member of the then majority I recognized, and recognize, this. And so did Anthony Eden, whose view of these honourable dissidents was always to be considerably different from the one he took of others who were so valiant at the outset and so unheroic when the crunch came.

Normal political allegiances were shivered into fragments. There were lifelong Conservatives who were opposed to the Government's action, and staunch Labour men and women who applauded it. This complete preoccupation with Suez was faithfully reflected in the House of Commons. Ministers went to the Dispatch Box to make speeches and statements; debates were held; Bills were passed; but so dominant was the one subject that I suspected that a wily minister could have passed almost any legislation without anyone noticing. It was, in fact, this calm conduct of business under Butler's shrewd and smooth guidance that was so impressive, and in such contrast to the uproar and tumult that now accompanied any statement, question or speech on Suez.

Those Conservative MPs who opposed the operation were few in number, were not an entity, and had no leader. There were eight of them who, it transpired, were wholeheartedly against the operation – Nutting, Boyle, Robert Boothby, J. J. Astor, Sir Frank Medlicott, Colonel Banks, William Yates and Nicolson. They were not so much a group as eight independent-minded MPs, but behind them there was another group, of which Sir Lionel Heald and Alexander Spearman were the most significant, whose concern was profound, and who were leaning towards abstention and might well break into open rebellion. Given the Government's relatively small majority, and the likely impact on international and Egyptian opinion of a split Government Party, every vote suddenly became vital.

Those Conservative MPs who were opposed to, or highly critical of, the Government's action did not lack courage. All indications were that Eden now enjoyed unparalleled support in the Conservative Party and a great deal outside it. The letters and telegrams of support deluged Downing Street and also MPs' resolutions of complete support were passed with acclamation by Conservative Associations. To stand against all this was brave indeed.

Eden appreciated this, and so did Heath. It must be left to Heath to give his account of how he handled the situation, but it was seen on all sides as masterly. One of the rebels has told me how sympathetically and fairly he was treated by Heath. Although there were times when the weight of the burden showed, Heath retained his aplomb and cool-headedness to a remarkable degree. He gave several the impression that he had his reservations about the entire enterprise, but his job was to keep the Parliamentary Party together in the storm. The fact that he achieved this was a remarkable political and personal performance. If Suez was, like Gallipoli, a mighty destroyer of reputations, it made Heath's. George Hutchinson has given an accurate assessment:

Outwardly, and in every practical way, he was at the Prime Minister's side, drumming up support for Eden in the House, robust in his defence of Government policy, sometimes berating his own back-bench critics, on other occasions appealing to them with honeyed words and reasoned phrase. No Chief Whip could have exerted himself more than Heath did in holding together, with some semblance of unity, a parliamentary party that was in part extravagantly warlike, in part apprehensive, in much lesser part opposed to its leader. What he really felt about the Suez policy he is not disposed to discuss. But I have reason to believe that his heart was not in it.*

But another conspicuous and admirable feature of this storm was the degree of self-control shown by the majority of MPs, and how cross-party friendships managed to survive unscathed. There were still periods of good-humour and courtesy when The Subject was not being discussed, and here the dignity and strength of Speaker Morrison and his Deputy, Sir Charles MacAndrew, were of priceless value.

The number of Labour MPs who actively supported the operation was very small, but there were a number whose sympathy for the Government was plain, and who in private left little doubt that they hoped the operation would succeed. Some were motivated by simple patriotism; British servicemen were at war, rightly or wrongly, and should be supported; the issues on the merits of their causes could come later. Others had been deeply impressed by the fervent positive reaction of their working-class supporters to Eden's action, and were nervous about the political costs. To this group, Gaitskell seemed to be going too far and was too passionate; Bevan's mixture of scorn and probing questions was considerably more to their taste, and in any event was far more effective. Thus the Labour Party had its troubles as well, and these were more acute than most outside commentators and observers appreciated, then or later.

In the Civil Service as a whole, but particularly in the Foreign Office, there was acute division, and in the case of the Foreign Office great passion. Nor was it simply a case of the 'Arabists' in protest; there were, indeed, several of these who strongly supported the operation, and fully shared Nuri's hostility to Nasser. As in all other instances, the causes for taking one side or the other were complex and personal.

It was not the case, as Professor Hugh Trevor-Roper, now Lord Dacre, claimed in a review in 1961 that the Foreign Office had supported Eden in 1938 but was against him in 1956. As Eden noted in 1961:

In 1938 Harvey & Caccia supported me; Cadogan was inclined my way, but would have liked compromise. Vansittart? Roger Makins was for appeasement and a

* George Hutchinson, *Edward Heath*, p. 85.

supporter of Munich, Strang inclined the same way. Sargent had a period of wishing to appease Mussolini, though he certainly was on my side in 1956 and against Munich. Our Embassy in Berlin (including Ivone Kirkpatrick) appeasement-inclined, but I.K. certainly in favour in 1956 in every conversation or meeting we had, and we had many. Therefore truer to say F.O. divided on both occasions.

But there was a very significant difference. As the letters he had received in 1938 demonstrated, Eden then had the warm support of the younger members of the service, whereas this was not the case in 1956 when the final crisis came. Any objective assessment of Foreign Office opinion in the two crises must conclude that in 1938 a very substantial majority supported Eden, whereas in 1956 it was the reverse, although the number who did support the Suez policy was rather greater than is generally believed, particularly during the early stages. Indeed, if the circle of those kept informed had been widened, this degree of support would probably have been larger; what ultimately distressed and angered many was that they had been kept in the dark by their political masters until the final crisis broke, and it is impossible not to feel strong sympathy with them. The junior Foreign Office ministers were in a particularly difficult position; until Nutting told them they had no knowledge of the circumstances behind the ultimatum, and found themselves deluged with messages and telephone calls from Foreign Office officials at home and abroad threatening resignation.

In considering their position, they came to the conclusion that, with British troops about to go into action, they should not resign and should put maximum pressure upon their officials to remain at their posts. There is no question that their decision was the right one, but it was not easy.

It is important to emphasize this intense polarization, as some accounts have concentrated entirely upon the opposition to Suez* and have ignored the strong support that Eden and the Government received. The travellers on my Number 11 bus from Chelsea to Westminster were staunchly pro-Government, and contemptuous of the unpatriotic Socialist 'intellectuals' who opposed it; Eden was told that the Queen's milkman left his eminent customer in no doubt of his views of the rightness of her Government; but there were many who were shocked and ashamed, and their anger was intense.

---

* A very good example is Paul Johnson's *The Suez War*, which describes 'the country ... in a ferment', protest meetings, and petitions against the Government, and says that 'there was a nine-hour delay in delivering telegrams to Downing Street.' This delay arose because the vast majority were *in favour* of the Government.

It was a novel and distressing experience for Eden, the pacifier and champion of One Nation, to find himself in this position. He had expected opposition, but not on this scale or of this intensity. Lloyd described him as 'tired, but very calm'. He made the same impression on those who worked closest with him. 'From the first', he later wrote, 'I was convinced that the course on which we had decided was the only acceptable one in a grim choice of difficulties. I did not expect it to be popular, but my colleagues and I had been grappling with the deteriorating situation for months and we were confident in our course. That makes for calm.'*

All this was true, but the price in fatigue, self-control and nervous tension was gradually being exacted, and, although Eden may not have been aware of this, others were. He seemed to age remarkably quickly, and to begin to look not only tired but drawn. The pressures on his time were daunting enough, in Downing Street and in the Commons, and to these were added inner strains on a delicate temperament which were in reality even more serious, although obviously closely related to the physical burdens. The emotional link between Eden's temperament and his eventual physical collapse are impossible to quantify, but they must have been of considerable significance. Thus for the time being he bore up with remarkable resilience to the storm – but for how long?

One Cabinet minister, summoned to Downing Street at a late hour, was concerned to hear Eden pacing in the flat above him, 'Up and down, up and down, talking incessantly; that worried me.' Clarissa's total support and love were vital to Eden at this crisis, and he had someone in whom he could confide everything. When Clarissa told a Conservative ladies' group that she felt as though 'the Suez Canal was flowing through the drawing-room', it was a heartfelt remark. There were meetings at impossible hours, incessant telephone calls and a mound of correspondence. When Clarissa Eden attended out of interest the major anti-Suez rally addressed by Bevan in Trafalgar Square, she was recognized and warmly cheered, but felt it politic to return home. She was totally staunch, and coped superbly with the chaotic situation at Downing Street. The fact that she was still recovering from her illness made her performance even more valiant.

The unhappy fact was that not all Eden's colleagues *were* 'confident in our course'. William Clark submitted his resignation, to Eden's genuine and deep regret. Theirs had not been a totally successful relationship, but Eden was saddened by his decision, and wrote Clark a personal handwritten note of regret and gratitude. To Clark's immense credit he refused all offers – and there were many – to speak or write of his time at Downing

* Avon, *Full Circle*, p. 550.

Street and his relations with Eden. He had his standards of loyalty, and they were very high.*

There could not be at the time any precise — or even approximately precise — measurement of British public opinion beyond impressions, anecdotal information or the press. That from the British Gallup organization reveals, for what it is worth, that on 1–2 November, in answer to the question, 'Speaking generally, do you agree or disagree with the way Eden has handled the Middle East situation since Israel marched into Egypt?' (as good an example of a loaded question as any), the response was 40 per cent in agreement, 46 per cent in disagreement and 14 per cent don't know (in Party terms, 76 per cent of Conservatives agreed, 16 per cent did not); in answer to the question, 'Do you think we were right or wrong to take military action against Egypt?', 37 per cent approved, 44 per cent disapproved and 19 per cent had no opinion. These figures were to change dramatically in favour of the Government, and on 10–11 November the 'approval' figure was 53 per cent, with disapproval 32 per cent, a proportion almost exactly repeated in another poll at the beginning of December. It has struck one particularly perceptive American observer and historian† that although on the poll figures 'there simply was not anything like a substantial majority in favour of the use of force ... neither the pros nor the cons were in a clear majority on any occasion.' What does emphasize the complexity of the divisions was that on the 1–2 November poll ('Do you think we were right or wrong to take military action in Egypt?') among those who approved were 68 per cent of Conservatives, 16 per cent Labour and 24 per cent Liberal voters; by the 1 2 December poll the respective figures were Conservative 81 per cent, Labour 22 per cent and Liberal 30 per cent. Thus, although a clear majority of Conservatives approved and a clear majority of Labour and Liberal voters did not, support for the Government was not confined to their own supporters — nor did all of the latter approve of what had been done.

With all the qualifications necessary for such polls, what is interesting about them is that they confirmed what one felt and heard at the time, that

---

* William Clark died of cancer in 1985 while this book was in its final stages. He had gone on to a very distinguished career on Third World issues, which were his dominant interest, and became a Vice-President of the World Bank. He was always immensely kind to me, and, although he had the reputation — well deserved — of being a 'name dropper' (the classic being his reply, when asked why he had this irritating habit: 'It's odd you should ask me that; the Queen Mother asked me exactly the same question yesterday'), he was highly reticent and discreet about his time in Downing Street. His posthumous autobiography was published in 1986. As his diaries and account demonstrate, he was never at the centre of events.

† Leon D. Epstein, *British Politics in the Suez Crisis*, ch. 7.

here was a truly divisive issue that crossed party boundaries to a remarkable extent.

Nor did the national press reveal any clear indications, there being an almost equal division between pro-Suez and anti-Suez, with some – including *The Times* – either neutral or undecided. The provincial press was overwhelmingly pro-Suez, the only exception being the *Glasgow Daily Record*; of the independent 'quality' papers only the *Observer* was totally hostile, and the reactions of most of the press could have been anticipated on party lines. Whether it mattered is highly questionable so far as British opinion was concerned; it will be a dark day when the British elector takes his politics from a newspaper, and it has not yet dawned. But it unquestionably *did* matter to opinion abroad, particularly in the United States and in the Soviet Union, where every evidence of division and dispute was eagerly seized upon and exploited; the Russians ensured that Nasser was fully informed, and the British press and the British Opposition, unwittingly and without any dishonour to themselves, gave immense comfort to those who were determined to resist the Anglo-French-Israeli successes. The opposition of the *Economist* and the *Spectator*, neither of which could remotely be described as left-wing journals, had a special impact abroad. It was abundantly plain that here was a nation totally divided about the policy of its Government, and this made a far deeper impression than reports of uproar in the Commons or mass demonstrations in Trafalgar Square or the signing of petitions in universities.

There had been a crucial shift of opinion within the Conservative Parliamentary Party since 30 October. One Parliamentary Private Secretary to a Cabinet minister – himself to be subsequently in the Cabinet – was a strong supporter of the operation until he discovered how long it would take for the main force to land. In this, he was not alone. Others discerned that, in spite of his overt support for the Government, Heath was profoundly troubled by what was being done; this realization was to be a key factor in Heath's ability to keep the Conservative Party together during the crisis and to prevent divisions that might well have brought the Government down, but it unquestionably fuelled the concern of the doubters. The Cabinet kept its counsel, and its collective loyalty to Eden was complete, but the unhappiness in certain faces could not be concealed. Gaitskell appears to have been well informed of these mounting doubts, which in the event he was to attempt to exploit with disastrous consequences. That they existed was the truth, although the motivations varied.

By 1 November, even those ministers who remained committed supporters of the operation were becoming severely rattled. It is not enjoyable to face a House of Commons in tumult, with an Opposition moving in relentlessly, without total support behind one – and the scenes in the House of Commons were beyond modern precedent. Some ministers became unashamedly frightened of the ordeal. Even worse was the feeling that it was the Opposition and not the Government that was winning the argument; this made what Eden called 'the weak sisters' even weaker and all but the most convinced uneasy. The delay in launching the invasion increased this tension. There was accordingly a very definite psychological change among several ministers, who began to cast around for some reasonable way out of this appalling situation. Thus, albeit almost invisibly, full support for Eden and the invasion began to dribble away at the top. The Suez Group below the gangway sensed this, and increased their own pressure. The national press was in total confusion and disarray, with pro-Suez journalists working in anti-Suez newspapers and vice versa; the *Observer* reported an alarmingly large number of subscription cancellations as a result of its strong opposition to the Government, but in most cases it was difficult to determine whether taking a particular stance gained or lost readers. Those papers and journals opposed to the operation gained in fierceness of comment while those in favour began to show a decline in self-confidence. What was obvious to everyone was that the country was completely divided, and that, although all known indications were that the Government had a majority of public support, it was by a perilously small margin. Those who recalled vividly that victory in the war could not have been achieved without total public and political support were particularly troubled.

Added to this unpleasant and demoralizing situation was the factor of physical and emotional fatigue. Ministers would go to bed exhausted, and wake up without having gained much benefit from sleep, to face the uproar again. It was not surprising that nerves and tempers were affected – indeed, it would have been very surprising if they were not.

Although back-benchers were not as badly affected, the toll on Conservative MPs coping with long hours in the House, in committees, in groups and cabals, and with a mountainous constituency mail, was not inconsiderable. It was a burden borne comparatively easily by those who were totally supportive of the Government or by the very small minority who were totally opposed to the action; but upon those who were torn by harshly conflicting loyalties it was very substantial. Everyone was in a high state of emotion, and the parliamentary atmosphere became poisonously charged. One felt that the House of Commons was close to a collective nervous collapse, so fraught was the temper of the time, and these are not the best circumstances for the calm and deliberate making of vital decisions. Rumours flew everywhere, and there were hot words between colleagues; as outside, many friendships abruptly and permanently ended. Michael Hughes-Young described it as 'a nightmare for the Whips' Office', and so it was; but it was a nightmare for everyone. It seemed, and probably was, impossible to continue living at such a frighteningly high condition of emotion and division. All of this seeped back from the frenzied House of Commons to ministerial offices and the Cabinet Room.

Subsequently, many MPs on both sides of the Commons felt ashamed of the uproar and their own participation in it. As I have emphasized, there were definite gradations of support and opposition in Conservative and Labour ranks. Also, in senior Conservative circles there was now serious alarm that it was not inconceivable that the Government might actually fall, or be fatally embarrassed as in May 1940, and the Conservative instinct for survival and for at least the appearance of unity can never be underestimated. Thus the chairman and officers of the 1922 Committee, although completely in support of the Government's actions, now smelt real danger, as did Heath, and they also, if subconsciously, began looking for a way out. The feeling that this could not go on indefinitely was common to all Conservative MPs, whatever their individual feelings.

So a very substantial majority of Conservatives wanted a swift military resolution, the capture of the Canal and the fall of Nasser; the minority wanted the operation stopped on reasonable terms. But both groups were united on the quick resolution of the crisis. All this was faithfully reported by the Whips, but ministers in the Commons could see and hear it for themselves – in itself a justification for the British system whereby ministers must be Members of Parliament, and the majority of them in the Commons.

It was in this context of high emotion, acute division and tension at home and abroad that the Anglo-French invasion fleet sailed slowly towards Port Said.

The Israelis had been too quick, the British too slow.

PART FOUR

Evening

14

Defeat

The decision to invade having been taken by the Governments of Britain and France, and the national and international political situations being so inflamed, everything now depended on the capacity of the Anglo-French forces to achieve a swift military result. Thus logistics and timing now became crucial, and both became more crucial to Eden's expectations with every hour. If the tensions at 10 Downing Street became almost unbearable, so did they elsewhere. It was the failure of anything to happen that was so acutely demoralizing.

The Israelis were especially indignant, having completed their part of the arrangement, that the Anglo-French invasion was so tardy. Even the 'ultimatum' was so late that the British Embassy in Tel Aviv was asked by the Israeli Foreign Office if it had received a copy, to the former's complete mystification.

After the Egyptian Air Force had been eliminated there could have been no other end to the Sinai campaign than a total Israeli victory. Although the Egyptians since the Anglo-French ultimatum had pulled forces back to the Canal, and hourly expected invasion – as did everyone else – nothing happened except more British air attacks which, because of the British insistence on the minimum of civilian casualties, were strictly limited, with the exception of the wholly successful – if very belated – destruction of Radio Cairo. The preparations of the military commanders had been meticulous, but the invasion fleet from Malta advanced slowly. When time was vital, the invasion forces ploughed on through the Mediterranean. Eden's reluctant agreement to Musketeer Revise now proved to have been his major error, although the blame lies more with Monckton and the military advisers. But Eden, as a former soldier himself, also desperately wanted the minimum of casualties and the maximum deployment of force. British hesitation was also emphasized when the Egypt Committee late in the evening of 1 November decided not to attack Egyptian oil installations for fear of Arab retaliation elsewhere, and also because it would conflict with the stated objectives of the intervention and wreck the Egyptian economy 'which we would subsequently need to repair during our occupation of parts of Egyptian territory'.

The delay gave further strength to international and national pressure. On 2 November, at a 4.30 p.m. meeting, the Cabinet on Eden's recommendation resolved that the United Nations should be informed that they and the French would be prepared to transfer the responsibility of policing the area to a UN force 'as soon as one could be effectively established in the area', but that the Anglo-French action could be suspended only if Israel and Egypt accepted such a force and if both accepted the presence on the Canal of the Anglo-French forces. Butler reported on the need for such a commitment for domestic political reasons, while Lloyd spoke alarmingly about the possibility of United States oil sanctions and the dire political consequences in the Middle East and the Gulf, which made a considerable impact on Macmillan. But it was agreed that the operations should not be suspended.

When the Cabinet met later on 2 November, Eden told his colleagues that the French agreed to the submission to the UN, but insisted that the military operations must continue. While this was still the majority view, some ministers very reasonably argued that to continue with invasion after promising to hand the issue to the UN would give rise to the charge that the offer had not been made in good faith. Eventually some form of compromise was reached, in that Eden should state that 'we were willing to stop military action as soon as (but not before) it was agreed that, until the United Nations force was constituted, detachments of Anglo-French troops should be stationed on Egyptian territory between the two combatants'.

But now the Chiefs of Staff and Head proposed further delays. The plan to land airborne troops at El Kantara on the 4th in advance of the general assault on Port Said on the 6th was now deemed too hazardous in view of the Egyptian build-up; also, there would have to be preliminary bombardment of Port Said which 'would cause considerable physical damage. Civilian casualties might also be heavy. ... Alternative landing places had therefore been considered.'

This was disclosed at a meeting of the Egypt Committee at 2.00 p.m. on Saturday 3 November in Eden's room at the House of Commons, as the House was still in turbulent session.

It almost defies belief that, after four months of planning for the operation, the Chiefs of Staff – all present at this meeting – should come up with major changes at this stage, especially as their original plans had not included the Israeli element. It was now seriously proposed that the landings should not be at Port Said, and Haifa was one of the alternatives! 'It had an excellent harbour and there were good roads leading southwards to the Suez Canal area.'

Eden listened to these amazing arguments with astonishment and anger. He said that 'it was politically desirable to establish Anglo-French forces at key points along the Suez Canal at the earliest possible date'. It was revealed that Keightley took the view that the Port Said operation was still 'militarily sound' and that the Egyptian forces in the area amounted to only a brigade; the poor performance of the Egyptians against the Israelis gave no indication that they would fight more resolutely than they had in the Sinai. (This was unfair on the Egyptian troops, but not on many of their commanders.) The only result of this extraordinary meeting was that it was agreed that Head and Templer should fly out immediately to Cyprus to see Keightley 'before final decisions were taken', and to confirm that the operation must go ahead as planned, with emphasis on limiting civilian casualties in the naval bombardment; all operations were to be strictly limited to the Canal Zone.

This was within three days of the invasion. With the United Nations, the House of Commons, British public opinion and the Arab world in turmoil, and with the force steaming towards Egypt, closely monitored by the American Sixth Fleet, the Egyptian Air Force destroyed without a declaration of war, it was now being seriously suggested that while the military operation should go forward, it should be totally changed!

On the next day, Sunday 4 November, at the Egypt Committee Lloyd warned of economic and other sanctions against Britain and France, but argued that it was essential to occupy the Canal;* however, he went on to say that heavy civilian casualties 'would finally alienate opinion in the United Nations'. But Head could now report Egyptian troop withdrawals from the Canal to Cairo, adding that Port Said could be secured by a parachute drop behind the town with a minimum sea bombardment. It was agreed, on Eden's urgings, that the operations should go forward, and as soon as possible, especially in view of 'the increasing disorder in the Canal area and the disintegration of authority in the region'.

That meeting had been at 12.30 at Downing Street; there was another at 3.30. Lloyd reported that the British Ambassador in Baghdad had cabled that unless the British condemned Israeli aggression the British position in Iraq would become 'untenable'; Lloyd also reported that in the UN sanctions were looming; and that the Israelis were now prepared to accept a cease-fire if the Egyptians were; the Egyptians had already agreed.

Thus the whole avowed purpose of the operation had been achieved! What was the point of going on? One minister (unnamed in the minutes,

* What is not recorded in the minutes is that when Lloyd reported Dixon's cable that there was now talk of oil sanctions, in Lloyd's account 'Macmillan threw his hands in the air and said, "Oil sanctions! That finishes it!"', an account confirmed from other sources.

almost certainly Amory, Monckton not being present) said, 'It would be difficult to counter the allegation that our real objective all along had been to attack Egypt. The censure would be particularly severe if the Anglo-French landings were resisted by the Egyptians and there were were heavy civilian casualties in Port Said.' But it was also agreed that the Israelis had only accepted a cease-fire, not a withdrawal, and had also rejected the proposed UN force, 'and unless some buffer were inserted between Israel and Egypt, hostilities might well break out again and become more wide-spread as a result of intervention by other Arab states on behalf of Egypt'.

The principal argument urged by Eden was that any further delays, even by twenty-four hours, 'would make it politically more difficult to resume military operations'. No UN force was in being, and the Anglo-French forces 'which would shortly be landed in Egypt would be regarded as advance elements of the international force or trustees on its behalf and ... the responsibility for policing the Middle East would be handed over to the international force as soon as possible. ... The United Kingdom and France would be in a stronger position when effective forces were firmly established in the Suez Canal area.' This was a clever way of appearing to meet the terms of the UN resolutions while going ahead with the invasion, but perhaps it was too clever for some ministers, as the only decision of the Committee was to refer the issues to the full Cabinet, which met at 6.30 p.m.

Calm deliberation was not assisted by the fact that ministers could hear the noise of the large anti-Government demonstration in Trafalgar Square, addressed by Bevan among others. In Lloyd's account, 'There was a steady. hum of noise and then every few minutes a crescendo and an outburst of howling or booing.'* Eden told his colleagues that there were three options before them: to proceed with the initial phase of the occupation, while informing the United States that, although this was imperative, they remained willing to transfer responsibility to a UN force in due course in which British and French units must be included; to suspend the parachute landings for twenty-four hours; or to delay military action indefinitely.

There was a very long discussion, at the end of which Eden asked his colleagues formally to indicate their views. The minutes do not give details of how ministers voted, but another record was being kept, which has been made available to me. It reveals that twelve were for going on; three (Butler, Kilmuir and Heathcoat Amory) were for postponement, and three (Salisbury, Buchan-Hepburn and Monckton) were for stopping. Amory then indicated he would accept the majority decision. Monckton, at long

---

* Lloyd, *Suez*, p. 207.

last, said that 'he must reserve his position'. Most disconcerting was that when the three Service ministers, Hailsham, Nigel Birch (Air) and John Hare (War), were asked for their views it transpired that only Hailsham was for going on, Hare actually favouring the third course.

There was then an adjournment as the Government was awaiting further information on the Israeli position. The vote, Butler later wrote, 'seemed to nonplus the Prime Minister. He said he must go upstairs and consider his position. If he could not have united support, the situation might arise in which someone else might have to take over from him.'* When this appeared in Butler's memoirs in 1971 Eden was considerably surprised, and asked for a copy of the full minutes; these are exceptionally full and make no reference to such a statement. What the minutes do state is that 'The Prime Minister, summing up the discussion, said that it was evident that the overwhelming balance of opinion in the Cabinet was in favour of allowing the initial phase of the military operation to go forward as planned.' Eden had no recollection of making the statement attributed to him by Butler, nor had Lennox-Boyd, Head or Lloyd when Eden consulted them after the publication of Butler's book. What actually happened was that Eden took Butler, Macmillan and Salisbury aside and, as Clarissa Eden's diaries describe the conversation, told them that 'if they wouldn't go on then he would have to resign. Rab said if he did resign no one else could form a Government.' Macmillan and Salisbury agreed. The adjournment was to await the Israeli response to the conditions of the UN.

When this was received, the Cabinet reconvened, to be told that, contrary to earlier reports, the Israelis had *not* accepted the conditions for the ceasefire and were *not* prepared to withdraw from occupied Egyptian territory. Clarissa Eden recorded that 'Everyone laughed & banged the table with relief – except Birch and Monckton, who looked glum.' The Cabinet therefore agreed that the initial phase should be put into effect, and on this no dissentients are recorded. Nor did Monckton resign. Unanimously, with whatever misgivings, the decision was taken. Eden sent a brief report to Churchill, who was asking to be kept informed, that 'These are tough days – but the alternative was a slow bleeding to death.'

Relations between London and Washington had become very considerably worse, but Eisenhower's preoccupation with his election and the terrible situation in Hungary, combined with Dulles' major operation,

---

* Butler, *The Art of the Possible*, p. 193. 'Like those colleagues whom you consulted I've no recollection of you proposing an adjournment and going upstairs to reconsider your position,' Lennox-Boyd wrote on 7 April 1972. 'Indeed, had you done so your colleagues who remained below would inevitably have discussed *their* position and the whole question, and I have no recollection whatever of such a discussion taking place in your absence.'

rendered the presidential pressure on Eden less than it might have been, although the tone of his telegrams and telephone conversations with Eden was clear enough. At an early stage in the crisis, Clark had answered the telephone to hear Eisenhower, thinking he was speaking to Eden, using 'barrack-room language' and demanding 'What the hell is going on?'* Reports reached London from the invasion fleet that the Sixth Fleet was not only shadowing it but was becoming deliberately interfering, and that an American submarine had hurriedly surfaced after it had been detected by British destroyers who were preparing to attack it – an event whose consequences would have been beyond calculation. American accounts strongly deny this version, but the American admiral commanding did move his ships away.

It was the break with the Americans that worried Eden's ministers more than any other single factor, while significantly it did not worry the French at all. Eden had already apologized to Eisenhower for the fact that he had heard of the ultimatum from the press, but there had been a notable absence of direct contact between the two capitals, and relations between Lloyd and Aldrich in London and Dixon and Lodge in New York were very bad indeed.

Late on the evening of 4 November Eden sent Eisenhower a long message expressing his 'great grief' that relations should have become so strained but strongly defending the Anglo–French action and their determination to occupy the key points on the Canal.

After a few days you will be in a position to act with renewed authority. I beg you to believe what we are doing now will in our view facilitate your action. I would most earnestly ask you to put the great weight of your authority behind the proposal which we are now making to the United Nations.

I believe as firmly as ever that the future of all of us depends on the closest Anglo–American co-operation. It has of course been a grief to me to have had to make a temporary breach into it which I cannot disguise, but I know that you are a man of big enough heart and vision to take up things again on the basis of fact. If you cannot approve, I would like you at least to understand the terrible decisions that we have had to make. I remember nothing like them since the days when we were comrades together in the war. History alone can judge whether we have made the right decision, but I do want to assure you that we have made it from a genuine sense of responsibility, not only to our country, but to all the world.

---

* This was Clark's version, to which he steadfastly adhered. There is, obviously, no evidence to dispute it, but when Eden asked Eisenhower about it in 1959 Eisenhower vehemently denied it. Clark had a habit of embellishing a good story without telling untruths, and my own judgement is that the episode did indeed occur, but became steadily better in the retelling.

One of the Government's major problems lay in what would now be called 'communication', which had worried Eden from the beginning of the crisis. The position of Cadogan was extraordinary; he was not only an old friend of Eden and chairman of the Governors of the BBC, but he was a Director of the Suez Canal Company. When a senior official of the BBC had refused a request that Menzies should broadcast on the crisis in August Eden had telephoned Cadogan to protest, and Cadogan had entirely agreed with him that the decision was 'nonsense' and had it changed. But Cadogan was never, as was claimed, a Government conspirator, and, although Eden urged that the BBC should bear in mind its 'very heavy responsibility . . . at this crucial time', there was no question of interference; indeed, on 14 September Cadogan saw Butler and Gaitskell to make it clear that if requests for ministerial broadcasts were made and accepted, so would requests to reply. There is no truth whatever in the canard that Eden instructed Kilmuir to prepare an instrument, in effect, to take over the BBC, but he was naturally concerned that the Government's case was fairly presented.

Eden's broadcast, on television and radio, on the evening of 3 November put the Government's case – and his personal one as 'a man of peace, a League of Nations man, a United Nations man – I am still the same man' – with considerable effectiveness. Gaitskell claimed the right of reply, but the Government strongly counter-claimed that a prime ministerial national broadcast was not in the same category as a party political broadcast, and therefore there was no right of reply. Although Cadogan was a supporter of the Government's policy there was no question of Gaitskell being denied his opportunity under the arrangements of 14 September. Downing Street certainly protested, but this is very different from planning to 'take over the BBC by legal manoeuvres which the directors and staff successfully resisted'.*

Gaitskell's broadcast on the evening of Sunday 4 November was regarded by many as outstanding, by others as disgraceful and even treasonable. The logic, that Britain should have formed part of a UN force to separate the belligerents, was indeed somewhat unrealistic, and the talk of Britain's moral standing in the world, delivered in a rather sanctimonious manner, was not convincing at all, but the key passage was an appeal to unhappy Conservatives to bring Eden down and to find a new Prime Minister who would halt the invasion and order an immediate cease-fire. The broadcast was powerful, but the immediate political result was to rally doubtful and hostile Conservatives to Eden and to incense others, including the troops steaming towards Port Said. One could be a friend and admirer of Gaitskell

* Williams, *Hugh Gaitskell*, p. 434.

and yet consider his broadcast to be maladroit; it certainly did the Government no harm, then or later, and was in contrast with the skill with which he and Bevan harried ministers in the Commons.

Gaitskell's real political offence, and one that undoubtedly drew doubters into the Government camp, was that he was broadcasting as British servicemen were about to enter battle, whose feelings – and those of their families – Gaitskell did not seem to take into account at all. If it was a brave speech, it was also remarkably insensitive, and made the Labour opposition look unpatriotic and politically opportunistic rather than acting on principle. His friends explain that it had to be prepared very hurriedly, and Gaitskell was also feeling the strain of the crisis. This was perfectly true, but the result was more helpful to the Government than to its enemies.

What the broadcast did do, at a time when the proceedings of the Commons were not broadcast, was to demonstrate internationally how acutely divided the British were. No one knows with exactitude why the Russians made their intervention on the following day, having been remarkably quiet throughout the crisis, but one factor in their calculations must have been to exploit the bitter division not only in the Atlantic Alliance but also in Britain. Gaitskell's supporters can reasonably claim that he had not created these divisions, and of his absolute sincerity there is no question; what was in question was his tactical judgement. As his biographer wrote of his broadcast, 'The appeal was counter-productive and rallied waverers to Eden. Gaitskell seems genuinely to have misjudged the likely reaction of the dissident Conservatives.' Also, Butler was not the only man who thought the appeal to bring Eden down was to him directly, and this did him no good at all in the Conservative Party. By Monday morning, 5 November, when the Anglo-French parachutists fell on Port Said and Port Fuad, the Government had unexpectedly regained the political initiative at home.

On 5 November Nutting's resignation was announced. He had warned Lloyd of his views on 22 October, which came as a very considerable surprise to Lloyd, and a great shock to Eden. Edward Boyle had also resigned, and there were strong rumours of others. Nutting gives a somewhat lachrymose account of his final meeting with Eden;* Eden, when he read it, vehemently denied that the meeting ever took place, and his own records support this contention. Nutting had agreed to postpone the announcement of his resignation, which he coupled with his resignation from Parliament, but the timing of the announcement as it happened – although not intentionally – was the most embarrassing of all times for Eden, Lloyd and the Government.

* Nutting, *No End of a Lesson*, p. 123.

In view of Nutting's previous statements, his fiery Conference speech, and his presence at some of the key meetings, his decision was bewildering.* Eden considered that personal as well as political factors played their part. But Eden's comments, then and later, were of pain and sadness rather than bitterness, although there were passages in the first proofs of Nutting's book that made him very angry. Nutting's was not a name to be used in Eden's company without a dark shadow falling. He had made Nutting; he had saved him at a very difficult moment; their correspondence and conversations had always been (as Eden thought) close and intimate; Nutting had privately and publicly denounced Nasser before as well as during the crisis – what on earth had happened to him? For the rest of his life Eden mused over this, without finding the solution. Others around him regarded it as an act of gross betrayal of a friend and patron; Eden regarded it as inexplicable except in terms of a man who had succumbed to pressure, and whom he had grievously overrated and over-promoted. Nutting's argument was that what was actually being done, and the circumstances under which it was being done, represented a major change from the previous policy; he saw it as a deliberate conspiracy, of a particularly obnoxious kind. He subsequently made this point passionately and eloquently, and there were many who agreed with him. Of his sincerity there is no question: what Eden questioned was his consistency. Few events in Eden's political career caused him greater mystification or sadness.

The landing of the British and French parachute regiments early on 5 November was an unpleasant and dangerous operation conducted with courage and determination, and resisted with spirit, a resistance overcome with severe Egyptian casualties and few among the French and British. It was a confused battle, which taxed the skills of subsequent historians, but the French capture of Port Fuad was a fierce affair, and the battle fought by the 3rd British Parachute Regiment in the cemetery at Port Said was not for the squeamish; the pent-up frustration of these elite soldiers, the perils of the drop and the sight of some of their comrades killed or injured had a cumulative effect which was not to the advantage of the Egyptian defenders. The ferocity of the French paras' attitude had much to do with their experiences in Algeria and Indo-China, and men are not recruited into 3 Para for the gentleness of their souls, as the Egyptians discovered to their cost.

By the afternoon the Anglo-French parachutists were in control, and the French commander, Chateau-Jobert, contacted the local Egyptian

* Nutting wrote to Lennox-Boyd in 1967 that he had resigned 'because the Government, having won an acceptable compromise in New York, threw it overboard, preferring to seek a "settlement" which I felt was unjust and was certainly not peaceful'.

commander, Brigadier El Moguy, by telephone to propose a cease-fire; this was refused, but as the afternoon continued El Moguy had second thoughts and was in touch with Chateau-Jobert through Colonel Rashdi, the local chief of police, to arrange a meeting with him and Brigadier Butler. This took place just after dark. Butler demanded an Egyptian surrender, which Rashdi, who seems to have taken charge on the Egyptian side,' at once refused, but a temporary cease-fire for the sake of tending the wounded and resuming the cut water supplies was agreed.

Unfortunately for Eden the report reached London via Cyprus in a mangled form in which Butler's emphasis on the brevity of the cease-fire was omitted. When it was handed to him he was in the House of Commons supporting Lloyd in a torrid debate about the British leaflets, Lloyd's position being made more uncomfortable by the fact that he had not seen the documents quoted at him by the Opposition. When he had read the note passed to him, Eden at once intervened to say that a cease-fire had been agreed and that surrender terms for Port Said were being discussed. The Conservative Members erupted in joy, and Labour looked nonplussed for the first time since 30 October. But within an hour the report was being denied; fortunately, the House had been prorogued, or Eden's position would have been even more embarrassing.

It is important to emphasize that the account in Keightley's despatch – that surrender terms were agreed and that El Moguy was overruled, which Eden repeated in his own account – is not correct, and, although the Russian Consul in Port Said, Tchikov, was very active in keeping Egyptian resistance going, Eden's belief that the Russian Government had intervened to break the 'surrender' was wrong.

The Russian dilemma had been acute, and the situation in Budapest remained bad, although their forces were gradually destroying the Hungarian resistance. There was nothing practical they could do to assist the Egyptians, but on the evening of 5 November they decided to resort to bluster by sending messages to Eden, Mollet and Ben-Gurion announcing Soviet determination 'to crush the aggressors and to restore peace in the East' together with threats of rocket attacks. A message to Eisenhower sought a joint Soviet and American involvement to stop the fighting. The tone of these messages revealed how deeply worried the Russians were: Budapest was in chaos, Poland was ominous, and now it seemed that their great hope of a major client-state in the Middle East was being destroyed, and Nasser with it. Few knew better than the Russian military and their agents the limitations of the Egyptian armed forces, and they almost certainly had good information about the size of the British armada now approaching Egypt.

On this matter Eisenhower was resolute. There would be no joint military action with the Russians, and if they intervened the Americans would respond, with force if necessary, 'with *everything* in the bucket', in his own words. All military personnel were recalled and American units put on full alert, a message which the Russian leaders could not miss, and did not. Eden's own reply was robust and firm, fortified by the knowledge that the Russians did not possess rockets remotely capable of hitting London, Paris or Tel Aviv. The only effects of the Russian intervention, which was only verbal, were to arouse Eisenhower and to increase Eden's personal standing, especially with his own Party.

The Anglo-French seaborne forces landed at first light on the morning of 6 November after a heavy naval barrage, and by 9 a.m. the British commanders heard – incorrectly – another request for surrender, inspired by the endeavours of the Italian Consul in Port Said. It was another false report, and, although casualties were not heavy, the landing forces experienced difficulty in moving forward rapidly, and there does seem to have been both confusion and lack of initiative in exploiting the situation, which was now entirely in favour of the invaders, so much so that many commentators believe that Qantara could have been taken by nightfall. As it was, in spite of these delays, the operation justified all the hard work of the planners, and by the afternoon there was little standing between the British and French forces and the seizure of the Canal.

But a far more potent force than the Russians had intervened. A run on the pound had developed, and with the Canal blocked and the Syrian pipeline severed the position of sterling had become critical. Some 15 per cent of the country's gold and dollar reserves went in November, and when Macmillan telephoned Washington early on the morning of 6 November to ask for assistance he was bluntly told that it would be available only if a cease-fire were arranged before midnight. Only in that eventuality would the United States support a loan from the International Monetary Fund and give other assistance. For Macmillan, this was decisive, but he in particular now realized that the public pretext for the invasion had collapsed. The alleged purposes of the operation had been achieved, and it was becoming impossible to provide any convincing defence for continuing it to the Americans and to Parliament. He was certainly the first Cabinet minister of the front rank to change his ground, but, although the economic pressure from the United States was now becoming unbearable, it was not the only factor in his *volte-face*.

The pressures on the British Government had become too strong. The Bulganin threats had stiffened the resolve of many Conservatives, but, although the threat of a missile attack on Britain could be dismissed, that of Soviet intervention in the area deeply worried others, including members of the Cabinet when it met at 9.45 a.m. on 6 November. The issue was stark and the situation menacing. The French were frantically urging that the operation must continue, but the majority of the Cabinet had now swung against this option, especially Macmillan, dismayed by the prospect of oil sanctions and by the sheer size of the rift with the Americans. It was on this point that most alarm concentrated, and the prospect of a viable United Nations force became increasingly attractive as a reasonable way out of the morass. Some ministers were now genuinely frightened that there could be a general war in the area that could be impossible to control. Others were deeply concerned by the acute divisions in the country, and by the possibility that the Conservative Party itself might split. All were very tired, and the strain on Eden himself had become intolerable. There was now a clear majority for an Anglo-French cease-fire if the Egyptians and Israelis agreed, which they were certain to do, 'at some point during the day, the exact time to be determined in the light of operational considerations.'

Eden, himself desperately tired and disillusioned, felt that he could no longer stand against the combined pressure of the Opposition, his own Cabinet and the United States. In retrospect it is easy to see and say that the operation should have been continued until the Canal was entirely occupied, which would almost certainly have been achieved within forty-eight hours. Also in retrospect, the near panic among ministers caused by the run on the pound and the withdrawal of sterling balances seems grossly exaggerated compared with the glittering opportunity of complete control of the Canal and negotiation from a position of considerable strength. But there was no question of the Cabinet accepting such a lead by this stage, and Eden had no doubts on this score. He was almost alone.

This was a political decision, made in the knowledge that the Egyptian military resistance was fading rapidly and that there was little to prevent the capture of the Canal. Although the build-up to the operation had been fatally slow, the actual execution had been very competently achieved, with relatively few casualties. The men were jubilant, knowing that they were in the presence of a totally defeated enemy. What they did not know was that the political resolve to continue had gone. Eden had been deserted by all his senior colleagues except Lloyd, Head and Stuart, and Macmillan's defection had been crucial. Butler and Salisbury now led the majority that in effect demanded acceptance of the Hammarskjöld offer under the Assembly resolution. The American pressure had become even more intense, and mounted during the day.

Eden telephoned Mollet to inform him of his decision; Pineau and Bourgès-Maunoury were for the French going on alone, but Mollet, supported by the majority, refused. The French were angry – very angry – at what they considered British weakness and even treachery, but few in Paris believed that continuation was now possible. At 1.43 p.m. Eden telephoned Eisenhower to tell him of what had been decided. Eisenhower's relief was intense.

There were ministers who found the decision heart-breaking, but they had to accept it. The pressure of the House of Commons itself had become unbearable. The booing and uproar and tension still existed, and Eden himself looked exhausted, although his self-control was extraordinary, and impressed even those most passionately opposed to his policies. As a performance of grace under fire it was admirable, but one could only estimate the physical and emotional cost. What we did not know was that he had now been abandoned by his own ministers, eager for a reasonable formula that would end the nightmare. For this is what it had become for everyone. The ghastly reports from Budapest of Russian savagery were merged with others from the Middle East. Pride in British military skill and courage was mingled with anxiety. The Russians may have been bluffing, and probably were, but the prospect, however remote, of them and the Americans becoming involved in the Middle East cauldron was a daunting one.

Eden now knew that he could not persuade his Cabinet to carry on with the military operation, and at six that evening he announced in the House of Commons that he had information from New York that Egypt and Israel had agreed to a cease-fire; in view of this, and the proposal to establish a United Nations international force, British and French forces would cease their operations at midnight.

There was then an extraordinary scene in that extraordinary week. There was a burst of sustained cheering from the Labour benches, but a considerable number of Conservatives leapt to their feet to wave order papers and applaud Eden. It was indeed difficult to judge whether this was out of the false belief that they had won, or relief that it was over, or simply loyalty to their leader, but it was also evident that many did not stand and cheer, and the members of the Suez Group were aghast and embittered. For Eden himself it was a black day and, although he conducted himself firmly and with the authority he had never lost in the House, he looked very much older than he was.

One who saw a great deal of Eden throughout the crisis, and who was very critical of certain aspects of Eden's personality, has said that in the last few days he seemed 'almost in a state of exaltation', and certainly his dignified and impressive responses to the tumult and disgraceful scenes in the Commons gives strong support to this description. If he had his enemies, he also had his friends. He believed, and rightly, that he had much support in the country and that the British serviceman would triumph over the enemy. He had done everything possible to meet American concerns; he had agreed to the international conference, to SCUA, and had been to the United Nations; he had exhausted all the possibilities of peaceful international control over the Canal. He had no doubts that Nasser was an evil brigand who imperilled British and Western power in the Middle East. He was not, as has been alleged, 'torn by pangs of conscience' or so ill that he was incapable of logical thought, although, as always, his moods had been mercurial during the crisis, and on occasions very mercurial indeed. He had no doubts that he had been right.

But to have to accept the cease-fire under duress from the United States and his colleagues was a shattering event. Having travelled so far, and on the verge of complete victory, it had been snatched away. The adrenalin that accompanies high tension and drama is dangerous when the drama ends, as this one had, so suddenly and harshly. Suddenly, he looked aged and ill, defeated and broken. 'The whole personality, if not prostrated, seemed completely withdrawn,' a Labour MP, J. P. W. Mallalieu, wrote in an especially vivid account. Looking sadly down on him from my seat in the Gallery, immediately opposite him, I thought Eden looked strangely alone. I did not, of course, then know how alone he really was.

Passing resolutions creating a United Nations force was a simple act, but creating one was more difficult, and there were no precedents or experience to guide Hammarskjöld and his very small staff. The British and French hope that it would include their forces was dashed by Eisenhower, who told Eden that it must not include any troops from the major powers, in order to exclude any possible Russian involvement. To this, Eden replied that although he personally agreed he must consult the Cabinet, which considered the matter at a long meeting that began at 11.30 on the morning of 7 November.

Eisenhower had been easily re-elected as President with a majority of nearly ten million votes on the previous evening, and, after the Egypt Committee meeting, Eden telephoned to congratulate him and suggest an immediate meeting in Washington between the President, himself and Mollet to discuss how matters could proceed after the cease-fire. Eisenhower was cordial – it is always a good time to telephone a politician on the morning immediately after an electoral victory – and was very willing to accept Eden's suggestion. But he added that he should consult others before making the matter definite, and promised to call back as soon as possible. Eden's active mind had already recovered from the shock of the cease-fire, and was concentrating hard upon capitalizing on the military position on the ground to achieve his purposes. He was elated by Eisenhower's reaction, and preparations were made for an immediate statement in the Commons and an early flight to Washington.

But Eisenhower consulted General Goodpaster, a particularly close confidant, and Hoover, who had spoken to Dulles in hospital. All were against the meeting, as it would give the impression of United States' willingness to discuss the future of the Middle East outside what they had achieved at the United Nations. All seem to have scented a trap, which was perhaps understandable, but was not the case. Eden was trying, once again, for a joint policy in the Middle East. But Eisenhower bowed to his advisers.

Eden, with an official by his side, had eagerly awaited Eisenhower's call. The first was for clarification that the topic would be a general discussion on the Middle East, which Eden confirmed. When the second one came Eden snatched the telephone excitedly, but as Eisenhower spoke the official could see Eden's face harden, and then sag. The whole tone had changed. The meeting would have to be 'postponed'. All Eden's arguments were politely but emphatically rejected. When Eden put down the instrument what remained of his spirit seemed to have gone.

Selwyn Lloyd, sent to the United Nations to attempt to restore the situation, reported to Eden on 15 November that 'More and more people are privately reproving me for our having ordered a cease-fire too soon. In spite of all this sort of talk I am sure that they would all join the hunt against us again given the chance.' On the 18th he cabled from Washington to Eden that 'there is no desire here to see Nasser built up, but there is no grip in the [US] Administration as to what is immediately involved, or what should speedily be done. It will be 1917 and 1941 all over again.' 'The plain fact', he told Eden on 19 November, 'is that, as Bedell [Smith] said, the President is the only man who matters and there is no one round him to give advice who is of the slightest use.'

Dulles' ambiguity remained to the end. When Lloyd went with Caccia to see him in hospital in Washington on 18 November – an act of notable kindness in the circumstances – Dulles asked him, 'Selwyn, why did you stop? Why didn't you go through with it and get Nasser down?' Lloyd replied that 'if you had so much as winked at us we might have gone on'.* The tantalizing possibility remains – although a very small one – that if Dulles had not had to go into hospital at the crucial moment there might

---

* Lloyd's cable to Eden after the meeting was less dramatic: 'He [Dulles] said that he had no complaint about our objectives in our recent operations. In fact they were the same as those of the United States but he still did not think that our methods of achieving them were the right ones. Even so, he deplored that we had not managed to bring down Nasser.'

have been an American 'wink', and matters *might* have been different. But Dulles could not have overridden the President, nor the much more vehement views of Hoover and Humphrey. By the evening of 6 November the essential political and military fact was that the operation had been stopped, and could not be started again. Nasser was triumphant, his standing and prestige now so high as to send waves of fear – fully justified – through the pro-Western governments of Iraq, Libya and Algeria. The Russians, having done hardly anything, could also look upon the results with deep, if surprised, satisfaction. Emotions in France were bitter against the Americans, and in some quarters against the British for having proved, when it came to the supreme test, that they were completely in the hands of the United States. De Gaulle, in exile, drew the lesson: from Suez there was to result the creation of the French independent nuclear deterrent, withdrawal from NATO, a foreign policy in Europe and towards the East based on perceptions of French national interests alone, and the tragically long delays before Britain was permitted to join the Common Market and come to be regarded by the French as truly European.

It was to be a long time before the United States Government appreciated the full extent of its own defeat in the area, or was prepared to admit it. With relentless morality, the Americans were to force the Israelis back to their original 1948 boundaries, having secured no guarantees or concessions at all from Egypt, Jordan or Syria. They opened the way for massively increased Soviet intervention in the Middle East, and a consequent destabilization, particularly in the Lebanon, that tragically lasts to this day. But, far from being hailed, as they had expected, as the saviours of people struggling against colonialism and of emerging Third World nations, they found that hostility against them remained, now augmented by a certain understandable contempt and incomprehension over what American foreign policy was. King Feisal and Nuri were to be among the first and the most conspicuous victims of the Western defeat, but many more were to follow.

Although Eden could not foresee all of this, he knew that the West had suffered a severe, indeed catastrophic, defeat. If, even at this stage, the Americans had realized this, it could have been possible to create a joint Anglo-American policy that made use of Nasser's military defeat and the overwhelming British, French and Israeli military position on the ground and in the air to fulfil some of the purposes of the operation, especially the establishment of a new form of international control over the Canal. For the reality was, in spite of the gloatings of the repaired Radio Cairo, that Nasser's immediate position was bad, and there could be little prospect of real Soviet assistance for some time, while the Anglo-French position was very strong indeed. On American insistence, all this was to be thrown away.

578

Eisenhower's refusal even to see the British and French leaders can now be seen as a gross abrogation of leadership, which was to have dire consequences, but at the time it was even more than that – it was a snub, a stinging rebuke, a punishment from the commander-in-chief to insubordinate juniors. Again, the impact upon the French was even greater, if that were possible, than on the British.

As events were to prove, the Anglo-American alliance could be repaired, but the opportunity of a joint Western policy in the Middle East based on strength had gone.

At the full Cabinet on 7 November, ministers were acutely, and very seriously, divided. There were some who agreed with Eden and Eisenhower about the involvement of major power contingents in the UN force; others who considered that if the British and French forces were withdrawn they would be throwing away their tangible gains; and some who considered that having a Soviet element in the UN force would be a positive advantage. What was common ground was that urgent steps must be taken to harmonize Middle East policy with the Americans, and the matter was referred to the Egypt Committee, which met again at 3.00 p.m. The Argentines had proposed a resolution that was generally acceptable except that it insisted that British and French forces should not be in the UN force and that it said nothing about settlement of the future of the Canal or the Egypt–Israel dispute. It was eventually decided that Dixon should vote for the resolution while making clear British reservations on certain aspects of it.

The Chiefs of Staff were now very concerned about the precarious military position of their men and about how matters could proceed. The 'tacit aims' of the operation – a settlement of the Canal situation on favourable terms and the downfall of Nasser – could not be achieved without further military action. They judged it likely that the Russians would reconstitute the Egyptian Air Force 'and thereby pose a serious threat to all our forces in the area'. They posed three alternatives – to renew the military action and occupy the entire Canal; to withdraw unconditionally; or to retain the present positions until they could be handed over to a UN force. The second alternative, they argued would be seen as a defeat for the West and a major victory for Nasser and the Soviet Union, and they favoured the third. To make their argument even stronger they set out a 'worst case' account of what would be required to fight a Russian-sponsored war in the Middle East. This was probably the most decisive paper of all, especially as Keightley was reporting a serious fall of morale after the cease-fire. But Eisenhower's continued refusal to discuss long-term issues until the British and French had withdrawn their forces – reported to the Cabinet on the 8th – gave added emphasis to the reports of Butler and Heath that 'the Government's political position in the House of Commons was vulnerable ... [and] their position would remain insecure so long as there appeared to be some divergence of policy between them and the Governments of the United States and other Commonwealth countries. In these circumstances it remained urgently necessary that we should re-establish close relations and understanding with the United States Government.' The decision was reached to initiate immediate staff talks with the Commander-designate of the UN force, General Burns of Canada, 'for the orderly and effective transfer of responsibility from the Anglo-French contingent' – namely, retreat.

The British, rather desperately, now put great emphasis on the importance of their clearing the Canal, which Eden stressed strongly in telegrams and telephone calls with Eisenhower, and which Caccia also pressed. There were certainly practical considerations: the British had the facilities on the spot and the experience to clear the Canal (the planners had certainly anticipated this eventuality), but the dominant considerations were political and psychological. The Egyptians, amazed and relieved by their unexpected rescue from disaster, refused to allow this clearance so long as foreign troops remained on their land. American salvage experts were convinced that an international team could be quickly assembled. The Egypt Committee on 9 November resolved that the British should clear that part of the Canal which they controlled, and should refuse to withdraw forces until the UN force arrived. Hailsham took a strong line on this issue, claiming that no other organization had the expertise to achieve the clearance, in which he was supported by Home, who had consulted the Commonwealth High Commissioners who agreed 'that some scheme should be evolved by the United Nations which would use the British machinery which was on the spot and competent to do the job'. Lloyd was instructed to press this point hard at the United Nations, but the fact was that most obstructions were in those parts of the Canal still held by the Egyptians; Nasser, his self-confidence now mightily restored, was implacable on his conditions, and the Americans would not support the British.

On 8 November there was another vote of confidence in the House of Commons in a mood of angry anti-climax. Now that the cease-fire had taken place, those Conservatives who had been opposed to the operation, and had been inhibited from speaking out publicly through a sense of responsibility to the servicemen going into action, could make their opposition known. It also seemed possible that the Suez Group, dismayed by the cease-fire would either abstain or even vote against the Government, and there was a real possibility that its majority would fall so low as to amount to a defeat. But feelings were running so high in the Conservative Party outside Westminster that even to abstain would have been regarded as treachery of the most unforgivable kind – as it was. This at least partly explains why only eight Conservatives, all critics of the operation, abstained in what was regarded as the most crucial division since the war. These were Nigel Nicolson,* Sir Frank Medlicott, Nutting, Cyril Banks, Boyle, J. J. Astor, Boothby and William Yates; although Spearman and Peter Kirk did vote with the Government, their known opposition to Suez caused them considerable difficulty in their Associations. Of the others, only Boothby, Yates and Boyle survived politically, evidence in itself of how deeply the Party outside Westminster felt about the matter. But neither ministers nor Whips had any illusions about the intense strains within the Parliamentary Party.

We now enter the shadows of the Suez crisis. By stopping when they did the British had incurred the maximum of odium and the minimum of advantage. The position of the Anglo–French forces was itself perilous; from clear victors, they had become vulnerable. Conservative MPs had, surprisingly, thought of the UN force in modern military terms, 'fully equipped as a fighting force with armour and aircraft', as the Egypt Committee was told on the 15th, and were now clamouring for no with-drawal until provision had been made for clearing the Canal, the inter-national settlement of the Canal and, even more ambitiously, a resolution of the Arab–Israeli dispute. But ministers had to deal with realities, the most important of which was that no support would be forthcoming from the United States 'until at least a start had been made on the withdrawal of the Anglo/French forces', as the Egypt Committee was sombrely in-formed on the 15th. At this meeting Eden fought hard, and successfully, for insisting on a phased withdrawal with conditions, of which the clearance of the Canal was the most crucial. But as Lloyd, now back in New York, realized only too well, the British had lost the opportunity of making any conditions.

The United Nations force was being drawn together, a remarkable example of ingenuity and improvisation, but with the difficulty that the Russians and Egyptians objected to the presence of a Canadian contingent. On 19 November the Egypt Committee, chaired by Eden for the last time, agreed to the arrival of a neutral-country UN company in Port Said, where tension was particularly acute, but faced the fact that the clearance of the Canal was dependent upon the withdrawal of the Anglo–French forces.

---

* When the initial voting lists appeared there was consternation when it was seen that Nigel Nicolson had voted for the Government but Godfrey Nicholson, the Member for Farnham, had not. This hideous error was the fault of the young Division Clerk, who in the confusion of the vote recorded the wrong man. Both forgave me, and I was so contrite at my mistake that I was not even rebuked by the then Clerk of the House, who knew very well the heavy burdens placed upon his staff in that turbulent week.

This was made very plain by Eisenhower, who refused a request by Lloyd to see him; what Eden did not know was that Butler and Macmillan were in touch with Washington by way of Aldrich. The retreat was on, but the Prime Minister, still trying vainly for a meeting with Eisenhower, did not realize it until many years later.

The combination of strain, physical exhaustion and bitter disappointment had exerted its eventual price on Eden. The brief period of exaltation had definitely passed. Now all was anti-climax, and a time for many regrets, the greatest of which was that he had agreed to the 6 November cease-fire. He himself was determined to go on, but those closest to him had become so worried by his condition that they persuaded him to see his doctors. They were wise to do so, but it marked another decisive moment in Eden's fortunes.

It is possible – although improbable – that under Eden's leadership the Government might have extricated itself from the situation on better terms than proved to be the case, but, although his fevers had not returned, his doctors were deeply concerned about his health. His fever in October had undoubtedly weakened him, and the immense strain of the previous months was now showing. His doctors could not decide whether he was seriously ill or merely suffering from exhaustion, but on 19 November they were adamant that he must have a complete rest, preferably in a warm climate. When they heard of this, Ian and Ann Fleming at once offered the Edens the use of their house in Jamaica, Goldeneye. It seemed the perfect solution to an apparently temporary problem, but in the event it had every possible disadvantage.

Butler, on whom the burden was now placed, was understandably amazed at the proposal, later writing with laudable restraint that 'it did seem the most extraordinarily remote suggestion in the middle of such unprecedented troubles. Harold Macmillan's strong character reacted in a fit of temper against Evans; he said that the Prime Minister could not possibly be withdrawn to that extent, leaving our troops in an uncertain predicament.'* The situation was made even more difficult by the fact that Goldeneye was a long way from the residence of the Governor, Sir Hugh Foot, to which all secret telegrams and messages had to be sent for security reasons. These then had to be taken by special messenger over poor roads to the Flemings' home. Evans wanted Eden to have a complete rest and to relax; ministers wanted to be in touch with him, and he with them. By agreeing to go to Goldeneye, none of these contradictory objectives could

* Butler, *The Art of the Possible*, p. 194.

be attained. It was to prove, from every point of view, a deeply unhappy compromise.

The position of Butler was the most unenviable of all. As he later wrote, with much feeling:

I was left in charge of the government, with the odious duty of withdrawing the troops, re-establishing the pound, salvaging our relations with the U.S. and the U.N., and bearing the brunt of the criticism from private members, constituency worthies and the general public for organizing a withdrawal, which was a collective responsibility.

The most serious results of the decision were political.

The announcement that the Prime Minister would fly on 23 November to a place so far from the country and the crisis was greeted with dismay and astonishment by the Conservative Party and the press, Randolph Churchill being especially sarcastic, writing in the *Manchester Guardian* that the only parallel to the position of the British troops in Egypt was Hitler's refusal to withdraw his army from Stalingrad, 'But even Hitler did not winter in Jamaica' - a jibe for which he was, rightly, never forgiven by the Edens, and which greatly embarrassed his father.

But press comment, which was mixed, and in many cases not at all unsympathetic, was of far less importance than the reactions in the Government and Party; there was serious renewed talk of Eden's resignation and a feeling that this was a situation that was both embarrassing and hopeless unless and until Eden's return to full health and activity could be guaranteed. On this point neither the doctors nor his colleagues could in all honesty give any assurances. It was assumed in Washington that Eden's days as Prime Minister were numbered, and direct dealings must be done with Butler, Macmillan and Salisbury. This was in itself perfectly reasonable; they were, after all, the key men in London, but the exclusion of Selwyn Lloyd – in New York – was significant. Eisenhower sent Eden a glowing telegram of friendship to Jamaica, but the American pressure on the British Government to withdraw now became even more fierce.

On 24 November, the day after the Edens left London for Jamaica, the General Assembly passed by 63 votes to 5 a resolution censuring Britain and France and demanding the immediate withdrawal of their forces from Egypt. A Belgian attempt to delete the censure and make the withdrawal gradual was defeated by 37 to 23; on this the Americans abstained, but they voted for the main resolution. The American attitude to this amendment was absolutely decisive; with their positive support they could have carried with them enough votes to have ensured its success. Although General Assembly resolutions are not mandatory, the passage of the Belgian amendment could have had very considerable significance. But it was also the case that Eisenhower was determined to use his power in other ways. The demands were brutal, and Butler and Macmillan – especially the latter – saw no alternative other than to comply. The stick was further assaults on sterling and the British economy and the denial of oil; the carrot was full assistance and oil supplies if the British and French withdrew unconditionally. It was the final point on which Eden would have struggled to resist had he been in London, but it is very doubtful that he would have been successful without a major, and probably terminal, crisis in the Cabinet. Conservative fury was directed against the Americans – over one hundred MPs signed a motion censuring the United States for 'gravely endangering the Atlantic Alliance' – but ministers had to deal with the actual, and grim, realities. Perhaps the President was bluffing, but the word from Washington and Aldrich was uncompromising, and the Cabinet capitulated.

The key figure in the surrender – or bowing to the inevitable, as it might be described by others – was, again, Macmillan. The economic pressure applied by the Americans was severe and the combination of events had made the run on sterling and the evaporation of reserves more frightening to the Treasury. Several of Macmillan's colleagues – and certainly Eden – considered that Macmillan saw the situation in excessively dire terms. Others thought that he was making a deliberate move for the leadership. On 27 November the Cabinet was told by him that 'It was urgently necessary that we should re-establish satisfactory political relations with the United States. We should have to announce, early in the following week, the extent of the drain on our reserves of gold and dollars during November; and it was desirable that we should have secured by then the support of the United States Government for the action which we should need to take to support sterling.' On the following day he was even more explicit: it was evident that American goodwill was essential and 'that this goodwill could not be obtained *without an immediate and unconditional undertaking to withdraw the Anglo-French force from Port Said'.* He therefore favoured a prompt announcement of our intention to withdraw this force, justifying this action on the ground that 'we have now achieved the purpose for which we had originally launched the Anglo-French military operation against Egypt and that we were content to leave to the United Nations, backed by the United States, the responsibility, which the General Assembly could now be deemed to have accepted, for settling the problems of the Middle East'.

This was a devastating statement. Macmillan may have been right in deducing that the situation was hopeless, but this, coming from formerly

---

* My italics.

the most fervent believer in the operation, caused consternation. There was a confused discussion in the Cabinet which centred on the acute difficulties certain to be experienced with Conservative MPs, and about conditions; a strong element in the Cabinet did not believe that all was lost, and that the presence of the Anglo-French forces on the spot and the rout of the Egyptian armed forces gave them an immensely powerful negotiating position. And what would the French say? The majority of the Cabinet accepted that withdrawal might be necessary, but not unconditionally. On this, however, Macmillan was adamant. American support was crucial to salvaging the economic crisis, and it was dependent upon *unconditional* withdrawal. There was no question of immediate withdrawal, as ministers pointed out at the next Cabinet, on the 29th. All soundings of back-benchers had disclosed that the Macmillan proposal – although it was such a well-kept secret that few knew he was the author – was wholly unacceptable to all but a few. The Cabinet resolved to seek more assurances and conditions, but at their meeting on 30 November it became clear that the decision was inevitable. What was now required was a formula that made withdrawal less odious to their supporters. Macmillan, who had played so strong a role as an initiator of the operation, was now the strongest participant in its ending. The gibe by Harold Wilson that Macmillan was 'First in, First out' was not literally true, but his part in the unconditional withdrawal had been decisive.

To the end of his days Eden believed that Macmillan had been excessively devoted to Anglo-American unity at all costs; had greatly exaggerated the reality of continued American pressure; had thrown away all the bargaining counters available to the British Government; and had used his authority as Chancellor of the Exchequer to intimidate and precipitate the Cabinet into a decision that was wholly unnecessary. This was also the view of Head and others, but it was Butler's conclusion that the preponderant view was with Macmillan. What is certain is that if Macmillan had taken a different course, the Cabinet – perhaps losing Monckton – would have bargained more toughly. As it was, they left Lloyd to make his statement of withdrawal on 3 December, after long discussions about how to dress up evacuation as victory.

Lloyd's statement to the House of Commons on the afternoon of 3 December was a terrible occasion. Lloyd unwisely endeavoured to claim that the operation had been such a success that the Anglo-French forces could now be withdrawn, which provoked the devastating sarcastic response from Bevan that 'We sympathize with the Rt Hon. and Learned gentleman in having to sound the bugle of advance to cover his retreat. . . . I am bound to say, in conclusion, that having regard to the obvious embarrassments of the Government, I feel I would be a bully if I proceeded any further.' The

Conservatives were torn between angry humiliation, fury against the United States and the Labour Party, and, in some quarters, relief. The Opposition enjoyed its day; the Government and its supporters writhed, utterly discomfited. The mood outside the Chamber after the exchanges even more graphically emphasized the contrasts of dejection and anger on the one side, exultation on the other. There were also strong feelings on the Conservative back benches that Butler should have made the statement, as Lloyd's credibility with the House had fallen so low.

There was much justification in this criticism, and it would have been far better for Butler's reputation, and his political future, if he had done so, but he could not be blamed for feeling that one of the key authors of the play should be made to speak the Epilogue. The decision did Butler much harm, with his Party in such an evil mood, casting around for scapegoats. There was little criticism of Eden, reflecting his huge popularity in the constituencies, and none whatever of Macmillan, whose precise roles throughout the crisis were not generally known. This left Butler isolated and vulnerable, and his enemies were swift to vent their own emotions upon him. It was very unjust, but justice in politics has an uncomfortable habit of being very rough.

The position of Butler was deeply unenviable. Unhappily for himself, he had not made matters easier by characteristically speaking freely at a private dinner of the Progress Trust at the House of Commons about the sterling crisis a few evenings before. Normally such meetings are sacrosanct, but what Butler said was totally new and electrifying to the twenty members. In his own words: 'The small private room became like a hornets' nest. They all hurried off to the Carlton Club to prepare representations to the government. Wherever I moved in the weeks that followed, I felt the party knives sticking into my back.'*

Thus the word went round that Butler was 'unsound'. He was lacking in devotion to the Government's policy and to the Prime Minister, it was alleged, and certain of the more unscrupulous Conservatives revived memories of Munich and Butler's alleged role in that tragedy. Not for the first – or last – time, Butler's flashing and unguarded tongue had created profound difficulties for himself and made new enemies. Thus, as he attempted to hold the position in a less frenzied but none the less heated House of Commons, the credibility of the Government ebbed remorselessly away. An eminent Member of Parliament (not a Conservative) described his performances in the House as 'pretty slippery'. If they were, they had to be. Meanwhile, Macmillan gave an admirable performance of calm

* Butler, *The Art of the Possible*, p. 194.

responsibility under stress, without actually carrying any of the responsibility for explaining the retreat that he had initiated. It was difficult to avoid the strong impression that some old political and personal debts were being settled with some ruthlessness during those turbulent days and nights.

Eden's departure to Jamaica had been a fatal mistake, but he did not give up his concern to be fully informed of events and to remain Prime Minister in fact rather than taking a temporary leave and entrusting the conduct of affairs to his deputy and colleagues. As one later remarked, 'Anthony simply could not let go.' This was very understandable, in the middle of a blazing national and international crisis, and was wholly in character, but it did not provide him with the complete physical and mental rest that his doctors had deemed essential, and certainly added to the already formidable difficulties of Butler and the Government.

Butler consistently tried to strike a cheerful note, as his first telegram emphasized: 'Everyone delighted to hear you arrived safely. All well here. Selwyn due Wednesday. Love to you both. Rab.' 'I still feel badly not being with you,' Eden cabled in reply, but on the 29th was asking for information about the Cabinet and 'general developments' and raising questions about a speech made in London by Makins which contained complimentary references to Dulles. Norman Brook replied by giving information about the accepted basis for withdrawal, but:

Main difficulty now foreseen is with Conservative opinion here, partly because these understandings cannot be presented as conditions of our withdrawal and partly because we have not yet obtained as firm an assurance as we should wish that work on clearance of Canal will begin without delay.

Brook added that Macmillan had approved Makins' speech, which did not mollify Eden, who felt strongly that officials should not make public speeches on political matters; on this issue, significantly, Butler, Macmillan and the Cabinet stood firm, and Eden's protests were politely rejected. Butler cabled that 'the political situation may be said to be in hand, despite the [Conservative] extremists'.

From Goldeneye Eden cabled alarm about the conditions for withdrawal and clearance of the Canal, and the composition of the UN force: 'I set out all this because I can well understand and share Conservative and National feelings on these matters. ... I am better and shall be available for any consultation over the weekend.' On 1 December Brook assured him that there was no weakening of the Cabinet's resolve: 'The movement, if any, has been in the opposite direction.' But on 2 December Eden was informed that the Cabinet had agreed to withdrawal on the basis of assurances given in New York; the major concession had been the agreement to put the Canal clearance in the hands of Hammarskjöld; hardly less major was the decision to accept Nasser's assurance that there would be no discrimination against British and French shipping after the clearance. It was obvious to Eden that the retreat was on, and Butler's cable continued:

You should also know that the November figure for the reserves, which must be announced on Tuesday, is worse than was feared when you left. To prevent confidence from being further shaken and something like a collapse of sterling taking place the Chancellor will need to announce that day the measures which he is taking to strengthen the position. But these depend for their efficacy on our political decision being announced on Monday. . . . There will be a Foreign Affairs debate on Wednesday and Thursday. I believe that we shall succeed in holding the Party steady through these four days. The Cabinet is united and firm, and I hope and think that our people in the House can be held.

I know how difficult it must be for you to form a judgement without full knowledge of all that has gone on since you left. But we believe that the policy on which we have decided is consistent with the course which you set for us. We hope you will feel that we have taken the right direction.

Eden was now becoming very restive indeed. In reply to an anxious query from Evans he replied that he was not seeing any doctors and was improving fast; to his PPS Robert Allan he cabled for information about the political situation: 'I am better and would return rather than let the side down or appear in flight' (2 December).

Eden also made plain his bitter disappointment at the settlement on clearing the Canal and wanted references to the eighteen-power proposals. 'I have never thought the six principles amounted to so much,' he cabled, but 'I will back you and my colleagues to the full in any statement you make. You will of course let me know if you want me to return.' Butler replied immediately that 'We of course considered very anxiously whether it was our duty to suggest to you that you should return. We concluded that you ought not to interrupt your rest. That remains our view at present. Best love to you both.' Allan, by separate cable, confirmed this strongly, adding:

Argument against immediate return runs thus:
(a) If you were sufficiently ill to go off when you did you can hardly be fully fit yet.
(b) If you are fully fit now, were you justified in going to Jamaica?
Because of this an immediate return would confuse your personal position, which is widely understood in country and Party.

This was unquestionably wise advice, but Eden was so alarmed that he now envisaged returning at once and speaking in the Thursday debate 'if this is a major crisis in the life of the Government and Party'; he added that 'I am better and look it for public but I cannot pretend to being fit yet. But I could manage' (3 December). This evidently was sent before Eden had received Butler's and Allan's telegrams of the same day, and on the 4th Salisbury telegraphed to warn that the Government's majority 'may fall very low' in the Thursday division and that 'your return is likely to be regarded as a sign of panic among your colleagues, which would be bad. We recognise that the decision must be yours; but on the whole, our advice would be that you should complete your cure. You will then be better able to pilot the country through the difficult times which must lie ahead.' Salisbury added that ministers had consulted Horace Evans, who entirely agreed. Eden cabled to Allan: 'I fully agree and will now pipe down.' 'I will follow your advice. As seen from here it seems right to me,' Butler cabled to Salisbury.

In fact, the information sent to Eden had been far from complete, and he had no knowledge of the Cabinet debates on Macmillan's unconditional withdrawal *démarche*. He was seriously unwell, and communications were fragmentary. In effect, he was ignored, and he himself recognized that it was impossible for him to run the Government from that distance, and that he had to rely upon the judgement of his ministers. What information he had made him very concerned indeed, but the key decisions were taken in his absence and without his full knowledge. The folly of going to a remote house so far away from his country at such a time was now clearly demonstrated.

But the cables continued to flow. Lennox-Boyd had to give and receive advice on how to handle the announcement of the postponement of Eden's visit to Australia and New Zealand, a visit which was now clearly out of the question, to Eden's deep regret. Allan felt he had to warn his master on 5 December that 'the Suez group are talking in terms of your resignation on grounds of failure of Middle East policy over past years. They may try to achieve this by voting tactics on Thursday though folly and dangers of this course are being pointed out. There is no serious alarm about this and no change in advice against immediate return. Rab is confident that you can play this hand when you get back. So am I.'

Eden was now very eager indeed to return, and Butler and Allan began the difficult arrangements. They strongly advised Eden against giving any press interviews and statements and told him they would prepare one for him to make when he arrived at London Airport on 14 December. On the 6th, Allan was able to report to Eden that the Government's majority on the Opposition censure amendment had been 67, and 52 on the main Question, so that the Suez Group rebellion had faded to fifteen Conservatives. Allan cabled to Eden on the 7th that:

The 15 Right Wing abstainers in last night's Division are much disliked in party as a whole. A number of other members are anxious about situation in which we find ourselves, and are talking of reconstruction of Government as a way out.

[Oliver] Poole insists and I am sure he is right that the public is far steadier than Parliament. A recent poll indicates drop of only one (repeat one) point in public support. Your position is unimpaired. Poole receives good reports from constituencies and publicity much improved under [Charles] Hill's guidance.

Some papers have carried rumours of your impending resignation. This was beginning to snowball but announcement of your return coupled with heavy background work has reversed this. Most papers now call for national unity and look forward to your return.

This was a kindly message, but not strictly accurate, and ministers were now very anxious to ensure that Eden said nothing publicly. In effect they vetoed him making any statements while abroad, and told the American network NBC, without his knowledge, that he was not available for interviews. 'You yourself are not giving interviews to the Press,' Allan and Bishop cabled Eden somewhat bluntly on 9 December, adding that 'You have been kept informed of the broad lines of policy, but might find difficulty over minor tricky questions. We all feel sure that a short statement on departure at the airport is the best course.' Eden agreed, but when he cabled his proposed statement at Heathrow on his return, with references to 'the Moscow–Cairo Axis', Nasser's dictatorial ambitions and the 1930s, and with some derision of the United Nations there was consternation in Downing Street. After consulting Butler, Eden's Private Secretary Guy Millard cabled to Eden that, rather than suggest amendments, they were sending the London-prepared draft: 'The Lord Privy Seal's view is that in the atmosphere in which we have been living here recently, a statement on the lines of the draft we have suggested would be wiser, if only for the reason that your draft might reopen issues which are closed or in the past.'

On 11 December Eden received from Frederick Bishop, his Principal Private Secretary, statements prepared in London for him to make on leaving Jamaica and arriving in London, of conspicuous blandness and optimism, which Eden disliked very much. Lloyd was called into the dispute, and Salisbury, who fully agreed with Butler that a vigorous self-justification that denounced the United States, the Soviet Union, China and the United Nations virtually in the same breath 'would create a bad impression. . . . People throughout the country are looking forward rather than back. In particular there is a growing wish to end the breach with the United States. It is important that your first pronouncement should be in tune with [the] changed atmosphere.' Harsh references to Nasser were also deleted 'as they support the contention that our real motive was to get rid of Nasser'. The atmosphere had indeed changed!

It is not at all unusual for a Prime Minister to consult colleagues and his Private Office about speeches, statements or answers to parliamentary questions; what *is* very unusual is for a prime ministerial speech or statement to be in effect overruled by his colleagues and officials, and this is what was happening in this instance. On the 12th Eden submitted another draft to take note of the objections made to the first, with the exception of the words 'We have been blamed for our action by the Russians, by Communist China, by the United States and by the United Nations. I regret that, but it cannot alter our view', a passage to which, Eden cabled, 'I am attached'. But even this watered-down draft was unacceptable to Butler, Salisbury and Lloyd, who put forward again their anodyne version, which Eden reluctantly accepted.

Eden returned to London to a friendly but notably cool reception, especially from the Parliamentary Party, and with his authority gravely diminished. Clarissa Eden wrote in her diary: 'Returned to find everyone looking at us with thoughtful eyes.' Even allowing for the difficulties of distance and communication, it was evident that Eden had not been in charge of events, that several actions had been taken to accelerate the British withdrawal of which he did not approve and on which either he had not been consulted or his views had simply been ignored by his colleagues. The incident, small in itself, of their rejection of his own planned statement at the airport was in fact immensely significant, as was the Cabinet's deliberate failure to inform him – let alone consult him – on Macmillan's economic proposals to halt the run on sterling. Indeed, in most respects Eden had been treated as a retired Prime Minister might be, given certain information out of courtesy to a former leader and friend, but with no executive role. It would have been very difficult indeed for any Prime Minister to have recovered his position after an episode such as this, but this was what Eden was determined to do. After he had seen Eden, Brendan Bracken wrote to Beaverbrook on 7 December:

Macmillan is telling journalists that he intends to retire from politics and go to the morgue [House of Lords]. He declares that he will never serve under Butler. His real intentions are to push his boss out of No. 10 and he has a fair following in the Tory Party. The so-called Canal die-hards think better of him than they do of Eden or Butler.

Eden has no intention of giving up No. 10. I should say he was the least rattled of all his ministers. . . . I still think you were right to back Eden. He is the best of the Tories. I don't say that is terrific praise, but it is something. The alternatives are the crackpot Macmillan or Butler.*

* Charles Lysaght, *Brendan Bracken*, p. 302.

It was not until Eden returned to the House of Commons on the Monday following his return that the full scale of the situation was made plain to him. It was indeed a melancholy occasion. Eden slipped into the House virtually without any attention being paid to him. One Conservative MP, Godfrey Lagden, leaped to his feet and waved his order paper; he looked around him, was stunned by the pervasive silence on the Conservative benches, and subsided with a thunderstruck look on his face. The Opposition just laughed. Eden looked hard at his shoes, and his colleagues shuffled papers and looked at each other meaningfully. At that moment one knew that it was all over.

At their meetings on 17, 19 and 20 December, the Cabinet dealt with the final details of the drama relating to Egyptian prisoners of war, British civilians in Egyptian hands, continuing difficulties with the United Nations over salvage operations, and casualty lists. On 18 December Eden addressed the 1922 Committee, where, although the reception was courteous and friendly, there were some pointed questions – notably by Nigel Nicolson – about collusion and the Tripartite Declaration, which Eden answered somewhat evasively. John Morrison assured Eden how well it had all gone – 'I hope you don't mind me saying "Very Well Done" at the 1922 Committee. Also Reactions all sound very Good' – but Eden was not so sure. On the 20th, more seriously, he was pressed in the House, and said that 'there were no plans to get together to attack Egypt ... there was no foreknowledge that Israel would attack Egypt'. In saying this he was sticking absolutely to the Sèvres agreement, for which Ben-Gurion was always grateful, but there were those present who knew that it was not true. Most seriously of all, Eden himself knew it was not true. He was speaking under pressure, and he was ill; the mood of the House, to which he was always acutely sensitive, was dismissive rather than hostile. His final declaration – destined to be his last words in the House of Commons – that 'I would be compelled ... if I had the same very disagreeable decisions to take again, to repeat them' simultaneously upset those Conservatives who had supported the operation but were humiliated by the cease-fire and retreat, those who had supported it but were now very critical of its conduct, and those who had disliked it. His absence in Jamaica cost him dearly not only in his popularity and political position but in his understanding of the new mood. It was a deeply painful experience for his friends, and even his critics, but even more painful for him.

Much has been written about Eden's role in the Suez crisis, but there has been no wiser nor more sensitive judgement than that of Martin Wight:

Eden's moral dilemma has a lasting significance. In trying to preserve the political conditions of international life he allowed himself to become unscrupulous. Was Brutus the hero of liberty, 'by awful virtue urg'd' to the last extremity in defence of principle, or a traitor in the senseless hope of restoring a regime past restoration? A clear-sighted resister against any power that set itself above the laws, or a blind rebel against the inevitability of monarchy? 'Events seemed to play with all the plans he had formed. His scruples about legality had caused him to lose the opportunity of saving the republic; his horror of civil war had only served to make him begin it too late. It was not enough that he found himself forced, in spite of himself, to violate the law and fight against his fellow-citizens, he was constrained to acknowledge, to his great regret, that in expecting too much of men he was mistaken' (Gaston Boissier, *Cicero And His Friends*).

Reduce the heroic scale; make it international society and not the Roman Republic; and Eden explored the same region of the moral universe of politics, with similar high-mindedness and self-righteousness, blindness and clear-sightedness, misjudgement and courage.*

At the Cabinet on 17 December Buchan-Hepburn, joined by all colleagues except James Stuart, had appealed to Eden not to give up, that the unity of the Party could not survive his resignation, and that it would be interpreted as signifying 'that the whole thing had been a tragic mistake'. He renewed this in a personal letter, reminding Eden that Baldwin had had his crises and that 'Winston's position was very uncertain indeed at the beginning of 1952, as I had to tell him. There are times when a leader has to battle through – one of the penalties of greatness.' But Buchan-Hepburn reduced the impact of his encouragement by holding out the possibility of a later resignation.

A more positive supporter and friend was Irene Ward, who wrote Eden a letter of glowing encouragement for Christmas, to which he replied on 28 December.

My dear Irene,

I was so grateful for your very understanding letter. I remember S.B. telling me years ago how very lonely it was at the top. I didn't know what he meant then. I do now.

I find it strange that so few, if any, have compared these events to 1936 – yet it is so like. Of course, Egypt is no Germany, but Russia is, and Egypt just her pawn. If we had let events drift until the spring I have little doubt that by then, or about then, Russia and Egypt would have been ready to pounce, with Israel as the apparent target and western interests as the real one. Russians don't give away all that equipment for fun.

Yet so many seem to fail to see this and give Nasser almost as much trust as others gave Hitler years ago.

* Martin Wight, 'Brutus in Foreign Policy', *International Affairs*, July 1960.

Forgive this diatribe, but after your courageous and heartening letter I wanted to say why I felt so unrepentant.

Every possible good wish for 1957 in which Clarissa joins me.

Yours ever,
Anthony

This, then, was Eden's mood as he spent Christmas quietly with his wife and Nicholas at Chequers. Nehru drove down from London, where he had stopped on his return journey from New York, with Mrs Pandit, who was also a welcome visitor, and the meeting reflected great credit on Nehru and Eden, and on the strength of their friendship. For it to have survived this supreme test was a remarkable tribute to its depth and durability.

Although Eden was determined to go on he was, not unnaturally, worried about his capacity to continue. On 27 December he and his wife entertained Butler, Kilmuir, Lennox-Boyd, Salisbury, Lloyd George and Head at Chequers. After a discussion about instructions to Dixon concerning clearance problems in the Canal, they had a late lunch, after which Eden asked Kilmuir to stay behind:

We went into the little 'white' sitting-room where Clarissa had arranged the Christmas cards – which owing to Suez had come in unusually large numbers – really charmingly. Then Anthony asked me my view as an old friend on the question whether he should stay on.

Of course, the principal factor was his health. He put it to me that it was not illness but an inability to get back his ordinary vigour. This was accompanied by bad nights and the fact that if he took anything to make him sleep then it did not suit his stomach. There was no suggestion on this day that the old trouble of 1953 had returned. Anthony was, however, afraid – and quite naturally – that he would be a Prime Minister at half-cock and therefore unable to give a lead over the grave questions which faced us.

I advised him strongly to carry on ... but I came away with the feeling that he was consumed with grave apprehensions about his personal position. He asked me to think the matter over and write to him. I wrote on Monday saying that I was of the same opinion still.*

Eden chaired a long Cabinet on 3 January, a joyless occasion that dealt with several matters unconnected with the Middle East. At the end, Eden turned to the senior official present and asked 'Is there anything more?' 'For a moment he was looking directly at me,' the official has told me, 'and I saw in his eyes a man pursued by every demon. I have never seen a look like it in any man's eyes, and I hope I never do again.'

The return of the cursed fevers and sleepless nights clearly required attention, and Evans was asked to come down to Chequers. Evans was so

* Lord Kilmuir, *Political Adventure*, pp. 283-4.

concerned by his examination that he arranged for Eden to come to London for a further examination by specialists early in January. Evans told Eden clearly that the fevers were very likely to recur; Eden asked for other opinions, but this was also the judgement of Sir Gordon Gordon-Taylor and of a third opinion, Dr Thomas Hunt. Eden, deeply unhappy at this unanimous verdict, asked Salisbury and Lord Scarbrough (formerly Roger Lumley) to see Evans, but they returned with the same message, and Salisbury in particular realized that Eden could not possibly continue as Prime Minister with such a recurring disability, liable to flare up on any occasion, and the memories of Jamaica were only too recent, and only too vivid. The implications that Eden used his medical condition as an excuse to leave, or even that colleagues had put political pressure on the doctors, are completely untrue. The doctors were adamant as well as unanimous in their professional judgement. Although Eden, by seeking other opinions, had hoped for another verdict, after Hunt had confirmed the opinions of his eminent colleagues Eden realized that he had no choice. It was a very hard decision to take, as all his instincts and ambitions pushed him in the opposite direction; but, as he came to recognize, there was no real choice. There was another, quite simple, but very human factor, vividly expressed by Clarissa, 'he wanted to stay alive'. Given the choice between his political life and the real one, he had no doubt which he preferred. Horace Evans' prognosis of what would happen if he remained Prime Minister, or even a back-bench Member of Parliament, was decisive. Eden was only fifty-nine, he was very happily married, and he wanted to live. The statement of Eden's doctors was as follows:

The Prime Minister's health gives cause for anxiety. In spite of the improvement which followed his rest before Christmas there has been a recurrence of abdominal symptoms. This gives us much concern because of the serious operations in 1953 and some subsequent attacks of fever. In our opinion his health will no longer enable him to sustain the heavy burdens inseparable from the office of Prime Minister.

Eden asked the Queen if she could receive his wife and himself at Sandringham, to which she at once agreed; the Edens drove there on 8 January.

Audiences between the Queen and her Prime Minister are virtually sacrosanct, as they are particularly private occasions. Eden made an immediate memorandum on this one, subsequently supplemented by two others, which cannot be published at this stage. What can be said is that the Queen expressed her deep personal sadness and offered Eden an earldom, not necessarily immediately but when he wished. Eden had also spoken to the Queen's Private Secretary, Sir Michael Adeane, about the succession, and tentatively suggested to him that a senior Cabinet minister not personally involved in the matter should be asked to take soundings in the Cabinet; not surprisingly, the name of Salisbury came up immediately. It need hardly be said, given the individuals involved, that the matter was handled with complete constitutional propriety and sensitiveness.

From Sandringham, Eden wrote to Churchill, for special and urgent delivery:

My dear Winston,

I have heavy news about health. The benefit of Jamaica is not significant. More troubling is that over Christmas & the New Year I have had a return of internal pain, which apart from its fatiguing effect worries the doctors in relation to my past operation.

In short they say firmly (and I have refused to accept one opinion and this is the outcome of 3 apart from my own doctor) that I am endangering my life by going on. But this is not the most troublesome. It is that all this results in a gradually increasing fatigue: in short I shall be less & less physically able to do my job as weeks go by.

This seems to me an impossible position, the more so since they give me little hope that I can continue as I am doing without collapse until Easter, & virtually no hope if I attempt to go on until the end of the Summer.

Bobbety & Norman Brook both agree that it will be of no use for me to drag on for such a short period of time. . . .

Yours ever,
Anthony

The Edens dined and slept at Sandringham, and returned to London on the morning of 9 January for a most painful day.

In the morning, Eden summoned Salisbury, Macmillan and Butler to Downing Street to see him individually to inform them in strict confidence that he was to resign, and that he had called a special Cabinet later that afternoon to inform all his colleagues. Salisbury had anticipated this, but Butler and Macmillan were surprised and shocked, and Salisbury realized that he would have to play a significant part in the choice of Eden's successor. He went to see Kilmuir, whose advice was emphatically that the Queen was fully entitled to seek and receive advice from anyone she wished in order to discover who could command the support of a majority in the House of Commons, and that she did not have to wait – indeed, ought not to wait – for the result of a Party meeting and election.

In giving this advice Kilmuir faithfully and accurately followed all precedents save that of 1922, when Bonar Law had insisted upon the Party's endorsement of his leadership before formally kissing hands. But the circumstances of 1922 had been very exceptional, and the Law precedent had not been followed on any occasion since then.

As Eden's papers make clear, if he had a preference it was for Butler – and very certainly not for Macmillan – but he was careful not to make any recommendations at all, being as strong a believer in the Queen's privilege as Kilmuir. What is new in his account is that it was he who suggested that Salisbury should be consulted. As will be seen, this advice was followed, and Salisbury's position became of critical importance.

So well had the secret been kept that the Cabinet members, apart from the four in the know, were mystified by the sudden calling of the Cabinet, and most assumed that some new crisis had developed in the Middle East. They were totally unprepared for what followed:

Eden had prepared some notes, which he now read out to his colleagues:

When I collapsed in November, I was told by my doctors that if I wanted to carry on as P.M. I must get right away at once. This I did as I was anxious not to have to resign.

When I returned from Jamaica I was depressed to find that my health, though improved, had not done so as much as had been hoped. It was decided that we should wait another two weeks to see if it had improved. It has not.

As you know, it is now nearly four years since I had a series of bad abdominal operations which left me with a largely artificial inside. It was not thought that I would lead an active life again. However, with the aid of [mild] drugs and stimulants, I have been able to do so.

During these last five months, since Nasser seized the Canal in July, I have been obliged to increase the drugs considerably and also increase the stimulants necessary to counteract the drugs. This has finally had an adverse effect on my rather precarious inside.

Naturally, the first thing I asked the doctors was whether I could last out till the summer, or Easter at the earliest. They tell me they doubt it, and think I would not last more than six weeks.

I know that many of you are genuinely tired and worn out by your work, but I can assure you that my past medical history puts me in a different class. I do not think I should be serving the best interests of my colleagues or of the country if I were to continue in my present condition.

In short, the doctors have told me that I cannot last long if I remain in office. As you know, I am quite prepared to risk my life by going on. This [prognosis] in itself would not influence me in the least.

Eden then formally, but also with much warmth, thanked his colleagues and bade them farewell, in a highly emotional atmosphere, and then did the same with the senior ministers outside the Cabinet, who had also been summoned to Downing Street. At six o'clock he drove to Buckingham Palace to submit his resignation formally, and to take leave of the Queen.

In such melancholy and dramatic circumstances did Anthony Eden's career end, and everything was done with dignity. The tears were shed by others, especially those who had worked with him so long.

From Chartwell there came by special messenger this letter:

My dear Anthony,

I am greatly grieved to learn yr news. It is important that only one reason shd be given – Health. Policy, & Spirit, will look after themselves. Anyhow one cannot do more than Health allows. You have my deepest sympathy.

All my heart goes out to one who always did his duty without fear, favour or affliction. I dare say a fine future lies before you both. Give my love to Clarissa.

Thank you so much for writing to me – little though I relished the contents.

I am so sorry.

Yours always,
Winston

Salisbury, also, was particularly distressed. 'You know my deep affection and admiration for you,' he wrote, 'which has grown with the years. I feel very very sad that I shall no longer be working with you after all those years. These things must be. They are God's will, however difficult they may be for us to understand. . . . I *do* feel so unhappy.'

There were to be many more letters, indeed, thousands of them, from colleagues, constituents, friends and complete strangers, each of which was valued, but perhaps these were the most important and warming of all. There was need of warmth on that bitter-black cold January evening.

15

Victory, 1957–77

Eden played no part in the developments that led to the appointment of his successor. Immediately after his farewell Cabinet, while Eden was meeting the senior ministers, Salisbury and Kilmuir asked Cabinet members, apart from Butler and Macmillan, to come individually to see them in Salisbury's room at the Privy Council offices, to which there was a direct internal route. Kilmuir was amused that virtually each began with the remarks, 'This is just like being called to the Headmaster's study.' To each Salisbury asked only one question: 'Well, which is it, Wab or Hawold?' The overwhelming majority recommended Macmillan.* This was also the advice of Heath, Poole and John Morrison. Although Eden had advised the Queen to consult Salisbury, and for the latter to take 'informal soundings', he had not proposed this somewhat odd procedure of counting Cabinet noses. It was also done surprisingly quickly.

Both Salisbury and Kilmuir were men of absolute integrity, and neither gave any hint of his personal views; they were simply the assessors, and indeed Salisbury had no interest in remaining in the Government, as he told Eden in his farewell from which an extract has been quoted. Also, he did not particularly like Macmillan. They honestly believed that the Queen must be in a position as soon as possible to receive advice that was soundly based, and that time was short. There was no intention of detailed canvassing of back-bench views, or even those of ministers outside the Cabinet; such information as was sought from these quarters was random, although several did telephone to give their opinion to the Whips when the news broke on radio and television. Hurriedly organized polls of Conservatives gave Butler a large advantage, which was why the national press on the following morning all assumed Butler would be chosen. It was a very reasonable assumption, and one that the Edens shared.

On the following morning Salisbury was summoned to the Palace. He meticulously reported the result of the Cabinet and Party soundings, and gave no views of his own. But the Queen also invited Churchill for his own views. This was in no sense a formality. Churchill revered the Queen, and her admiration and affection for her greatest and most experienced subject

---

* Lord Kilmuir told me that only Buchan-Hepburn was definitely for Butler.

were immense. Their audience must remain strictly confidential, but Churchill himself later revealed that he had 'gone for the older man', namely Macmillan. Churchill had strong reservations about Macmillan, and liked Butler personally more, but he doubted Butler's decisiveness; also, Macmillan had been on the right side over Munich, and although Churchill admired Butler's brain and political skills, he was temperamentally closer to Macmillan. In any event, whatever the motivations, Churchill recommended Macmillan.

In spite of the expectations of the press – Randolph Churchill in the *Evening Standard* being the solitary exception, his source being not his father but Beaverbrook – Macmillan was summoned to the Palace at 2 p.m. and accepted the Queen's invitation to form a Government as Prime Minister. The reaction of the Edens to this was vividly expressed by Clarissa, who wrote to Butler at Eden's request:

Dear Rab
Just a line to say what a beastly profession I think politics are – and how greatly I admire your dignity and good humour.
Yours ever
Clarissa

Among the letters of regret and loyalty that poured in to the Edens – some from somewhat surprising quarters, Cyril Connolly writing that 'I am 100% behind the Prime Minister' – was a very characteristic one to Clarissa from Tim:

Anthony and I have never really agreed on politics – chiefly because I am out of date and do not believe in universal democracy! – and, therefore, it is a great deal to me (and may mean something to him) to know and feel that I am extremely proud of my brother.

It did mean a lot, as did others, but none more than this, in her own hand, from the Queen, who has graciously permitted me to reproduce it, as it meant so much to Eden:

My dear Anthony,
I hope this letter will reach you in time to bring you and Clarissa my most sincere good wishes....
You know already how very deeply I felt your resignation last week, and how much I sympathize in the tragic turn of fate which laid you low at the moment when our country is beginning to see the possibility of some brightening in the international sky.
There is no doubt that you took the only possible course after the doctors had given you their verdict, but one can only guess at what it must have cost you to do it.

I want to thank you, not only for the loyal and distinguished service you have given to me, first as Foreign Secretary and then as Prime Minister, but for the many years' work, both in and out of office, which you have devoted to the greatness and prosperity of our country.

Much has been said and written during the last week about your record in the House of Commons and as a Statesman; I am only anxious that you should realize that that record, which has indeed been written in tempestuous times, is highly valued and will never be forgotten by your Sovereign.

With renewed good wishes for your speedy return to health and I hope you will have a really good rest.

I am,

Yours very sincerely,

ELIZABETH R

Eden replied on the 17th:

Madam,

With my humble duty, I was more grateful than I can express for Your Majesty's generous words.

I will not pretend that this decision has been other than odious, not I hope for entirely selfish reasons, but because out of the turmoil I was sure that some joint plan to check Russian plans could be worked out. And without a turmoil neither U.N. nor the U.S.A. would move. As it turned out the Americans preferred to play their hand regardless of their allies and their interests. As a result it will take longer to make safe the right flank of NATO. I pray that they will not be too late. Syria looks ominous.

But it is not of all this, with which Your Majesty is only too familiar, that I want to write. It is rather to try to express what my Sovereign's understanding and encouragement has meant at a time of exceptional ordeal. It is the bare truth to say that I looked forward to my weekly audience, knowing that I should receive from Your Majesty a wise and impartial reaction to events, which was quite simply the voice of our land.

Years ago Baldwin told me that the post of Prime Minister was the most lonely in the world. That may be true in respect of colleagues. That I have not found it so is due to Your Majesty's unfailing sympathy and understanding.

Tonight it is sad in one sense to leave this scene of so many meetings and decisions. On the other hand, as I pursue health across the world I can never forget Your Majesty's kindness to me, and I count myself proud and happy to have served as your First Minister.

I remain, with my humble duty, Your Majesty's devoted subject and servant,

ANTHONY EDEN

The Edens had no plans. Indeed, apart from Clarissa Eden's Wiltshire cottage, they did not even have a home. The new Prime Minister willingly gave them permission to use Chequers, but this obviously could only be a very short-term arrangement. As Eden had decided to leave Parliament as well as the premiership, to the moving distress of his ever-loyal Conservative Association and the constituents of Warwick and Leamington, he now had no income beyond the small sum paid to former Prime Ministers and a hardly generous parliamentary pension after thirty-three years of continuous service as a Member of Parliament. Their financial predicament worried their friends greatly, and Eden had, once again, to face a bleak and uncertain financial future in addition to his other manifold troubles. There was serious talk by his friends of setting up a special voluntary fund for him. Eden was very touched, but refused. He had little idea of how he was going to manage, but he felt he could not possibly live on the generosity of others. The offers that came in moved him very much, and if he had accepted them he would have been financially independent and without care. But it was not only pride that made him refuse; he did not accept that the story was over.

Among the messages he had received on his resignation was one from the New Zealand Prime Minister, Holland, inviting him to come to New Zealand. The prospect cheered Eden, and he gratefully accepted, although the doctors and Clarissa were dubious. They eventually agreed that a long sea voyage might well be beneficial, and gave their uneasy consent.

The Edens sailed on the *Rangitata* from Tilbury on 18 January. Eden gave a final statement that 'The difference between the West and Egypt has not been colonialism – it is the difference between democracies and a dictatorship. The British people, with their instinctive good sense, have understood that. I am sure they will always understand.'

Their departure, on a bleak and foggy day, was triumphal as well as melancholy, with many friends present, their cabin filled with flowers and the cadets of the training ship *Worcester*, at their own request, manning ship and cheering them off. As the ship began to move the Edens saw the unmistakable figure of Brendan Bracken emerging from the mist on the Thames shore; he had missed their departure, and had ordered his driver to chase the ship until they reached a vantage-point from which he could wave his hat and cheer. What they did not know was that in his hurry he had fallen over a railway line in the fog, and had badly bruised and shaken himself, but would not permit such a triviality to stop him from loudly bidding adieu, and running along the quay with a box of Havana cigars as a farewell present which he handed over and which Clarissa still has. Truly, Bracken was a friend for all seasons, as he was to prove again.

The apprehensions of Eden's doctors proved to have been justified. The five-week voyage was not a success, Clarissa writing of 'the hellship *Rangitata*', but their reception in New Zealand was ecstatic, and Eden was deeply moved by the huge crowds. But the fevers returned, and Eden felt wretchedly ill in New Zealand; Cattell was consulted, and realized that the bile duct insertion was not working and yet another operation would be necessary. Eden had to abandon his New Zealand visit and fly to Boston, where the operation was conducted on 14 April. Eden took it well, but did not conceal from himself how sick he was, and Cattell was not optimistic about the future. Clarissa Eden wrote to Beaverbrook that her husband

is terribly enfeebled and has relapses when he really feels like hell. The doctors say they cannot predict if and when the same complaint will not start again. They think it pretty well inevitable that it will – maybe in months, maybe years. When it does, the operation will have to be repeated. They say he will only be capable of leading a very quiet life, because of this threat. At the moment, he will feel too weak to wish for anything else – and I suppose for months to come.

They returned to Britain early in June, to begin a new life.

There is nothing in Anthony Eden's life more remarkable and admirable than the manner in which he rebuilt his shattered reputation and health after this year of catastrophe. With the heartlessness of politics it was generally assumed that he was finished, and with all attention on his successor and his eventually highly successful work to restore the Anglo-American relationship and the morale of the Conservative Party, little notice was given to Eden by politicians or press, although Beaverbrook and Bracken were especially faithful. His medical prognosis was not good, and there was a general assumption in medical circles that the damage he had suffered was so severe that he could never hope to resume anything like an active life. His financial situation was bad, and huge medical bills loomed. These dismal realities added to a very understandable depression.

It was Brendan Bracken who came to the rescue immediately after the Edens returned.

My dear Anthony

Mathew, the General Manager of *The Times*, was lunching here the other day and told us that he was casting about for ideas as to how *The Times* could launch a big campaign for new readers. I told him that one of the ways he might do this would be to try to persuade you to write your memoirs and sell the world rights to the *Times* of London and New York.

I added that I had no reason to believe that you would write your memoirs or would use *The Times* as the basis for their serialization. I also contributed the constructive suggestion that the only way to do this was to offer £100,000 to the author and that it must be done in such a way that this global figure would not be badly dented by tax. The worthy Mr Mathew seemed a bit surprised by the magnitude of the sum I threw out, but as I had to go back to work I had no more talk with him. I didn't actually attach much importance to the conversation because it was a very hot day and I was bored by Mathew's Wellsian ideas for getting electronics to print papers like *The Times* and the *Financial Times* in five or six parts of Britain. That may come, but neither the weather or the company encouraged me to listen to any more scientific predictions.

I was, therefore, surprised this morning by a telephone message from Mathew telling me that the memoirs suggestion was acceptable and asking me if I would be willing to put it to you. Having told him that I had no idea whether you would be at all willing to consider it, I felt no harm could be done by passing it on and I leave you to do some ruminating.

The essence of the whole matter is tax. Mathew seems to think that this can be arranged. I don't know what reason he has for saying this. But since he spoke to me an idea has come into my mind which might dissolve all tax worries.

If this idea were to prove sound I could do something useful by lending you Alan Hodge to help you in putting the book together. Hodge has all the grace of style and nicety of perspective which is wanted for a book dealing with many complicated historical events.

Winston can tell you the measure of Hodge's worth to him in getting out his *History of the English-Speaking Peoples.* And I believe that Hodge would be willing to help.

On a hot day it is always desirable to stress the obvious. *The Times'* tentative offer might well be improved by Printing House Square or bettered by some of their competitors. Let me add by way of peroration that I can see some considerable advantages in Clarissa and you having £100,000 to do what you like with. I could add that you owe it to what is loosely called history to write a record of all the great doings in which you had a part. I also think you might get a lot of interest out of doing this work in a leisurely way in your garden. As your health improves you would have an occupation which you could control yourself. Whatever resolution you make at this moment about leading a quiet private life you will be conscribed by public opinion to get into some sort of Government harness. Meanwhile I see advantages in your making a little fortune.

Yours ever
Brendan

Eden replied that he was 'intrigued' but could not contemplate any serious work until much later in the year. Bracken offered more sage advice on the advantages of syndication, serialization and the eagerness of newspapers to increase their circulations: 'It would pay *The Times* to offer you £100,000 as it would pay Kemsley and the *Telegraph* to offer even more' (12 July 1957). He was also seeking houses for the Edens – 'Housing is a question of paramount importance to Clarissa and you (and the book) and if you make a deal with *The Times* or any other paper you can well afford to pay a good sum for a house' (18 July 1957). Beaverbrook offered them his house in Somerset for August, and Bracken eagerly advised house-hunting there – 'Somerset is a lovely county and hidden away in it are many delightful small houses which are comparatively inexpensive' (26 July 1957).

The Edens contemplated buying Compton Chamberlayne, where they found the retired Lord Chief Justice, Lord Goddard. When Bracken heard what happened he wrote this splendid letter:

My dear Anthony   5th December 1957

Knowing how much thought you gave to the acquirement of Compton Park and the normal arrangements you had made to send your surveyor to inspect it, the arrogance of the old Lord Chief Justice in saying you must blindly buy the house without any surveyor's report is indeed astonishing. That you should be told the 'reason' for asking you to throw caution to the winds and cancel the arrangements you had made for your surveyor is even more extraordinary. The Lord Chief Justice says he intends to eat his Christmas dinner at Compton Park as the guest of his daughter and he will not run the risk of the cook's sensitive feelings being upset by your surveyor inspecting the house.

Goddard has sat on the Bench for more than twenty-five years and this performance of his shows the full measure of judicial arrogance. It would be good for him to have to undergo the experience of a greater Lord Chief Justice, Russell of Killowen, who was in his spare time a bridge addict. One of his cronies at the St James's Club whom he expected to make up a four fell ill and so old LCJ looked about the dining room, which was practically empty, in the hope of inducing someone to act as his partner. A young officer of the Blues who had nothing else to do felt it was polite to assent to Russell's wish. This youth was not a good bridge player and after he had lost a succession of sets, Russell exploded and made some scathing comments about his intelligence. The young man promptly ended the partnership by saying 'Look, you're not in your bloody old Police Court now and so you should try to make yourself fit for the society of gentlemen'....

There was another difficulty. *The Times* in 1957 had become increasingly hostile to Eden's policies in the Middle East and his record as Prime Minister, while at the same time bidding eagerly for his memoirs. Eden was genuinely puzzled, and indignant; in a very long letter Bracken explained that '*The Times* is a sprawling organization' and that the editor William Haley had supported Suez; 'Haley is no more like Dawson than Winston Churchill is like Neville Chamberlain' (15 January 1958).

Bracken hurled himself into these tasks with great energy and enthusiasm, seeking National Trust properties, buttonholing friends, putting Eden in touch with Churchill's lawyer and American publishers, and giving wise advice on taxation matters. Then Beaverbrook entered with a bid of a million pounds for Eden's papers and memoirs! Eden demurred, but Bracken wrote (30 August 1957), 'your attitude to your literary wares should be the same as if you were sending a picture for sale to Christies. The biggest offer should be accepted.'

Bracken's letters and suggestions about the memoirs and houses were voluminous and frequent; Eden was very touched, but also nervous about dealing with friends. Bracken, although sympathetic, was considerably more robust. The Beaverbrook proposal turned out, on closer examination, to be for articles rather than a book, and the sum proposed fell far short of Bracken's expectations, although it was a formidable one. Eden did not like the idea, nor did Bracken.

This was Bracken at his very best. Other friends wrote Eden consoling and kind letters, which were greatly appreciated, but Bracken and Oliver Chandos flung themselves into the twin tasks of tracking down suitable houses for sale or rent and negotiating the best deal possible for the unwritten and unplanned memoirs. 'We have plenty of reasons for delighting in this work,' Bracken wrote on 26 September 1957. 'I shall say nothing about what friendship means to us, but remembering all you have done for the country during a score of years in great places, we urge you to let us relieve you of any business work during your time of recovery. . . . Your broad-shouldered friends can take care of these troubles without you being dragged into them.'

Bracken was particularly upset by the fact that the Edens still did not have their own home:

I feel very depressed about Clarissa and you having to live in furnished homes. The possession of an attractive little place of your own where you can cultivate your own garden, put your books and pictures in position and generally feel you have an agreeable home of your own would, I think, do more for your health than Horace [Evans] or any other doctor can do. It is a wretched existence having to live in somebody else's house. (17 January 1958)

Bracken lived to see Eden's arrangement with *The Times* successfully completed, but not his housing quest. In January 1958 he went into hospital, and cancer of the throat was diagnosed. 'The treatment itself is rather interesting,' he wrote to Eden on 7 February 1958. In reality, it was agonizing, but although Bracken faded fast he never lost his keen concern to see the Edens properly and permanently housed. 'I have finished for the time being with my harrowing treatment,' he added in an afterthought to another long letter about houses.

The doctors who looked at the recent X-rays told me they were pleased, but immediately added, You must find it very much easier to swallow now? Winston is given to explosive blasts, but he never blasted more explosively than I did at the doctors because I told them truly that all their labours haven't given me the slightest relief. They then fell back on the old saw that time will prove the value of the treatment and I cannot be bothered to find an answer to that platitude. (28 March 1958)

Eden's last letter to his old friend was written on 20 July, to tell him that he and Clarissa had found Fyfield, in Wiltshire, and had made an offer which had been accepted. One of Bracken's last letters to him expressed his astonishment that the French should turn to de Gaulle, 'that fishwife Joan of Arc' – a subject on which they were not likely to agree.*

Bracken's ordeal ended in August 1958. By then he had ended Eden's immediate financial concerns, and although the Edens and not he had found Fyfield, he was happy that their long search had at last ended in success.

Eden had always loved the sun, and his health now required that he should, if at all possible, spend part of the winter abroad. Ronald and Marietta Tree were enthusiastic hosts at their beautiful house in Heron Bay in Barbados, but while the Edens were staying with Colin Tennant on Mustique in the Grenadines they saw a derelict house on the island of Bequia. It had no facilities, and could only be reached by boat, but the Edens bought it and restored it to a home. On reflection, it was hardly a wise choice for a man in poor health, and there was a particularly comic episode when Clarissa sent a note to the administrator on St Vincent after Eden had complained of chest pains, asking for a doctor. He and Clarissa were relaxing in the sun on the following morning when a white uniformed British naval officer arrived to inform them smartly that HMS *Belfast* had been urgently summoned to take him to hospital! And there, in the bay, was HMS *Belfast*. The hospital confirmed that Eden had merely strained himself while swimming. The Edens found this highly embarrassing, but the episode revealed how unsuitable Bequia was, and they then bought Villa Nova, in Barbados. This was to be their winter home until 1973, and played an important part in the fact that, against all expectations, Eden lived in reasonably good health for twenty years after his resignation from politics. For the last three winters of his life, after Villa Nova had to be sold, the Edens were the honoured guests of Averell and Pamela Harriman at Hobe Sound, Florida.

* * *

* On what was to be his own death-bed, Bracken wrote to Eden to seek his support for a scholarship for the twelve-year-old son of a Minister of the Church of Scotland for whom he had a particularly high regard, whose wife had died, and who was himself dying. Eden was a trustee for a special fund for Loretto School scholarships, and at once agreed. The boy was Peter Fraser, subsequently to be Conservative Member of Parliament for Angus South and Solicitor-General for Scotland. Until I showed him the correspondence in 1985 he had no idea that his benefactors had been Bracken and Eden, and the latter died before Fraser was elected to Parliament in 1979. It was absolutely characteristic of Bracken, so close to death himself, to go to such trouble over a boy who was about to become an orphan, with no means whatever for his education: it was also characteristic of Eden to ensure that the boy, of whom he knew nothing beyond Bracken's recommendation, should receive the money that was so vital to him. The distinction of Peter Fraser's career as a lawyer, politician and minister would have gratified them both, but Bracken had an eerie capacity for spotting talent, which Eden had come to respect. This is a story that reflects credit on everyone involved, and with the happiest of endings.

Eden watched the events of the first period of the Macmillan Government closely, and not always approvingly. When Salisbury resigned early in 1957 in protest at the decision to return Makarios to Cyprus, writing to Eden to say that he found Macmillan 'very uncongenial' to work with, although he still had no doubts about his advice to the Queen, Eden strongly sympathized with him. There was an extraordinary correspondence with Macmillan in 1959, when Macmillan first asked him, and then in a series of handwritten letters almost begged him, to give him a personal endorsement for the general election. Eden was prepared to issue a statement supporting the Conservative Party, but baulked at one endorsing Macmillan personally, which was what Macmillan eagerly sought. Eden would not do it, and was angry at Macmillan's persistence. After many drafts he issued a general statement of support for the Conservative Government and Party in which there was no reference to Macmillan personally except an oblique reference that fell far short of what Macmillan had asked for. An objective observer might comment that it was remarkably insensitive of Macmillan to seek Eden's personal accolade, but that Eden should have made some gesture to help his successor, however uncongenial it would have been. Yet it would have been hypocritical, and Eden would not do it. The lengthy correspondence makes sad reading for an admirer of both men, but it revealed how deep were Eden's feelings about Macmillan. My own view is that both were in the wrong – Macmillan to ask, and Eden to refuse – but too much had happened, and memories were too close.

Eden's retirement, the labour of writing his memoirs, travels and country life reduced neither his keen interest in politics nor his desire to return to them. But health barred the door. Eden wrote to Beaverbrook on 20 October 1958:

Health can still be damnable. Last week I had an attack of a severity I have not had for several months. It is over now, but reconciles me [to] Ulysses' speech in *Troilus and Cressida* Act III (I think Scene 3, but my Shakespeare is still packed). I hang

> Quite out of fashion, like a rusting mail
> In monumental mockery.*

He had found that he missed politics more than he had anticipated, and until late 1960 did not give up the idea of standing again for the House of Commons. 'The whole country is now well aware of the wisdom of your

---

*Eden was right that it is Act III, scene III, but the full and correct quotation is:
> Perseverence, dear my lord,
> Keeps honour bright: to have done, is to hang
> Quite out of fashion, like a rusty mail
> In monumental mockery.

policy when you were Prime Minister,' Beaverbrook wrote warmly on 6 April 1961. 'And those of your colleagues who opposed you and brought your plans to nothing will in the end be held accountable.' Others, notably de Gaulle, wrote in similar terms, and Eden was very tempted. He wrote to Beaverbrook on 1 April:

First I must tell you of our meeting with Winston at Bequia. We saw him in bed in the morning and agreed at once that he could not come ashore. He looked very frail. We came back to the boat for luncheon and stayed with him until after four. The general state of his health, however, and the setting made us very sad. There were occasional moments of the real Winston.

Looking abroad, he was alarmed by the American-inspired invasion of Cuba that month. 'My own fear', he wrote again to Beaverbrook, 'is that the Americans have launched their partisans in insufficient numbers and with insufficient power. They may be faced with a choice of backing them with American forces or letting them fail' (20 April 1961). The latter proved to be the decision of the new President Kennedy.

But any ambitions, however forlorn, of an active return to politics were destroyed by a speaking tour in Yorkshire. 'Yorkshire was stimulating,' Eden wrote to Beaverbrook, 'but exhausting, and I feel 100 today. I expect that I shall take your advice and join your House. It provides a platform with less trouble.'

This was emphatically the opinion of Clarissa Eden and the doctors, and Eden had to accept their advice. On 3 July he wrote to Beaverbrook:

I have now decided to go ahead and take this advice. Had I been strong enough, I would have preferred to go back to the Commons, but I am quite sure that I am not, and so is Clarissa and, what matters less, so are the doctors. This is not caution for fear of getting ill, but simply the fact that I am sure my strength would not last for more than a few weeks.

The decision to accept the Queen's gracious offer of an earldom was not reached lightly or quickly. He regretted that he had given up Warwick and Leamington, and always enjoyed his visits to Birmingham University, where he took his responsibilities as Chancellor seriously, and where he was always warmly welcomed. He considered – with good reason – that if his health recovered he would have no difficulty in finding a seat in the House of Commons, and there were Conservative MPs who let it be known that they would be prepared to resign their seats on his behalf if this were necessary. But although the Conservative hierarchy was ambivalent about the prospect of Eden's return to active politics, his doctors were not. He might only be sixty-three, which by political standards is not old, but he was in no condition to fight an election, let alone be as good and as active a Member of Parliament as he would undoubtedly try to be. The thing was impossible, but it was with much reluctance that Eden accepted yet another medical verdict.

Some misunderstanding then arose, for when Eden formally wrote to Macmillan the Prime Minister replied that he would be glad to recommend Eden for a viscountcy! This was almost certainly an unintentional error, but it met with a stinging rejection and a reminder of the Queen's offer, which settled the matter. But it certainly did nothing to warm relations between the two men, Eden taking it as a calculated insult, although later he laughed at it. He became the first Earl of Avon, but although he held this fine title for nearly seventeen years he always obstinately remained 'Anthony Eden' to his admirers and correspondents.

In the event, his health prevented him from much attendance in the Lords, and although he spoke from time to time, and was always listened to attentively, he never found the atmosphere as stimulating as the Commons. Peers who go to the Commons are amazed by the noise, the almost constant movement and the irreverence of that House; those who graduate from the Commons to the Lords usually find the silence of the Upper Chamber, broken only by the occasional murmured 'Hear, hear', unnerving. Avon never really made his mark in the Lords that many expected, but his ill health and other preoccupations would have made that difficult, even if he had found the Lords a congenial audience, which he did not.

The Macmillan Government ran into a series of misfortunes in the winter of 1962 and the spring and early summer of 1963, some of its own making, others sheer bad luck of the type with which Avon was himself not unfamiliar. Macmillan's own authority, which for so long had seemed unshakeable, was now so undermined that the chances of his leading the Conservatives to victory in the next general election appeared increasingly remote. But on the night of 7 October he suffered much pain through a serious inflammation of the prostate gland, which required an operation. To augment this ill fortune, the Conservative Conference was being held in Blackpool, and, once again, Butler had to assume responsibility as acting Head of Government. Macmillan's resignation was announced to the shocked Conference by Home, and a brief but highly dramatic crisis ensued that has often been described, and from which Home emerged as Prime Minister.

'As for the Conservative Party and its leadership', Avon wrote to Beaverbrook on 10 October, 'the changes are so kaleidoscopic that I will not discuss them here, for they would all be out of date by the time we meet. I would only set down that I wish Butler were a man I could respect.

L.G. once called him "the artful dodger", but if this is important in politics, it is also not enough.' This was harsh, but Butler's essential fault in Avon's eyes was, as he wrote to Beaverbrook again on 14 October, 'he has too little faith for me, and too much the habit of supporting one policy to one set of men, and then opposite to another a few hours later'.

The Avons followed the drama with intense interest and participation, being strong supporters of Hailsham, who had rather theatrically announced he would renounce his peerage – an option only very recently provided by legislation initiated by Anthony Wedgwood Benn after a long and ultimately successful battle to renounce his peerage after the death of his father Lord Stansgate. Avon used his strong contacts in the Party, especially Oliver Poole, to urge this course on Hailsham, although his enthusiasm for him faded somewhat when he learned that Randolph Churchill was lobbying hard for him. As it happened, the Hailsham cause was of short duration, and the one candidate few had taken seriously, Home, emerged. Butler could have refused to serve, which would have precipitated an even worse crisis, but he did not, although Iain Macleod and Enoch Powell refused to join the Home Government.

When the dust settled, Avon wrote that 'Home was not my first choice, but he may do better than anyone expects, as he did at Dominions Office and has done, on the whole, at Foreign Office. I shall certainly pray that he succeeds, for the country needs its head a little higher in the world.'

Eden had dedicated himself to his memoirs with typical application. He had the resources for first-rate assistance, Alan Hodge for the first volume, and on the advice of Bill Deakin, Bryan Cartledge, a Fellow of St Antony's College, Oxford, and Robin Furneaux, the son of Freddy Birkenhead. The pattern was that the two young men worked during the week in the Foreign Office library and came down for weekends with papers and drafts. The latter were subjected to detailed, and often fierce, criticism, and it was not unusual for papers to be hurled furiously away, with the young men searching for them in the flowerbeds, followed by abject apologies. What saddened his young assistants was that in relaxation Avon was very amusing, with a stream of anecdotes about men and events; but he refused to put these in his book, which, they thought, was becoming a diplomatic record rather than a true autobiography. On this they were absolutely right, and as Avon relaxed and the project went forward more lightness was permitted. For the last volume the historian David Dilks was an especially admirable adviser and assistant. *Full Circle*, dealing with the years 1951–6, appeared in 1960, *Facing the Dictators* in 1962, and *The Reckoning* (1938–45) in 1965, this chronology caused by the eagerness of *The Times* and Eden himself to have the volume covering Suez published first. This was unfortunate, as the revelations about Sèvres came shortly afterwards, and by 1966 there was a move, initiated by Michael Foot in the Commons, for a full enquiry on the lines of the Dardanelles Commission in the First War. Avon and Norman Brook (by now Lord Normanbrook) corresponded at length about this, preparing statements and drawing together material, but Harold Wilson and his Cabinet colleagues did not share Foot's enthusiasm for raking over the ashes, and the matter was quietly dropped.

The principal criticism of Avon's memoirs was that they were immensely long and dry, but their quality and importance were recognized, and the reviews got better with every publication day. It would have been a massive undertaking for a qualified historian in good health; for someone who had neither advantage it was remarkable, and in its own way a personal triumph. For eight years of his retirement the memoirs dominated almost everything else, but he retained his keen interest in international affairs, particularly in Indo-China as the American commitment deepened and became more perilous.

Then, in June 1967, the all-confident Nasser demanded the withdrawal of the UN Emergency Force from the Sinai. Under the secret protocol signed by Hammarskjöld in 1957 the new Secretary-General, U Thant, had little choice but to comply, and the Israelis had no status as they had unwisely refused to have UNEF troops on their side of the border. Avon considered, as did many others, that U Thant could have at least stalled before removing the troops. But it proved to be not the Israelis but Nasser who had made the fatal error, and this time Hussein and the Syrians joined him. The Israelis first eliminated the Egyptian Air Force, again on the ground, and utterly destroyed the Egyptian Army in the Sinai before turning on Jordan and seizing Jerusalem and the entire West Bank. It took six days, at the end of which the Israelis were on the east bank of the Canal and on the Jordan, with the vital formerly Syrian-held Golan Heights also in their possession. The map of the Middle East had again been redrawn. Nasser survived again, but his dreams of Arab hegemony had at last gone.

Avon not only watched all this with understandable satisfaction but also received a huge mail whose unanimous theme was that he had been right in 1956 to go for Nasser and that if he had succeeded none of this need have happened. Historians might cavil at this, but perceptions of Suez were definitely altered, and Avon's standing significantly raised. He had never lost the support of ordinary people; now others, who had been bitterly against Suez, began to think again, not least in the United States. He felt, and so did many others, that he had been justified by events, by the revelation of what Nasser was and what he had done in Iraq, Syria and the Yemen, and by his continued and closer affiliation with the Russians since 1957. This marked a very real and enduring point in Eden's rehabilitation.

This was also the case in the United States, France and Israel. In America there had been a remarkable change in perceptions of the Eisenhower–Dulles performance in 1956 as the true character of the Nasser regime had become apparent. Nasser was never the complete Soviet lackey that has been depicted, but the realization that he was a menace to stability and Western and American interests in the Middle East had now been grasped. In this context, American regret for what happened in 1956 had succeeded self-satisfaction. In France, there had never been any doubts of American perfidy and Nasser's evil, and de Gaulle's triumph in extricating France from Algeria was also marked by much bitterness and division. There was no denying that this was another defeat, for which the French held Nasser principally responsible. De Gaulle's old suspicions of the Americans had been fortified; France would never again be dependent upon cross-Atlantic, or even cross-Channel, goodwill; France moved towards military self-sufficiency, its own nuclear deterrent and withdrawal from NATO; British entry into the Common Market would be blocked so long as Britain regarded herself as closer to the United States than to Europe. This was another major and enduring result of what had happened in 1956.

One of the balms of Avon's retirement was de Gaulle's friendship and respect. De Gaulle had never forgotten his kindness and understanding in the war, and now he repaid it with warm letters, birthday and Christmas greetings, and invitations to the Élysée, where Avon was treated as a major political figure as well as a valued friend. France now rejoiced at Nasser's humiliation; the Israelis, counting the human cost of their victory, reflected with much feeling on how this might have been avoided if matters had taken a different turn in 1956. Avon had always had many friends in Israel; now he had many more. Also, as the Americans plunged even deeper into the Vietnam quagmire, Avon's advice and experience were increasingly sought in the United States. He resisted the strong temptation to point to the errors made since the Geneva Agreement by the Americans, and his essay in 1966 *Towards Peace in Indo-China* deserved closer attention than in fact it received, but by this point the situation had deteriorated far beyond diplomatic skills.

In these years Avon dug his hands deep into the English countryside, his wife and friends seeing him – sometimes with amusement, at others with surprise – change into a farmer and stockbreeder, gaining endless pleasure from long walks and conversations with all who worked on the land. His true home was at first Fyfield, and then, after 1968, the Manor House at Alvediston, where Clarissa Avon created another beautiful garden of surprises, vistas, attention to detail, and colour. His health remained variable. When he attended Churchill's funeral* as one of the chief pall-bearers in February 1965 on a memorable but bitterly cold day he looked gaunt and unwell. But there were, blessedly, far more good days than bad and he remained the best of hosts. His visits to London became increasingly infrequent, but whenever he and his wife travelled by train they received what was on occasions almost a hero's welcome from travellers, commuters and station staff, especially after the 1967 Six Day War. All talk of special enquiries into Suez faded away.

Avon was acutely conscious of his own reputation, and could react with anger and fierceness when he considered that it was being impugned. When Kilmuir's forthcoming autobiography was serialized in 1964 he took great exception to Kilmuir's account of the 1951 Rome press conference, to the point of instructing solicitors. It so happened that I had edited these memoirs – which, in their original form, had been inordinately long – but was not, of course, responsible for his opinions and recollections. I was summoned to David Kilmuir's flat in Westminster to find him very agitated indeed at the prospect of being sued for libel by his old friend and leader, to whom he had been staunchly loyal throughout Suez. Close inspection of Kilmuir's full text, as opposed to the serialized extract, revealed that Avon had a point, but so had Kilmuir. Although I am not a lawyer I drafted some relatively minor changes for future editions which were accepted by the former Prime Minister and former Lord Chancellor, and the storm almost immediately ended. My various careers have had some odd moments, but acting at the age of thirty as intermediary between these very eminent men was one of the oddest, as I especially reflected when I read my conciliatory formula in Eden's papers nearly twenty years later. I felt at the time that Eden had over-reacted, but David Kilmuir's distress was so real that I was glad to play some part in healing the rift.

More considerable difficulties arose over Nutting's proposed book *No End of a Lesson* early in 1967. Nutting had undertaken to deliver the typescript to the Cabinet Office, but in the event Burke Trend was confronted with bound page proofs, on which Eden was consulted. Eden read this version of events with considerable amazement, his copy marked with comments such as 'I have no recollection of this meeting', 'I never said this', 'Check the Cabinet Minutes', 'How can he get away with this?' Changes were made, but Eden considered that the revised version was if anything 'even worse', and his copy is peppered with 'not true', and many

---

* At the reception for foreign dignatories after the ceremonies Eden was talking to the Queen – who had broken all precedent by attending the service in St Paul's – when he saw Ben-Gurion. Excusing himself, he went to talk to him. Ben-Gurion was overwhelmed. When Bar-On, visiting him in his last days, again asked for permission to publish his account of Sèvres the old man flashed out, 'No! He left his Queen to talk to me!'

even less complimentary observations. But although there was some talk, and correspondence about, action for defamation of character it was decided to insist upon certain additional changes and let the book go ahead. Antony Lambton, briefed by Avon, dealt with it vehemently in a memorably destructive review, but the impact of the book was more effectively reduced by the advent of the Six Day War.

In Nutting's case there was certainly anger in the Avon household, but Avon's reaction was more of sadness and mystification that someone he had built up and trusted could have behaved like this, and Nutting must have realized that Avon had in his possession documents which, if revealed, would have done him great harm. He was also given clear and written warning from the Cabinet Office that his book 'will be liable to damage the international relationships of this country ... [and] involves a very serious breach of the principle of collective Ministerial responsibility and of the conventions which are normally accepted as regulating the disclosure of the confidential exchanges between colleagues in a Government'. In addition to Avon, Macmillan, Normanbrook and Edward Heath, in his capacity as leader of the Conservative Party, had to be involved, as well as the Permanent Under-Secretary of the Foreign Office, Sir Paul Gore-Booth, and a number of senior officials who had other things to do. For his part, Avon had to return to his official papers and telegrams and his own correspondence with, and about, Nutting. A considerable amount of work was involved, and much correspondence, but indignation with Nutting was much greater among current and former officials than it was among the politicians, and Avon's role was limited to comments on particular episodes. When he enquired what had happened to the Privy Councillor's Oath there was no satisfactory reply. Avon considered, as did many others, that Nutting had put himself beyond the pale by his conduct, and when his book coincided with the Six Day War there was much quiet satisfaction. But Avon was deeply wounded by what Nutting had done.

In contrast, Avon had not been particularly annoyed when Randolph Churchill published his singularly offensive and inaccurate *The Rise and Fall of Sir Anthony Eden* in 1959, but his friends were, and he received a considerable number of anxious letters from them seeking to console him. He certainly did appreciate one of Attlee's most acerbic reviews, which tartly remarked that 'Readers of this book will not learn much about Sir Anthony Eden, but they should get a full appreciation of Mr Randolph Churchill.' Most upset of all were Winston and Clementine Churchill, acutely embarrassed and angry by their son's vilification of their old friend and ally. Eden brushed this effusion off rather more lightly than he normally treated criticism, but when he met Attlee at a dinner given by Macmillan for Eisenhower he thanked him, to which Attlee replied that he always hated denigration, adding that 'Winston spoke to me about it too and said that he wished that I had made it stronger.' Churchill himself saw Eden about the book, and told him he could do nothing about it. As Eden noted of Churchill's comments: 'He rarely saw Randolph nowadays. What was the use? When he did they only had a flaming row. Clemmie nodded sad assent to this.'

There was another new event in his life. Not even the perennially optimistic Bracken had expected that Eden's memoirs would be the huge financial success they proved to be. The arrangement was that Eden and *The Times* would share equally any profits after *The Times* had received the £100,000 it had paid Eden, but there were many – including Bracken and Eden – who doubted whether *The Times* would even recover its investment. In fact, by 1970 Avon wonderingly recorded that income had already totalled £185,000, and royalties were still coming in at a healthy rate; *The Times* made a large and satisfying profit, and Avon, for the first time in his life, had no serious money worries. He was also deeply happy. 'A lovely day,' he recorded in August 1966. 'C. and I spent it happily in the garden. Alone all day which we much enjoy. Nobody is better company than C. whatever she is doing or not doing. A first walk over newly harvested stubble with C. & a talk to the Wiltshire boy driving tractor and trailer. Delightful contrast to press and politics.' Or, on 1 February 1973: 'Randolph & I agreed on one judgement for sure: that his cousin Clarissa was a winner to beat all winners.'

In February 1972, Salisbury, the truest and best of his political friends, died, and Avon represented the Queen at his funeral. It was an event that especially saddened him.

In 1975 his doctors told him that his health could not permit him to keep his beloved Herefords. Obviously, Eden did not do all the work, but he was a devoted owner, proud of his successes, disappointed by failures, and very upset on market days. On one, having reluctantly seen his charges off to their fate, he wrote that 'Animals are so much nicer than humans.' The sale depressed him greatly, although he knew that the doctors were right; what did please him was that they fetched an average of £298 a head, double the auctioneer's valuation. 'It is a wrench, & I shall miss the animals terribly,' he lamented, and his pride when 'Avon Priam' was first at the Royal Highland Show and reserve Supreme Champion at the Royal itself was manifest and touching. One special cow was called My Friend, a particularly devoted animal who made an instant impact by her affection to Eden, who called out to Clarissa 'Come and meet my friend.' When My Friend had to go the diary entry was very gloomy and sad. If Eden lacked ruthlessness as a politician, he certainly demonstrated the same admirable qualities as owner of a herd.

In 1966, after the Conservative defeat and the triumphant re-election of Labour he was very 'depressed about the outlook for my poor country. It is not, as I believe, the ordinary people who are still loyal & true & of good quality, the majority of them, but there is unsavoury stuff in authority in many places, I fear. Also too much "too clever by half". Maybe we miss too much the dead of two wars.' When the Conservatives won in 1970 he was very touched when the new Prime Minister, Edward Heath, called him to ask 'how things looked from outside' after he had formed his Government, and then arranged a dinner in his honour at Number 10. Avon had not expected speeches, but after Heath had made a witty and moving brief speech in his honour he made an impromptu reply to hope that Britain would discover 'a lake of oil' in the North Sea, an expectation which, to his own very considerable surprise, was fulfilled – although not in time for Heath to have the advantage.

Inevitably, and naturally, even after the memoirs were completed, there was much thought about the past, and the more he learned the more severe were his judgements on certain individuals, particularly Dulles, Macmillan and Mountbatten. Dulles, he noted one day, was 'as tortuous as a wounded snake, with much less excuse', and as for Macmillan, 'he should have been a cardinal in the Middle Ages, under a strong Pope'. But there were those – Salisbury, Chandos, Alan Lennox-Boyd, 'Bomber' Harris, de Gaulle, Tony Lambton and Acheson among them – who were welcomed particularly warmly, and for whom there was much praise. When Heath lost the Conservative leadership in February 1975 and was being excoriated, Avon wrote that 'The media can never forgive anyone who cares or acts for our own people.'

He gave few press interviews, and protected his privacy, which was respected, but in September 1974 Bel Money interviewed him for the *Radio Times* at Alvediston.

Eden explained that his morning was spent principally on letters, and the rest of the day in the garden and on the farm, Clarissa Avon principally in the garden and he on the farm. The garden was his wife's creation, which Eden admired immensely, and with good reason. But his pride was his Hereford herd of sixty head, one of whom was called Churchill, and some of whom were exported 'to countries with very diverse political activities – Russia, Portugal, and Kenya'. He deplored, if gently, 'the ungentlemanly politics of today with regretful surprise' and regretted international anarchy. He was 'remarkably content' with his home, his wife, his farm and his books, remarking that 'the one thing about being old is you go back to the things you used to enjoy'.

And this was wholly genuine. There was no shortage of friends who wrote or visited, and the only shadows were caused by physical pains, and the need to be careful.

One day I invited myself to Alvediston to talk about Churchill. The Manor House is not easy to find, and I arrived rather late and immensely nervous. I was fascinated by Eden's pictures, Sir William's watercolours, and his books, and the way in which he spoke about them, each clearly being an old friend. I had brought a number of vital questions to ask him, but what enthralled me was the ease with which he ranged on other subjects, with the result that I began to forget Churchill and to become more interested in my host. At one point he said, 'You must talk to the man who came here some weeks ago – a very nice man, in the Guards, I believe, with a moustache. I can never remember his name.' I was blank. Lady Avon stared at her husband and said, 'Do you mean Harold Macmillan?' 'Oh yes, that's the man's name!' Eden replied, his eyes twinkling.

Throughout his life Anthony Eden had toiled as a writer, and if there is such an individual as a natural writer – which, short of genius, is highly questionable – he would not have claimed to have been one. As the last volume of his official memoirs have shown, to the surprise of some reviewers, he had the capacity to give flashes of style and insight before the reader was dragged down into another international conference. In his memoirs he was immensely conscientious, tending to follow the Churchill format in which little is omitted. They were hard work to write, and hard work to read. As he was ill for so much of the time they were being prepared and laboriously written, his achievement was remarkable, but Avon would not have claimed they were great literature. He was immensely modest about his writing, and envied those with greater skills, ancient and modern.

But in 1975, greatly encouraged by Clarissa Avon and friends who were intrigued by the early life about which he had written virtually nothing in his official memoirs, he began to draw together papers and memories of his childhood, Windlestone and the war. He dipped not only into his own papers at Alvediston, but into old photograph albums; he got in touch with old friends. Consistent illness may have damaged his body, but not his mind or memory.

If the memoirs had been a chore, written principally for money, this fragment of autobiography was sheer pleasure, although the research was, as ever, immensely thorough, and the files of letters and notes and drafts are dauntingly large. But the result was a book of 150 pages, published in the last year of his life, which he entitled *Another World*.

He had enjoyed writing it, although it had not been easy as the deepening shadows of ill health gathered, and he was, after all, in his late seventies. But the venture exhilarated him, and gave him immense pleasure.

What genuinely amazed him was that it was at once hailed as a minor masterpiece of autobiography by literary critics who could have been expected to be deeply hostile to his politics and career. The style as well as the content were lauded, and to his real astonishment the praises flowed flowed upon him from very improbable sources, even his friends and family – sometimes with tactless surprise – expressing delight.

Another World, from which I have already quoted, is the work of an artist unconscious of his artistry, which gives it so much of its charm and vigour. It is vivid and moving, without in any way being sentimental. It is honest, and it is funny. It is a self-portrait, with, to those who knew Anthony Eden only as a politician, wholly unexpected aspects.

Another World was published when Eden was seventy-nine, yet it is the book of a young man. Only his wife and those closest to him knew how hard it had been to write, but it was its freshness and youthfulness that dazzled reviewers and multitudes of readers. The only comparable modern autobiography by a major politician was Churchill's *My Early Life*, but Churchill had been a stripling in his early fifties when that classic was written. Eden was a dying man when he wrote *Another World*. In a lifetime of achievement against the odds, perhaps this was the most wonderful of all.

Eden had tasted success and failure throughout his long life. This particular success, so close at the end, had a special flavour, all the more so because it was so unexpected. What he called 'my little book' soared into justified fame, which has proved enduring.

In what was destined to be the last year of Avon's life, Robert and Joan Carr came to see him at Alvediston. Robert Carr was astonished to see how well he looked, and after lunch, when they were alone, told him he had not seen him so fit since 1951. Avon replied that 'This is the first time I have felt well for thirty years.'

For the last years of his life Avon's health had been variable, but the combination of his own spirit, his wife's devotion and care, and the skill of his doctors had given him many more years of health and pleasure than could have been imagined in 1957. In these years he had written four books – three of them of formidable length, and one a minor classic – and followed local, national and international affairs with keen interest. His real friends had not deserted him, and his public popularity was as great as ever. For all the pangs of memories, and physical annoyances, these had been the happiest years of his life, for which he was grateful beyond description.

There are very few diary entries for 1976. In January he was dealing, somewhat angrily, with Sir Martin Charteris over a *Sunday Times* article by Robert Lacey and a book that contained the Queen's alleged views on Suez, commenting that Mountbatten, who was the source of this canard, was 'ga-ga [and] a congenital liar'. On 10 June: 'First peas & beans – early, but drought is worrisome.' On 5 September: 'Very beautiful day. Soft sunshine, gentle light and breeze. Enjoyed it.' And then, on 11 September the last diary entry of all:

Exquisite small vase of crimson glory buds & mignonette from beloved C.

He was so used to pain and illness that a new onset of both in the late summer of 1976 did not cause him or others much anxiety. He and Clarissa spent their last Christmas together in Bermuda, and then were the guests of the Harrimans at Hobe Sound, Florida, until it was obvious that there was something very seriously wrong. As always, Clarissa Avon sought the best advice, which was forthcoming from both sides of the Atlantic, everyone at first assuming that it was another recurrence of the old bile duct problem. Closer investigation, when he did not respond as quickly as usual to treatment, revealed that he had cancer of the liver, which was inoperable and incurable. The cold records of his last battle make sad reading, and are too personal to relate, not least because the pain itself was so acute, relieved only by heavy doses of morphia.

When he realized he was dying Avon wanted desperately to return to England. Alerted by Randolph Churchill's son, Winston, the Prime Minister, James Callaghan, immediately and willingly arranged for an RAF VC-10 with doctors and nurses to fly to fetch him, and to bring him back to Alvediston, an action deeply appreciated by Avon, his family and friends. The end was mercifully peaceful and painless. With Clarissa and Nicholas at his bedside, Robert Anthony Eden, first Earl of Avon, died on 14 January 1977. On the 17th his coffin took the familiar road under the tall trees, through the farm gate and across the field to Alvediston Church, in whose graveyard, in the peace of the Wiltshire valley he so loved, he was buried.

With speeches of rare eloquence, the leading members of the House of Commons moved and approved the Adjournment of the House in honour of him. The art of writing obituaries is never an easy one, and in the case of Eden some anti-Suez authors clearly found it especially difficult, but the tributes were characterized by a warmth and generosity which may have surprised a generation that knew of him only through his premiership and Suez, and those only by unkind legend. Even more moving were the letters that poured into Alvediston from heads of state, Prime Ministers, old friends and so many unknown people. These files are very copious and their contents very moving. Each one was read; each one replied to; each one has been kept. Each is in Eden's archives in Birmingham University, and each testifies to the character and impact of Anthony Eden upon those who knew him and those who, from close or afar, had admired and followed him.

For Anthony Eden belongs to that small group of British politicians who were regarded with deep and widespread affection as well as admiration, which have long survived his death, making his grave at Alvediston a place of pilgrimage for people from abroad as well as his fellow countrymen. It is unusual indeed to find anyone who speaks of him with rancour, and many who opposed him so vehemently over Suez almost invariably speak of it with regretful sadness, often mingled with incomprehension, rather than with anger.

What was the secret of this remarkable durability of popular regard and warmth? Those who disparage him ascribe it to good looks, blandness, and luck that eventually ran out, all surface and no substance. This will not do; there is far more to it.

As this biography has demonstrated, Anthony Eden was an exceptionally complex and sensitive man, of varying moods. Eden 'up' was a delight; Eden 'down' was less attractive, however short and explosive such occasions might have been. One of the best modern parliamentarians, it was in Office that he was most content. His relationship with the Conservative Party was always uneasy so far as the House of Commons was concerned, but not in Warwick and Leamington. Clarissa Eden wrote in her diary in February 1953: 'I'm not really a Conservative, A. says, I have more sympathy with the opposition. I am an old-fashioned Liberal.' In reality he was a Conservative whose real education had been in the First World War, the precursor and champion of modern One Nation Conservatism, and whose relationship with the Conservative Party had been as complex as that of Churchill, seeking to emphasize the best aspects and despising the worst.

Those who ascribed his success to good luck did not appreciate the extent to which he had experienced the reverse. The deaths of his brothers, the disaster that befell Windlestone, the sadness of his first marriage, the death of Simon, and, perhaps most important of all, the debilitating impact of poor health, may be especially cited; the responsibility for the ultimate failure over Suez, as I have demonstrated, should be apportioned more broadly, and he certainly had ill luck virtually throughout that melancholy episode.

It was especially ironical that the greatest source of Anthony Eden's ill luck had been Winston Churchill, the object of his scorn – and worse – as a schoolboy, soldier and young politician; his closest political friend and leader in the most terrible of all wars; and the man under whose shadow he had worked for so long. If Churchill had succumbed to any of his serious wartime ailments, Eden would have automatically succeeded him as Britain's leader; if Churchill had retired in 1945, Eden would have become the uncontested leader of the Conservative Party, and would have reached the political summit at the height of his powers; if he had not been so desperately ill himself, he would almost certainly have been Prime Minister in 1953. Instead, he did so under lowering circumstances that were, unhappily, stronger than he could survive.

Although Churchill had many supreme qualities that Eden lacked, Eden had others that Churchill did not have, which made them such a uniquely powerful combination in war, but which made Eden the stronger and more attractive in peace. With Churchill, one always had the vivid emotion of being carried back nostalgically to more glorious days; with Anthony Eden, one looked to a better future. But, when Churchill reluctantly departed in 1955, too much had happened to ensure a successful inheritance. It was not calculated, but it happened. If Churchill had acted differently, this biography would have had a very different ending. But Churchill acted as he did, and events occurred as they did.

The British people understood this much better than most politicians. From the beginning Eden had seemed different, as indeed he was. His kindness, his warmth and erudition were genuine, as was his shyness. He was also palpably honest and brave, with that precious, unusual, but crucial quality of sincerity. Historians may question some of his judgements and actions; but it will be difficult indeed for them to discover turpitude, even in the 1956 Anglo-French-Israeli agreement. This action can be criticized, but it was done sincerely in the national interest. Again, I am sure that this was also widely recognized, and the swiftly aborted venture in 1966 to reopen the Suez issue is good evidence of this.

Winston Churchill loved the phrase 'An English Worthy', his highest form of praise. It applies perfectly to Anthony Eden, for the 'secret' of his success and regard was that he was a highly intelligent, good, honest, sincere and decent man who was worthy of trust. Of all the honours he received, the greatest of all was the most rare of all – the confidence and love of the British people.

One who worked closely with Eden at one stage of his career in the Foreign Office has mused on why Eden was in politics at all, and that surely there would have been other opportunities for his remarkable talents as a diplomat and negotiator. As I have related, Eden made a deliberate choice to emulate Curzon by approaching foreign affairs through politics rather than becoming a career Foreign Office diplomat, but it was also the case that he was fascinated by politics at an unusually early age, and was in reality throughout his life a politician by inclination rather than calculated choice. For those who have never succumbed to the political virus this absorption with 'the great game' is difficult to explain; for those who have it is very understandable. Eden was an instinctive politician who worked hard at his profession, and yet who was never obsessed by personal ambition or expediency, a combination that politicians of stronger wills and of a more calculating nature found incomprehensible; others found it attractive.

'I sometimes felt', a close colleague has remarked, 'that I was dealing with two men. One was cultivated, highly intelligent, wise, dedicated to his country and calling, kind, generous, and immensely courageous – the best of hosts, great fun, and clearly a great man whom it was an honour to know and work for. But then one would meet someone totally different – bad-tempered, unfair, petulant, and even petty. One never knew which man one was going to meet. I know which one I preferred.' A senior member of his Private Office, who was devoted to him, has said that 'as I went through the door first thing in the morning I sniffed the air to deduce whether this was going to be a good or a bad day'. Another has told me that 'it was an interesting test of character to see those who tolerated and ignored Eden's bad moods, knowing his great virtues, and those who could not, and did not. I always believed that the virtues far outweighed the other side, but there were those who did not.'

This phrase 'two men' recurs so often in the comments of those who knew and worked for Eden that it has made his portrait difficult to draw. We are all complex, but few major British politicians of modern times have been as complex as Eden. It is fruitless to speculate whether the circumstances of his childhood and young manhood were decisive, or his disappointment in his first marriage, or his ill health. No doubt, each made its contribution to the negative side of his personality. But what of the positive? That also stemmed from heredity, childhood and early experiences, and was then tested by harsh experiences from which he emerged triumphantly. It is surely the positive that was the more important, and which a fair and objective portrait must emphasize and honour.

In the best brief essay on Eden that has been written, Oliver Chandos wrote:

Anthony Eden is not an easy man to know. Added to a natural reserve, he sets high store upon good manners and they sometimes concealed the depth of his convictions. His elegant appearance and ease of manner, his disregard of men's clubs, his appreciation of painting, his liking of female society and his hobby of gardening perhaps concealed from the superficial observer the inflexible nature of his principles on high matters of State....

... In all the many years in which I have served in the same Cabinet, I can never recall an occasion when he abandoned for expediency a principle in which he believed. Sometimes he fought his corner with impatience and even petulance but rarely, if ever, gave any rein to anger.

Physically, his slim figure gave some impression that his constitution was delicate. The impression at that time was false. Few of my colleagues showed less signs of fatigue: he appeared to carry the burdens of the Foreign Office as easily as he fell in at times with the diet and régime of his leader [Churchill]. He could smoke a long cigar after midnight without flinching, and his digestion was robust.

The effect upon the House of Commons of his sober and unexaggerated mode and his sense of balance, which led him away from phrase-making, often as far as undistinguished language, was cumulative. Until the crisis of Suez, I can think of no occasion when he was not listened to with the deepest attention and respect.

He had in my opinion a greater hold on the House – day by day – than even the Prime Minister himself. The words 'day by day' are necessary because on the very greatest occasions, Mr Churchill dominated the assembly by his stature and by his eloquence, but on some others his combative nature and love of argument aroused the House to anger, even to bitterness.

Anthony never overstated a case: his reproofs were always concealed by apparent mildness and by impeccable Parliamentary manners. 'I hope I didn't put so-and-so down too hard,' he said to me one day. 'My dear,' I replied, 'I thought that your commination was more like a caress.' He smiled and saw no harm in that.

John McGovern, the Clydesider and a friend of mine, once said to me in the smoking-room: 'Anthony is our idea of a gentleman. We respect him, but we shan't ever match him.'*

The myth that Eden was a potentially great civil servant or ambassador who had wandered into politics by mistake is as inaccurate as the charge that he lacked the political gifts. As Chandos noted: 'Politics are his dominant interest.' He had deliberately formed his own style of speaking and writing to sacrifice drama and arresting phrases for reasoned argument in language everyone could understand; his approach to the Labour Party and the House of Commons had matured in the 1920s from crude beginnings, deeply influenced by Baldwin's style and approach. He was good on the public platform, outstanding in the House of Commons, where he has been described by Harold Macmillan as the most brilliant man to wind up a debate he had heard throughout his long period as a Member of Parliament. He was never interested in the small talk of politics and the House of Commons and had few strong political friends, seeking his companionship outside Parliament. But in the Chamber he was consistently the master of the Commons, even if there were times when it seemed that he, like Baldwin, was more highly regarded on the Labour than on the Conservative benches. As I have emphasized, this was not surprising.

The weakness of his political position lay in the fact that his experience was so limited to foreign affairs. In retrospect we can see very clearly that he was wrong to ignore the advice of his friends and colleagues to insist

---

* Chandos, *Memoirs*, pp. 291–2.

upon a period in a home department to grapple with domestic problems
for a change. For, when he became Prime Minister at last, he had held
only one of the great Offices of State, and there is no substitute for direct
personal experience. Although he knew what he wanted to happen in
Britain, and immersed himself in domestic problems, the reality was that
he had never had to put through Parliament any substantive domestic
legislation – indeed, any legislation at all – which is a task that concentrates
the politician's mind very notably. In one area, accordingly, his knowledge
and skill was deeper than that of any of his contemporaries; in all others
they were disturbingly shallow. This had been a deliberate decision, but
we can now see that it had been the wrong one.

Yet, through all vicissitudes, the genuine charm, kindness and warmth
had survived. One of the most cultivated of all British Prime Ministers, he
lacked hardness and ruthlessness – which is very different from the false
charge of indecisiveness. His career ended in defeat – which is very different
from failure. It had been a great career, and a remarkable life, and there
had been much sunshine in the later years. It can be described most
faithfully in the words used by Churchill of George Curzon:

These heavy reverses were supported after the initial shocks with goodwill and
dignity. But undoubtedly they invested the long and strenuous career with ultimate
disappointment. The morning had been golden; the noontide was bronze; and the
evening lead. But all were solid, and each was polished till it shone after its fashion.

Windlestone, after so many vicissitudes, has now become a residential
school and is the property of, and well administered by, Durham County
Council. The structure is sound, although the stone is in need of attention,
and in places is crumbling badly. Inside, with the exception of the library,
which, although shelfless and bookless, still has the gallery and secret
staircase that the young Anthony Eden so loved, there are few reminders
of what it was once like, and it requires imagination to visualize its former
character. Partitions and changes inside, new buildings outside and a
modern wing have changed it greatly, although not totally.

Outside, Sir William Eden's gardens have gone, as have his statues,
fountain, hedges and even his lake. Trees have been allowed to grow so
close to the house that it has lost much of its former majestic position. The
stable clock remains, but the stables are now class-rooms, and the iron
gates have gone. So has the chapel; it is now a mound discovered with
difficulty through a thick wood badly in need of thinning. One can appreciate how depressed Eden was in his old age to see his birthplace and home
thus changed.

None the less, it still stands in an age that has seen so much destruction
of so many fine country houses. The park and surrounding country still

have the mark of Sir William Eden's planting and pruning, and it hardly seems possible that so much serene beauty lies so close to industrialization and urban sprawl. 'Windles' has not lost its magical quality, and there is still the laughter of children down the corridors and across the lawns. So, not all has been lost.

In 1984 John Eden, son of Tim and nephew of Anthony, and now himself a peer of the realm in his own right, realized that the condition of the chapel had deteriorated so terribly that it was essential in all decency and reverence to remove the bodies of his family to consecrated ground elsewhere. They were accordingly reburied in Bishop Auckland, where the Edens had originated.

And, thus, the long tenure of Windlestone Hall by the Eden family finally ended. Windlestone survives, a mute, golden memorial to a saga that contained much happiness, much sadness and tragedy, and a family still remembered and honoured by the kind and good people of County Durham.

Few people appreciated, knowledge of Shakespeare not being what it was, the significance of Eden's choice of the title *Full Circle* for the last volume of his official memoirs. The words he had in mind are these, from Act v of *King Lear*:

> Thou hast spoken right, 'tis true.
> The wheel is come full circle: I am here.

Select Bibliography

The late A. G. Macdonell, whose fame rests somewhat unfairly upon only one of his many books and literary achievements – *England Their England* – remarked that he was profoundly suspicious of all bibliographies, as 'Nothing is easier than to hire someone to visit the British Museum and make a most impressive list of authorities, which will persuade the non-suspecting that the author is a monument of erudition and laboriousness.' Eden's career was so long that he frequently appears in a very considerable number of memoirs, biographies, specialist studies and general histories, so that a reasonably full list of these would be of formidable length and of doubtful informative value.

In Eden's lifetime four biographies of him were published, by Denis Bardens and Lewis Broad in 1955, by William Rees-Mogg in 1956, and by Sidney Aster in 1976, the last being the only one that covers his full life and career; although relatively brief, it is characterized by considerable skill and fairness. Elisabeth Barker's *Churchill and Eden at War* (1978) is of good quality; Randolph Churchill's diatribe, *The Rise and Fall of Sir Anthony Eden* (1959), is best forgotten. The most substantial book is by Dr David Carlton, published in 1981, but which can hardly be described as sympathetic. Sir Anthony Nutting's essay in Herbert van Thal's *The Prime Ministers*, volume two (1975), repeats the portrait of Eden given in his account of the Suez crisis, *No End of a Lesson* (1967), with which I also find myself in strong disagreement.

Eden's own books are *Places in the Sun* (1926), his three long and detailed volumes of memoirs, published in 1960, 1962 and 1965, and, by far his best book, *Another World, 1897–1917* (1976). Selected speeches were published in *Foreign Affairs* (1939), *Freedom and Order* (1947) and *Days for Decision* (1949). The portrait of Sir William Eden by Eden's brother, Tim, *The Tribulations of a Baronet* (1933), deserves to be reprinted in its own right, as does *Another World*.

To a somewhat surprising extent several of Eden's closest official advisers and associates kept diaries or wrote their memoirs, notably Sir Alexander Cadogan (edited by David Dilks and published in 1971); Oliver Harvey (edited by John Harvey and published in two volumes in 1970 and 1978);

Sir John Colville, whose *The Fringes of Power* (1985) is incomparable; 'Chips' Channon (edited by myself and first published in 1967); and Harold Nicolson (edited by Nigel Nicolson and published in 1966, 1967 and 1968). Sir Evelyn Shuckburgh also kept a diary, to which I have not sought access, but from which Dr Carlton makes quotations.

In 1968 Piers Dixon published the biography of his father, Sir Pierson Dixon, who worked closely with Eden for so long; Lord Gladwyn (1972), Vansittart (1943 and 1958), Ismay (1960), Lord Gore-Booth (1974), Lord Trevelyan (1973), Sir Ivone Kirkpatrick (1959) and Sir Charles Mott-Radclyffe (1975) have published their memoirs. Sir Nicholas Henderson's *The Private Office* (1984) has a brief but delightful portrait of Eden.

Of the memoirs of Eden's principal political contemporaries special note must be taken of those of Sir Winston Churchill, de Gaulle (1959), Ivan Maisky (1967), John G. Winant (1947), Averell Harriman (1976), Robert Murphy (1964) and Lord Woolton (1959). Those of Lord Stockton (Harold Macmillan) (1967 and 1969), Duff Cooper (1953) and Lord (R. A.) Butler (1971) are of such outstanding quality that they merit attention in their own right, as does A. J. P. Taylor's biography of Beaverbrook (1972), one of the enduring joys of modern biography.

Biographies of other important figures in Eden's career must include Martin Gilbert's epic biography of Winston Churchill, especially *Finest Hour* (1983), Lord Bullock's *Ernest Bevin* (1969 and 1983), Kenneth Harris' *Attlee* (1982), the late Lord Birkenhead on Halifax (1965) and Walter Monckton (1969), Philip Ziegler's biography of Mountbatten (1985) and Stephen Ambrose's of Eisenhower (*Eisenhower The President*, 1984). Iain Macleod on Neville Chamberlain (1961) was a severe disappointment, and David Dilks' monumental study (1984) only takes the story to 1929. Keith Middlemas and John Barnes on Baldwin (1961) has the defect of excessive length, although many qualities. Of the several studies of John Foster Dulles, Townsend Hoopes' *The Devil and John Foster Dulles* (1974) is the most convincing.

The bibliography on Suez seems likely to rival that on Gallipoli. An excellent selection is contained in Roy Fullick's and Geoffrey Powell's *Suez: The Double War* (1979), which also contains references to specialist articles on the military aspects. General André Beaufre's *The Suez Expedition* (English translation, 1967) is particularly useful on the French military side as is Christian Pineau's account (1976) on the French political; for the Israeli versions the most important are Moshe Dayan's *Diary of the Sinai Campaign* (1966) and his memoirs (1976), and Michael Bar-Zohar's biography of Ben-Gurion (1978). Anthony Moncrieff's BBC broadcasts published under the title *Suez – Ten Years Later* (1967) are valuable;

Selwyn Lloyd's version, published after his death (1978), requires cautious handling, as do the Suez chapters in the late Philip Williams' biography of Hugh Gaitskell (1979). It can be safely assumed that as time elapses and more material becomes available the Suez literature will be considerably augmented.

The literature on the inter-war political and diplomatic history is also considerable. F. S. Northedge's *The Troubled Giant: Britain among the Great Powers, 1916–1939* (1966) is a characteristically well-informed and thoughtful analysis, as is his posthumously published study of the League of Nations (1986), which complements rather than replaces F. P. Walters' history (1952). A. J. P. Taylor's *English History 1914–1939* is superb literature but controversial, as is his *Origins of the Second World War* (1961). Keith Middlemas' *Diplomacy of Illusion* (1972) is a work of considerable distinction, and of all the studies of Hitler, that of Allan Bullock (first published in 1962 and subsequently frequently revised and republished) still holds the field, as does C. L. Mowat's *Britain between the Wars* (1955). F. Lipson's *Europe in the Nineteenth and Twentieth Centuries* (eighth edition 1960) is a superb example of the fact that weighty scholarship should not necessarily involve weighty books.

Wartime politics have been covered copiously in memoirs and biographies of the principal participants on the British, American and French side, and Gabriel Kolko's *The Politics of War, 1943–45* (1968) is profoundly well informed and stimulating, as is James MacGregor Burns' *Roosevelt: The Soldier of Freedom 1940–1945* (1960). Two admirable brief books, which also cover the post-war period, are Henry Pelling's *Modern Britain, 1885–1955* (1960) and T. L. Jarman's *Democracy and World Conflict 1868–1962* (1963). D. C. Watt, Frank Spencer and Neville Brown's *A History of the World in the Twentieth Century* (1967) is not brief, but is formidably comprehensive and takes the sad story up to 1963.

Index

With the exception of the entries for Anthony Eden and his immediate family, the arrangement of sub-headings in the index is chronological, following the order in which subjects first occur in the text. Reference to the diaries, letters, relationships and views of those indexed are grouped at the end of the sequence of sub-headings, in the entry for each person.

Many people mentioned in the biography succeeded to titles or were created life peers after the events described; they are indexed either by surname or by their title at the time. Those who entered into their titles during the period covered will be found under their latest title, with the appropriate cross-reference(s) from their surname or previous title. To avoid overloading an already long index, the prefix 'Rt Hon.' has been omitted throughout.

The abbreviation 'AE' is used for Anthony Eden and 'E' for Eden.

Simonds, 1st Viscount, 358
Simpson, Wallis (*later* Duchess of Windsor), 169
Sinai Peninsula, 520, 521, 522; UN Emergency Force withdrawn from, 612; Israeli attack on, 612
Sinclair, Sir Archibald (*later* 1st Viscount Thurso), 227, 239
Singapore, fall of, 260
Six Day War (1967), 612, 614, 615
Sixtieth Rifles, 2nd Battalion (1st Armoured Division): AE in, 220, 223; in defence of Calais, 230
Skelton, Noel, 101, 105
Sledgehammer, Operation, 268
Slim, General Sir William, 298
Smith, F.E., *see* Birkenhead, 1st Earl of
Smuts, Field Marshal Jan, 221; AE meets, 241, 251
Snowden, Philip (1st Viscount Snowden), 88, 108, 111
Sobolev, Arkady (Soviet Ambassador to UN), 308, 545
Somme, Battle of the: AE in, 45, 46–7
'Souls, The', 14–17
South Africa, 221, 468; AE meets Prime Minister of, 92; and Suez crisis, 550, 551
South-East Asia Defence Organization: proposed by Dulles, 377, 380
South-East Asia Treaty Organization (SEATO), 380, 386, 395
Soviet citizens, order for repatriation of, 290–1
Soviet Union, *see* Russia
Spaak, Paul-Henri, 388, 552
Spanish Civil War, 167–8, 170, 175, 179, 192, 209
Spearman, Sir Alexander, 553, 581
Spectator, The: and Suez, 558
Spence, Private, 42
Spender-Clay, H.H., 107
Spennymoor (Co. Durham): AE commands defence force detachment at, 62; fights election at (1922), 63–5; remains in contact with, 66
Stalin, Marshal Josef, 218, 225, 254, 255, 256, 285, 289, 295; AE's first meeting with, 144; later meetings with: (1941), 258–60; (1943), 276–

7; his good relations with, 264; Churchill's visit to (1942), 266, 267; Churchill's near-infatuation with, 288; at Tehran Conf., 280; at Yalta Conf., 289–92; at Potsdam Conf., 307–8; stroke, 359; AE on, 144, 277, 288, 307; *mentioned*, 257, 274, 275
Stalingrad, 276
Stanhope, 7th Earl, 155
Stanley, Oliver, 101, 103, 133, 181, 222, 226, 228, 318, 326, 343
Stansgate, 1st Viscount, 493, 611
Stark, Sir Andrew, 389
Stavisky Affair, 134
sterling crisis (1956), 573, 586; Cabinet failure to inform AE of, 591
Stettinius, Edward R., 289
Stevenson, Adlai, 548
Stikker, Dr U., 352
Stimson, Henry, 121, 122, 274
Stockwell, General Sir Hugh, 487, 488, 508, 509
Strand Magazine, The, 216
Strang, William (*later* Baron Strang), 166, 218, 361, 555; on Br. foreign policy, 114; on N. Chamberlain, 173
Stresa, Anglo–French–Italian conference at, 146
Stresemann, Gustav, 92
Stuart, James (*later* 1st Viscount), 201, 295, 319, 392, 393, 537n, 574; intrigues against AE, 194, 261; Chief Whip, 245
Studholme, Sir Henry, 59
Sudan, 237, 242, 354, 398, 447; 1899 Condominium abrogated, 354; independence, 383
Sudeten Germans, issue of, 184, 206, 207, 209, 210
Suez: Six Day War in, 612
Suez Canal: 1888 Convention, *see* Constantinople Convention; AE in (1925), 86; Anglo-Egypt. Treaty on (1936), 169, 354; importance of, in WWII, 233; threatened, 237, 252; US endorses principle of freedom of passage in, 360, 380, 383; AE proposes international milit. force

Wavell, General Sir Archibald—*contd*
confidence in, 252; C. in C., India,
252; Viceroy, 273; discusses Indian
policy with Churchill, Simon and
AE, 295
Weizmann, Chaim, 301
Welles, Sumner, 187, 214, 225, 265, 464
Wellesley, Sir Victor, 121
Wells, 'Bombardier' Billy, 20
West Auckland (Co. Durham), 4; Eden
baronetcy of, 8
West Indian immigrants, 418–19
Western European Union, 384, 389
Westminster Bank, AE joins Board of,
317
Weygand, General Maxime, 233
Wheeler-Bennett, Sir John: on AE,
161
Whibley, Charles, 15
Wight, Martin, 592–3
Wigram, Sir Clive, 133
Wilkie, Wendell, 247
Williams, Philip, 481, 482
Willoughby de Broke, 20th Baron, 72
Wilson, Charles, *see* Moran, 1st Baron
Wilson, Harold (*later* Baron Wilson),
318, 337, 585, 612
Wilson, General Sir Henry Maitland,
250
Wilson, Sir Horace, 173, 175, 183, 187,
188, 190, 193, 195, 209
Wilson, Woodrow, 464
Winant, John G., 256, 257, 264, 265,
274, 313; on AE, 157
Windlestone (Co. Durham), Eden
family estate, 4, 5, 6–7, 304; AE
revisits, in old age, 3; Sir William
E and, 10, 11, 19–20, 625, 626;
AE christened at, 11–12, 13; his
childhood appreciation of life and
treasures at, 19–20, 22; memorial
service for Jack E at, 31; Sir William E buried at, 32; inherited by
Timothy E, 33; AE on leave at, 40,
49; memorial service for Nicholas
E at, 42; Timothy E and, 51, 55,
61, 89, 94, 95, 96, 171; watercolours of, 60; AE bored at, 65, 66,
67; family rows over, 85, 89; sold,
171; as residential school, 625–6;

family graves transferred from,
626; AE on, 3, 7, 10, 13, 19, 22,
30, 95–6; *mentioned*, 8, 16, 17, 18,
24, 26, 29, 31, 32, 40, 46, 119, 292,
314, 618, 621
Wingate, General Orde, 235
Winterton, 6th Earl, 208, 316
Wood, Sir Kingsley, 165, 168, 181, 190,
194, 208, 271; at lunch meeting
with Churchill and AE, 225–6;
Chancellor of the Exchequer, 240;
Cadogan on, 226n
Woolton, 1st Earl of: Chairman of Con-
serv. Party, 315, 316, 324, 325,
332; at 1950 Party Conf., 338; minister in second Churchill Govt,
344; in Eden Govt, 404, 407;
retires, 424; *mentioned*, 319, 355,
392, 408
Wootton, Captain, 37, 38
World Bank: and Aswan High Dam
project, 426, 430, 445, 447, 448,
449, 450, 451
World War I, 29–54; AE on active service in, 36–54
World War II, 220–312 *passim*; ends: in
Europe, 294; in Japan, 312
Wright, Sir Michael, 551
Wyndham, George, 15–16, 20, 21, 171;
Sybil E on, 16; letter and poem to
her, 17; AE's resemblance to, 18;
death, 18; AE reads 'Recognita',
52; Churchill compares AE with,
216
Wyndham, Mary, *see* Elcho, Lady

Yalta Conference, 248, 280, 288, 289–
92
Yates, William, 526, 553, 581
Yeoman Rifles, 21st Battalion, 35–6; AE
in, 36–51; AE on life in, 54
Yorkshire Post: AE writes articles for,
77, 81, 82, 86, 94, 104, 108; rep-
resents paper at Empire Press
Conf., 85; on AE's resignation as
Foreign Secretary, 196; on Cabinet
reshuffle, 425
Younger, Kenneth, 318
Ypres offensive, AE in, 48, 49–51
Yugoslavia, 248, 249, 251, 253, 254,